W9-ANZ-362

 *Oracle Press*™

Oracle8 PL/SQL Programming

Scott Urman

Osborne **McGraw-Hill**

Berkeley New York St. Louis
San Francisco Auckland Bogotá Hamburg London Madrid
Mexico City Milan Montreal New Delhi Panama City
Paris São Paulo Singapore Sydney Tokyo Toronto

Osborne/**McGraw-Hill**
2600 Tenth Street
Berkeley, California 94710
U.S.A.

For information on translations or book distributors outside the U.S.A., or to
arrange bulk purchase discounts for sales promotions, premiums, or
fund-raisers, please contact Osborne/**McGraw-Hill** at the above address.

Oracle8 PL/SQL Programming

Copyright © 1997 by The McGraw-Hill Companies. All rights reserved.
Printed in the United States of America. Except as permitted under the
Copyright Act of 1976, no part of this publication may be reproduced or
distributed in any form or by any means, or stored in a database or retrieval
system, without the prior written permission of the publisher, with the
exception that the program listings may be entered, stored, and executed in
a computer system, but they may not be reproduced for publication.

34567890 AGM 998

ISBN 0-07-882305-6

Publisher	**Copy Editor**
Brandon A. Nordin	Judith Brown
Editor-in-Chief	**Proofreader**
Scott Rogers	Jeff Barash
Acquisitions Editor	**Indexer**
Wendy Rinaldi	James Minkin
Project Editor	**Computer Designer**
Nancy McLaughlin	Sylvia Brown
Editorial Assistant	**Illustrator**
Ann Sellers	Roberta Steele
Technical Editor	**Cover Design**
Tim Smith	Lisa Schultz

Information has been obtained by Osborne/**McGraw-Hill** from sources believed to be
reliable. However, because of the possibility of human or mechanical error by our sources,
Osborne/**McGraw-Hill**, or others, Osborne/**McGraw-Hill** does not guarantee the accuracy,
adequacy, or completeness of any information and is not responsible for any errors or omissions
or the results obtained from use of such information.

This book is dedicated to the memory of my grandmother.

Contents
at a Glance

1	Introduction to PL/SQL	1
2	PL/SQL Basics	23
3	Records and Tables	81
4	SQL Within PL/SQL	97
5	Built-in SQL Functions	129
6	Cursors	203
7	Subprograms: Procedures and Functions	241
8	Packages	283
9	Triggers	317
10	Error Handling	353
11	Objects	395
12	Collections	433
13	PL/SQL Execution Environments	463
14	Testing and Debugging	503

15	Dynamic PL/SQL	. . . .	549
16	Intersession Communication	. . . .	617
17	Oracle Advanced Queuing	. . . .	651
18	Database Jobs and File I/O	. . . .	699
19	Oracle's WebServer Program	. . . .	731
20	External Procedures	. . . .	779
21	Large Objects	. . . .	815
22	Performance and Tuning	. . . .	855
A	PL/SQL Reserved Words	. . . .	881
B	Guide to Supplied Packages	. . . .	887
C	Glossary of PL/SQL Features	. . . .	913
D	The Data Dictionary	. . . .	937
	Index	. . . .	961
	License Terms for Oracle Software	. . . .	983

Contents

Acknowledgments, xxiii
Introduction, xxv

1 Introduction to PL/SQL 1
Why PL/SQL?   2
        Client-Server Model   4
        Standards   4
Features of PL/SQL   5
        Block Structure   5
        Variables and Types   7
        Looping Constructs   8
Conventions Used in This Book   10
        PL/SQL and Oracle Versions   10
        Oracle Documentation   12
        Online Code   12
Example Tables   13
Summary   21

2 PL/SQL Basics 23
The PL/SQL Block   24
        Basic Block Structure   28

Lexical Units   30
        Identifiers   31
        Delimiters   34
        Literals   34
        Comments   38
Variable Declarations   39
        Declaration Syntax   40
        Variable Initialization   41
PL/SQL Types   42
        Scalar Types   43
        Composite Types   50
        Reference Types   50
        LOB Types   51
        Using %TYPE   51
        User-Defined Subtypes   52
        Converting Between Datatypes   53
        Variable Scope and Visibility   56
Expressions and Operators   58
        Assignment   58
        Expressions   59
PL/SQL Control Structures   62
        IF-THEN-ELSE   63
        Loops   67
        GOTOs and Labels   71
        Pragmas   75
PL/SQL Style Guide   75
        Style of Comments   76
        Style of Variable Names   77
        Style of Capitalization   78
        Style of Indentation   78
        Style in General   79
Summary   79

3 Records and Tables **81**
PL/SQL Records   82
        Record Assignment   84
        Using %ROWTYPE   85
Tables   86
        Tables vs. Arrays   87
        Table Attributes   90
        Guidelines for Using PL/SQL Tables   94
Summary   95

4 SQL Within PL/SQL **97**
SQL Statements   98
    Using SQL in PL/SQL   98
DML in PL/SQL   100
    SELECT   102
    INSERT   105
    UPDATE   106
    DELETE   107
    The WHERE Clause   108
    Table References   112
    Database Links   113
    Synonyms   113
Pseudocolumns   114
    CURRVAL and NEXTVAL   115
    LEVEL   116
    ROWID   116
    ROWNUM   117
GRANT, REVOKE, and Privileges   118
    Object vs. System Privileges   118
    GRANT and REVOKE   118
    Roles   121
Transaction Control   122
    COMMIT vs. ROLLBACK   123
    Savepoints   125
    Transactions vs. Blocks   126
Summary   127

5 Built-in SQL Functions **129**
Introduction   130
Character Functions
  Returning Character Values   131
    CHR   131
    CONCAT   132
    INITCAP   132
    LOWER   133
    LPAD   133
    LTRIM   134
    NLS_INITCAP   135
    NLS_LOWER   136
    NLS_UPPER   136
    REPLACE   137
    RPAD   138
    RTRIM   138

SOUNDEX 139
SUBSTR 140
SUBSTRB 141
TRANSLATE 142
UPPER 143
Character Functions
Returning Numeric Values 143
ASCII 143
INSTR 144
INSTRB 145
LENGTH 146
LENGTHB 146
NLSSORT 147
Numeric Functions 147
ABS 147
ACOS 148
ASIN 148
ATAN 149
ATAN2 149
CEIL 150
COS 150
COSH 151
EXP 151
FLOOR 152
LN 152
LOG 153
MOD 153
POWER 154
ROUND 154
SIGN 155
SIN 155
SINH 156
SQRT 156
TAN 157
TANH 157
TRUNC 158
Date Functions 158
ADD_MONTHS 158
LAST_DAY 159
MONTHS_BETWEEN 160
NEW_TIME 160
NEXT_DAY 161

ROUND   162
SYSDATE   162
TRUNC   163
Conversion Functions   165
CHARTOROWID   166
CONVERT   166
HEXTORAW   167
RAWTOHEX   168
ROWIDTOCHAR   168
TO_CHAR (dates)   169
TO_CHAR (labels)   171
TO_CHAR (numbers)   172
TO_DATE   175
TO_LABEL   175
TO_MULTI_BYTE   176
TO_NUMBER   176
TO_SINGLE_BYTE   177
Group Functions   177
AVG   178
COUNT   178
GLB   179
LUB   179
MAX   180
MIN   180
STDDEV   181
SUM   181
VARIANCE   182
Other Functions   183
BFILENAME   183
DECODE   183
DUMP   184
EMPTY_CLOB/EMPTY_BLOB   186
GREATEST   186
GREATEST_LB   187
LEAST   187
LEAST_UB   188
NVL   188
UID   188
USER   189
USERENV   190
VSIZE   190

PL/SQL at Work: Printing Numbers as Text Words   192
Summary   201

6 Cursors **203**
What Is a Cursor?   204
    Processing Explicit Cursors   205
    Processing Implicit Cursors   215
Cursor Fetch Loops   217
    Simple Loops   217
    WHILE Loops   219
    Cursor FOR Loops   221
    NO_DATA_FOUND vs. %NOTFOUND   222
    SELECT FOR UPDATE Cursors   223
Cursor Variables   227
    Declaring a Cursor Variable   228
    Allocating Storage for
        Cursor Variables   230
    Opening a Cursor
        Variable for a Query   231
    Closing Cursor Variables   232
    Cursor Variable Example 1   232
    Cursor Variable Example 2   235
    Restrictions on
        Using Cursor Variables   237
Summary   237

7 Subprograms: Procedures and Functions **241**
Creating Procedures and Functions   242
    Creating a Procedure   243
    Creating a Function   257
    Exceptions Raised Inside Subprograms   261
    Dropping Procedures and Functions   262
Subprogram Locations   263
    Stored Subprograms
        and the Data Dictionary   263
    Local Subprograms   266
Subprogram Dependencies   269
    How Dependencies Are Determined   272
Privileges and
   Stored Subprograms   275
    EXECUTE Privilege   276
    Stored Subprograms and Roles   278
Summary   281

8 Packages **283**
Packages   284
    Package Specification   284
    Package Body   286
    Packages and Scope   288
    Overloading Packaged Subprograms   289
    Package Initialization   292
    Packages and Dependencies   294
Using Stored
  Functions in SQL Statements   297
    Purity Levels   297
    Default Parameters   303
PL/SQL at Work:
  A PL/SQL Schema Exporter   303
Summary   314

9 Triggers **317**
Creating Triggers   318
    Trigger Components   320
    Triggers and the Data Dictionary   324
    Order of Trigger Firing   326
    Using :old and :new in Row-Level Triggers   328
    Using Trigger Predicates: INSERTING, UPDATING, and
      DELETING   332
Mutating Tables   334
    Mutating Table Example   336
    Workaround for the Mutating Table Error   337
PL/SQL at Work:
  Implementing Update Cascade   340
    Contents of this Utility   342
    How It Works   347
Summary   351

10 Error Handling **353**
What Is an Exception?   354
    Declaring Exceptions   356
    Raising Exceptions   360
    Handling Exceptions   362
    The EXCEPTION_INIT Pragma   368
    Using RAISE_APPLICATION_ERROR   369
Exception Propagation   372
    Exceptions Raised in the Executable Section   373
    Exceptions Raised in the Declarative Section   376
    Exceptions Raised in the Exception Section   378

Exception Guidelines   380
    Scope of Exceptions   380
    Avoiding Unhandled Exceptions   382
    Masking Location of the Error   382
PL/SQL at Work: A General Error Handler   384
Summary   393

11 Objects **395**
Background   396
    Basis of Object-Oriented Programming   396
    Object-Relational Databases   398
Object Types   399
    Defining Object Types   400
    Declaring and Initializing Objects   403
    Methods   405
    Altering and Dropping Types   413
    Object Dependencies   416
Objects in the Database   417
    Object Locations   417
    Objects in DML Statements   421
    MAP and ORDER Methods   427
Summary   430

12 Collections **433**
Nested Tables   434
    Declaring a Nested Table   434
    Nested Tables in the Database   438
    Nested Tables vs. Index-by Tables   444
Varrays   445
    Declaring a Varray   445
    Varrays in the Database   447
    Varrays vs. Nested Tables   449
Collection Methods   450
    EXISTS   450
    COUNT   452
    LIMIT   452
    FIRST and LAST   453
    NEXT and PRIOR   453
    EXTEND   454
    TRIM   457
    DELETE   459
Summary   461

13 PL/SQL Execution Environments **463**

Different PL/SQL Engines   464
   Implications of Client-side PL/SQL   466
Server-side PL/SQL   468
   SQL*Plus   468
   Oracle Precompilers   475
   OCI   482
   SQL-Station   486
Client-side PL/SQL   489
   Why a Client-side Engine Is Provided   490
   Oracle Forms   493
   Procedure Builder   495
The PL/SQL Wrapper   498
   Running the Wrapper   498
   Input and Output Files   499
   Checking Syntax and Semantics   499
   Guidelines for the Wrapper   500
Summary   501

14 Testing and Debugging **503**

Problem Diagnosis   504
   Debugging Guidelines   504
   The Debug Package   505
Inserting into a Test Table   506
   Problem 1   506
DBMS_OUTPUT   517
   The DBMS_OUTPUT Package   517
   Problem 2   522
PL/SQL Debuggers   530
Procedure Builder   530
   Problem 3   530
SQL-Station   537
   Problem 4   538
Comparison Between Procedure Builder and SQL-Station   543
Programming Methodologies   543
   Modular Programming   544
   Top-Down Design   545
   Data Abstraction   546
Summary   547

15 Dynamic PL/SQL **549**

Introduction   550
   Static vs. Dynamic SQL   550
   Overview of DBMS_SQL   551

Executing Non-Query DML and DDL Statements   556
    Open the Cursor   557
    Parse the Statement   557
    Bind Any Input Variables   559
    Execute the Statement   562
    Close the Cursor   563
    Example   563
    Executing DDL Statements   564
    Executing Queries   566
    Parse the Statement   567
    Define the Output Variables   567
    Fetch the Rows   570
    Return the Results to
      PL/SQL Variables   571
    Example   575
Executing PL/SQL   577
    Parse the Statement   578
    Retrieve the Value of
      Any Output Variables   579
    Example   581
    Using out_value_size   583
PL/SQL at Work: Executing Arbitrary Stored Procedures   584
DBMS_SQL Enhancements
  for PL/SQL 8.0   592
    Parsing Large SQL Strings   592
    DBMS_SQL Array Processing   594
    Describing the Select List   600
Miscellaneous Procedures   604
    Fetching LONG Data   604
    Additional Error Functions   606
PL/SQL At Work:
  Writing a LONG to a FILE   608
Privileges and DBMS_SQL   611
    Privileges Required for DBMS_SQL   611
    Roles and DBMS_SQL   611
Comparison Between DBMS_SQL and Other
  Dynamic Methods   612
    Describing the Select List   613
    Array Processing   614
    Piecewise Operations on LONG Data   614
    Interface Differences   614

Tips and Techniques   615
    Reusing Cursors   615
    Permissions   615
    DDL Operations and Hanging   615
Summary   615

16 Intersession Communication **617**
DBMS_PIPE   618
    Sending a Message   623
    Receiving a Message   625
    Creating and Managing Pipes   627
    Privileges and Security   630
    Establishing a Communications Protocol   632
    Example   633
DBMS_ALERT   641
    Sending an Alert   641
    Receiving an Alert   642
    Other Procedures   645
    Alerts and the Data Dictionary   646
Comparing DBMS_PIPE
   and DBMS_ALERT   648
Summary   649

17 Oracle Advanced Queuing **651**
Introduction   652
    Components of Advanced Queuing   653
    Implementation of Advanced Queuing   655
Queue Operations   656
    Supporting Types   656
    ENQUEUE   665
    DEQUEUE   666
Queue Administration   667
    DBMS_AQADM Subprograms   668
    Queue Privileges   678
    Queues and the Data Dictionary   678
Extended Examples   681
    Creating Queues and Queue Tables   681
    Simple Enqueue and Dequeue   683
    Clearing a Queue   685
    Enqueue and Dequeue by Priority   686
    Enqueue and Dequeue by Correlation or
      Message Identifier   688
    Browsing a Queue   691

Using Exception Queues   694
Dropping Queues   697
Summary   697

18   Database Jobs and File I/O **699**
Database Jobs   700
Background Processes   700
Running a Job   702
Broken Jobs   707
Removing a Job   707
Altering a Job   708
Viewing Jobs in the Data Dictionary   708
Job Execution Environments   709
File I/O   709
Security   709
Exceptions Raised by UTL_FILE   712
Opening and Closing Files   712
File Output   716
File Input   719
Examples   720
Summary   729

19   Oracle's WebServer Program **731**
The WebServer Environment   732
The PL/SQL Agent   734
Specifying Procedure Parameters   736
PL/SQL Web Toolkit   739
HTP and HTF   740
OWA_UTIL   757
OWA_IMAGE   767
OWA_COOKIE   769
Development Environments
for OWA Procedures   774
OWA_UTIL.SHOWPAGE   774
SQL-Station Coder   775
Summary   776

20   External Procedures **779**
What Is an External Procedure?   780
Required Steps   782
Parameter Mappings   791
External Functions and Packaged Procedures   800
Callbacks to the Database   802
Service Routines   803

Executing SQL in an External Procedure 807
Tips, Guidelines, and Restrictions 808
Debugging External Procedures 808
Guidelines 810
Restrictions 811
Summary 812

21 Large Objects **815**
What Is a LOB? 816
LOB Storage 817
LOBs in DML 818
Manipulating BFILEs 821
Directories 822
Opening and Closing BFILEs 823
BFILEs in DML 824
The DBMS_LOB Package 826
DBMS_LOB Routines 826
Exceptions Raised by
DBMS_LOB Routines 846
DBMS_LOB vs. OCI 847
PL/SQL at Work: Copying LONG Data into a LOB 849
Summary 852

22 Performance and Tuning **855**
The Shared Pool 856
Structure of an Oracle Instance 856
How the Shared Pool Works 861
Estimating the Size of the Shared Pool 863
Pinning Objects 865
SQL Statement Tuning 867
Determining the Execution Plan 867
Using the Plan 875
Network Issues 876
Using Client-side PL/SQL 877
Avoiding Unnecessary Reparsing 877
Array Processing 878
Summary 878

A PL/SQL Reserved Words **881**

B Guide to Supplied Packages **887**
Creating the Packages 888
Package Descriptions 888
DBMS_ALERT 888
DBMS_APPLICATION_INFO 890

DBMS_AQ and DBMS_AQADM   892

DBMS_DEFER, DBMS_DEFER_SYS and
    DBMS_DEFER_QUERY   892

DBMS_DDL   892

DBMS_DESCRIBE   894

DBMS_JOB   896

DBMS_LOB   897

DBMS_LOCK   897

DBMS_OUTPUT   901

DBMS_PIPE   902

DBMS_REFRESH and DBMS_SNAPSHOT   902

DBMS_REPCAT, DBMS_REPCAT_AUTH and
    DBMS_REPCAT_ADMIN   902

DBMS_ROWID   902

DBMS_SESSION   902

DBMS_SHARED_POOL   905

DBMS_SQL   905

DBMS_TRANSACTION   905

DBMS_UTILITY   908

UTL_FILE   911

C   Glossary of PL/SQL Features **913**

D   The Data Dictionary **937**

What Is the Data Dictionary?   938

    Naming Conventions   938

    Permissions   939

All/User/DBA Dictionary Views   939

    Dependencies   939

       941

    Collections   941

    Compile Errors   942

    Directories   943

    Jobs   943

    Libraries   945

    LOBs   945

    Object Methods   946

    Object Method Parameters   947

    Object Method Results   948

    Object References   949

    Object Type Attributes   949

    Schema Objects   950

    Source Code   951

    Tables   952

Table Columns   954
Triggers   956
Trigger Columns   958
Views   958
Other Dictionary Views   959
dbms_alert_info   959
dict_columns   959

Index 961
License Terms for Oracle Software 983

Acknowledgments

project like this book takes quite a lot of time to do properly. Although this is technically a revision of the second edition of *Oracle PL/SQL Programming,* I took the time to examine every chapter to add improvements and additions, and I think that this is virtually a new book. Six months (and of course the obligatory caffeine) later, I think that my time was well spent. If you've already purchased the first edition, I hope you will take a look at this one as well I'm very proud of this book, and I hope that you will enjoy it and find it useful.

There were a number of people who should be acknowledged for their invaluable help with this project. Thanks to Tim Smith from Oracle for his insightful and detailed review—it is still interesting switching roles with you. As with the first edition, you helped out tremendously by catching the errors I did not, and suggesting ways to better organize the material. Thanks also to Wendy Rinaldi, Lisa Lucas, and Nancy McLaughlin from Osborne for cajoling me into finishing on time. And of course thanks to my family and friends (you know who you are) for their comments and advice.

I would also like to mention here the sources for several of the "PL/SQL at Work" examples. Although the ideas for many of the examples came from you (the readers of the first edition), four people in particular gave me complete source code and permission to use it. Paul Narth from Oracle UK Customer Support supplied the example in Chapter 15,

"Writing a LONG to a File." Pamela Rothman from Oracle US Customer Support supplied the basis for the other PL/SQL at Work example in Chapter 15, "Executing Arbitrary Stored Procedures." David L. Hunt from Oracle Education supplied the code for the "Printing Numbers as Text Words" example from Chapter 5. Finally, thanks to Tom Kyte from Oracle Government for the cascade update example in Chapter 9 and for many Oracle Web Server examples.

I used a number of resources during the development of this book, including several Oracle manuals. These include the *PL/SQL User's Guide and Reference, Oracle Server Application Developer's Guide, Oracle Server Administrator's Guide, Oracle Server SQL Reference, Oracle Server Concepts Manual,* and the *Programmer's Guide to the Pro*C Precompiler.*

If you have any comments about this book, I can be reached via email at **surman@us.oracle.com**. I have really enjoyed hearing your comments and suggestions on the first edition, and welcome your thoughts on this version.

Introduction

racle is an extremely powerful and flexible relational database system. Along with this power and flexibility, however, comes complexity. In order to design useful applications that are based on Oracle, it is necessary to understand how Oracle manipulates the data stored within the system. PL/SQL is an important tool that is designed for data manipulation, both internally within Oracle and externally in your own applications.

PL/SQL is available in a variety of environments, each of which has different advantages.

This book is meant to help you understand PL/SQL and appreciate the power of this unique language. After reading it, you should be able to use PL/SQL in your own applications easily and effectively. Once you are familiar with the basics of PL/SQL, this book can also serve as a reference manual for day-to-day questions and topics about PL/SQL.

What's New?

This is the second edition of *Oracle PL/SQL Programming*. So what is different about this edition, and why should you read it if you have already read the first edition? The first difference is that this edition includes material on Oracle8, such as object types and external procedures.

Even if you are not using Oracle8, however, there are still improvements over the first edition. I have reorganized the presentation of the material in the first edition to better illustrate different PL/SQL constructs. The new edition also includes "PL/SQL at Work" examples, as well as an accompanying CD.

PL/SQL at Work

You are probably reading this book because you plan on using PL/SQL for a real-world application. That is good, since it is what the language was designed for. To assist with this, I have added many examples throughout the book which are called "PL/SQL at Work." These examples are designed either to be used as-is in your own applications or to serve as a starting point. The ideas for these examples came mainly from you—the readers of the first edition—so I think they will be very applicable to real-world PL/SQL.

The Accompanying CD

The source code used in the first edition was available for download from the Oracle Press web site at **http://www.osborne.com/oracle**. Likewise, the code for this edition is available there. However, I chose to include a CD directly with the book as well. This CD contains all of the examples, plus demo versions of two products that use PL/SQL—Oracle's WebServer and Platinum's SQL-Station™, which are also discussed in the text. I hope that you try these tools, and find them valuable. You can find more information about SQL-Station at Platinum's web site at **http://www .platinum.com** and information about the Oracle Web Server at Oracle's web site at **http://www.oracle.com**.

Intended Audience

This book is designed to be both a user's guide and a reference to PL/SQL. It is appropriate for both experienced programmers who need to know just the syntax for PL/SQL and its advanced features, and for novice programmers who are not familiar with other third-generation languages. It is helpful, but not required, for the reader to be familiar with Oracle in general (connecting to and using the database, basic SQL, etc.) before reading.

How to Use This Book

This book is divided into 22 chapters and 4 appendices. Chapter 1 is an introduction, and Chapters 2 through 12 describe the syntax and semantics for PL/SQL. Chapter 12 also covers performance and tuning. Chapters 13 and 14 describe execution environments and debugging techniques, and Chapters 15 through 21 discuss the advanced features of the language, including the built-in packages. The appendices provide a reference for many of the material as well.

Chapter 1: Introduction to PL/SQL

This chapter introduces PL/SQL and describes some of the major features of the language. It also discusses the versions of PL/SQL and which database versions they correspond to. The chapter concludes with a description of the database schema used as an example throughout the book.

Chapter 2: PL/SQL Basics

This chapter describes the syntax of PL/SQL. Topics included are the structure of a PL/SQL program, variables and types, expressions and operator, and control structures (loops and conditional statements). This chapter concludes with advice on PL/SQL style and how to write more readable and maintainable code.

Chapter 3: Records and Tables

The user-defined types available with PL/SQL version 2 and Oracle7 are records, which allow related variables to be manipulated as a unit, and tables, which allow array-like access to data. Chapter 3 discusses how to use these datatypes.

Chapter 4: SQL Within PL/SQL

This chapter covers the SQL statements available within PL/SQL—the data manipulation commands that are used to manage Oracle data. It also describes transaction control and privileges.

Chapter 5: Built-in SQL Functions

This chapter discusses the built-in SQL functions that are available from PL/SQL.

Chapter 6: Cursors

This chapter contains a detailed discussion of cursors and how they are used to manipulate large amounts of data. It includes the syntax for cursor declaration and usage, a description of cursor attributes, and examples of how to use cursor variables.

Chapter 7: Subprograms: Procedures and Functions

Chapters 7 through 9 discuss the four different kinds of named PL/SQL blocks. Chapter 7 introduces this discussion by describing procedures and functions. The syntax and meaning of each are discussed, along with the differences between them. The chapter also includes details on using functions in SQL statements, how roles and procedures interact, and the relationship of stored subprograms and the data dictionary.

Chapter 8: Packages

Packages allow related subprograms to be grouped together as a unit. Many of the advanced features of PL/SQL are implemented as packages, which also promote good application design through data abstraction.

Chapter 9: Triggers

Triggers are the final type of named PL/SQL block. Triggers are automatically fired when Oracle data is modified, so they allow you to enforce complicated business rules that can't be done with referential integrity constraints.

Chapter 10: Error Handling

Error handing is crucial to any well-designed application. This chapter describes how to use PL/SQL exceptions to insure that your program is robust and able to handle runtime exception conditions. Guidelines for using exceptions effectively are also included.

Chapter 11: Objects

 Object types, introduced with Oracle8, provide a different programming methodology. This chapter discusses how the Oracle8

object-relational database model works, including how to create object types and methods.

Chapter 12: Collections

PL/SQL **8.0** ...and **HIGHER** This chapter discusses collections, which include nested tables and varrays. These new datatypes available with Oracle8 extend the functionality of the PL/SQL tables discussed in Chapter 2. This chapter discusses how to use these datatypes, including the collection methods.

Chapter 13: PL/SQL Execution Environments

PL/SQL can be run from a variety of environments. This chapter contains a discussion of the merits of client versus server side PL/SQL, and detailed information about using PL/SQL in SQL*Plus, the Oracle precompilers, OCI, the Developer 2000 suite of tools, and third-party tools like SQL-Station.

Chapter 14: Testing and Debugging

This chapter describes several different methods of debugging your PL/SQL applications, including SQL-Station Debugger. The techniques described in this chapter are illustrated by solving three common PL/SQL problems, and are applicable to your own development. The chapter concludes with a discussion of the software development process and how it can be used effectively in PL/SQL.

Chapter 15: Dynamic PL/SQL

Dynamic PL/SQL is a very powerful programming technique that allows you to write very flexible programs. This chapter discusses the DBMS_SQL package, which implements dynamic PL/SQL. This package can also be used to overcome the restriction that only DML statements are allowed in PL/SQL.

Chapter 16: Intersession Communication

This chapter describes the two built-in packages available for communicating directly between database sessions—database pipes (DBMS_PIPE) and database alerts (DBMS_ALERT). Specific examples are included, as well as a comparison between these two packages.

Chapter 17: Oracle Advanced Queuing

PL/SQL **8.0** ...and HIGHER Oracle/AQ (the Advanced Queuing option) implements a robust queuing system similar to that found in transaction processing monitors. This chapter discusses how to use Oracle/AQ and provides a comprehensive example.

Chapter 18: Database Jobs and File I/O

The DBMS_JOB package allows you to schedule PL/SQL jobs (in the form of stored procedures) to run automatically at specified times. The UTL_FILE package allows PL/SQL to read from and write to operating system files. Both packages are discussed in detail, with examples.

Chapter 19: Oracle's WebServer Program

This chapter discusses how PL/SQL fits into the Oracle web server environment, and how you can generate HTML output from a PL/SQL-stored procedure. Using PL/SQL in this way allows you to create dynamic web pages from information in the database.

Chapter 20: External Procedures

PL/SQL **8.0** ...and HIGHER PL/SQL version 8 (with Oracle8) allows you to directly call a procedure or function written in C from PL/SQL. This valuable enhancement allows PL/SQL to be extended easily to include all the functionality available in C, and is the topic of this chapter. Topics discussed include the mapping between PL/SQL and C datatypes.

Chapter 21: Large Objects

PL/SQL **8.0** ...and HIGHER LOBs (Large OBjects) can contain up to 4 gigabytes of text or binary data. Oracle8 allows you to manipulate large objects with the DBMS_LOB package, described in this chapter. DBMS_LOB allows random read and write access to large objects, which is a significant improvement over the Oracle7 LONG and LONG RAW types. The storage for binary data can also be kept outside the database, if desired.

Chapter 22: Performance and Tuning

A properly written PL/SQL program should not only produce the correct result, but it should determine this result as efficiently as possible. Several performance and tuning techniques are discussed in this chapter, including the use of the shared pool, how to tune SQL statements, and how to use the Oracle array interface.

Appendix A: PL/SQL Reserved Words

This appendix lists the keywords reserved by PL/SQL and by the database itself.

Appendix B: Guide to Supplied DBMS Packages

This appendix describes all of the built-in packages available in PL/SQL. These packages implement such things as file I/O, job scheduling, inter-session communication, dynamic programming, and management of the shared pool.

Appendix C: Glossary of PL/SQL Features

This appendix contains an alphabetical list of the features of PL/SQL, organized for easy reference. A brief description of each is included, with a reference to the chapter that describes the topic in detail.

Appendix D: The Data Dictionary

This appendix describes the data dictionary views that are relevant to the PL/SQL programmer.

CHAPTER
1

Introduction to PL/SQL

L/SQL is a sophisticated programming language used to access an Oracle database from various environments. PL/SQL is integrated with the database server, so that the PL/SQL code can be processed quickly and efficiently. It is also available in some client-side Oracle tools. In this chapter we will discuss the reasons for development of PL/SQL, the major features of the language, and the importance of knowing the PL/SQL and database versions. The chapter concludes with descriptions of some conventions used in the book and the database tables that are used as examples throughout the book.

Why PL/SQL?

Oracle is a relational database. The language used to access a relational database is *Structured Query Language* (*SQL*—often pronounced *sequel*). SQL is a flexible, efficient language, with features designed to manipulate and examine relational data. For example, the following SQL statement will delete all students who are majoring in nutrition from the database:

```
DELETE FROM students
   WHERE major = 'Nutrition';
```

(The database tables used in this book, including the **students** table, are described at the end of this chapter.)

SQL is a *fourth-generation language*. This means that the language describes what should be done, but not how to do it. In the DELETE statement just shown, for example, we don't know how the database will actually determine which students are majoring in nutrition. Presumably, the server will loop through all the students in some order to determine the proper entries to delete. But the details of this are hidden from us.

Third-generation languages, such as C and COBOL, are more procedural in nature. A program in a third-generation language (3GL) implements a step-by-step algorithm to solve the problem. For example, we could accomplish the DELETE operation with something like this:

```
LOOP over each student record
   IF this record has major = 'Nutrition' THEN
      DELETE this record;
   END IF;
END LOOP;
```

Each language has advantages and disadvantages. Fourth-generation languages such as SQL are generally fairly simple (compared to third-generation languages) and have fewer commands. They also insulate the user from the underlying data structures and algorithms. In some cases, however, the procedural constructs available in 3GLs are useful to express a desired program. This is where PL/SQL comes in—it combines the power and flexibility of SQL (a 4GL) with the procedural constructs of a 3GL.

PL/SQL stands for Procedural Language/SQL. As its name implies, PL/SQL extends SQL by adding constructs found in other procedural languages, such as:

- Variables and types (both predefined and user-defined)

- Control structures such as IF-THEN-ELSE statements and loops

- Procedures and functions

- Object types and methods (PL/SQL version 8 and higher)

Procedural constructs are integrated seamlessly with Oracle SQL, resulting in a structured, powerful language. For example, suppose we want to change the major for a student. If the student doesn't exist, then we want to create a new record. We could do this with the following PL/SQL code:

```
-- Available online as 3gl_4gl.sql
DECLARE
  /* Declare variables which will be used in SQL statements */
  v_NewMajor VARCHAR2(10) := 'History';
  v_FirstName VARCHAR2(10) := 'Scott';
  v_LastName VARCHAR2(10) := 'Urman';
BEGIN
  /* Update the students table. */
  UPDATE students
    SET major = v_NewMajor
    WHERE first_name = v_FirstName
    AND last_name = v_LastName;
  /* Check to see if the record was found. If not, then we need
     to insert this record. */
  IF SQL%NOTFOUND THEN
    INSERT INTO students (ID, first_name, last_name, major)
      VALUES (student_sequence.NEXTVAL, v_FirstName, v_LastName,
              v_NewMajor);
  END IF;
END;
```

This example contains two different SQL statements (UPDATE and INSERT) as well as several variable declarations and the conditional IF statement.

NOTE
In order to run the preceding example, you first need to create the database objects referenced (the **students** *table and the* **student_sequence** *sequence). This can be done with the* **tables.sql** *script, provided as part of the online code. For more information about creating these objects and the online distribution, see the section "Online Code" later in this chapter.*

PL/SQL is unique in that it combines the flexibility of SQL with the power and configurability of a 3GL. Both the necessary procedural constructs and the database access are there, integrated with the language. This results in a robust, powerful language well suited for designing complex applications.

Client-Server Model

Many database applications are built using the client-server model. The program itself resides on a client machine and sends requests to a database server for information. The requests are done using SQL. Typically, this results in many network trips, one for each SQL statement. This is illustrated by the diagram on the left side of Figure 1-1. Compare this with the situation on the right, however. Several SQL statements can be bundled together into one PL/SQL block and sent to the server as a single unit. This results in less network traffic and a faster application.

Even when the client and the server are both running on the same machine, performance is increased. In this case, there isn't any network, but packaging SQL statements still results in a simpler program that makes fewer calls to the database.

Standards

Oracle supports the ANSI (American National Standards Institute) standard for the SQL language, as defined in ANSI document X3.135-1992 "Database Language SQL." This standard, commonly known as SQL92

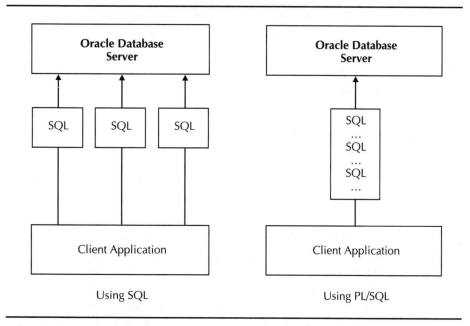

FIGURE I-I. *PL/SQL in a client-server environment*

(or SQL2), defines the SQL language only. It does not define the 3GL extensions to the language that PL/SQL provides. SQL92 has three compliance levels: Entry, Intermediate, and Full. Oracle7 Release 7.2 (and all higher versions, including Oracle8) complies with Entry SQL92 standards, as certified by the National Institute for Standards and Technology (NIST). Oracle is working with ANSI to ensure that future versions of Oracle and PL/SQL comply with the full standard.

Features of PL/SQL

PL/SQL's many different features and capabilities are best illustrated by example. The following sections describe some of the main features of the language. We will be examining these in detail throughout the book.

Block Structure

The basic unit in PL/SQL is a *block*. All PL/SQL programs are made up of blocks, which can be nested within each other. Typically, each block performs a logical unit of work in the program, thus separating different tasks from each other. A block has the following structure:

```
DECLARE
    /* Declarative section - PL/SQL variables, types, cursors,
       and local subprograms go here. */
BEGIN
    /* Executable section - procedural and SQL statements go here.
       This is the main section of the block and the only one
       that is required. */
EXCEPTION
    /* Exception handling section - error-handling statements go
       here. */
END;
```

Only the executable section is required; the declarative and exception handling sections are optional. The executable section must also contain at least one executable statement. The different sections of the block separate different functions of a PL/SQL program.

The design for PL/SQL is modeled after the Ada third-generation language. Many of the constructs available in Ada can also be found in PL/SQL. These include the block structure. Other Ada features found in PL/SQL include exception handling, the syntax for declaring procedures and functions, and packages. Throughout this book, we will see examples of the similarities between Ada and PL/SQL.

Error Handling

The exception handling section of the block is used to respond to run-time errors encountered by your program. By separating the error-handling code from the main body of the program, the structure of the program itself is clear. For example, the following PL/SQL block demonstrates an exception handling section that logs the error received along with the current time and the user who encountered the error:

```
-- Available online as error.sql
DECLARE
    v_ErrorCode NUMBER;            -- Code for the error
    v_ErrorMsg  VARCHAR2(200);     -- Message text for the error
    v_CurrentUser VARCHAR2(8);     -- Current database user
    v_Information VARCHAR2(100);   -- Information about the error
BEGIN
    /* Code that processes some data here */
```

```
EXCEPTION
  WHEN OTHERS THEN
    -- Assign values to the log variables, using built-in
    -- functions.
    v_ErrorCode := SQLCODE;
    v_ErrorMsg := SQLERRM;
    v_CurrentUser := USER;
    v_Information := 'Error encountered on ' ||
      TO_CHAR(SYSDATE) || ' by database user ' || v_CurrentUser;
    -- Insert the log message into log_table.
    INSERT INTO log_table (code, message, info)
      VALUES (v_ErrorCode, v_ErrorMsg, v_Information);
END;
```

NOTE
The previous example, like many others in the book, can be found in the online distribution. For more information, see the section "Online Code" at the end of this chapter.

Variables and Types

Information is transmitted between PL/SQL and the database with *variables*. A variable is a storage location that can be read from or assigned to by the program. In the previous example, **v_CurrentUser**, **v_ErrorCode**, and **v_Information** are all variables. Variables are declared in the declarative section of the block.

Every variable has a specific *type* associated with it. The type defines what kind of information the variable can hold. PL/SQL variables can be of the same type as database columns,

```
DECLARE
  v_StudentName  VARCHAR2(20);
  v_CurrentDate  DATE;
  v_NumberCredits NUMBER(3);
```

or they can be of additional types:

```
DECLARE
  v_LoopCounter BINARY_INTEGER;
  v_CurrentlyRegistered BOOLEAN;
```

PL/SQL also supports user-defined types: tables and records. User-defined types allow you to customize the structure of the data your program manipulates:

```
DECLARE
  TYPE t_StudentRecord IS RECORD (
    FirstName  VARCHAR2(10),
    LastName   VARCHAR2(10),
    CurrentCredits NUMBER(3)
  );
  v_Student t_StudentRecord;
```

PL/SQL 8.0 ...and HIGHER Oracle8 (with PL/SQL 8) supports object types as well. An object type has attributes and methods, and can be stored in a database table. The following example creates an object type:

```
-- Available online as part of tables8.sql
CREATE OR REPLACE TYPE StudentObj AS OBJECT (
  ID               NUMBER(5),
  first_name       VARCHAR2(20),
  last_name        VARCHAR2(20),
  major            VARCHAR2(30),
  current_credits  NUMBER(3),

  -- Returns the first and last names, separated by a space.
  MEMBER FUNCTION FormattedName
    RETURN VARCHAR2,
  PRAGMA RESTRICT_REFERENCES(FormattedName, RNDS, WNDS, RNPS, WNPS),

  -- Updates the major to the specified value in p_NewMajor.
  MEMBER PROCEDURE ChangeMajor(p_NewMajor IN VARCHAR2),
  PRAGMA RESTRICT_REFERENCES(ChangeMajor, RNDS, WNDS, RNPS, WNPS),

  -- Updates the current_credits by adding the number of
  -- credits in p_CompletedClass to the current value.
  MEMBER PROCEDURE UpdateCredits(p_CompletedClass IN ClassObj),
  PRAGMA RESTRICT_REFERENCES(UpdateCredits, RNDS, WNDS, RNPS, WNPS)
);
```

Looping Constructs

PL/SQL supports different kinds of loops. A *loop* allows you to execute the same sequence of statements repeatedly. For example, the following block uses a *simple loop* to insert the numbers 1 through 50 into **temp_table**:

```
-- Available online as simple.sql
DECLARE
  v_LoopCounter BINARY_INTEGER := 1;
BEGIN
  LOOP
    INSERT INTO temp_table (num_col)
      VALUES (v_LoopCounter);
    v_LoopCounter := v_LoopCounter + 1;
    EXIT WHEN v_LoopCounter > 50;
  END LOOP;
END;
```

Another type of loop, a *numeric FOR loop,* can be used as well. This looping construct provides a simpler syntax. We can accomplish the same thing as the preceding example with

```
-- Available online as numeric.sql
BEGIN
  FOR v_LoopCounter IN 1..50 LOOP
    INSERT INTO temp_table (num_col)
      VALUES (v_LoopCounter);
  END LOOP;
END;
```

Cursors

A *cursor* is used to process multiple rows retrieved from the database (with a SELECT statement). Using a cursor, your program can step through the set of rows returned one at a time, processing each one. For example, the following block will retrieve the first and last names of all students in the database:

```
-- Available online as cursor.sql
DECLARE
  v_FirstName VARCHAR2(20);
  v_LastName  VARCHAR2(20);
  -- Cursor declaration. This defines the SQL statement to
  -- return the rows.
  CURSOR c_Students IS
    SELECT first_name, last_name
      FROM students;
BEGIN
  -- Begin cursor processing.
  OPEN c_Students;
```

```
LOOP
  -- Retrieve one row.
  FETCH c_Students INTO v_FirstName, v_LastName;
  -- Exit the loop after all rows have been retrieved.
  EXIT WHEN c_Students%NOTFOUND;
  /* Process data here */
END LOOP;
-- End processing.
CLOSE c_Students;
END;
```

Conventions Used in This Book

I use several conventions throughout the remainder of the book, which are discussed here. These include the icons used to delineate differences between PL/SQL versions, how I refer to the Oracle documentation, and the location for the online examples.

PL/SQL and Oracle Versions

PL/SQL is contained within the Oracle server. The first version of PL/SQL, 1.0, was released with Oracle version 6. Oracle7 contains PL/SQL 2.0. With Oracle8, the PL/SQL version number was increased to 8 as well. Each subsequent release of the database contains an associated version of PL/SQL, as illustrated in Table 1-1. This table also describes the major new features incorporated in each release. This book discusses PL/SQL versions 2.0 through 8.0. Features available only in specific releases are highlighted by icons, as in:

 This paragraph discusses a feature available with PL/SQL 2.1 and higher, such as the DBMS_SQL package.

 This paragraph discusses a feature available with PL/SQL 2.2 and higher, such as cursor variables.

 This paragraph discusses a feature available with PL/SQL 2.3 and higher, such as the UTL_FILE package.

 This paragraph discusses a feature available with PL/SQL 8.0 and higher, such as object types.

Oracle Version	PL/SQL Version	Features Added or Changed
6	1.0	Initial version
7.0	2.0	CHAR datatype changed to fixed length Subprograms (procedures, functions, packages, and triggers) User-defined composite types—tables and records Intersession communication with the DBMS_PIPE and DBMS_ALERT packages Output in SQL*Plus or Server Manager with the DBMS_OUTPUT package
7.1	2.1	User-defined subtypes Ability to use user-defined functions in SQL statements Dynamic PL/SQL with the DBMS_SQL package
7.2	2.2	Cursor variables User-defined constrained subtypes Ability to schedule PL/SQL batch processing with the DBMS_JOB package
7.3	2.3	Enhancements to cursor variables (allow fetch on server) File I/O with the UTL_FILE package PL/SQL table attributes and tables of records Triggers stored in compiled form
8.0	8.0	Object types and methods Collection types—nested tables and varrays Advanced Queuing option External procedures LOB enhancements

TABLE 1-1. *Oracle and PL/SQL Versions*

It is important to be aware of the PL/SQL release you are using so you can take advantage of the appropriate features. When you connect to the database, the initial string will contain the database version. For example,

```
Connected to:
Personal Oracle7 Release 7.3.2.1.1 - Production Release
With the distributed and replication options
PL/SQL Release 2.3.2.0.0 - Production
```

and

```
Connected to:
Oracle8 Server Release 8.0.3.0.0 - Production
With the distributed, heterogeneous, replication, objects,
parallel query and Spatial Data options
PL/SQL Release 8.0.3.0.0 - Production
```

are both valid initial strings. Note that the PL/SQL release corresponds to the database release.

The majority of the examples in this book were done with Personal Oracle 7.3.2.1.1, running under Microsoft Windows 95. The examples for PL/SQL 8.0 were done against an Oracle8 database running on a Unix system. All of the screen shots were taken under Windows with Personal Oracle running as the database server.

Oracle Documentation

In many sections of the book, I refer you to the Oracle documentation for more information. Because the names of the manuals change with versions, I generally use a shortened version. For example, the *Oracle Server Reference* refers to either the *Oracle7 Server Reference* or the *Oracle8 Server Reference*, depending on which version of Oracle you are using.

Online Code

The CD accompanying this book has three different kinds of information on it:

> 1. A demo version of Platinum's SQL-Station, which runs on Windows 95 or NT. SQL-Station is a PL/SQL development environment that includes a PL/SQL debugger; it is described in Chapters 13, 14, and 22.

2. A demo version of Oracle's WebServer program. The CD includes both a Solaris and NT version. WebServer uses PL/SQL extensively and is described in Chapter 19.

3. The code for the examples used in the book. This code can also be found on Osborne's Oracle Press web page at **http://www.osborne.com/oracle**.

For more information on the CD contents, see the README file in the root directory.

Example Locations

The examples included in the online distribution are identified by a comment on the first line indicating the filename. All of these examples are in the directory named *code* on the CD (and the web page as well), in a subdirectory with the chapter number. For example, consider the following looping example, which we saw earlier in this chapter:

```
-- Available online as simple.sql
DECLARE
  v_LoopCounter BINARY_INTEGER := 1;
BEGIN
  LOOP
    INSERT INTO temp_table (num_col)
      VALUES (v_LoopCounter);
    v_LoopCounter := v_LoopCounter + 1;
    EXIT WHEN v_LoopCounter > 50;
  END LOOP;
END;
```

This example can be found online in the file code/ch01/simple.sql. The file code/readme.txt describes all of the examples.

Example Tables

The examples used in this book operate on a common set of database tables that implement a registration system for a college. There are three main tables: **students**, **classes**, and **rooms**. These contain the main entities necessary for the system. In addition to these main tables, the **registered_students** table contains information about students who have signed up for classes. The following sections detail the structure of these tables, with the SQL necessary to create them.

NOTE
These tables can all be created using the **tables.sql** *script, found in the online distribution. The Oracle8 tables can be found in* **tables8.sql**. *Both scripts are located in the code/ch01 subdirectory. This section documents the Oracle7 tables only; see* **tables8.sql** *for the Oracle8 versions.*

student_sequence

The **student_sequence** sequence is used to generate unique values for the primary key of **students**.

```
CREATE SEQUENCE student_sequence
   START WITH 10000
   INCREMENT BY 1;
```

students

The **students** table contains information about students attending the school.

```
CREATE TABLE students (
   id               NUMBER(5) PRIMARY KEY,
   first_name       VARCHAR2(20),
   last_name        VARCHAR2(20),
   major            VARCHAR2(30),
   current_credits  NUMBER(3)
   );

INSERT INTO students (id, first_name, last_name, major,
                      current_credits)
   VALUES (student_sequence.NEXTVAL, 'Scott', 'Smith',
           'Computer Science', 0);

INSERT INTO students (id, first_name, last_name, major,
                      current_credits)
   VALUES (student_sequence.NEXTVAL, 'Margaret', 'Mason',
           'History', 0);
```

```
INSERT INTO students (id, first_name, last_name, major,
                 current_credits)
  VALUES (student_sequence.NEXTVAL, 'Joanne', 'Junebug',
        'Computer Science', 0);

INSERT INTO students (id, first_name, last_name, major,
                 current_credits)
  VALUES (student_sequence.NEXTVAL, 'Manish', 'Murgratroid',
        'Economics', 0);

INSERT INTO students(id, first_name, last_name, major,
                 current_credits)
  VALUES(student_sequence.NEXTVAL, 'Patrick', 'Poll',
        'History', 0);

INSERT INTO students(id, first_name, last_name, major,
                 current_credits)
  VALUES (student_sequence.NEXTVAL, 'Timothy', 'Taller',
        'History', 0);

INSERT INTO students(id, first_name, last_name, major,
                 current_credits)
  VALUES (student_sequence.NEXTVAL, 'Barbara', 'Blues',
        'Economics', 0);

INSERT INTO students(id, first_name, last_name, major,
                 current_credits)
  VALUES (student_sequence.NEXTVAL, 'David', 'Dinsmore',
        'Music', 0);

INSERT INTO students(id, first_name, last_name, major,
                 current_credits)
  VALUES (student_sequence.NEXTVAL, 'Ester', 'Elegant',
        'Nutrition', 0);

INSERT INTO students(id, first_name, last_name, major,
                 current_credits)
  VALUES (student_sequence.NEXTVAL, 'Rose', 'Riznit',
        'Music', 0);

INSERT INTO STUDENTS(id, first_name, last_name, major,
                 current_credits)

  VALUES (student_sequence.NEXTVAL, 'Rita', 'Razmataz',
        'Nutrition', 0);
```

major_stats
The **major_stats** table holds statistics generated about different majors.

```
CREATE TABLE major_stats (
  major            VARCHAR2(30),
  total_credits    NUMBER,
  total_students   NUMBER);
```

rooms
The **rooms** table holds information about the classrooms available.

```
CREATE TABLE rooms (
  room_id          NUMBER(5) PRIMARY KEY,
  building         VARCHAR2(15),
  room_number      NUMBER(4),
  number_seats     NUMBER(4),
  description      VARCHAR2(50)
  );

INSERT INTO rooms
  (room_id, building, room_number, number_seats, description)
  VALUES (99999, 'Building 7', 310, 1000, 'Large Lecture Hall');

INSERT INTO rooms
  (room_id, building, room_number, number_seats, description)
  VALUES (99998, 'Building 6', 101, 500, 'Small Lecture Hall');

INSERT INTO rooms
  (room_id, building, room_number, number_seats, description)
  VALUES (99997, 'Building 6', 150, 50, 'Discussion Room A');

INSERT INTO rooms
  (room_id, building, room_number, number_seats, description)
  VALUES (99996, 'Building 6', 160, 50, 'Discussion Room B');

INSERT INTO rooms
  (room_id, building, room_number, number_seats, description)
  VALUES (99995, 'Building 6', 170, 50, 'Discussion Room C');

INSERT INTO rooms
  (room_id, building, room_number, number_seats, description)
  VALUES (99994, 'Music Building', 100, 10, 'Music Practice Room');

INSERT INTO rooms
```

```
     (room_id, building, room_number, number_seats, description)
  VALUES (99993, 'Music Building', 200, 1000, 'Concert Room');

INSERT INTO rooms
     (room_id, building, room_number, number_seats, description)
  VALUES (99992, 'Building 7', 300, 75, 'Discussion Room D');

INSERT INTO rooms
     (room_id, building, room_number, number_seats, description)
  VALUES (99991, 'Building 7', 310, 50, 'Discussion Room E');
```

classes

The **classes** table describes the classes available for students to take.

```
CREATE TABLE classes (
   department        CHAR(3),
   course            NUMBER(3),
   description       VARCHAR2(2000),
   max_students      NUMBER(3),
   current_students  NUMBER(3),
   num_credits       NUMBER(1),
   room_id           NUMBER(5),
   CONSTRAINT classes_department_course
     PRIMARY KEY (department, course),
   CONSTRAINT classes_room_id
     FOREIGN KEY (room_id) REFERENCES rooms (room_id)
   );

INSERT INTO classes
   (department, course, description, max_students,
    current_students, num_credits, room_id)
   VALUES ('HIS', 101, 'History 101', 30, 0, 4, 99999);

INSERT INTO classes
   (department, course, description, max_students,
    current_students, num_credits, room_id)
   VALUES ('HIS', 301, 'History 301', 30, 0, 4, 99995);

INSERT INTO classes
   (department, course, description, max_students,
    current_students, num_credits, room_id)
   VALUES ('CS', 101, 'Computer Science 101', 50, 0, 4, 99998);
```

```
INSERT INTO classes
   (department, course, description, max_students,
    current_students, num_credits, room_id)
   VALUES ('ECN', 203, 'Economics 203', 15, 0, 3, 99997);

INSERT INTO classes
   (department, course, description, max_students,
    current_students, num_credits, room_id)
   VALUES ('CS', 102, 'Computer Science 102', 35, 0, 4, 99996);

INSERT INTO classes
   (department, course, description, max_students,
    current_students, num_credits, room_id)
   VALUES ('MUS', 410, 'Music 410', 5, 0, 3, 99994);

INSERT INTO classes
   (department, course, description, max_students,
    current_students, num_credits, room_id)
   VALUES ('ECN', 101, 'Economics 101', 50, 0, 4, 99992);

INSERT INTO classes
   (department, course, description, max_students,
    current_students, num_credits, room_id)
   VALUES ('NUT', 307, 'Nutrition 307', 20, 0, 4, 99991);
```

registered_students

The **registered_students** table contains information about the classes students are currently taking.

```
CREATE TABLE registered_students (
   student_id NUMBER(5) NOT NULL,
   department CHAR(3)   NOT NULL,
   course     NUMBER(3) NOT NULL,
   grade      CHAR(1),
   CONSTRAINT rs_grade
     CHECK (grade IN ('A', 'B', 'C', 'D', 'E')),
   CONSTRAINT rs_student_id
     FOREIGN KEY (student_id) REFERENCES students (id),
   CONSTRAINT rs_department_course
     FOREIGN KEY (department, course)
     REFERENCES classes (department, course)
   );
```

```
INSERT INTO registered_students
  (student_id, department, course, grade)
  VALUES (10000, 'CS', 102, 'A');

INSERT INTO registered_students
  (student_id, department, course, grade)
  VALUES (10002, 'CS', 102, 'B');

INSERT INTO registered_students
  (student_id, department, course, grade)
  VALUES (10003, 'CS', 102, 'C');

INSERT INTO registered_students
  (student_id, department, course, grade)
  VALUES (10000, 'HIS', 101, 'A');

INSERT INTO registered_students
  (student_id, department, course, grade)
  VALUES (10001, 'HIS', 101, 'B');

INSERT INTO registered_students
  (student_id, department, course, grade)
  VALUES (10002, 'HIS', 101, 'B');

INSERT INTO registered_students
  (student_id, department, course, grade)
  VALUES (10003, 'HIS', 101, 'A');

INSERT INTO registered_students
  (student_id, department, course, grade)
  VALUES (10004, 'HIS', 101, 'C');

INSERT INTO registered_students
  (student_id, department, course, grade)
  VALUES (10005, 'HIS', 101, 'C');

INSERT INTO registered_students
  (student_id, department, course, grade)
  VALUES (10006, 'HIS', 101, 'E');

INSERT INTO registered_students
  (student_id, department, course, grade)
  VALUES (10007, 'HIS', 101, 'B');
```

```
INSERT INTO registered_students
  (student_id, department, course, grade)
  VALUES (10008, 'HIS', 101, 'A');

INSERT INTO registered_students
  (student_id, department, course, grade)
  VALUES (10009, 'HIS', 101, 'D');

INSERT INTO registered_students
  (student_id, department, course, grade)
  VALUES (10010, 'HIS', 101, 'A');

INSERT INTO registered_students
  (student_id, department, course, grade)
  VALUES (10008, 'NUT', 307, 'A');

INSERT INTO registered_students
  (student_id, department, course, grade)
  VALUES (10010, 'NUT', 307, 'A');

INSERT INTO registered_students
  (student_id, department, course, grade)
  VALUES (10009, 'MUS', 410, 'B');

INSERT INTO registered_students
  (student_id, department, course, grade)
  VALUES (10006, 'MUS', 410, 'E');
```

RS_audit

The **RS_audit** table is used to record changes made to **registered_students**.

```
CREATE TABLE RS_audit (
  change_type     CHAR(1)      NOT NULL,
  changed_by      VARCHAR2(8)  NOT NULL,
  timestamp       DATE         NOT NULL,
  old_student_id  NUMBER(5),
  old_department  CHAR(3),
  old_course      NUMBER(3),
  old_grade       CHAR(1),
  new_student_id  NUMBER(5),
  new_department  CHAR(3),
  new_course      NUMBER(3),
  new_grade       CHAR(1)
  );
```

log_table

The **log_table** table is used to record Oracle errors.

```
CREATE TABLE log_table (
   code            NUMBER,
   message         VARCHAR2(200),
   info            VARCHAR2(100)
   );
```

temp_table

The **temp_table** table is used to store temporary data that is not necessarily relevant to the other information.

```
CREATE TABLE temp_table (
   num_col    NUMBER,
   char_col   VARCHAR2(60)
   );
```

debug_table

The **debug_table** table is used by the Debug package in Chapter 14 to hold PL/SQL debugging information.

```
CREATE TABLE debug_table (
   linecount   NUMBER,
   debug_str   VARCHAR2(100)
   );
```

Summary

In this chapter, we saw a broad overview of PL/SQL, including the purpose of the language and the major features. We also discussed the importance of PL/SQL and database versions and how they correspond. The chapter concluded with a description of the accompanying CD and the example tables used in this book. In the next chapter, we will begin our detailed discussion of the language, with the syntax and constructs of PL/SQL.

CHAPTER
2

PL/SQL Basics

efore talking about the advanced features of PL/SQL, we must cover the basic syntax. The syntax rules form the building blocks for any programming language, PL/SQL included. This chapter discusses the components of a PL/SQL block, explains variable declarations and datatypes, presents the basic procedural constructs, and gives you a brief introduction to cursors and subprograms. It also covers PL/SQL programming style and shows you handy techniques that will help you write elegant, easily understandable code.

All PL/SQL statements are either procedural or SQL statements. *Procedural statements* include variable declarations, procedure calls, and looping constructs. *SQL statements* are used to access the database. This chapter and Chapter 3 focus on the procedural statements of PL/SQL, while Chapters 4, 5, and 6 cover SQL statements.

The PL/SQL Block

The basic unit in any PL/SQL program is the block. All PL/SQL programs are composed of blocks, which can occur sequentially (one after the other) can be or nested (one inside the other). There are several different kinds of blocks:

- *Anonymous blocks* are generally constructed dynamically and executed only once.

- *Named blocks* are anonymous blocks with a label that gives the block a name. These are also generally constructed dynamically and executed only once.

- *Subprograms* are procedures, packages, and functions that are stored in the database. These blocks generally don't change once they are constructed, and they are executed many times. Subprograms are executed explicitly via a call to the procedure, package, or function.

- *Triggers* are named blocks that are also stored in the database. They also generally don't change once they are constructed and are executed many times. Triggers are executed implicitly whenever the triggering event occurs. The triggering event is a data manipulation language (DML) statement executed against a table in the database. DML statements include INSERT, UPDATE, and DELETE.

For example, the following is an anonymous PL/SQL block that inserts two rows into the **temp_table** database table, and selects them back, and echoes them to the screen:

```
-- Available online as anon.sql
DECLARE
  /* Declare variables to be used in this block. */
  v_Num1      NUMBER := 1;
  v_Num2      NUMBER := 2;
  v_String1   VARCHAR2(50) := 'Hello World!';
  v_String2   VARCHAR2(50) := '-- This message brought to you
                              by PL/SQL!';
  v_OutputStr VARCHAR2(50);
BEGIN
  /* First, insert two rows into temp_table, using the values of
     the variables. */
  INSERT INTO temp_table (num_col, char_col)
    VALUES (v_Num1, v_String1);
  INSERT INTO temp_table (num_col, char_col)
    VALUES (v_Num2, v_String2);

  /* Now query temp_table for the two rows we just inserted, and
     output them to the screen using the DBMS_OUTPUT package. */
  SELECT char_col
    INTO v_OutputStr
  FROM temp_table
  WHERE num_col = v_Num1;
  DBMS_OUTPUT.PUT_LINE(v_OutputStr);

  SELECT char_col
    INTO v_OutputStr
  FROM temp_table
  WHERE num_col = v_Num2;
  DBMS_OUTPUT.PUT_LINE(v_OutputStr);
END;
```

NOTE
*In order to run the above example, along with most of the other examples in this book, you need to create several database tables, including **temp_table**. These can all be created using the tables.sql script, which can be found on the accompanying CD. Furthermore, many of the examples are online as well. The filenames are indicated at the beginning of each example, and can also be found in the README file on the CD. For more information on the CD and its contents, including a description of the sample tables, see Chapter 1. For more information on the DBMS_OUTPUT package, see Chapter 14.*

In order to name this block, we put a label before the DECLARE keyword, as in the next example. The label can optionally appear after the END keyword as well. Labels will be discussed in more detail later in this chapter.

```
-- Available online as labeled.sql
<<l_InsertIntoTemp>>
DECLARE
  /* Declare variables to be used in this block. */
  v_Num1      NUMBER := 3;
  v_Num2      NUMBER := 4;
  v_String1   VARCHAR2(50) := 'Hello World!';
  v_String2   VARCHAR2(50) := '-- This message brought to you
                              by PL/SQL!';
  v_OutputStr VARCHAR2(50);
BEGIN
  /* First, insert two rows into temp_table, using the values of
     the variables. */
  INSERT INTO temp_table (num_col, char_col)
    VALUES (v_Num1, v_String1);
  INSERT INTO temp_table (num_col, char_col)
    VALUES (v_Num2, v_String2);

  /* Now query temp_table for the two rows we just inserted, and
```

```
    output them to the screen using the DBMS_OUTPUT package. */
  SELECT char_col
    INTO v_OutputStr
  FROM temp_table
  WHERE num_col = v_Num1;
  DBMS_OUTPUT.PUT_LINE(v_OutputStr);

  SELECT char_col
    INTO v_OutputStr
  FROM temp_table
  WHERE num_col = v_Num2;
  DBMS_OUTPUT.PUT_LINE(v_OutputStr);
END l_InsertIntoTemp;
```

We can make this block into a stored procedure by replacing the DECLARE keyword with the CREATE OR REPLACE PROCEDURE keywords. Procedures are discussed in more detail in Chapter 7. Again, note that the procedure name is used after the END keyword.

```
-- Available online as proc.sql
CREATE OR REPLACE PROCEDURE InsertIntoTemp AS
  /* Declare variables to be used in this block. */
  v_Num1      NUMBER := 5;
  v_Num2      NUMBER := 6;
  v_String1   VARCHAR2(50) := 'Hello World!';
  v_String2   VARCHAR2(50) := '-- This message brought to you
                              by PL/SQL!';
  v_OutputStr VARCHAR2(50);
BEGIN
  /* First, insert two rows into temp_table, using the values of
     the variables. */
  INSERT INTO temp_table (num_col, char_col)
    VALUES (v_Num1, v_String1);
  INSERT INTO temp_table (num_col, char_col)
    VALUES (v_Num2, v_String2);

  /* Now query temp_table for the two rows we just inserted, and
     output them to the screen using the DBMS_OUTPUT package. */
  SELECT char_col
    INTO v_OutputStr
  FROM temp_table
  WHERE num_col = v_Num1;
  DBMS_OUTPUT.PUT_LINE(v_OutputStr);
```

```
SELECT char_col
  INTO v_OutputStr
FROM temp_table
WHERE num_col = v_Num2;
DBMS_OUTPUT.PUT_LINE(v_OutputStr);
END InsertIntoTemp;
```

Finally, we can construct a trigger on the **temp_table** table to ensure that only positive values are put into **num_col**. Triggers are discussed in more detail in Chapter 9. This trigger will be called whenever a new row is inserted into **temp_table** or an existing row is updated.

```
-- Available online as trigger.sql
CREATE OR REPLACE TRIGGER OnlyPositive
  BEFORE INSERT OR UPDATE OF num_col
  ON temp_table
  FOR EACH ROW
BEGIN
  IF :new.num_col < 0 THEN
    RAISE_APPLICATION_ERROR(-20100, 'Please insert a positive
value');
  END IF;
END OnlyPositive;
```

Basic Block Structure

All blocks have three distinct sections—the declarative section, executable section, and exception section. Only the executable section is required; the other two are optional. For example, here is an anonymous block with all three sections:

```
-- Available online as allthree.sql
DECLARE
  /* Start of declarative section */
  v_StudentID NUMBER(5) := 10000;   -- Numeric variable initialized
                                    -- to 10,000
  v_FirstName VARCHAR2(20);         -- Variable length character
                                    -- string
                                    -- with maximum length of 20
BEGIN
  /* Start of executable section */
  -- Retrieve first name of student with ID 10,000
  SELECT first_name
    INTO v_FirstName
```

```
      FROM students
       WHERE id = v_StudentID;
   EXCEPTION
     /* Start of exception section */
     WHEN NO_DATA_FOUND THEN
        -- Handle the error condition
        INSERT INTO log_table (info)
           VALUES ('Student 10,000 does not exist!');
   END;
```

NOTE
This example references two additional tables which are created by tables.sql — **students** *and* **log_table**. *Again, see Chapter 1 for the complete description of the sample schema.*

The *declarative section* is where all variables, cursors, and types used by this block are located. Local procedures and functions can also be declared in this section. These subprograms will be available for this block only. We will discuss the components of the declarative section in more detail in the rest of this chapter and Chapter 3.

The *executable section* is where the work of the block is done. Both SQL statements and procedural statements can appear in this section. Chapters 4, 5, and 6 cover the contents of the executable section.

Errors are handled in the *exception section*. Code in this section is not executed unless an error occurs. Chapter 10 deals with the exception section and how it is used to detect and handle errors.

The keywords DECLARE, BEGIN, EXCEPTION, and END delimit each section. The final semicolon is also required—this is a syntactic part of the block. Based on this, the skeleton of an anonymous block looks like this:

```
DECLARE
    /* Declarative section is here */
BEGIN
    /* Executable section is here */
EXCEPTION
    /* Exception section is here */
END;
```

NOTE
The DECLARE keyword is not necessary when creating a procedure. In fact, it is an error to use it. However, DECLARE is required when creating a trigger. See Chapters 7-9 for more information.

If the declarative section is absent, the block starts with the BEGIN keyword. If the exception section is absent, the EXCEPTION keyword is omitted, and the END keyword followed by a semicolon finishes the block. So a block with just the executable section would be structured as,

```
BEGIN
    /* Executable section is here */
END;
```

while a block with declarative and executable sections, but no exception section, would look like this:

```
DECLARE
    /* Declarative section is here */
BEGIN
    /* Executable section is here */
END;
```

NOTE
The statements in the preceding blocks delimited by /* and */ are comments. Comments are discussed in more detail in the following section.

Lexical Units

Any PL/SQL program is made up of lexical units—the building blocks of a language. Essentially, a *lexical unit* is a sequence of characters, in the character set allowed for the PL/SQL language. This character set includes

- Upper- and lowercase letters: A-Z and a-z
- Digits: 0-9

- ■ White space: tabs, spaces, and carriage returns
- ■ Mathematical symbols: + − * / < > =
- ■ Punctuation symbols: ( ) { } [ ] ? ! ~ ; : . ' " @ # % $ ^ & _ |

Any symbol in the character set, and only the symbols in the character set, can be used as part of a PL/SQL program. Like SQL, PL/SQL is not case-sensitive. Thus, upper- and lowercase letters are equivalent, except inside quoted strings.

The standard PL/SQL character set is part of the ASCII character set. ASCII is a single-byte character set, which means that every character can be represented as one byte of data. This limits the total number of characters to 256. Oracle does have support for other multibyte character sets, which have more than 256 characters. These are necessary to represent languages that do not use the English alphabet. A full discussion of multibyte characters is beyond the scope of this book—consult the Oracle documentation for more information.

Lexical units can be classified as identifiers, delimiters, literals, and comments.

Identifiers

Identifiers are used to name PL/SQL objects, such as variables, cursors, types, and subprograms. Identifiers consist of a letter optionally followed by any sequence of characters, including letters, numbers, dollar signs, underscores, and pound signs. Other characters are illegal. The maximum length for an identifier is 30 characters, and all characters are significant. For example, here are some legal identifiers:

```
x
v_StudentID
TempVar
v1
v2_
social_security_#
```

Here are some illegal identifiers:

```
x+y                         -- Illegal character +
_temp_                      -- Must start with a letter,
```

```
                                     not an underscore
First Name                        -- Illegal space
This_is_a_really_long_identifier  -- More than 30 characters
1_variable                        -- Can't start with a digit
```

Since PL/SQL is not case-sensitive, the following identifiers all mean the same thing to PL/SQL:

```
Room_Description
room_description
ROOM_DESCRIPTION
rOOm_DEscriPTIOn
```

It is good programming practice to have a consistent naming scheme for identifiers and to make them descriptive. See the "PL/SQL Style Guide" at the end of this chapter for more information.

Reserved Words

Many identifiers, known as *reserved words* (or keywords), have special meaning to PL/SQL. It is illegal to use these words to name your own identifiers. For example, BEGIN and END are used to delimit PL/SQL blocks. Thus you cannot use them as variable names. The following declarative section is illegal and will generate a compile error, since "begin" is a reserved word:

```
DECLARE
  begin NUMBER;
```

These words are only reserved when used as identifiers by themselves. They can appear within other identifiers. For example, the following declarative section is legal, even though 'date' is reserved:

```
DECLARE
  v_BeginDate DATE;
```

In this book, reserved words are written in uppercase to improve readability. See the "PL/SQL Style Guide" at the end of this chapter for more information. Appendix A contains a complete list of reserved words.

Quoted Identifiers

If you want to make an identifier case-sensitive, include characters such as spaces, or use a reserved word, you can enclose the identifier in double quotation marks. For example, all of the following are legal and distinct identifiers:

```
"A number"
"Linda's variable"
"x/y"
"X/Y"
```

Like nonquoted identifiers, the maximum length of a quoted identifier is 30 characters (not including the double quotes). Any printable character is legal as part of a quoted identifier except a double quote.

Quoted identifiers can be useful when you want to use a PL/SQL reserved word in an SQL statement. PL/SQL reserves more words than SQL (this is also indicated by the chart in Appendix A). For example, if you wanted to query a table with a column called "exception" (a reserved word), you could access it with

```
DECLARE
  v_Exception    VARCHAR2(10);
BEGIN
  SELECT "EXCEPTION"
    INTO v_Exception
    FROM exception_table;
END;
```

Note that **"EXCEPTION"** is in uppercase. All identifiers are stored in uppercase in the data dictionary, unless explicitly created as a quoted lowercase identifier in the table CREATE statement.

I don't recommend using reserved words for identifiers, even though it is legal. It is poor programming style and can make the program more difficult to understand. The only case where this may become necessary is when a database table uses a PL/SQL reserved word for a column name. Because PL/SQL has more reserved words than SQL, a table may have a column that is a PL/SQL reserved word, but not an SQL reserved word. The **exception_table** table in the previous example illustrates this case.

TIP
Although the **exception_table** *table can still be used in PL/SQL, it is better to rename the offending column. If the table definition cannot be changed, a view can be created with an alternate name for the column. This view can then be used in PL/SQL. For example, suppose we create* **exception_table** *as follows:*

```
-- Available online as part of tables.sql
CREATE TABLE exception_table (
  exception       VARCHAR2(20),
  date_occurred   DATE);
```

Given this definition, we can create a view with

```
CREATE VIEW exception_view AS
  SELECT exception  exception_description,
         date_occurred
    FROM exception_table;
```

We can now use **exception_view** *instead of* **exception_table***, and the column can now be referred to as* **exception_description***, which is not reserved.*

Delimiters

Delimiters are symbols (either a single character or a sequence of characters) that have special meaning to PL/SQL. They are used to separate identifiers from each other. Table 2-1 lists the delimiters available to PL/SQL.

Literals

A *literal* is a character, numeric, or boolean value that is not an identifier. As an example, −23.456 and NULL are both literals. The boolean,

Symbol	Description	Symbol	Description
+	Addition operator	-	Subtraction operator
*	Multiplication operator	/	Division operator
=	Equality operator	<	Less-than operator
>	Greater-than operator	(	Initial expression delimiter
)	Final expression delimiter	;	Statement terminator
%	Attribute indicator	,	Item separator
.	Component selector	@	Database link indicator
'	Character string delimiter	"	Quoted string delimiter
:	Bind variable indicator	**	Exponentiation operator
<>	Not-equal-to operator	!=	Not-equal-to operator (equivalent to <>)
~=	Not-equal-to operator (equivalent to !=)	^=	Not-equal-to operator (equivalent to ~=)
<=	Less-than-or-equal-to operator	>=	Greater-than-or-equal-to operator
:=	Assignment operator	=>	Association operator
..	Range operator	||	String concatenation operator
<<	Begin label delimiter	>>	End label delimiter
—	Single line comment indicator	/*	Initial multiline comment indicator
*/	Final multiline comment indicator	<space>	Space
<tab>	Tab character	<cr>	Carriage return

TABLE 2-1. *PL/SQL Delimiters*

character, and numeric types are discussed in the section "PL/SQL Types" later in this chapter.

Character Literals

Character literals, also known as string literals, consist of one or more characters delimited by single quotes. Character literals can be assigned to variables of type CHAR or VARCHAR2 without conversion. For example, all of the following are legal string literals:

```
'12345'
'Four score and seven years ago...'
'100%'
'"'
```

All string literals are considered to have the datatype CHAR. Any printable character in the PL/SQL character set can be part of a literal, including another single quote. Since a single quote is also used to delimit the literal, to include a single quote as part of the string, place two single quotes next to each other. For example, to put the string "Mike's string" into a literal, we would use

```
'Mike''s string'
```

Thus, in PL/SQL, the string that consists of just a single quote would be identified by

```
''''
```

The first single quote delimits the start of the string, the next two identify the single character in the string (which happens to be a single quote), and the fourth quote delimits the end of the string. Note that this is different from the literal

```
''
```

which denotes a zero-length string. In PL/SQL, the zero-length string literal is considered identical to NULL.

Numeric Literals

A numeric literal represents either an integer or real value. Numeric literals can be assigned to variables of type NUMBER without conversion. These are the only literals that are valid as part of arithmetic expressions. Integer literals consist of an optional sign (+ or -) followed by digits. No decimal point is allowed for an integer literal. The following are legal integer literals:

```
123
-7
+12
0
```

A real literal consists of an optional sign followed by digits containing one decimal point. The following are all legal real literals:

```
-17.1
23.0
3.
```

Even though **23.0** and **3.** actually contain numbers with no fractional part, they are still considered real literals by PL/SQL. Real literals can also be written using scientific notation if desired. The following are also legal real literals:

```
1.345E7
9.87E-3
-7.12e+12
```

After the **E** or **e**, there can be only an integer literal. The **E** stands for "exponent" and can be interpreted as "times 10 to the power of." So the preceding three values can also be read as

```
1.345E7 = 1.345 times 10 to the power of 7
        = 1.345 x 10,000,000 = 13,450,000
9.87E-3 = 9.87 times 10 to the power of -3
        = 9.87 x .001 = 0.00987
-7.12e+12 = -7.12 times 10 to the power of 12
        = -7.12 x 1,000,000,000,000
        = -7,120,000,000,000
```

(The commas are included for readability—commas are not allowed in numeric literals.)

Boolean Literals

There are only three possible boolean literals: TRUE, FALSE, and NULL. These values can only be assigned to a boolean variable. Boolean literals represent the truth or falsity of conditions and are used in IF and LOOP statements.

Comments

Comments improve readability and make your programs more understandable. They are ignored by the PL/SQL compiler. There are two kinds of comments: single-line comments and multiline or C-style comments.

Single-line Comments

A single-line comment starts with two dashes and continues until the end of the line (delimited by a carriage return). Given the PL/SQL block

```
-- Available online as part of comments.sql
DECLARE
  v_Department  CHAR(3);
  v_Course      NUMBER;
BEGIN
  INSERT INTO classes (department, course)
    VALUES (v_Department, v_Course);
END;
```

we can add single-line comments to make this block more understandable. For example:

```
-- Available online as part of comments.sql
DECLARE
  v_Department  CHAR(3);   -- Variable to hold the 3 character
                           -- department code
  v_Course      NUMBER;    -- Variable to hold the course number
BEGIN
  -- Insert the course identified by v_Department and v_Course
  -- into the classes table in the database.
  INSERT INTO classes (department, course)
    VALUES (v_Department, v_Course);
END;
```

NOTE
If the comment extends over more than one line, the double dash (– –) is necessary at the start of each line.

Multiline Comments

Multiline comments start with the **/*** delimiter and end with the ***/**
delimiter. This is the comment style as used in the C language. For example:

```
-- Available online as part of comments.sql
DECLARE
  v_Department   CHAR(3);   /* Variable to hold the 3 character
                              department name */
  v_Course       NUMBER;    /* Variable to hold the course
                              number */
BEGIN
  /* Insert the course identified by v_Department and v_Course
     into the classes table in the database. */
  INSERT INTO classes (department, course)
    VALUES (v_Department, v_Course);
END;
```

Multiline comments can extend over as many lines as desired.
However, they cannot be nested. One comment has to end before another
can begin. The following block is illegal because it contains nested
comments.

```
-- Available online as part of comments.sql
BEGIN
  /* We are now inside a comment. If we were to begin another
     comment such as /* this */ it would be illegal. */
  NULL;
END;
```

Variable Declarations

Communication with the database takes place through variables in the
PL/SQL block. *Variables* are memory locations, which can store data
values. As the program runs, the contents of variables can and do change.
Information from the database can be assigned to a variable, or the contents
of a variable can be inserted into the database. These variables are declared
in the declarative section of the block. Every variable has a specific type as
well, which describes what kind of information can be stored in it. Types
are discussed shortly.

Declaration Syntax

Variables are declared in the declarative section of the block. The general syntax for declaring a variable is

> *variable_name type* [CONSTANT] [NOT NULL] [:= *value*];

where *variable_name* is the name of the variable, *type* is the type, and *value* is the initial value of the variable. For example, the following are all legal variable declarations:

```
DECLARE
    v_Description     VARCHAR2(50);
    v_NumberSeats     NUMBER := 45;
    v_Counter         BINARY_INTEGER := 0;
```

Any legal PL/SQL identifier (as defined earlier in the section "Lexical Units") can be used as a variable name. **VARCHAR2**, **NUMBER**, and **BINARY_INTEGER** are valid PL/SQL types. In this example, **v_NumberSeats** and **v_Counter** are both initialized, to 45 and 0, respectively. If a variable is not initialized, such as **v_Description**, it is assigned NULL by default. If NOT NULL is present in the declaration, then the variable must be initialized. Furthermore, it is illegal to assign NULL to a variable constrained to be NOT NULL in the executable or exception section of the block. The following declaration is illegal because **v_TempVar** is constrained to be NOT NULL, but is not initialized:

```
DECLARE
    v_TempVar  NUMBER NOT NULL;
```

We can correct this by assigning a default value to **v_TempVar**, for example:

```
DECLARE
    v_TempVar  NUMBER NOT NULL := 0;
```

If CONSTANT is present in the variable declaration, the variable must be initialized, and its value cannot be changed from this initial value. A constant variable is treated as read-only for the remainder of the block.

Constants are often used for values that are known when the block is written, for example:

```
DECLARE
  c_MinimumStudentID  CONSTANT NUMBER(5) := 10000;
```

If desired, the keyword DEFAULT can be used instead of := as well. For example:

```
DECLARE
  v_NumberSeats   NUMBER DEFAULT 45;
  v_Counter       BINARY_INTEGER DEFAULT 0;
  v_FirstName     VARCHAR2(20) DEFAULT 'Scott';
```

There can be only one variable declaration per line in the declarative section. The following section is illegal, since two variables are declared on the same line:

```
DECLARE
  v_FirstName, v_LastName  VARCHAR2(20);
```

The correct version of this block would be

```
DECLARE
  v_FirstName VARCHAR2(20);
  v_LastName  VARCHAR2(20);
```

Variable Initialization

Many languages do not define what uninitialized variables contain. As a result, uninitialized variables can contain random or unknown values at run time. In a language such as this, leaving uninitialized variables is not good programming style. In general, it is best to initialize a variable if its value can be determined.

PL/SQL, however, does define what an uninitialized variable contains—it is assigned NULL. NULL simply means "missing or unknown value." As a result, it is logical that NULL be assigned by default to any uninitialized variable. This is a unique feature of PL/SQL. Many other programming languages (C and Ada included) do not define the value for uninitialized variables.

PL/SQL Types

PL/SQL versions 1 and 2 have three categories of types—scalar, composite, and reference. PL/SQL 8.0 defines an additional type category—the LOB types. Scalar datatypes do not have any components within the type, while composite types do. A reference type is a pointer to another type. Figure 2-1 lists all of the PL/SQL types, and they are described in the following sections.

PL/SQL types are defined in a package called STANDARD. The contents of this package are available to any PL/SQL block. Besides types, package STANDARD defines the built-in SQL and conversion functions available in PL/SQL.

SCALAR TYPES	
Numeric Family:	Character Family:
BINARY_INTEGER	CHAR
DEC	CHARACTER
DECIMAL	LONG
DOUBLE PRECISION	NCHAR[1]
FLOAT	NVARCHAR2[1]
INT	STRING
INTEGER	VARCHAR
N ATURAL	VARCHAR2
NATURALN1	
NUMBER	Boolean Family:
NUMERIC	BOOLEAN
PLS_INTEGER[2]	
POSITIVE	Date Family:
POSITIVEN[1]	DATE
REAL	
SIGNTYPE[1]	Trusted Family
SMALLINT	MLSLABEL

COMPOSITE TYPES
RECORD
TABLE
VARRAY[1]

REFERENCE TYPES
REF CURSOR
REF *object type*[1]

LOB TYPES
BFILE
LOB
CLOB
NLOB

FIGURE 2-1.   *PL/SQL Types*

[1]This type is available in PL/SQL 3.0 and higher
[2]This type is available in PL/SQL 2.3 and higher

Scalar Types

The legal scalar types consist of the same types valid for a database column, with a number of additions. Scalar types can be divided into seven families—numeric, character, raw, date, rowid, boolean, and trusted—each of which is described in the following sections.

Numeric Family

Types in the numeric family store integer or real values. There are three basic types—NUMBER, PLS_INTEGER, and BINARY_INTEGER. Variables of type NUMBER can hold either an integer or real quantity, and variables of type BINARY_INTEGER or PLS_INTEGER can hold only integers.

NUMBER   This type can hold a numeric value, either integer or floating point. It is the same as the NUMBER database type. The syntax for declaring a number is

NUMBER (*P,S*);

where *P* is the precision and *S* is the scale. The precision is the number of digits in the value, and the scale is the number of digits to the right of the decimal point. Both precision and scale are optional, but if scale is present, precision must be present as well. Table 2-2 shows different combinations of precision and scale and their meanings.

The maximum precision is 38, and the scale ranges from −84 to 127.

A *subtype* is an alternate name for a type, which can optionally constrain the legal values for a variable of the subtype. Subtypes are explained in detail in the "User-Defined Subtypes" section later in this chapter. There are a number of subtypes that are equivalent to NUMBER, which essentially rename the NUMBER datatype, since none of them are constrained. You may want to use an alternate name for readability, or for compatibility with datatypes from other databases. The equivalent types are

- DEC
- DECIMAL
- DOUBLE PRECISION
- INTEGER

- INT
- NUMERIC
- REAL
- SMALLINT

BINARY_INTEGER The NUMBER type is stored in a decimal format, which is optimized for accuracy and storage efficiency. Because of this, arithmetic operations can't be performed directly on NUMBERs. In order to compute using numeric quantities, NUMBERs must be converted into a binary type. The PL/SQL engine will do this automatically if you have an arithmetic expression involving NUMBERs, and will convert the result back to NUMBER if necessary.

However, if you have a value that won't be stored in the database, but will only be used for computations, the BINARY_INTEGER datatype is available. This datatype is used to store signed integer values, which range from ™2147483647 to +2147483647. It is stored in a 2's complement binary format, which means that it is available for computations without conversion. Loop counters are often of type BINARY_INTEGER.

Declaration	Assigned Value	Stored Value
NUMBER;	1234.5678	1234.5678
NUMBER(3);	123	123
NUMBER(3);	1234	Error—exceeds precision
NUMBER(4,3);	123.4567	Error—exceeds precision
NUMBER(4,3);	1.234567	1.235[1]
NUMBER(7,2)	12345.67	12345.67
NUMBER(3,™3)	1234	1000[2]
NUMBER(3, ™1)	1234	1230[2]

TABLE 2-2. *Precision and Scale Values*

[1] If the assigned value exceeds the scale, the store value is rounded to the number of digits specified by the scale.

[2] If the scale is negative, the stored value is rounded to the number of digits specified by the scale.

Like NUMBER, there are subtypes defined for BINARY_INTEGER. Unlike the NUMBER subtypes, however, the BINARY_INTEGER subtypes are *constrained*, which means that they can only hold restricted values. These constrained subtypes of BINARY_INTEGER are listed in Table 2-3.

PLS_INTEGER   PLS_INTEGERs have the same range as BINARY_INTEGERs, from –2147483647 to +2147483647, and are also implemented using the native 2's complement format. However, when a calculation involving a PLS_INTEGER overflows, an error is raised. If a calculation involving a BINARY_INTEGER overflows, the result can be assigned to a NUMBER variable (which has a greater range) with no error.

Character Family

Variables in the character family are used to hold strings, or character data. The types in the character family are VARCHAR2, CHAR, and LONG, along with NCHAR and NVARCHAR2 (the latter two available with PL/SQL 8.0 and higher).

VARCHAR2   This type behaves similarly to the VARCHAR2 database type. Variables of type VARCHAR2 can hold variable length character strings, with a maximum length. The syntax for declaring a VARCHAR2 variable is

        VARCHAR2(*L*);

Subtype	Constraint
NATURAL	0..2147483647
NATURALN	0..2147483647 NOT NULL
POSITIVE	1..2147483647
POSITIVEN	1..2147483647 NOT NULL
SIGNTYPE	–1, 0, 1

TABLE 2-3.   *BINARY_INTEGER Subtypes*

where *L* is the maximum length of the variable. The length is required—there is no default. The maximum length for a VARCHAR2 variable is 32,767 bytes. Note that a VARCHAR2 database column can only hold 2,000 bytes. If a VARCHAR2 PL/SQL variable is more than 2,000 bytes, it can only be inserted into a database column of type LONG, which has a maximum length of 2 gigabytes. Likewise, LONG data cannot be selected into a VARCHAR2 variable unless it is 2,000 bytes or less in length.

NOTE
In Oracle8, a VARCHAR2 database column can hold 4,000 bytes. Thus a PL/SQL VARCHAR2 can be inserted into an Oracle8 VARCHAR2 column only if it is less than or equal to 4,000 bytes in length.

The length of a VARCHAR2 is specified in bytes, not in characters. The actual data is stored in the character set for your database, which could be ASCII or EBCDIC Code Page 500, for example. If the database character contains multibyte characters, the maximum number of characters that a VARCHAR2 variable can hold may be less than the length specified. This is because a single character may take more than one byte to represent.

The subtype VARCHAR is equivalent to VARCHAR2.

CHAR   Variables of this type are fixed-length character strings. The syntax for declaring a CHAR variable is

    CHAR(*L*);

where *L* is the maximum length, in bytes. Unlike VARCHAR2, however, specifying the length is optional. If it is not specified, it defaults to 1. If the length isn't specified, then the parenthesis shouldn't be included, either. Since CHAR variables are fixed-length, they are blank-padded if necessary to fill out the maximum length. Because they are blank-padded, CHAR variables won't necessarily match in a character comparison. See the section "Boolean Expressions" later in this chapter for more information on character comparisons.

The maximum length of a CHAR variable is 32,767 bytes. The maximum length of a CHAR database column is 255 bytes. Therefore, if a

CHAR variable contains more than 255 bytes, it can only be inserted into a VARCHAR2 or LONG database column. Similarly, LONG data can only be selected into a CHAR variable if it is less than 32,767 bytes.

NOTE
In Oracle8, CHAR database columns can hold up to 2,000 bytes.

Like VARCHAR2, the length of a CHAR variable is specified in bytes, not characters. If the database character set contains multibyte characters, the maximum number of characters a CHAR variable can hold may be less than the length specified.

CHARACTER is a subtype for CHAR, with the same restrictions. VARCHAR2 and CHAR variables have significantly different semantics (see the section "Boolean Expressions" later in this chapter for more information).

LONG   Unlike the database LONG type, which can hold up to 2 gigabytes of data, the PL/SQL LONG type is a variable length string with a maximum length of 32,760 bytes. LONG variables are very similar to VARCHAR2 variables. Similar to the behavior for VARCHAR2 variables, if a LONG database column contains more than 32,760 bytes of data, it cannot be selected into a PL/SQL LONG variable. However, since the maximum length of a PL/SQL LONG is less than a database LONG, a PL/SQL LONG can be inserted into a database column of type LONG with no restrictions.

PL/SQL 8.0 ...and HIGHER **NCHAR AND NVARCHAR2**   Oracle8 provides two additional database types, which are included in PL/SQL 8.0. These are the NLS character types NCHAR and NVARCHAR2. *NLS character types* are used to store character strings in a different character set from the PL/SQL language itself. This character set is known as the *national character set*.

NCHARs and NVARCHAR2s are specified the same way as CHARs and VARCHAR2s. However, the specification for the length can vary depending on the national character set. If the national character set is fixed width, the length is specified in characters. If the national character set is variable width, the length is specified in bytes.

For more information on NCHAR, NVARCHAR2, and NLS in general, see the *Oracle8 Server SQL Reference*.

Raw Family

The types in the raw family are used to store binary data. Character variables are automatically converted between character sets by Oracle if necessary. This can happen if the data is being passed via a database link between two databases, each using different character sets. This will not happen for raw variables.

RAW   RAW variables are similar to CHAR variables, except that they are not converted between character sets. The syntax for specifying a RAW variable is

    RAW(L);

where L is the length in bytes of the variable. RAW is used to store fixed-length binary data. Unlike character data, RAW data is not converted between character sets when transmitted between two different databases. The maximum length of a RAW variable is 32,767 bytes. The maximum length of a RAW database column is 255 bytes. So if the data is more than 255 bytes in length, it cannot be inserted into a RAW database column. It can be inserted, however, into a LONG RAW database column; which has a maximum length of 2 gigabytes. Similarly, if the data in a LONG RAW database column is more than 32,767 bytes in length, it cannot be selected into a PL/SQL RAW variable.

LONG RAW   LONG RAW data is similar to LONG data, except that PL/SQL will not convert between character sets. The maximum length of a LONG RAW variable is 32,760 bytes. Again, since the maximum length of a database LONG RAW column is 2 gigabytes, if the actual length of the data is more than 32,760 bytes in length, it cannot be selected into a PL/SQL LONG RAW variable. But since the maximum length of a PL/SQL LONG RAW will fit into a database LONG RAW, there are no restrictions on insertion of a PL/SQL LONG RAW into a database LONG RAW.

Date Family

There is only one type in the date family—DATE. The DATE PL/SQL type behaves the same way as the DATE database type. The DATE type is used to store both date and time information, including the century, year, month, day, hour, minute, and second. A DATE variable is 7 bytes, with one byte for each component (century through second).

Values are usually assigned to DATE variables via the TO_DATE built-in function. This allows character variables to be converted to DATE variables with ease. Likewise, the TO_CHAR function can convert from DATE to character. The built-in conversion functions are described in the "Converting Between Datatypes" section later in this chapter, and also in Chapter 3.

Rowid Family

The only type in the rowid family is ROWID. The ROWID PL/SQL type is the same as the database ROWID pseudocolumn type. It can hold a *rowid*, which can be thought of as a unique key for every row in the database. Rowids are stored internally as a fixed-length binary quantity, whose length varies between operating systems. In order to manipulate rowids, they can be converted to character strings via the built-in function ROWIDTOCHAR. The output of this function is an 18-character string with format

```
BBBBBBBB.RRRR.FFFF
```

where BBBBBBBB identifies the block within a database file, RRRR the row within the block, and FFFF the file number. Each component of a rowid is represented as a hexadecimal number. For example, the rowid

```
0000001E.00FF.0001
```

identifies the 30th block, the 255th row within this block, in file 1. Rowids are not generally constructed by a PL/SQL program; they are selected from the ROWID pseudocolumn of a table. This value can then be used in the where clause of a subsequent UPDATE or DELETE statement.

PL/SQL 8.0 ...and HIGHER Oracle8 provides an extended ROWID type, which includes support for partitioned tables and indexes. This is done by including a *data object number*, which identifies the database segment. This extended ROWID format is manipulated with the DBMS_ROWID package, described in Appendix B.

Boolean Family

The only datatype in the boolean family is BOOLEAN. Boolean variables are used in PL/SQL control structures, such as IF-THEN-ELSE and LOOP statements. A BOOLEAN value can hold TRUE, FALSE, or NULL only. Thus, the following declarative section is illegal since 0 is not a valid BOOLEAN value:

```
DECLARE
  v_ContinueFlag  BOOLEAN := 0;
```

Trusted Family

The only datatype in the trusted family is MLSLABEL. This datatype is used in Trusted Oracle to store variable length binary labels. With standard Oracle, variables and table columns of type MLSLABEL can only hold the value NULL. Internally, MLSLABEL variables are between 2 and 5 bytes in length. However, they can be converted to and from a character variable automatically. The maximum length of a character representation of an MLSLABEL is 255 bytes.

Composite Types

The three composite types available in PL/SQL are records, tables, and varrays. A *composite type* is one that has components within it. A variable of a composite type contains one or more scalar variables. The composite types are discussed in detail in the next chapter.

Reference Types

PL/SQL **2.2** ...and HIGHER Once a variable is declared of a scalar or composite type in PL/SQL, the memory storage for this variable is allocated. The variable names this storage and is used to refer to it later in the program. However, there is no way to deallocate the storage and still have the variable remain available—the memory is not freed until the variable is no longer in scope. (See the section "Variable Scope and Visibility" later in this chapter for information on scope.) A reference type does not have this restriction. A reference type in PL/SQL is the same as a pointer in C. A variable that is declared of a reference type can point to different storage locations over the life of the program.

The only reference type available with PL/SQL 2.2 is REF CURSOR. This type, also known as a cursor variable, will be discussed in detail in

Chapter 4. PL/SQL 8.0 introduces the REF object type, which can point to an object. REF objects are described in Chapter 11.

LOB Types

PL/SQL 8.0 ...and HIGHER The LOB types are used to store large objects. A *large object* can be either a binary or character value up to 4 gigabytes in size. Large objects can contain unstructured data, which is accessed more efficiently than LONG or LONG RAW data, with fewer restrictions. LOB types are manipulated using the DBMS_LOB package; they are discussed in detail in Chapter 21.

Using %TYPE

In many cases, a PL/SQL variable will be used to manipulate data stored in a database table. In this case, the variable should have the same type as the table column. For example, the **first_name** column of the **students** table has type VARCHAR2(20). Based on this, we can declare a variable as follows:

```
DECLARE
  v_FirstName    VARCHAR2(20);
```

This is fine, but what happens if the definition of **first_name** is changed? Say the table is altered and **first_name** now has type VARCHAR2(25). Any PL/SQL code that uses this column would have to be changed, as in

```
DECLARE
  v_FirstName  VARCHAR2(25);
```

If you have a large amount of PL/SQL code, this can be a time-consuming and error-prone process. Rather than hardcode the type of a variable in this way, you can use the %TYPE attribute. This attribute is appended to a table column reference, or another variable, and returns its type. For example:

```
DECLARE
  v_FirstName  students.first_name%TYPE;
```

By using %TYPE, **v_FirstName** will have whatever type the **first_name** column of the **students** table has. The type is determined each time the block is run for anonymous and named blocks, and whenever stored objects (procedures, functions, and so on) are compiled. %TYPE can also be applied to an earlier PL/SQL variable declaration. The following example shows various applications of the %TYPE attribute.

```
DECLARE
  v_RoomID      classes.room_id%TYPE;   -- Returns NUMBER(5)
  v_RoomID2     v_RoomID%TYPE;          -- Returns NUMBER(5)
  v_TempVar     NUMBER(7,3) NOT NULL := 12.3;
  v_AnotherVar  v_TempVar%TYPE;         -- Returns NUMBER(7,3)
```

If %TYPE is applied to a variable or column that is constrained to be NOT NULL (such as **classes.room_id** or **v_TempVar**), the type it returns does not have this restriction. The preceding block is still legal even though **v_RoomID**, **v_RoomID2**, and **v_AnotherVar** are not initialized, because they can hold NULL values.

It is good programming style to use %TYPE, since it makes a PL/SQL program more flexible and able to adapt to changing database definitions.

User-Defined Subtypes

PL/SQL **2.1** ...and HIGHER A subtype is a PL/SQL type that is based on an existing type. A subtype can be used to give an alternate name for a type, which describes its intended use. PL/SQL defines several subtypes (for example, DECIMAL and INTEGER are subtypes of NUMBER) in package STANDARD. With PL/SQL 2.1 and higher, you can define subtypes as well, in addition to the predefined subtypes. The syntax is

SUBTYPE *new_type* IS *original_type*;

where *new_type* is the name of the new subtype, and *original type* refers to the base type. The base type can be a predefined type or subtype, or a %TYPE reference. For example:

```
DECLARE
  SUBTYPE t_LoopCounter IS NUMBER;  -- Define the new subtype
  v_LoopCounter    t_LoopCounter;   -- Declare a variable of the
                                    -- subtype
  SUBTYPE t_NameType IS students.first_name%TYPE;
```

The SUBTYPE definition cannot be constrained directly in the definition. The following block is illegal:

```
DECLARE
    SUBTYPE T_LoopCounter IS NUMBER(4);  -- Illegal constraint
```

There is a workaround for this, however. You can declare a dummy variable of the desired type (with the constraint) and use %TYPE in the SUBTYPE definition:

```
DECLARE
    v_DummyVar  NUMBER(4)       -- Dummy variable, won't be used
    SUBTYPE t_LoopCounter is v_DummyVar%TYPE;  -- Returns NUMBER(4)
    v_Counter   t_LoopCounter;
```

Variable declarations using an unconstrained subtype can also constrain the type:

```
DECLARE
    SUBTYPE  t_Numeric IS NUMBER; -- Define unconstrained subtype,
    v_Counter is t_Numeric(5);    -- but a constrained variable
```

A subtype is considered to be in the same family as its base type.

Converting Between Datatypes

PL/SQL can handle conversions between different families among the scalar datatypes. Within a family, you can convert datatypes with no restrictions, except for constraints imposed on the variables. For example, a CHAR(10) variable cannot be converted into a VARCHAR2(1) variable, since there is not enough room. Likewise, precision and scale constraints may prohibit conversion between NUMBER(3,2) and NUMBER(3). In cases of constraint violations, the PL/SQL compiler will not issue an error, but you may get a run-time error, depending on the values in the variables to be converted.

In general, the composite datatypes cannot be converted between each other, since they are too dissimilar. You can write a function to perform this conversion if necessary, however, based on the meaning of the datatypes in your program.

There are two types of conversions, regardless of the type: implicit and explicit.

Explicit Datatype Conversion

The built-in conversion functions available in SQL are also available in PL/SQL. Table 2-4 gives brief descriptions of these functions. When desired,

Function	Description	Families Available for Conversion
TO_CHAR	Converts its argument to a VARCHAR2 type, depending on the optional format specifier.	Numeric, date
TO_DATE	Converts its argument to a DATE type, depending on the optional format specifier.	Character
TO_NUMBER	Converts its argument to a NUMBER type, depending on the optional format specifier.	Character
RAWTOHEX	Converts a RAW value to a hexadecimal representation of the binary quantity.	Raw
HEXTORAW	Converts a hexadecimal representation into the equivalent binary quantity.	Character (must be in a hexadecimal representation)
CHARTOROWID	Converts a character representation of a ROWID into the internal binary format.	Character (must be in the 18-character rowid format)
ROWIDTOCHAR	Converts an internal binary ROWID variable into the 18-character external format.	Rowid

TABLE 2-4. *PL/SQL and SQL Datatype Conversion Functions*

you can use these functions to convert explicitly between variables in different datatype families. For more information and examples on using these conversion functions, see Chapter 5.

Implicit Datatype Conversion

PL/SQL will automatically convert between datatype families when possible. For example, the following block retrieves the current number of credits for student 10002:

```
DECLARE
   v_CurrentCredits  VARCHAR2(5);
BEGIN
   SELECT current_credits
     INTO v_CurrentCredits
     FROM students
     WHERE id = 10002;
END;
```

In the database, **current_credits** is a NUMBER(3) field. But **v_CurrentCredits** is a VARCHAR2(5) variable. PL/SQL will automatically convert the numeric data into a character string and then assign it to the character variable. PL/SQL can convert between

- Characters and numbers
- Characters and dates

Even though PL/SQL will implicitly convert between datatypes, it is good programming practice to use an explicit conversion function. In the next example, this is done with the TO_CHAR function.

```
DECLARE
   v_CurrentCredits  VARCHAR2(5);
BEGIN
   SELECT TO_CHAR(current_credits)
     INTO v_CurrentCredits
     FROM students
     WHERE id = 10002;
END;
```

The advantage of this is that an explicit format string can also be used in the TO_CHAR function, if desired. It also makes the intent of the program clearer and emphasizes the type conversion.

Automatic datatype conversion can also take place when PL/SQL is evaluating expressions, which are described fully in the section "Expressions and Operators" later in this chapter. The same guidelines apply there as well; however, use of an explicit conversion function is recommended.

Variable Scope and Visibility

The *scope* of a variable is the portion of the program in which the variable can be accessed. For a PL/SQL variable, this is from the variable declaration until the end of the block. When a variable goes out of scope, the PL/SQL engine will free the memory used to store the variable, since it can no longer be referenced. Figure 2-2 illustrates this. **v_Character** is in scope only in the inner block; after the END of the inner block, it is out of scope. The scope of **v_Number** ranges until the END of the outer block. Both variables are in scope in the inner block.

The *visibility* of a variable is the portion of the program where the variable can be accessed without having to qualify the reference. The visibility is always within the scope; if a variable is out of scope, it is not visible. Consider Figure 2-3. At location 1, both **v_AvailableFlag** and **v_SSN** are in scope and are visible. At location 2, the same two variables are in scope, but only **v_AvailableFlag** is still visible. The redeclaration of **v_SSN** as a CHAR(11) variable has hidden the NUMBER(9) declaration. All four variables are in scope at location 2, but only three are visible— **v_AvailableFlag**, **v_StartDate**, and the CHAR(11) **v_SSN**. By location 3, **v_StartDate** and the CHAR(11) **v_SSN** are no longer in scope and hence are no longer visible. The same two variables are in scope and visibility as in location 1—**v_AvailableFlag** and the NUMBER(9) **v_SSN**.

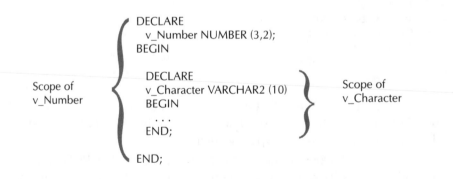

FIGURE 2-2. *Variable scope*

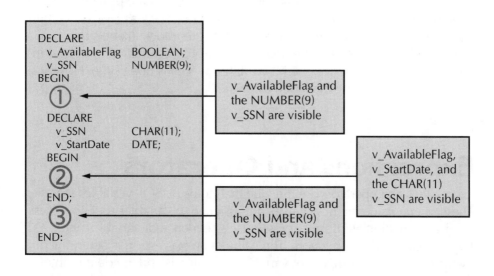

FIGURE 2-3. *Scope and visibility*

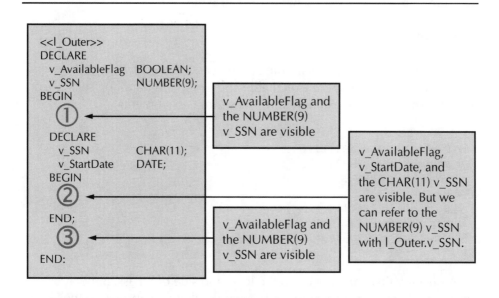

FIGURE 2-4. *Using a label to reference a variable*

If a variable is in scope but is not visible, how does the program reference it? Consider Figure 2-4. This is the same block as Figure 2-3, but a label **<<l_Outer>>** has been added to the outer block. (Labels are discussed in more detail in the "PL/SQL Control Structures" section later in this chapter.) At location 2, the NUMBER(9) **v_SSN** is not visible. However, we can refer to it, using the label, as

```
l_Outer.v_SSN
```

Expressions and Operators

Expressions and operators are the glue that holds PL/SQL variables together. These operators define how values are assigned to variables and how these values are manipulated. An *expression* is a sequence of variables and literals, separated by *operators*. The value of an expression is determined by the values of its component variables and literals and the definition of the operators.

Assignment

The most basic operator is assignment. The syntax is

> *variable* := *expression*;

where *variable* is a PL/SQL variable and *expression* is a PL/SQL expression. Assignments are legal in the executable and exception handling sections of a block. The following example illustrates some assignments.

```
DECLARE
  v_String1  VARCHAR2(10);
  v_String2  VARCHAR2(15);
  v_Numeric  NUMBER;
BEGIN
  v_String1 := 'Hello';
  v_String2 := v_String1;
  v_Numeric := -12.4;
END;
```

A quantity that can appear on the left-hand side of an assignment operator is known as an *lvalue*, and a quantity that can appear on the right-hand side is known as an *rvalue*. An lvalue must refer to an actual storage location, since the rvalue will be written into it. In the preceding example, all of the lvalues are variables. The PL/SQL engine will allocate storage for variables, and the values **'Hello'** and **-12.4** can be put into this storage. An rvalue can be the contents of a storage location (referenced by a variable) or a literal. The example illustrates both cases: **'Hello'** is a literal, and **v_String1** is a variable. An rvalue will be read from, while an lvalue will be written to. All lvalues are also rvalues.

In a given PL/SQL statement, there can be only one assignment. Unlike languages such as C, the following assignment is illegal:

```
DECLARE
  v_Val1 NUMBER;
  v_Val2 NUMBER;
  v_Val3 NUMBER;
BEGIN
  v_Val1 := v_Val2 := v_Val3 := 0;
END;
```

Expressions

PL/SQL expressions are rvalues. As such, an expression is not valid as a statement by itself—it must be part of another statement. For example, an expression can appear on the right-hand side of an assignment operator or as part of an SQL statement. The operators that make up an expression, together with the type of their operands, determine the type of the expression.

An *operand* is the argument to an operator. PL/SQL operators take either one argument (unary) or two arguments (binary). For example, the negation operator (-) is a unary operand, while the multiplication operator (*) is a binary operand. Table 2-5 classifies the PL/SQL operators according to their precedence, or priority. Operators with the highest precedence are listed first.

The *precedence* of the operators in an expression determines the order of evaluation. Consider the following numeric expression:

```
3 + 5 * 7
```

Since multiplication has a higher precedence than addition, this expression evaluates to 38 (3 + 35) rather than 56 (8 * 7). You use parentheses in the expression to override the default order of precedence. For example, in the following form, the expression evaluates to 56:

```
(3 + 5) * 7
```

Character Expressions

The only character operator is concatenation (||). This operator attaches two or more strings (or arguments which can be converted implicitly to a string) together. For example, the expression

```
'Hello ' || 'World' || '!'
```

evaluates to

```
'Hello World!'
```

If all of the operands in a concatenation expression are of type CHAR, then the expression is of type CHAR. If any operand is of type VARCHAR2, then the expression is of type VARCHAR2. String literals are considered to be of type CHAR, so the preceding example evaluates to a CHAR value. The expression assigned to **v_Result** in the following block, however, evaluates to a VARCHAR2 value.

```
DECLARE
  v_TempVar  VARCHAR2(10) := 'PL';
  v_Result   VARCHAR2(20);
BEGIN
  v_Result := v_TempVar || '/SQL';
END;
```

Boolean Expressions

All of the PL/SQL control structures (except GOTO) involve boolean expressions, also known as conditions. A *boolean expression* is any expression that evaluates to a boolean value (TRUE, FALSE, or NULL). For example, all of the following are boolean expressions:

```
X > Y
NULL
(4 > 5) OR (-1 != Z)
```

Three operators—AND, OR, and NOT—take boolean arguments and return boolean values. Their behavior is described by the truth tables in

Figure 2-5. These operators implement standard three-valued logic. Essentially, AND returns TRUE only if both of its operands are TRUE, and OR returns FALSE only if both of its operands are FALSE.

NULLs add complexity to boolean expressions. (Recall that NULL means "missing or unknown value.") The expression

```
TRUE AND NULL
```

evaluates to NULL because we don't know whether the second operand is TRUE or not. For more information, see the section "Null Conditions" later in this chapter.

Comparison, or *relational,* operators take numeric, character, or data operands and return a boolean value. These operators are defined according to the following table.

Operator	Definition
=	Is equal to (equality)
!=	Is not equal to (inequality)
<	Is less than
>	Is greater than
<=	Is less than or equal to
>=	Is greater than or equal to

NOT	TRUE	FALSE	NULL
	FALSE	TRUE	NULL

AND	TRUE	FALSE	NULL
TRUE	TRUE	FALSE	NULL
FALSE	FALSE	FALSE	FALSE
NULL	NULL	FALSE	NULL

OR	TRUE	FALSE	NULL
TRUE	TRUE	TRUE	TRUE
FALSE	TRUE	FALSE	NULL
NULL	TRUE	NULL	NULL

FIGURE 2-5. *Truth tables*

The IS NULL operator returns TRUE only if its operand is NULL. NULLs cannot be tested using the relational operators because any relational expression with a NULL operand returns NULL.

The LIKE operator is used for pattern matching in character strings, similar to regular expressions in Unix. The underscore character (_) matches exactly one character, and the percent character (%) matches zero or more characters. The following expressions all return TRUE.

```
'Scott' LIKE 'Sc%t'

'Scott' LIKE 'Sc_tt'

'Scott' LIKE '%'
```

The BETWEEN operator combines <= and >= in one expression. For example, the following expression returns FALSE,

```
100 BETWEEN 110 AND 120
```

while this expression returns TRUE:

```
100 BETWEEN 90 and 110
```

The IN operator returns TRUE if its first operand is contained in the set identified by the second operand. For example, the following expression returns FALSE:

```
'Scott' IN ('Mike', 'Pamela', 'Fred')
```

If the set contains NULLs, they are ignored, since a comparison with NULL will always return NULL.

PL/SQL Control Structures

PL/SQL, like other third generation languages, has a variety of control structures that allow you to control the behavior of the block as it runs. These structures include conditional statements and loops. It is these structures, combined with variables, that give PL/SQL its power and flexibility.

IF-THEN-ELSE

The syntax for an IF-THEN-ELSE statement is

> IF *boolean_expression1* THEN
>   *sequence_of_statements1*;
> [ELSIF *boolean_expression2* THEN
>   *sequence_of_statements2*;]
> ...
> [ELSE
>   *sequence_of_statements3*;]
> END IF;

where *boolean_expression* is any expression that evaluates to a boolean value, defined in the previous section, "Boolean Expressions." The ELSIF and ELSE clauses are optional, and there can be as many ELSIF clauses as desired. For example, the following block shows an IF-THEN-ELSE statement with one ELSIF clause and one ELSE clause:

```
-- Available online as if1.sql
DECLARE
  v_NumberSeats rooms.number_seats%TYPE;
  v_Comment VARCHAR2(35);
BEGIN
  /* Retrieve the number of seats in the room identified
     by ID 99999. Store the result in v_NumberSeats. */
  SELECT number_seats
    INTO v_NumberSeats
    FROM rooms
    WHERE room_id = 99999;
  IF v_NumberSeats < 50 THEN
    v_Comment := 'Fairly small';
  ELSIF v_NumberSeats < 100 THEN
    v_Comment := 'A little bigger';
  ELSE
    v_Comment := 'Lots of room';
  END IF;
END;
```

The behavior of the preceding block is the same as the keywords imply. If the first condition evaluates to TRUE, then the first sequence of statements is executed. In this case, the first condition is

```
v_NumberSeats < 50
```

and the first sequence of statements is

```
v_Comment := 'Fairly small';
```

If the number of seats is not less than 50, then the second condition

```
v_NumberSeats < 100
```

is evaluated. If this evaluates to TRUE, then the second sequence of statements

```
v_Comment := 'A little bigger';
```

is executed. Finally, if the number of seats is not less than 100, the final sequence of statements

```
v_Comment := 'Lots of room';
```

is executed. Each sequence of statements is executed only if its associated boolean condition evaluates to TRUE.

In the example, each sequence of statements has only one procedural statement. However, in general, you can have as many statements (procedural or SQL) as desired. The following block illustrates this.

```
-- Available online as if2.sql
DECLARE
  v_NumberSeats rooms.number_seats%TYPE;
  v_Comment VARCHAR2(35);
BEGIN
  /* Retrieve the number of seats in the room identified
     by ID 99999. Store the result in v_NumberSeats. */
  SELECT number_seats
    INTO v_NumberSeats
    FROM rooms
    WHERE room_id = 99999;
  IF v_NumberSeats < 50 THEN
    v_Comment := 'Fairly small';
    INSERT INTO temp_table (char_col)
      VALUES ('Nice and cozy');
  ELSIF v_NumberSeats < 100 THEN
    v_Comment := 'A little bigger';
    INSERT INTO temp_table (char_col)
      VALUES ('Some breathing room');
```

```
  ELSE
    v_Comment := 'Lots of room';
  END IF;
END;
```

NOTE
*Be aware of the spelling of ELSIF—there is
no E and no space. This syntax comes from
the Ada language.*

Null Conditions

A sequence of statements in an IF-THEN-ELSE statement is executed only if
its associated condition evaluates to TRUE. If the condition evaluates to
FALSE or NULL, then the sequence of statements is not executed. Consider
the following two blocks as an example:

```
/* Block 1 */
DECLARE
  v_Number1 NUMBER;
  v_Number2 NUMBER;
  v_Result  VARCHAR2(7);
BEGIN
  ...
  IF v_Number1 < v_Number2 THEN
    v_Result := 'Yes';
  ELSE
    v_Result := 'No';
  END IF;
END;

/* Block 2 */
DECLARE
  v_Number1 NUMBER;
  v_Number2 NUMBER;
  v_Result VARCHAR2(7);
BEGIN
  ...
  IF v_Number1 >= v_Number2 THEN
    v_Result := 'No';
  ELSE
    v_Result := 'Yes';
  END IF;
END;
```

Do these blocks behave the same? Suppose that **v_Number1** = 3 and **v_Number2** = 7. The condition in block 1 (3 < 7) will thus evaluate to TRUE, and **v_Result** will be set to 'Yes'. Similarly, the condition in block 2 (3 >= 7) will evaluate to FALSE, and **v_Result** will also be set to 'Yes'. For any non-NULL values of **v_Number1** and **v_Number2**, the blocks have the same behavior.

Now suppose that **v_Number1** = 3 but **v_Number2** is NULL. What happens now? The condition in block 1 (3 < NULL) will evaluate to NULL, so the ELSE clause will be executed, assigning 'No' to **v_Result**. The condition in block 2 (3 >= NULL) will also evaluate to NULL, so the ELSE clause will be executed, assigning 'Yes' to **v_Result**. If either **v_Number1** or **v_Number2** is NULL, the blocks behave differently.

If we add a check for NULL to the preceding blocks, we can make them behave the same:

```
/* Block 1 */
DECLARE
  v_Number1 NUMBER;
  v_Number2 NUMBER;
  v_Result  VARCHAR2(7);
BEGIN
  ...
  IF v_Number1 IS NULL OR
      v_Number2 IS NULL THEN
    v_Result := 'Unknown';
  ELSIF v_Number1 < v_Number2 THEN
    v_Result := 'Yes';
  ELSE
    v_Result := 'No';
  END IF;
END;

/* Block 2 */
DECLARE
  v_Number1 NUMBER;
  v_Number2 NUMBER;
  v_Result VARCHAR2(7);
BEGIN
  ...
  IF v_Number1 IS NULL OR
      v_Number2 IS NULL THEN
    v_Result := 'Unknown';
  ELSIF v_Number1 >= v_Number2 THEN
```

```
     v_Result := 'No';
   ELSE
     v_Result := 'Yes';
   END IF;
 END;
```

The **IS NULL** condition will evaluate to TRUE only if the variable it is checking is NULL. If the variable is not NULL, the condition will evaluate to FALSE. By adding this check to the preceding blocks, we assign 'Unknown' to **v_Result** if either variable is NULL. The block will only check whether **v_Number1** is greater than **v_Number2** if it is assured that both are non-NULL, in which case the remainder of the blocks behave the same.

Loops

PL/SQL provides a facility for executing statements repeatedly, via *loops.* Loops are divided into four categories. Simple loops, WHILE loops, and numeric FOR loops are discussed in the following sections. Cursor FOR loops are discussed in Chapter 6.

Simple Loops

The most basic kind of loops, simple loops, have the syntax

```
LOOP
  sequence_of_statements;
END LOOP;
```

The *sequence_of_statements* will be executed infinitely, since this loop has no stopping condition. However, we can add one with the EXIT statement, which has the syntax:

```
EXIT [WHEN condition];
```

For example, the following block inserts 50 rows into **temp_table**.

```
-- Available online as simple.sql
DECLARE
  v_Counter BINARY_INTEGER := 1;
```

```
BEGIN
  LOOP
    -- Insert a row into temp_table with the current value of
    -- the loop counter.
    INSERT INTO temp_table
      VALUES (v_Counter, 'Loop index');
    v_Counter := v_Counter + 1;
    -- Exit condition - when the loop counter > 50 we will
    -- break out of the loop.
    IF v_Counter > 50 THEN
      EXIT;
    END IF;
  END LOOP;
END;
```

The statement

EXIT WHEN *condition*;

is equivalent to:

IF *condition* THEN
   EXIT;
END IF;

So we can rewrite the example with the following block, which behaves exactly the same way.

-- **Available online as exitwhen.sql**

```
DECLARE
  v_Counter BINARY_INTEGER := 1;
BEGIN
  LOOP
    -- Insert a row into temp_table with the current value of
    -- the loop counter.
    INSERT INTO temp_table
      VALUES (v_Counter, 'Loop index');
    v_Counter := v_Counter + 1;
    -- Exit condition - when the loop counter > 50 we will
    -- break out of the loop.
    EXIT WHEN v_Counter > 50;
  END LOOP;
END;
```

WHILE Loops

The syntax for a WHILE loop is

WHILE *condition* LOOP
  sequence_of_statements;
END LOOP;

The *condition* is evaluated before each iteration of the loop. If it evaluates to TRUE, *sequence_of_statements* is executed. If *condition* evaluates to FALSE or NULL, the loop is finished and control resumes after the END LOOP statement. Now we can rewrite the example using a WHILE loop, as follows:

```
-- Available online as while1.sql
DECLARE
  v_Counter BINARY_INTEGER := 1;
BEGIN
  -- Test the loop counter before each loop iteration to
  -- insure that it is still less than or equal to 50.
  WHILE v_Counter <= 50 LOOP
    INSERT INTO temp_table
      VALUES (v_Counter, 'Loop index');
    v_Counter := v_Counter + 1;
  END LOOP;
END;
```

The EXIT or EXIT WHEN statement can still be used inside a WHILE loop to exit the loop prematurely, if desired.

Keep in mind that if the loop condition does not evaluate to TRUE the first time it is checked, the loop is not executed at all. If we remove the initialization of **v_Counter** in our example, the condition **v_Counter < = 50** will evaluate to NULL, and no rows will be inserted into temp_table:

```
-- Available online as while2.sql
DECLARE
  v_Counter BINARY_INTEGER;
BEGIN
  -- This condition will evaluate to NULL, since v_Counter
  -- is initialized to NULL by default.
  WHILE v_Counter <= 50 LOOP
    INSERT INTO temp_table
      VALUES (v_Counter, 'Loop index');
```

```
    v_Counter := v_Counter + 1;
  END LOOP;
END;
```

Numeric FOR Loops

The number of iterations for simple loops and WHILE loops is not known in advance—it depends on the loop condition. Numeric FOR loops, on the other hand, have a defined number of iterations. The syntax is

> FOR *loop_counter* IN [REVERSE] *low_bound .. high_bound LOOP*
>   *sequence_of_statements'*
> END LOOP;

where *loop_counter* is the implicitly declared index variable, *low_bound* and *high_bound* specify the number of iterations, and *sequence_of_statements* is the content of the loop.

The bounds of the loop are evaluated once. This determines the total number of iterations that *loop_counter* will take on the values ranging from *low_bound* to *high_bound*, incrementing by 1 each time, until the loop is complete. We can rewrite our looping example using a FOR loop as follows:

```
-- Available online as forloop.sql
BEGIN
  FOR v_Counter IN 1..50 LOOP
    INSERT INTO temp_table
      VALUES (v_Counter, 'Loop Index');
  END LOOP;
END;
```

Scoping Rules   The loop index for a FOR loop is implicitly declared as a BINARY_INTEGER. It is not necessary to declare it prior to the loop. If it is declared, the loop index will hide the outer declaration in the same way that a variable declaration in an inner block can hide a declaration in an outer block. For example:

```
-- Available online as forscope.sql
DECLARE
  v_Counter  NUMBER := 7;
BEGIN
```

```
-- Inserts the value 7 into temp_table.
INSERT INTO temp_table (num_col)
  VALUES (v_Counter);
-- This loop redeclares v_Counter as a BINARY_INTEGER,
-- which hides the NUMBER declaration of v_Counter.
FOR v_Counter IN 20..30 LOOP
  -- Inside the loop, v_Counter ranges from 20 to 30.
  INSERT INTO temp_table (num_col)
    VALUES (v_Counter);
END LOOP;
-- Inserts another 7 into temp_table.
  INSERT INTO temp_table (num_col)
    VALUES (v_Counter);
END;
```

USING REVERSE   If the REVERSE keyword is present in the FOR loop, then the loop index will iterate from the high value to the low value. Note that the syntax is the same—the low value is still referenced first. For example:

```
BEGIN
  FOR v_Counter in REVERSE 10..50 LOOP
    -- v_Counter will start with 50, and will be decremented
    -- by 1 each time through the loop.
    NULL;
  END LOOP;
END;
```

LOOP RANGES   The high and low values don't have to be numeric literals. They can be any expression that can be converted to a numeric value. Here is an example:

```
DECLARE
  v_LowValue  NUMBER := 10;
  v_HighValue NUMBER := 40;
BEGIN
  FOR v_Counter IN REVERSE v_LowValue .. v_HighValue LOOP
    INSERT INTO temp_table
      VALUES (v_Counter, 'Dynamically specified loop ranges');
  END LOOP;
END;
```

GOTOs and Labels

PL/SQL also includes a GOTO statement. The syntax is

GOTO *label*;

where *label* is a label defined in the PL/SQL block. Labels are enclosed in double angle brackets. When a GOTO statement is evaluated, control immediately passes to the statement identified by the label. For example, we can implement our looping example with:

```
-- Available online as goto.sql
DECLARE
  v_Counter  BINARY_INTEGER := 1;
BEGIN
  LOOP
    INSERT INTO temp_table
      VALUES (v_Counter, 'Loop count');
    v_Counter := v_Counter + 1;
    IF v_Counter > 50 THEN
      GOTO l_EndOfLoop;
    END IF;
  END LOOP;

  <<l_EndOfLoop>>
  INSERT INTO temp_table (char_col)
    VALUES ('Done!');
END;
```

Restrictions on GOTO

PL/SQL enforces restrictions on the use of GOTO. It is illegal to branch into an inner block, loop, or IF statement. The following illegal example illustrates this.

```
BEGIN
    GOTO l_InnerBlock;  -- Illegal, cannot branch to an
                        -- inner block.
    BEGIN
      ...
      <<l_InnerBlock>>
      ...
    END;

    GOTO l_InsideIf;  -- Illegal, cannot branch into an
                      -- IF statement.
    IF x > 3 THEN
      ...
```

```
    <<l_InsideIf>>
    INSERT INTO ...
  END IF;
END;
```

If these were legal, statements inside the IF statement could be executed even if the IF condition did not evaluate to TRUE. In the preceding example, the INSERT statement could be executed if x = 2.

It is also illegal for a GOTO to branch from one IF clause to another:

```
BEGIN
  IF x > 3 THEN
    ...
    GOTO l_NextCondition;
  ELSE
    <<l_NextCondition>>
    ...
  END IF;
END;
```

Finally, it is illegal to branch from an exception handler back into the current block. Exceptions are discussed in Chapter 10.

```
DECLARE
  v_Room    rooms%ROWTYPE;
BEGIN
  -- Retrieve a single row from the rooms table.
  SELECT *
    INTO v_Room
    FROM rooms
    WHERE rowid = 1;
  <<l_Insert>>
  INSERT INTO temp_table (char_col)
    VALUES ('Found a row!');
EXCEPTION
  WHEN NO_DATA_FOUND THEN
    GOTO l_Insert;  -- Illegal, cannot branch into current block
END;
```

Labeling Loops

Loops themselves can be labeled. If so, the label can be used on the EXIT statement to indicate which loop is to be exited. For example:

```
BEGIN
  <<l_Outer>>
  FOR v_OuterIndex IN 1..50 LOOP
    ...
    <<l_Inner>>
    FOR v_InnerIndex IN 2..10 LOOP
      ...
      IF v_OuterIndex > 40 THEN
        EXIT l_Outer;  -- Exits both loops
      END IF;
    END LOOP l_Inner;
END LOOP l_Outer;
```

If a loop is labeled, the label name can optionally be included after the END LOOP statement, as the preceding example indicates.

GOTO Guidelines

Be careful when using GOTO. Unnecessary GOTO statements can create *spaghetti code*—code that jumps around from place to place with no apparent reason and is very difficult to understand and maintain.

Just about all cases where a GOTO could be used can be rewritten using other PL/SQL control structures, such as loops or conditionals. Exceptions can also be used to exit out of a deeply nested loop, rather than branching to the end.

NULL as a Statement

In some cases, you may want to explicitly indicate that no action is to take place. This can be done via the NULL statement. The NULL statement does not do anything; it just serves as a placeholder. For example:

```
-- Available online as null.sql
DECLARE
  v_TempVar  NUMBER := 7;
BEGIN
  IF v_TempVar < 5 THEN
    INSERT INTO temp_table (char_col)
      VALUES ('Too small');
  ELSIF v_TempVar < 10 THEN
    INSERT INTO temp_table (char_col)
      VALUES ('Just right');
  ELSE
    NULL;  -- Do nothing
```

```
    END IF;
END;
```

Pragmas

Pragmas are compiler directives, similar to **#pragma** or **#define** directives in
C. They serve as instructions to the PL/SQL compiler. The compiler will act
on the pragma during the compilation of the block. For example, the
RESTRICT_REFERENCES pragma places restrictions on what kinds of SQL
statements can be in a function. In addition to compiling the function as
normal, the compiler needs to verify that the restrictions are met. The
RESTRICT_REFERENCES pragma is described in Chapter 8. PL/SQL has a
number of pragmas, which we will see throughout this book.

Pragmas are another concept that PL/SQL and Ada have in common.

PL/SQL Style Guide

There are no absolute rules for the style of a program. Program style
includes things such as variable names, use of capitalization and white
space, and the use of comments. These are not things that will necessarily
affect how a program runs—two different styles for the same program
will still do the same thing. However, a program that is written with
good style will be much easier to understand and maintain than a poorly
written program.

Good style means that it will take less time to understand what the
program is doing when seeing it for the first time. Also, it will help you
understand what the program is doing, both as you write it and when you
see it a month later.

As an example, consider the following two blocks. Which one is easier
to understand?

```
declare
x number;
y number;
begin if x < 10 then y := 7; else y := 3; end if; end;

DECLARE
  v_Test   NUMBER;   -- Variable which will be examined
  v_Result NUMBER;   -- Variable to store the result
BEGIN
  -- Examine v_Test, and assign 7 to v_Result if v_Test < 10.
```

```
  IF v_Test < 10 THEN
    v_Result := 7;
  ELSE
    v_Result := 3;
  END IF;
END;
```

Both blocks accomplish the same thing. However, the program flow in the second one is significantly easier to understand.

This section covers several points of style. I feel that if you follow these recommendations, you will produce better code. All of the examples in this book follow these guidelines and serve as illustrations of this style of PL/SQL programming.

Style of Comments

Comments are the main mechanism for informing the reader what the purpose of a program is and how it works. I recommend putting comments:

■ At the start of each block and/or procedure. These comments should explain what the block or procedure is supposed to do. Especially for procedures, it is important to list which variables or parameters will be read by the procedure (input) and which variables or parameters will be written to by the procedure (output). Also, it is a good idea to list the database tables accessed.

■ By each variable declaration. Describe what the variable will be used for. Often, these can simply be one-line comments, such as

```
v_SSN CHAR(11);    -- Social Security Number
```

■ Before each major section of the block. You don't necessarily need comments around every statement, but a comment explaining the purpose of the next group of statements is useful. The algorithm used may be apparent from the code itself, so it is better to describe the purpose of the algorithm and what the results will be used for, rather than the details of the method.

It's possible to have too many comments, which just get in the way of the code. When deciding on whether or not a comment is appropriate, ask yourself, "What would a programmer seeing this for the first time want to know?" Remember that the programmer may be yourself a month or two after you write the code!

Comments should be meaningful and not restate what the PL/SQL code itself says. For example, the following comment doesn't tell us anything more than the PL/SQL does and thus isn't really useful.

```
DECLARE
    v_Temp NUMBER := 0;   -- Assign 0 to v_Temp
```

However, this comment is better, because it tells us the purpose of the **v_Temp** variable:

```
DECLARE
    v_Temp NUMBER := 0;   -- Temporary variable used in main loop
```

Style of Variable Names

The key to variable names is to make them descriptive. The declaration

```
x number;
```

doesn't tell us anything about what x will be used for. However,

```
v_StudentID  NUMBER(5);
```

tells us that this variable will probably be used for a student ID number, even without an explanatory comment by the declaration. Remember the maximum length of a PL/SQL identifier is 30 characters, and all of them are significant. Thirty characters is generally enough for a descriptive name.

The variable name can also tell us the use of the variable. I use a one-letter code separated by an underscore from the rest of the variable to indicate this. For example:

```
v_VariableName      Program variable
e_ExceptionName     User-defined exception
t_TypeName          User-defined type
p_ParameterName     Parameter to a procedure or function
c_ConstantValue     Variable constrained with the CONSTANT clause
```

Style of Capitalization

PL/SQL is not case-sensitive. However, I feel that proper use of upper- and lowercase significantly increases program readability. I generally follow these rules:

- Reserved words are in uppercase (BEGIN, DECLARE, ELSIF, for example).

- Built-in functions are in uppercase (SUBSTR, COUNT, TO_CHAR).

- Predefined types are in uppercase (NUMBER(7,2), BOOLEAN, DATE).

- SQL keywords are in uppercase (SELECT, INTO, UPDATE, WHERE).

- Database objects are in lowercase (log_table, classes, students).

- Variable names are in mixed case, with a capital letter for each word in the name (v_HireDate, e_TooManyStudents, t_StudentRecordType).

Style of Indentation

Use of *white space* (carriage returns, spaces, and tabs) is one of the simplest things you can do, and it can have the largest effect on program readability. Compare the two identical nested IF-THEN-ELSE constructs shown here:

```
IF x < y THEN IF z IS NULL THEN x := 3; ELSE x := 2; END IF; ELSE
x := 4; END IF;

IF x < y THEN
  IF z IS NULL THEN
    x := 3;
  ELSE
    x := 2;
  END IF;
ELSE
  x := 4;
END IF;
```

I generally indent each line within a block by two spaces. I indent the contents of a block from the DECLARE..END keywords, and I indent loops

and IF-THEN-ELSE statements. SQL statements that are continued over
multiple lines are also indented, as in

```
SELECT id, first_name, last_name
  INTO v_StudentID, v_FirstName, v_LastName
  FROM STUDENTS
  WHERE id = 10002;
```

Style in General

As you write more PL/SQL code, you will probably develop your own
programming style. These guidelines are by no means required, but I have
found them useful in my own PL/SQL development, and I use them in the
examples in this book. It is a good idea to show your code to another
programmer and ask him or her what it does. If another programmer can
describe what the program does and the outline of how it works, then you
have documented it well and written in a good style.

In addition, many development organizations have guidelines for good
code documentation and style, which can apply to other languages besides
PL/SQL. The converse is also true: if you have an established C coding
style, you can probably adapt it for use in PL/SQL.

Summary

In this chapter, we have covered the basic building blocks of PL/SQL: the
structure of a PL/SQL block, variables and datatypes (scalar, composite, and
reference), expressions and operators, datatype conversion rules, and the
basic control structures. We also discussed PL/SQL style, which can help
you write more understandable and manageable code. Now that we
understand these fundamental concepts, we can continue in Chapter 3 by
discussing the composite types, and then in Chapter 4 by adding SQL to the
procedural constructs we have discussed.

CHAPTER
3

Records and Tables

n the last chapter, we looked at the PL/SQL scalar types. As we saw, these types are predefined by PL/SQL and provide the foundation for the type system. In this chapter, we will examine the composite types available with PL/SQL version 2—records and tables. We will discuss object types in Chapter 11 and the composite types available with PL/SQL version 8.0 in Chapter 12.

PL/SQL Records

The scalar types (NUMBER, VARCHAR2, DATE, and so on) are already predefined in package STANDARD. Therefore, in order to use one of these types in your program, you need only declare a variable of the required type. Composite types, on the other hand, are user-defined. In order to use a composite type, you must first define the type, then declare variables of that type. We will see this in the following sections.

PL/SQL records are similar to C structures. A record provides a way to deal with separate but related variables as a unit. Consider the following declarative section:

```
DECLARE
   v_StudentID   NUMBER(5);
   v_FirstName   VARCHAR2(20);
   v_LastName    VARCHAR2(20);
```

All three of these variables are logically related, since they refer to common fields in the **students** table. Once a record type is declared for these variables, the relationship between them is apparent, and they can be manipulated as a unit. Consider this example:

```
DECLARE
   /* Define a record type to hold common student information */
   TYPE t_StudentRecord IS RECORD (
     StudentID   NUMBER(5),
     FirstName   VARCHAR2(20),
     LastName    VARCHAR2(20));

   /* Declare a variable of this type. */
   v_StudentInfo   t_StudentRecord;
```

The general syntax for defining a record type is

TYPE *record_type* IS RECORD (
    field1 type1 [NOT NULL] [:= *expr1*],
    field2 type2 [NOT NULL] [:= *expr2*],
    ...
    fieldn typen [NOT NULL] [:= *exprn*]);

Here, *record_type* is the name of the new type, *field1* through *fieldn* are
the names of the fields within the record, and *type1* through *typen* are the
types of the associated fields. A record can have as many fields as desired.
Each field declaration looks essentially the same as a variable declaration
outside a record, including NOT NULL constraints and initial values. *expr1*
through *exprn* represent the initial value of each field. Like a variable
declaration outside a record, the initial value and NOT NULL constraint
are optional. The following declare section first defines the record type
t_SampleRecord, and then declares two records of that type.

```
DECLARE
   TYPE t_SampleRecord IS RECORD (
     Count          NUMBER(4),
     Name           VARCHAR2(10) := 'Scott',
     EffectiveDate  DATE,
     Description    VARCHAR2(45) NOT NULL := 'Unknown');
   v_Sample1  t_SampleRecord;
   v_Sample2  t_SampleRecord;
```

Similar to declarations that are not inside record definitions, if a field is
constrained to be NOT NULL, then it must have an initial value. Any field
without an initial value is initialized to NULL. You can use either the
DEFAULT keyword or := to specify the default value.
    In order to refer to a field within a record, dot notation is used. The
syntax is

    record_name.field_name

The following example shows how fields in **v_Sample1** and **v_Sample2**
are referenced:

```
BEGIN
   /* SYSDATE is a built-in function which returns the current
      date and time. */
   v_Sample1.EffectiveDate := SYSDATE;
   v_Sample2.Description := 'Pesto Pizza';
END;
```

A reference like this is an rvalue, so it can be used on either side of an assignment operator.

Record Assignment

In order for one record to be assigned to another, both records must be of the same type. For example, given the previous declarations of **v_Sample1** and **v_Sample2**, the following assignment is legal:

```
v_Sample1 := v_Sample2;
```

A record assignment like this one will use *copy semantics*—the values of the fields in **v_Sample1** will be assigned the values of the corresponding fields in **v_Sample2**. Even if you have two different types that happen to have the same field definitions, the records cannot be assigned to each other. The following example is illegal, and raises the error "PLS-382: expression is of wrong type".

```
-- Available online as assign.sql
DECLARE
  TYPE t_Rec1Type IS RECORD (
    Field1 NUMBER,
    Field2 VARCHAR2(5));
  TYPE t_Rec2Type IS RECORD (
    Field1 NUMBER,
    Field2 VARCHAR2(5));
  v_Rec1 t_Rec1Type;
  v_Rec2 t_Rec2Type;
BEGIN
   /* Even though v_Rec1 and v_Rec2 have the same field names
      and field types, the record types themselves are different.
      This is an illegal assignment which raises PLS-382. */
   v_Rec1 := v_Rec2;

   /* However, the fields are the same type, so the following
      are legal assignments. */
   v_Rec1.Field1 := v_Rec2.Field1;
   v_Rec2.Field2 := v_Rec2.Field2;
END;
```

A record can also be assigned to with a SELECT statement. This will retrieve data from the database and store it in the record. The fields in the record should match the fields in the select list of the query. Chapter 4 describes the SELECT statement in more detail. The following example illustrates this:

```
-- Available online as select.sql
DECLARE
    -- Define a record to match some fields in the students table.
    -- Note the use of %TYPE for the fields.
    TYPE t_StudentRecord IS RECORD (
      FirstName   students.first_name%TYPE,
      LastName    students.last_name%TYPE,
      Major       students.major%TYPE);

    -- Declare a variable to receive the data.
    v_Student   t_StudentRecord;
BEGIN
    -- Retrieve information about student with ID 10,000.
    -- Note how the query is returning columns which match the
    -- fields in v_Student.
    SELECT first_name, last_name, major
      INTO v_Student
      FROM students
      WHERE ID = 10000;
END;
```

Using %ROWTYPE

It is common in PL/SQL to declare a record with the same types as a database row. PL/SQL provides the %ROWTYPE operator to facilitate this. Similar to %TYPE, %ROWTYPE will return a type based on the table definition. For example, a declaration such as

```
DECLARE
    v_RoomRecord   rooms%ROWTYPE;
```

will define a record whose fields correspond to the columns in the **rooms** table. Specifically, **v_RoomRecord** will look like this:

```
(room_id        NUMBER(5),
 building       VARCHAR2(15),
 room_number    NUMBER(4),
 number_seats   NUMBER(4),
 description    VARCHAR2(50))
```

As with %TYPE, any NOT NULL constraint defined on the column is not included. However, the length of VARCHAR2 and CHAR columns and the precision and scale for NUMBER columns are included.

If the table definition changes, then %ROWTYPE changes along with it. Like %TYPE, %ROWTYPE is evaluated each time an anonymous block is submitted to the PL/SQL engine, and each time a stored object is compiled.

Tables

PL/SQL tables are similar to arrays in C. Syntactically, they are treated like arrays. However, they are implemented differently. In order to declare a PL/SQL table, you first need to define the table type, and then you declare a variable of this type, as the following declarative section illustrates:

```
DECLARE
    /* Define the table type. Variables of this type can hold
       character strings with a max of 10 characters each. */
    TYPE t_CharacterTable IS TABLE OF VARCHAR2(10)
      INDEX BY BINARY_INTEGER;

    /* Declare a variable of this type. This is what actually
       allocates the storage. */
    v_Characters t_CharacterTable;
```

The general syntax for defining a table type is

TYPE *tabletype* IS TABLE OF *type* INDEX BY BINARY_INTEGER;

where *tabletype* is the name of the new type being defined, and *type* is a predefined scalar type, or a reference to a scalar type via %TYPE. In the previous example, *tabletype* is **t_CharacterTable**, and *type* is **VARCHAR2(10)**. The following declarative section illustrates several different PL/SQL table types and variable declarations:

```
DECLARE
    TYPE t_NameTable IS TABLE OF students.first_name%TYPE
      INDEX BY BINARY_INTEGER;
    TYPE t_DateTable IS TABLE OF DATE
      INDEX BY BINARY_INTEGER;
    v_Names t_NameTable;
    v_Dates t_DateTable;
```

NOTE
PL/SQL version 2 requires the **INDEX BY**
BINARY_INTEGER *clause as part of the*
table definition. This clause is not necessary
for a version 8 table. These tables are
discussed in Chapter 12.

Once the type and the variable are declared, we can refer to an
individual element in the PL/SQL table by using the syntax

tablename(*index*)

where *tablename* is the name of a table and *index* is either a variable of
type BINARY_INTEGER or a variable or expression that can be converted to
a BINARY_INTEGER. Given the declarations for the different table types,
we could continue the PL/SQL block with

```
BEGIN
  v_Names(1) := 'Scott';
  v_Dates(-4) := SYSDATE - 1;  /* SYSDATE -1 evaluates to the time
                                  24 hours ago */
END;
```

Note that a table reference, like a record or variable reference, is
an lvalue since it points to storage that has been allocated by the
PL/SQL engine.

Tables vs. Arrays

Syntactically, PL/SQL tables are treated like arrays. However, the actual
implementation of a table differs from an array. A PL/SQL table is similar to
a database table, with two columns—KEY and VALUE. The type of KEY is
BINARY_INTEGER, and the type of VALUE is whatever type is specified in
the definition (*type* in the syntax shown earlier).

Given the definition of **t_NameTable** and **v_Names** in the declarative
section shown in the previous section, suppose the following sequence of
statements is executed:

```
v_Names(0) := 'Harold';
v_Names(-7) := 'Susan';
v_Names(3) := 'Steve';
```

The data structure will then look like this one:

Key	Value
0	Harold
–7	Susan
3	Steve

There are several things to note about PL/SQL tables that are illustrated by this example:

■ Tables are unconstrained. The only limit on the number of rows is the values that can be represented by the BINARY_INTEGER type.

■ The elements in a PL/SQL table are not necessarily in any particular order. Since they are not stored contiguously in memory like an array, elements can be inserted under arbitrary keys.

■ The keys used for a PL/SQL table don't have to be sequential. Any BINARY_INTEGER value or expression can be used for a table index.

An assignment to element *i* in a PL/SQL table actually creates this element. It is very similar to an INSERT operation on a database table. If element *i* is referenced before it has been created, the PL/SQL engine will return the error

```
ORA-1403: no data found
```

Memory for the table is allocated as data is inserted, and grows as the number of rows in the table grows. It is not dependent on the values used for the key.

PL/SQL 2.3 ...and HIGHER Prior to version 2.3 of PL/SQL, tables can only hold scalar types. However, version 2.3 lifts this restriction and allows tables of records. The following block is legal in PL/SQL 2.3 and higher only:

`-- Available online as tabrec.sql`

```
DECLARE
  TYPE t_StudentTable IS TABLE OF students%ROWTYPE
    INDEX BY BINARY_INTEGER;
  /* Each element of v_Students is a record */
  v_Students t_StudentTable;
BEGIN
  /* Retrieve the record with id = 10,001 and store it into
     v_Students(10001) */
  SELECT *
    INTO v_Students(10001)
    FROM students
    WHERE id = 10001;
END;
```

Since each element of this table is a record, we can refer to fields within this record via the syntax

table(*index*)*.field*

For example, we can continue the previous block with

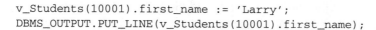

```
v_Students(10001).first_name := 'Larry';
DBMS_OUTPUT.PUT_LINE(v_Students(10001).first_name);
```

Here, **v_Students(10001)** refers to a record of type **students**%ROWTYPE, and a field within this record is **first_name**. A period separates the record and field reference.

> **NOTE**
> *The previous example uses the DBMS_OUTPUT.PUT_LINE procedure. This procedure can be used to output text to the screen in a SQL*Plus session. See Chapter 14 for more information on DBMS_OUTPUT.*

Tables of records significantly enhance the functionality of PL/SQL tables, since only one table definition is required to hold information about all the fields of a database table. Prior to version 2.3, a separate table definition is required for each database field.

Attribute	Type Returned	Description
COUNT	NUMBER	Returns the number of rows in the table.
DELETE	N/A	Deletes rows in a table.
EXISTS	BOOLEAN	Returns TRUE if the specified entry exists in the table.
FIRST	BINARY_INTEGER	Returns the index of the first row in the table.
LAST	BINARY_INTEGER	Returns the index of the last row in the table.
NEXT	BINARY_INTEGER	Returns the index of the next row in the table after the specified row.
PRIOR	BINARY_INTEGER	Returns the index of the previous row in the table before the specified row.

TABLE 3-1.   *PL/SQL 2.3 Table Attributes*

Table Attributes

PL/SQL 2.3 ...and HIGHER   Besides allowing tables of records, PL/SQL 2.3 extends the functionality of PL/SQL tables through *table attributes*. The syntax for using an attribute is

   table.attribute

where *table* is a PL/SQL table reference, and *attribute* is the attribute desired. PL/SQL table attributes are described in Table 3-1 and in the

following sections.

COUNT

This attribute returns the current number of rows in a PL/SQL table. Consider the following block:

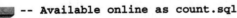

```
-- Available online as count.sql
DECLARE
  TYPE t_NumberTable IS TABLE OF NUMBER
    INDEX BY BINARY_INTEGER;
```

```
   v_Numbers t_NumberTable;
   v_Total NUMBER;
BEGIN
  -- Insert 50 rows into the table.
  FOR v_Counter IN 1..50 LOOP
    v_Numbers(v_Counter) := v_Counter;
  END LOOP;


  v_Total := v_Numbers.COUNT;
END;
```

v_Numbers.COUNT returns 50, and this value is assigned to **v_Total**.

DELETE

The DELETE attribute removes rows from a PL/SQL table. It is used as follows:

- ■ *table*.DELETE removes all rows in the table.
- ■ *table*.DELETE(*i*) removes the row with index *i* from the table.
- ■ *table*.DELETE(*i,j*) removes all rows with indices between *i* and *j* from the table.

These are illustrated in the following example:

```
-- Available online as delete.sql
DECLARE
  TYPE t_ValueTable IS TABLE OF VARCHAR2(10)
    INDEX BY BINARY_INTEGER;
  v_Values t_ValueTable;
BEGIN
  -- Insert rows into the table.
  v_Values(1) := 'One';
  v_Values(3) := 'Three';
  v_Values(-2) := 'Minus Two';
  v_Values(0) := 'Zero';
  v_Values(100) := 'Hundred';

  DBMS_OUTPUT.PUT_LINE('Before DELETE, COUNT=' || v_Values.COUNT);
  v_Values.DELETE(100);  -- Removes 'Hundred'
  DBMS_OUTPUT.PUT_LINE('After first DELETE, COUNT=' ||
                       v_Values.COUNT);
  v_Values.DELETE(1,3);  -- Removes 'One' and 'Three'
```

```
    DBMS_OUTPUT.PUT_LINE('After second DELETE, COUNT=' ||
                        v_Values.COUNT);
    v_Values.DELETE;        -- Removes all remaining values
    DBMS_OUTPUT.PUT_LINE('After last DELETE, COUNT=' ||
                        v_Values.COUNT);
END;
```

Note that the DELETE attribute is an entire statement by itself; it is not called as part of an expression like the other attributes.

EXISTS

table.EXISTS(*i*) returns TRUE if a row with index *i* is in the table and FALSE otherwise. This attribute is useful to avoid the ORA-1403 error, which is raised when referring to a nonexistent table element. Here is an example:

```
-- Available online as exists.sql
DECLARE
  TYPE t_FirstNameTable IS TABLE OF students.first_name%TYPE
    INDEX BY BINARY_INTEGER;
  FirstNames  t_FirstNameTable;
BEGIN
  -- Insert rows into the table.
  FirstNames(1) := 'Scott';
  FirstNames(3) := 'Joanne';

  -- Check to see if rows exist.
  IF FirstNames.EXISTS(1) THEN
    INSERT INTO temp_table (char_col) VALUES
      ('Row 1 exists!');
  ELSE
    INSERT INTO temp_table (char_col) VALUES
      ('Row 1 doesn''t exist!');
  END IF;
  IF FirstNames.EXISTS(2) THEN
    INSERT INTO temp_table (char_col) VALUES
      ('Row 2 exists!');
  ELSE
    INSERT INTO temp_table (char_col) VALUES
      ('Row 2 doesn''t exist!');
  END IF;
END;
```

After execution of this block, "Row 1 exists!" and "Row 2 doesn't exist" would be inserted into **temp_table**.

FIRST and LAST

FIRST and LAST return the index of the first and last rows in the PL/SQL table, respectively. Note that they don't return the value contained for these rows, just the index. The first row is defined as the row with the lowest index, and the last row is the row with the highest index. Here is an example:

```
-- Available online as frstlast.sql
DECLARE
   TYPE t_LastNameTable IS TABLE OF students.last_name%TYPE
      INDEX BY BINARY_INTEGER;
   v_LastNames   t_LastNameTable;
   v_Index   BINARY_INTEGER;
BEGIN
   -- Insert rows in the table.
   v_LastNames(43) := 'Mason';
   v_LastNames(50) := 'Junebug';
   v_LastNames(47) := 'Taller';

   -- Assigns 43 to v_Index.
   v_Index := v_LastNames.FIRST;

   -- Assigns 50 to v_Index.
   v_Index := v_LastNames.LAST;
END;
```

NEXT and PRIOR

NEXT and PRIOR each take a single argument, similar to DELETE. They return the index of the next element in the table, or the previous element, respectively. They can be used in a loop that iterates over the entire table, regardless of the values used in the indices. Here is an example:

```
-- Available online as nxtprior.sql
DECLARE
   TYPE t_MajorTable IS TABLE OF students.major%TYPE
      INDEX BY BINARY_INTEGER;
   v_Majors t_MajorTable;
   v_Index   BINARY_INTEGER;
BEGIN
   -- Insert values into the table.
   v_Majors(-7) := 'Computer Science';
   v_Majors(4) := 'History';
   v_Majors(5) := 'Economics';
```

```
-- Loop over all the rows in the table, and insert them into
-- temp_table.
v_Index := v_Majors.FIRST;
LOOP
  INSERT INTO temp_table (num_col, char_col)
    VALUES (v_Index, v_Majors(v_Index));
  EXIT WHEN v_Index = v_Majors.LAST;
  v_Index := v_Majors.NEXT(v_Index);
  END LOOP;
END;
```

Guidelines for Using PL/SQL Tables

The following list of guidelines should make dealing with PL/SQL tables a little more straightforward.

1. Keep a separate variable as a row count. This is not quite as necessary in PL/SQL 2.3 since the COUNT table attribute is available, but it is still a good idea. Since the size of a table is unconstrained, your program should keep track of how many rows have been added to the table.

2. Start with index value 1, and increment by 1 for each new element. The next element would have index 2, the following 3, and so on. This way, it is easy to loop through the elements in the table in a controlled manner. Indexing a table this way also makes it possible for the table to be bound to a C array, when the PL/SQL block is called from, or embedded in, a Pro*C or OCI program. See Chapter 13 for information on using PL/SQL in Pro*C or OCI.

3. Remember that an element in a table is not defined until it is explicitly assigned. If you refer to a table element before it has been assigned to, then the ORA–1403 error will be raised.

4. Except for the DELETE attribute in PL/SQL 2.3, there is no way to delete all the rows in a table. However, when a table is first created,

it has no rows. Thus if you need to delete an entire PL/SQL table, you can assign such an empty table to it:

```
-- Available online as nulltab.sql
DECLARE
  TYPE t_NameTable IS TABLE OF students.first_name%TYPE
    INDEX BY BINARY_INTEGER;
  v_Names t_NameTable;
  v_EmptyTable t_NameTable;
BEGIN
  /* Assign some rows to v_Names. */
  v_Names(1) := 'Scott';
  v_Names(2) := 'Lefty';
  v_Names(3) := 'Susan';
  /* Delete everything in v_Names */
  v_Names := v_EmptyTable;
END;
```

Summary

In this chapter, we have explored some of the composite user-defined types available to the PL/SQL programmer. We will see the remainder of these types in Chapters 11 and 12. First, however, we need to examine other PL/SQL fundamentals, starting with the interaction between PL/SQL and SQL in the next chapter.

CHAPTER
4

SQL Within PL/SQL

tructured Query Language (SQL) defines how data in Oracle is manipulated. The procedural constructs we examined in Chapters 2 and 3 become significantly more useful when combined with the processing power of SQL, since they allow PL/SQL programs to manipulate data in Oracle. This chapter discusses the SQL statements that are permitted in PL/SQL and the transaction control statements that guarantee consistency of the data. Chapter 5 discusses the built-in SQL functions.

SQL Statements

SQL statements can be divided into six categories, as listed here. Table 4-1 gives some example statements. The *Server SQL Reference* manual describes all of the SQL statements in detail.

■ *Data manipulation language* (DML) statements change the data in tables, or query data in a database table, but do not change the structure of a table or other object.

■ *Data definition language* (DDL) statements create, drop, or alter the structure of a schema object. Commands that change permissions on schema objects are also DDL.

■ *Transaction control* statements guarantee the consistency of the data by organizing SQL statements into logical transactions, which either succeed or fail as a unit.

■ *Session control* statements change the settings for a single database connection, for example, to enable SQL tracing.

■ *System control* statements change the settings for the entire database, for example, to enable or disable archiving.

■ *Embedded SQL* commands are used in Oracle precompiler programs.

Using SQL in PL/SQL

The only SQL statements allowed in a PL/SQL program are DML and transaction control statements. Specifically, DDL statements are illegal.

EXPLAIN PLAN, although classified as DML, is also illegal. In order to explain why this is the case, we need to look at the way PL/SQL is designed.

In general, a programming language can bind variables in two ways—early or late. *Binding* a variable is the process of identifying the storage location associated with an identifier in the program. In PL/SQL, binding also involves checking the database for permission to access the schema object referenced. A language that uses *early binding* does the bind during the compile phase, while a language that uses *late binding* postpones the bind until run time. Early binding means that the compile phase will take longer (since the work of binding has to be done), but execution will be faster, since the bind has already been completed. Late binding shortens the compile time but lengthens the execution time.

PL/SQL was intentionally designed to use early binding. This decision was made so that execution of a block would be as fast as possible, because all of the database objects have been verified by the compiler. This makes sense, since PL/SQL blocks can be stored in the database via procedures, functions, packages, and triggers. These objects are stored in compiled form, so that when needed they can be loaded from the database

Category	Sample SQL Statements
Data manipulation language (DML)	SELECT, INSERT, UPDATE, DELETE, SET TRANSACTION, EXPLAIN PLAN
Data definition language (DDL)	DROP, CREATE, ALTER, GRANT, REVOKE
Transaction control	COMMIT, ROLLBACK, SAVEPOINT
Session control	ALTER SESSION, SET ROLE
System control	ALTER SYSTEM
Embedded SQL	CONNECT, DECLARE CURSOR, ALLOCATE[1]

TABLE 4-1. *Categories of SQL Statements*

[1] The ALLOCATE embedded SQL command is available with Oracle 7.2 and higher.

into memory and run. For more information on stored objects, see Chapters 7, 8, and 9. As a result of this design decision, DDL statements are prohibited. Since a DDL statement will modify a database object, the permissions must be validated again. Validating the permissions would require that the identifiers be bound, and this has already been done during the compile.

To further illustrate this, consider the following hypothetical PL/SQL block:

```
BEGIN
  CREATE TABLE temp_table (
    num_value    NUMBER,
    char_value   CHAR(10));
  INSERT INTO temp_table (num_value, char_value)
    VALUES (10, 'Hello');
END;
```

In order to compile this, the **temp_table** identifier needs to be bound. This process will check to see whether this table exists. However, the table won't exist until the block is run. But since the block can't even compile, there is no way that it can run.

DML and transaction control statements are the only SQL statements that don't have the potential to modify schema objects or permissions on schema objects, thus they are the only legal SQL statements in PL/SQL.

Using DDL

PL/SQL **2.1** ...and HIGHER There is, however, an alternative. The built-in package DBMS_SQL is available with PL/SQL 2.1 and higher. This package allows you to create a SQL statement dynamically at run time, and then parse and execute it. Since the statement doesn't actually get created until run time, the PL/SQL compiler doesn't have to bind the identifiers in the statement, which allows the block to compile. Chapter 15 describes the DBMS_SQL package in detail. We could use the DBMS_SQL package to execute the CREATE TABLE statement in the preceding block, for example. However, the INSERT statement would fail to compile since the table wouldn't exist until the block is run. The solution to this problem is to use DBMS_SQL to execute the INSERT statement as well.

DML in PL/SQL

The allowable DML statements are SELECT, INSERT, UPDATE, and DELETE. Each of these commands operates as its name implies: SELECT

returns rows from a database table that match the criteria given by its
WHERE clause, INSERT adds rows to a database table, UPDATE modifies
the rows in a database table that match the WHERE clause, and DELETE
removes rows identified by the WHERE clause. Besides the WHERE clause,
these statements can have other clauses, which are described later in
this section.

When SQL statements are executed from SQL*Plus, the results are
returned to the screen, as shown in Figure 4-1. For an UPDATE, INSERT, or
DELETE statement, SQL*Plus returns the number of rows processed. For a
SELECT statement, the rows that match the query are echoed to the screen.

Notice the UPDATE statement in Figure 4-1:

```
UPDATE CLASSES
   SET num_credits = 3
   WHERE department = 'HIS'
   AND course = 101;
```

All of the values that are used to change the contents of **classes** are
hardcoded—they are known at the time this statement is written. PL/SQL

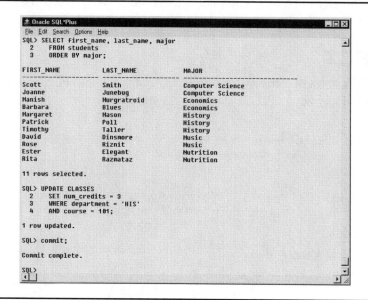

FIGURE 4-1.   *Results of executing SQL statements in SQL*Plus*

removes this restriction with variables. Variables are allowed wherever an expression is allowed in the SQL statement. When used in this manner, they are known as *bind variables*. For example, in the preceding UPDATE statement, we could replace the hardcoded value for the number of credits with a bind variable:

```
-- Available online as bindvar.sql
DECLARE
  v_NumCredits  classes.num_credits%TYPE;
BEGIN
  /* Assign to v_NumCredits */
  v_NumCredits := 3;
  UPDATE CLASSES
    SET num_credits = v_NumCredits
    WHERE department = 'HIS'
    AND course = 101;
END;
```

Not everything in a SQL statement can be replaced by a variable—only expressions. Notably, the table and column names have to be known. This is required because of early binding—names of Oracle objects have to be known at compile time. By definition, the value of a variable is not known until run time. The DBMS_SQL package can be used to overcome this restriction as well.

SELECT

A SELECT statement retrieves data from the database into PL/SQL variables. The general form of a SELECT statement is shown here:

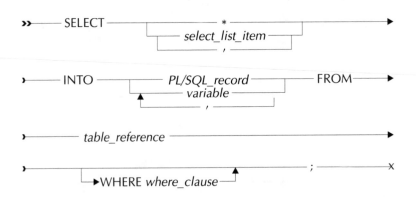

Each component is described in the following table:

Select Clause	Description
select_list_item	Column (or expression) to be selected. Each *select list item* is separated by a comma and can optionally be identified by an alias. The complete set of select list items is known as the *select list*. The * syntax is shorthand for the entire row. This will bring back every field in the table, in the order in which the fields were defined.
variable	PL/SQL variable into which a select list item will go. Each variable should be compatible with its associated select list item, and there should be the same number of select list items and output variables.
PL/SQL_record	Can be used instead of a list of variables. The record should contain fields that correspond to the select list, but allows easier manipulation of the returned data. Records combine related fields in one syntactic unit, so they can be manipulated as a group as well as individually. Records are described in more detail later in this chapter. If the select list is just *, then this record could be defined as *table_reference*%ROWTYPE.
table_reference	Identifies the table from which to get the data. Can be a synonym, or a table at a remote database specified with a database link. See the section on table references later in this chapter for more information.
where_clause	Criteria for the query. This clause identifies the row that will be returned by the query. It is made up of boolean conditions joined by the boolean operators, and is also described in more detail later in this chapter.

NOTE
In general, more clauses are available for a SELECT statement. These include the ORDER BY and GROUP BY clauses, for example. We will discuss these in more detail in Chapter 6. For more information, see the Server SQL Reference.

The form of the SELECT statement described here should return no more than one row. The WHERE clause will be compared against each row in the table. If it matches more than one row, PL/SQL will return this error message:

 ORA-1427: Single-row query returns more than one row

In this case, you should use a cursor to retrieve each row individually. See Chapter 6 for information about cursors.

The following example illustrates two different SELECT statements:

```
-- Available online as select.sql
DECLARE
  v_StudentRecord   students%ROWTYPE;
  v_Department      classes.department%TYPE;
  v_Course          classes.course%TYPE;
BEGIN
  -- Retrieve one record from the students table, and store it
  -- in v_StudentRecord. Note that the WHERE clause will only
  -- match one row in the table.
  -- Note also that the query is returning all of the fields in
  -- the students table (since we are selecting *). Thus the
  -- record into which we fetch is defined as students%ROWTYPE.
  SELECT *
    INTO v_StudentRecord
    FROM students
    WHERE id = 10000;

  -- Retrieve two fields from the classes table, and store them
  -- in v_Department and v_Course. Again, the WHERE clause will
  -- only match one row in the table.
  SELECT department, course
    INTO v_Department, v_Course
    FROM classes
    WHERE room_id = 99997;
END;
```

INSERT

The syntax for the INSERT statement is shown here. Note that there is no WHERE clause directly in the statement (although there could be one in the subquery).

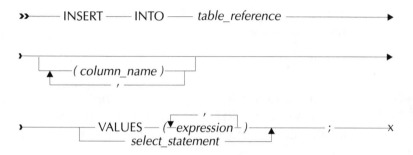

The *table_reference* clause refers to an Oracle table, *column_name* refers to a column in this table, and *expression* is a SQL or PL/SQL expression, as defined in the previous chapter. Table references are discussed in more detail later in this chapter. If the INSERT statement contains a *select_statement*, the select list should match the columns to be inserted.

The following example includes several valid INSERT statements:

```
-- Available online as insert.sql
DECLARE
  v_StudentID   students.id%TYPE;
BEGIN
  -- Retrieve a new student ID number.
  SELECT student_sequence.NEXTVAL
    INTO v_StudentID
    FROM dual;

  -- Add a row to the students table.
  INSERT INTO students (id, first_name, last_name)
    VALUES (v_StudentID, 'Timothy', 'Taller');

  -- Add a second row, but use the sequence number directly
  -- in the INSERT statement.
  INSERT INTO students (id, first_name, last_name)
    VALUES (student_sequence.NEXTVAL, 'Patrick', 'Poll');
END;
```

The following example is invalid, since the select list of the subquery does not match the columns to be inserted. This statement returns the Oracle error ORA-913: too many values.

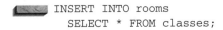

```
INSERT INTO rooms
   SELECT * FROM classes;
```

This next example, however, is legal. It doubles the size of the classes table by inserting a second copy of each row.

```
INSERT INTO classes
   SELECT * FROM classes;
```

PL/SQL 8.0 **...and HIGHER** Oracle8 with the objects option provides an additional clause for INSERT statements—the REF INTO clause. When used with object tables, this will return a reference to the object inserted. See Chapter 11 for more information.

UPDATE

The syntax for the UPDATE statement is shown here:

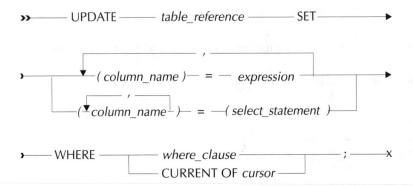

The *table_reference* clause refers to the table being updated, *column* is a column whose value will be changed, and *expression* is a SQL expression as defined in Chapter 2. If the statement contains a *select_statement*, the select list should match the columns in the SET clause.

The following block shows an example of an UPDATE statement:

```
-- Available online as update.sql
DECLARE
  v_Major             students.major%TYPE;
  v_CreditIncrease   NUMBER := 3;
BEGIN
  -- This UPDATE statement will add 3 to the current_credits
  -- field of all students who are majoring in History.
  v_Major := 'History';
  UPDATE students
    SET current_credits = current_credits + v_CreditIncrease
    WHERE major = V_Major;
END;
```

DELETE

The DELETE statement removes rows from a database table. The WHERE clause of the statement indicates which rows are to be removed. Here is the syntax for the DELETE statement:

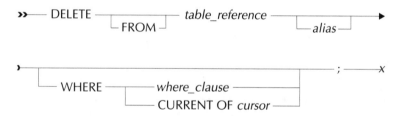

The *table_reference* clause refers to an Oracle table, and the *where_clause* defines the set of rows to be deleted. The special syntax CURRENT OF *cursor* is used with a cursor definition, and will be discussed in Chapter 6. Table references and the WHERE clause are discussed in detail in the sections that follow.

The following block illustrates some different DELETE statements:

```
-- Available online as delete.sql
DECLARE
  v_StudentCutoff  NUMBER;
BEGIN
  v_StudentCutoff := 10;
  -- Delete any classes which don't have enough
```

```
  -- students registered.
  DELETE FROM classes
    WHERE current_students < v_StudentCutoff;

  -- Delete any Economics students who don't have
  -- any credits yet.
  DELETE FROM students
    WHERE current_credits = 0
    AND   major = 'Economics';
END;
```

The WHERE Clause

The SELECT, UPDATE, and DELETE statements all include the WHERE clause as an integral part of their operations. This clause defines which statements make up the *active set*—the set of rows returned by a query (SELECT) or acted upon by an UPDATE or DELETE statement.

A WHERE clause consists of conditions, joined together by the boolean operators AND, OR, and NOT. Conditions usually take the form of comparisons, for example, in the following DELETE statement:

```
DECLARE
  v_Department  CHAR(3);
BEGIN
  v_Department := 'CS';
  -- Remove all Computer Science classes
  DELETE FROM classes
    WHERE department = v_Department;
END;
```

The preceding block will remove all rows in the **classes** table for which the condition evaluates to TRUE (those in which the **department** column = 'CS'). There are several things to note about comparisons such as these, including the importance of variable names and how characters are compared.

Variable Names

Suppose we change the name of the variable in the preceding block from **v_Department** to **department**:

```
DECLARE
  Department  CHAR(3);
BEGIN
  Department := 'CS';
  -- Remove all Computer Science classes
  DELETE FROM classes
    WHERE department = Department;
END;
```

This simple change has a dramatic effect on the results of the statement—the modified block will remove *all* rows in the classes table, not just the ones in which department = 'CS'! This happens because of the way the identifiers in a SQL statement are parsed. When the PL/SQL engine sees a condition such as

$$expr1 = expr2$$

expr1 and *expr2* are first checked to see if they match columns in the table being operated upon, then checked to see if they are variables in the PL/SQL block. PL/SQL is not case sensitive, so in the preceding block both **department** and **Department** are associated with the column in the **classes** table, rather than the variable. This condition will evaluate to TRUE for every row in the table; thus all rows will be deleted.

If the block has a label, we can still use the same name for a variable as a table column by prepending the label to the variable reference. This block has the desired effect, namely, to delete only those rows where **department** = 'CS':

```
<<l_DeleteBlock>>
DECLARE
  Department  CHAR(3);
BEGIN
  Department := 'CS';
  -- Remove all Computer Science classes
  DELETE FROM classes
    WHERE department = l_DeleteBlock.Department;
END;
```

Although this method can be used to get the desired behavior, it is still not good programming style to use the same name for a PL/SQL variable as for a table column. This and other PL/SQL style guidelines are discussed at the end of Chapter 2.

Character Comparisons

When two character values are being compared, as in the previous
example, Oracle can use two different kinds of comparison semantics:
blank-padded or non-blank-padded. These comparison semantics differ in
how character strings of different lengths are compared. Suppose we are
comparing two character strings, **string1** and **string2**. For *blank-padded*
semantics, the following algorithm is used:

1. If **string1** and **string2** are of different lengths, pad the shorter value
   with blanks first so that they are both the same length.

2. Compare each string, character by character, starting from the left.
   Suppose the character in **string1** is **char1**, and the character in
   string2 is **char2**.

3. If ASCII(**char1**) < ASCII(**char2**), **string1** < **string2**. If ASCII(**char1**) >
   ASCII(**char2**), **string1** > **string2**. If ASCII(**char1**) = ASCII(**char2**),
   continue to the next character in **string1** and **string2**.

4. If the ends of **string1** and **string2** are reached, then the strings
   are equal.

Using blank-padded semantics, the following conditions will all return
TRUE:

```
'abc' = 'abc'
'abc   ' = 'abc'   -- Note the trailing blanks in the first string
'ab' < 'abc'
'abcd' > 'abcc'
```

The *non-blank-padded* comparison algorithm is a little different:

1. Compare each string, character by character, starting from the left.
   Suppose the character in **string1** is **char1**, and the character in
   string2 is **char2**.

2. If ASCII(**char1**) < ASCII(**char2**), **string1** < **string2**. If ASCII(**char1**) >
   ASCII(**char2**), **string1** > **string2**. If ASCII(**char1**) = ASCII(**char2**),
   continue to the next character in **string1** and **string2**.

3. If **string1** ends before **string2**, then **string1** < **string2**. If **string2** ends before **string1**, then **string1** > **string2**.

Using non-blank-padded character comparison semantics, the following comparisons will return TRUE:

```
'abc' = 'abc'
'ab' < 'abc'
'abcd' > 'abcc'
```

However, the following comparison will return FALSE since the strings are of different lengths. This is the basic difference between the two comparison methods.

```
'abc   ' = 'abc'   -- Note the trailing blanks in the first string
```

Having defined these two different methods, when is each one used? PL/SQL will use blank-padded semantics only when both values being compared are *fixed-length* values. If either value is variable length, non-blank-padded semantics are used. The CHAR datatype is fixed length, and the VARCHAR2 datatype is variable length. Character literals (enclosed in single quotes) are always considered to be fixed length.

If a statement isn't acting upon the correct rows, check the datatypes used in the WHERE clause. The following block will *not* delete any rows, since the **v_Department** variable is VARCHAR2 rather than CHAR:

```
DECLARE
  v_Department  VARCHAR2(3);
BEGIN
  v_Department := 'CS';
  -- Remove all Computer Science classes
  DELETE FROM classes
    WHERE department = v_Department;
END;
```

The **department** column of the **classes** table is CHAR. Any computer science classes will thus have a value of 'CS ' for **department** (note the trailing blank). Since **v_Department** = 'CS' (no trailing blank) and is of a variable length datatype, the DELETE statement does not affect any rows.

To ensure that your WHERE clauses have the desired effect, make sure that the variables in the PL/SQL block have the same datatype as the database columns to which they are compared. Using %TYPE can guarantee this.

Table References

All of the DML operations reference a table. This reference can in general look like

>   [*schema.*]*table*[*@dblink*]

where *schema* identifies the owner of the table, and *dblink* identifies a table at a remote database.

In order to establish a database connection, the user's name and password for a particular schema must be provided. Subsequent SQL statements issued during the session will reference this schema by default. If a table reference is unqualified, as in

```
UPDATE students
   SET major = 'Music'
   WHERE id = 10005;
```

then the table name (**students** in this example) must name a table in the default schema. If it does not, then an error such as

```
ORA-942: table or view does not exist
```

or

```
PLS-201: identifier must be declared
```

will be reported. The default schema is the one to which you connect before executing any SQL or PL/SQL commands. If the table is in another schema, then it can be qualified by the schema name, as in:

```
UPDATE example.students
   SET major = 'Music'
   WHERE id = 10005;
```

The preceding UPDATE will work if the connection is made to the **example** schema, or to another schema that has been granted the UPDATE privilege on the **students** table.

Database Links

If you have SQL*Net installed on your system, you can take advantage of database links. A *database link* is a reference to a remote database, which can be located on a completely different system from the local database. The following DDL statement creates a database link:

```
CREATE DATABASE LINK link_name
  CONNECT TO username IDENTIFIED BY password
  USING sqlnet_string;
```

The name of the database link, *link_name*, follows the usual rules for a database identifier. *username* and *password* identify a schema on the remote database, and *sqlnet_string* is a valid connect string for the remote database. Assuming that the appropriate schemas have been created and SQL*Net version 2 is installed, the following is an example of a database link creation:

```
CREATE DATABASE LINK example_backup
   CONNECT TO example IDENTIFIED BY example
   USING 'backup_database';
```

For more information on how to install and configure SQL*Net, consult the *SQL*Net User's Guide and Reference*. Given the preceding link, we can now update the students table remotely with

```
UPDATE students@example_backup
   SET major = 'Music'
   WHERE id = 10005;
```

When a database link is used as part of a transaction, the transaction is said to be a *distributed transaction*, since it modifies more than one database. For more information on distributed transactions and their administration and implications, consult the *Server SQL Reference*.

Synonyms

Table references can be complicated, especially if a schema and/or database link is included. In order to make maintenance easier, Oracle allows you to create a synonym for a complicated reference. The *synonym* essentially renames the table reference, similar to an alias for a select list item. A synonym is a data dictionary object and is created by the CREATE SYNONYM DDL statement:

> CREATE SYNONYM *synonym_name* FOR *reference*;

Replace *synonym_name* with the name of your synonym and *reference* with the schema object that is referenced. Note that this schema object can be a table, as in the following example, or it could be a procedure, sequence, or other database object.

```
CREATE SYNONYM backup_students
    FOR students@example_backup;
```

Given this synonym, we can rewrite our distributed UPDATE statement with

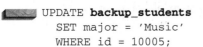

```
UPDATE backup_students
    SET major = 'Music'
    WHERE id = 10005;
```

NOTE
Creating a synonym does not grant any privileges on the referenced object—it just provides an alternate name for the object. If the object needs to be referenced from another schema, access to the object should be granted either explicitly or via a role (using the GRANT statement).

Pseudocolumns

Pseudocolumns are additional functions that can be called only from SQL statements. Syntactically, they are treated like columns in a table. However, they don't actually exist in the same way that table columns do. Rather, they are evaluated as part of the SQL statement execution.

CURRVAL and NEXTVAL

These two pseudocolumns, CURRVAL and NEXTVAL, are used with sequences. A *sequence* is an Oracle object that is used to generate unique numbers. A sequence is created with the CREATE SEQUENCE DDL command. Once a sequence is created, you can access it with

> *sequence.*CURRVAL

and

> *sequence.*NEXTVAL

where *sequence* is the name of the sequence. CURRVAL returns the current value of the sequence, and NEXTVAL increments the sequence and returns the new value. Both CURRVAL and NEXTVAL return NUMBER values.

Sequence values can be used in the select list of a query, in the VALUES clause of an INSERT statement, and in the SET clause of an UPDATE statement. They cannot be used in the WHERE clause or in a PL/SQL procedural statement, however. The following are legal examples of using CURRVAL and NEXTVAL:

```
CREATE SEQUENCE student_sequence
  START WITH 10000;

-- This statement will use 10,000 as the id value
INSERT INTO students (id, first_name, last_name)
  VALUES (student_sequence.NEXTVAL, 'Scott', 'Smith');

-- This statement will use 10,001 as the id value
INSERT INTO students (id, first_name, last_name)
  VALUES (student_sequence.NEXTVAL, 'Margaret', 'Mason');

SELECT student_sequence.NEXTVAL "Value"
  FROM dual;  -- Increments the sequence number first
Value
----------
10002
```

```
SELECT student_sequence.CURRVAL "Value"
  FROM dual;  -- Returns the current value
Value
----------
10002
```

LEVEL

LEVEL is used only inside a SELECT statement that implements a hierarchical tree walk over a table, using the START WITH and CONNECT BY clauses. The LEVEL pseudocolumn will return the current level of the tree as a NUMBER value. For more information, see the *Server SQL Reference.*

ROWID

The ROWID pseudocolumn is used in the select list of a query. It returns the row identifier of that particular row. The external format of a ROWID is an 18-character string, as described in Chapter 2. The ROWID pseudocolumn returns a value of type ROWID. For example, the following query returns all of the rowids in the **rooms** table:

```
SELECT ROWID
  FROM rooms;

ROWID
------------------
00000045.0000.0002
00000045.0001.0002
00000045.0002.0002
00000045.0003.0002
00000045.0004.0002
```

NOTE
The format of a ROWID is different in Oracle8 from the format in Oracle7. However, the external format for both is still an 18-character string. See Chapter 2 for more information.

ROWNUM

ROWNUM will return the current row number in a query. It is useful for limiting the total number of rows, and it is used primarily in the WHERE clause of queries and the SET clause of UPDATE statements. ROWNUM returns a NUMBER value. For example, the following query returns only the first two rows from the **students** table:

```
SELECT *
  FROM students
  WHERE ROWNUM < 3;
```

The first row has ROWNUM 1, the second has ROWNUM 2, and so on.

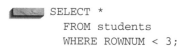

NOTE
The ROWNUM value is assigned to a row before a sort is done (via the ORDER BY clause). As a result, you cannot use ROWNUM to retrieve the n highest rows in the search order. Consider this statement:

```
SELECT first_name, last_name
  FROM students
  WHERE ROWNUM < 3
  ORDER BY first_name;
```

*While this statement will return two rows from the **students** table, sorted by **first_name**, they won't necessarily be the first two rows in the entire sort order. To guarantee this, it is best to declare a cursor for this query and only fetch the first two rows. Chapter 6 discusses cursors and how to use them.*

GRANT, REVOKE, and Privileges

While DDL statements such as GRANT and REVOKE can't be used directly in PL/SQL, they do have an effect on which SQL statements are legal. In order to perform an operation such as INSERT or DELETE on an Oracle table, you need permission to perform the operation. These permissions are manipulated via the GRANT and REVOKE SQL commands.

Object vs. System Privileges

There are two different kinds of privileges—object and system. An *object privilege* allows an operation on a particular object (such as a table). A *system privilege* allows operations on an entire class of objects.

Table 4-2 describes the available object privileges. The DDL object privileges (ALTER, INDEX, REFERENCES) can't be utilized directly in PL/SQL (except for the DBMS_SQL package), since they allow DDL operations on the object in question.

There are many system privileges for just about any DDL operation possible. For example, the CREATE TABLE system privilege allows the grantee to create tables. The CREATE ANY TABLE system privilege allows the grantee to create tables in other schemas. The *Server SQL Reference* documents all of the available system privileges.

GRANT and REVOKE

The GRANT statement is used to allow another schema access to a privilege, and the REVOKE statement is used to remove the access allowed by GRANT. Both statements can be used for object and system privileges.

GRANT
The basic syntax of GRANT for object privileges is

GRANT *privilege* ON *object* TO *grantee* [WITH GRANT OPTION];

where *privilege* is the desired privilege, *object* is the object to which access is granted, and *grantee* is the user who will receive the privilege. For

Object Privilege	Description	Types of Schema Objects
ALTER	Allows grantee to issue an ALTER statement (such as ALTER TABLE) on the object.	Tables, sequences
DELETE	Allows grantee to issue a DELETE statement against the object.	Tables, views
EXECUTE	Allows grantee to execute the stored PL/SQL object. (Stored objects are discussed in Chapters 7-9.)	Procedures, functions, packages
INDEX	Allows grantee to create an index on the table via the CREATE INDEX command.	Tables
INSERT	Allows grantee to issue an INSERT statement against the object.	Tables, views
REFERENCES	Allows grantee to create a constraint that refers to the table.	Tables
SELECT	Allows grantee to issue a SELECT statement against the object.	Tables, views, sequences, snapshots
UPDATE	Allows grantee to issue an UPDATE statement against the object.	Tables, views

TABLE 4-2. *SQL Object Privileges*

example, assuming that **userA** is a valid database schema, the following GRANT statement is legal:

```
GRANT SELECT ON classes TO userA;
```

If the WITH GRANT OPTION is specified, then **userA** can in turn grant the privilege to another user. More than one privilege can be specified in one GRANT statement, for example:

```
GRANT UPDATE, DELETE ON students TO userA;
```

For system privileges, the syntax is

GRANT *privilege* TO *grantee* [WITH ADMIN OPTION];

where *privilege* is the system privilege to be granted, and *grantee* is the user receiving the privilege. If WITH ADMIN OPTION is included, then *grantee* can grant the privilege to other users as well. For example:

```
GRANT CREATE TABLE, ALTER ANY PROCEDURE to userA;
```

Similar to the GRANT statement for object privileges, more than one system privilege can be specified in the same statement.

Since GRANT is a DDL statement, it takes effect immediately and issues an implicit COMMIT after execution.

REVOKE

The syntax for REVOKE for object privileges is

REVOKE *privilege* ON *object* FROM *grantee* [CASCADE CONSTRAINTS];

where *privilege* is the privilege to be revoked, *object* is the object on which the privilege is granted, and *grantee* is the recipient of the privilege. For example, the following is a legal REVOKE command:

```
REVOKE SELECT ON classes FROM userA;
```

If the CASCADE CONSTRAINTS clause is included and the REFERENCES privilege is being revoked, all referential integrity constraints created by *grantee* with this privilege are dropped as well. Multiple privileges can also be revoked with one statement, as in

```
REVOKE UPDATE, DELETE, INSERT ON students FROM userA;
```

To revoke a system privilege, the syntax is

REVOKE *privilege* FROM *grantee*;

where *privilege* is the system privilege to be revoked, and *grantee* is the user who will no longer have this privilege. For example:

```
REVOKE ALTER TABLE, EXECUTE ANY PROCEDURE FROM userA;
```

Roles

In a large Oracle system, with many different user accounts, administrating privileges can be a challenge. To ease this, Oracle provides a facility known as roles. A *role* is essentially a collection of privileges, both object and system. Consider the following series of statements:

```
CREATE ROLE table_query;
GRANT SELECT ON students TO table_query;
GRANT SELECT ON classes TO table_query;
GRANT SELECT ON rooms TO table_query;
```

The **table_query** role has SELECT privileges on three different tables. We can now grant this role to additional users with

```
GRANT table_query TO userA;
GRANT table_query TO userB;
```

Now, **userA** and **userB** have SELECT privileges on the three tables. This is easier to administer than the six separate grants that would otherwise have been required.

The role PUBLIC is predefined by Oracle. Every user has been automatically granted this role. Thus, you can issue a statement such as,

```
GRANT privilege TO PUBLIC;
```

which grants the privilege to every Oracle user at once.

Oracle predefines several other roles, which include common system privileges. These are listed in Table 4-3. The predefined Oracle user SYSTEM is automatically granted all of these roles.

Typically, the CONNECT and RESOURCE roles are granted to the database users who will be creating schema objects, and just the CONNECT role is granted to users who query schema objects. Users with just CONNECT would need additional object privileges on the schema objects that they will need to access.

Role Name	Privileges Granted
CONNECT	ALTER SESSION, CREATE CLUSTER, CREATE DATABASE LINK, CREATE SEQUENCE, CREATE SESSION, CREATE SYNONYM, CREATE TABLE, CREATE VIEW
RESOURCE	CREATE CLUSTER, CREATE PROCEDURE, CREATE SEQUENCE, CREATE TABLE, CREATE PROCEDURE
DBA	All system privileges (with the ADMIN OPTION, so they can be granted again), plus EXP_FULL_DATABASE and IMP_FULL_DATABASE
EXP_FULL_DATABASE	SELECT ANY TABLE, BACKUP ANY TABLE, plus INSERT, UPDATE, DELETE on the system tables **sys.incexp**, **sys.incvid**, and **sys.incfil**
IMP_FULL_DATABASE	BECOME USER

TABLE 4-3. *Predefined System Roles*

Transaction Control

A *transaction* is a series of SQL statements that either succeeds or fails as a unit. Transactions are a standard part of relational databases and prevent inconsistent data. The classic example of this is a bank transaction: consider the following two SQL statements, which implement a transfer of **transaction_amount** dollars between two bank accounts identified as **from_acct** and **to_acct**.

```
UPDATE accounts
  SET balance = balance - transaction_amount
  WHERE account_no = from_acct;
UPDATE accounts
  SET balance = balance + transaction_amount
  WHERE account_no = to_acct;
```

Suppose the first UPDATE statement succeeds, but the second statement fails due to an error (perhaps the database or network went down). The data is now inconsistent—**from_acct** has been debited, but **to_acct** has not been credited. Needless to say, this is not a good situation, especially if you are the owner of **from_acct**. We prevent this by combining the two statements into a transaction, whereby either both statements will succeed, or both statements will fail. This prevents inconsistent data.

A transaction begins with the first SQL statement issued after the previous transaction, or the first SQL statement after connecting to the database. The transaction ends with the COMMIT or ROLLBACK statement.

COMMIT vs. ROLLBACK

When a COMMIT statement is issued to the database, the transaction is ended, and:

- All work done by the transaction is made permanent.

- Other sessions can see the changes made by this transaction.

- Any locks acquired by the transaction are released.

The syntax for the COMMIT statement is

COMMIT [WORK];

The optional WORK keyword is available for increased readability. Until a transaction is committed, only the session executing that transaction can see the changes made by that session. This is illustrated in Figure 4-2. Session A issues the INSERT statement first. Session B issues a query against the **rooms** table, but does not see the INSERT done by session A, since it hasn't been committed. Session A then commits, and the second SELECT by session B will see the new inserted row.

When a ROLLBACK statement is issued to the database, the transaction is ended, and:

- All work done by the transaction is undone, as if it hadn't been issued.

- Any locks acquired by the transaction are released.

Session A	Session B	

INSERT INTO rooms
   (room_id, building, room_number,
   number_seats, description)
   VALUES (99991, 'Building 7', 310,
   50, 'Discussion Room E');		

	SELECT *
	   FROM rooms
	   WHERE building = 'Building 7';
		TIME

COMMIT;		

	SELECT *
	   FROM rooms
	   WHERE building = 'Building 7';	

FIGURE 4-2. *Two sessions*

The syntax for the ROLLBACK statement is

ROLLBACK [WORK];

Just like COMMIT, the WORK keyword is optional and is available for increased readability. An explicit ROLLBACK statement is often used when an error is detected by the program that prevents further work. If a session disconnects from the database without ending the current transaction with COMMIT or ROLLBACK, the transaction is automatically rolled back by the database.

NOTE
*SQL*Plus will automatically issue a COMMIT when you exit. The **autocommit** option will issue a COMMIT after every SQL statement, as well. This does not affect the SQL statements inside a PL/SQL block, since SQL*Plus doesn't have control until the block finishes.*

Savepoints

The ROLLBACK statement undoes the entire transaction, as we have seen. With the SAVEPOINT command, however, only part of the transaction need be undone. The syntax for SAVEPOINT is

SAVEPOINT *name*;

where *name* is the savepoint's name. Savepoint names follow the usual rules for SQL identifiers (see Chapter 2). Note that savepoints are not declared in the declarative section, since they are global to a transaction, and the transaction can continue past the end of the block. Once a savepoint is defined, the program can roll back to the savepoint via the following syntax:

ROLLBACK [WORK] TO SAVEPOINT *name*;

When a ROLLBACK TO SAVEPOINT is issued, the following things occur:

- Any work done since the savepoint is undone. The savepoint remains active, however. It can be rolled back to again, if desired.

- Any locks and resources acquired by the SQL statements since the savepoint will be released.

- The transaction is *not* finished, since SQL statements are still pending.

Consider the following fragment of a PL/SQL block:

```
BEGIN
  INSERT INTO temp_table (char_col) VALUES ('Insert One');
  SAVEPOINT A;
  INSERT INTO temp_table (char_col) VALUES ('Insert Two');
  SAVEPOINT B;
  INSERT INTO temp_table (char_col) VALUES ('Insert Three');
  SAVEPOINT C;
  /* Missing statements here */
  COMMIT;
END;
```

If we put

```
ROLLBACK TO B;
```

in for the missing statements, the third INSERT and savepoint C will be undone. But the first two INSERTs will be processed. If, on the other hand, we put

```
ROLLBACK TO A;
```

in for the missing statements, the second and third INSERTs will be undone, leaving only the first INSERT.

SAVEPOINT is often used before a complicated section of a transaction. If this part of the transaction fails, it can be rolled back, allowing the earlier part to continue.

Transactions vs. Blocks

It is important to note the distinction between transactions and PL/SQL blocks. When a block starts, it does not mean that a transaction starts. Likewise, the start of a transaction need not coincide with the start of a block. For example, suppose we issue the following statements from the SQL*Plus prompt:

```
-- Available online as 1trans.sql
INSERT INTO classes
    (department, course, description, max_students,
    current_students, num_credits, room_id)
  VALUES ('CS', 101, 'Computer Science 101', 50, 10, 4, 99998);

BEGIN
  UPDATE rooms
    SET room_id = room_id - 1000;
  ROLLBACK WORK;
END;
```

Note that we have issued an INSERT statement and then an anonymous PL/SQL block. The block issues an UPDATE and then a ROLLBACK. This ROLLBACK undoes not only the UPDATE statement, but the prior INSERT as well. Both the INSERT statement and the block are part of the same database session, thus the same transaction.

Similarly, a single PL/SQL block can contain multiple transactions. Consider the following:

```
-- Available online as 1block.sql
DECLARE
  v_NumIterations    NUMBER;
BEGIN
  -- Loop from 1 to 500, inserting these values into temp_table.
  -- Commit every 50 rows.
  FOR v_LoopCounter IN 1..500 LOOP
    INSERT INTO temp_table (num_col) VALUES (v_LoopCounter);
    v_NumIterations := v_NumIterations + 1;
    IF v_NumIterations = 50 THEN
      COMMIT;
      v_NumIterations := 0;
    END IF;
  END LOOP;
END;
```

This block will insert the numbers 1 through 500 into **temp_table** and will commit after every 50 rows. So there will be a total of 10 transactions during the execution of 1 block.

Summary

In this chapter, we have discussed the SQL language in general, and the DML and transaction control statements allowed in PL/SQL in particular. We've also explored privileges and roles, and we've seen how transactions prevent inconsistent data. In the next chapter, we will discuss the built-in SQL functions. Chapter 6 discusses cursors, which are used for multirow queries. It will build on the concepts in this and the next chapter.

CHAPTER
5

Built-in SQL Functions

he basic SQL commands that we saw in Chapter 4 are enhanced by many predefined functions. In this chapter, we will examine the different kinds of functions and discuss some of their uses.

Introduction

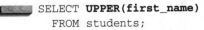

SQL provides a number of predefined functions that can be called from a SQL statement. For example, the following SELECT statement uses the UPPER function to return the first names of students, in all uppercase, rather than the case in which they were stored:

```
SELECT UPPER(first_name)
   FROM students;
```

Many SQL functions can be called from PL/SQL procedural statements as well. For example, the following block also uses the UPPER function, but in an assignment statement:

```
DECLARE
   v_FirstName  students.first_name%TYPE;
BEGIN
   v_FirstName := UPPER('Charlie');
END;
```

SQL functions can be divided into categories based on the type of arguments each function expects. The UPPER function, for example, expects a character argument. If you supply an argument that is not in the correct family, it is converted automatically by PL/SQL before the function is called, in accordance with the datatype conversion rules which we saw in Chapter 2. SQL functions can also be classified as group or single-row functions. A *group function* operates on many rows of data and returns a single result. Group functions are valid only in the select list or HAVING clause of a query. They are not allowed in PL/SQL procedural statements. COUNT is an example of a group function. *Single-row functions*, such as UPPER, operate on one value and return another value. They are allowed anywhere an expression is allowed in SQL statements, and also in PL/SQL procedural statements.

The following sections describe built-in functions in detail. Each section lists the syntax, purpose, and where a function is allowed. Examples are also provided. The functions are listed in alphabetical order within each section. Some of the functions take optional arguments. These are indicated by square brackets ([]) in the function's syntax.

Character Functions
Returning Character Values

These functions all take arguments in the character family (except CHR) and return character values. The majority of the functions return a VARCHAR2 value, except where noted. The return type of character functions is subject to the same restrictions as the base database type, namely that VARCHAR2 values are limited to 2,000 characters (4,000 in Oracle8), and CHAR values are limited to 255 characters (2,000 in Oracle8). When used in procedural statements, they can be assigned to either VARCHAR2 or CHAR PL/SQL variables.

CHR
Syntax

CHR(*x*)

PURPOSE   Returns the character that has the value equivalent to *x* in the database character set. CHR and ASCII are opposite functions. CHR returns the character given the character number, and ASCII returns the character number given the character.

WHERE ALLOWED   Procedural and SQL statements.

Example

```
SQL> SELECT CHR(37) a, CHR(100) b, CHR(101) c
  2    FROM dual;

A B C
- - -
% d e
```

CONCAT

Syntax

CONCAT(*string1, string2*)

PURPOSE   Returns *string1* concatenated with *string2*. This function is identical to the II operator.

WHERE ALLOWED   Procedural and SQL statements.

Example

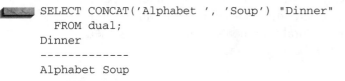

```
SELECT CONCAT('Alphabet ', 'Soup') "Dinner"
   FROM dual;
Dinner
-------------
Alphabet Soup
```

INITCAP

Syntax

INITCAP(*string*)

PURPOSE   Returns *string* with the first character of each word capitalized and the remaining characters of each word in lowercase. Words are separated by spaces or nonalphanumeric characters. Characters that are not letters are unaffected.

WHERE ALLOWED   Procedural and SQL statements.

Example

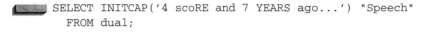

```
SELECT INITCAP('4 scoRE and 7 YEARS ago...') "Speech"
   FROM dual;
```

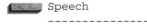

```
Speech
--------------------------
4 Score And 7 Years Ago...
```

LOWER

Syntax

LOWER(*string*)

PURPOSE   Returns *string* with all characters in lowercase. Any characters that are not letters are left intact. If *string* has the CHAR datatype, the result is also CHAR. If *string* is VARCHAR2, the result is VARCHAR2.

WHERE ALLOWED   Procedural and SQL statements.

Example

```
SELECT LOWER('4 scoRE and 7 YEARS ago...') "Speech"
  FROM dual;
Speech
-------------------------
4 score and 7 years ago...
```

LPAD

Syntax

LPAD(*string1*, *x* [,*string2*])

PURPOSE   Returns *string1* padded on the left to length *x* with the characters in *string2*. If *string2* is fewer than *x* characters, it is duplicated as necessary. If *string2* is more than *x* characters, only the first *x* characters of *string2* are used. If *string2* is not specified, it defaults to a single blank. Note that *x* is specified in terms of display length, rather than actual length. If the database character set is multibyte, the display length can be longer than the actual length of the string in bytes. LPAD behaves similarly to RPAD, except that it pads on the left rather than the right.

WHERE ALLOWED   Procedural and SQL statements.

Example

```
SELECT LPAD('Short String', 15) "First"
   FROM dual;
First
---------------
    Short String

SELECT LPAD('Short String', 20, 'XY') "Second"
   FROM dual;
Second
--------------------
XYXYXYXYShort String

SELECT LPAD('Short String', 13, 'XY') "Third"
   FROM dual;
Third
-------------
XShort String
```

LTRIM

Syntax

LTRIM(*string1, string2*)

PURPOSE   Returns *string1* with the leftmost characters appearing in *string2* removed. *string2* defaults to a single blank. The database will scan *string1*, starting from the leftmost position. When the first character not in *string2* is encountered, the result is returned. LTRIM behaves similarly to RTRIM.

WHERE ALLOWED   Procedural and SQL statements.

Example

```
SELECT LTRIM('   End of the string') "First"
   FROM dual;
First
----------------
End of the string
```

```
SELECT LTRIM('xxxEnd of the string', 'x') "Second"
  FROM dual;
Second
-----------------
End of the string

SELECT LTRIM('xyxyxyEnd of the string', 'xy') "Third"
  FROM dual;
Third
-----------------
End of the string

SELECT LTRIM('xyxyxxxyEnd of the string', 'xy') "Fourth"
  FROM dual;
Fourth
-----------------
End of the string
```

NLS_INITCAP

Syntax

NLS_INITCAP(*string* [,*nlsparams*])

PURPOSE   Returns *string* with the first character of each word capitalized and the remaining characters of each word in lowercase. *nlsparams* specifies a different sorting sequence than the default for the session. If it is not specified, NLS_INITCAP behaves the same as INITCAP. *nlsparams* should be of the form

'NLS_SORT = *sort*'

where *sort* specifies a linguistic sort sequence. For more information on NLS parameters and how they are used, see the *Server SQL Reference*.

WHERE ALLOWED   Procedural and SQL statements.

Example

```
SELECT NLS_INITCAP('ijsbeer', 'NLS_SORT = Xdutch') "Result"
  FROM dual;
```

```
Result
------
IJsbeer
```

NLS_LOWER
Syntax

NLS_LOWER(*string* [,*nlsparams*])

PURPOSE   Returns *string* with all letters in lowercase. Characters that are not letters are left intact. *nlsparams* has the same form and serves the same purpose as in NLS_INITCAP. If *nlsparams* is not included, NLS_LOWER behaves the same as LOWER.

WHERE ALLOWED   Procedural and SQL statements.

Example

```
SELECT NLS_LOWER('CITA''DEL', 'NLS_SORT = Xgerman') "Result"
   FROM dual;
Result
---------
citàdel
```

NLS_UPPER
Syntax

NLS_UPPER(*string*, [,*nlsparams*])

PURPOSE   Returns *string* with all letters in uppercase. Characters that are not letters are left intact. *nlsparams* has the same form and behaves the same as in NLS_INITCAP. If *nlsparams* isn't specified, NLS_UPPER behaves the same as UPPER.

WHERE ALLOWED   Procedural and SQL statements.

Example

```
SELECT NLS_UPPER('große', 'NLS_SORT = Xgerman') "Result"
   FROM dual;
Result
------
GROSS
```

REPLACE
Syntax

REPLACE (*string, search_str* [,*replace_str*])

PURPOSE   Returns *string* with every occurrence of *search_str* replaced with *replace_str*. If *replace_str* is not specified, all occurrences of *search_str* are removed. REPLACE is a subset of the functionality provided by TRANSLATE.

WHERE ALLOWED   Procedural and SQL statements.

Example

```
SELECT REPLACE('This and That', 'Th', 'B') "First"
   FROM dual;
First
-----------
Bis and Bat

SELECT REPLACE('This and That', 'Th') "Second"
   FROM dual;
Second
---------
is and at

SELECT REPLACE('This and That', NULL) "Third"
   FROM dual;
Third
-------------
This and That
```

RPAD
Syntax

RPAD(*string1*, *x* [,*string2*])

PURPOSE   Returns *string1* padded on the right to length *x* with the characters in *string2*. If *string2* is fewer than *x* characters, it is duplicated as necessary. If *string2* is more than *x* characters, only the first *x* are used. If *string2* is not specified, it defaults to a single blank. Note that *x* is specified in terms of display length rather than actual length. If the database character set is multibyte, the display length can be longer than the actual length of the string in bytes. RPAD behaves similarly to LPAD, except that it pads on the right rather than the left.

WHERE ALLOWED   Procedural and SQL statements.

Example

```
SELECT RPAD('Nifty', 10, '!') "First"
  FROM dual;
First
----------
Nifty!!!!!

SELECT RPAD('Nifty', 10, 'AB') "Second"
  FROM dual;
Second
----------
NiftyABABA
```

RTRIM
Syntax

RTRIM(*string1* [,*string2*])

PURPOSE   Returns *string1* with the rightmost characters appearing in *string2* removed. *string2* defaults to a single blank. The database will scan *string1* , starting from the rightmost position. When the first character not in *string2* is encountered, the result is returned. RTRIM behaves similarly to LTRIM.

WHERE ALLOWED   Procedural and SQL statements.

Example

```
SELECT RTRIM('This is a stringxxxxx', 'x') "First"
   FROM dual;
First
----------------
This is a string

SELECT RTRIM('This is also a stringxxXXxx', 'x') "Second"
   FROM dual;
Second
------------------------
This is also a stringxxXX

SELECT RTRIM('This is a string as well', 'well') "Third"
   FROM dual;
Third
-------------------
This is a string as
```

SOUNDEX
Syntax

SOUNDEX(*string*)

PURPOSE   Returns the phonetic representation of *string*. This is useful for comparing words that are spelled differently but sound alike. The phonetic representation is defined in *The Art of Computer Programming, Volume 3: Sorting and Searching,* by Donald E. Knuth. The algorithm for developing the phonetic spelling is as follows:

■ Keep the first letter of the string, but remove occurrences of a, e, h, i, o, w, and y.

■ Assign numbers to the remaining letters as follows:

1. a, e, h, i, o, w, y

2. b, f, p, v

3. c, e, g, j, k, q, s, x, z

4. d, t

5. l

6. m, n

7. r

- If two or more numbers are in sequence, remove all but the first.

- Return the first 4 bytes padded with 0.

WHERE ALLOWED   Procedural and SQL statements.

Example

```
SELECT first_name, SOUNDEX(first_name)
  FROM students;
FIRST_NAME              SOUN
-------------------     ----
Scott                   S300
Margaret                M626
Joanne                  J500
Manish                  M520
Patrick                 P362
Timothy                 T530

SELECT first_name
  FROM students
  WHERE SOUNDEX(first_name) = SOUNDEX('skit');
FIRST_NAME
--------------------
Scott
```

SUBSTR
Syntax

SUBSTR(*string, a* [,*b*])

PURPOSE   Returns a portion of *string* starting at character *a*, *b* characters long. If *a* is 0, it is treated as 1 (the beginning of the string). If *b* is positive, characters are returned counting from the left. If *b* is negative, characters are returned starting from the end of *string*, and counting from the right. If *b* is not present, it defaults to the entire string. If *b* is less than 1, NULL is returned. If a floating point value is passed for either *a* or *b*, the value is truncated to an integer first.

WHERE ALLOWED   Procedural and SQL statements.

Example

```
SELECT SUBSTRB('abc123def', 4, 4) "First"
   FROM dual;
First
-----
123d

SELECT SUBSTR('abc123def', -4, 4) "Second"
   FROM dual;
Second
------
3def

SELECT SUBSTR('abc123def', 5) "Third"
   FROM dual;

Third
-----
23def
```

SUBSTRB
Syntax

SUBSTRB(*string, a* [,*b*])

PURPOSE   Behaves the same as SUBSTR, except that *a* and *b* are expressed in bytes rather than characters. For a single-byte character string, such as ASCII, SUBSTRB behaves the same as SUBSTR.

WHERE ALLOWED   Procedural and SQL statements.

Example (Assuming a Double-Byte Character Set)

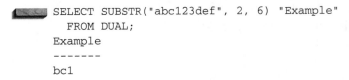

```
SELECT SUBSTR("abc123def", 2, 6) "Example"
   FROM DUAL;
Example
-------
bc1
```

TRANSLATE
Syntax

> TRANSLATE(*string, from_str, to_str*)

PURPOSE   Returns *string* with all occurrences of each character in *from_str* replaced by the corresponding character in *to_str*. TRANSLATE is a superset of the functionality provided by REPLACE. If *from_str* is longer than *to_str*, any extra characters in *from_str* not in *to_str* are removed from *string*, since they have no corresponding characters. *to_str* cannot be empty. Oracle interprets the empty string to be the same as NULL, and if any argument to TRANSLATE is NULL, the result is NULL as well.

WHERE ALLOWED   Procedural and SQL statements.

Example

```
SELECT TRANSLATE('abcdefghij', 'abcdef', '123456')
   FROM dual;
TRANSLATE(
----------
123456ghij

SELECT TRANSLATE('abcdefghij', 'abcdefghij', '123456')
   FROM dual;
TRANSL
------
123456
```

UPPER
Syntax

UPPER(*string*)

PURPOSE Returns *string* with all letters in uppercase. If string has datatype CHAR, the return value is also CHAR. If string has datatype VARCHAR2, the return value is VARCHAR2. Characters that are not letters are left intact in the returned value.

WHERE ALLOWED Procedural and SQL statements.

Example

```
SELECT UPPER('THE quick bROwn Fox jumped over THE LAZY dOg...') "Result"
  FROM dual;
Result
------------------------------------------------
THE QUICK BROWN FOX JUMPED OVER THE LAZY DOG...
```

Character Functions Returning Numeric Values

These functions take character arguments and return numeric results. The arguments can be either CHAR or VARCHAR2. Although many results are in fact integer values, the return value is simply NUMBER, with no precision or scale defined.

ASCII
Syntax

ASCII(*string*)

PURPOSE Returns the decimal representation of the first byte of *string* in the database character set. Note that the function is still called ASCII even if the character set is not 7-bit ASCII. CHR and ASCII are opposite functions. CHR returns the character given the character number, and ASCII returns the character number given the character.

WHERE ALLOWED   Procedural and SQL statements.

Example

```
SELECT ASCII(' ')
  FROM dual;
ASCII('')
---------
       32

SELECT ASCII('a')
  FROM dual;
ASCII('A')
----------
       97
```

INSTR

Syntax

INSTR(*string1*, *string2* [,*a* [,*b*]])

PURPOSE   Returns the position within *string1* where *string2* is contained. *string1* is scanned from the left, starting at position *a*. If *a* is negative, then *string1* is scanned from the right. The position of the *b*th occurrence is returned. Both *a* and *b* default to 1, which would return the first occurrence of *string2* within *string1*. If *string2* isn't found subject to *a* and *b*, 0 is returned. Positions are relative to the beginning of *string1* regardless of the values of *a* and *b*.

WHERE ALLOWED   Procedural and SQL statements.

Example

```
SELECT INSTR('Scott''s spot', 'ot', 1, 2) "First"
  FROM dual;
```

```
        First
---------
       11

SELECT INSTR('Scott''s spot', 'ot', -1, 2) "Second"
  FROM dual;
   Second
---------
        3

SELECT INSTR('Scott''s spot', 'ot', 5) "Third"
  FROM dual;
    Third
---------
       11

SELECT INSTR('Scott''s spot', 'ot', 12) "Fourth"
  FROM dual;
   Fourth
---------
        0
```

INSTRB

Syntax

INSTRB(*string1, string2* [,a [,b]])

PURPOSE   Behaves the same as INSTR, except that *a* and the return value are expressed as bytes. Similar to SUBSTRB, INSTRB behaves the same as INSTR for single-byte character sets.

WHERE ALLOWED   Procedural and SQL statements.

Example (Assuming a Double-Byte Character Set)

```
SELECT INSTRB('Scott''s spot', 'ot', 1, 2) "INSTRB"
  FROM dual;
   INSTRB
---------
       21
```

LENGTH

Syntax

LENGTH(*string*)

PURPOSE   Returns the length of *string* in characters. Since CHAR values are blank-padded, if *string* has datatype CHAR, the trailing blanks are included in the length. If *string* is NULL, the function returns NULL.

WHERE ALLOWED   Procedural and SQL statements.

Example

```
SELECT LENGTH('Mary had a little lamb') "Length"
  FROM dual;
  Length
---------
      22
```

LENGTHB

Syntax

LENGTHB(*string*)

PURPOSE   Behaves the same as LENGTH, except that the return value is expressed in bytes rather than characters. Similar to INSTRB, LENGTHB behaves the same as LENGTH for single-byte character sets.

WHERE ALLOWED   Procedural and SQL statements.

Example (Assuming a Double-Byte Character Set)

```
SELECT LENGTHB('Mary had a little lamb') "Length"
  FROM dual;
  Length
---------
      44
```

NLSSORT
Syntax

NLSSORT(*string* [,*nlsparams*])

PURPOSE   Returns the string of bytes used to sort *string*. All character values are converted into byte strings such as this for consistency among different database character sets. *nlsparams* behaves the same as it does for NLS_INITCAP. If *nlsparams* is omitted, the default sort sequence for your session is used. For more information on sort sequences, see the "National Language Support" section of the *Server SQL Reference*.

WHERE ALLOWED   Procedural and SQL statements.

Example

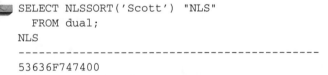

```
SELECT NLSSORT('Scott') "NLS"
   FROM dual;
NLS
---------------------------------------------
53636F747400
```

Numeric Functions

These functions take NUMBER arguments and return NUMBER values. The return values of the transcendental and trigonometric functions are accurate to 36 decimal digits. ACOS, ASIN, ATAN, and ATAN2 (all new in Oracle8) are accurate to 30 decimal digits.

ABS
Syntax

ABS(*x*)

PURPOSE   Returns the absolute value of *x*.

WHERE ALLOWED   Procedural and SQL statements.

Example

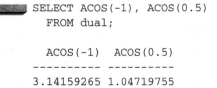

```
SELECT ABS(-7), ABS(7)
  FROM dual;
  ABS(-7)    ABS(7)
--------- ---------
        7         7
```

ACOS
Syntax

ACOS(*x*)

PURPOSE   Returns the arc cosine of *x*. *x* should range from -1 to 1, and the output ranges from 0 to Π, expressed in radians.

WHERE ALLOWED   Procedural and SQL statements.

Example

```
SELECT ACOS(-1), ACOS(0.5)
  FROM dual;

  ACOS(-1)   ACOS(0.5)
---------- ----------
3.14159265 1.04719755
```

ASIN
Syntax

ASIN(*x*)

PURPOSE   Returns the arc sine of *x*. *x* should range from -1 to 1, and the output ranges from -Π/2 to Π/2, expressed in radians.

WHERE ALLOWED   Procedural and SQL statements.

Example

```
SELECT ASIN(1), ASIN(0.5)
  FROM dual;

   ASIN(1)  ASIN(0.5)
---------- ----------
1.57079633 .523598776
```

ATAN

Syntax

ATAN(x)

PURPOSE   Returns the arc tangent of x. The output ranges from −Π/2 to Π/2, expressed in radians.

WHERE ALLOWED   Procedural and SQL statements.

Example

```
SELECT ATAN(0), ATAN(0.5)
  FROM dual;

  ATAN(0)  ATAN(0.5)
---------- ----------
        0 .463647609
```

ATAN2

Syntax

ATAN2(x, y)

PURPOSE   Returns the arc tangent of x and y. The output ranges from -Π to Π, depending on the signs of x and y, and is expressed in radians. ATAN2(x, y) is the same as ATAN(x/y).

WHERE ALLOWED   Procedural and SQL statements.

Example

```
SELECT ATAN2(1, 2)
  FROM dual;

ATAN2(1,2)
----------
.463647609
```

CEIL
Syntax

CEIL(*x*)

PURPOSE   Returns the smallest integer greater than or equal to *x*.

WHERE ALLOWED   Procedural and SQL statements.

Example

```
SELECT CEIL(18.1), CEIL(-18.1)
  FROM dual;
CEIL(18.1) CEIL(-18.1)
---------- -----------
        19         -18
```

COS
Syntax

COS(*x*)

PURPOSE   Returns the cosine of *x*. *x* is an angle expressed in radians.

WHERE ALLOWED   Procedural and SQL statements.

Example

```
SELECT COS(0), COS(90 * 3.14159265359/180)
  FROM dual;
  COS(0) COS(90*3.14159265359/180)
--------- -------------------------
        1                        -1
```

COSH
Syntax

COSH(*x*)

PURPOSE   Returns the hyperbolic cosine of *x*.

WHERE ALLOWED   Procedural and SQL statements.

Example

```
SELECT COSH(0), COSH(90 * 3.14159265359/180)
  FROM dual;
  COSH(0) COSH(90*3.14159265359/180)
--------- -------------------------
        1                 2.5091785
```

EXP
Syntax

EXP(*x*)

PURPOSE   Returns *e* raised to the *x*th power. $e = 2.71828183...$

WHERE ALLOWED   Procedural and SQL statements.

Example

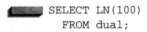

```
SELECT EXP(1), EXP(2.7)
  FROM dual;
   EXP(1)   EXP(2.7)
--------- ---------
2.7182818 14.879732
```

FLOOR

Syntax

FLOOR(*x*)

PURPOSE   Returns the largest integer equal to or less than *x*.

WHERE ALLOWED   Procedural and SQL statements.

Example

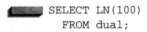

```
SELECT FLOOR(-23.5), FLOOR(23.5)
  FROM dual;
FLOOR(-23.5) FLOOR(23.5)
------------ -----------
        -24          23
```

LN

Syntax

LN(*x*)

PURPOSE   Returns the natural logarithm of *x*. *x* must be greater than 0.

WHERE ALLOWED   Procedural and SQL statements.

Example

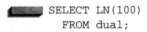

```
SELECT LN(100)
  FROM dual;
```

```
LN(100)
---------
4.6051702
```

LOG
Syntax

LOG(*x, y*)

PURPOSE   Returns the logarithm base *x* of *y*. The base must be a positive number other than 0 or 1, and *y* can be any positive number.

WHERE ALLOWED   Procedural and SQL statements.

Example

```
SELECT LOG(2, 32), LOG(5, 25)
   FROM dual;
LOG(2,32) LOG(5,25)
--------- ---------
        5         2
```

MOD
Syntax

MOD(*x, y*)

PURPOSE   Returns the remainder of *x* divided by *y*. If *y* is 0, *x* is returned.

WHERE ALLOWED   Procedural and SQL statements.

Example

```
SELECT MOD(23, 5), MOD(4, 1.3)
   FROM dual;
MOD(23,5) MOD(4,1.3)
--------- ----------
        3         .1
```

NOTE
The MOD function behaves differently from classic modulus function when x *is negative. The classic modulus can be defined as*

$$x - y * FLOOR(x/y)$$

POWER
Syntax

POWER(*x, y*)

PURPOSE   Returns *x* raised to the *y*th power. The base *x* and the exponent *y* need not be positive integers, but if *x* is negative, then *y* must be an integer.

WHERE ALLOWED   Procedural and SQL statements.

Example

```
SELECT POWER(4, 3), POWER(1.1, 2.6), POWER(25, -2), POWER(-2, 3)
   FROM dual;
POWER(4,3) POWER(1.1,2.6) POWER(25,-2) POWER(-2,3)
---------- -------------- ------------ ----------
        64       1.281212        .0016         -8
```

ROUND
Syntax

ROUND(*x* [*,y*])

PURPOSE   Returns *x* rounded to *y* places to the right of the decimal point. *y* defaults to 0, which rounds *x* to the nearest integer. If *y* is negative, digits left of the decimal point are rounded. *y* must be an integer.

WHERE ALLOWED   Procedural and SQL statements.

Example

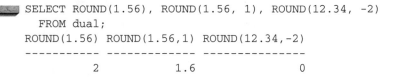

```
SELECT ROUND(1.56), ROUND(1.56, 1), ROUND(12.34, -2)
  FROM dual;
ROUND(1.56) ROUND(1.56,1) ROUND(12.34,-2)
----------- ------------- ---------------
          2           1.6               0
```

SIGN
Syntax

SIGN(*x*)

PURPOSE   If *x* < 0, returns −1. If *x* = 0, returns 0. If *x* > 0, returns 1.

WHERE ALLOWED   Procedural and SQL statements.

Example

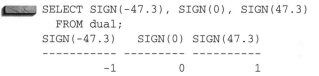

```
SELECT SIGN(-47.3), SIGN(0), SIGN(47.3)
  FROM dual;
SIGN(-47.3)    SIGN(0) SIGN(47.3)
----------- --------- ----------
         -1         0          1
```

SIN
Syntax

SIN(*x*)

PURPOSE   Returns the sine of *x*, which is an angle expressed in radians.

WHERE ALLOWED   Procedural and SQL statements.

Example

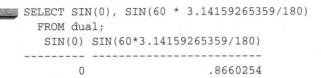

```
SELECT SIN(0), SIN(60 * 3.14159265359/180)
  FROM dual;
  SIN(0) SIN(60*3.14159265359/180)
--------- -------------------------
        0                  .8660254
```

SINH
Syntax

   SINH(*x*)

PURPOSE   Returns the hyperbolic sine of *x*.

WHERE ALLOWED   Procedural and SQL statements.

Example

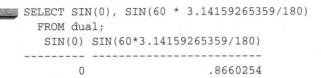

```
SELECT SINH(0), SINH(60 * 3.14159265359/180)
  FROM dual;
  SINH(0) SINH(60*3.14159265359/180)
--------- -------------------------
        0                 1.2493671
```

SQRT
Syntax

   SQRT(*x*)

PURPOSE   Returns the square root of *x*. *x* cannot be negative.

WHERE ALLOWED   Procedural and SQL statements.

Example

```
SELECT SQRT(64), SQRT(97.654)
  FROM dual;
 SQRT(64) SQRT(97.654)
--------- ------------
        8    9.8820038
```

TAN
Syntax

TAN(*x*)

PURPOSE   Returns the tangent of *x*, which is an angle expressed in radians.

WHERE ALLOWED   Procedural and SQL statements.

Example

```
SELECT TAN(0), TAN(-60 * 3.14159265359/180)
  FROM dual;
   TAN(0) TAN(-60*3.14159265359/180)
--------- ---------------------------
        0                   -1.732051
```

TANH
Syntax

TANH(*x*)

PURPOSE   Returns the hyperbolic tangent of *x*.

WHERE ALLOWED   Procedural and SQL statements.

Example

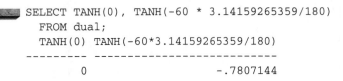

```
SELECT TANH(0), TANH(-60 * 3.14159265359/180)
   FROM dual;
   TANH(0) TANH(-60*3.14159265359/180)
--------- --------------------------
        0                   -.7807144
```

TRUNC
Syntax

TRUNC(x [,y])

PURPOSE   Returns x truncated (as opposed to rounded) to y decimal places. y defaults to 0, which truncates x to an integer value. If y is negative, digits left of the decimal point are truncated.

WHERE ALLOWED   Procedural and SQL statements.

Example

```
SELECT TRUNC(-123.456), TRUNC(-123.456, 1), TRUNC(-123.456, -1)
   FROM dual;
TRUNC(-123.456) TRUNC(-123.456,1) TRUNC(-123.456,-1)
--------------- ----------------- ------------------
           -123            -123.4               -120
```

Date Functions

The date functions take arguments of type DATE. Except for the MONTHS_BETWEEN function, which returns a NUMBER, all of the functions return DATE values. Date arithmetic is also discussed in this section.

ADD_MONTHS
Syntax

ADD_MONTHS(d, x)

PURPOSE   Returns the date *d* plus *x* months. *x* can be any integer. If the resultant month has fewer days than the month of *d,* the last day of the resultant month is returned. If not, the result has the same day component as *d.* The time component of *d* and the result are the same.

WHERE ALLOWED   Procedural and SQL statements.

Example

```
SELECT ADD_MONTHS('02-FEB-91', 1), ADD_MONTHS('19-JAN-87', 1),
       ADD_MONTHS('30-JAN-87', 13)
   FROM dual;
ADD_MONTH ADD_MONTH ADD_MONTH
--------- --------- ---------
02-MAR-91 19-FEB-87 29-FEB-88
```

LAST_DAY

Syntax

LAST_DAY(*d*)

PURPOSE   Returns the date of the last day of the month that contains *d.* This function can be used to determine how many days are left in the current month.

WHERE ALLOWED   Procedural and SQL statements.

Example

```
SELECT LAST_DAY('12-APR-71') "Current",
       LAST_DAY('12-APR-71') - TO_DATE('12-APR-71') "Days Left"
   FROM dual;
Current   Days Left
--------- ---------
30-APR-71        18
```

MONTHS_BETWEEN
Syntax

MONTHS_BETWEEN(*date1, date2*)

PURPOSE   Returns the number of months between *date1* and *date2*. If both *date1* and *date2* have the same day component, or if both are the last days of their respective months, then the result is an integer. Otherwise, the result will contain the fractional portion of a 31-day month.

WHERE ALLOWED   Procedural and SQL statements.

Example

```
SELECT MONTHS_BETWEEN('12-APR-71', '12-MAR-97') "First",
       MONTHS_BETWEEN('12-APR-71', '22-MAR-60') "Second"
  FROM dual;
First     Second
--------- ---------
    -311 132.67742
```

NEW_TIME
Syntax

NEW_TIME(*d, zone1, zone2*)

PURPOSE   Returns the date and time in time zone *zone2* when the date and time in time zone *zone1* are *d. zone1* and *zone2* are character strings with meanings described in the following table:

String	Time Zone
AST	Atlantic Standard Time
ADT	Atlantic Daylight Time
BST	Bering Standard Time
BDT	Bering Daylight Time
CST	Central Standard Time

String	Time Zone
CDT	Central Daylight Time
EST	Eastern Standard Time
EDT	Eastern Daylight Time
GMT	Greenwich Mean Time
HST	Alaska-Hawaii Standard Time
HDT	Alaska-Hawaii Daylight Time
MST	Mountain Standard Time
MDT	Mountain Daylight Time
NST	Newfoundland Standard Time
PST	Pacific Standard Time
PDT	Pacific Daylight Time
YST	Yukon Standard Time
YDT	Yukon Daylight Time

WHERE ALLOWED   Procedural and SQL statements.

Example

```
SELECT TO_CHAR(NEW_TIME(TO_DATE('12-APR-71 12:00:00',
                               'DD-MON-YY HH24:MI:SS'),
                     'PST', 'EST'),
               'DD-MON-YY HH24:MI:SS') "Pacific -> Eastern"
  FROM dual;
Pacific -> Eastern
------------------
12-APR-71 15:00:00
```

NEXT_DAY
Syntax

NEXT_DAY(*d, string*)

PURPOSE   Returns the date of the first day named by *string* that is later than the date *d*. *string* specifies a day of the week in the language of the current session. The time component of the returned value is the same as the time component of *d*. The case of *string* is not significant.

WHERE ALLOWED   Procedural and SQL statements.

Example
This example returns the next Thursday after April 12, 1971.

```
SELECT NEXT_DAY('12-APR-71', 'thursday') "Result"
   FROM dual;
Result
--------
15-APR-71
```

ROUND
Syntax

ROUND(*d* [,*format*])

PURPOSE   Rounds the date *d* to the unit specified by *format*. The available formats (as specified in Table 3-11 of the *SQL Language Reference*) for ROUND and TRUNC are described in Table 5-1. If *format* is not specified, it defaults to 'DD', which rounds *d* to the nearest day.

WHERE ALLOWED   Procedural and SQL statements.

Example

```
SELECT ROUND(TO_DATE('12-APR-71'), 'MM') "Nearest Month"
   FROM dual;
Nearest Month
-------------
01-APR-71
```

SYSDATE
Syntax

SYSDATE

PURPOSE   Returns the current date and time, of type DATE. Takes no arguments. When used in distributed SQL statements, SYSDATE returns the date and time of the local database.

WHERE ALLOWED   Procedural and SQL statements.

Example

```
SELECT TO_CHAR(SYSDATE, 'Month DD, YYYY HH24:MI:SS') "Now"
   FROM dual;
Now
---------------------------

April     13, 1997 23:31:17
```

TRUNC
Syntax

> TRUNC(*d* [,*format*])

PURPOSE   Returns the date *d* truncated to the unit specified by *format*. The available format models and their effects are the same as ROUND, described in Table 5-1. If *format* is omitted, it defaults to 'DD', which truncates *d* to the nearest day.

WHERE ALLOWED   Procedural and SQL statements.

Example

```
SELECT TRUNC(TO_DATE('12-APR-71 13:21:00',
              'DD-MON-YY HH24:MI:SS'),
              'Year') "First Day"
   FROM dual;
First Day
---------
01-JAN-71
```

Format Model	Rounding or Truncating Unit
CC, SCC	Century
SYYYY, YYYY, YEAR, SYEAR, YYY, YY, Y	Year (rounds up on July 1)
IYYY, IY, IY, I	ISO year
Q	Quarter (rounds up on the sixteenth day of the second month of the quarter)
MONTH, MON, MM, RM	Month (rounds up on the sixteenth day)
WW	Same day of the week as the first day of the year
IW	Same day of the week as the first day of the ISO year
W	Same day of the week as the first day of the month
DDD, DD, J	Day
Day, DY, D	Starting day of the week
HH, HH12, HH24	Hour
MI	Minute

TABLE 5-1. *ROUND and TRUNC Date Formats*

Date Arithmetic

Applying the arithmetic operators to dates and numbers is described according to Table 5-2. Note that when subtracting two date values, the result is a number.

Examples of valid date arithmetic expressions follow:

```
SELECT SYSDATE "Today", SYSDATE + 1 "Tomorrow"
  FROM dual;

Today     Tomorrow
--------- ---------
29-MAR-97 30-MAR-97
```

```
SELECT TO_DATE('12-APR-71 12:00:00', 'DD-MON-YY HH24:MI:SS') -
       TO_DATE('15-MAR-71 15:00:00',
                 'DD-MON-YY HH24:MI:SS') "Difference"
  FROM dual
Difference
----------
    27.875
```

Conversion Functions

The conversion functions are used to convert between PL/SQL datatypes. PL/SQL will do many of these conversions automatically, with an implicit call to a conversion function. However, you have no control over the format specifiers used in implicit calls, and it can make your code more difficult to understand. Consequently, it is good programming style to use an explicit conversion function rather than relying on PL/SQL's implicit conversions.

Operation	Type of Returned Value	Result
$d1 - d2$	NUMBER	Returns the difference in days between $d1$ and $d2$. This value is expressed as a number, with the real part representing a fraction of a day.
$d1 + d2$	N/A	Illegal—can only subtract two dates.
$d1 + n$	DATE	Adds n days to $d1$ and returns the result, as a DATE. n can be a real number, including a fraction of a day.
$d1 - n$	DATE	Subtracts n days from $d1$ and returns the result, as a DATE. n can be a real number, including a fraction of a day.

TABLE 5-2.   *Semantics of Date Arithmetic*

CHARTOROWID

Syntax

CHARTOROWID(*string*)

PURPOSE   Converts a CHAR or VARCHAR2 value containing the external format of a ROWID into the internal binary format. The argument *string* must be an 18-character string containing the external format of a ROWID, as described in Chapter 2. The external format is different in Oracle7 and Oracle8. CHARTOROWID is the inverse of ROWIDTOCHAR.

WHERE ALLOWED   Procedural and SQL statements.

Example (Using the Oracle7 rowid Format)

```
SELECT description
  FROM classes
  WHERE rowid = CHARTOROWID('0000002D.0002.0002');
DESCRIPTION
-------------
Economics 203
```

CONVERT

Syntax

CONVERT(*string, dest_set* [,*source_set*])

PURPOSE   Converts the character string *string* from the character set identified by *source_set* to the character set identified by *dest_set*. If *source_set* is not specified, it defaults to the character set of the database. Common character sets include those listed here:

Character Set Identifier	Description
US7ASCII	U.S. 7-bit ASCII. This is the character set used by most Unix operating systems and Oracle databases on Unix.

Character Set Identifier	Description
WE8DEC	DEC West European 8-bit.
WE8HP	HP West European LaserJet 8-bit.
F7DEC	DEC French 7-bit.
WE8EBCDIC500	IBM West European EBCDIC Code Page 500.
WE8PC850	IBM PC Code Page 500. This is the character set used by most PC systems and by Oracle running on PCs.
WE8ISO8859P1	ISO-8859-1 West European 8-bit.

For complete conversion, the destination character set should contain a representation of all the characters in the source character set. If not, then a replacement character set is used in the destination. This replacement character is part of the character set definition itself.

WHERE ALLOWED   Procedural and SQL statements.

Example (from the *Server SQL Reference*)

```
SELECT CONVERT('Groß', 'WE8HP', 'WE8DEC') "Conversion"
  FROM dual;
Conversion
----------
Groß
```

HEXTORAW
Syntax

HEXTORAW(*string*)

PURPOSE   Converts the binary value represented by *string* to a RAW value. *string* should contain hexadecimal values. Every two characters in *string* represent one byte of the resultant RAW. HEXTORAW and RAWTOHEX are inverse functions.

WHERE ALLOWED   Procedural and SQL statements.

Example

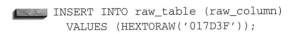

```
INSERT INTO raw_table (raw_column)
  VALUES (HEXTORAW('017D3F'));
```

RAWTOHEX

Syntax

> RAWTOHEX(*rawvalue*)

PURPOSE   Converts the RAW *rawvalue* to a character string containing the hexadecimal representation. Each byte of *rawvalue* is converted into a two-character string. RAWTOHEX and HEXTORAW are inverse functions.

WHERE ALLOWED   Procedural and SQL statements.

Example

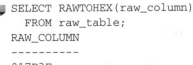

```
SELECT RAWTOHEX(raw_column)
  FROM raw_table;
RAW_COLUMN
----------
017D3F
```

ROWIDTOCHAR

Syntax

> ROWIDTOCHAR(*rowid*)

PURPOSE   Converts the ROWID value *rowid* to its external 18-character string representation, which differs between Oracle7 and Oracle8. ROWIDTOCHAR and CHARTOROWID are inverse functions.

WHERE ALLOWED   Procedural and SQL statements.

Example (Using the Oracle7 rowid Format)

```
SELECT ROWIDTOCHAR(rowid)
  FROM classes;

ROWIDTOCHAR(ROWID)
------------------
0000002D.0000.0002
0000002D.0002.0002
0000002D.0003.0002
```

TO_CHAR (dates)
Syntax

TO_CHAR(*d* [,*format* [,*nlsparams*]])

PURPOSE   Converts the date *d* to a VARCHAR2 character string. If *format* is specified, it is used to control how the result is structured. A format string is made up of *format elements*. Each element returns a portion of the date value, such as the month. The date format elements are described in Table 5-3. If *format* is not specified, the default date format for your session is used. If *nlsparams* is specified, it controls the language for the month and day components of the returned string. The format of *nlsparams* is

'NLS_DATE_LANGUAGE = *language*'

where *language* represents the desired language. For more information on TO_CHAR and date format elements, see the *Server SQL Reference*.

WHERE ALLOWED   Procedural and SQL statements.

Example

```
SELECT TO_CHAR(SYSDATE, 'DD-MON-YY HH24:MI:SS') "Right Now"
  FROM dual;
Right Now
------------------
15-NOV-95 01:17:14
```

Date Format Element	Description
punctuation	All punctuation symbols are reproduced in the result string.
"text"	Text contained in double quotes is likewise reproduced.
AD, A.D.	AD indicator, with or without periods.
AM, A.M.	Ante meridiem indicator, with or without periods.
BC, B.C.	BC indicator, with or without periods.
CC, SCC	Century. SCC returns BC dates as negative values.
D	Day of week (1-7).
DAY[1]	Name of day, padded with blanks to length of nine characters.
DD	Day of month (1-31).
DDD	Day of year (1-366).
DY[1]	Abbreviated name of day.
IW	Week of year (1-52, 1-53) based on the ISO standard.
IYY, IY, I	Last three, two, or one digits of the ISO year.
IYYY	Four-digit year based on the ISO standard.
HH, HH12	Hour of day (1-12).
HH24	Hour of day (0-23).
J	Julian day. The number of days since January 1, 4712 BC. The corresponding output will be an integer value.
MI	Minute (0-59).
MM	Month (1-12). JAN=1, DEC=12.
MONTH[1]	Name of month, padded with blanks to nine characters.
MON[1]	Abbreviated name of month.
PM, P.M.	Post meridiem indicator, with and without periods.

TABLE 5-3. *Valid Date Format Elements*

Date Format Element	Description
Q	Quarter of year (1-4). JAN-MAR = 1.
RM	Roman numeral month (I-XII). JAN=I, DEC=XII.
RR	Last two digits of year for years in other centuries.
SS	Second (0-59).
SSSSS	Seconds past midnight (0-86399). The format model 'J.SSSSS' will always yield a numeric value.
WW	Week of year (1-53). Week 1 starts on the first day of the year and continues to the seventh day. Thus, the weeks do not necessarily start on Sunday.
W	Week of month (1-5). Weeks are defined as they are for the WW element.
Y, YYY	Year with comma in this position.
YEAR, SYEAR[1]	Year spelled out. SYEAR returns BC dates as negative.
YYYY, SYYYY	Four-digit year. SYYYY returns BC dates as negative.
YYY, YY, Y	Last three, two, or one digit(s) of year.

TABLE 5-3.   *Valid Date Format Elements (continued)*

[1]These elements are case-sensitive. For example, 'MON' will return 'JAN', and 'Mon' will return 'Jan'.

TO_CHAR (labels)
Syntax

TO_CHAR(*label* [,*format*])

PURPOSE   Converts the MLSLABEL *label* to a VARCHAR2 type. If specified, the label format *format* is used for the conversion. If not specified, the default label *format* is used. This function is only relevant when using Trusted Oracle. The TO_LABEL function and this version of TO_CHAR are inverse functions.

WHERE ALLOWED   Procedural and SQL statements in a trusted database.

Example
See the *Trusted Oracle Server Administrator's Guide*.

TO_CHAR (numbers)
Syntax

TO_CHAR(*num* [,*format* [,*nlsparams*]])

PURPOSE   Converts the NUMBER argument *num* to a VARCHAR2. If specified, *format* governs the conversion. Available number formats are described in Table 5-4. If *format* is not specified, the resultant string will have exactly as many characters as necessary to hold the significant digits of *num*. *nlsparams* is used to specify the decimal and group separator, along with the currency symbol. It can have the format

'NLS_NUMERIC_CHARS = "*dg*" NLS_CURRENCY = "*string*"

where *d* and *g* represent the decimal and group separators, respectively. *string* represents the currency symbol. For example, in the United States the decimal separator is typically a period (.), the group separator is a comma (,), and the currency symbol is $. See the *Oracle Server SQL Reference* for complete details on National Language Support.

WHERE ALLOWED   Procedural and SQL statements.

Example

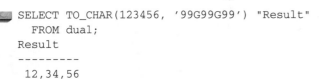

```
SELECT TO_CHAR(123456, '99G99G99') "Result"
  FROM dual;
Result
---------
 12,34,56
```

```
SELECT TO_CHAR(123456, 'L99G99D99',
               'NLS_NUMERIC_CHARACTERS = '',.''
               NLS_CURRENCY = ''Money'' ') "Result 2"
  FROM dual;
Result 2
------------
Money12,34.56
```

Format Element	Sample Format String	Result
9	99	Each 9 represents a significant digit in the result. The return value has the number of significant digits equal to the number of 9s, with a leading minus if negative. Any leading zeros are left blank.
0	0999	Returns leading zeros rather than blanks.
0	9990	Returns trailing zeros rather than blanks.
$	$999	Returns value with a leading dollar sign, regardless of the currency symbol. This can be used in addition to leading or trailing zeros.
B	B999	Returns blanks for the integer part of a decimal number when the integer part is zero.
MI	999MI	Returns a negative value with a trailing minus sign rather than a leading minus. A positive value will have a trailing blank.
S	S9999	Returns a leading sign: + for positive numbers, − for negative numbers.
S	9999S	Returns a trailing sign: + for positive numbers, − for negative numbers.

TABLE 5-4. *Number Format Elements*

Format Element	Sample Format String	Result
PR	99PR	Returns a negative value in \<angle brackets\>. A positive value will have a leading and trailing blank.
D	99D9	Returns a decimal point in the specified position. The number of 9s on either side specifies the maximum number of digits.
G	9G999	Returns a group separator in the position specified. G can appear more than once in the format string.
C	C99	Returns the ISO currency symbol in the specified position. C can also appear more than once in the format string.
L	L999	Returns the local currency symbol in the specified position.
,	999,999	Returns a comma in the specified position, regardless of the group separator.
.	99.99	Returns a decimal point in the specified position, regardless of the decimal separator.
V	99V999	Returns a value multiplied by 10^n, where n is the number of 9s after the V. The value is rounded if necessary.
EEEE	9.99EEEE	Returns the value using scientific notation.
RM	RM	Returns the value using uppercase Roman numerals.

TABLE 5-4. *Number Format Elements (continued)*

TO_DATE
Syntax

TO_DATE(*string* [,*format* [,*nlsparams*]])

PURPOSE   Converts the CHAR or VARCHAR2 *string* into a DATE.
format is a date format string, as described in Table 5-3. If *format* is not
specified, the default date format for the session is used. *nlsparams* is used
the same way for TO_DATE as it is for TO_CHAR. TO_DATE and
TO_CHAR are inverse functions.

WHERE ALLOWED   Procedural and SQL statements.

Example

```
DECLARE
  v_CurrentDate  DATE;
BEGIN
  v_CurrentDate := TO_DATE('January 7, 1973', 'Month DD, YYYY');
END;
```

TO_LABEL
Syntax

TO_LABEL(*string* [,*format*])

PURPOSE   Converts *string* to a MLSLABEL. *string* can be either
VARCHAR2 or CHAR. If specified, *format* is used for the conversion.
If *format* is not specified, the default conversion format is used. This
function is only relevant in Trusted Oracle. TO_LABEL and TO_CHAR
are inverse functions.

WHERE ALLOWED   Procedural and SQL statements in a trusted
database.

Example
See the *Trusted Oracle Server Administrator's Guide.*

TO_MULTI_BYTE
Syntax

TO_MULTI_BYTE(*string*)

PURPOSE   Returns *string* with all single-byte characters replaced by their equivalent multibyte characters. This function is only relevant if the database character set contains both single-byte and multibyte characters. If not, *string* is returned without change. TO_MULTI_BYTE and TO_SINGLE_BYTE are inverse functions.

WHERE ALLOWED   Procedural and SQL statements.

Example

```
SELECT TO_MULTI_BYTE('Hello') "Multi"
  FROM dual;
Multi
----------
Hello
```

TO_NUMBER
Syntax

TO_NUMBER(*string* [,*format* [,*nlsparams*]])

PURPOSE   Converts the CHAR or VARCHAR2 *string* to a NUMBER value. If *format* is specified, *string* should correspond to the number format. *nlsparams* behaves the same as it does for TO_CHAR. TO_NUMBER and TO_CHAR are inverse functions.

WHERE ALLOWED   Procedural and SQL statements.

Example

```
DECLARE
  v_Num   NUMBER;
BEGIN
  v_Num := TO_NUMBER('$12345.67', '$99999.99');
END;
```

TO_SINGLE_BYTE
Syntax

TO_SINGLE_BYTE(*string*)

PURPOSE   Converts all multibyte characters found in *string* to their equivalent single-byte characters. This function is only relevant if the database character set contains both single-byte and multibyte characters. If not, *string* is returned unchanged. TO_SINGLE_BYTE and TO_MULTI_BYTE are inverse functions.

WHERE ALLOWED   Procedural and SQL statements.

Example

```
SELECT TO_SINGLE_BYTE('Greetings') "Single"
  FROM dual;
Single
----------
Greetings
```

Group Functions

Group functions return a single result based on many rows, as opposed to single-row functions, which return one result for each row. For example, the COUNT group function returns the number of rows returned. These functions are valid in the select list of a query and the GROUP BY clause only.

Most of these functions can accept qualifiers on their arguments. These qualifiers are DISTINCT and ALL. If the DISTINCT qualifier is passed, then only distinct values returned by the query are considered. The ALL qualifier causes the function to consider all of the values returned by the query. If none is specified, ALL is the default.

AVG

Syntax

AVG([DISTINCT | ALL] *col*)

PURPOSE Returns the average of the column values.

WHERE ALLOWED Query select lists and GROUP BY clauses only.

Example

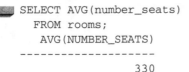

```
SELECT AVG(number_seats)
  FROM rooms;
  AVG(NUMBER_SEATS)
-------------------
             330
```

COUNT

Syntax

COUNT(* | [DISTINCT | ALL] *col*)

PURPOSE Returns the number of rows in the query. If * is passed, then the total number of rows is returned. If a select list item is passed instead, the non-null values are counted.

WHERE ALLOWED Query select lists and GROUP BY clauses only.

Example

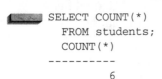

```
SELECT COUNT(*)
  FROM students;
  COUNT(*)
----------
         6
```

```
SELECT COUNT(DISTINCT major) "Majors"
  FROM students;
    Majors
----------
         3
SQL> SELECT major, COUNT(major)
  2     FROM students
  3     GROUP BY major;

MAJOR                            COUNT(MAJOR)
------------------------------   ------------
Computer Science                            2
Economics                                   2
History                                     3
Music                                       2
Nutrition                                   2
```

GLB

Syntax

GLB([DISTINCT | ALL] *label*)

PURPOSE   Returns the greatest lower bound of *label*. This function is meaningful in Trusted Oracle only.

WHERE ALLOWED   Query select lists and GROUP BY clauses only, in a trusted database.

Example

See the *Trusted Oracle Server Administrator's Guide* for examples and the definition of greatest lower bound.

LUB

Syntax

LUB([DISTINCT | ALL] *label*)

PURPOSE   Returns the least upper bound of *label*. This function is meaningful in Trusted Oracle only.

WHERE ALLOWED   Query select lists and GROUP BY clauses only.

Example
See the *Trusted Oracle Server Administrator's Guide* for examples and the definition of least upper bound.

MAX
Syntax

    MAX([DISTINCT | ALL] *col*)

PURPOSE   Returns the maximum value of the select list item. Note that DISTINCT and ALL have no effect, since the maximum value would be the same in either case.

WHERE ALLOWED   Query select lists and GROUP BY clauses only.

Example
This example returns the length of the longest name in the students table.

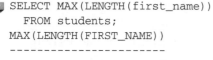

```
SELECT MAX(LENGTH(first_name))
   FROM students;
MAX(LENGTH(FIRST_NAME))
-----------------------
                      8
```

MIN
Syntax

    MIN([DISTINCT | ALL] *col*)

PURPOSE   Returns the minimum value of the select list item. Note that DISTINCT and ALL have no effect, since the minimum value would be the same in either case.

WHERE ALLOWED   Query select lists and GROUP BY clauses only.

Example

```
SELECT MIN(id)
  FROM students;
  MIN(ID)
---------
    10000
```

STDDEV
Syntax

STDDEV([DISTINCT | ALL] *col*)

PURPOSE   Returns the standard deviation of the select list item. This is defined as the square root of the variance.

WHERE ALLOWED   Query select lists and GROUP BY clauses only.

Example

```
SELECT STDDEV(number_seats)
  FROM rooms;
STDDEV(NUMBER_SEATS)
--------------------
         422.19664
```

SUM
Syntax

SUM([DISTINCT | ALL] *col*)

PURPOSE   Returns the sum of the values for the select list item.

WHERE ALLOWED   Query select lists and GROUP BY clauses only.

Example

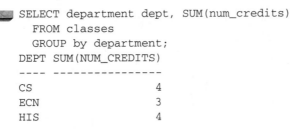

```
SELECT department dept, SUM(num_credits)
  FROM classes
  GROUP by department;
DEPT SUM(NUM_CREDITS)
---- ----------------
CS                  4
ECN                 3
HIS                 4
```

VARIANCE

Syntax

VARIANCE([DISTINCT | ALL] *col*)

PURPOSE   Returns the statistical variance of the select list item. Oracle calculates the variance using the formula shown here:

$$\frac{\displaystyle\sum_{i=1}^{n} x_i^2 - \frac{1}{n} \left[\sum_{i=1}^{n} x_i\right]^2}{n-1}$$

In the formula, x_i is a single row value, and n is the total number of elements in the set. If $n = 1$, the variance is defined to be 0.

WHERE ALLOWED   Query select lists and GROUP BY clauses only.

Example

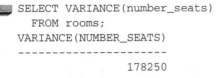

```
SELECT VARIANCE(number_seats)
  FROM rooms;
VARIANCE(NUMBER_SEATS)
----------------------
                178250
```

Other Functions

This section lists the remaining functions that do not fit in the previous categories.

BFILENAME

Syntax

BFILENAME(*directory*, *file_name*)

PURPOSE   Returns the BFILE locator associated with the physical file *file_name* on the operating system. *directory* must be a DIRECTORY object in the data dictionary.

WHERE ALLOWED   Procedural and SQL statements.

Example

See Chapter 21 for more information on LOBs and the DBMS_LOB package, including BFILEs.

DECODE

Syntax

DECODE(*base_expr, compare1, value1,*
               compare2, value2,
               ...
               default)

PURPOSE   The DECODE function is similar to a series of nested IF-THEN-ELSE statements. The *base_expr* is compared to each of *compare1*, *compare2*, etc., in sequence. If *base_expr* matches the *i*th *compare* item, the *i*th *value* is returned. If *base_expr* doesn't match any of the *compare* values, *default* is returned.

Each *compare* value is evaluated in turn. If a match is found, the remaining *compare* values, if any, are not evaluated. A NULL *base_expr* is considered equivalent to a NULL *compare* value.

WHERE ALLOWED   SQL statements only.

Example

```
SELECT DECODE('abc', 'a', 1,
                     'b', 2,
                     'abc', 3,
                     'd', 4,
                     -1) "Decode 1"
  FROM dual;
 Decode 1
---------
        3

SELECT DECODE(NULL, 'a', 1,
                    NULL, 2) "Decode 2"
  FROM dual;
 Decode 2
---------
        2
```

DUMP
Syntax

DUMP(*expr* [,*number_format* [,*start_position*] [,*length*]]])

PURPOSE   Returns a VARCHAR2 value that contains information about the internal representation of *expr*. *number_format* specifies the base of the values returned according to the following table:

number_format	Result Returned In
8	Octal notation
10	Decimal notation
16	Hexadecimal notation
17	Single characters

If *number_format* is not specified, the result is returned in decimal notation.

If *start_position* and *length* are specified, *length* bytes starting at *start_position* are returned. The default is to return the entire representation. The datatype is returned as a number corresponding to internal datatypes according to the following table:

Code	Datatype
1	VARCHAR2
2	NUMBER
8	LONG
12	DATE
23	RAW
24	LONG RAW
69	ROWID
96	CHAR
106	MLSLABEL

WHERE ALLOWED   SQL statements only.

Example

```
SELECT first_name, DUMP(first_name) "Dump"
    FROM students
FIRST_NAME              Dump
------------------      -------------------------------------------
Scott                   Typ=1 Len=5: 83,99,111,116,116
Margaret                Typ=1 Len=8: 77,97,114,103,97,114,101,116
Joanne                  Typ=1 Len=6: 74,111,97,110,110,101
Manish                  Typ=1 Len=6: 77,97,110,105,115,104
Patrick                 Typ=1 Len=7: 80,97,116,114,105,99,107
Timothy                 Typ=1 Len=7: 84,105,109,111,116,104,121

SELECT first_name, DUMP(first_name, 17) "Dump"
   FROM students
FIRST_NAME              Dump
------------------      -------------------------------------
Scott                   Typ=1 Len=5: S,c,o,t,t
Margaret                Typ=1 Len=8: M,a,r,g,a,r,e,t
```

```
Joanne              Typ=1 Len=6: J,o,a,n,n,e
Manish              Typ=1 Len=6: M,a,n,i,s,h
Patrick             Typ=1 Len=7: P,a,t,r,i,c,k
Timothy             Typ=1 Len=7: T,i,m,o,t,h,y

SELECT first_name, DUMP(first_name, 17, 2, 4) "Dump"
  FROM students;
FIRST_NAME          Dump
------------------- ------------------------------------
Scott               Typ=1 Len=5: c,o,t,t
Margaret            Typ=1 Len=8: a,r,g,a
Joanne              Typ=1 Len=6: o,a,n,n
Manish              Typ=1 Len=6: a,n,i,s
Patrick             Typ=1 Len=7: a,t,r,i
```

EMPTY_CLOB/EMPTY_BLOB
Syntax

    EMPTY_CLOB
    EMPTY_BLOB

PURPOSE   Returns an empty LOB locator. EMPTY_CLOB returns a character locator, and EMPTY_BLOB returns a binary locator.

WHERE ALLOWED   Procedural and SQL statements.

Example
See Chapter 21 for more information on LOBs and the DBMS_LOB package.

GREATEST
Syntax

    GREATEST(expr1 [,expr2] ...)

PURPOSE   Returns the greatest expression of its arguments. Each expression is implicitly converted to the type of expr1 before the comparisons are made. If expr1 is a character type, non-blank-padded character comparisons are used, and the result has datatype VARCHAR2.

WHERE ALLOWED   Procedural and SQL statements.

Example

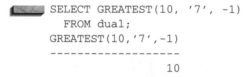
```
SELECT GREATEST(10, '7', -1)
   FROM dual;
GREATEST(10,'7',-1)
-------------------
                 10
```

GREATEST_LB
Syntax

GREATEST_LB(*label1* [,*label2*] ...)

PURPOSE   Returns the greatest lower bound of the list of labels. Each label must have datatype MLSLABEL, RAW MLSLABEL, or be a quoted string literal. This function is valid in Trusted Oracle only.

For more information, including examples and the definition of the greatest lower bound, see the *Trusted Oracle Server Administrator's Guide*.

LEAST
Syntax

LEAST(*expr1* [,*expr2*] ...)

PURPOSE   Returns the least value in the list of expressions. LEAST behaves similarly to GREATEST, in that all expressions are implicitly converted to the datatype of the first. All character comparisons are done with non-blank-padded character comparison semantics.

WHERE ALLOWED   Procedural and SQL statements.

Example

```
SELECT LEAST('abcd', 'ABCD', 'a', 'xyz') "Least"
   FROM dual;
Least
-----
ABCD
```

LEAST_UB
Syntax

> LEAST_UB(*label1* [,*label2*] ...)

PURPOSE   Similar to GREATEST_LB, LEAST_UB returns the least upper bound of the list of labels. The labels must have datatype MLSLABEL or be quoted literals. The return value is RAW MLSLABEL. For more information, including examples and the definition of the least upper bound, see the *Trusted Oracle Server Administrator's Guide*.

NVL
Syntax

> NVL(*expr1*, *expr2*)

PURPOSE   If *expr1* is NULL, returns *expr2*; otherwise, returns *expr1*. The return value has the same datatype as *expr1* unless *expr1* is a character string, in which case the return value has datatype VARCHAR2. This function is useful to ensure that the active set of a query contains no NULL values.

WHERE ALLOWED   Procedural and SQL statements.

Example

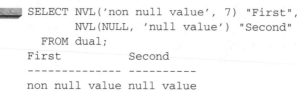

```
SELECT NVL('non null value', 7) "First",
       NVL(NULL, 'null value') "Second"
  FROM dual;
First          Second
-------------- ----------
non null value null value
```

UID
Syntax

> UID

PURPOSE   Returns an integer that uniquely identifies the current database user. UID takes no arguments.

WHERE ALLOWED   Procedural and SQL statements.

Example
This example shows a sample SQL*Plus session.

```
SQL> connect scott/tiger
Connected.
SQL> SELECT UID
  2    FROM dual;
     UID
---------
       8
SQL> connect system/manager
Connected.
SQL> SELECT UID
  2    FROM dual;
     UID
---------
       5
```

USER
Syntax

```
USER
```

PURPOSE   Returns a VARCHAR2 value containing the name of the current Oracle user. USER takes no arguments.

WHERE ALLOWED   Procedural and SQL statements.

Example
This example shows a sample SQL*Plus session.

```
SQL> connect scott/tiger
Connected.
SQL> SELECT USER
  2    FROM dual;
```

```
USER
------------------------------
SCOTT
SQL> connect sys/change_on_install
Connected.
SQL> SELECT USER
  2    FROM dual;
USER
------------------------------
SYS
```

USERENV

Syntax

USERENV(*option*)

PURPOSE   Returns a VARCHAR2 value containing information about the current session, based on *option*. The behavior is described in Table 5-5.

WHERE ALLOWED   Procedural and SQL statements.

Example

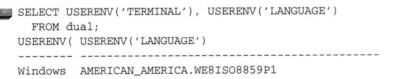

```
SELECT USERENV('TERMINAL'), USERENV('LANGUAGE')
  FROM dual;
USERENV( USERENV('LANGUAGE')
-------- --------------------------------------------
Windows  AMERICAN_AMERICA.WE8ISO8859P1
```

VSIZE

Syntax

VSIZE(*value*)

PURPOSE   Returns the number of bytes in the internal representation of *value*. This information is also returned by the DUMP function. If *value* is NULL, the return value is also NULL.

Value of *option*	Behavior of **USERENV** Function
'OSDBA'[1]	If the current session has the OSDBA role enabled, returns 'TRUE'; otherwise, returns 'FALSE'. Note that the return value is VARCHAR2, not BOOLEAN.
'LABEL'	Valid in Trusted Oracle only. Returns the current session label. For more information, see the *Trusted Oracle Server Administrator's Guide.*
'LANGUAGE'	Returns the language and territory currently used by your session, along with the database character set. These are NLS parameters. The returned value has the form *language_territory.characterset.*
'TERMINAL'	Returns an operating system-dependent identifier for the current session's terminal. For distributed SQL statements, the identifier for the local session is returned.
'SESSIONID'	Returns the auditing session identifier, if the initialization parameter AUDIT_TRAIL is set to TRUE. USERENV('SESSIONID') is not valid in distributed SQL statements.
'ENTRYID'	Returns the available auditing entry identifier, if the initialization parameter AUDIT_TRAIL is set to TRUE. USERENV('ENTRYID') is not valid in distributed SQL statements.
'LANG'[2]	Returns the ISO abbreviation for the language name. This is a shorter format than USERENV('LANGUAGE').

TABLE 5-5. *Results of Different* option *Values*

[1]USERENV('OSDBA') is valid in PL/SQL 2.2 (Oracle 7.2) and higher.
[2]USERENV('LANG') is valid in PL/SQL 8.0 (Oracle 8.0) and higher.

WHERE ALLOWED   Procedural and SQL statements.

Example

```
SELECT last_name, VSIZE(last_name) "Size"
  FROM students;
LAST_NAME                Size
-------------------- ---------
Smith                       5
Mason                       5
Junebug                     7
Murgratroid                11
Poll                        4
Taller                      6
```

PL/SQL at Work: Printing Numbers as Text Words

This example uses the character and conversion functions to spell out numbers as text strings. The DH_UTIL package contains two public functions—SPELL and CHECK_PROTECT.

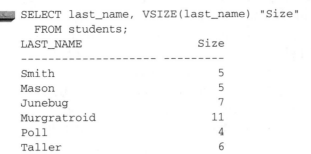

NOTE
Packages and their usage are discussed in Chapter 8.

The SPELL function will return a string with its argument spelled out. The following SQL*Plus session (which also uses the DBMS_OUTPUT package, described in Chapter 14) demonstrates its use.

```
SQL> set serveroutput on
SQL> BEGIN
  2    DBMS_OUTPUT.PUT_LINE('12340: ' || DH_UTIL.SPELL(12340));
  3    DBMS_OUTPUT.PUT_LINE('987.123: ' || DH_UTIL.SPELL(987.123));
  4    DBMS_OUTPUT.PUT_LINE('10000: ' || DH_UTIL.SPELL(10000));
  5  END;
  6  /
12340: Twelve Thousand Three Hundred Forty
```

```
987.123: Nine Hundred Eighty-Seven and One Hundred
         Twenty-Three / Thousandths
10000: Ten Thousand

PL/SQL procedure successfully completed.
```

The CHECK_PROTECT function takes a numeric dollar amount and spells it out, as used on a printed check. For example:

```
SQL> set serveroutput on
SQL> BEGIN
  2     DBMS_OUTPUT.PUT_LINE('12340: ' ||
                            DH_UTIL.CHECK_PROTECT(12340));
  3     DBMS_OUTPUT.PUT_LINE('987.12: ' ||
                            DH_UTIL.CHECK_PROTECT(987.12));
  4     DBMS_OUTPUT.PUT_LINE('10000: ' ||
                            DH_UTIL.CHECK_PROTECT(10000));
  5  END;
  6  /
12340: Twelve Thousand Three Hundred Forty Dollars and Zero Cents
987.12: Nine Hundred Eighty-Seven Dollars and Twelve Cents
10000: Ten Thousand Dollars and Zero Cents

PL/SQL procedure successfully completed.
```

The script that follows can be run from SQL*Plus to create the DH_UTIL package.

```
-- Available online as spelchek.sql
REM ***********************************************************
REM David L. Hunt (file author) distributes this and other
REM files/scripts for educational purposes only, to illustrate the
REM use or application of various computing techniques. Neither the
REM author nor Oracle Corporation makes any warranty regarding this
REM script's fitness for any industrial application or purpose nor is
REM there any claim that this or any similarly-distributed scripts
REM are error free or should be used for any purpose other than
REM illustration.
REM
REM Please contact the author via email (see address below) when
REM you have comments, suggestions, and/or difficulties with this
REM packages functions.
REM
REM [Please keep the above disclaimer and the embedded electronic
REM  documentation with this script.]
```

```
REM ***************************************************************
REM About this script/file:
REM
REM NAME: SPELCHEK.SQL - PL/SQL code to create a package (DH_UTIL)
REM       providing 1) Number spelling and 2) Bank Draft/Checking
REM       protection via spelled amounts.
REM
REM AUTHOR: Dave Hunt, Senior Principal Instructor
REM         Oracle Eduction Services
REM         170 South Main Street, Suite 1150
REM         Salt Lake City, Utah, USA  84101
REM         dhunt@us.oracle.com
REM
REM ***************************************************************
REM Maintenance History:
REM
REM 24-APR-96: Original Code
REM 03-MAR-96: Enhanced to handle 1) negative numbers and 2) zero
REM 16-JAN-97: Enhanced to translate non-integer decimal numbers
REM 20-JAN-97: Enhanced to handle numbers in the range:
REM            (-10 ** 100)+1 to (10 ** 100) -1 with precision to
REM            40 digits. Up to 40 digits behind the decimal point
REM            can be spelled.
REM 25-JAN-97: Added additional documentation and remarks.
REM ***************************************************************
REM This package contains two GLOBAL functions:
REM   1) DH_UTIL.SPELL: Translates a number into English words.
REM      [Note: This version contains "American" (vs. "British")
REM             numeric-magnitude wordings:
REM
REM                       Number American      British
REM     ------------------------- ----------   -----------------
REM             1,000,000,000 Billion      Milliard
REM         1,000,000,000,000 Trillion     Billion
REM     1,000,000,000,000,000 Quadrillion  Thousand Billion
REM 1,000,000,000,000,000,000 Quintillion  Trillion
REM
REM     For British system spellings, modify the table as needed
REM     at the end of the Package Body.]
REM
REM ***************************************************************
REM     Function 1 Usage: "DH_UTIL.SPELL(any-number)"
REM     SQL Example:
REM        SELECT last_name,
REM          salary, DH_UTIL.SPELL(salary) Worded
```

```
REM         FROM s_emp;"
REM
REM         LAST_NAME     SALARY WORDED
REM         -----------   ------ --------------------------------
REM         Velasquez       2500 Two Thousand Five Hundred
REM         Ngao            1450 One Thousand Four Hundred Fifty
REM         Nagayama        1400 One Thousand Four Hundred
REM
REM ***********************************************************
REM     PL/SQL Example:
REM         BEGIN
REM            DBMS_OUTPUT.PUT_LINE
REM                (dh_util.spell(-123456789.123456789));
REM         END;
REM         /
REM         Negative One Hundred Twenty-Three Million Four
REM         Hundred Fifty-Six Thousand Seven Hundred Eighty-Nine
REM         and One Hundred Twenty-Three Million Four
REM         Hundred Fifty-Six Thousand Seven Hundred
REM         Eighty-Nine / Billionths
REM
REM ***********************************************************
REM ***********************************************************
REM   2) DH_UTIL.CHECK_PROTECT: Translates a number into spelled
REM         "Dollars & Cents".
REM      Function 2 Usage: "DH_UTIL.CHECK_PROTECT(any-number)"
REM ***********************************************************
REM      SQL Example:
REM         select 'Pay to the order of: '||
REM            rpad(ltrim(first_name||' '||last_name||' '),22,'*')
REM            ||' '||lpad(rtrim(' '||ltrim(nvl(
REM            to_char(salary,'$99,999,990.00'),'Null Amount')
REM                )),16,'*')||chr(10)||
REM            rpad('** '||
REM            dh_util.check_protect(SALARY)||' ',56,'*') " "
REM         from s_emp
REM         where rownum <= 3;
REM
REM  Pay to the order of: Carmen Velasquez *****  ****** $2,500.00
REM  ** Two Thousand Five Hundred Dollars and Zero Cents ********
REM
REM  Pay to the order of: LaDoris Ngao ********  ****** $1,450.00
REM  ** One Thousand Four Hundred Fifty Dollars and Zero Cents ***
REM
REM  Pay to the order of: Midori Nagayama ******  ****** $1,400.00
```

```
REM  ** One Thousand Four Hundred Dollars and Zero Cents *********
REM
REM ************************************************************
REM      PL/SQL Example:
REM          begin
REM              dbms_output.put_line
REM                  (dh_util.check_protect(123456789.56));
REM          end;
REM          /
REM      One Hundred Twenty-Three Million Four Hundred
REM      Fifty-Six Thousand Seven Hundred Eighty-Nine Dollars
REM      and Fifty-Six Cents
REM
REM ************************************************************
REM DH_UTIL Package Specification
REM ************************************************************
create or replace package dh_util is
   function spell (x in number) return varchar2;
   function check_protect (x in number) return varchar2;
   pragma restrict_references(spell,WNDS);
   pragma restrict_references(check_protect,WNDS);
end;
/


REM ************************************************************
REM DH_UTIL Package Body
REM ************************************************************
create or replace package body dh_util is
   result    varchar2(2000);
   working_integer          number;
   working_decimal          varchar2(100);
   working_dec_mag          number;
   working_integer_spell    varchar2(2000);
   working_decimal_spell    varchar2(2000);
   working_fraction_spell   varchar2(2000);
   type number_stencil is table of number
        index by binary_integer;
   type varchar2_stencil is table of varchar2(2000)
        index by binary_integer;
   denom varchar2_stencil;
   pad_factor number_stencil;
   hold varchar2_stencil;


   --  ************************************************************


   --  Packaged Global Function Definition: DH_UTIL.SPELL
```

```
-- ***************************************************************
function spell (x in number) return varchar2 is
-- ***************************************************************

-- Local Function Specification: WORDING

-- ***************************************************************
  function wording (x in number) return varchar2 is
  begin
    if x = 0 then
       return 'Zero';
    else
       return to_char(to_date(x,'j'),'Jsp'); -- Numbers-to-words
    end if;
  end wording;


-- ***************************************************************

-- Local Function Specification: INTEGER_TRANSLATION

-- ***************************************************************
  function integer_translation (working_x in number)
         return varchar2 is
    x_char varchar2(128);
    denoms_to_do number;
    start_byte    number;
    pointer       binary_integer;
    interim_spelling varchar2(2000);
  begin
    if working_x is null then
       return 'Null';
    elsif working_x = 0 then
       return 'Zero';
    end if;
    x_char := abs(working_x);
    pointer := 3-mod(length(x_char),3);
    x_char :=
lpad(x_char,length(x_char)+pad_factor(pointer),'0');
    denoms_to_do := length(x_char)/3;
    result := null;
    for i in 1..denoms_to_do loop
        start_byte := ((i-1)*3)+1;
        interim_spelling := wording(substr(x_char,start_byte,3));
        pointer := (denoms_to_do+1)-i;
```

```
           if upper(interim_spelling) <> 'ZERO' then
              result := rtrim(ltrim(result||' '||interim_spelling||
                 ' '||denom(pointer)));
           end if;
           hold(i) := result;
      end loop;
      return result;
  end integer_translation;


--   ************************************************************

--   Global Function SPELL Procedural Section

--   ************************************************************
begin
  working_integer_spell := null;
  working_decimal_spell := null;
  working_fraction_spell := null;
  working_integer := trunc(x);
  if abs(x) > abs(working_integer) then
     working_decimal :=
        substr(rtrim(to_char(abs(x)-abs(working_integer),
        '.000000000000000000000000000000000000000'),
        '0'),3);
  else
     working_decimal := null;
     working_dec_mag := null;
  end if;
  working_integer_spell := integer_translation(working_integer);
  if working_decimal is not null then
     working_dec_mag := 10 ** length(working_decimal);
     working_decimal_spell :=
        ' and '||integer_translation(working_decimal);
     working_fraction_spell :=
        integer_translation(working_dec_mag)||'th';
     if working_decimal > 1 then
        working_fraction_spell := working_fraction_spell||'s';
     end if;
     if upper(substr(working_fraction_spell,1,3))='ONE' then
        working_fraction_spell :=
substr(working_fraction_spell,5);
     end if;
     working_fraction_spell := ' / '||working_fraction_spell;
  end if;
  if working_integer = 0 and working_decimal_spell is not null then
```

```
      result := substr(working_decimal_spell,5)||
         working_fraction_spell;
   else
      result := working_integer_spell||
         working_decimal_spell||working_fraction_spell;
   end if;
   if x < 0 then
      result := 'Negative '||result;
   end if;
   result := replace(result,'  ',' ');
   return result;
end spell;


--   ****************************************************************


--   End of Global Function: SPELL


--   ****************************************************************


--   ****************************************************************


--   Global Function Specification: CHECK_PROTECT


--   ****************************************************************

function check_protect (x in number) return varchar2 is
   hold_dollar number;
   hold_cents  number;
   function check_for_single (y in number, currency in varchar2)
      return varchar2 is
   begin
      if y = 1 then
         return 'One '||currency;
      else
         return spell(y) ||' '||currency||'s';
      end if;
   end;
begin
   if x is null then
      return 'Non Negotiable';
   end if;
   hold_dollar := trunc(x);
   hold_cents  := (abs(x) - trunc(abs(x)))*100;
   return check_for_single(hold_dollar,'Dollar')||' and '||
          check_for_single(hold_cents,'Cent');
end check_protect;
```

```
--   ****************************************************************

--   "First-time-only" Package Initialization activities

--   ****************************************************************
begin
   pad_factor(1) := 1;
   pad_factor(2) := 2;
   pad_factor(3) := 0;
   denom(1) := null;
   denom(2) := 'Thousand';
   denom(3) := 'Million';
   denom(4) := 'Billion';
   denom(5) := 'Trillion';
   denom(6) := 'Quadrillion';
   denom(7) := 'Quintillion';
   denom(8) := 'Sextillion';
   denom(9) := 'Septillion';
   denom(10) := 'Octillion';
   denom(11) := 'Nonillion';
   denom(12) := 'Decillion';
   denom(13) := 'Undecillion';
   denom(14) := 'Duodecillion';
   denom(15) := 'Tredecillion';
   denom(16) := 'Quattuordecillion';
   denom(17) := 'Quindecillion';
   denom(18) := 'Sexdecillion';
   denom(19) := 'Septendecillion';
   denom(20) := 'Octodecillion';
   denom(21) := 'Novemdecillion';
   denom(22) := 'Vigintillion';
   denom(23) := 'Unvigintillion';
   denom(24) := 'Duovigintillion';
   denom(25) := 'Trevigintillion';
   denom(26) := 'Quattuorvigintillion';
   denom(27) := 'Quinvigintillion';
   denom(28) := 'Sexvigintillion';
   denom(29) := 'Septenvigintillion';
   denom(30) := 'Octovigintillion';
   denom(31) := 'Novemvigintillion';
   denom(32) := 'Tregintillion';
```

```
   denom(33) := 'Untregintillion';
   denom(34) := 'Duotregintillion';
end dh_util;

--   **************************************************************

--   End of Global Function: SPELL

--   **************************************************************
/
```

Summary

In this chapter, we have discussed the different types of built-in functions in detail, pointing out where each type is approprate. In the next chapter, we will discuss cursors, which are used for multirow queries. That discussion will build on the concepts that we have examined so far.

CHAPTER
6

Cursors

n Chapters 4 and 5, we discussed how SQL statements can be used in PL/SQL. This functionality is enhanced through the use of cursors, which allow a program to take explicit control of SQL statement processing. In this chapter, we will see how cursors are used for multirow queries and other SQL statements. We will also discuss cursor variables, one of the main new features of PL/SQL 2.2, and enhanced in version 2.3.

What Is a Cursor?

In order to process a SQL statement, Oracle will allocate an area of memory known as the *context area*. The context area contains information necessary to complete the processing, including the number of rows processed by the statement, a pointer to the parsed representation of the statement, and in the case of a query, the *active set*, which is the set of rows returned by the query.

A *cursor* is a handle, or pointer, to the context area. Through the cursor, a PL/SQL program can control the context area and what happens to it as the statement is processed. The following PL/SQL block illustrates a cursor fetch loop, in which multiple rows of data are returned from a query.

```
-- Available online as curexamp.sql
DECLARE
  /* Output variables to hold the results of the query */
  v_StudentID    students.id%TYPE;
  v_FirstName    students.first_name%TYPE;
  v_LastName     students.last_name%TYPE;

  /* Bind variable used in the query */
  v_Major        students.major%TYPE := 'Computer Science';

  /* Cursor declaration */
  CURSOR c_Students IS
    SELECT id, first_name, last_name
      FROM students
      WHERE major = v_Major;
BEGIN
  /* Identify the rows in the active set, and prepare for further
     processing of the data */
  OPEN c_Students;
  LOOP
    /* Retrieve each row of the active set into PL/SQL variables */
```

```
   FETCH c_Students INTO v_StudentID, v_FirstName, v_LastName;

   /* If there are no more rows to fetch, exit the loop */
   EXIT WHEN c_Students%NOTFOUND;
 END LOOP;

 /* Free resources used by the query */
 CLOSE c_Students;
END;
```

This example illustrates an *explicit* cursor, in which the cursor name is explicitly assigned to a SELECT statement via the CURSOR..IS statement. An *implicit* cursor is used for all other SQL statements. Processing an explicit cursor involves four steps, which are described in the next section. Processing an implicit cursor, on the other hand, is taken care of automatically by PL/SQL.

Processing Explicit Cursors

The four PL/SQL steps necessary for explicit cursor processing are as follows:

1. Declare the cursor.

2. Open the cursor for a query.

3. Fetch the results into PL/SQL variables.

4. Close the cursor.

The cursor declaration is the only step that goes in the declarative section of a block—the other three steps are found in the executable or exception sections.

Declaring a Cursor

Declaring a cursor defines the name of the cursor and associates it with a SELECT statement. The syntax is

   CURSOR *cursor_name* IS *SELECT_statement*;

where *cursor_name* is the name of the cursor, and *SELECT_statement* is the query that it will process. Cursor names follow the usual scope and visibility rules for PL/SQL identifiers, as described in Chapter 2. Since a cursor name is a PL/SQL identifier, it must be declared before it is referenced. Any SELECT statements are legal, including joins and statements with the UNION or MINUS clause.

NOTE
SELECT_statement contains no INTO clause. The INTO clause is part of the FETCH statement.

A cursor declaration can reference PL/SQL variables in the WHERE clause. These variables are considered bind variables, as discussed in Chapter 3. Since the usual scoping rules apply, these variables must be visible at the point of the cursor declaration. For example, the following declarative section is legal.

```
DECLARE
  v_Department    classes.department%TYPE;
  v_Course        classes.course%TYPE;
  CURSOR c_Classes IS
    SELECT * from classes
      WHERE department = v_Department
      AND course = v_Course;
```

The next declarative section is illegal, because **v_Department** and **v_Course** are not declared before they are referenced.

```
DECLARE
  CURSOR c_Classes IS
    SELECT * from classes
      WHERE department = v_Department
      AND course = v_Course;
  v_Department    classes.department%TYPE;
  v_Course        classes.course%TYPE;
```

To ensure that all variables referenced in a cursor declaration are declared before the reference, you can declare all cursors at the end of a declarative section. This is the convention used in this book. The only exception to this is when the cursor name itself is used in a reference, such as the %ROWTYPE attribute. In this case, the cursor must be declared before a reference to it.

Opening a Cursor

The syntax for opening a cursor is

OPEN *cursor_name*;

where *cursor_name* identifies a cursor that has previously been declared. When a cursor is opened, the following things happen:

- The values of the bind variables are examined.

- Based on the values of the bind variables, the active set is determined.

- The active set pointer is set to the first row.

Bind variables are examined at cursor open time, and only at cursor open time. For example, consider the following PL/SQL block:

```
--Available online as binds.sql
DECLARE
  v_RoomID       classes.room_id%TYPE;
  v_Building     rooms.building%TYPE;
  v_Department   classes.department%TYPE;
  v_Course       classes.course%TYPE;
  CURSOR c_Buildings IS
    SELECT building
      FROM rooms, classes
      WHERE rooms.room_id = classes.room_id
      and department = v_Department
      and course = v_Course;
BEGIN
  -- Assign to bind variables before the cursor OPEN.
  v_Department := 'HIS';
  v_Course := 101;

  -- Open the cursor.
  OPEN c_Buildings;

  -- Reassign the bind variables - this has no effect,
  -- since the cursor is already open.
  v_Department := 'XXX';
  v_Course := -1;
END;
```

When **c_Buildings** is opened, **v_Department** and **v_Course** contain 'HIS' and 101, respectively. These are the values used in the query. Even though **v_Department** and **v_Course** are changed after the OPEN, the active set of the query does not change. This fact is known as *read-consistency* and is designed to ensure the integrity of the data. Read-consistency is discussed in more detail in the section "SELECT FOR UPDATE Cursors" later in this chapter. In order for the new values to be examined, the cursor would have to be closed and reopened. The query will see changes made to the database that have been committed prior to the OPEN statement. If another session has made data changes, but has not yet committed them, those changes will not be visible.

The active set, or the set of rows that match the query, is determined at cursor open time. The previous query, for example, returns one row ('Building Seven'). The WHERE clause is evaluated against the table or tables referenced in the FROM clause of the query, and any rows for which the condition evaluates to TRUE are added to the active set. A pointer into the set is also established at cursor open time. This pointer indicates which row is to be fetched next by the cursor.

It is legal to open a cursor that is already open. Before the second OPEN, PL/SQL will implicitly issue a CLOSE statement before reopening the cursor. More than one cursor can be open at a time, as well.

Fetching from a Cursor

The INTO clause for the query is part of the FETCH statement. The FETCH statement has two forms,

    FETCH *cursor_name* INTO *list_of_variables*;

and

    FETCH *cursor_name* INTO *PL/SQL_record*;

where *cursor_name* identifies a previously declared and opened cursor, *list_of_variables* is a comma-separated list of previously declared PL/SQL variables, and *PL/SQL_record* is a previously declared PL/SQL record. In either case, the variable or variables in the INTO clause must be type

compatible with the select list of the query. Given the preceding
c_Buildings cursor declaration, the following FETCH statement is legal:

```
FETCH c_Buildings INTO v_Building;
```

The following example illustrates legal and illegal FETCH statements:

```
-- Available online as badfetch.sql
DECLARE
  v_Department  classes.department%TYPE;
  v_Course      classes.course%TYPE;
  CURSOR c_AllClasses IS
    SELECT *
      FROM classes;
  v_ClassesRecord  c_AllClasses%ROWTYPE;
BEGIN
  OPEN c_AllClasses;

  -- This is a legal FETCH statement, returning the first
  -- row into a PL/SQL record which matches the select list
  -- of the query.
  FETCH c_AllClasses INTO v_ClassesRecord;

  -- This FETCH statement is illegal, since the select list
  -- of the query returns all 7 columns in the classes table
  -- but we are only fetching into 2 variables.
  -- This will raise the error "PLS-394: wrong number of values
  -- in the INTO list of a FETCH statement".
  FETCH c_AllClasses INTO v_Department, v_Course;
END;
```

After each FETCH, the active set pointer is increased to the next row. Thus, each FETCH will return successive rows in the active set, until the entire set is returned.

The %NOTFOUND attribute, described in the "Cursor Attributes" section, is used to determine when the entire active set has been retrieved. The last FETCH will not assign values to the output variables; they will still contain their prior values.

Closing a Cursor
When all of the active set has been retrieved, the cursor should be closed. This tells PL/SQL that the program is finished with the cursor, and the

resources associated with it can be freed. These resources include the storage used to hold the active set, as well as any temporary space used for determining the active set. The syntax for closing a cursor is

   CLOSE *cursor_name*;

where *cursor_name* identifies a previously opened cursor. Once a cursor is closed, it is illegal to fetch from it. Doing so will yield the Oracle error

ORA-1001: Invalid Cursor

or

ORA-1002: Fetch out of Sequence

Similarly, it is illegal to close an already closed cursor, which will also raise the ORA-1001 error.

Cursor Attributes

There are four attributes available in PL/SQL that can be applied to cursors. Cursor attributes are appended to a cursor name in a PL/SQL block, similar to %TYPE and %ROWTYPE. However, instead of returning a type, cursor attributes return a value that can be used in expressions. The attributes are %FOUND, %NOTFOUND, %ISOPEN, and %ROWCOUNT. They are described in the following sections, each of which refers to the listing in Figure 6-1. For this example, assume that **temp_table** has two rows. The data for these rows is listed here:

num_col	char_col
10	'Hello'
20	'There'

%FOUND   %FOUND is a boolean attribute. It returns TRUE if the previous FETCH returned a row and FALSE if it didn't. If %FOUND is checked while the cursor isn't open, ORA-1001 (invalid cursor) is returned.

```
DECLARE
    -- Cursor declaration
        CURSOR c_TempData IS
        SELECT * from temp_table;
    -- Record to store the fetched data
    v_TempRecord c_TempData%ROWTYPE;
BEGIN
    -- location ①
    OPEN c_Tempdata;                          -- Open cursor
    -- location ②
    FETCH c_TempData INTO v_TempRecord;  -- Fetch first row
    -- location ③
    FETCH c_TempData INTO v_TempRecord;  -- Fetch second row
    -- location ④
    FETCH c_TempData INTO v_TempRecord;  -- Third fetch
    -- location ⑤
    CLOSE c_TempData;
    -- location ⑥
END;
```

FIGURE 6-1.   *Code for cursor attribute example*

The following table uses the numbered locations in Figure 6-1 to illustrate the behavior of %FOUND.

Location	Value of c_TempData%FOUND	Explanation
1	Error: ORA-1001	**c_TempData** hasn't been opened yet. There is no active set associated with it.
2	NULL	Although **c_TempData** has been opened, no fetch has been done. The value of the attribute can't be determined.
3	TRUE	The prior fetch returned the first row in **temp_table**.
4	TRUE	The prior fetch returned the second row in **temp_table**.

Location	Value of c_TempData%FOUND	Explanation
5	FALSE	The prior fetch didn't return any data, since all rows in the active set have been retrieved.
6	Error: ORA-1001	**c_TempData** has been closed, clearing all stored information about the active set.

%NOTFOUND   %NOTFOUND behaves opposite to %FOUND—if the prior fetch returns a row, then %NOTFOUND is FALSE. %NOTFOUND returns TRUE only if the prior fetch does not return a row. It is often used as the exit condition for a fetch loop. The following table describes the behavior of %NOTFOUND for the example in Figure 6-1.

Location	Value of c_TempData%NOTFOUND	Explanation
1	Error: ORA-1001	**c_TempData** hasn't been opened yet. There is no active set associated with it.
2	NULL	Although **c_TempData** has been opened, no fetch has been done. The value of the attribute can't be determined.
3	FALSE	The prior fetch returned the first row in **temp_table**.
4	FALSE	The prior fetch returned the second row in **temp_table**.
5	TRUE	The prior fetch didn't return any data, since all rows in the active set have been retrieved.
6	Error: ORA-1001	**c_TempData** has been closed, clearing all stored information about the active set.

%ISOPEN   This boolean attribute is used to determine whether or not the associated cursor is open. If so, %ISOPEN returns TRUE; otherwise, it returns FALSE. This is illustrated in the next table.

Location	Value of c_TempData%ISOPEN	Explanation
1	FALSE	c_TempData hasn't been opened yet.
2	TRUE	c_TempData has been opened.
3	TRUE	c_TempData is still open.
4	TRUE	c_TempData is still open.
5	TRUE	c_TempData is still open.
6	FALSE	c_TempData has been closed.

%ROWCOUNT   This numeric attribute returns the number of rows fetched by the cursor so far. If referenced when its associated cursor is not open, ORA-1001 is returned. The behavior of %ROWCOUNT is described in the following table.

Location	Value of c_TempData%ROWCOUNT	Explanation
1	Error: ORA-1001	c_TempData hasn't been opened yet. There is no active set associated with it.
2	0	c_TempData has been opened, but no fetch has been done.
3	1	The first row from temp_table has been fetched.
4	2	The second row from temp_table has been fetched.
5	2	Two rows have been fetched from temp_table so far.
6	Error: ORA-1001	c_TempData has been closed, removing all information about the active set.

CURSOR ATTRIBUTE COMPARISON Table 6-1 shows the value of all four cursor attributes as the block progresses, for comparison.

Parameterized Cursors

There is an additional way of using bind variables in a cursor. A *parameterized* cursor takes arguments, similar to a procedure. (Procedures are discussed in more detail in Chapter 7.) Consider the **c_Classes** cursor, which we examined earlier in this chapter:

```
DECLARE
  v_Department    classes.department%TYPE;
  v_Course        classes.course%TYPE;
  CURSOR c_Classes IS
    SELECT *
      FROM classes
      WHERE department = v_Department
      AND course = v_Course;
```

c_Classes contains two bind variables, **v_Department** and **v_Course**. We can modify **c_Classes** into a parameterized cursor that is equivalent, as follows:

```
DECLARE
  CURSOR c_Classes(p_Department classes.department%TYPE,
                   p_Course classes.course%TYPE) IS
    SELECT *
      FROM classes
      WHERE department = p_Department
      AND course = p_Course;
```

Location	c_TempData %FOUND	c_TempData %NOTFOUND	c_TempData %ISOPEN	c_TempData %ROWCOUNT
1	ORA-1001	ORA-1001	FALSE	ORA-1001
2	NULL	NULL	TRUE	0
3	TRUE	FALSE	TRUE	1
4	TRUE	FALSE	TRUE	2
5	FALSE	TRUE	TRUE	2
6	ORA-1001	ORA-1001	FALSE	ORA-1001

TABLE 6-1. *Behavior of All Cursor Attributes*

With a parameterized cursor, the OPEN statement is used to pass the actual values into the cursor. We could open **c_Classes** with

```
OPEN c_Classes('HIS', 101);
```

In this case, 'HIS' would be passed in for **p_Department**, and 101 for **p_Course**. Parameters can be passed using positional or named notation, as well. For more information on parameter passing in general, see Chapter 7.

Processing Implicit Cursors

Explicit cursors are used to process SELECT statements that return more than one row, as we have seen in the previous sections. However, all SQL statements are executed inside a context area and thus have a cursor that points to this context area. This cursor is known as the *SQL cursor*. Unlike explicit cursors, the SQL cursor is not opened or closed by the program. PL/SQL implicitly opens the SQL cursor, processes the SQL statement in it, and closes the cursor afterwards.

The implicit cursor is used to process INSERT, UPDATE, DELETE, and single-row SELECT..INTO statements. Since the SQL cursor is opened and closed by the PL/SQL engine, the OPEN, FETCH, and CLOSE commands are not relevant. However, the cursor attributes can be applied to the SQL cursor. For example, the following block will perform an INSERT statement if the UPDATE statement does not match any rows:

```
-- Available online as nomatch1.sql
BEGIN
  UPDATE rooms
    SET number_seats = 100
    WHERE room_id = 99980;
  -- If the previous UPDATE statement didn't match any rows,
  -- insert a new row into the rooms table.
  IF SQL%NOTFOUND THEN
    INSERT INTO rooms (room_id, number_seats)
      VALUES (99980, 100);
  END IF;
END;
```

We can also accomplish the same thing by using SQL%ROWCOUNT:

```
-- Available online as nomatch2.sql
BEGIN
  UPDATE rooms
    SET number_seats = 100
    WHERE room_id = 99980;
  -- If the previous UPDATE statement didn't match any rows,
  -- insert a new row into the rooms table.
  IF SQL%ROWCOUNT = 0 THEN
    INSERT INTO rooms (room_id, number_seats)
      VALUES (99980, 100);
  END IF;
END;
```

Although SQL%NOTFOUND can be used with SELECT..INTO statements, it is not really useful to do so. This is because a SELECT..INTO statement will raise the Oracle error

```
ORA-1403: no data found
```

when it does not match any rows. This error causes control to pass immediately to the exception handling section of the block, preventing the check for SQL%NOTFOUND. This is illustrated by the following example:

```
-- Available online as nodata.sql
DECLARE
  -- Record to hold room information.
  v_RoomData    rooms%ROWTYPE;
BEGIN
  -- Retrieve information about room ID -1.
  SELECT *
    INTO v_RoomData
    FROM rooms
    WHERE room_id = -1;

  -- The following statement will never be executed, since
  -- control passes immediately to the exception handler.
  IF SQL%NOTFOUND THEN
    INSERT INTO temp_table (char_col)
      VALUES ('Not found!');
  END IF;
EXCEPTION
  WHEN NO_DATA_FOUND THEN
    INSERT INTO temp_table (char_col)
      VALUES ('Not found, exception handler');
END;
```

Exception handling is discussed in detail in Chapter 10. Note that SQL%NOTFOUND can be checked inside a NO_DATA_FOUND exception handler, but it will always evaluate to TRUE at this point.

SQL%ISOPEN is also valid; however, it will always evaluate to FALSE since the implicit cursor is automatically closed after the statement within it has been processed.

Cursor Fetch Loops

The most common operation with cursors is to fetch all of the rows in the active set. This is done with a *fetch loop*, which is simply a loop that processes each of the rows in the active set, one by one. The following sections examine several different kinds of cursor fetch loops and their uses.

Simple Loops

In this first style of fetch loop, the simple loop syntax (LOOP..END LOOP) is used for the cursor processing. Explicit cursor attributes are used to control how many times the loop executes. An example of this type of fetch loop is given here:

```
-- Available online as simple.sql
DECLARE
  -- Declare variables to hold information about the students
  -- majoring in History.
  v_StudentID    students.id%TYPE;
  v_FirstName    students.first_name%TYPE;
  v_LastName     students.last_name%TYPE;

  -- Cursor to retrieve the information about History students
  CURSOR c_HistoryStudents IS
    SELECT id, first_name, last_name
      FROM students
      WHERE major = 'History';
BEGIN
  -- Open the cursor and initialize the active set
  OPEN c_HistoryStudents;
  LOOP
    -- Retrieve information for the next student
    FETCH c_HistoryStudents INTO v_StudentID, v_FirstName,
                                 v_LastName;
```

```
  -- Exit loop when there are no more rows to fetch
  EXIT WHEN c_HistoryStudents%NOTFOUND;

  -- Process the fetched rows.  In this case sign up each
  -- student for History 301 by inserting them into the
  -- registered_students table. Record the first and last
  -- names in temp_table as well.
  INSERT INTO registered_students (student_id, department,
                                  course)
    VALUES (v_StudentID, 'HIS', 301);

  INSERT INTO temp_table (num_col, char_col)
    VALUES (v_StudentID, v_FirstName || ' ' || v_LastName);

END LOOP;

-- Free resources used by the cursor
CLOSE c_HistoryStudents;

-- Commit our work
COMMIT;
END;
```

Note the placement of the EXIT WHEN statement immediately after the FETCH statement. After the last row has been retrieved, **c_HistoryStudents%NOTFOUND** becomes TRUE, and the loop is exited. The EXIT WHEN statement is also before the processing of the data. This is done to ensure that the processing will not handle any duplicate rows.

Consider the following loop, which is very similar to the previous one, except that the EXIT WHEN statement has been moved to the end of the loop.

```
-- Available online as exitwhen.sql
DECLARE
  -- Declare variables to hold information about the students
  -- majoring in History.
  v_StudentID    students.id%TYPE;
  v_FirstName    students.first_name%TYPE;
  v_LastName     students.last_name%TYPE;

  -- Cursor to retrieve the information about History students
  CURSOR c_HistoryStudents IS
    SELECT id, first_name, last_name
```

```
      FROM students
      WHERE major = 'History';
BEGIN
  -- Open the cursor and initialize the active set
  OPEN c_HistoryStudents;
  LOOP
    -- Retrieve information for the next student
    FETCH c_HistoryStudents INTO v_StudentID, v_FirstName,
                                      v_LastName;

    -- Process the fetched rows, in this case sign up each
    -- student for History 301 by inserting them into the
    -- registered_students table. Record the first and last
    -- names in temp_table as well.
    INSERT INTO registered_students (student_id, department,
                                  course)
      VALUES (v_StudentID, 'HIS', 301);

    INSERT INTO temp_table (num_col, char_col)
      VALUES (v_StudentID, v_FirstName || ' ' || v_LastName);

    -- Exit loop when there are no more rows to fetch
    EXIT WHEN c_HistoryStudents%NOTFOUND;

  END LOOP;

  -- Free resources used by the cursor
  CLOSE c_HistoryStudents;

  -- Commit our work
  COMMIT;
END;
```

The last FETCH will not modify **v_StudentID**, **v_FirstName**, and
v_LastName, since there are no more rows in the active set. The output
variables will thus still have the values for the prior FETCHed rows. Since
the check is after the processing, however, these duplicate values are
inserted into the **registered_students** and **temp_table** tables, which is not
the desired effect.

WHILE Loops

A cursor fetch loop can also be constructed using the WHILE..LOOP
syntax, as illustrated by the following example.

```
-- Available online as while.sql
DECLARE
  -- Cursor to retrieve the information about History students
  CURSOR c_HistoryStudents IS
    SELECT id, first_name, last_name
      FROM students
      WHERE major = 'History';

  -- Declare a record to hold the fetched information.
  v_StudentData  c_HistoryStudents%ROWTYPE;
BEGIN
  -- Open the cursor and initialize the active set
  OPEN c_HistoryStudents;

  -- Retrieve the first row, to set up for the WHILE loop
  FETCH c_HistoryStudents INTO v_StudentData;

  -- Continue looping while there are more rows to fetch
  WHILE c_HistoryStudents%FOUND LOOP
    -- Process the fetched rows, in this case sign up each
    -- student for History 301 by inserting them into the
    -- registered_students table. Record the first and last
    -- names in temp_table as well.
    INSERT INTO registered_students (student_id, department,
                                     course)
      VALUES (v_StudentData.ID, 'HIS', 301);

    INSERT INTO temp_table (num_col, char_col)
      VALUES (v_StudentData.ID,
              v_StudentData.first_name || ' ' ||
              v_StudentData.last_name);

    -- Retrieve the next row. The %FOUND condition will be checked
    -- before the loop continues again.
    FETCH c_HistoryStudents INTO v_StudentData;
  END LOOP;

  -- Free resources used by the cursor
  CLOSE c_HistoryStudents;

  -- Commit our work
  COMMIT;
END;
```

This fetch loop behaves the same as the LOOP..END LOOP example in the previous section. Note that the FETCH statement appears twice—once before the loop and once after the loop processing. This is necessary so that the loop condition (**c_HistoryStudents%FOUND**) will be evaluated for each loop iteration.

Cursor FOR Loops

Both of the FETCH loops just described require explicit processing of the cursor, with OPEN, FETCH, and CLOSE statements. PL/SQL provides a simpler type of loop, which implicitly handles the cursor processing. This is known as a cursor FOR loop. An example, which again is equivalent to the previous two examples, is given here:

```
-- Available online as forloop.sql
DECLARE
   -- Cursor to retrieve the information about History students
   CURSOR c_HistoryStudents IS
     SELECT id, first_name, last_name
       FROM students
       WHERE major = 'History';
BEGIN
   -- Begin the loop. An implicit OPEN of c_HistoryStudents
   -- is done here.
   FOR v_StudentData IN c_HistoryStudents LOOP
     -- An implicit FETCH is done here.

     -- Process the fetched rows, in this case sign up each
     -- student for History 301 by inserting them into the
     -- registered_students table. Record the first and last
     -- names in temp_table as well.
     INSERT INTO registered_students (student_id, department,
                                      course)
       VALUES (v_StudentData.ID, 'HIS', 301);

     INSERT INTO temp_table (num_col, char_col)
       VALUES (v_StudentData.ID,
               v_StudentData.first_name || ' ' ||
               v_StudentData.last_name);
```

```
    -- Before the loop will continue, an implicit check of
    -- c_HistoryStudents%NOTFOUND is done here.
  END LOOP;
  -- Now that the loop is finished, an implicit CLOSE of
  -- c_HistoryStudents is done.

  -- Commit our work.
  COMMIT;
END;
```

There are two important things to note about this example. First, the record **v_StudentData** is *not* declared in the declarative section of the block. This variable is *implicitly* declared by the PL/SQL compiler, similar to the loop index for a numeric FOR loop. The type of this variable is **c_HistoryStudents%ROWTYPE**, and the scope of **v_StudentData** is only the FOR loop itself. The implicit declaration of the loop index, and the scope of this declaration, is the same behavior as a numeric FOR loop, as described in Chapter 2. Because of this, you cannot assign to a loop variable inside a cursor FOR loop.

Second, **c_HistoryStudents** is implicitly opened, fetched from, and closed by the loop at the places indicated by the comments. Before the loop starts, the cursor is opened. Before each loop iteration, the %FOUND attribute is checked to make sure there are remaining rows in the active set. When the active set is completely fetched, the cursor is closed as the loop ends.

Cursor FOR loops have the advantage of providing the functionality of a cursor fetch loop simply and cleanly, with a minimum of syntax.

NO_DATA_FOUND vs. %NOTFOUND

The NO_DATA_FOUND exception is raised only for SELECT..INTO statements, when the WHERE clause of the query does not match any rows. When the WHERE clause of an explicit cursor does not match any rows, the %NOTFOUND attribute is set to TRUE instead. If the WHERE clause of an UPDATE or DELETE statement does not match any rows, SQL%NOTFOUND is set to TRUE, rather than raising NO_DATA_FOUND. Because of this, all of the fetch loops shown so far use %NOTFOUND or %FOUND to determine the exit condition for the loop, rather than the NO_DATA_FOUND exception.

SELECT FOR UPDATE Cursors

Very often, the processing done in a fetch loop modifies the rows that have been retrieved by the cursor. PL/SQL provides a convenient syntax for doing this. This method consists of two parts—the FOR UPDATE clause in the cursor declaration and the WHERE CURRENT OF clause in an UPDATE or DELETE statement.

FOR UPDATE

The FOR UPDATE clause is part of a SELECT statement. It is legal as the last clause of the statement, after the ORDER BY clause (if it is present). The syntax is

SELECT ... FROM ... FOR UPDATE [OF *column_reference*] [NOWAIT]

where *column_reference* is a column in the table against which the query is performed. A list of columns can also be used. For example, the following declarative section defines two cursors that are both legal forms of the SELECT..FOR UPDATE syntax.

```
DECLARE
  -- This cursor lists two columns for the UPDATE clause.
  CURSOR c_AllStudents IS
    SELECT *
      FROM students
      FOR UPDATE OF first_name, last_name;

  -- This cursor does not list any columns.
  CURSOR c_LargeClasses IS
    SELECT department, course
      FROM classes
      WHERE max_students > 50
      FOR UPDATE;
```

Normally, a SELECT operation will not take any locks on the rows being accessed. This allows other sessions connected to the database to change the data being selected. The result set is still consistent, however. At OPEN time, when the active set is determined, Oracle takes a snapshot of the table. Any changes that have been committed prior to this point are reflected in the active set. Any changes made after this point, even if they are committed, are not reflected unless the cursor is reopened, which will evaluate the active set again. This is the read-consistency process mentioned at the beginning of the chapter. However, if the FOR UPDATE clause is present, exclusive row locks are taken on the rows in the active set before the OPEN returns. These locks prevent other sessions from changing the rows in the active set until the transaction is committed.

If another session already has locks on the rows in the active set, then the SELECT FOR UPDATE operation will wait for these locks to be released by the other session. There is no time-out for this waiting period—the SELECT FOR UPDATE will hang until the other session releases the lock. To handle this situation, the NOWAIT clause is available. If the rows are locked by another session, then the OPEN will return immediately with the Oracle error

```
ORA-54: resource busy and acquire with NOWAIT specified
```

In this case, you may want to retry the OPEN later or change the active set to fetch unlocked rows.

WHERE CURRENT OF

If the cursor is declared with the FOR UPDATE clause, the WHERE CURRENT OF clause can be used in an UPDATE or DELETE statement. The syntax for this clause is

WHERE CURRENT OF *cursor*

where *cursor* is the name of a cursor that has been declared with a FOR UPDATE clause. The WHERE CURRENT OF clause evaluates to the row that was just retrieved by the cursor. For example, the following block will update the current credits for all students registered in HIS 101.

```
-- Available online as forupdat.sql
DECLARE
  -- Number of credits to add to each student's total
  v_NumCredits  classes.num_credits%TYPE;

  -- This cursor will select only those students who are currently
  -- registered for HIS 101.
  CURSOR c_RegisteredStudents IS
    SELECT *
      FROM students
      WHERE id IN (SELECT student_id
```

```
                       FROM registered_students
                       WHERE department= 'HIS'
                       AND course = 101)
        FOR UPDATE OF current_credits;

  BEGIN
    -- Set up the cursor fetch loop.
    FOR v_StudentInfo IN c_RegisteredStudents LOOP
    -- Determine the number of credits for HIS 101.
    SELECT num_credits
      INTO v_NumCredits
      FROM classes
      WHERE department = 'HIS'
      AND course = 101;

    -- Update the row we just retrieved from the cursor.
    UPDATE students
      SET current_credits = current_credits + v_NumCredits
      WHERE CURRENT OF c_RegisteredStudents;
    END LOOP;

    -- Commit our work.
    COMMIT;
  END;
```

Note that the UPDATE statement updates only the column listed in the FOR UPDATE clause of the cursor declaration. If no columns are listed, then any column can be updated.

It is legal to execute a query with a FOR UPDATE clause, but not reference the rows fetched via WHERE CURRENT OF. In this case, the rows are still locked and thus can only be modified by the current session (which holds the lock). UPDATE and DELETE statements that modify these rows will not block if they are executed by the session holding the lock.

Fetching Across COMMITS

Note that the COMMIT in the example in the previous section is done after the fetch loop is complete. This is done because a COMMIT will release any locks held by the session. Since the FOR UPDATE clause acquires locks, these will be released by the COMMIT. When this happens, the cursor is invalidated. Any subsequent fetches will return the Oracle error

```
ORA-1002: fetch out of sequence
```

Consider the following example, which raises this error.

--Available online as commit1.sql
```
DECLARE
  -- Cursor to retrieve all students, and lock the rows as well.
  CURSOR c_AllStudents IS
    SELECT *
      FROM students
      FOR UPDATE;

  -- Variable for retrieved data.
  v_StudentInfo  c_AllStudents%ROWTYPE;
BEGIN
  -- Open the cursor. This will acquire the locks.
  OPEN c_AllStudents;

  -- Retrieve the first record.
  FETCH c_AllStudents INTO v_StudentInfo;

  -- Issue a COMMIT. This will release the locks, invalidating
  -- the cursor.
  COMMIT WORK;

  -- This FETCH will raise the ORA-1002 error.
  FETCH c_AllStudents INTO v_StudentInfo;
END;
```

Thus, if there is a COMMIT inside a SELECT FOR UPDATE fetch loop, any fetches done after the COMMIT will fail. So it is not advisable to use a COMMIT inside the loop. If the cursor is not defined as a SELECT FOR UPDATE, there is no problem.

What do you do if you want to update the row just fetched from the cursor and use a COMMIT inside the fetch loop? The WHERE CURRENT OF clause isn't available, since the cursor can't be defined with a FOR UPDATE clause. However, you can use the primary key of the table in the WHERE clause of the UPDATE, as illustrated by the following example.

-- Available online as commit2.sql
```
DECLARE
  -- Number of credits to add to each student's total
  v_NumCredits  classes.num_credits%TYPE;

  -- This cursor will select only those students who are currently
  -- registered for HIS 101.
```

```
CURSOR c_RegisteredStudents IS
  SELECT *
    FROM students
    WHERE id IN (SELECT student_id
                   FROM registered_students
                   WHERE department= 'HIS'
                   AND course = 101);

BEGIN
  -- Set up the cursor fetch loop.
  FOR v_StudentInfo IN c_RegisteredStudents LOOP
  -- Determine the number of credits for HIS 101.
  SELECT num_credits
    INTO v_NumCredits
    FROM classes
    WHERE department = 'HIS'
    AND course = 101;

  -- Update the row we just retrieved from the cursor.
  UPDATE students
    SET current_credits = current_credits + v_NumCredits
    WHERE id = v_Studentinfo.id;

  -- We can commit inside the loop, since the cursor is
  -- not declared FOR UPDATE.
  COMMIT;
  END LOOP;
END;
```

This example essentially simulates the WHERE CURRENT OF clause, but does not create locks on the rows in the active set. As a result, it may not perform as expected if other sessions are accessing the data concurrently.

Cursor Variables

All of the explicit cursor examples we have seen so far are examples of *static cursors*—the cursor is associated with one SQL statement, and this statement is known when the block is compiled. A *cursor variable*, on the other hand, can be associated with different statements at run time. Cursor variables are analogous to PL/SQL variables, which can hold different values at run time. Static cursors are analogous to PL/SQL constants, since they can only be associated with one run-time query.

PL/SQL 2.2 ...and HIGHER Cursor variables are not available in PL/SQL versions prior to 2.2. They were introduced in version 2.2, and their functionality has been enhanced for PL/SQL 2.3. This section describes the features available in both versions. All of the examples in this section will work with 2.2, and, where indicated, with 2.3 and higher.

In order to use a cursor variable, it must first be declared. Storage for it must then be allocated at run time, since a cursor variable is a REF type. It is then opened, fetched, and closed similarly to a static cursor.

Declaring a Cursor Variable

A cursor variable is a reference type. With versions 2.2 and 2.3 of PL/SQL, it is the only reference type available. As discussed in Chapter 2, a reference type is the same as a pointer in C or Pascal. It can name different storage locations as the program runs. In order to use a reference type, first the variable has to be declared, and then the storage has to be allocated. Reference types in PL/SQL are declared using the syntax

REF *type*

where *type* is a previously defined type. The REF keyword indicates that the new type will be a pointer to the defined type. The type of a cursor variable is therefore REF CURSOR. This is the only legal REF type up to version 2.3 of PL/SQL. (PL/SQL 8.0 allows REFs to objects, described in Chapter 11.) The complete syntax for defining a cursor variable type is

TYPE *type_name* IS REF CURSOR RETURN *return_type*;

where *type_name* is the name of the new reference type, and *return_type* is a record type indicating the types of the select list that will eventually be returned by the cursor variable.

The return type for a cursor variable must be a record type. It can be declared explicitly as a user-defined record, or implicitly using %ROWTYPE. Once the reference type is defined, the variable can be declared. The following declarative section shows different declarations for cursor variables.

```
DECLARE
  -- Definition using %ROWTYPE.
  TYPE t_StudentsRef IS REF CURSOR
    RETURN students%ROWTYPE;

  -- Define a new record type,
  TYPE t_NameRecord IS RECORD (
    first_name  students.first_name%TYPE,
    last_name   students.last_name%TYPE);

  -- a variable of this type,
  v_NameRecord  t_NameRecord;

  -- And a cursor variable using the record type.
  TYPE t_NamesRef IS REF CURSOR
    RETURN t_NameRecord;

  -- We can declare another type, using %TYPE for the previously
  -- defined record.
  TYPE t_NamesRef2 IS REF CURSOR
    RETURN v_NameRecord%TYPE;

  -- Declare cursor variables using the above types.
  v_StudentCV t_StudentsRef;
  v_NameCV    t_NamesRef;
```

Constrained and Unconstrained Cursor Variables

The cursor variables in the previous section are *constrained*—they are declared for a specific return type only. When the variable is later opened, it must be opened for a query whose select list matches the return type of the cursor. If not, the predefined exception ROWTYPE_MISMATCH is raised.

PL/SQL 2.3 ...and HIGHER PL/SQL 2.3, however, allows the declaration of *unconstrained* cursor variables. An unconstrained cursor variable does not have a RETURN clause. When an unconstrained cursor variable is later opened, it can be opened for any query. The following declarative section declares an unconstrained cursor variable.

```
DECLARE
    -- Define an unconstrained reference type.
    -- TYPE t_FlexibleRef IS REF CURSOR;

    -- and a variable of that type.
    v_CursorVar t_FlexibleRef;
```

Allocating Storage for Cursor Variables

Since a cursor variable is a reference type, no storage is allocated for it when it is declared. Before it can be used, it needs to point to a valid area of memory. This memory can be created in two ways—by allocating it in an OCI or precompiler program, or automatically by the PL/SQL engine.

NOTE
PL/SQL 2.2 cannot automatically allocate storage for reference variables. Therefore, in order to use cursor variables with release 2.2, either these OCI or a precompiler is required, since these are the only tools that can allocate the necessary memory. PL/SQL 2.3 can allocate storage for cursor variables, and thus the precompiler or OCI is no longer necessary.

Using EXEC SQL ALLOCATE

In order to allocate storage when using the Pro*C precompiler, you need to declare a variable of type SQL_CURSOR. This variable should be declared in the DECLARE section of the Pro*C program, since it is a host variable. It is then allocated with the EXEC SQL ALLOCATE command. For example, the following Pro*C fragment declares and allocates a cursor variable:

```
EXEC SQL BEGIN DECLARE SECTION;
    SQL_CURSOR v_CursorVar;
EXEC SQL END DECLARE SECTION;

EXEC SQL ALLOCATE :v_CursorVar;
```

Using PL/SQL in Pro*C and other precompilers is discussed in more detail in Chapter 13. A host cursor variable is unconstrained, since it has no return type associated with it. This is the only way to declare an unconstrained cursor variable in PL/SQL 2.2.

Automatic Allocation

PL/SQL 2.3 ...and HIGHER With PL/SQL 2.3, cursor variables are automatically allocated when necessary. When the variable goes out of scope and thus no longer references the storage, it is de-allocated.

Opening a Cursor Variable for a Query

In order to associate a cursor variable with a particular SELECT statement, the OPEN syntax is extended to allow the query to be specified. This is done with the OPEN FOR syntax,

    OPEN *cursor_variable* FOR *select_statement*;

where *cursor_variable* is a previously declared cursor variable, and *select_statement* is the desired query. If the cursor variable is constrained, then the select list must match the return type of the cursor. If it is not constrained, the error

```
ORA-6504: PL/SQL: return types of result set variables or query
          do not match
```

is returned. For more information on PL/SQL errors and how to handle them, see Chapter 10. For example, given a cursor variable declaration like this,

```
DECLARE
   TYPE t_ClassesRef IS REF CURSOR RETURN classes%ROWTYPE;
   v_ClassesCV t_ClassesRef;
```

we can open **v_ClassesCV** with:

```
OPEN v_ClassesCV FOR
   SELECT * FROM CLASSES;
```

If, on the other hand, we attempt to open **v_ClassesCV** this way,

```
OPEN v_ClassesCV FOR
   SELECT department, course FROM CLASSES
```

we would receive ORA-6504, since the select list of the query does not match the return type of the cursor variable.

OPEN..FOR behaves the same way as OPEN—any bind variables in the query are examined and the active set is determined. Following the OPEN..FOR, the cursor variable is fetched from using the FETCH statement. The fetch must be done on the client with version 2.2, or it can be done on the server with version 2.3.

Closing Cursor Variables

Cursor variables are closed just like static cursors—with the CLOSE statement. This frees the resources used for the query. It does not necessarily free the storage for the cursor variable itself, however. The storage for the variable is freed when the variable goes out of scope. It is illegal to close a cursor or cursor variable that is already closed. Cursor variables can be closed on either the client or the server.

Cursor Variable Example 1

The following is a complete Pro*C program that demonstrates the use of cursor variables. It uses an embedded PL/SQL block to select from either the **classes** or the **rooms** table, depending on user input. For the benefit of those who may not be familiar with C, the code is more heavily commented than usual. This program will work with PL/SQL 2.2 and higher.

```
-- Available online as cursor1.pc
/* Include C and SQL header files. */
#include <stdio.h>
EXEC SQL INCLUDE SQLCA;

/* SQL Declare section. All host variables must be declared
   here. */
EXEC SQL BEGIN DECLARE SECTION;
   /* Character string to hold the username and password. */
   char *v_Username = "example/example";

   /* SQL Cursor variable */
```

```
    SQL_CURSOR v_CursorVar;

    /* Integer variable used to control table selection. */
    int v_Table;

    /* Output variables for rooms. */
    int v_RoomID;
    VARCHAR v_Description[2001];

    /* Output variables for classes. */
    VARCHAR v_Department[4];
    int v_Course;
EXEC SQL END DECLARE SECTION;


/* Error handling routine. Print out the error, and exit. */
void handle_error() {
  printf("SQL Error occurred!\n");
  printf("%.*s\n", sqlca.sqlerrm.sqlerrml,
sqlca.sqlerrm.sqlerrmc);
  EXEC SQL ROLLBACK WORK RELEASE;
  exit(1);
}

int main() {
  /* Character string to hold user input. */
  char v_Choice[20];

  /* Set up the error handling. Whenever a SQL error occurs, we
     will call the handle_error() routine. */
  EXEC SQL WHENEVER SQLERROR DO handle_error();

  /* Connect to the database. */
  EXEC SQL CONNECT :v_Username;
  printf("Connected to Oracle.\n");

  /* Allocate the cursor variable. */
  EXEC SQL ALLOCATE :v_CursorVar;

  /* Print a message asking the user for input, and retrieve their
     selection into v_Choice. */
  printf("Choose from (C)lasses or (R)ooms. Enter c or r: ");
  gets(v_Choice);

  /* Determine the correct table. */
```

```
if (v_Choice[0] == 'c')
  v_Table = 1;
else
  v_Table = 2;

/* Open the cursor variable using an embedded PL/SQL block. */
EXEC SQL EXECUTE
  BEGIN
    IF :v_Table = 1 THEN
      /* Open variable for the classes table. */
      OPEN :v_CursorVar FOR
        SELECT department, course
          FROM classes;
    ELSE
      /* Open variable for the rooms table. */
      OPEN :v_CursorVar FOR
        SELECT room_id, description
          FROM rooms;
    END IF;
  END;
END-EXEC;

/* Exit the loop when we are done fetching. */
EXEC SQL WHENEVER NOT FOUND DO BREAK;

/* Begin the fetch loop. */
for (;;) {
  if (v_Table == 1) {
    /* Fetch class info. */
    EXEC SQL FETCH :v_CursorVar
      INTO :v_Department, :v_Course;

    /* Display it to the screen. Since v_Department is a
       VARCHAR, use the .len field for the actual length
       and the .arr field for the data. */
    printf("%.*s %d\n", v_Department.len, v_Department.arr,
                        v_Course);
  }
  else {
    /* Fetch room info. */
    EXEC SQL FETCH :v_CursorVar
      INTO :v_RoomID, v_Description;

    /* Display it to the screen. Since v_Description is a
       VARCHAR, use the .len field for the actual length
```

```
          and the .arr field for the data. */
      printf("%d %.*s\n", v_RoomID, v_Description.len,
                      v_Description.arr);
   }
}

/* Close the cursor. */
EXEC SQL CLOSE :v_CursorVar;

/* Disconnect from the database. */
EXEC SQL COMMIT WORK RELEASE;
}
```

In the preceding program, the cursor is opened on the server (via the embedded anonymous block), and fetched from and closed back on the client. Since the cursor variable is declared as a host variable, it is unconstrained. Thus, we were able to use the same variable for selecting both from **classes** and from **rooms**.

Cursor Variable Example 2

PL/SQL 2.3 ...and HIGHER The following example is similar to the Pro*C example in the previous section, but is written entirely in PL/SQL. It is a stored procedure that selects from **classes** or **rooms** depending on its input. Since the fetch is done in the procedure and therefore on the server, it will only work in PL/SQL 2.3. For more information on stored procedures, see Chapter 7.

```
-- Available online as cursor2.sql
CREATE OR REPLACE PROCEDURE ShowCursorVariable
   /* Demonstrates the use of a cursor variable on the server.
      If p_Table is 'classes', then information from the classes
      table is inserted into temp_table.  If p_Table is 'rooms'
      then information from rooms is inserted. */
   (p_Table IN VARCHAR2) AS

   /* Define the cursor variable type */
   TYPE t_ClassesRooms IS REF CURSOR;

   /* and the variable itself. */
   v_CursorVar t_ClassesRooms;

   /* Variables to hold the output. */
   v_Department   classes.department%TYPE;
```

```
  v_Course      classes.course%TYPE;
  v_RoomID      rooms.room_id%TYPE;
  v_Description rooms.description%TYPE;
BEGIN
  -- Based on the input parameter, open the cursor variable.
  IF p_Table = 'classes' THEN
    OPEN v_CursorVar FOR
      SELECT department, course
        FROM classes;
  ELSIF p_table = 'rooms' THEN
    OPEN v_CursorVar FOR
      SELECT room_id, description
        FROM rooms;
  ELSE
    /* Wrong value passed as input - raise an error */
    RAISE_APPLICATION_ERROR(-20000,
      'Input must be ''classes'' or ''rooms''');
  END IF;

  /* Fetch loop.  Note the EXIT WHEN clause after the FETCH -
     with PL/SQL 2.3 we can use cursor attributes with cursor
     variables. */
  LOOP
    IF p_Table = 'classes' THEN
      FETCH v_CursorVar INTO
        v_Department, v_Course;
      EXIT WHEN v_CursorVar%NOTFOUND;

      INSERT INTO temp_table (num_col, char_col)
        VALUES (v_Course, v_Department);
    ELSE
      FETCH v_CursorVar INTO
        v_RoomID, v_Description;
      EXIT WHEN v_CursorVAR%NOTFOUND;

      INSERT INTO temp_table (num_col, char_col)
        VALUES (v_RoomID, SUBSTR(v_Description, 1, 60));
    END IF;
  END LOOP;

  /* Close the cursor. */
  CLOSE v_CursorVar;

  COMMIT;
END ShowCursorVariable;
```

Restrictions on Using Cursor Variables

Cursor variables are a powerful feature, and they can greatly simplify processing, since they allow different kinds of data to be returned in the same variable. However, there are a number of restrictions associated with their use. Some of the restrictions have been lifted in versions 2.3 and 8.0. The restrictions are listed here:

- In PL/SQL 2.2, cursor variables cannot be declared in a package. This is because the storage for a cursor variable has to be allocated using Pro*C or OCI. With version 2.2, the only mechanism for passing a cursor variable to a PL/SQL block is via a bind variable or a procedure parameter. This has been lifted in PL/SQL 2.3.

- Remote subprograms cannot return the value of a cursor variable. This restriction still exists between database servers in 2.3, but cursor variables can be passed between client- and server-side PL/SQL.

- Cursor attributes cannot be used with cursor variables with PL/SQL 2.2. This has been lifted for version 2.3. The %ROWTYPE attribute cannot be applied to a cursor variable with either version, however.

- With version 2.2, all fetches from cursor variables have to be done on the client, written in Pro*C or OCI. With version 2.3, cursor variables can be fetched from on the server.

- PL/SQL tables cannot store cursor variables in either version.

- You cannot use cursor variables with dynamic SQL in Pro*C.

- The query associated with a cursor variable in the OPEN..FOR statement cannot be FOR UPDATE.

Summary

In this chapter, we discussed the steps necessary for processing cursors, which allow explicit control of SQL statement processing. For explicit cursors, the steps include declaring, opening, fetching, and closing the cursor. Cursor attributes are used to determine the current state of a cursor, and thus how to manipulate it. In addition, we discussed different kinds of fetch loops. The chapter concluded with a discussion of cursor variables and the difference between their implementation in PL/SQL 2.2 and 2.3. In the next three chapters, we will continue the basics of PL/SQL by examining procedures, functions, packages, and triggers.

CHAPTER
7

Subprograms:
Procedures and
Functions

he PL/SQL blocks that we have seen so far have been anonymous ones. An anonymous block is compiled each time it is issued. In addition, an anonymous block is not stored in the database, and it cannot be called directly from other PL/SQL blocks. The constructs that we will look at in the next three chapters—procedures, functions, packages, and triggers—are all named blocks and thus do not have these restrictions. They can be stored in the database and run when appropriate. In this chapter, we will explore procedures and functions.

Creating Procedures and Functions

PL/SQL procedures and functions behave very much like procedures and functions in other third-generation languages. They share many of the same properties. Collectively, procedures and functions are also known as *subprograms*. As an example, the following code creates a procedure in the database:

```
-- Available online as addstud.sql
CREATE OR REPLACE PROCEDURE AddNewStudent (
  p_FirstName   students.first_name%TYPE,
  p_LastName    students.last_name%TYPE,
  p_Major       students.major%TYPE) AS
BEGIN
  -- Insert a new row in the students table. Use
  -- student_sequence to generate the new student ID, and
  -- 0 for current_credits.
  INSERT INTO students (ID, first_name, last_name,
                        major, current_credits)
    VALUES (student_sequence.nextval, p_FirstName, p_LastName,
            p_Major, 0);

  COMMIT;
END AddNewStudent;
```

Once this procedure is created, we can call it from another PL/SQL block, as in this example:

```
BEGIN
  AddNewStudent('David', 'Dinsmore', 'Music');
END;
```

This example illustrates several notable points:

- The **AddNewStudent** procedure is created first, with the CREATE OR REPLACE PROCEDURE statement. When a procedure is created, it is first compiled, then stored in the database in compiled form. This compiled code can then be run later, from another PL/SQL block.

- When the procedure is called, parameters can be passed. In the preceding example, the new student's first name, last name, and major are passed to the procedure at run time. Inside the procedure, the parameter **p_FirstName** will have the value 'David', **p_LastName** will have the value 'Dinsmore', and **p_Major** will have the value 'Music', since these literals are passed to the procedure when it is called.

- A procedure call is a PL/SQL statement by itself. It is not called as part of an expression. When a procedure is called, control passes to the first executable statement inside the procedure. When the procedure finishes, control resumes at the statement following the procedure call. In this regard, PL/SQL procedures behave the same as procedures in other 3GLs (third-generation languages).

- A procedure is a PL/SQL block, with a declarative section, executable section, and exception handling section. As in an anonymous block, only the executable section is required. **AddNewStudent** only has an executable section.

Creating a Procedure

The syntax for the CREATE OR REPLACE PROCEDURE statement is

```
CREATE [OR REPLACE] PROCEDURE procedure_name
    [(argument [{IN | OUT | IN OUT}] type,
       ...
       argument[{IN | OUT | IN OUT}] type)] {IS | AS}
    procedure_body
```

where *procedure_name* is the name of the procedure to be created, *argument* is the name of a procedure parameter, *type* is the type of the associated parameter, and *procedure_body* is a PL/SQL block that makes up the code of the procedure.

In order to change the code of a procedure, the procedure must be dropped and then re-created. Since this is a common operation while the procedure is under development, the OR REPLACE keywords allow this to be done in one operation. If the procedure exists, it is dropped first, without a warning message. To drop a procedure, use the DROP PROCEDURE command, described in the "Dropping Procedures and Functions" section later in this chapter. If the procedure does not already exist, then it is simply created. If the procedure exists and the OR REPLACE keywords are not present, the CREATE statement will return the Oracle error:

```
ORA-00955: name is already used by an existing object
```

As in other CREATE statements, creating a procedure is a DDL operation, so an implicit COMMIT is done both before and after the procedure is created. Either the IS or the AS keyword can be used—they are equivalent.

Parameters and Modes

Given the **AddNewStudent** procedure shown earlier, we can call this procedure from the following anonymous PL/SQL block:

```
-- Available online as callproc.sql
DECLARE
    -- Variables describing the new student
    v_NewFirstName    students.first_name%TYPE := 'Margaret';
    v_NewLastName     students.last_name%TYPE := 'Mason';
    v_NewMajor        students.major%TYPE := 'History';
BEGIN
    -- Add Margaret Mason to the database.
    AddNewStudent(v_NewFirstName, v_NewLastName, v_NewMajor);
END;
```

The variables declared in the preceding block (**v_NewFirstName**, **v_NewLastName**, **v_NewMajor**) are passed as arguments to **AddNewStudent**. In this context, they are known as *actual parameters*, while the parameters in the procedure declaration (**p_FirstName**, **p_LastName**, **p_Major**) are known as *formal parameters*. Actual parameters contain the values passed to the procedure when it is called, and they receive results from the procedure when it returns. The values of the actual parameters are the ones that will be used in the procedure. The formal parameters are the placeholders for the values of the actual parameters. When the procedure is called, the formal parameters are assigned the values of the actual parameters. Inside the procedure, they are referred to by the formal parameters. When the procedure returns, the actual parameters are assigned the value of the formal parameters. These assignments follow the normal rules for PL/SQL assignment, including type conversion if necessary.

Formal parameters can have three modes—IN, OUT, or IN OUT. If the mode is not specified for a formal parameter, it defaults to IN. The differences between each mode are described in Table 7-1 and illustrated in the following example:

```
-- Available online as modetest.sql
CREATE OR REPLACE PROCEDURE ModeTest (
  p_InParameter    IN NUMBER,
  p_OutParameter   OUT NUMBER,
  p_InOutParameter IN OUT NUMBER) IS

  v_LocalVariable  NUMBER;
BEGIN
  /* Assign p_InParameter to v_LocalVariable. This is legal,
     since we are reading from an IN parameter and not writing
     to it. */
  v_LocalVariable := p_InParameter;  -- Legal

  /* Assign 7 to p_InParameter. This is ILLEGAL, since we
     are writing to an IN parameter. */
  p_InParameter := 7;  -- Illegal

  /* Assign 7 to p_OutParameter. This is legal, since we
     are writing to an OUT parameter and not reading from
     it. */
  p_OutParameter := 7;  -- Legal

  /* Assign p_OutParameter to v_LocalVariable. This is
     ILLEGAL, since we are reading from an OUT parameter. */
  v_LocalVariable := p_outParameter;  -- Illegal

  /* Assign p_InOutParameter to v_LocalVariable. This is legal,
     since we are reading from an IN OUT parameter. */
```

```
v_LocalVariable := p_InOutParameter;   -- Legal

/* Assign 7 to p_InOutParameter. This is legal, since we
   are writing to an IN OUT parameter. */
p_InOutParameter := 7;   -- Legal
END ModeTest;
```

NOTE

*The **ModeTest** example shows legal and illegal PL/SQL assignments. A SELECT..INTO or a FETCH..INTO statement also assigns to the variables in the INTO clause, and these variables are subject to the same restrictions.*

Mode	Description
IN	The value of the actual parameter is passed into the procedure when the procedure is invoked. Inside the procedure, the formal parameter is considered *read-only*—it cannot be changed. When the procedure finishes and control returns to the calling environment, the actual parameter is not changed.
OUT	Any value the actual parameter has when the procedure is called is ignored. Inside the procedure, the formal parameter is considered *write-only*—it can only be assigned to and cannot be read from. When the procedure finishes and control returns to the calling environment, the contents of the formal parameter are assigned to the actual parameter.
IN OUT	This mode is a combination of IN and OUT. The value of the actual parameter is passed into the procedure when the procedure is invoked. Inside the procedure, the formal parameter can be read from and written to. When the procedure finishes and control returns to the calling environment, the contents of the formal parameter are assigned to the actual parameter.

TABLE 7-1. *Parameter Modes*

PL/SQL will check for legal assignments when the procedure is created. For example, **ModeTest** generates the following errors if we attempt to compile it, since it does contain illegal assignments:

```
PLS-363: expression 'P_INPARAMETER' cannot be used as an
         assignment target
PLS-365: 'P_OUTPARAMETER' is an OUT parameter and cannot be read
```

An IN parameter is an rvalue inside a procedure; it can only appear on the right-hand side of an assignment statement. An OUT parameter is an lvalue; it can only appear on the left-hand side of an assignment statement, and not on the right-hand side, even if it has been assigned to in the procedure. (For more information on lvalues and rvalues, see Chapter 2.) An IN OUT parameter is both an rvalue and an lvalue, and thus can appear on either side of an assignment statement.

If a parameter is OUT or IN OUT, the actual parameter will be written into by the procedure. When the procedure finishes, the contents of the formal parameters are written to their corresponding actual parameters. Because of this, the actual parameter must be an lvalue. A literal is an rvalue and thus cannot be used for OUT or IN OUT parameters, since there is no permanent memory allocated for a literal. For example, the following would be a legal call to **ModeTest**, since the actual parameters for **p_OutParameter** and **p_InOutParameter** are variable declarations:

```
DECLARE
  v_Variable1 NUMBER;
  v_Variable2 NUMBER;
BEGIN
  ModeTest(12, v_Variable1, v_Variable2);
END;
```

If we were to replace **v_Variable2** with a literal, however, we would get the following illegal example:

```
DECLARE
  v_Variable1 NUMBER;
BEGIN
  ModeTest(12, v_Variable1, 11);
END;
```

The preceding block produces the following errors:

```
ERROR at line 4:
ORA-06550: line 4, column 29:
PLS-00363: expression '11' cannot be used as an assignment target
ORA-06550: line 4, column 3:
PL/SQL: Statement ignored
```

If there are no parameters for a procedure, there are no parentheses in either the procedure declaration or the procedure call. This is also true for functions, described later in this chapter.

The Procedure Body

The body of a procedure is a PL/SQL block with declarative, executable, and exception sections. The declarative section is located between the IS or AS keyword and the BEGIN keyword. The executable section (the only one that is required) is located between the BEGIN and EXCEPTION keywords. The exception section is located between the EXCEPTION and END keywords.

> **NOTE**
> *There is no DECLARE keyword in a procedure or function declaration. The IS or AS keyword is used instead. This again is similar to the Ada syntax.*

The structure of a procedure therefore looks like this:

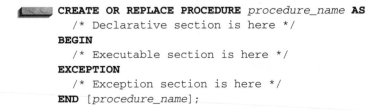
```
CREATE OR REPLACE PROCEDURE procedure_name AS
   /* Declarative section is here */
BEGIN
   /* Executable section is here */
EXCEPTION
   /* Exception section is here */
END [procedure_name];
```

The procedure name can optionally be included after the final END statement in the procedure declaration. If there is an identifier after the END, it must match the name of the procedure. It is good style to include this, since it emphasizes the END statement, which matches the CREATE statement.

Constraints on Formal Parameters

When a procedure is called, the values of the actual parameters are passed in, and they are referred to using the formal parameters inside the procedure. Not only the values are passed, but the constraints on the variables are passed as well, as part of the parameter passing mechanism. In a procedure declaration, it is illegal to constrain CHAR and VARCHAR2 parameters with a length, and NUMBER parameters with a precision and/or scale. For example, the following procedure declaration is illegal and will generate a compile error:

```
-- Available online as part of plength.sql
CREATE OR REPLACE PROCEDURE ParameterLength (
  p_Parameter1 IN OUT VARCHAR2(10),
  p_Parameter2 IN OUT NUMBER(3,2)) AS
BEGIN
  p_Parameter1 := 'abcdefghijklm';
  p_Parameter2 := 12.3;
END ParameterLength;
```

The correct declaration for this procedure would be

```
-- Available online as part of plength.sql
CREATE OR REPLACE PROCEDURE ParameterLength (
  p_Parameter1 IN OUT VARCHAR2,
  p_Parameter2 IN OUT NUMBER) AS
BEGIN
  p_Parameter1 := 'abcdefghijklmno';
  p_Parameter2 := 12.3;
END ParameterLength;
```

So, what are the constraints on **p_Parameter1** and **p_Parameter2**? They come from the actual parameters. If we call **ParameterLength** with

```
-- Available online as part of plength.sql
DECLARE
  v_Variable1 VARCHAR2(40);
  v_Variable2 NUMBER(3,4);
BEGIN
  ParameterLength(v_Variable1, v_Variable2);
END;
```

then **p_Parameter1** will have a maximum length of 40 (coming from the actual parameter **v_Variable1**) and **p_Parameter2** will have precision 3 and scale 4 (coming from the actual parameter **v_Variable2**). It is important to be aware of this. Consider the following block, which also calls **ParameterLength**:

```
-- Available online as part of plength.sql
DECLARE
  v_Variable1 VARCHAR2(10);
  v_Variable2 NUMBER(3,4);
BEGIN
  ParameterLength(v_Variable1, v_Variable2);
END;
```

The only difference between this block and the prior one is that **v_Variable1**, and hence **p_Parameter1**, has a length of 10 rather than 40. Since **ParameterLength** assigns a character string of length 15 to **p_Parameter1** (and hence **v_Variable1**), there is not enough room in the string. This will result in the following Oracle error when the procedure is called:

```
ORA-6502: numeric or value error
```

The source of the error is not in the procedure, it is in the code that calls the procedure.

TIP
In order to avoid errors such as ORA-6502, document any constraint requirements of the actual parameters when the procedure is created. This documentation should consist of comments stored with the procedure, and should include a description of what the procedure does in addition to any parameter definitions.

%TYPE AND PROCEDURE PARAMETERS   The only way to get constraints on a formal parameter is to use %TYPE. If a formal parameter is declared using %TYPE, and the underlying type is constrained, then the constraint will be on the formal parameter rather than the actual parameter. If we declare **ParameterLength** with

```
-- Available online as part of plength.sql
CREATE OR REPLACE PROCEDURE ParameterLength (
  p_Parameter1 IN OUT VARCHAR2,
  p_Parameter2 IN OUT students.current_credits%TYPE) AS
BEGIN
  p_Parameter2 := 12345;
END ParameterLength;
```

p_Parameter2 will be constrained with precision of 3, since that is the precision of the **current_credits** column. Even if we call **ParameterLength** with an actual parameter of enough precision, the formal precision is taken. The following example will generate the ORA-6502 error:

```
-- Available online as part of plength.sql
DECLARE
  v_Variable1 VARCHAR2(1);
  v_Variable2 NUMBER;  -- Declare v_Variable2 with no constraints
BEGIN
  -- Even though the actual parameter has room for 12345, the
  -- constraint on the formal parameter is taken and we get
  -- ORA-6502 on this procedure call.
  ParameterLength(v_Variable1, v_Variable2);
END;
```

Positional and Named Notation

In all of the examples shown so far in this chapter, the actual arguments are associated with the formal arguments by position. Given a procedure declaration such as

```
-- Available online as part of callme.sql
CREATE OR REPLACE PROCEDURE CallMe (
  p_ParameterA VARCHAR2,
  p_ParameterB NUMBER,
  p_ParameterC BOOLEAN,
  p_ParameterD DATE) AS
BEGIN
  NULL;
END CallMe;
```

and a calling block such as

```
-- Available online as part of callme.sql
DECLARE
  v_Variable1 VARCHAR2(10);
  v_Variable2 NUMBER(7,6);
  v_Variable3 BOOLEAN;
  v_Variable4 DATE;
BEGIN
  CallMe(v_Variable1, v_Variable2, v_Variable3, v_Variable4);
END;
```

the actual parameters are associated with the formal parameters by position: **v_Variable1** is associated with **p_ParameterA**, **v_Variable2** is associated with **p_ParameterB**, and so on. This is known as *positional notation*. Positional notation is more commonly used, and it is also the notation used in other third-generation languages such as C.

Alternatively, we can call the procedure using *named notation*:

```
Available online as part of callme.sql
DECLARE
  v_Variable1 VARCHAR2(10);
  v_Variable2 NUMBER(7,6);
  v_Variable3 BOOLEAN;
  v_Variable4 DATE;
BEGIN
  CallMe(p_ParameterA => v_Variable1,
         p_ParameterB => v_Variable2,
         p_ParameterC => v_Variable3,
         p_ParameterD => v_Variable4);
END;
```

In named notation, the formal parameter and the actual parameter are both included for each argument. This allows us to rearrange the order of the arguments, if desired. For example, the following block also calls **CallMe**, with the same arguments:

```
-- Available online as part of callme.sql
DECLARE
  v_Variable1 VARCHAR2(10);
```

```
    v_Variable2 NUMBER(7,6);
    v_Variable3 BOOLEAN;
    v_Variable4 DATE;
BEGIN
  CallMe(p_ParameterB => v_Variable2,
         p_ParameterC => v_Variable3,
         p_ParameterD => v_Variable4,
         p_ParameterA => v_Variable1);
END;
```

Positional and named notation can be mixed in the same call as well, if desired. The first arguments must be specified by position, and the remaining arguments can be specified by name. The following block illustrates this method:

```
-- Available online as part of callme.sql
DECLARE
  v_Variable1 VARCHAR2(10);
  v_Variable2 NUMBER(7,6);
  v_Variable3 BOOLEAN;
  v_Variable4 DATE;
BEGIN
  -- First 2 parameters passed by position, the second 2 are
  -- passed by name.
  CallMe(v_Variable1, v_Variable2,
         p_ParameterC => v_Variable3,
         p_ParameterD => v_Variable4);
END;
```

Named notation is another feature of PL/SQL that comes from Ada. When should you use positional notation, and when should you use named notation? Neither is more efficient than the other, so the only preference is one of style. Some of the style differences are illustrated in Table 7-2.

I generally use positional notation, as I prefer to write succinct code. It is important to use good names for the actual parameters, however. On the other hand, if the procedure takes a large number of arguments (more than ten is a good measure), then named notation is desirable, since it is easier to match the formal and actual parameters. Procedures with this many arguments are fairly rare, however.

Positional Notation	Named Notation
Relies more on good names for the actual parameters to illustrate what each is used for.	Clearly illustrates the association between the actual and formal parameters.
Names used for the formal and actual parameters are independent; one can be changed without modifying the other.	Can be more difficult to maintain because all calls to the procedure using named notation must be changed if the names of the formal parameters are changed.
Can be more difficult to maintain because all calls to the procedure using positional notation must be changed if the order of the formal parameters is changed.	The order used for the formal and actual parameters is independent; one can be changed without modifying the other.
More succinct than named notation.	Requires more coding, since both the formal and actual parameters are included in the procedure call.
Parameters with default values must be at the end of the argument list.	Allows default values[1] for formal parameters to be used, regardless of which parameter has the default.

TABLE 7-2.   *Positional vs. Named Notation*

[1]Default parameters are discussed in the next section.

TIP
The more parameters a procedure has, the more difficult it is to call and make sure that all of the required parameters are present. If you have a significant number of parameters that you would like to pass to or from a procedure, consider defining a record type with the parameters as fields within the record. Then you can use a single parameter of the record type. PL/SQL has no explicit limit on the number of parameters.

Parameter Default Values

Similar to variable declarations, the formal parameters to a procedure or function can have default values. If a parameter has a default value, it does not have to be passed from the calling environment. If it is passed, the value of the actual parameter will be used instead of the default. A default value for a parameter is included using the syntax

parameter_name [*mode*] *parameter_type* {:= | DEFAULT} *initial_value*

where *parameter_name* is the name of the formal parameter, *mode* is the parameter mode (IN, OUT, or IN OUT), *parameter_type* is the parameter type (either predefined or user-defined), and *initial_value* is the value to be assigned to the formal parameter by default. Either := or the DEFAULT keyword can be used. For example, we can rewrite the **AddNewStudent** procedure to assign the economics major by default to all new students, unless overridden by an explicit argument:

```
-- Available online as default.sql
CREATE OR REPLACE PROCEDURE AddNewStudent (
  p_FirstName   students.first_name%TYPE,
  p_LastName    students.last_name%TYPE,
  p_Major       students.major%TYPE DEFAULT 'Economics') AS
BEGIN
  -- Insert a new row in the students table. Use
  -- student_sequence to generate the new student ID, and
  -- 0 for current_credits.
  INSERT INTO students VALUES (student_sequence.nextval,
    p_FirstName, p_LastName, p_Major, 0);

  COMMIT;
END AddNewStudent;
```

The default value will be used if the **p_Major** formal parameter does not have an actual parameter associated with it in the procedure call. We can do this with positional notation,

```
BEGIN
  AddNewStudent('Barbara', 'Blues');
END;
```

or with named notation:

```
BEGIN
  AddNewStudent(p_FirstName => 'Barbara',
                p_LastName => 'Blues');
END;
```

If positional notation is used, all parameters with default values that don't have an associated actual parameter must be at the end of the parameter list. Consider the following example:

```
CREATE OR REPLACE PROCEDURE DefaultTest (
  p_ParameterA NUMBER DEFAULT 10,
  p_ParameterB VARCHAR2 DEFAULT 'abcdef',
  p_ParameterC DATE DEFAULT sysdate) AS
BEGIN
  ...
END DefaultTest;
```

All three parameters to **DefaultTest** take default arguments. If we wanted to take the default value for **p_ParameterB** only, but specify values for **p_ParameterA** and **p_ParameterC**, we would have to use named notation, as follows:

```
BEGIN
  DefaultTest(p_ParameterA => 7, p_ParameterC => '30-DEC-95');
END;
```

If we wanted to use the default value for **p_ParameterB**, we would also have to use the default value for **p_ParameterC** when using positional notation. When using positional notation, all default parameters for which there are no associated actual parameters must be at the end of the parameter list, as in the following example:

```
BEGIN
  /* Uses the default value for both p_ParameterB and
     p_ParameterC. */
  DefaultTest(7);
END;
```

TIP
When using default values, make them the last parameters in the argument list if possible. This way, either positional or named notation can be used.

Creating a Function

A function is very similar to a procedure. Both take arguments, which can be of any mode. Both are different forms of PL/SQL blocks, with a declarative, executable, and exception section. Both can be stored in the database or declared within a block. (Procedures and functions not stored in the database are discussed later in this chapter, in the section "Subprogram Locations".) However, a procedure call is a PL/SQL statement by itself, while a function call is called as part of an expression.

A function call is an rvalue. For example, the following function returns TRUE if the specified class is more than 90 percent full and FALSE otherwise:

```sql
-- Available online as almostfl.sql
CREATE OR REPLACE FUNCTION AlmostFull (
  p_Department classes.department%TYPE,
  p_Course     classes.course%TYPE)
  RETURN BOOLEAN IS

  v_CurrentStudents NUMBER;
  v_MaxStudents     NUMBER;
  v_ReturnValue     BOOLEAN;
  v_FullPercent     CONSTANT NUMBER := 90;
BEGIN
  -- Get the current and maximum students for the requested
  -- course.
  SELECT current_students, max_students
    INTO v_CurrentStudents, v_MaxStudents
    FROM classes
    WHERE department = p_Department
    AND course = p_Course;

  -- If the class is more full than the percentage given by
  -- v_FullPercent, return TRUE. Otherwise, return FALSE.
  IF (v_CurrentStudents / v_MaxStudents * 100) > v_FullPercent
  THEN
    v_ReturnValue := TRUE;
  ELSE
    v_ReturnValue := FALSE;
  END IF;

  RETURN v_ReturnValue;
END AlmostFull;
```

The **AlmostFull** function returns a boolean value. It can be called from the following PL/SQL block. Note that the function call is not a statement by itself—it is used as part of the IF statement inside the loop.

```
-- Available online as callfunc.sql
DECLARE
  CURSOR c_Classes IS
    SELECT department, course
      FROM classes;
BEGIN
  FOR v_ClassRecord IN c_Classes LOOP
    -- Record all classes which don't have very much room left
    -- in temp_table.
    IF AlmostFull(v_ClassRecord.department, v_ClassRecord.course)
    THEN
       INSERT INTO temp_table (char_col) VALUES
         (v_ClassRecord.department || ' ' || v_ClassRecord.course
         || ' is almost full!');
    END IF;
  END LOOP;
END;
```

Function Syntax

The syntax for creating a stored function is very similar to the syntax for a procedure. It is

```
CREATE [OR REPLACE] FUNCTION function_name
  [(argument [{IN | OUT | IN OUT}] type,
   ...
   argument [{IN | OUT | IN OUT}] type)]
  RETURN return_type {IS | AS}
  function_body
```

where *function_name* is the name of the function, *argument* and *type* are the same as for procedures, *return_type* is the type of the value that the function returns, and *function_body* is a PL/SQL block containing the code for the function.

Similar to procedures, the argument list is optional. In this case, there are no parentheses either in the function declaration or in the function call. However, the function return type is required, since the function call is part of an expression. The type of the function is used to determine the type of the expression containing the function call.

The RETURN Statement

Inside the body of the function, the RETURN statement is used to return control to the calling environment with a value. The general syntax of the RETURN statement is

RETURN *expression*;

where *expression* is the value to be returned. The value *expression* will be converted to the type specified in the RETURN clause of the function definition, if it is not already of that type. When the RETURN statement is executed, control immediately returns to the calling environment.

There can be more than one RETURN statement in a function, although only one of them will be executed. It is an error for a function to end without executing a RETURN. The following example illustrates multiple RETURN statements in one function. Even though there are five different RETURN statements in the function, only one of them is executed. Which one is executed depends on how full the class specified by **p_Department** and **p_Course** is.

```
-- Available online as clasinfo.sql
CREATE OR REPLACE FUNCTION ClassInfo (
  /* Returns 'Full' if the class is completely full,
     'Some Room' if the class is over 80% full,
     'More Room' if the class is over 60% full,
     'Lots of Room' if the class is less than 60% full, and
     'Empty' if there are no students registered. */
  p_Department classes.department%TYPE,
  p_Course     classes.course%TYPE)
  RETURN VARCHAR2 IS

  v_CurrentStudents NUMBER;
  v_MaxStudents     NUMBER;
  v_PercentFull     NUMBER;
BEGIN
  -- Get the current and maximum students for the requested
  -- course.
  SELECT current_students, max_students
    INTO v_CurrentStudents, v_MaxStudents
```

```
   FROM classes
   WHERE department = p_Department
   AND course = p_Course;

-- Calculate the current percentage.
v_PercentFull := v_CurrentStudents / v_MaxStudents * 100;

IF v_PercentFull = 100 THEN
   RETURN 'Full';
ELSIF v_PercentFull > 80 THEN
   RETURN 'Some Room';
ELSIF v_PercentFull > 60 THEN
   RETURN 'More Room';
ELSIF v_PercentFull > 0 THEN
   RETURN 'Lots of Room';
ELSE
   RETURN 'Empty';
END IF;
END ClassInfo;
```

When used in a function, the RETURN statement must have an expression associated with it. RETURN can also be used in a procedure, however. In this case, it has no arguments, which causes control to pass back to the calling environment immediately. The current values of the formal parameters declared as OUT or IN OUT are passed back to the actual parameters, and execution continues from the statement following the procedure call.

Function Style

Functions share many of the same features as procedures:

- Functions can return more than one value via OUT parameters.

- Function code has declarative, executable, and exception handling sections.

- Functions can accept default values.

- Functions can be called using positional or named notation.

So when is a function appropriate, and when is a procedure appropriate? It generally depends on how many values the subprogram is expected to return and how those values will be used. The rule of thumb is that if there is more than one return value, use a procedure. If there is only one return value, a function can be used. Although it is legal for a function to have OUT parameters (and thus return more than one value), it is poor style, and I don't recommend it.

Exceptions Raised Inside Subprograms

If an error occurs inside a subprogram, an exception is raised. This exception may be user-defined or predefined. If the procedure has no exception handler for this error, control immediately passes out of the procedure to the calling environment, in accordance with the exception propagation rules. (Exceptions and propagation rules are discussed in detail in Chapter 10.) However, in this case, the values of OUT and IN OUT formal parameters are *not* returned to the actual parameters. The actual parameters will have the same values as they would had the procedure not been called. For example, suppose we create the following procedure:

```
-- Available online as part of error.sql
CREATE OR REPLACE PROCEDURE RaiseError (
  /* Illustrates the behavior of unhandled exceptions and
     OUT variables. If p_Raise is TRUE, then an unhandled
     error is raised. If p_Raise is FALSE, the procedure
     completes successfully. */
  p_Raise IN BOOLEAN := TRUE,
  p_ParameterA OUT NUMBER) AS
BEGIN
  p_ParameterA := 7;

  IF p_Raise THEN
    /* Even though we have assigned 7 to p_ParameterA, this
       unhandled exception causes control to return immediately
       without returning 7 to the actual parameter associated
       with p_ParameterA. */
    RAISE DUP_VAL_ON_INDEX;
  ELSE
    /* Simply return with no error. This will return 7 to the
       actual parameter. */
    RETURN;
  END IF;
END RaiseError;
```

If we call **RaiseError** with the following block,

```
-- Available online as part of error.sql
DECLARE
  v_TempVar NUMBER := 1;
BEGIN
  INSERT INTO temp_table (num_col, char_col)
    VALUES (v_TempVar, 'Initial value');
  RaiseError(FALSE, v_TempVar);

  INSERT INTO temp_table (num_col, char_col)
    VALUES (v_TempVar, 'Value after successful call');

  v_TempVar := 2;
  INSERT INTO temp_table (num_col, char_col)
    VALUES (v_TempVar, 'Value before 2nd call');
  RaiseError(TRUE, v_TempVar);
EXCEPTION
  WHEN OTHERS THEN
    INSERT INTO temp_table (num_col, char_col)
      VALUES (v_TempVar, 'Value after unsuccessful call');
END;
```

and select from **temp_table**, we get the following results:

```
SQL> SELECT * FROM temp_table;

  NUM_COL CHAR_COL
--------- -------------------------------
        1 Initial value
        7 Value after successful call
        2 Value before 2nd call
        2 Value after unsuccessful call
```

Before the first call to **RaiseError**, **v_TempVar** contained 1. The first call was successful, and **v_TempVar** was assigned the value 7. The block then changed **v_TempVar** to 2 before the second call to **RaiseError**. This second call did not complete successfully, and **v_TempVar** was unchanged at 2 (rather than being changed to 7 again).

Dropping Procedures and Functions

Similar to dropping a table, procedures and functions can also be dropped. This removes the procedure or function from the data dictionary. The syntax for dropping a procedure is

DROP PROCEDURE *procedure_name*;

and the syntax for dropping a function is

DROP FUNCTION *function_name*;

where *procedure_name* is the name of an existing procedure, and *function_name* is the name of an existing function. For example, the following statement drops the **AddNewStudent** procedure:

```
DROP TABLE AddNewStudent;
```

If the object to be dropped is a function, you must use DROP FUNCTION, and if the object is a procedure, you must use DROP PROCEDURE. DROP is a DDL command, so an implicit COMMIT is done both before and after the statement.

Subprogram Locations

Subprograms can be stored in the data dictionary, as all of the examples in this chapter have shown. The subprogram is created first via the CREATE OR REPLACE command, and then it is called from another PL/SQL block. A subprogram can also be defined within the declarative section of a block, in which case, it is known as a *local subprogram*.

Stored Subprograms and the Data Dictionary

When a subprogram is created via the CREATE OR REPLACE command, it is stored in the database. The subprogram is stored in compiled form, which is known as *p-code*. The p-code has all of the references in the subprogram evaluated, and the source code is translated into a form that is easily readable by the PL/SQL engine. When the subprogram is called, the p-code is read from disk, if necessary, and executed. P-code is analogous to the object code generated by other 3GL compilers. Since the p-code has the object references in the subprogram evaluated (this is a property of early binding, as defined in Chapter 4), executing the p-code is a comparatively inexpensive operation.

Information about the subprogram is accessible through various data dictionary views. The **user_objects** view contains information about all objects, including stored subprograms. This information includes when the object was created and last modified, the type of the object (table, sequence, function, and so on), and the validity of the object. The **user_source** view contains the original source code for the object. The **user_errors** view contains information about compile errors.

Consider the following simple procedure:

```
CREATE OR REPLACE PROCEDURE Simple AS
   v_Counter NUMBER;
BEGIN
   v_Counter := 7;
END Simple;
```

After this procedure is created, **user_objects** shows it as valid, and **user_source** contains the source code for it. **User_errors** has no rows, since the procedure was compiled successfully. This is illustrated in Figure 7-1.

If, however, we change the code of **Simple** so that it has a compile error (note the missing semicolon), such as

```
CREATE OR REPLACE PROCEDURE Simple AS
   v_Counter NUMBER;
BEGIN
   v_Counter := 7
END Simple;
```

and examine the same three data dictionary views (as shown in Figure 7-2), we see several differences. **User_source** still shows the source code for the procedure. However, in **user_objects** the status is listed as 'INVALID' rather than 'VALID'. And **user_errors** contains the compilation error PLS-103.

TIP

*In SQL*Plus, the SHOW ERRORS command will query **user_errors** for you and format the output for readability. You can use SHOW ERRORS after receiving the message "Warning: Procedure created with compilation errors." For more information, see Chapter 13.*

```
± Oracle SQL*Plus                                            _ □ X
File  Edit  Search  Options  Help
SQL> SELECT object_name, object_type, status
  2    FROM user_objects WHERE object_name = 'SIMPLE';

OBJECT_NAME          OBJECT_TYPE    STATUS
-------------------- -------------- -------
SIMPLE               PROCEDURE      VALID

SQL> SELECT text FROM user_source
  2    WHERE name = 'SIMPLE' ORDER BY line;

TEXT
--------------------------------------------
PROCEDURE Simple AS
  v_Counter NUMBER;
BEGIN
  v_Counter := 7;
END Simple;

SQL> SELECT line, position, text
  2    FROM user_errors
  3    WHERE name = 'SIMPLE'
  4    ORDER BY sequence;

no rows selected

SQL>
```

FIGURE 7-1.   *Data dictionary views after successful compilation*

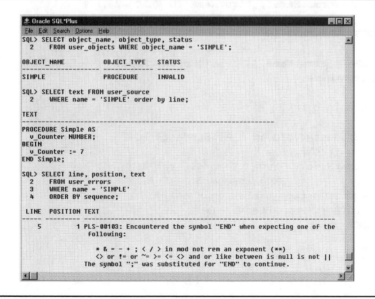

FIGURE 7-2.   *Data dictionary views after unseccessful compilation*

A stored subprogram that is invalid is still stored in the database. However, it cannot be called successfully until the error is fixed. If an invalid procedure is called, the following error is returned:

```
PLS-905: object is invalid
```

The data dictionary is discussed in more detail in Appendix D.

Local Subprograms

A local subprogram, declared in the declarative section of a PL/SQL block, is illustrated in the following example:

```
-- Available online as local.sql
DECLARE
  CURSOR c_AllStudents IS
    SELECT first_name, last_name
      FROM students;

  v_FormattedName VARCHAR2(50);

  /* Function which will return the first and last name
     concatenated together, separated by a space. */
  FUNCTION FormatName(p_FirstName IN VARCHAR2,
                      p_LastName IN VARCHAR2)
    RETURN VARCHAR2 IS
  BEGIN
    RETURN p_FirstName || ' ' || p_LastName;
  END FormatName;

-- Begin main block.
BEGIN
  FOR v_StudentRecord IN c_AllStudents LOOP
    v_FormattedName :=
      FormatName(v_StudentRecord.first_name,
                 v_StudentRecord.last_name);
    INSERT INTO temp_table (char_col)
      VALUES (v_FormattedName);
  END LOOP;

  COMMIT;
END;
```

The **FormatName** function is declared in the declarative section of the anonymous block. The function name is a PL/SQL identifier and thus follows the same scope and visibility rules as any other PL/SQL identifier. Specifically, it is only visible in the block in which it is declared. Its scope extends from the point of declaration until the end of the block. No other block can call **FormatName**, since it would not be visible from another block. Scope and visibility rules are discussed in more detail in Chapter 2.

Any local subprogram must be declared at the end of the declarative section. If we were to move **FormatName** above the declaration for **c_AllStudents**, as the following illegal example illustrates, we would get a compile error.

```
-- Available online as local2.sql
DECLARE
  /* Declare FormatName first. This will generate a compile
     error, since all other declarations have to be before
     any local subprograms. */
  FUNCTION FormatName(p_FirstName IN VARCHAR2,
                      p_LastName IN VARCHAR2)
    RETURN VARCHAR2 IS
  BEGIN
    RETURN p_FirstName || ' ' || p_LastName;
  END FormatName;

  CURSOR c_AllStudents IS
    SELECT first_name, last_name
      FROM students;

  v_FormattedName VARCHAR2(50);
-- Begin main block
BEGIN
  NULL;
END;
```

Forward Declarations

Since the names of local PL/SQL subprograms are identifiers, they must be declared before they are referenced. This is normally not a problem. However, in the case of mutually referential subprograms, this does present a difficulty. Consider the following example:

```
-- Available online as mutual.sql
DECLARE
  v_TempVal BINARY_INTEGER := 5;

  -- Local procedure A. Note that the code of A calls procedure B.
  PROCEDURE A(p_Counter IN OUT BINARY_INTEGER) IS
  BEGIN
    IF p_Counter > 0 THEN
      B(p_Counter);
      p_Counter := p_Counter - 1;
    END IF;
  END A;

  -- Local procedure B. Note that the code of B calls procedure A.
  PROCEDURE B(p_Counter IN OUT BINARY_INTEGER) IS
  BEGIN
    p_Counter := p_Counter - 1;
    A(p_Counter);
  END B;
BEGIN
  B(v_TempVal);
END;
```

This example is impossible to compile. Since procedure **A** calls procedure **B**, **B** must be declared prior to **A** so that the reference to **B** can be resolved. Since procedure **B** calls procedure **A**, **A** must be declared prior to **B** so that the reference to **A** can be resolved. Both of these can't be true at the same time. In order to rectify this, we can use a *forward declaration*. This is simply a procedure name and its formal parameters, which allows mutually referential procedures to exist. The following example illustrates this technique:

```
-- Available online as forward.sql
DECLARE
  v_TempVal BINARY_INTEGER := 5;

  -- Forward declaration of procedure B.
  PROCEDURE B(p_Counter IN OUT BINARY_INTEGER);

  PROCEDURE A(p_Counter IN OUT BINARY_INTEGER) IS
  BEGIN
    IF p_Counter > 0 THEN
      B(p_Counter);
      p_Counter := p_Counter - 1;
```

```
    END IF;
  END A;

  PROCEDURE B(p_Counter IN OUT BINARY_INTEGER) IS
  BEGIN
    p_Counter := p_Counter - 1;
    A(p_Counter);
  END B;
BEGIN
  B(v_TempVal);
END;
```

Stored vs. Local Subprograms

Stored subprograms and local subprograms behave differently, and they have different properties. When should they each be used? I generally prefer to use stored subprograms. If you develop a useful subprogram, chances are that you will want to call it from more than one block. In order to do this, the subprogram must be stored in the database. The size and complexity benefits are also usually a factor. The only procedures and functions that I would declare local to a block would tend to be short ones, which are only called from one specific section of the program (their containing block). Table 7-3 summarizes the differences between stored and local subprograms.

Subprogram Dependencies

When a procedure or function is compiled, all of the Oracle objects that it references are recorded in the data dictionary. The procedure is *dependent* on these objects. We have seen that a subprogram that has compile errors is marked as invalid in the data dictionary. A stored subprogram can also become invalid if a DDL operation is performed on one of its dependent objects. The best way to illustrate this is by example. The **AlmostFull** function (defined earlier in this chapter) queries the **classes** table. The dependencies of **AlmostFull** are illustrated in Figure 7-3. **AlmostFull** depends on only one object—**classes**. This is indicated by the arrow in the figure.

Stored Subprograms	**Local Subprograms**
Stored in compiled p-code in the database; when the procedure is called, it does not have to be compiled.	The local subprogram is compiled as part of its containing block. If the block is run multiple times, the subprogram has to be compiled each time.
Can be called from any block submitted by a user who has EXECUTE privileges on the subprogram.	Can be called only from the block containing the subprogram.
By keeping the subprogram code separate from the calling block, the calling block is shorter and easier to understand. The subprogram and calling block can also be maintained separately, if desired.	The subprogram and the calling block are one and the same, which can lead to confusion. If a change to the calling block is made, the subprogram has to be recompiled.
The compiled p-code can be pinned in the shared pool using the DBMS_SHARED_POOL.KEEP packaged procedure.[1] This can improve performance.	Local subprograms cannot be pinned in the shared pool by themselves.

TABLE 7-3.   *Stored vs. Local Subprograms*

[1] The shared pool and the DBMS_SHARED_POOL package are discussed in Chapter 22.

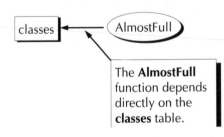

FIGURE 7-3.   *AlmostFull dependencies*

Now suppose we create a procedure that calls **AlmostFull** and inserts the results into **temp_table**. This procedure is **RecordFullClasses**:

```
-- Available online as rfclass.sql
CREATE OR REPLACE PROCEDURE RecordFullClasses AS
  CURSOR c_Classes IS
    SELECT department, course
      FROM classes;
BEGIN
  FOR v_ClassRecord IN c_Classes LOOP
    -- Record all classes which don't have very much room left
    -- in temp_table.
    IF AlmostFull(v_ClassRecord.department,
    THEN
v_ClassRecord.course)
      INSERT INTO temp_table (char_col) VALUES
        (v_ClassRecord.department || ' ' || v_ClassRecord.course
        || ' is almost full!');
    END IF;
  END LOOP;
END RecordFullClasses;
```

The dependency information is illustrated by the arrows in Figure 7-4. **RecordFullClasses** depends both on **AlmostFull** and on **temp_table**. These are *direct* dependencies, since **RecordFullClasses** refers directly to both **AlmostFull** and **temp_table**. **AlmostFull** depends on **classes**, so **RecordFullClasses** has an *indirect* dependency on **classes**.

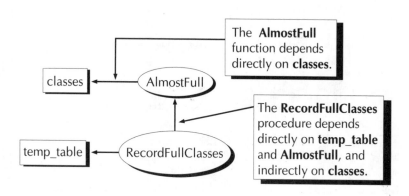

FIGURE 7-4. *RecordFullClasses dependencies*

If a DDL operation is performed on **classes**, all objects that depend on **classes** (directly or indirectly) are invalidated. Suppose we alter the **classes** table in our example by adding an extra column:

```
ALTER TABLE classes ADD (
  student_rating  NUMBER(2));  -- Difficulty rating from 1 to 10
```

This will cause both **AlmostFull** and **RecordFullClasses** to become invalid, since they depend on **classes**. This is illustrated by the SQL*Plus session in Figure 7-5.

How Dependencies Are Determined

To determine when objects should be evaluated, the timestamps of their last modification are compared. The LAST_DDL_TIME field of **user_objects** contains this timestamp. This method works fine when comparing two objects on the same database, but it raises some issues when the objects are contained within different PL/SQL engines.

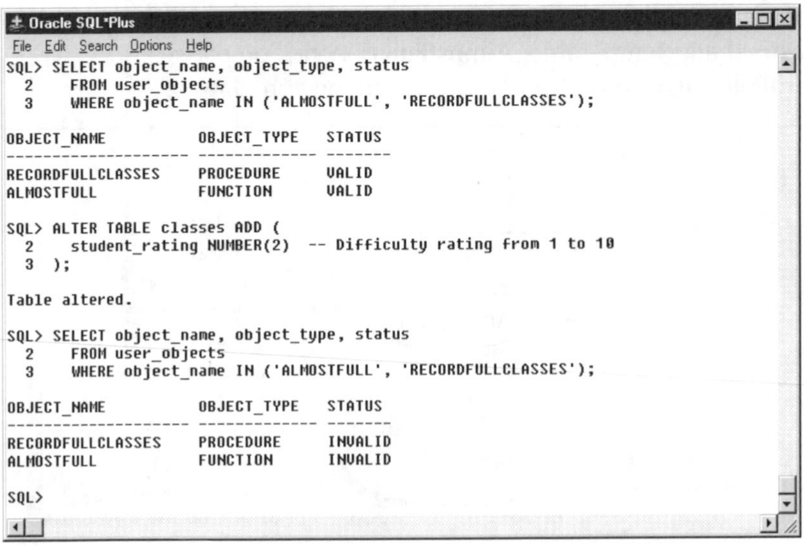

FIGURE 7-5. *Invalidation as a result of a DDL operation*

Suppose we have two procedures, **P1** and **P2**. **P1** calls **P2** over a database link, as shown in Figure 7-6. These two procedures are located in two different PL/SQL engines, in different databases. **P1** could also be located in a client-side PL/SQL engine, while **P2** is on the server. (For more information on client-side versus server-side PL/SQL, see Chapter 13.) If a DDL operation is then performed on **P2**, when should **P1** get invalidated? There are two methods for determining this—the timestamp and signature methods.

Timestamp Model

The timestamp model works the same way as it would if **P1** and **P2** were in the same PL/SQL engine. When **P2** is altered, **P1** is invalidated the next time it is called. This can cause unnecessary compilations, however. If only the body of **P2** is altered, and not its specification, then **P1** doesn't really have to be recompiled, since the call

```
P2(...)@DBLINK
```

in **P1** wouldn't have to change. However, with the timestamp model, **P1** would be recompiled.

Slightly more serious is when **P1** is contained in a client-side PL/SQL engine, such as Oracle Forms. In this case, it may not be possible to

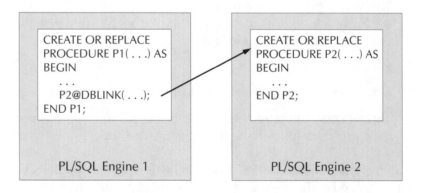

```
CREATE OR REPLACE
PROCEDURE P1(...) AS
BEGIN
   ...
   P2@DBLINK(...);
END P1;
```

```
CREATE OR REPLACE
PROCEDURE P2(...) AS
BEGIN
   ...
END P2;
```

PL/SQL Engine 1   PL/SQL Engine 2

FIGURE 7-6. *A remote procedure call*

recompile **P1**, since the source for it may not be included with the run-time version of Forms.

Signature Model

PL/SQL **2.3** PL/SQL 2.3 provides a different method for determining when
...and HIGHER remote dependent objects need to be recompiled, called the
signature model. When a procedure is created, a *signature* is stored as well.
The signature encodes the procedure specification, including the types and
order of the parameters. With this model, the signature of **P2** will change
only when the specification changes. When **P1** is compiled, the signature
of **P2** is included (rather than the timestamp). Thus **P1** only needs to be
recompiled when the signature of **P2** changes.

In order to use the signature model, the parameter
REMOTE_DEPENDENCIES_MODE must be set to SIGNATURE. This is a
parameter in the database initialization file, which is by default called
INIT.ORA. It can also be set interactively. There are three ways of setting
this mode:

1. Add the line REMOTE_DEPENDENCIES_MODE=SIGNATURE to
   the INIT.ORA file. The next time the database is started, the mode
   will be set to SIGNATURE for all sessions.

2. Issue the command

   ```
   ALTER SYSTEM SET REMOTE_DEPENDENCIES_MODE = SIGNATURE;
   ```

   This will affect the entire database (all sessions) from the time the
   statement is issued. You must have the ALTER SYSTEM system
   privilege to issue this command.

3. Issue the command

   ```
   ALTER SESSION SET REMOTE_DEPENDENCIES_MODE = SIGNATURE;
   ```

   This will only affect your session. Objects created after this point in
   the current session will use the signature method.

In all of these options, TIMESTAMP can be used instead of SIGNATURE
to get the 2.2 and earlier behavior. TIMESTAMP is the default, so if you
don't change REMOTE_DEPENDENCIES_MODE, the system will behave
the old way.

There are several things to be aware of when using the signature method:

- Signatures don't get modified if the default values of formal parameters are changed. Suppose **P2** has a default value for one of its parameters, and **P1** is using this default value. If the default value in the specification for **P2** is changed, **P1** will not be recompiled by default. The old value for the default parameter will still be used until **P1** is manually recompiled. This applies for IN parameters only.

- If **P1** is calling a packaged procedure **P2**, and a new overloaded version of **P2** is added to the remote package, the signature is not changed. **P1** will still use the old version (not the new overloaded one) until **P1** is recompiled manually. (Packages and overloading are discussed in the next chapter.)

- To manually recompile a procedure, use the command

    ALTER PROCEDURE *procedure_name* COMPILE;

where *procedure_name* is the name of the procedure to be compiled. For functions, use

    ALTER FUNCTION *function_name* COMPILE;

For more information on the signature model, see the *Oracle Server Application Developer's Guide*, release 7.3 or later.

Privileges and Stored Subprograms

Stored subprograms and packages are objects in the data dictionary, and as such, they are owned by a particular database user, or schema. Other users can access these objects if they are granted the correct privileges on them. Privileges and roles also come into play when creating a stored object, with regard to the access available inside the subprogram.

EXECUTE Privilege

In order to allow access to a table, the SELECT, INSERT, UPDATE, and
DELETE object privileges are used. The GRANT statement gives these
privileges to a database user or a role (see Chapter 4 for more information
on GRANT). For stored subprograms and packages, the relevant privilege is
EXECUTE. Consider the **RecordFullClasses** procedure, which we examined
earlier in this chapter:

```
-- Available online as rfclass.sql
CREATE OR REPLACE PROCEDURE RecordFullClasses AS
  CURSOR c_Classes IS
    SELECT department, course
      FROM classes;
BEGIN
  FOR v_ClassRecord IN c_Classes LOOP
    -- Record all classes which don't have very much room left
    -- in temp_table.
    IF AlmostFull(v_ClassRecord.department, v_ClassRecord.course) THEN
      INSERT INTO temp_table (char_col) VALUES
        (v_ClassRecord.department || ' ' || v_ClassRecord.course
         || ' is almost full!');
    END IF;
  END LOOP;
END RecordFullClasses;
```

Suppose that the objects on which **RecordFullClasses** depends (the
function **AlmostFull** and tables **classes** and **temp_table**) are all owned by
the database user **UserA**. **RecordFullClasses** is owned by **UserA** as well. If
we grant the EXECUTE privilege on **RecordFullClasses** to another database
user, say **UserB**, with

```
GRANT EXECUTE ON RecordFullClasses TO UserB;
```

then **UserB** can execute **RecordFullClasses** with the following block:

```
BEGIN
  UserA.RecordFullClasses;
END;
```

In this scenario, all of the database objects are owned by **UserA**. This
situation is illustrated in Figure 7-7. The dotted line signifies the GRANT

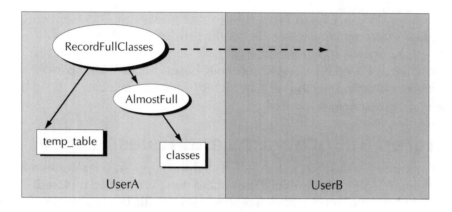

FIGURE 7-7.   *Database objects owned by UserA*

statement from **UserA** to **UserB**, while the solid lines signify object dependencies.

Now suppose that **UserB** has another table, also called **temp_table**, as illustrated in Figure 7-8. If **UserB** calls **UserA.RecordFullClasses**, which

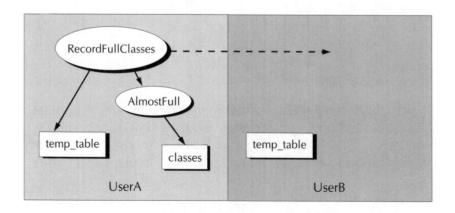

FIGURE 7-8.   *Temp_table owned by UserB and UserA*

table gets modified? The table in **UserA** does. This concept can be expressed as follows:

■ A subprogram executes under the privilege set of its owner.

Even though **UserB** is calling **RecordFullClasses**, **RecordFullClasses** is owned by **UserA**. Thus the identifier **temp_table** will evaluate to the table belonging to **UserA**, *not* **UserB**.

Stored Subprograms and Roles

Let's modify the situation in Figure 7-8 slightly. Suppose **UserA** does not own **temp_table** or **RecordFullClasses**, and these are owned by **UserB**. Furthermore, suppose we have modified **RecordFullClasses** to explicitly refer to the objects in **UserA**. This is illustrated by the following listing and Figure 7-9.

```
CREATE OR REPLACE PROCEDURE RecordFullClasses AS
  CURSOR c_Classes IS
    SELECT department, course
      FROM UserA.classes;
BEGIN
  FOR v_ClassRecord IN c_Classes LOOP
    -- Record all classes which don't have very much room left
    -- in temp_table.
    IF UserA.AlmostFull(v_ClassRecord.department,
                        v_ClassRecord.course) THEN
      INSERT INTO temp_table (char_col) VALUES
        (v_ClassRecord.department || ' ' || v_ClassRecord.course
         || ' is almost full!');
    END IF;
  END LOOP;
END RecordFullClasses;
```

In order for **RecordFullClasses** to compile correctly, **UserA** must have granted the SELECT privilege on **classes** and the EXECUTE privilege on **AlmostFull** to **UserB**. The dotted lines in Figure 7-9 show this. Furthermore, this grant must be done explicitly and *not* through a role. The following

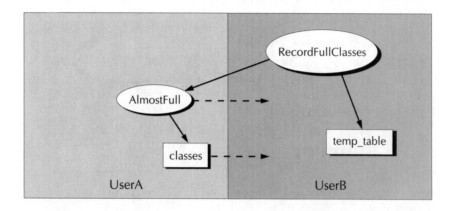

FIGURE 7-9. *RecordFullSlasses owned by UserB*

grants, executed by **UserA**, would allow a successful compilation of
UserB.RecordFullClasses:

```
GRANT SELECT ON classes TO UserB;
GRANT EXECUTE ON AlmostFull TO UserB;
```

A grant done through an intermediate role, as in

```
CREATE ROLE UserA_Role;
GRANT SELECT ON classes TO UserA_Role;
GRANT EXECUTE ON AlmostFull TO UserA_Role;
GRANT UserA_Role to UserB;
```

will not work. The role is illustrated in Figure 7-10.
So we can clarify the rule in the previous section with:

■ A subprogram executes under the privileges that have been granted
explicitly to its owner, not via a role.

If the grants had been done via a role, we would have received PLS-201
errors when we tried to compile **RecordFullClasses**:

```
PLS-201: identifier 'CLASSES' must be declared
PLS-201: identifier 'ALMOSTFULL' must be declared
```

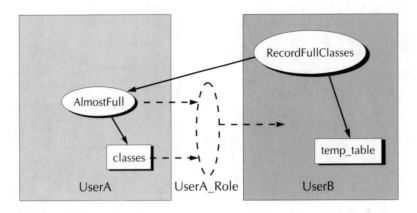

FIGURE 7-10. *Grants done via a role*

This rule also applies for triggers and packages, which are stored in the database as well. Essentially, *the only objects available inside a stored procedure, function, package, or trigger are the ones owned by the owner of the subprogram, or explicitly granted to the owner.*

Why is this? To explain this restriction, we need to examine binding again. Remember that PL/SQL uses early binding—references are evaluated when a subprogram is compiled, not when it is run. GRANT and REVOKE are both DDL statements. They take effect immediately, and the new privileges are recorded in the data dictionary. All database sessions will see the new privilege set. However, this is not necessarily true for roles. A role can be granted to a user, and that user can then choose to disable the role with the SET ROLE command. The distinction is that SET ROLE applies to one database session only, while GRANT and REVOKE apply to all sessions. A role can be disabled in one session but enabled in other sessions.

In order to allow privileges granted via a role to be used inside stored subprograms and triggers, the privileges would have to be checked every time the procedure is run. The privileges are checked as part of the binding process. But early binding means that the privileges are checked at compile time, not run time. In order to maintain early binding, *all roles are disabled inside stored procedures and triggers.*

Summary

Subprograms are essential to PL/SQL development. In this chapter, we have discussed the differences between procedures and functions, including how each is created, and how they are called. We also discussed how dependencies between PL/SQL objects are maintained and their effects on subprogram development. We concluded with a discussion of roles and procedures. In Chapter 8, we will see how PL/SQL procedures and functions, along with other objects such as variables, types, and cursors, can be grouped together into packages.

CHAPTER
8

Packages

ackages are the third type of named PL/SQL blocks, after procedures and functions. They are a very useful feature for PL/SQL, and they provide a mechanism for extending the language. In this chapter, we will first examine the syntax of package creation, and then discuss some of the advantages of using packages.

Packages

Another Ada feature incorporated in the design of PL/SQL is the *package*. A package is a PL/SQL construct that allows related objects to be stored together. A package has two separate parts—the specification and the body. Each of them is stored separately in the data dictionary. Unlike procedures and functions, which can be contained locally in a block or stored in the database, a package can only be stored; it cannot be local. Besides allowing related objects to be grouped together, packages are useful because they are less restrictive with respect to dependencies.. They also have a number of performance advantages, which are discussed in Chapter 22.

   A package is essentially a named declarative section. Anything that can go in the declarative part of a block can go in a package. This includes procedures, functions, cursors, types, and variables. One advantage of putting these objects into a package is the ability to reference them from other PL/SQL blocks, so packages also provide global variables for PL/SQL.

Package Specification

The *package specification* (also known as the *package header*) contains information about the contents of the package. However, it does not contain the code for any procedures. Consider the following example:

```
-- Available online as part of clpack.sql
CREATE OR REPLACE PACKAGE ClassPackage AS
   -- Add a new student into the specified class.
   PROCEDURE AddStudent(p_StudentID  IN students.id%TYPE,
                        p_Department IN classes.department%TYPE,
                        p_Course     IN classes.course%TYPE);

   -- Removes the specified student from the specified class.
   PROCEDURE RemoveStudent(p_StudentID  IN students.id%TYPE,
```

```
                       p_Department IN classes.department%TYPE,
                       p_Course     IN classes.course%TYPE);

  -- Exception raised by RemoveStudent.
  e_StudentNotRegistered EXCEPTION;

  -- Table type used to hold student info.
  TYPE t_StudentIDTable IS TABLE OF students.id%TYPE
    INDEX BY BINARY_INTEGER;

  -- Returns a PL/SQL table containing the students currently
  -- in the specified class.
  PROCEDURE ClassList(p_Department  IN  classes.department%TYPE,
                      p_Course      IN  classes.course%TYPE,
                      p_IDs         OUT t_StudentIDTable,
                      p_NumStudents IN OUT BINARY_INTEGER);
END ClassPackage;
```

ClassPackage contains three procedures, a type, and an exception. (Exceptions are used for PL/SQL error handling and are discussed in more detail in Chapter 10.) The general syntax for creating a package header is

```
CREATE [OR REPLACE] PACKAGE package_name {IS | AS}
  procedure_specification |
  function_specification |
  variable_declaration |
  type_definition |
  exception_declaration |
  cursor_declaration
END [package_name];
```

where *package_name* is the name of the package. The *elements* within the package (procedure and function specifications, variables, and so on) are the same as they would be in the declarative section of an anonymous block. The same syntax rules apply for a package header as for a declarative section, except for procedure and function declarations. These rules are as follows:

■ Package elements can appear in any order. However, as in a declarative section, an object must be declared before it is referenced. If a cursor contains a variable as part of the WHERE clause, for example, the variable must be declared before the cursor declaration.

■ All types of elements do not have to be present. A package can contain only procedure and function specifications, for example, without declaring any exceptions or types.

■ Any declarations for procedures and functions must be forward declarations. This is different from the declarative section of a block, where both forward declarations and the actual code for procedures or functions may be found. The code which implements the package's procedures and functions is found in the package body.

Package Body

The *package body* is a separate data dictionary object from the package header. It cannot be successfully compiled unless the package header has already been successfully compiled. The body contains the code for the forward subprogram declarations in the package header. The following example shows the package body for **ClassPackage**:

```
-- Available online as part of clpack.sql
CREATE OR REPLACE PACKAGE BODY ClassPackage AS
  -- Add a new student for the specified class.
  PROCEDURE AddStudent(p_StudentID  IN students.id%TYPE,
                       p_Department IN classes.department%TYPE,
                       p_Course     IN classes.course%TYPE) IS

  BEGIN
    INSERT INTO registered_students (student_id, department, course)
      VALUES (p_StudentID, p_Department, p_Course);
    COMMIT;
  END AddStudent;



  -- Removes the specified student from the specified class.
  PROCEDURE RemoveStudent(p_StudentID  IN students.id%TYPE,
                          p_Department IN classes.department%TYPE,
                          p_Course     IN classes.course%TYPE) IS
  BEGIN
    DELETE FROM registered_students
      WHERE student_id = p_StudentID
      AND department = p_Department
      AND course = p_Course;
```

```
  -- Check to see if the DELETE operation was successful. If
  -- it didn't match any rows, raise an error.
  IF SQL%NOTFOUND THEN
    RAISE e_StudentNotRegistered;
  END IF;

  COMMIT;
END RemoveStudent;


-- Returns a PL/SQL table containing the students currently
-- in the specified class.
PROCEDURE ClassList(p_Department  IN  classes.department%TYPE,
                    p_Course      IN  classes.course%TYPE,
                    p_IDs         OUT t_StudentIDTable,
                    p_NumStudents IN OUT BINARY_INTEGER) IS

  v_StudentID  registered_students.student_id%TYPE;

  -- Local cursor to fetch the registered students.
  CURSOR c_RegisteredStudents IS
    SELECT student_id
      FROM registered_students
      WHERE department = p_Department
      AND course = p_Course;
BEGIN
  /* p_NumStudents will be the table index. It will start at
     0, and be incremented each time through the fetch loop.
     At the end of the loop, it will have the number of rows
     fetched, and therefore the number of rows returned in
     p_IDs. */
  p_NumStudents := 0;

  OPEN c_RegisteredStudents;
  LOOP
    FETCH c_RegisteredStudents INTO v_StudentID;
    EXIT WHEN c_RegisteredStudents%NOTFOUND;

    p_NumStudents := p_NumStudents + 1;
    p_IDs(p_NumStudents) := v_StudentID;
  END LOOP;
  END ClassList;
END ClassPackage;
```

The package body contains the code for the forward declarations in the package header. Objects in the header that are not forward declarations (such as the **e_StudentNotRegistered** exception) can be referenced in the package body without being redeclared.

The package body is optional. If the package header does not contain any procedures or functions (only variable declarations, cursors, types, and so on), then the body does not have to be present. This technique is valuable for declaring global variables, since all objects in a package are visible outside the package. (Scope and visibility of packaged elements are discussed in the next section.)

Any forward declaration in the package header must be fleshed out in the package body. The specification for the procedure or function must be the same in both. This includes the name of the subprogram, the names of its parameters, and the mode of the parameters. For example, the following package header does not match the package body, since the body uses a different parameter list for **FunctionA**.

```
CREATE OR REPLACE PACKAGE PackageA AS
    FUNCTION FunctionA(p_Parameter1 IN NUMBER,
                       p_Parameter2 IN DATE)
      RETURN VARCHAR2;
END PackageA;

CREATE OR REPLACE PACKAGE BODY PackageA AS
    FUNCTION FunctionA(p_Parameter1 IN CHAR)
      RETURN VARCHAR2;
END PackageA;
```

If we try to create **PackageA** as above, we get the following errors:

```
PLS-00328: A subprogram body must be defined for the forward
declaration of FUNCTIONA.

PLS-00323: subprogram or cursor 'FUNCTIONA' is declared in a
package specification and must be defined in the package body.
```

Packages and Scope

Any object declared in a package header is in scope and is visible outside the package, by qualifying the object with the package name. For example, we can call **ClassPackage.RemoveStudent** from the following PL/SQL block:

```
BEGIN
    ClassPackage.RemoveStudent(10006, 'HIS', 101);
END;
```

The procedure call is the same as it would be for a stand-alone procedure. The only difference is that it is prefixed by the package name. Packaged procedures can have default parameters, and they can be called using either positional or named notation, just like stand-alone stored procedures.

This also applies to user-defined types defined in the package. In order to call **ClassList**, for example, we need to declare a variable of **ClassPackage.t_StudentIDTable**:

```
-- Available online as cllist.sql
DECLARE
    v_HistoryStudents ClassPackage.t_StudentIDTable;
    v_NumStudents     BINARY_INTEGER := 20;
BEGIN
    -- Fill the PL/SQL table with the first 20 History 101
    -- students.
    ClassPackage.ClassList('HIS', 101, v_HistoryStudents,
                            v_NumStudents);

    -- Insert these students into temp_table.
    FOR v_LoopCounter IN 1..v_NumStudents LOOP
      INSERT INTO temp_table (num_col, char_col)
        VALUES (v_HistoryStudents(v_LoopCounter),
                'In History 101');
    END LOOP;
END;
```

Inside the package body, objects in the header can be referenced without the package name. For example, the **RemoveStudent** procedure can reference the exception with simply **e_StudentNotRegistered**, not **ClassPackage.e_StudentNotRegistered**. The fully qualified name can be used if desired, however.

Overloading Packaged Subprograms

Inside a package, procedures and functions can be *overloaded*. This means that there is more than one procedure or function with the same name, but with different parameters. This is a very useful feature, since it allows the same operation to be applied to objects of different types. For example, suppose we want to add a student to a class either by specifying the student ID or by specifying the first and last names. We could do this by modifying **ClassPackage** as follows:

```
-- Available online as overload.sql
CREATE OR REPLACE PACKAGE ClassPackage AS
  -- Add a new student into the specified class.
  PROCEDURE AddStudent(p_StudentID  IN students.id%TYPE,
                       p_Department IN classes.department%TYPE,
                       p_Course     IN classes.course%TYPE);

  -- Also adds a new student, by specifying the first and last
  -- names, rather than ID number.
  PROCEDURE AddStudent(p_FirstName IN students.first_name%TYPE,
                       p_LastName  IN students.last_name%TYPE,
                       p_Department IN classes.department%TYPE,
                       p_Course     IN classes.course%TYPE);
  ...
END ClassPackage;

CREATE OR REPLACE PACKAGE BODY ClassPackage AS
  -- Add a new student for the specified class.
  PROCEDURE AddStudent(p_StudentID  IN students.id%TYPE,
                       p_Department IN classes.department%TYPE,
                       p_Course     IN classes.course%TYPE) IS
  BEGIN
    INSERT INTO registered_students (student_id, department, course)
      VALUES (p_StudentID, p_Department, p_Course);
    COMMIT;
  END AddStudent;

  -- Add a new student by name, rather than ID.
  PROCEDURE AddStudent(p_FirstName IN students.first_name%TYPE,
                       p_LastName  IN students.last_name%TYPE,
                       p_Department IN classes.department%TYPE,
                       p_Course     IN classes.course%TYPE) IS
    v_StudentID students.ID%TYPE;
  BEGIN
    /* First we need to get the ID from the students table. */
    SELECT ID
      INTO v_StudentID
      FROM students
      WHERE first_name = p_FirstName
      AND last_name = p_LastName;
```

```
    -- Now we can add the student by ID.
    INSERT INTO registered_students (student_id, department, course)
      VALUES (v_StudentID, p_Department, p_Course);
    COMMIT;
  END AddStudent;
  ...
END ClassPackage;
```

We can now add a student to Music 410 with either

```
BEGIN
  ClassPackage.AddStudent(10000, 'MUS', 410);
END;
```

or

```
BEGIN
  ClassPackage.AddStudent('Barbara', 'Blues', 'MUS', 410);
END;
```

Overloading can be a very useful technique, when the same operation can be done on arguments of different types. Overloading is subject to several restrictions, however.

1. You cannot overload two subprograms if their parameters differ only in name or mode. The following two procedures cannot be overloaded, for example:

```
PROCEDURE OverloadMe(p_TheParameter IN NUMBER);
PROCEDURE OverloadMe(p_TheParameter OUT NUMBER);
```

2. You cannot overload two functions based only on their return type. For example, the following functions cannot be overloaded:

```
FUNCTION OverloadMeToo RETURN DATE;
FUNCTION OverloadMeToo RETURN NUMBER;
```

3. Finally, the parameters of overloaded functions must differ by type family—you cannot overload on the same family. (See Chapter 2 for information on type families.) For example, since both CHAR and VARCHAR2 are in the same family, you can't overload the following procedures:

```
PROCEDURE OverloadChar(p_TheParameter IN CHAR);
PROCEDURE OverloadChar(p_TheParameter IN VARCHAR2);
```

NOTE
The PL/SQL compiler will actually allow you to create a package that has subprograms that violate the preceding restrictions. However, the run-time engine will not be able to resolve the references and will always generate the error:
"PLS-307: too many declarations of 'subprogram' match this call."

Package Initialization

The first time a package is called, it is *instantiated*. This means that the package is read from disk into memory, and the p-code is run. At this point, memory is allocated for all variables defined in the package. Each session will have its own copy of packaged variables, insuring that two sessions executing subprograms in the same package use different memory locations.

In many cases, initialization code needs to be run the first time the package is instantiated. This can be done by adding an initialization section to the package body, after all other objects, with the syntax

```
CREATE OR REPLACE PACKAGE BODY package_name {IS | AS}
  ...
BEGIN
  initialization_code;
END [package_name];
```

where *package_name* is the name of the package, and *initialization_code* is the code to be run. For example, the following package implements a random number function.

 -- **Available online as random.sql**
```
CREATE OR REPLACE PACKAGE Random AS
/* Random number generator.  Uses the same algorithm as the
   rand() function in C. */

  -- Used to change the seed.  From a given seed, the same
  -- sequence of random numbers will be generated.
  PROCEDURE ChangeSeed(p_NewSeed IN NUMBER);
```

```
  -- Returns a random integer between 1 and 32767.
  FUNCTION Rand RETURN NUMBER;

  -- Same as Rand, but with a procedural interface.
  PROCEDURE GetRand(p_RandomNumber OUT NUMBER);

  -- Returns a random integer between 1 and p_MaxVal.
  FUNCTION RandMax(p_MaxVal IN NUMBER) RETURN NUMBER;

  -- Same as RandMax, but with a procedural interface.
  PROCEDURE GetRandMax(p_RandomNumber OUT NUMBER,
                       p_MaxVal IN NUMBER);
END Random;

CREATE OR REPLACE PACKAGE BODY Random AS

  /* Used for calculating the next number. */
  v_Multiplier  CONSTANT NUMBER := 22695477;
  v_Increment   CONSTANT NUMBER := 1;

  /* Seed used to generate random sequence. */
  v_Seed        number := 1;

  PROCEDURE ChangeSeed(p_NewSeed IN NUMBER) IS
  BEGIN
    v_Seed := p_NewSeed;
  END ChangeSeed;

  FUNCTION Rand RETURN NUMBER IS
  BEGIN
    v_Seed := MOD(v_Multiplier * v_Seed + v_Increment,
              (2 ** 32));
    RETURN BITAND(v_Seed/(2 ** 16), 32767);
  END Rand;

  PROCEDURE GetRand(p_RandomNumber OUT NUMBER) IS
  BEGIN
    -- Simply call Rand and return the value.
    p_RandomNumber := Rand;
  END GetRand;

  FUNCTION RandMax(p_MaxVal IN NUMBER) RETURN NUMBER IS
  BEGIN
    RETURN MOD(Rand, p_MaxVal) + 1;
  END RandMax;
```

```
PROCEDURE GetRandMax(p_RandomNumber OUT NUMBER,
                     p_MaxVal IN NUMBER) IS
BEGIN
  -- Simply call RandMax and return the value.
  p_RandomNumber := RandMax(p_MaxVal);
END GetRandMax;

BEGIN
  /* Package initialization.  Initialize the seed to the current
     time in seconds. */
  ChangeSeed(TO_NUMBER(TO_CHAR(SYSDATE, 'SSSSS')));
END Random;
```

In order to retrieve a random number, you can simply call
Random.Rand. The sequence of random numbers is controlled by the
initial seed—the same sequence is generated for a given seed. Thus, in
order to provide more random values, we need to initialize the seed to a
different value each time the package is instantiated. To accomplish this,
the **ChangeSeed** procedure is called from the package initialization section.
The **Debug** package, examined in Chapter 14, also contains an
initialization section.

Packages and Dependencies

The dependency picture for **ClassPackage** is shown in Figure 8-1. The
package body depends on **registered_students** and the package header.
The package header does *not* depend on anything. This is the advantage of
packages. We can change the package body without having to change the

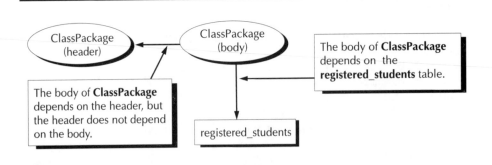

FIGURE 8-1. *ClassPackage dependencies*

header. Therefore, other objects that depend on the header won't have to be recompiled at all, since they never get invalidated. If the header is changed, this automatically invalidates the body, since the body depends on the header.

We can also see this behavior from the following SQL*Plus session.

```
-- Available online as depend.sql
SQL> -- First create a simple table.
SQL> CREATE TABLE simple_table (f1 NUMBER);

Table created.

SQL>
SQL> -- Now create a packaged procedure which references the table.
SQL> CREATE OR REPLACE PACKAGE Dependee AS
  2     PROCEDURE Example(p_Val IN NUMBER);
  3  END Dependee;
  4  /

Package created.

SQL>
SQL> CREATE OR REPLACE PACKAGE BODY Dependee AS
  2     PROCEDURE Example(p_Val IN NUMBER) IS
  3     BEGIN
  4       INSERT INTO simple_table VALUES (p_Val);
  5     END Example;
  6  END Dependee;
  7  /

Package body created.

SQL>
SQL> -- Now create a procedure which references Dependee.
SQL> CREATE OR REPLACE PROCEDURE Depender(p_Val IN NUMBER) AS
  2  BEGIN
  3     Dependee.Example(p_Val + 1);
  4  END Depender;
  5  /

Procedure created.

SQL>
SQL> -- Query user_objects to see that all objects are valid.
SQL> SELECT object_name, object_type, status
```

```
  2    FROM user_objects
  3    WHERE object_name IN ('DEPENDER', 'DEPENDEE', 'SIMPLE_TABLE');
```

OBJECT_NAME	OBJECT_TYPE	STATUS
SIMPLE_TABLE	TABLE	**VALID**
DEPENDEE	PACKAGE	**VALID**
DEPENDEE	PACKAGE BODY	**VALID**
DEPENDER	PROCEDURE	**VALID**

```
SQL>
SQL> -- Change the package body only.  Note that the header is
unchanged.
SQL> CREATE OR REPLACE PACKAGE BODY Dependee AS
  2    PROCEDURE Example(p_Val IN NUMBER) IS
  3    BEGIN
  4     INSERT INTO simple_table VALUES (p_Val - 1);
  5    END Example;
  6  END Dependee;
  7  /

Package body created.

SQL>
SQL> -- Now user_objects shows that Depender is still valid.
SQL> SELECT object_name, object_type, status
  2    FROM user_objects
  3    WHERE object_name IN ('DEPENDER', 'DEPENDEE',
'SIMPLE_TABLE');
```

OBJECT_NAME	OBJECT_TYPE	STATUS
SIMPLE_TABLE	TABLE	**VALID**
DEPENDEE	PACKAGE	**VALID**
DEPENDEE	PACKAGE BODY	**VALID**
DEPENDER	PROCEDURE	**VALID**

```
SQL>
SQL> -- Even if we drop the table, it only invalidates the package body.
SQL> DROP TABLE simple_table;

Table dropped.

SQL> SELECT object_name, object_type, status
  2    FROM user_objects
  3    WHERE object_name IN ('DEPENDER', 'DEPENDEE', 'SIMPLE_TABLE');
```

```
OBJECT_NAME                            OBJECT_TYPE    STATUS
----------------------------------     -------------  -------
DEPENDEE                               PACKAGE        VALID
DEPENDEE                               PACKAGE BODY   INVALID
DEPENDER                               PROCEDURE      VALID
```

PL/SQL 8.0 ...and HIGHER Note: Oracle8 provides data dictionary views **user_dependencies**, **all_dependencies**, and **dba_dependencies**. These views directly list the relationships between schema objects. For more information on these views, see Chapter 11 and Appendix D.

Using Stored Functions in SQL Statements

PL/SQL 2.1 ...and HIGHER In Chapter 4, we addressed the differences between procedural and SQL statements. Since calls to subprograms are procedural, they cannot in general be done in SQL statements. PL/SQL 2.1, however, lifts this restriction for stored functions. If a stand-alone or package function meets certain restrictions, it can be called during execution of a SQL statement. This feature is available with PL/SQL 2.1 (Oracle7 Release 7.1) and higher.

The user-defined function is called the same way as the built-in functions we examined in Chapter 4, such as TO_CHAR, UPPER, or ADD_MONTHS. A function must meet different restrictions depending on where it is used. These restrictions are defined in terms of purity levels.

Purity Levels

There are four different *purity levels* for functions. A purity level defines what kinds of data structures the function reads or modifies. The available levels are listed in Table 8-1.

Depending on the purity level of a function, it is subject to the following restrictions:

■ Any function called from a SQL statement cannot modify any database tables (WNDS).

■ In order to be executed remotely (via a database link) or in parallel, a function must not read or write the value of packaged variables (RNPS and WNPS).

■ Functions called from the SELECT, VALUES, or SET clauses can write packaged variables. Functions in all other clauses must have the WNPS purity level.

■ A function is only as pure as the subprograms it calls. If a function calls a stored procedure that does an UPDATE, for example, the function does not have the WNDS purity level and thus cannot be used inside a SQL statement.

■ Regardless of their purity level, stored PL/SQL functions cannot be called from a CHECK constraint clause of a CREATE TABLE or ALTER TABLE command, or be used to specify a default value for a column, because these situations require an unchanging definition.

Purity Level	Meaning	Description
WNDS	Writes no database state	The function does not modify any database tables (using DML statements).
RNDS	Reads no database state	The function does not read any database tables (using the SELECT statement).
WNPS	Writes no package state	The function does not modify any packaged variables (no packaged variables are used on the left side of an assignment, or in a FETCH statement).
RNPS	Reads no package state	The function does not examine any packaged variables (no packaged variables appear on the right side of an assignment, or as part of a procedural or SQL expression).

TABLE 8-1. *Function Purity Levels*

In addition to the preceding restrictions, a user-defined function must also meet the following requirements to be callable from a SQL statement. Note that all the built-in functions meet these requirements as well.

- The function has to be stored in the database, either alone or as part of a package. It must not be local to another block.

- The function can take only IN parameters, no IN OUT or OUT.

- The formal parameters must use only database types, not PL/SQL types such as BOOLEAN or RECORD. Database types are NUMBER, CHAR, VARCHAR2, ROWID, LONG, LONG RAW, and DATE.

- The return type of the function must also be a database type.

As an example, the **FullName** function takes a student ID number as input and returns the concatenated first and last names:

```
-- Available online as fullname.sql
CREATE OR REPLACE FUNCTION FullName (
  p_StudentID  students.ID%TYPE)
  RETURN VARCHAR2 IS

  v_Result  VARCHAR2(100);
BEGIN
  SELECT first_name || ' ' || last_name
    INTO v_Result
    FROM students
    WHERE ID = p_StudentID;

  RETURN v_Result;
END FullName;
```

FullName meets all of the restrictions, so we can call it from SQL statements, as follows:

```
SQL> SELECT ID, FullName(ID) "Full Name"
  2    FROM students;

    ID Full Name
--------- -------------------------------
    10000 Scott Smith
    10001 Margaret Mason
```

```
    10002 Joanne Junebug
    10003 Manish Murgratroid
    10004 Patrick Poll
    10005 Timothy Taller
    10006 Barbara Blues
    10007 David Dinsmore
    10008 Ester Elegant
    10009 Rose Riznit
    10010 Rita Razmataz

11 rows selected.
SQL> INSERT INTO temp_table (char_col)
  2     VALUES (FullName(10010));

1 row created.
```

RESTRICT_REFERENCES

The PL/SQL engine can determine the purity level of stand-alone functions. When the function is called from a SQL statement, the purity level is checked. If it does not meet the restrictions, an error is returned. For packaged functions, however, the RESTRICT_REFERENCES pragma is required. This pragma specifies the purity level of a given function, with the syntax

PRAGMA RESTRICT_REFERENCES(*function_name*,
    WNDS [, WNPS] [, RNDS] [, RNPS]);

where *function_name* is the name of a packaged function. Since WNDS is required for all functions used in SQL statements, it is also required for the pragma. The other purity levels can be specified in any order. The pragma goes in the package header, with the specification for the function. For example, the **StudentOps** package uses RESTRICT_REFERENCES twice:

```
-- Available online as studops.sql
CREATE OR REPLACE PACKAGE StudentOps AS
  FUNCTION FullName(p_StudentID IN students.ID%TYPE)
    RETURN VARCHAR2;
  PRAGMA RESTRICT_REFERENCES(FullName, WNDS, WNPS, RNPS);
```

```
  /* Returns the number of History majors. */
  FUNCTION NumHistoryMajors
    RETURN NUMBER;
  PRAGMA RESTRICT_REFERENCES(NumHistoryMajors, WNDS, WNPS, RNPS);
END StudentOps;

CREATE OR REPLACE PACKAGE BODY StudentOps AS

  -- Packaged variable to hold the number of history majors.
  v_NumHist NUMBER;

  FUNCTION FullName(p_StudentID IN students.ID%TYPE)
    RETURN VARCHAR2 IS
    v_Result  VARCHAR2(100);
  BEGIN
    SELECT first_name || ' ' || last_name
      INTO v_Result
      FROM students
      WHERE ID = p_StudentID;
    RETURN v_Result;
  END FullName;

  FUNCTION NumHistoryMajors RETURN NUMBER IS
    v_Result NUMBER;
  BEGIN
    IF v_NumHist IS NULL THEN
      /* Determine the answer. */
      SELECT COUNT(*)
        INTO v_Result
        FROM students
        WHERE major = 'History';
      /* And save it for future use. */
      v_NumHist := v_Result;
    ELSE
      v_Result := v_NumHist;
    END IF;

    RETURN v_Result;
  END NumHistoryMajors;
END StudentOps;
```

NOTE
The WNPS and RNPS purity levels apply to variables in other packages. **NumHistoryMajors** *does modify the* **v_NumHist** *packaged variable, but* **v_NumHist** *is contained in the same package as* **StudentOps**. *So we can still assert the WNPS and RNPS purity levels for* **NumHistoryMajors**.

RATIONALE FOR RESTRICT_REFERENCES   Why is the pragma required for packaged functions, but not for stand-alone functions? The answer lies in the relationship between the package header and package body. Remember that PL/SQL blocks calling a packaged function will depend only on the package header, and not the body. Furthermore, the body may not even exist when the calling block is created. Consequently, the PL/SQL compiler needs the pragma to determine the purity levels of the packaged function, to verify that it is being used correctly in the calling block. Whenever the package body is subsequently modified (or created for the first time) the function code is also checked against the pragma.

INITIALIZATION SECTION   The code in the initialization section of a package can have a purity level as well. The first time any function in the package is called, the initialization section is run. Thus a packaged function is only as pure as its initialization section. The purity level for a package is also done with RESTRICT_REFERENCES, but with the package name rather than a function name:

```
CREATE OR REPLACE PACKAGE StudentOps AS
  PRAGMA RESTRICT_REFERENCES (StudentOps, WNDS, WNPS, RNPS);
  ...
END StudentOps;
```

OVERLOADED FUNCTIONS   RESTRICT_REFERENCES can appear anywhere in the package specification, after the function declaration. It can apply to only one function definition, however. Thus, for overloaded functions, the pragma applies to the nearest definition prior to the pragma. In the following example, the function applies to the second declaration of **F**:

```
CREATE OR REPLACE PACKAGE TestPackage AS
  FUNCTION F(p_ParameterOne IN NUMBER) RETURN VARCHAR2;
  FUNCTION F RETURN DATE;
  PRAGMA RESTRICT_REFERENCES(F, WNDS, RNDS);
END TestPackage;
```

BUILT-IN PACKAGES   Packages supplied with PL/SQL are not considered pure as of PL/SQL 2.3. This includes DBMS_OUTPUT, DBMS_PIPE, DBMS_ALERT, DBMS_SQL, and UTL_FILE. Because of this, any function that uses these packages is also not pure, and thus can't be used in SQL statements. These packages are discussed in more detail in later chapters.

Default Parameters

When calling a function from a procedural statement, you can use the default values for formal parameters, if they are present. When calling a function from a SQL statement, however, all parameters must be specified. Furthermore, you have to use positional notation and not named notation. The following call to **FullName** is illegal:

```
SELECT FullName(p_StudentID => 10000) FROM dual;
```

PL/SQL at Work: A PL/SQL Schema Exporter

PL/SQL 2.3 ...and HIGHER   The source code for PL/SQL objects stored in the database is available from the data dictionary. We can query these data dictionary views to retrieve the source, and then use the UTL_FILE package to write it out to a file along with the necessary CREATE OR REPLACE statements. What results is a file which contains all the statements necessary to recreate the PL/SQL objects, that can be run from SQL*Plus.

Because the **Export** package uses both the UTL_FILE package (described in Chapter 18) and cursor variables (described in Chapter 6), it requires PL/SQL version 2.3 or higher. Before examining how to use **Export**, we need to note several things about this package:

■ **Export** uses UTL_FILE to create the output file. Consequently, the owner of **Export** must have EXECUTE permission on the UTL_FILE package. In addition, the UTL_FILE_DIR init.ora parameter must be set appropriately to allow the file to be created. For more information on UTL_FILE_DIR and how it is used, see Chapter 18.

■ **Export** uses the data dictionary views all_objects, all_source, and all_triggers to determine the source. These views will show information about objects on which the owner of **Export** has EXECUTE privileges. Thus, if the **Export** owner can't run a PL/SQL object, they won't be able to export it.

■ If the PL/SQL wrapper was used to encrypt the object's source code, then only the encrypted code will be available in the data dictionary. This is what **Export** will put into the file.

Export has two procedures—**OneObj** and **AllObjs**. **OneObj** is used to export the code for one object only, and **AllObjs** can export all objects owned by a particular owner of a particular type (or all types). The code for **Export** follows, with an example afterwards.

```
-- Available online as export.sql
CREATE OR REPLACE PACKAGE Export AS
  /* Exports one object.  The parameters are used as follows:
   * p_Schema:   Specifies the owner of the object to be exported
   * p_ObjType:  Specifies the type of the object.  Valid values
   *             are 'PACKAGE', 'PACKAGE BODY', 'PROCEDURE',
   *             'FUNCTION', or 'TRIGGER'.  If NULL, then the
   *             object type is determined by selecting from
   *             all_objects.
   * p_BothTypes: If TRUE, when p_ObjType = 'PACKAGE' both the
   *             package and package body will be exported.
   * p_FileDir:  Directory where the output file should be created.
   * p_FileName: Name of the output file.
   * p_Mode:     Mode (either 'A' to append or 'W' to write) of
   *             the output file.
   */
  PROCEDURE OneObj(p_Schema IN VARCHAR2,
                   p_ObjName IN VARCHAR2,
                   p_ObjType IN VARCHAR2 DEFAULT NULL,
                   p_BothTypes IN BOOLEAN DEFAULT TRUE,
                   p_FileDir IN VARCHAR2,
                   p_FileName IN VARCHAR2,
                   p_Mode IN VARCHAR2);
```

```
    /* Exports all objects of a given type.  The parameters are
     * used as follows:
     * p_Schema:    Specifies the owner of the objects to be exported
     * p_ObjType:   Specifies the type of the object.  Valid values
     *              are 'PACKAGE',
     *              'PACKAGE BODY', 'PROCEDURE', 'FUNCTION', or
     *              'TRIGGER'.  If specified, than all objects
     *              owned by p_Schema of the given type will be
     *              exported. If NULL, then all PL/SQL objects owned by
     *              p_Schema will be exported.
     * p_FileDir:   Directory where the output file should be created.
     * p_FileName:  Name of the output file.
     * p_Mode:      Mode (either 'A' to append or 'W' to write) of
     *              the output file.
     */
    PROCEDURE AllObjs(p_Schema IN VARCHAR2,
                      p_ObjType IN VARCHAR2 DEFAULT NULL,
                      p_FileDir IN VARCHAR2,
                      p_FileName IN VARCHAR2,
                      p_Mode IN VARCHAR2);
END Export;

CREATE OR REPLACE PACKAGE BODY Export AS
    /* This is the work horse procedure for the package.
     * OutputObj will output one object, specified by p_Schema,
     * p_ObjName, and p_ObjType, to the file specified by
     * p_FileHandle.  The file must have already been opened
     * for writing (in 'W' or 'A' mode).
     */
    PROCEDURE OutputObj(p_FileHandle IN OUT UTL_FILE.FILE_TYPE,
                        p_Schema IN VARCHAR2,
                        p_ObjName IN VARCHAR2,
                        p_ObjType IN VARCHAR2) IS

    /* These variables are used to retreive the trigger text.
     * Since all_triggers stores a trigger body as a LONG, we
     * have to use DBMS_SQL to fetch the long in chunks. */
    v_SQLStmt VARCHAR2(200) :=
      'SELECT description, trigger_body
         FROM all_triggers
         WHERE owner = :v_owner
         AND trigger_name = :v_name';
    v_Cursor        INTEGER;
    v_NumRows       INTEGER;
    v_Dummy         INTEGER;
```

```
  v_Description    all_triggers.description%TYPE;
  v_BodyChunk      VARCHAR2(100);
  v_ChunkSize      NUMBER := 100;
  v_CurPos         NUMBER := 0;
  v_ReturnedLength NUMBER := 0;

  /* These variables are used to retrieve the source for other
   * types of objects.
   * DBMS_SQL is not necessary here, since all_source stores
   * each line of source separately.
   */
  v_TextLine all_source.text%TYPE;
  CURSOR c_ObjCur IS
    SELECT text
      FROM all_source
      WHERE owner = p_Schema
      AND name = p_ObjName
      AND type = p_ObjType
      ORDER BY line;

BEGIN
  -- First, write the 'CREATE OR REPLACE ' to the file.
  UTL_FILE.PUT(p_FileHandle, 'CREATE OR REPLACE ');

  IF (p_ObjType = 'TRIGGER') THEN
    BEGIN
      -- Output the object type (TRIGGER in this case) to the file.
      UTL_FILE.PUT(p_FileHandle, 'TRIGGER ');

      -- Open the cursor and parse the statement.
      v_Cursor := DBMS_SQL.OPEN_CURSOR;
      DBMS_SQL.PARSE(v_Cursor, v_SQLStmt, DBMS_SQL.V7);

      -- Bind the input variables to the placeholders.
      DBMS_SQL.BIND_VARIABLE(v_Cursor, ':v_owner', p_Schema);
      DBMS_SQL.BIND_VARIABLE(v_Cursor, ':v_name', p_Objname);

      -- Define the output variables.  Note the use of
      -- DEFINE_COLUMN_LONG for the trigger body text.
      DBMS_SQL.DEFINE_COLUMN(v_Cursor, 1, v_Description, 2000);
      DBMS_SQL.DEFINE_COLUMN_LONG(v_Cursor, 2);

      -- Execute the statement, and fetch the row.  We don't
      -- have to fetch in a loop since there is only one row
```

```
per trigger.
v_Dummy := DBMS_SQL.EXECUTE(v_Cursor);
v_NumRows := DBMS_SQL.FETCH_ROWS(v_Cursor);

-- Retreive the value for the trigger description, and
-- output it to the file.
-- Note that we can use UTL_FILE.PUT rather than
-- UTL_FILE.PUT_LINE, since the
-- table contains the trailing newline character.
-- DBMS_SQL.COLUMN_VALUE(v_Cursor, 1, v_Description);

UTL_FILE.PUT(p_FileHandle, v_Description);

-- Loop until we've retrieved the entire trigger body.
-- We will retrieve v_ChunkSize characters each loop iteration.
LOOP
  DBMS_SQL.COLUMN_VALUE_LONG(v_Cursor, 2, v_ChunkSize,
                            v_CurPos, v_BodyChunk,
                            v_ReturnedLength);

  IF v_ReturnedLength < v_ChunkSize THEN
    -- We've just retrieved the last chunk.  For some
    -- reason, an extra NULL character is stored in the
    -- table after the newline.  So we need toremove it first.
    v_BodyChunk := SUBSTR(v_BodyChunk, 1, LENGTH(v_BodyChunk) - 1);

    -- Output the trimmed chunk, and exit the loop.
    UTL_FILE.PUT(p_FileHandle, v_BodyChunk);
    EXIT;
  ELSE
    -- We've retrieved a chunk from the middle of the
    -- long.  Output it to the file, and update the
    -- current position for the next loop iteration.
    UTL_FILE.PUT(p_FileHandle, v_BodyChunk);
    v_CurPos := v_CurPos + v_ReturnedLength;
  END IF;
END LOOP;

-- Close the cursor, since we're finished the processing.
DBMS_SQL.CLOSE_CURSOR(v_Cursor);
EXCEPTION
  WHEN OTHERS THEN
    -- For all errors, first close the cursor, then re-raise
    -- the exception for handling in the calling environment.
    DBMS_SQL.CLOSE_CURSOR(v_Cursor);
```

```
            RAISE;
          END;
      ELSE
        -- If we get here, we are not outputting a trigger.  So we
        -- can just loop through the source lines in all_source,
        -- and output each one. Note that the first line will be
        -- the type and object name, plus 'IS' or 'AS'.
        OPEN c_ObjCur;
        LOOP
          FETCH c_ObjCur INTO v_TextLine;
          EXIT WHEN c_ObjCur%NOTFOUND;

          -- Each line already contains a trailing newline
          -- character, so we can just use
          -- UTL_FILE.PUT rather than UTL_FILE.PUT_LINE.
          UTL_FILE.PUT(p_FileHandle, v_TextLine);
        END LOOP;
        CLOSE c_ObjCur;
      END IF;

    -- Output the final '/'.
    UTL_FILE.PUT_LINE(p_FileHandle, '/');
  END OutputObj;

  PROCEDURE OneObj(p_Schema IN VARCHAR2,

                   p_ObjName IN VARCHAR2,
                   p_ObjType IN VARCHAR2 DEFAULT NULL,
                   p_BothTypes IN BOOLEAN DEFAULT TRUE,
                   p_FileDir IN VARCHAR2,
                   p_FileName IN VARCHAR2,
                   p_Mode IN VARCHAR2) IS
    v_FileHandle UTL_FILE.FILE_TYPE;
    v_ObjType all_objects.object_type%TYPE;
  BEGIN
    -- Validate the input parameters.
    IF p_BothTypes AND (p_ObjType != 'PACKAGE') THEN
      RAISE_APPLICATION_ERROR(-20000,
        'Export.OneObj: BothTypes set but type != PACKAGE');
    ELSIF p_ObjType IS NOT NULL AND p_ObjType NOT IN
          ('PACKAGE', 'PACKAGE BODY', 'PROCEDURE', 'FUNCTION',
         'TRIGGER') THEN RAISE_APPLICATION_ERROR(-20001,
          'Export.OneObj: Illegal value ' || p_ObjType || ' for object type');
    ELSIF p_FileDir IS NULL OR p_FileName IS NULL or p_Mode IS
NULL THEN
      RAISE_APPLICATION_ERROR(-20002,
```

```
          'Export.OneObj: Directory, Filename and Mode must be non-NULL');
ELSIF p_Mode NOT IN ('A', 'a', 'W', 'w') THEN
    RAISE_APPLICATION_ERROR(-20003,
      'Export.OneObj: Mode ' || p_Mode || ' not ''A'' or ''W''');
END IF;

-- Determine the correct object type, and insure that the object
-- exists.
BEGIN
  IF p_ObjType IS NULL THEN
    -- No object type specified - check for existence without
    -- specifying the type.
    SELECT object_type
      INTO v_ObjType
      FROM all_objects
      WHERE owner = UPPER(p_Schema)
      AND object_name = UPPER(p_Objname)
      AND object_type IN ('PROCEDURE', 'FUNCTION', 'PACKAGE',
                          'PACKAGE BODY', 'TRIGGER');
  ELSIF p_BothTypes THEN
    -- BothTypes specified - check for existence of package header
    -- first.
    SELECT object_type
      INTO v_ObjType
      FROM all_objects
      WHERE owner = UPPER(p_Schema)
      AND object_name = UPPER(p_Objname)
      AND object_type = 'PACKAGE';

    -- Now check for the package body.

    BEGIN
      SELECT object_type
        INTO v_ObjType
        FROM all_objects
        WHERE owner = UPPER(p_Schema)
        AND object_name = UPPER(p_Objname)
        AND object_type = 'PACKAGE BODY';
    EXCEPTION
      WHEN NO_DATA_FOUND THEN
        RAISE_APPLICATION_ERROR(-20006,
          'Export.ObjObj: BothTypes set but package body ' ||
        p_Schema || '.' || p_Objname || ' not found');
    END;
  ELSE
```

```
        -- Object type specified, Bothtypes not specified - check for
        -- existence using object type.
        SELECT object_type
          INTO v_ObjType
          FROM all_objects
          WHERE owner = UPPER(p_Schema)
          AND object_name = UPPER(p_Objname)
          AND object_type = p_ObjType;
      END IF;
    EXCEPTION
      WHEN NO_DATA_FOUND THEN
        RAISE_APPLICATION_ERROR(-20004,
          'Export.OneObj: Object ' || p_Schema || '.' || p_Objname ||
          ' not found');
      WHEN TOO_MANY_ROWS THEN
        RAISE_APPLICATION_ERROR(-20005,
          'Export.OneObj: More than one match for ' || p_Schema || '.' ||
          p_Objname);
    END;

    -- If we get to this point, we know that the object exists,
    --  so we can open the file and write to it.  If the mode is
    --  'A', then write 2 blank lines first.
    v_FileHandle := UTL_FILE.FOPEN(p_FileDir, p_FileName, p_Mode);
    IF p_Mode IN ('A', 'a') THEN
      UTL_FILE.NEW_LINE(v_FileHandle, 2);
    END IF;

    -- Output the object.
    IF p_ObjType = 'PACKAGE' AND p_BothTypes THEN
      OutputObj(v_FileHandle, p_Schema, p_ObjName, 'PACKAGE');
      UTL_FILE.NEW_LINE(v_FileHandle, 2);
      OutputObj(v_FileHandle, p_Schema, p_ObjName, 'PACKAGE BODY');
    ELSE
      OutputObj(v_FileHandle, p_Schema, p_ObjName, v_ObjType);
    END IF;

    -- Close the output file.
    UTL_FILE.FCLOSE(v_FileHandle);
  EXCEPTION
    -- Handle the UTL_FILE exceptions meaningfully, and make sure
    -- that the file is properly closed.
    WHEN UTL_FILE.INVALID_PATH THEN
      UTL_FILE.FCLOSE(v_FileHandle);
```

```
        RAISE_APPLICATION_ERROR(-20010,
                                'Export.OneObj: Invalid Path');
   WHEN UTL_FILE.INVALID_OPERATION THEN

     UTL_FILE.FCLOSE(v_FileHandle);
     RAISE_APPLICATION_ERROR(-20010,
                                'Export.OneObj: Invalid Operation');
   WHEN UTL_FILE.INVALID_FILEHANDLE THEN
     UTL_FILE.FCLOSE(v_FileHandle);
     RAISE_APPLICATION_ERROR(-20010,
                                'Export.OneObj: Invalid File Handle');
   WHEN UTL_FILE.WRITE_ERROR THEN
     UTL_FILE.FCLOSE(v_FileHandle);
     RAISE_APPLICATION_ERROR(-20010,
                                'Export.OneObj: Write Error');
   WHEN UTL_FILE.INTERNAL_ERROR THEN
     UTL_FILE.FCLOSE(v_FileHandle);
     RAISE_APPLICATION_ERROR(-20010,
                                'Export.OneObj: Internal Error');
   WHEN OTHERS THEN
     UTL_FILE.FCLOSE(v_FileHandle);
     RAISE;
END OneObj;


PROCEDURE AllObjs(p_Schema IN VARCHAR2,
                  p_ObjType IN VARCHAR2 DEFAULT NULL,
                  p_FileDir IN VARCHAR2,
                  p_FileName IN VARCHAR2,
                  p_Mode IN VARCHAR2) IS
  v_FileHandle UTL_FILE.FILE_TYPE;
  v_ObjName all_objects.object_name%TYPE;
  v_ObjType all_objects.object_type%TYPE;
  v_ObjectFound BOOLEAN := FALSE;

  -- Use a cursor variable for the query, since it can take two forms.
  TYPE t_AllObjs IS REF CURSOR;
  c_AllObjsCur t_AllObjs;

BEGIN
  -- Validate the input parameters.
  IF p_ObjType IS NOT NULL AND p_ObjType NOT IN
          ('PACKAGE', 'PACKAGE BODY', 'PROCEDURE', 'FUNCTION',
           'TRIGGER') THEN
     RAISE_APPLICATION_ERROR(-20001,
```

```
       'Export.AllObjs: Illegal value ' || p_ObjType || ' for object type');
  ELSIF p_FileDir IS NULL OR p_FileName IS NULL or p_Mode IS NULL THEN
    RAISE_APPLICATION_ERROR(-20002,
       'Export.AllObjs: Directory, Filename and Mode must be non-NULL');
  ELSIF p_Mode NOT IN ('A', 'a', 'W', 'w') THEN

    RAISE_APPLICATION_ERROR(-20003,
       'Export.AllObjs: Mode ' || p_Mode || ' not ''A'' or ''W''');
  END IF;

  -- If the object type isn't specified, then open the cursor for
  -- querying all objects owned by p_Schema.  If it is, then open the
  -- cursor for querying only that type of object.
  IF p_ObjType IS NULL THEN
    OPEN c_AllObjsCur FOR
      SELECT object_name, object_type
        FROM all_objects
        WHERE owner = UPPER(p_Schema)
        AND object_type in ('PACKAGE', 'PACKAGE BODY',
                             'PROCEDURE', 'FUNCTION', 'TRIGGER');
  ELSE
    OPEN c_AllObjsCur FOR
      SELECT object_name, object_type
        FROM all_objects
        WHERE owner = UPPER(p_Schema)
        AND object_type = p_ObjType;
  END IF;

  -- Loop over all objects matching the selection criteria, and output
  -- each one, with 2 blank lines in between.
  LOOP
    FETCH c_AllObjsCur INTO v_ObjName, v_ObjType;
    EXIT WHEN c_AllObjsCur%NOTFOUND;

    IF NOT v_ObjectFound THEN
      -- We've found at least one object matching the input parameters.
      -- Open the file, and if the mode is 'A' write 2
      -- blank lines first.
      v_ObjectFound := TRUE;
      v_FileHandle := UTL_FILE.FOPEN(p_FileDir, p_FileName, p_Mode);
      IF p_Mode IN ('A', 'a') THEN
        UTL_FILE.NEW_LINE(v_FileHandle, 2);
      END IF;
    END IF;
```

```
        OutputObj(v_FileHandle, p_Schema, v_ObjName, v_ObjType);
        UTL_FILE.NEW_LINE(v_FileHandle, 2);
      END LOOP;

      -- Check for a found object, and close the cursor and file handle.
      CLOSE c_AllObjsCur;
      IF NOT v_ObjectFound THEN
        RAISE_APPLICATION_ERROR(-20004,
            'Export.AllObjs: No objects found');
      END IF;
      UTL_FILE.FCLOSE(v_FileHandle);
    EXCEPTION
      -- Handle the UTL_FILE exceptions meaningfully, and make sure
      -- that the file is properly closed.
      WHEN UTL_FILE.INVALID_PATH THEN
        UTL_FILE.FCLOSE(v_FileHandle);
        RAISE_APPLICATION_ERROR(-20010,
                                'Export.AllObjs: Invalid Path');
      WHEN UTL_FILE.INVALID_OPERATION THEN
        UTL_FILE.FCLOSE(v_FileHandle);
        RAISE_APPLICATION_ERROR(-20010,
                                'Export.AllObjs: Invalid Operation');
      WHEN UTL_FILE.INVALID_FILEHANDLE THEN
        UTL_FILE.FCLOSE(v_FileHandle);
        RAISE_APPLICATION_ERROR(-20010,
                                'Export.AllObjs: Invalid File Handle');
      WHEN UTL_FILE.WRITE_ERROR THEN
        UTL_FILE.FCLOSE(v_FileHandle);
        RAISE_APPLICATION_ERROR(-20010,
                                'Export.AllObjs: Write Error');
      WHEN OTHERS THEN
        UTL_FILE.FCLOSE(v_FileHandle);
        RAISE;
    END AllObjs;
  END Export;
```

For example, we could use **Export.OneObj** to export the
AddNewStudent procedure (created in Chapter 7) by running the following
block:

```
BEGIN
    Export.OneObj('EXAMPLE', 'ADDNEWSTUDENT', 'PROCEDURE', FALSE,
                  'c:\temp', 'addstud.sql', 'W');
END;
```

This would then create a file c:\temp\addstud.sql, which would contain the following:

```
CREATE OR REPLACE PROCEDURE AddNewStudent (
  p_FirstName   students.first_name%TYPE,
  p_LastName    students.last_name%TYPE,
  p_Major       students.major%TYPE) AS
BEGIN
  -- Insert a new row in the students table. Use
  -- student_sequence to generate the new student ID, and
  -- 0 for current_credits.
  INSERT INTO students (ID, first_name, last_name,
                        major, current_credits)
    VALUES (student_sequence.nextval, p_FirstName, p_LastName,
            p_Major, 0);
  COMMIT;
END AddNewStudent;
/
```

This file can be run directly from SQL*Plus to recreate the procedure.

Summary

In this chapter, we have examined packages in detail, including both the syntax and the rationale for using them. This includes taking advantage of the dependency features of packages. In the next chapter, we will discuss the final type of named PL/SQL blocks—triggers.

CHAPTER

9

Triggers

he fourth type of named PL/SQL block is the trigger. Triggers share many of the same characteristics as subprograms, but they have some significant differences. In this chapter, we will examine how to create triggers and discuss some possible applications.

Creating Triggers

Triggers are similar to procedures or functions, in that they are named PL/SQL blocks with declarative, executable, and exception handling sections. Like packages, triggers must be stored in the database and cannot be local to a block. However, a procedure is executed explicitly from another block via a procedure call, which can also pass arguments. A trigger is executed implicitly whenever the triggering event happens, and a trigger doesn't accept arguments. The act of executing a trigger is known as *firing* the trigger. The triggering event is a DML (INSERT, UPDATE, or DELETE) operation on a database table.

Triggers can be used for many things, including

- Maintaining complex integrity constraints not possible through declarative constraints enabled at table creation

- Auditing information in a table, by recording the changes made and who made them

- Automatically signaling other programs that action needs to take place, when changes are made to a table

As an example, suppose we want to track statistics about different majors, including the number of students registered and the total credits taken. We are going to store these results in the **major_stats** table:

```
-- Available online as part of tables.sql
CREATE TABLE major_stats (
  major          VARCHAR2(30),
  total_credits  NUMBER,
  total_students NUMBER);
```

In order to keep **major_stats** up-to-date, we can create a trigger on **students** that will update **major_stats** every time **students** is modified. The **UpdateMajorStats** trigger, shown next, does this. After any DML operation on **students**, the trigger will execute. The body of the trigger queries **students** and updates **major_stats** with the current statistics.

```
-- Available online as updateMS.sql
CREATE OR REPLACE TRIGGER UpdateMajorStats
  /* Keeps the major_stats table up-to-date with changes made
     to the students table. */
  AFTER INSERT OR DELETE OR UPDATE ON students
DECLARE
  CURSOR c_Statistics IS
    SELECT major, COUNT(*) total_students,
           SUM(current_credits) total_credits
      FROM students
      GROUP BY major;
BEGIN
  /* Loop through each major. Attempt to update the statistics
     in major_stats corresponding to this major. If the row
     doesn't exist, create it. */
  FOR v_StatsRecord in c_Statistics LOOP
    UPDATE major_stats
      SET total_credits = v_StatsRecord.total_credits,
          total_students = v_StatsRecord.total_students
      WHERE major = v_StatsRecord.major;
    /* Check to see if the row exists. */
    IF SQL%NOTFOUND THEN
      INSERT INTO major_stats (major, total_credits, total_students)
        VALUES (v_StatsRecord.major, v_StatsRecord.total_credits,
                v_StatsRecord.total_students);
    END IF;
  END LOOP;
END UpdateMajorStats;
```

The general syntax for creating a trigger is

CREATE [OR REPLACE] TRIGGER *trigger_name*
{BEFORE | AFTER} *triggering_event* ON *table_reference*
[FOR EACH ROW [WHEN *trigger_condition*]]
trigger_body;

where *trigger_name* is the name of the trigger, *triggering_event* specifies when the trigger fires (in the case of **UpdateMajorStats**, after any DML operation), *table_reference* is the table for which the trigger is defined, and *trigger_body* is the main code for the trigger. The *trigger_condition* in the

WHEN clause, if present, is evaluated first. The body of the trigger is executed only when this condition evaluates to TRUE.

Trigger Components

The required components of a trigger are the trigger name, triggering event, and the body. The WHEN clause is optional.

Trigger Names

The namespace for trigger names is different from that of other subprograms. A *namespace* is the set of legal identifiers available for use as the names of an object. Procedures, packages, and tables all share the same namespace. This means that, within one database schema, all objects in the same namespace must have unique names. For example, it is illegal to give the same name to a procedure and a package.

Triggers, however, exist in a separate namespace. This means that a trigger can have the same name as a table or procedure. Within one schema, however, a given name can be used for only one trigger. Trigger names are database identifiers and as such follow the same rules as other identifiers, as described in Chapter 2. For example, we can create a trigger called **major_stats** on the **major_stats** table, but it is illegal to create a procedure also called **major_stats**, as the following SQL*Plus session shows.

```
-- Available online as samename.sql
SQL> CREATE OR REPLACE TRIGGER major_stats
  2    BEFORE INSERT ON major_stats
  3  BEGIN
  4    INSERT INTO temp_table (char_col)
  5      VALUES ('Trigger fired!');
  6  END major_stats;
  7  /

Trigger created.

SQL> CREATE OR REPLACE PROCEDURE major_stats AS
  2  BEGIN
  3    INSERT INTO temp_table (char_col)
  4      VALUES ('Procedure called!');
  5  END major_stats;
  6  /
CREATE OR REPLACE PROCEDURE major_stats AS
```

```
*
ERROR at line 1:
ORA-00955: name is already used by an existing object
```

TIP
Although it is possible to use the same name for a trigger and a table, I don't recommend it. It is better to give each trigger a unique name that identifies its function as well as the table on which it is defined.

Types of Triggers

The triggering event determines the type of the trigger. Triggers can be defined for INSERT, UPDATE, or DELETE operations. They can be fired before or after the operation, and they can also fire on row or statement operations. Table 9-1 summarizes the various options.

The values for the statement, timing, and level determine the type of the trigger. There are a total of 12 possible types: 3 statements ö 2 timing ö 2 levels. For example, all of the following are valid trigger types:

- Before update statement level

- After insert row level

- Before delete row level

PL/SQL 2.1 ...and HIGHER A table can have up to 12 triggers defined on it—one of each type. Starting with PL/SQL 2.1 (Oracle7 release 7.1), however, a table can have more than one trigger of each type. This capability allows you to define as many triggers as you want for one table. The order in which the triggers are fired is described in the "Order of Trigger Firing" section later in this chapter.

A trigger can also be fired for more than one type of triggering statement. For example, the **UpdateMajorStats** trigger is fired on INSERT, UPDATE, and DELETE statements. The triggering event specifies one or more of the DML operations that should fire the trigger.

Category	Values	Comments
Statement	INSERT, DELETE, UPDATE	Defines which kind of DML statement causes the trigger to fire.
Timing	BEFORE or AFTER	Defines whether the trigger fires before the statement is executed or after the statement is executed.
Level	Row or statement	If the trigger is a row-level trigger, it fires once for each row affected by the triggering statement. If the trigger is a statement-level trigger, it fires once, either before or after the statement. A row-level trigger is identified by the FOR EACH ROW clause in the trigger definition.

TABLE 9-1. *Types of Triggers*

Instead-of Triggers

PL/SQL 8.0 ...and HIGHER

PL/SQL 8.0 provides one additional kind of trigger. *Instead-of* triggers can be defined on views (either relational or object) only, and they will fire instead of the DML statement that fired them. Instead-of triggers must be row level. Instead-of triggers are necessary because the view on which one is defined could be based on a join, and not all joins are updatable. The trigger would allow the update to take place in a reasonable manner. For example, consider the **room_summary** view:

```
-- Available online as part of instead.sql
CREATE VIEW room_summary AS
  SELECT building, sum(number_seats) total_seats
    FROM rooms
  GROUP BY building;
```

It is illegal to delete from this view directly:

```
SQL> DELETE FROM room_summary where building = 'Building 7';
DELETE FROM room_summary where building = 'Building 7'
                  *
ERROR at line 1:
ORA-01732: data manipulation operation not legal on this view
```

However, we can create an instead-of trigger which does the correct thing for a DELETE, namely, to delete all of the underlying rows in **rooms**:

```
-- Available online as part of instead.sql
CREATE TRIGGER room_summary_delete
  INSTEAD OF DELETE ON room_summary
  FOR EACH ROW
BEGIN
  -- Delete all of the rows in rooms which match this single row
  -- in room_summary
  DELETE FROM rooms
    WHERE building = :old.building;
END room_summary_delete;
```

With the **room_summary_delete** trigger in place, the DELETE statement succeeds and does the correct thing. For more information on instead-of triggers, see Chapter 11.

Restrictions on Triggers

The body of a trigger is a PL/SQL block. Any statement that is legal in a PL/SQL block is legal in a trigger body, subject to the following restrictions:

- A trigger may not issue any transaction control statements—COMMIT, ROLLBACK, or SAVEPOINT. The trigger is fired as part of the execution of the triggering statement and is in the same transaction as the triggering statement. When the triggering statement is committed or rolled back, the work in the trigger is committed or rolled back as well.

- Likewise, any procedures or functions that are called by the trigger body cannot issue any transaction control statements.

- The trigger body cannot declare any LONG or LONG RAW variables. Also, :new and :old (described later) cannot refer to a LONG or LONG RAW column in the table for which the trigger is defined.

■ There are restrictions on which tables a trigger body may access. Depending on the type of trigger and the constraints on the tables, tables may be mutating. This situation is discussed in detail in the section "Mutating Tables" later in this chapter.

Triggers and the Data Dictionary

Similar to stored subprograms, certain data dictionary views contain information about triggers and their status. These views are updated whenever a trigger is created or dropped.

Data Dictionary Views

When a trigger is created, its source code is stored in the data dictionary view **user_triggers**. This view includes the trigger body, WHEN clause, triggering table, and the trigger type. For example, the following query returns information about **UpdateMajorStats**:

```
SQL> SELECT trigger_type, table_name, triggering_event
  2    FROM user_triggers
  3    WHERE trigger_name = 'UPDATEMAJORSTATS';

TRIGGER_TYPE      TABLE_NAME      TRIGGERING_EVENT
----------------  --------------  --------------------------
AFTER STATEMENT   STUDENTS        INSERT OR UPDATE OR DELETE
```

For more information on data dictionary views, see Appendix E.

Dropping and Disabling Triggers

Similar to procedures and packages, triggers can be dropped. The command to do this has the syntax

    DROP TRIGGER *triggername*;

where *triggername* is the name of the trigger to be dropped. This permanently removes the trigger from the data dictionary. Similar to subprograms, the OR REPLACE clause can be specified in the trigger CREATE statement. In this case, the trigger is dropped first, if it already exists.

Unlike procedures and packages, however, a trigger can be disabled without dropping it. When a trigger is disabled, it still exists in the data dictionary but is never fired. To disable a trigger, use the ALTER TRIGGER statement,

ALTER TRIGGER *triggername* {DISABLE | ENABLE};

where *triggername* is the name of the trigger. All triggers are enabled by default when they are created. ALTER TRIGGER can disable, and then reenable, any trigger. For example, the following code disables and then reenables **UpdateMajorStats**:

```
SQL> ALTER TRIGGER UpdateMajorStats DISABLE
Trigger altered.

SQL> ALTER TRIGGER UpdateMajorStats ENABLE;
Trigger altered.
```

All triggers for a particular table can be enabled or disabled using the ALTER TABLE command as well, by adding the ENABLE ALL TRIGGERS or the DISABLE ALL TRIGGERS clause. For example:

```
SQL> ALTER TABLE students
  2    ENABLE ALL TRIGGERS;
Table altered.

SQL> ALTER TABLE students
  2    DISABLE ALL TRIGGERS;
Table altered.
```

The **status** column of **user_triggers** contains either 'ENABLED' or 'DISABLED', indicating the current status of a trigger. Disabling a trigger does not remove it from the data dictionary, like dropping it would do.

Trigger P-Code

When a package or subprogram is stored in the data dictionary, the compiled p-code is stored in addition to the source code for the object. This is not the case for triggers, however. The only item stored in the data dictionary is the source code for the trigger, not the p-code. As a result, the trigger must be compiled each time it is read from the dictionary. This doesn't have any effect on the way triggers are defined and used, but it can have an effect on trigger performance. For more information on performance and tuning, see Chapter 22.

PL/SQL 2.3 PL/SQL 2.3, with Oracle7 Release 7.3, stores triggers in compiled **...and HIGHER** form, like procedures, functions, and packages. This allows triggers to be called without recompilation. However, since triggers are stored objects just like packages and subprograms, they do have dependency information stored as well. Thus they can be automatically invalidated in the same manner as packages and subprograms. When a trigger is invalidated, it will be recompiled the next time it is fired.

Order of Trigger Firing

Triggers are fired as the DML statement is executed. The algorithm for executing a DML statement is given here:

1. Execute the BEFORE statement-level trigger, if present.

2. For each row affected by the statement:

   a. Execute the BEFORE row-level trigger, if present.

   b. Execute the statement itself.

   c. Execute the AFTER row-level trigger, if present.

3. Execute the AFTER statement-level trigger, if present.

To illustrate this, suppose we create all four kinds of UPDATE triggers on the **classes** table—before and after, statement and row level as follows:

```
-- Available online as order.sql
CREATE SEQUENCE trigger_seq
  START WITH 1
  INCREMENT BY 1;

CREATE OR REPLACE TRIGGER classes_BStatement
  BEFORE UPDATE ON classes
BEGIN
  INSERT INTO temp_table (num_col, char_col)
    VALUES (trigger_seq.NEXTVAL, 'Before Statement trigger');
END classes_BStatement;

CREATE OR REPLACE TRIGGER classes_AStatement
  AFTER UPDATE ON classes
```

```
BEGIN
  INSERT INTO temp_table (num_col, char_col)
    VALUES (trigger_seq.NEXTVAL, 'After Statement trigger');
END classes_AStatement;

CREATE OR REPLACE TRIGGER classes_BRow
  BEFORE UPDATE ON classes
  FOR EACH ROW
BEGIN
  INSERT INTO temp_table (num_col, char_col)
    VALUES (trigger_seq.NEXTVAL, 'Before Row trigger');
END classes_BRow;

CREATE OR REPLACE TRIGGER classes_ARow
  AFTER UPDATE ON classes
  FOR EACH ROW
BEGIN
  INSERT INTO temp_table (num_col, char_col)
    VALUES (trigger_seq.NEXTVAL, 'After Row trigger');
END classes_ARow;
```

Suppose we now issue the following UPDATE statement:

```
UPDATE classes
  SET num_credits = 4
  WHERE department IN ('HIS', 'CS');
```

This statement affects four rows. The before and after statement-level triggers are each executed once, and the before and after row-level triggers are each executed four times. If we then select from **temp_table**, we get:

```
-- Available online as part of order.sql
SQL> SELECT * FROM temp_table
  2    ORDER BY num_col;

  NUM_COL CHAR_COL
--------- ------------------------
        1 Before Statement trigger
        2 Before Row trigger
        3 After Row trigger
        4 Before Row trigger
        5 After Row trigger
        6 Before Row trigger
        7 After Row trigger
        8 Before Row trigger
```

```
 9 After Row trigger
10 After Statement trigger
```

As each trigger is fired, it will see the changes made by the earlier triggers, as well as any database changes made by the statement so far. The order in which triggers of the same type are fired is not defined. If the order is important, combine all of the operations into one trigger.

Using :old and :new in Row-Level Triggers

A row-level trigger fires once per row processed by the triggering statement. Inside the trigger, you can access the row that is currently being processed. This is accomplished through two *pseudo-records*—:old and :new. :old and :new are not true records. Although syntactically they are treated as records, in reality they are not (this is discussed below in more detail). Thus they are known as pseudo-records, with meanings as described in Table 9-2. The type of both is

    triggering_table%ROWTYPE;

where *triggering_table* is the table for which the trigger is defined.

NOTE
:old is undefined for INSERT statements, and :new is undefined for DELETE statements. The PL/SQL compiler will not generate an error if you use :old in an INSERT or :new in a DELETE, but the field values of both will be NULL. The colon in front of :new and :old is required. This is the only place within PL/SQL where colons are used to delimit bind variables. The reason is that :new and :old are actually implemented as bind variables (in the sense of host variables used in embedded PL/SQL). Like other bind variables, the colon delimits them from regular PL/SQL variables. Bind variables are used in different PL/SQL execution environments (see Chapter 13 for more information). A reference such as new.field will be valid only if field is a field in the triggering table.

CAUTION
Although :new and :old are syntactically treated as records of triggering_table%ROWTYPE, in reality they are not. As a result, operations that would normally be valid on records are not valid for :new and :old. For example, they cannot be assigned as entire records. Only the individual fields within them may be assigned. The following example illustrates this:

```
-- Available online as pseudo.sql
CREATE OR REPLACE TRIGGER TempDelete
BEFORE DELETE ON temp_table
FOR EACH ROW
DECLARE
  v_TempRec temp_table%ROWTYPE;
BEGIN
  /* This is not a legal assignment, since :old is not truly
     a record. */
  v_TempRec := :old;

  /* We can accomplish the same thing, however, by assigning
     the fields individually. */
  v_TempRec.char_col := :old.char_col;
  v_TempRec.num_col := :old.num_col;
END TempDelete;
```

In addition, old and new cannot be passed to procedures or functions that take arguments of triggering_table%ROWTYPE.

The **GenerateStudentID** trigger shown next uses :new. It is a before INSERT or UPDATE trigger, and its purpose is to fill in the **ID** field of **students** with a value generated from the **student_sequence** sequence.

Triggering Statement	:old	:new
INSERT	Undefined—all fields are NULL.	Values that will be inserted when the statement is complete.
UPDATE	Original values for the row before the update.	New values that will be updated when the statement is complete.
DELETE	Original values before the row is deleted.	Undefined—all fields are NULL.

TABLE 9-2.   *:old and :new*

```
-- Available online as studID.sql
CREATE OR REPLACE TRIGGER GenerateStudentID
  BEFORE INSERT OR UPDATE ON students
  FOR EACH ROW
BEGIN
  /* Fill in the ID field of students with the next value from
     student_sequence. Since ID is a column in students, :new.ID
     is a valid reference. */
  SELECT student_sequence.nextval
    INTO :new.ID
    FROM dual;
END GenerateStudentID;
```

GenerateStudentID actually modifies the value of **:new.ID**. This is one of the useful features of :new—when the statement is actually executed, whatever values are in :new will be used. With **GenerateStudentID**, we can issue an INSERT statement such as

```
INSERT INTO students (first_name, last_name)
  VALUES ('Lolita', 'Lazarus');
```

without generating an error. Even though we haven't specified a value for the primary key column **ID** (which is required), the trigger will supply it. In fact, if we do specify a value for **ID**, it will be ignored, since the trigger changes it. If we issue

```
INSERT INTO students (ID, first_name, last_name)
  VALUES (-7, 'Lolita', 'Lazarus');
```

we get the same behavior. In either case, **student_sequence.nextval** will be used for the **ID** column.

As a result of this, you cannot change :new in an after row-level trigger, since the statement has already been processed. In general, :new is modified only in a before row-level trigger, and :old is never modified, only read from.

The :new and :old records are only valid inside row-level triggers. If you try to reference either inside a statement-level trigger, you will get a compile error. Since a statement-level trigger executes once—even if there are many rows processed by the statement—:old and :new have no meaning. Which row would they refer to?

The WHEN Clause

The WHEN clause is valid for row-level triggers only. If present, the trigger body will be executed only for those rows that meet the condition specified by the WHEN clause. The WHEN clause looks like

> WHEN *condition*

where *condition* is a boolean expression. It will be evaluated for each row. The :new and :old records can be referenced inside *condition* as well, but the colon is *not* used there. The colon is only valid in the trigger body. For example, the body of the **CheckCredits** trigger is only executed if the current credits being taken by a student are more than 20:

```
CREATE OR REPLACE TRIGGER CheckCredits
  BEFORE INSERT OR UPDATE OF current_credits ON students
  FOR EACH ROW
  WHEN (new.current_credits > 20)
BEGIN
  /* Trigger body goes here. */
END;
```

CheckCredits could also be written as follows:

```
CREATE OR REPLACE TRIGGER CheckCredits
   BEFORE INSERT OR UPDATE OF current_credits ON students
   FOR EACH ROW
BEGIN
   IF :new.current_credits > 20 THEN
      /* Trigger body goes here. */
   END IF;
END;
```

Using Trigger Predicates: INSERTING, UPDATING, and DELETING

The **UpdateMajorStats** trigger earlier in this chapter is an INSERT, UPDATE, and a DELETE trigger. Inside a trigger of this type (that will fire for different kinds of DML statements), there are three boolean functions that you can use to determine what the operation is. These predicates are INSERTING, UPDATING, and DELETING. Their behavior is described in the following table.

Predicate	Behavior
INSERTING	TRUE if the triggering statement is an INSERT; FALSE otherwise.
UPDATING	TRUE if the triggering statement is an UPDATE; FALSE otherwise.
DELETING	TRUE if the triggering statement is a DELETE; FALSE otherwise.

The **LogRSChanges** trigger uses these predicates to record all changes made to the **registered_students** table. In addition to the change, it records the user who makes the change. The records are kept in the **RS_audit** table, which looks like:

```
--Available online as part of tables.sql
CREATE TABLE RS_audit (
   old_student_id NUMBER(5),
   old_department CHAR(3),
   old_course     NUMBER(3),
   old_grade      CHAR(1),
```

```
  new_student_id NUMBER(5),
  new_department CHAR(3),
  new_course     NUMBER(3),
  new_grade      CHAR(1),
  changed_by     VARCHAR2(8),
  timestamp      DATE
  );
```

LogRSChanges is created with:

```
-- Available online as RSchange.sql
CREATE OR REPLACE TRIGGER LogRSChanges
  BEFORE INSERT OR DELETE OR UPDATE ON registered_students
  FOR EACH ROW
DECLARE
  v_ChangeType CHAR(1);
BEGIN
  /* Use 'I' for an INSERT, 'D' for DELETE, and 'U' for UPDATE. */
  IF INSERTING THEN
    v_ChangeType := 'I';
  ELSIF UPDATING THEN
    v_ChangeType := 'U';
  ELSE
    v_ChangeType := 'D';
  END IF;

  /* Record all the changes made to registered_students in
     RS_audit. Use SYSDATE to generate the timestamp, and
     USER to return the userid of the current user. */
  INSERT INTO RS_audit
    (change_type, changed_by, timestamp,
     old_student_id, old_department, old_course, old_grade,
     new_student_id, new_department, new_course, new_grade)
  VALUES
    (v_ChangeType, USER, SYSDATE,
     :old.student_id, :old.department, :old.course, :old.grade,
     :new.student_id, :new.department, :new.course, :new.grade);
END LogRSChanges;
```

Triggers are commonly used for auditing, as in **LogRSChanges**. Oracle provides auditing as part of the database, but triggers allow for more flexible auditing. **LogRSChanges** could be modified, for example, to record changes only made by certain people. It could also check to see if users have permission to make changes and raise an error (with RAISE_APPLICATION_ERROR) if they don't.

Mutating Tables

There are restrictions on the tables and columns that a trigger body may access. In order to define these restrictions, it is necessary to understand mutating and constraining tables. A *mutating table* is a table that is currently being modified by a DML statement. For a trigger, this is the table on which the trigger is defined. Tables that may need to be updated as a result of DELETE CASCADE referential integrity constraints are also mutating. (For more information on referential integrity constraints, see the *Oracle Server Reference*.) A *constraining table* is a table that might need to be read from for a referential integrity constraint. To illustrate these definitions, consider the **registered_students** table, which is created with

```
-- Available online as part of tables.sql
CREATE TABLE registered_students (
  student_id NUMBER(5) NOT NULL,
  department CHAR(3)   NOT NULL,
  course     NUMBER(3) NOT NULL,
  grade      CHAR(1),
  CONSTRAINT rs_grade
    CHECK (grade IN ('A', 'B', 'C', 'D', 'E')),
  CONSTRAINT rs_student_id
    FOREIGN KEY (student_id) REFERENCES students (id),
  CONSTRAINT rs_department_course
    FOREIGN KEY (department, course)
    REFERENCES classes (department, course)
);
```

Registered_students has two declarative referential integrity constraints. As such, both **students** and **classes** are constraining tables for **registered_students**. **Registered_students** itself is mutating during execution of a DML statement against it. Because of the constraints, **classes** and **students** also need to be modified and/or queried by the DML statement.

SQL statements in a trigger body may not:

- Read from or modify any mutating table of the triggering statement. This includes the triggering table itself.

- Read from or modify the primary, unique, or foreign key columns of a constraining table of the triggering table. They may, however, modify the other columns if desired.

These restrictions apply to all row-level triggers. They apply for statement triggers only when the statement trigger would be fired as a result of a DELETE CASCADE operation.

NOTE
If an INSERT statement affects only one row, then the before and after row triggers for that row do not treat the triggering table as mutating. This is the only case where a row-level trigger may read from or modify the triggering table. Statements such as

```
INSERT INTO table SELECT ...
```

always treat the triggering table as mutating, even if the subquery returns only one row.

As an example, consider the **CascadeRSInserts** trigger shown next. Even though it modifies both **students** and **classes**, it is legal because the columns in **students** and **classes** that are modified are not key columns. In the next section, we will examine an illegal trigger.

```
-- Available online as RSinsert.sql
CREATE OR REPLACE TRIGGER CascadeRSInserts
   /* Keep the registered_students, students, and classes
      tables in synch. */
   BEFORE INSERT ON registered_students
   FOR EACH ROW
DECLARE
   v_Credits classes.num_credits%TYPE;
BEGIN
   -- Determine the number of credits for this class.
   SELECT num_credits
     INTO v_Credits
     FROM classes
     WHERE department = :new.department
     AND course = :new.course;

   -- Modify the current credits for this student.
   UPDATE students
     SET current_credits = current_credits + v_Credits
```

```
    WHERE ID = :new.student_id;

  -- Add one to the number of students in the class.
  UPDATE classes
    SET current_students = current_students + 1
    WHERE department = :new.department
    AND course = :new.course;
END CascadeRSInserts;
```

In order to be complete, triggers to update **students** and **classes** when **registered_students** is deleted from or updated should be written as well. They would be very similar to **CascadeRSInserts**.

Mutating Table Example

Suppose we want to limit the number of students in each major to 5. We could accomplish this with a before insert or update row-level trigger on **students**, given here:

```
-- Available online as limMajor.sql
CREATE OR REPLACE TRIGGER LimitMajors
  /* Limits the number of students in each major to 5.
     If this limit is exceeded, an error is raised through
     raise_application_error. */
  BEFORE INSERT OR UPDATE OF major ON students
  FOR EACH ROW
DECLARE
  v_MaxStudents CONSTANT NUMBER := 5;
  v_CurrentStudents NUMBER;
BEGIN
  -- Determine the current number of students in this
  -- major.
  SELECT COUNT(*)
    INTO v_CurrentStudents
    FROM students
    WHERE major = :new.major;

  -- If there isn't room, raise an error.
  IF v_CurrentStudents + 1 > v_MaxStudents THEN
    RAISE_APPLICATION_ERROR(-20000,
      'Too many students in major ' || :new.major);
  END IF;
END LimitMajors;
```

The RAISE_APPLICATION_ERROR procedure is a standard procedure, which is discussed in more detail in Chapter 10. At first glance, this trigger seems to accomplish the desired result. However, if we update **students** and fire the trigger, we get

```
SQL> UPDATE students
  2    SET major = 'History'
  3    WHERE ID = 10003;
UPDATE students
  *
ERROR at line 1:
ORA-04091: table EXAMPLE.STUDENTS is mutating, trigger/function
          may not see it
ORA-06512: at line 7
ORA-04088: error during execution of trigger 'EXAMPLE.LIMITMAJORS'
```

The ORA-4091 error results because **LimitMajors** queries its own triggering table, which is mutating. ORA-4091 is raised when the trigger is fired, not when it is created.

Workaround for the Mutating Table Error

Students is mutating only for a row-level trigger. This means that we cannot query it in a row-level trigger, but we can in a statement-level trigger. However, we cannot simply make **LimitMajors** into a statement trigger, since we need to use the value of **:new.major** in the trigger body. The solution for this is to create two triggers—a row and a statement level. In the row-level trigger, we record the value of **:new.major**, but we don't query **students**. The query is done in the statement-level trigger and uses the value recorded in the row trigger.

How do we record this value? The best way is to use a PL/SQL table inside a package. This way, we can save multiple values per update. Also, each session gets its own instantiation of packaged variables, so we don't have to worry about simultaneous updates by different sessions. This solution is implemented with the **student_data** package and the **RLimitMajors** and **SLimitMajors** triggers:

```
-- Available online as mutating.sql
CREATE OR REPLACE PACKAGE StudentData AS
  TYPE t_Majors IS TABLE OF students.major%TYPE
    INDEX BY BINARY_INTEGER;
```

```
    TYPE t_IDs IS TABLE OF students.ID%TYPE
      INDEX BY BINARY_INTEGER;

    v_StudentMajors t_Majors;
    v_StudentIDs    t_IDs;
    v_NumEntries    BINARY_INTEGER := 0;
  END StudentData;

CREATE OR REPLACE TRIGGER RLimitMajors
  BEFORE INSERT OR UPDATE OF major ON students
  FOR EACH ROW
BEGIN
  /* Record the new data in StudentData. We don't make any
     changes to students, to avoid the ORA-4091 error. */
  StudentData.v_NumEntries := StudentData.v_NumEntries + 1;
  StudentData.v_StudentMajors(StudentData.v_NumEntries) :=
    :new.major;
  StudentData.v_StudentIDs(StudentData.v_NumEntries) := :new.id;
END RLimitMajors;

CREATE OR REPLACE TRIGGER SLimitMajors
  AFTER INSERT OR UPDATE OF major ON students
DECLARE
  v_MaxStudents     CONSTANT NUMBER := 5;
  v_CurrentStudents NUMBER;
  v_StudentID       students.ID%TYPE;
  v_Major           students.major%TYPE;
BEGIN
  /* Loop through each student inserted or updated, and verify
     that we are still within the limit. */
  FOR v_LoopIndex IN 1..StudentData.v_NumEntries LOOP
    v_StudentID := StudentData.v_StudentIDs(v_LoopIndex);
    v_Major := StudentData.v_StudentMajors(v_LoopIndex);

    -- Determine the current number of students in this major.
    SELECT COUNT(*)
      INTO v_CurrentStudents
      FROM students
      WHERE major = v_Major;

    -- If there isn't room, raise an error.
    IF v_CurrentStudents > v_MaxStudents THEN
      RAISE_APPLICATION_ERROR(-20000,
        'Too many students for major ' || v_Major ||
        ' because of student ' || v_StudentID);
```

```
  END IF;
END LOOP;

  -- Reset the counter so the next execution will use new data.
  StudentData.v_NumEntries := 0;
END LimitMajors;
```

NOTE
*Be sure to drop the incorrect **LimitMajors***
trigger before running the above script.

We can now test this series of triggers by updating **students** until we have too many history majors:

```
SQL> UPDATE students
  2     SET major = 'History'
  3     WHERE ID = 10003;
1 row updated.

SQL> UPDATE students
  2     SET major = 'History'
  3     WHERE ID = 10002;
1 row updated.

SQL> UPDATE students
  2     SET major = 'History'
  3     WHERE ID = 10009;
UPDATE students
  *
ERROR at line 1:
ORA-20000: Too many students for major History because of student
          10009
ORA-06512: at line 20
ORA-04088: error during execution of trigger
          'EXAMPLE.SLIMITMAJORS'
```

This is the desired behavior. This technique can be applied to occurrences of ORA-4091 when a row-level trigger reads from or modifies a mutating table. Instead of doing the illegal processing in the row-level trigger, we defer the processing to an after statement-level trigger, where it is legal. The packaged PL/SQL tables are used to store the rows that were changed.

There are several things to note about this technique:

■ The PL/SQL tables are contained in a package so that they will be visible to both the row- and the statement-level trigger. The only way to ensure that variables are global is to put them in a package.

■ A counter variable, **StudentData.v_NumEntries**, is used. This is initialized to zero when the package is created. It is incremented by the row-level trigger. The statement-level trigger references it and then resets it to zero after processing. This is necessary so that the next UPDATE statement issued by this session will have the correct value.

■ The check in **SLimitMajors** for the maximum number of students had to be changed slightly. Since this is now an after statement trigger, **v_CurrentStudents** will hold the number of students in the major after the insert or update, not before. Thus the check for **v_CurrentStudents + 1**, which we did in **LimitMajors**, is replaced by **v_CurrentStudents**.

■ A database table could have been used instead of PL/SQL tables. I don't recommend this technique, since simultaneous sessions issuing an UPDATE would interfere with each other. Packaged PL/SQL tables are unique among sessions, which avoids the problem.

PL/SQL at Work: Implementing Update Cascade

Oracle7 has the ability to perform a *delete cascade*. With delete cascade, when a row is deleted from a parent table, the related rows are also deleted from a child table that depends on the parent with a foreign key. However, there is no update cascade implemented by default. This package removes this restriction by generating the needed packages and triggers to support update cascade, without infringing on declarative referential integrity constraints.

This example is from the Oracle Government Products group, and is used by permission. For more information (and other useful utilities), see the Government Products home page at **http://govt.us.oracle.com**.

This package supports the following features:

- Tables with multi-part primary keys (primary key(a,c,b))

- Update cascade to many child tables from one parent

- Self-referencing integrity such as that found in the SCOTT.EMP table (mgr->empno)

- Application that is transparent—the application does not know it is happening

- Versions 7.0 and above of the database

- Tuned and optimized to fully avoid full table scans on all tables (complete with utility to show you un-indexed foreign keys in a schema. Cascading an update to un-indexed foreign keys can be bad)

However, this solution has the following restrictions:

- All foreign keys to the parent table must point to the primary key constraint of the parent table. They cannot point to a unique constraint on the parent table, they must point to the primary key.

- No other unique constraints/indexes may be in place on the parent table other than the primary key constraint.

- Updates to primary keys that do not generate 'new' primary keys are not currently supported. For example, look at the standard **dept** table. The update statement

```
UPDATE dept SET deptno = deptno + 10;
```

will not work, whereas the update

```
UPDATE dept SET deptno = deptno + 1;
```

will work. The first update will change 10->20, 20->30, and so on. The problem is that 10->20 is not generating a 'new' primary key, because 20 is already a valid department. On the other hand, "UPDATE dept SET deptno = deptno + 1" does not have this problem since 10->11, 20->21, and so on. Note that an update that affects a single row will never suffer from this problem.

- The owner of the parent table must also be the owner of the child tables.

- The owner of the parent table must run the following package in their schema. This package must be installed for each user that wants to generate update cascade support. It may be dropped after the cascade support has been generated.

- The owner of the parent table must have been granted create procedure and create trigger. Since this package uses DBMS_SQL to generate the required objects, these privileges may not be inherited from a role.

This utility uses both DBMS_SQL and DBMS_OUTPUT. For more information on DBMS_SQL, see Chapter 15. For more information on DBMS_OUTPUT, see Chapter 14.

Contents of this Utility

The cascade update utility consists of four SQL scripts, described in the following table and in subsequent sections. They can all be found online.

Script Name	Purpose
uc.sql	Creates the **update_cascade** package.
demobld.sql	Creates a sample schema for demonstration.
unindex.sql	Shows indexes that should be created to avoid full table scans.
generate.sql	Creates calls to **update_cascade** for all parent tables in a given schema.

uc.sql

The uc.sql script will create the **update_cascade** package and package body in the current schema. **update_cascade** has one procedure, **on_table**, that has the following specification:

```
PROCEDURE on_table(
table_name IN VARCHAR2,
p_preserve_rowid IN BOOLEAN DEFAULT TRUE,
p_use_dbms_output IN BOOLEAN DEFAULT FALSE);
```

How It Works

The **update_cascade** package generates three triggers that perform the update cascade:

- A before update trigger; used to reset some package variables

- A before update, for each row trigger; used to capture the before and after images of the primary keys in PL/SQL tables. It also 'undoes' the update to the primary key.

- An after update trigger that performs the following steps:

    1. 'Clones' the parent records with their new primary key by issuing a statement similar to

    ```
    INSERT INTO parent
      SELECT NEW_KEY, other_cols
        FROM parent
        WHERE CURRENT_KEY = ( SELECT OLD_KEY FROM dual );
    ```

    For example, given "UPDATE dept SET deptno = deptno + 1", this would insert the values of 11, 21, 31, 41 into the **dept** table. 11 would have the values in the rest of the columns that 10 had. 21 would look like 20 and so on.

    2. If **p_preserve_rowids** = TRUE, then the primary keys of the row that was cloned and the clone are flip-flopped. For example, if you issue: "UPDATE dept SET deptno = 11 WHERE deptno = 10", we would make 10 become the new value 11 and 11 become the old value 10.

    3. Re-parents the child records in all subordinate tables. Performs the equivalent of:

    ```
    UPDATE child
      SET fkey = ( SELECT new_key FROM dual )
      WHERE fkey = ( SELECT old_key FROM dual );
    ```

    4. It then removes the 'cloned' parent records or the record with the old primary key value.

The generated code from issuing "update_cascade.on_table('dept', TRUE, TRUE)" follows. This code is commented to explain each part. The actual generated code, however, doesn't have comments.

This generated code preserves rowids and will be in bold. This code would not be present in the generated package if rowid preservation were disabled.

The package spec name is always u || TABLE_NAME || p. The package name is in mixed case (to prevent collisions with other user objects).

```
create or replace package "uDEPTp"
as
   -- Rowcnt is used to collect the number of rows processed by a
   -- given update statement. It is reset in the uDEPTp.reset
   -- routine in a before update trigger. The 'inTrigger' variable
   -- is used to prevent recursive firing of triggers when
   -- p_preserve_rowid = TRUE.
   rowCnt     number default 0;
   inTrigger boolean default FALSE;

   -- For each element in the primary key, a table type will be
   -- declared and then an array of that type will be declared
   -- to hold 1.) the before image, 2.) the after image, and 3.) an
   -- empty array used to zero out the previous two arrays.

   type C1_type is table of "DEPT"."DEPTNO"%type
     index by binary_integer;

   empty_C1 C1_type;
   old_C1   C1_type;
   new_C1   C1_type;

   -- Reset is the routine fired by the BEFORE UPDATE trigger that
   -- resets the rowcnt variable and empties out the
   -- arrays from the previous invocation.
   procedure reset;

   -- Do_cascade is the workhorse routine. It performs the actual
   -- cascade when fired from an AFTER UPDATE trigger.
   procedure do_cascade;

   -- Add_entry simply increments the rowcnt and collects the
   -- before/after images of the primary keys. It also 'undoes' the
   -- update to the primary key by accessing the :new and :old
   -- variables.
   procedure add_entry
     (
      p_old_C1 in "DEPT"."DEPTNO"%type,
```

```
    p_new_C1 in out "DEPT"."DEPTNO"%type
    );
end "uDEPTp";
```

This is the generated package body that implements the above specification:

```
create or replace package body "uDEPTp"
as
  procedure reset is
  begin
    -- This line is present in all routines when p_preserve_rowids
    -- = TRUE. It prevents recursive firing of the triggers.
    if ( inTrigger ) then return; end if;

    rowCnt := 0;
    old_C1 := empty_C1;
    new_C1 := empty_C1;
  end reset;

  procedure add_entry
  (
    p_old_C1 in "DEPT"."DEPTNO"%type,
    p_new_C1 in out "DEPT"."DEPTNO"%type
  ) is
  begin
    if ( inTrigger ) then return; end if;
    -- This code saves the before and after images in pl/sql tables
    -- and 'undoes' the primary key update by setting the new
    -- columns back to the old columns.
    if (
        p_old_C1 <> p_new_C1
        ) then
      rowCnt := rowCnt + 1;
      old_C1( rowCnt ) := p_old_C1;
      new_C1( rowCnt ) := p_new_C1;
      p_new_C1 := p_old_C1;
    end if;
  end add_entry;

  procedure do_cascade is
  begin
    if ( inTrigger ) then return; end if;
    inTrigger := TRUE;
    -- For every row that was updated we will perform the clone,
```

```
-- cascade and delete....
for i in 1 .. rowCnt loop
  -- This insert clones the parent row, duping the old values
  -- with the new primary key.
  insert into DEPT ("DEPTNO", "DNAME", "LOC")
    select new_C1(i), "DNAME", "LOC"
      from "DEPT" a
        where ( "DEPTNO" ) =
          ( select old_C1(i) from dual );

  -- This code is generated only when p_preserve_rowids=true
  -- and will flip-flop the old and new primary keys, hence
  -- preserving the rowid of the original parent.
  update "DEPT" set
    ( "DEPTNO" ) =
    ( select
        decode( "DEPTNO", old_c1(i), new_c1(i), old_c1(i) )
      from dual )
    where ( "DEPTNO" ) =
          ( select  new_C1(i)
              from dual )
        OR ( "DEPTNO" ) =
          ( select  old_C1(i)
              from dual );

  -- Do a cascade update to all children tables.
  update "EMP" set
  ( "DEPTNO" ) =
  ( select   new_C1(i)
      from dual )
  where ( "DEPTNO" ) =
        ( select   old_C1(i)
            from dual );

  -- Removing the old primary key value.
  delete from "DEPT"
   where ( "DEPTNO" ) =
         ( select  old_C1(i)
             from dual);
end loop;
inTrigger := FALSE;
reset;
exception
when others then
  inTrigger := FALSE;
```

```
        reset;
        raise;
    end do_cascade;
end "uDEPTp";
```

Lastly, we have the three triggers placed on the parent table to effect the update cascade. The first trigger simply 'resets' the package variables above.

```
create or replace trigger "uc$DEPT_bu"
before update of
    "DEPTNO"
on "DEPT"
begin "uDEPTp".reset; end;
```

The next trigger, the for each row trigger, simply calls **add_entry** for each changed row.

```
create or replace trigger "uc$DEPT_bufer"
before update of
    "DEPTNO"
on "DEPT"
for each row
begin
    "uDEPTp".add_entry(
        :old."DEPTNO"
        ,:new."DEPTNO"
        );
end;
```

The last trigger calls **do_cascade** to effect the change.

```
create or replace trigger "uc$DEPT_au"
after update of
    "DEPTNO"
on "DEPT"
begin "uDEPTp".do_cascade; end;
```

Summary

As we have seen, triggers are a valuable addition to PL/SQL and Oracle. They can be used to enforce data constraints that are much more complex than normal referential integrity constraints. Triggers complete our discussion of named PL/SQL blocks in the past three chapters. In the next chapter, we move on to error handling in PL/SQL.

CHAPTER
10

Error Handling

ny well-written program must have the ability to handle errors intelligently and recover from them if possible. PL/SQL implements error handling with *exceptions* and *exception handlers.* Exceptions can be associated with Oracle errors or with your own user-defined errors. In this chapter, we will discuss the syntax of exceptions and exception handlers, how exceptions are raised and handled, and the rules of exception propagation. The chapter closes with guidelines on using exceptions.

What Is an Exception?

In Chapter 1 we discussed how PL/SQL is based on the Ada language. One of the features of Ada that is also incorporated into PL/SQL is the exception mechanism. By using exceptions and exception handlers, you can make your PL/SQL programs robust and able to deal with both unexpected and expected errors during execution.

What kinds of errors can occur in a PL/SQL program? Errors can be classified as described in Table 10-1. Exceptions are designed for run-time error handling, rather than compile-time error handling. Errors that occur during the compilation phase are detected by the PL/SQL engine and reported back to the user. The program cannot handle these, since the program has yet to run. For example, the following block will raise the compilation error:

```
PLS-201: identifier 'SSTUDENTS' must be declared
```

because 'students' is misspelled in the select statement:

```
DECLARE
   v_NumStudents NUMBER;
BEGIN
   SELECT COUNT(*)
     INTO v_NumStudents
     FROM sstudents;
END;
```

Exceptions and exception handlers are the method by which the program reacts and deals with run-time errors. Run-time errors include SQL errors such as

```
ORA-1: unique constraint violated
```

Error Type	When Reported	How Handled
Compile-time	PL/SQL compiler	Interactively: compiler reports errors, and you have to correct them.
Run-time	PL/SQL run-time engine	Programmatically: exceptions are raised and caught by exception handlers.

TABLE 10-1. *Types of PL/SQL Errors*

and procedural errors such as

```
ORA-06502: PL/SQL: numeric or value error
```

When an error occurs, an exception is *raised*. When this happens, control is passed to the exception handler, which is a separate section of the program. This separates the error handling from the rest of the program, which makes the logic of the program easier to understand. This also ensures that all errors will be trapped.

In a language that doesn't use the exception model for error handling (such as C), in order to ensure that your program can handle errors in all cases, you must explicitly insert error-handling code. For example:

```
int x, y, z;
f(x);  /* Function call, passing x as an argument. */
if <an error occurred>
  handle_error(...);
y = 1 / z;
if <an error occurred>
  handle_error(...);
z = x + y;
if <an error occurred>
  handle_error(...);
```

Note that a check for errors must occur after each statement in the program. If you forget to insert the check, the program will not properly handle an error situation. In addition, the error handling can clutter up the program, making it difficult to understand the program's logic. Compare the preceding example to the similar example in PL/SQL:

```
DECLARE
  x NUMBER;
  y NUMBER;
  z NUMBER;
BEGIN
  f(x);
  y := 1 / z;
  z := x + y;
EXCEPTION
  WHEN OTHERS THEN
    /* Handler to execute for all errors */
    handle_error(...);
END;
```

Note that the error handling is separated from the program logic. This solves both problems with the C example, namely:

- Program logic is easier to understand, since it is clearly visible.

- No matter which statement fails, the program will detect and handle the error.

Declaring Exceptions

Exceptions are declared in the declarative section of the block, raised in the executable section, and handled in the exception section. There are two types of exceptions—*user-defined* and *predefined*.

User-Defined Exceptions

A user-defined exception is an error that is defined by the program. The error that it signifies is not necessarily an Oracle error—it could be an error with the data, for example. Predefined exceptions, on the other hand, correspond to common SQL errors.

User-defined exceptions are declared in the declarative section of a PL/SQL block. Just like variables, exceptions have a type (EXCEPTION) and scope. For example:

```
DECLARE
  e_TooManyStudents EXCEPTION;
```

e_TooManyStudents is an identifier that will be visible until the end of this block. Note that the scope of an exception is the same as the scope of any other variable or cursor in the same declarative section. See Chapter 2 for information on the scope and visibility rules for PL/SQL identifiers.

Predefined Exceptions

Oracle has predefined several exceptions that correspond to the most common Oracle errors. Like the predefined types (NUMBER, VARCHAR2, and so on), the identifiers for these exceptions are defined in package STANDARD (see Chapter 2 for more information on predefined types and package STANDARD). Because of this, they are already available to the program—it is not necessary to declare them in the declarative section like a user-defined exception. These predefined exceptions are described in Table 10-2.

Short descriptions of some of the predefined exceptions follow. For more information on these errors, see Appendix C.

Oracle Error	Equivalent Exception	Description
ORA-0001	DUP_VAL_ON_INDEX	Unique constraint violated.
ORA-0051	TIMEOUT_ON_RESOURCE	Time-out occurred while waiting for resource.
ORA-0061	TRANSACTION_BACKED_OUT[1]	The transaction was rolled back due to deadlock.
ORA-1001	INVALID_CURSOR	Illegal cursor operation.
ORA-1012	NOT_LOGGED_ON	Not connected to Oracle.
ORA-1017	LOGIN_DENIED	Invalid user name/password.
ORA-1403	NO_DATA_FOUND	No data found.
ORA-1422	TOO_MANY_ROWS	A SELECT..INTO statement matches more than one row.

1. This exception is predefined only in PL/SQL 2.0 and 2.1.

TABLE 10-2. *Predefined Oracle Exceptions*

Oracle Error	Equivalent Exception	Description
ORA-1476	ZERO_DIVIDE	Division by zero.
ORA-1722	INVALID_NUMBER	Conversion to a number failed; for example, '1A' is not valid.
ORA-6500	STORAGE_ERROR	Internal PL/SQL error raised if PL/SQL runs out of memory.
ORA-6501	PROGRAM_ERROR	Internal PL/SQL error.
ORA-6502	VALUE_ERROR	Truncation, arithmetic, or conversion error.
ORA-6504	ROWTYPE_MISMATCH[2]	Host cursor variable and PL/SQL cursor variable have incompatible row types.
ORA-6511	CURSOR_ALREADY_OPEN	Attempt to open a cursor that is already open.
ORA-6530	ACCESS_INTO_NULL[3]	Attempt to assign values to the attributes of a NULL object.
ORA-6531	COLLECTION_IS_NULL[3]	Attempt to apply collection methods other than EXISTS to a NULL PL/SQL table or varray.
ORA-6532	SUBSCRIPT_OUTSIDE_LIMIT[3]	Reference to a nested table or varray index outside the declared range (such as -1).
ORA-6533	SUBSCRIPT_BEYOND_COUNT[3]	Reference to a nested table or varray index higher than the number of elements in the collection.

2. This exception is predefined in PL/SQL 2.2 and higher.
3. This exception is predefined in PL/SQL 8.0 and higher.

TABLE 10-2. *Predefined Oracle Exceptions* (continued)

INVALID_CURSOR   This error is raised when an illegal cursor operation is performed, such as attempting to close a cursor that is already closed. The analogous situation of attempting to open a cursor that is already open causes CURSOR_ALREADY_OPEN to be raised.

NO_DATA_FOUND   This exception can be raised in two different situations. The first is when a SELECT..INTO statement does not return any rows. If the statement returns more than one row, TOO_MANY_ROWS is raised. The second situation is an attempt to reference a PL/SQL table element that has not been assigned a value. For example, the following anonymous block will raise NO_DATA_FOUND:

```
DECLARE
  TYPE t_NumberTableType IS TABLE OF NUMBER
    INDEX BY BINARY_INTEGER;
  v_NumberTable t_NumberTableType;
  v_TempVar NUMBER;
BEGIN
  v_TempVar := v_NumberTable(1);
END;
```

INVALID_NUMBER   This exception is raised in an SQL statement when an attempted conversion from a character string to a number fails. In a procedural statement, VALUE_ERROR is raised instead. For example, the following statement raises INVALID_NUMBER since 'X' is not a valid number:

```
INSERT INTO students (id, first_name, last_name)
  VALUES, ('X', 'SCOTT', 'Smith');
```

STORAGE_ERROR and PROGRAM_ERROR   These are internal exceptions, which are not normally raised. If they occur, either your machine has run out of memory (STORAGE_ERROR) or a PL/SQL internal error occurred (PROGRAM_ERROR). Internal errors are often caused by bugs in the PL/SQL engine and should be reported to Oracle Technical Support.

VALUE_ERROR   This exception is raised when an arithmetic, conversion, truncation, or constraint error occurs in a procedural statement. If the error occurs in an SQL statement, an error such as INVALID_

NUMBER is raised instead. The error can occur either as a result of an assignment statement or a SELECT..INTO statement. Both of the following examples will raise VALUE_ERROR:

```
DECLARE
  v_TempVar VARCHAR2(3);
BEGIN
  v_TempVar := 'ABCD';
END;
```

```
DECLARE
  v_TempVar NUMBER(2);
BEGIN
  SELECT id
    INTO v_TempVar
    FROM students
    WHERE last_name = 'Smith';
END;
```

ROWTYPE MISMATCH

PL/SQL 2.2 ...and HIGHER This exception is raised when the types of a host cursor variable and a PL/SQL cursor variable do not match. For example, if the actual and formal return types don't match for a procedure that takes a cursor variable as an argument, ROWTYPE_MISMATCH is raised. See Chapter 6 for more information on cursor variables and an example that raises this exception.

Raising Exceptions

When the error associated with an exception occurs, the exception is raised. User-defined exceptions are raised explicitly via the RAISE statement, while predefined exceptions are raised implicitly when their associated Oracle error occurs. Predefined exceptions can be raised explicitly via the RAISE statement as well, if desired. Continuing the example started earlier in the "User-Defined Exceptions" section, we have:

```
-- Available online as handle.sql
DECLARE
  e_TooManyStudents EXCEPTION;     -- Exception to indicate an error condition
  v_CurrentStudents NUMBER(3);     -- Current number of students registered
                                   -- for HIS-101
```

```
   v_MaxStudents NUMBER(3);         -- Maximum number of students allowed for
                                    -- HIS-101
BEGIN
  /* Find the current number of registered students, and the maximum number of
     students allowed. */
  SELECT current_students, max_students
    INTO v_CurrentStudents, v_MaxStudents
    FROM classes
    WHERE department = 'HIS' AND course = 101;
  /* Check the number of students in this class. */
  IF v_CurrentStudents > v_MaxStudents THEN
    /* Too many students registered -- raise exception. */
    RAISE e_TooManyStudents;
  END IF;
END;
```

When an exception is raised, control immediately passes to the exception section of the block. If there is no exception section, the exception is propagated to the enclosing block (see the section "Exception Propagation" later in the chapter for more information). Once control passes to the exception handler, there is *no* way to return to the executable section of the block. This is illustrated in Figure 10-1.

Predefined exceptions are automatically raised when the associated Oracle error occurs. For example, the following PL/SQL block will raise the DUP_VAL_ON_INDEX exception:

```
BEGIN
    INSERT INTO students (id, first_name, last_name)
      VALUES (10001, 'John', 'Smith');
    INSERT INTO students (id, first_name, last_name)
      VALUES (10001, 'Susan', 'Ryan');
END;
```

The exception is raised because the **id** column of the students table is a primary key and therefore has a unique constraint defined on it. When the second INSERT statement attempts to insert 10001 into this column, the error

```
ORA-0001: unique constraint violated
```

is raised. This corresponds to the DUP_VAL_ON_INDEX exception.

Handling Exceptions

When an exception is raised, control passes to the exception section of the block, as illustrated in Figure 10-1. The exception section consists of *handlers* for all the exceptions. An exception handler contains the code that is executed when the error associated with the exception occurs, and the exception is raised. The syntax for the exception section is as follows:

```
EXCEPTION
  WHEN exception_name THEN
    sequence_of_statements1;
  WHEN exception_name THEN
    sequence_of_statements2;
  WHEN OTHERS THEN
    sequence_of_statements3;
END;
```

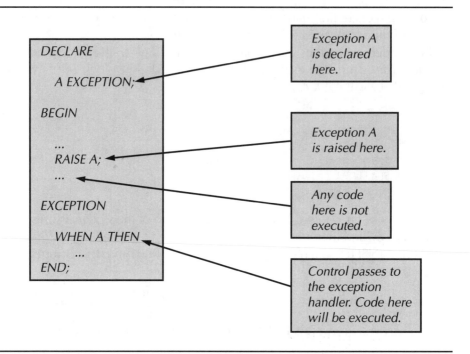

FIGURE 10-1. *Control passing to exception handler*

Each exception handler consists of the WHEN clause and statements to execute when the exception is raised. The WHEN clause identifies which exception this handler is for. Continuing the example started earlier, we have:

```
DECLARE
    e_TooManyStudents EXCEPTION;    -- Exception to indicate an error condition
    v_CurrentStudents NUMBER(3);    -- Current number of students registered
                                    -- for HIS-101
    v_MaxStudents NUMBER(3);        -- Maximum number of students allowed for
                                    -- HIS-101
BEGIN
  /* Find the current number of registered students, and the maximum number of
     students allowed. */
  SELECT current_students, max_students
    INTO v_CurrentStudents, v_MaxStudents
    FROM classes
    WHERE department = 'HIS' AND course = 101;
  /* Check the number of students in this class. */
  IF v_CurrentStudents > v_MaxStudents THEN
    /* Too many students registered - raise exception. */
    RAISE e_TooManyStudents;
  END IF;
EXCEPTION
  WHEN e_TooManyStudents THEN
    /* Handler which executes when there are too many students registered
       for HIS-101. We will insert a log message explaining what has happened. */
    INSERT INTO log_table (info) VALUES ('History 101 has ' || v_CurrentStudents ||
      'students: max allowed is ' || v_MaxStudents);
END;
```

A single handler can also be executed for more than one exception. Simply list the exception names in the WHEN clause separated by the keyword OR:

```
EXCEPTION
  WHEN NO_DATA_FOUND OR TOO_MANY_ROWS THEN
    INSERT INTO log_table (info) VALUES ('A select error occurred.');
END;
```

The OTHERS Exception Handler

The OTHERS handler will execute for all raised exceptions. It should always be the last handler in the block. It is good programming practice to have an

OTHERS handler at the top level of your program (the outermost block) to ensure that no errors go undetected. The next listing continues the previous example by adding an OTHERS handler:

```
-- Available online as others.sql
DECLARE
  e_TooManyStudents EXCEPTION;    -- Exception to indicate an error condition
  v_CurrentStudents NUMBER(3);    -- Current number of students registered
                                  -- for HIS-101
  v_MaxStudents NUMBER(3);        -- Maximum number of students allowed for
                                  -- HIS-101
BEGIN
  /* Find the current number of registered students, and the maximum number of
     students allowed. */
  SELECT current_students, max_students
    INTO v_CurrentStudents, v_MaxStudents
    FROM classes
    WHERE department = 'HIS' AND course = 101;
  /* Check the number of students in this class. */
  IF v_CurrentStudents > v_MaxStudents THEN
    /* Too many students registered - raise exception. */
    RAISE e_TooManyStudents;
  END IF;
EXCEPTION
  WHEN e_TooManyStudents THEN
    /* Handler which executes when there are too many students registered
       for HIS-101. We will insert a log message explaining what has happened. */
    INSERT INTO log_table (info) VALUES ('History 101 has ' || v_CurrentStudents ||
      'students: max allowed is ' || v_MaxStudents);
  WHEN OTHERS THEN
    /* Handler which executes for all other errors. */
    INSERT INTO log_table (info) VALUES ('Another error occurred');
END;
```

The OTHERS exception handler in this example simply records the fact that an error occurred. However, it doesn't record which error. We can determine which error raised the exception that is being handled by an OTHERS handler through the predefined functions SQLCODE and SQLERRM, described next.

SQLCODE and SQLERRM   Inside an OTHERS handler, it is often useful to know which Oracle error raised the exception. One reason would be to log which error occurred, rather than the fact that an error happened.

Or, you may want to do different things depending on which error was raised. PL/SQL provides this information via two built-in functions, SQLCODE and SQLERRM. SQLCODE returns the current error code, and SQLERRM returns the current error message text.

NOTE
*The DBMS_UTILITY.FORMAT_ERROR_
STACK function also returns the current
error message and can be used in addition
to SQLERRM. The "PL/SQL at Work"
example later in this chapter illustrates this.*

Here is the complete PL/SQL block that we have developed so far, with a complete OTHERS exception handler:

```
-- Available online as sqlrrm.sql
DECLARE
    e_TooManyStudents EXCEPTION;    -- Exception to indicate an error condition
    v_CurrentStudents NUMBER(3);    -- Current number of students registered
                                    -- for HIS-101
    v_MaxStudents NUMBER(3);        -- Maximum number of students allowed for
                                    -- HIS-101

    v_ErrorCode NUMBER;             -- Variable to hold the error message code
    v_ErrorText VARCHAR2(200);      -- Variable to hold the error message text

BEGIN
  /* Find the current number of registered students, and the maximum number of
     students allowed. */
  SELECT current_students, max_students
    INTO v_CurrentStudents, v_MaxStudents
    FROM classes
    WHERE department = 'HIS' AND course = 101;
  /* Check the number of students in this class. */
  IF v_CurrentStudents > v_MaxStudents THEN
    /* Too many students registered - raise exception. */
    RAISE e_TooManyStudents;
  END IF;
EXCEPTION
  WHEN e_TooManyStudents THEN
    /* Handler which executes when there are too many students registered
```

```
          for HIS-101. We will insert a log message explaining what has happened. */
       INSERT INTO log_table (info) VALUES ('History 101 has ' || v_CurrentStudents ||
          'students: max allowed is ' || v_MaxStudents);
   WHEN OTHERS THEN
       /* Handler which executes for all other errors. */
       v_ErrorCode := SQLCODE;
       v_ErrorText := SUBSTR(SQLERRM, 1, 200);  -- Note the use of SUBSTR here.
       INSERT INTO log_table (code, message, info) VALUES
          (v_ErrorCode, v_ErrorText, 'Oracle error occurred');
   END;
```

The maximum length of an Oracle error message is 512 characters. In the preceding listing, **v_ErrorText** is only 200 characters (to match the **code** field of the log_table table). If the error message text is longer than 200 characters, the assignment

```
v_ErrorText := SQLERRM;
```

will itself raise the predefined exception VALUE_ERROR. To prevent this, we use the SUBSTR built-in function to ensure that at most 200 characters of the error message text are assigned to **v_ErrorText**. For more information on SUBSTR and other predefined PL/SQL functions, see Chapter 5.

Note that the values of SQLCODE and SQLERRM are assigned to local variables first; then these variables are used in an SQL statement. Because these functions are procedural, they cannot be used directly inside an SQL statement.

SQLERRM can also be called with a single number argument. In this case, it returns the text associated with the number. This argument should always be negative. If SQLERRM is called with zero, the message

```
ORA-0000: normal, successful completion
```

is returned. If SQLERRM is called with any positive value other than +100, the message

```
User-Defined Exception
```

is returned. SQLERRM(100) returns

```
ORA-1403: no data found
```

When called from an exception handler, SQLCODE will return a negative value indicating the Oracle error. The only exception to this is the error "ORA-1403: no data found," in which case SQLCODE returns +100.

If SQLERRM (with no arguments) is called from the executable section of a block, it always returns

ORA-0000: normal, successful completion

and SQLCODE returns 0. All of these situations are shown in the following listing.

```
-- Available online as sqlerrmz.sql
DECLARE
  v_ErrorText    log_table.message%TYPE;  -- Variable to hold error message text
BEGIN
  /* SQLERRM(0) */
  v_ErrorText := SUBSTR(SQLERRM(0), 1, 200);
  INSERT INTO log_table (code, message, info)
    VALUES (0, v_ErrorText, 'SQLERRM(0)');

  /* SQLERRM(100) */
  v_ErrorText := SUBSTR(SQLERRM(100), 1, 200);
  INSERT INTO log_table (code, message, info)
    VALUES (100, v_ErrorText, 'SQLERRM(100)');

  /* SQLERRM(10) */
  v_ErrorText := SUBSTR(SQLERRM(10), 1, 200);
  INSERT INTO log_table (code, message, info)
    VALUES (10, v_ErrorText, 'SQLERRM(10)');

  /* SQLERRM with no argument */
  v_ErrorText := SUBSTR(SQLERRM, 1, 200);
  INSERT INTO log_table (code, message, info)
    VALUES (NULL, v_ErrorText, 'SQLERRM with no argument');

  /* SQLERRM(-1) */
  v_ErrorText := SUBSTR(SQLERRM(-1), 1, 200);
  INSERT INTO log_table (code, message, info)
    VALUES (-1, v_ErrorText, 'SQLERRM(-1)');

  /* SQLERRM(-54) */
  v_ErrorText := SUBSTR(SQLERRM(-54), 1, 200);
  INSERT INTO log_table (code, message, info)
    VALUES (-54, v_ErrorText, 'SQLERRM(-54)');

END;
```

If we were to run the preceding example, the log_table table would contain the values in Table 10-3.

The EXCEPTION_INIT Pragma

You can associate a named exception with a particular Oracle error. This gives you the ability to trap this error specifically, rather than via an OTHERS handler. This is done via the EXCEPTION_INIT pragma. For more information on pragmas and how they are used, see Chapter 2. The EXCEPTION_INIT pragma is used as follows:

        PRAGMA EXCEPTION_INIT (*exception_name, Oracle_error_number*);

where *exception_name* is the name of an exception declared prior to the pragma, and *Oracle_error_number* is the desired error code to be associated with this named exception. This pragma must be in the declarative section.

Code	Message	SQLERRM Function Used
0	ORA-0000: normal, successful completion	SQLERRM(0)
+100	ORA-01403: no data found	SQLERRM(100)
+10	User-Defined Exception	SQLERRM(10)
NULL	ORA-0000: normal, successful completion	SQLERRM with no argument
-1	ORA-00001: unique constraint (.) violated	SQLERRM(-1)
-54	ORA-00054: resource busy and acquire with NOWAIT specified	SQLERRM(-54)

TABLE 10-3. *Log_table Contents*

The following example will raise the **e_MissingNull** user-defined exception if the "ORA-1400: mandatory NOT NULL column missing or NULL during insert" error is encountered at run time:

```
-- Available online as pragma.sql
DECLARE
  e_MissingNull EXCEPTION;
  PRAGMA EXCEPTION_INIT(e_MissingNull, -1400);
BEGIN
  INSERT INTO students (id) VALUES (NULL);
EXCEPTION
  WHEN e_MissingNull then
    INSERT INTO log_table (info) VALUES ('ORA-1400 occurred');
END;
```

Only one user-defined exception can be associated with an Oracle error with each occurrence of PRAGMA EXCEPTION_INIT. Inside the exception handler, SQLCODE and SQLERRM will return the code and message for the Oracle error which occurred, rather than the user-defined message.

Using RAISE_APPLICATION_ERROR

You can use the built-in function RAISE_APPLICATION_ERROR to create your own error messages, which can be more descriptive than named exceptions. User-defined errors are passed out of the block the same way as Oracle errors to the calling environment. The syntax of RAISE_APPLICATION_ERROR is

RAISE_APPLICATION_ERROR(*error_number, error_message,* [*keep_errors*]);

where *error_number* is a parameter between -20,000 and -20,999, *error_message* is the text associated with this error, and *keep_errors* is a boolean value. The *error_message* parameter must be fewer than 512 characters. The boolean parameter, *keep_errors*, is optional. If *keep_errors* is TRUE, the new error is added to the list of errors already raised (if one exists). If it is FALSE, which is the default, the new error will replace the current list of errors. For example, the following procedure checks to see if there is enough room in a class before registering a student:

```
-- Available online as register.sql
CREATE OR REPLACE PROCEDURE Register (
  /* Registers the student identified by the p_StudentID parameter in the class
     identified by the p_Department and p_Course parameters. Before calling
     ClassPackage.AddStudent, which actually adds the student to the class, this
     procedure verifies that there is room in the class, and that the class
     exists. */
  p_StudentID IN students.id%TYPE,
  p_Department IN classes.department%TYPE,
  p_Course IN classes.course%TYPE) AS

  v_CurrentStudents NUMBER;  -- Current number of students in the class
  v_MaxStudents NUMBER;      -- Maximum number of students in the class

BEGIN
  /* Determine the current number of students registered, and the maximum
     number of students allowed to register. */
  SELECT current_students, max_students
    INTO v_CurrentStudents, v_MaxStudents
    FROM classes
    WHERE course = p_Course
    AND department = p_Department;

  /* Make sure there is enough room for this additional student. */
  IF v_CurrentStudents + 1 > v_MaxStudents THEN
    RAISE_APPLICATION_ERROR(-20000, 'Can''t add more students to ' ||
      p_Department || ' ' || p_Course);
  END IF;

  /* Add the student to the class. */
  ClassPackage.AddStudent(p_StudentID, p_Department, p_Course);

EXCEPTION
  WHEN NO_DATA_FOUND THEN
    /* Class information passed to this procedure doesn't exist. Raise an error
       to let the calling program know of this. */
    RAISE_APPLICATION_ERROR(-20001, p_Department || ' ' || p_Course ||
      ' doesn''t exist!');
END Register;
```

The **Register** procedure uses RAISE_APPLICATION_ERROR in two different places. The first thing the procedure does is to determine the current number of students registered for the class. This is done via the SELECT..INTO statement. If this statement returns NO_DATA_FOUND, control passes to the exception handler, and RAISE_APPLICATION_ERROR is used to notify the user that the class doesn't exist. If the class does exist, the procedure then verifies that there is room for the new student. If there isn't, RAISE_APPLICATION_ERROR is again used to notify the user that there isn't enough room. Finally, if there is enough room, the student is actually added to the class. The packaged procedure **ClassPackage.AddStudent**, described in Chapter 8, does this.

Figure 10-2 shows the output when we call the **Register** procedure from SQL*Plus. Note the select statement in the figure—this shows that History 101 is full (**max_students = current_students**). So when the procedure is called, we should get an error indicating that there is no more room. This is in fact what happens, and the error is returned as:

```
ORA-20000: Can't add more students to HIS 101
```

Compare the output in Figure 10-2 to the output shown in Figure 10-3, which illustrates an anonymous block executed via SQL*Plus. This block simply raises the NO_DATA_FOUND exception. Note that predefined exceptions can also be raised explicitly, if desired. The error is returned to the screen as:

```
ORA-1403: no data found
```

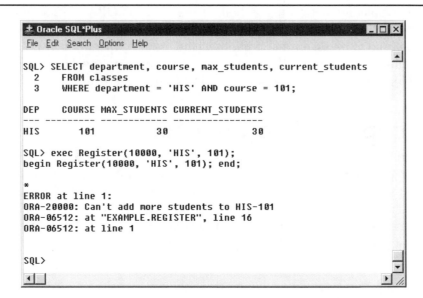

```
± Oracle SQL*Plus                                          _ □ ×
File  Edit  Search  Options  Help

SQL> SELECT department, course, max_students, current_students
  2      FROM classes
  3      WHERE department = 'HIS' AND course = 101;

DEP    COURSE MAX_STUDENTS CURRENT_STUDENTS
---    ------- ------------ ----------------
HIS       101           30               30

SQL> exec Register(10000, 'HIS', 101);
begin Register(10000, 'HIS', 101); end;

*
ERROR at line 1:
ORA-20000: Can't add more students to HIS-101
ORA-06512: at "EXAMPLE.REGISTER", line 16
ORA-06512: at line 1

SQL>
```

FIGURE 10-2.   *Results of calling the Register procedure*

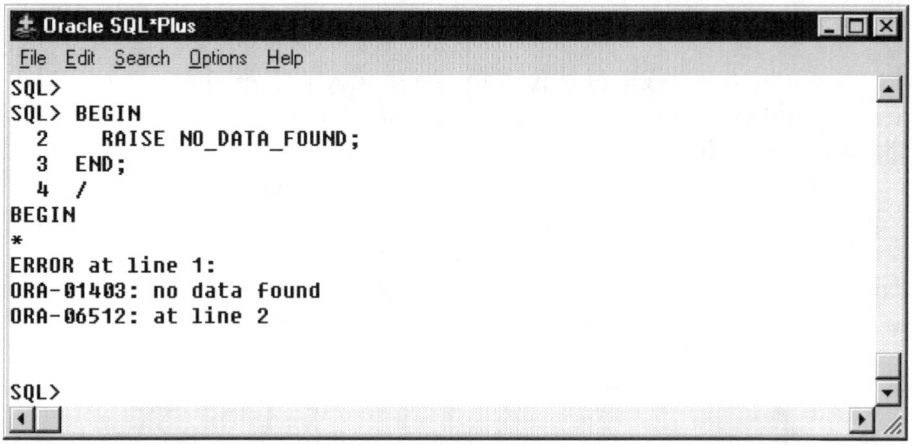

```
Oracle SQL*Plus                                    _ □ ✕
File  Edit  Search  Options  Help
SQL>                                                  ▲
SQL> BEGIN
  2     RAISE NO_DATA_FOUND;
  3  END;
  4  /
BEGIN
*
ERROR at line 1:
ORA-01403: no data found
ORA-06512: at line 2


SQL>                                                  ▼
◄ ▌                                                 ► ▌
```

FIGURE 10-3. *Results of an anonymous block that raises NO_DATA_FOUND*

The format of both outputs is the same—an Oracle error number and text associated with it. Note that both also include an ORA-6512 statement indicating the line that caused the error. So RAISE_APPLICATION_ERROR can be used to return error conditions to the user in a manner consistent with other Oracle errors. This is very useful, because no special error handling is necessary for user-defined errors versus predefined ones.

Exception Propagation

Exceptions can occur in the declarative, executable, or the exception section of a PL/SQL block. We have seen in the previous section what happens when exceptions are raised in the executable portion of the block, and there is a handler for the exception. But what if there isn't a handler, or the exception is raised from a different section of the block? The process that governs this is known as *exception propagation*.

Exceptions Raised in the Executable Section

When an exception is raised in the executable section of a block, PL/SQL uses the following algorithm to determine which exception handler to invoke.

1. If the current block has a handler for the exception, execute it and complete the block successfully. Control then passes to the enclosing block.

2. If there is no handler for the current exception, propagate the exception by raising it in the enclosing block. Step 1 will then be executed for the enclosing block.

Before we can examine this algorithm in detail, we need to define an *enclosing block*. A block can be embedded inside another block. In this case, the outer block encloses the inner block. For example:

```
DECLARE
    -- Begin outer block.
    ...
BEGIN
    ...
    DECLARE
      -- Begin inner block 1. This is embedded in the outer block.
    ...
    BEGIN
      ...
    END;
    ...
    BEGIN
      -- Begin inner block 2. This is also embedded in the outer block.
      -- Note that this block doesn't have a declarative part.
      ...
    END;
    ...
    -- End outer block.
END;
```

In the preceding listing, inner blocks 1 and 2 are both enclosed by the outer block. Any unhandled exceptions in blocks 1 and 2 will be propagated to the outer block.

A procedure call will also create an enclosing block, and is illustrated in the following example.

```
BEGIN
    -- Begin outer block.
    -- Call a procedure. The procedure will be enclosed by this outer block.
    F(...);
END;
```

If procedure **F** raises an unhandled exception, it will be propagated to the outer block, since it encloses the procedure.

Different cases for the exception propagation algorithm are illustrated in examples 1, 2, and 3, in the following sections.

Propagation Example 1

The example shown here illustrates application of rule 1. Exception A is raised and handled in the sub-block. Control then returns to the outer block.

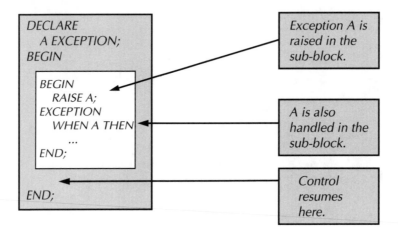

Propagation Example 2

In this example, rule 2 is applied for the sub-block. The exception is propagated to the enclosing block, where rule 1 is applied. The enclosing block then completes successfully.

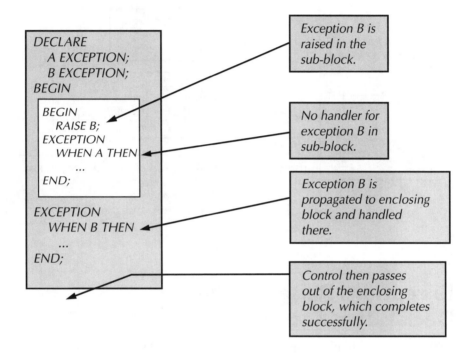

```
DECLARE
    A EXCEPTION;
    B EXCEPTION;
BEGIN

    BEGIN
        RAISE B;
    EXCEPTION
        WHEN A THEN
            ...
    END;

EXCEPTION
    WHEN B THEN
        ...
END;
```

Exception B is raised in the sub-block.

No handler for exception B in sub-block.

Exception B is propagated to enclosing block and handled there.

Control then passes out of the enclosing block, which completes successfully.

Propagation Example 3

Here, rule 2 is applied for the sub-block. The exception is propagated to the enclosing block, where there is still no handler for it. Rule 2 is applied again, and the enclosing block completes unsuccessfully with an unhandled exception.

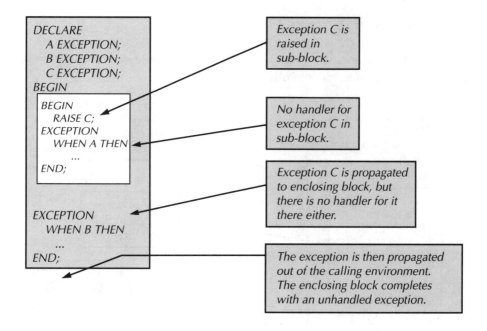

Exceptions Raised in the Declarative Section

If an assignment in the declarative section raises an exception, the exception is immediately propagated to the enclosing block. Once there, the rules given in the previous section are applied to propagate the exception further. Even if there is a handler in the current block, it is *not* executed. Examples 4 and 5 illustrate this.

Propagation Example 4

In this example, the VALUE_ERROR exception is raised by the declaration

```
v_Number NUMBER(3) := 'ABC';
```

This exception is immediately propagated to the enclosing block. Even though there is an OTHERS exception, it is not executed. If this block had been enclosed in an outer block, the outer block would have been able to catch this exception. (Example 5 illustrates this scenario.)

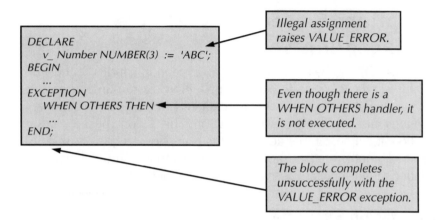

Propagation Example 5

Similar to example 4, the VALUE_ERROR exception is raised in the declarative section of the inner block. The exception is immediately propagated to the outer block. Since the outer block has an OTHERS exception handler, the exception is handled and the outer block completes successfully.

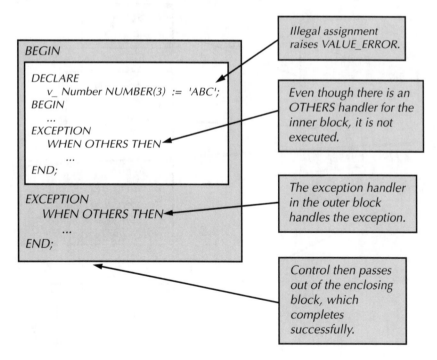

Exceptions Raised in the Exception Section

Exceptions can also be raised while in an exception handler, either explicitly via the RAISE statement or implicitly via a run-time error. In either case, the exception is propagated immediately to the enclosing block, like exceptions raised in the declarative section. This is done because only one exception at a time can be "active" in the exception section. As soon as one is handled, another can be raised. But there cannot be more than one exception raised simultaneously. Examples 6, 7, and 8 illustrate this scenario.

Propagation Example 6

In this example, exception A is raised and then handled. But in the exception handler for A, exception B is raised. This exception is immediately propagated to the outer block, bypassing the handler for B. Similar to example 5, if this block had been enclosed in an outer block, this outer block could have caught exception B. (Example 7 illustrates the latter case.)

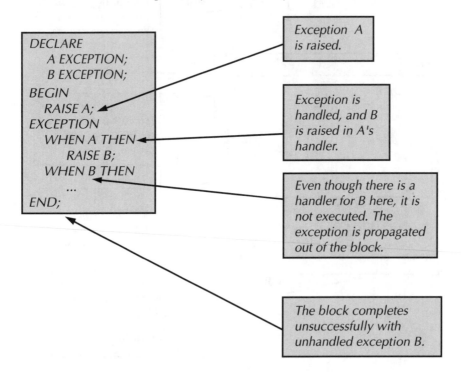

Propagation Example 7

Similar to example 6, exception B is raised in the handler for exception A. This exception is immediately propagated to the enclosing block, bypassing the inner handler for B. However, in example 7 we have an outer block that handles exception B and completes successfully.

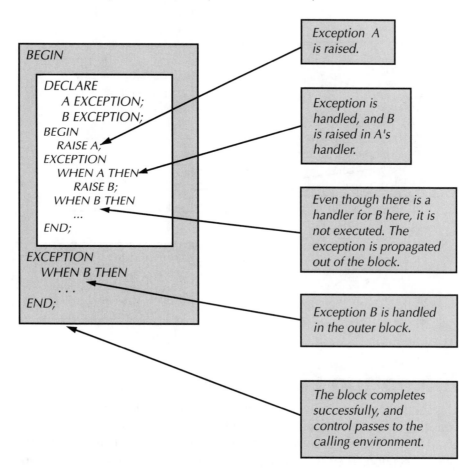

```
BEGIN

    DECLARE
        A EXCEPTION;
        B EXCEPTION;
    BEGIN
        RAISE A;
    EXCEPTION
        WHEN A THEN
            RAISE B;
        WHEN B THEN
            ...
    END;

EXCEPTION
    WHEN B THEN
        . . .
END;
```

*Exception A
is raised.*

*Exception is
handled, and B
is raised in A's
handler.*

*Even though there is a
handler for B here, it is
not executed. The
exception is propagated
out of the block.*

*Exception B is handled
in the outer block.*

*The block completes
successfully, and
control passes to the
calling environment.*

Propagation Example 8

As examples 6 and 7 illustrate, RAISE can be used to raise another exception inside a handler. In an exception handler, RAISE can also be used without an argument. If RAISE doesn't have an argument, the current exception is propagated to the enclosing block. This technique is useful for logging the error and/or doing any necessary cleanup because of it, and then notifying the enclosing block that it occurred. We will see this technique again in Chapter 18, with the UTL_FILE package. Example 8 illustrates this final scenario.

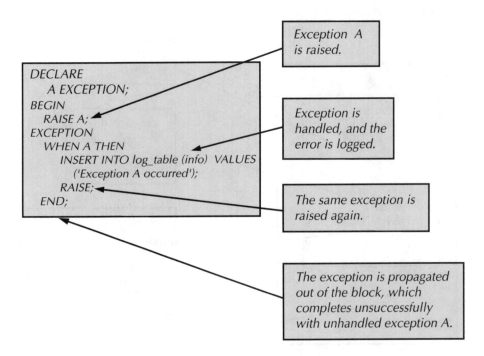

```
DECLARE
    A EXCEPTION;
BEGIN
    RAISE A;
EXCEPTION
    WHEN A THEN
        INSERT INTO log_table (info)  VALUES
        ('Exception A occurred');
    RAISE;
END;
```

Exception A is raised.

Exception is handled, and the error is logged.

The same exception is raised again.

The exception is propagated out of the block, which completes unsuccessfully with unhandled exception A.

Exception Guidelines

This section contains guidelines and tips on how best to use exceptions in your programs. These guidelines include the scope of exceptions, how to avoid unhandled exceptions, and how to identify which statement raised a given exception. They should help you use exceptions more effectively in your own programs, and avoid some common pitfalls.

Scope of Exceptions

Exceptions are scoped just like variables. If a user-defined exception is propagated out of its scope, it can no longer be referenced by name. The next listing illustrates this.

```
DECLARE
  ...
BEGIN
  ...
  DECLARE
    e_UserDefinedException EXCEPTION;
  BEGIN
    RAISE e_UserDefinedException;
  END;
EXCEPTION
  /* e_UserDefinedException is out of scope here - can only be handled
     by an OTHERS handler */
  WHEN OTHERS THEN
    /* Handle error */
END;
```

In general, if a user-defined error is to be propagated out of a block, it is best to define the exception in a package so that it will still be visible outside the block, or to use RAISE_APPLICATION_ERROR instead. See the section "Using RAISE_APPLICATION_ERROR" earlier in this chapter for more information. If we create a package called **Globals** and define **e_UserDefinedException** in this package, the exception will still be visible in the outer block. For example:

```
CREATE OR REPLACE PACKAGE Globals
  /* This package contains global declarations. Objects declared here will be
     visible via qualified references for any other blocks or procedures.
     Note that this package does not have a package body. */

  /* A user-defined exception. */
  e_UserDefinedException EXCEPTION;
END Globals;
```

Given package **Globals**, we can rewrite the preceding listing as:

```
DECLARE
  ...
BEGIN
  ...
  BEGIN
    /* Note that we must qualify e_UserDefinedException with the package name */
    RAISE Globals.e_UserDefinedException;
  END;
EXCEPTION
```

```
    /* Since e_UserDefinedException is still visible, we can handle it explicitly */
    WHEN Globals.e_UserDefinedException THEN
      /* Handle error */
END;
```

Package **Globals** can also be used for common PL/SQL tables, variables, and types, in addition to exceptions. See Chapter 8 for more information on packages.

Avoiding Unhandled Exceptions

It is good programming practice to avoid unhandled exceptions. This can be done via an OTHERS handler at the topmost level of your program. This handler may simply log the error and where it occurred. This way, you ensure that no error will go undetected. For example:

```
DECLARE
    v_ErrorNumber NUMBER;        -- Variable to hold the error number
    v_ErrorText VARCHAR2(200);   -- Variable to hold the error message text
BEGIN
  /* Normal PL/SQL processing */
  ...
EXCEPTION
  WHEN OTHERS THEN
    /* Log all exceptions so we complete successfully */
    v_ErrorNumber := SQLCODE;
    v_ErrorText := SUBSTR(SQLERRM, 1, 200);
    INSERT INTO log_table (code, message, info) VALUES
      (v_ErrorNumber, v_ErrorText, 'Oracle error occurred at ' ||
      TO_CHAR(SYSDATE, 'DD-MON-YY HH24:MI:SS'));
END;
```

Masking Location of the Error

Since the same exception section is examined for the entire block, it can be difficult to determine which SQL statement caused the error. Consider the following example:

```
BEGIN
    SELECT ...
    SELECT ...
    SELECT ...
```

```
EXCEPTION
  WHEN NO_DATA_FOUND THEN
    -- Which select statement raised the exception?
END;
```

There are two methods to solve this. The first is to increment a counter identifying the SQL statement:

```
DECLARE
  v_SelectCounter NUMBER := 1;  -- Variable to hold the select statement number
BEGIN
  SELECT ...
  v_SelectCounter := 2;
  SELECT ...
  v_SelectCounter := 3;
  SELECT ...
EXCEPTION
  WHEN NO_DATA_FOUND THEN
    INSERT INTO log_table (info) VALUES ('No data found in select ' ||
      v_SelectCounter);
END;
```

The second method is to put each statement into its own sub-block:

```
BEGIN
  BEGIN
    SELECT ...
  EXCEPTION
    WHEN NO_DATA_FOUND THEN
      INSERT INTO log_table (info) VALUES ('No data found in select 1;);
  END;
  BEGIN
    SELECT ...
  EXCEPTION
    WHEN NO_DATA_FOUND THEN
      INSERT INTO log_table (info) VALUES ('No data found in select 2');
  END;
  BEGIN
    SELECT ...
  EXCEPTION
    WHEN NO_DATA_FOUND THEN
      INSERT INTO log_table (info) VALUES ('No data found in select 3');
  END;
END;
```

PL/SQL at Work: A General Error Handler

One problem with exceptions is that when an exception occurs, there is no easy way to tell what part of the code was executing at the time. PL/SQL does provide a solution to this, with the DBMS_UTILITY.FORMAT_CALL_ STACK function. This built-in function will return the current call stack, as a VARCHAR2 value. Consider the following example, with procedures **A**, **B**, and **C**:

```
-- Available online as abc1.sql
CREATE OR REPLACE PROCEDURE C AS
  v_CallStack VARCHAR2(2000);
BEGIN
    v_CallStack := DBMS_UTILITY.FORMAT_CALL_STACK;
    INSERT INTO temp_table (char_col) VALUES (v_CallStack);
    INSERT INTO temp_table (num_col)
      VALUES (-1);
END C;
CREATE OR REPLACE PROCEDURE B AS
BEGIN
  C;
END B;
CREATE OR REPLACE PROCEDURE A AS
BEGIN
  B;
END A;
```

Note that **A** calls **B**, which calls **C**. If we call procedure **A**, and select from temp_table, we get:

```
----- PL/SQL Call Stack -----
  object     line  object
  handle   number  name
  16998f0       4  procedure EXAMPLE.C
  1699ca0       3  procedure EXAMPLE.B
  169f918       3  procedure EXAMPLE.A
  1667ef0       1  anonymous block
```

Similar to CALL_STACK, DBMS_UTILITY_FORMAT_ERROR_STACK will return the current sequence of errors. Given these two functions, we can write a general error handler that will record both the location of an error and what the error is.

Here are the table definitions necessary for this package:

```
-- Available online as e_tables.sql
CREATE TABLE errors (
  module        VARCHAR2(50),
  seq_number    NUMBER,
  error_number  NUMBER,
  error_mesg    VARCHAR2(100),
  error_stack   VARCHAR2(2000),
  call_stack    VARCHAR2(2000),
  timestamp     DATE,
  PRIMARY KEY (module, seq_number));

CREATE TABLE call_stacks (
  module        VARCHAR2(50),
  seq_number    NUMBER,
  call_order    NUMBER,
  object_handle VARCHAR2(10),
  line_num      NUMBER,
  object_name   VARCHAR2(80),
  PRIMARY KEY (module, seq_number, call_order),
  FOREIGN KEY (module, seq_number) REFERENCES errors ON DELETE CASCADE);

DROP TABLE error_stacks;
CREATE TABLE error_stacks (
  module        VARCHAR2(50),
  seq_number    NUMBER,
  error_order   NUMBER,
  facility      CHAR(3),
  error_number  NUMBER(5),
  error_mesg    VARCHAR2(100),
  PRIMARY KEY (module, seq_number, error_order),
  FOREIGN KEY (module, seq_number) REFERENCES errors ON DELETE CASCADE);


CREATE SEQUENCE error_seq
  START WITH 1
  INCREMENT BY 1;
```

Given the above definitions, here is the **ErrorPkg** package:

```
-- Available online as e.pkg.sql
CREATE OR REPLACE PACKAGE ErrorPkg AS
  /* Generic error-handling package, using DBMS_UTILITY.FORMAT_ERROR_STACK
     and DBMS_UTILITY.FORMAT_CALL_STACK.  This package will store general
     error information in the errors table, with detailed call stack and
     error stack information in the call_stacks and error_stacks tables,
     respectively. */

  - Entry point for handling errors.  HandleAll should be called from all
  - exception handlers where you want the error to be logged.  p_Top should be
  - TRUE only at the topmost level of procedure nesting.  It should be FALSE
  - at other levels.  See error_readme.txt for details on usage.
  PROCEDURE HandleAll(p_Top BOOLEAN);

  - Prints the error and call stacks (using DBMS_OUTPUT) for the given
  - module and sequence number.
  PROCEDURE PrintStacks(p_Module IN errors.module%TYPE,
                        p_SeqNum IN errors.seq_number%TYPE);

  - Unwinds the call and error stacks, and stores them in the errors and
  - call_stacks tables.  Returns the sequence number under which the
  - error is stored.
  - If p_CommitFlag is TRUE, then the inserts are committed.
  - In order to use StoreStacks, an error must have been handled.  Thus
  - HandleAll should have been called with p_Top = TRUE.
  PROCEDURE StoreStacks(p_Module IN errors.module%TYPE,
                        p_SeqNum OUT errors.seq_number%TYPE,
                        p_CommitFlag BOOLEAN DEFAULT FALSE);
END ErrorPkg;


CREATE OR REPLACE PACKAGE BODY ErrorPkg AS

  v_NewLine    CONSTANT CHAR(1) := CHR(10);

  v_Handled    BOOLEAN := FALSE;
  v_ErrorStack VARCHAR2(2000);
  v_CallStack  VARCHAR2(2000);

  PROCEDURE HandleAll(p_Top BOOLEAN) IS
  BEGIN
    IF p_Top THEN
      v_Handled := FALSE;
    ELSIF NOT v_Handled THEN
      v_Handled := TRUE;
```

```
      v_ErrorStack := DBMS_UTILITY.FORMAT_ERROR_STACK;
      v_CallStack := DBMS_UTILITY.FORMAT_CALL_STACK;
   END IF;
END HandleAll;

PROCEDURE PrintStacks(p_Module IN errors.module%TYPE,
                      p_SeqNum IN errors.seq_number%TYPE) IS
   v_TimeStamp errors.timestamp%TYPE;
   v_ErrorMsg  errors.error_mesg%TYPE;

   CURSOR c_CallCur IS
     SELECT object_handle, line_num, object_name
       FROM call_stacks
       WHERE module = p_Module
       AND seq_number = p_SeqNum
       ORDER BY call_order;

   CURSOR c_ErrorCur IS
     SELECT facility, error_number, error_mesg
       FROM error_stacks
       WHERE module = p_Module
       AND seq_number = p_SeqNum
       ORDER BY error_order;
BEGIN
   SELECT timestamp, error_mesg
     INTO v_TimeStamp, v_ErrorMsg
     FROM errors
     WHERE module = p_Module
     AND seq_number = p_SeqNum;

   -- Output general error information.
   DBMS_OUTPUT.PUT(TO_CHAR(v_TimeStamp, 'DD-MON-YY HH24:MI:SS'));
   DBMS_OUTPUT.PUT('  Module: ' || p_Module);
   DBMS_OUTPUT.PUT('  Error #' || p_SeqNum || ':  ');
   DBMS_OUTPUT.PUT_LINE(v_ErrorMsg);

   -- Output the call stack.
   DBMS_OUTPUT.PUT_LINE('Complete Call Stack:');
   DBMS_OUTPUT.PUT_LINE('  Object Handle  Line Number  Object Name');
   DBMS_OUTPUT.PUT_LINE('  -------------  -----------  -----------');
   FOR v_CallRec in c_CallCur LOOP
     DBMS_OUTPUT.PUT(RPAD('  ' || v_CallRec.object_handle, 15));
     DBMS_OUTPUT.PUT(RPAD('  ' || TO_CHAR(v_CallRec.line_num), 13));
     DBMS_OUTPUT.PUT_LINE('  ' || v_CallRec.object_name);
   END LOOP;
```

```
  — Output the error stack.
  DBMS_OUTPUT.PUT_LINE('Complete Error Stack:');
  FOR v_ErrorRec in c_ErrorCur LOOP
    DBMS_OUTPUT.PUT('  ' || v_ErrorRec.facility || '-');
    DBMS_OUTPUT.PUT(TO_CHAR(v_ErrorRec.error_number) || ': ');
    DBMS_OUTPUT.PUT_LINE(v_ErrorRec.error_mesg);
  END LOOP;

END PrintStacks;

PROCEDURE StoreStacks(p_Module IN errors.module%TYPE,
                      p_SeqNum OUT errors.seq_number%TYPE,
                      p_CommitFlag BOOLEAN DEFAULT FALSE) IS
  v_SeqNum      NUMBER;

  v_Index       NUMBER;
  v_Length      NUMBER;
  v_End         NUMBER;

  v_Call        VARCHAR2(100);
  v_CallOrder   NUMBER := 1;
  v_Handle      call_stacks.object_handle%TYPE;
  v_LineNum     call_stacks.line_num%TYPE;
  v_ObjectName  call_stacks.object_name%TYPE;

  v_Error       VARCHAR2(120);
  v_ErrorOrder  NUMBER := 1;
  v_Facility    error_stacks.facility%TYPE;
  v_ErrNum      error_stacks.error_number%TYPE;
  v_ErrMsg      error_stacks.error_mesg%TYPE;

  v_FirstErrNum errors.error_number%TYPE;
  v_FirstErrMsg errors.error_mesg%TYPE;
BEGIN
  — First get the error sequence number.
  SELECT error_seq.nextval
    INTO v_SeqNum
    FROM dual;

  p_SeqNum := v_SeqNum;

  — Insert the first part of the header information into the errors table.
  INSERT INTO errors
    (module, seq_number, error_stack, call_stack, timestamp)
  VALUES
```

```
     (p_Module, v_SeqNum, v_ErrorStack, v_CallStack, SYSDATE);

— Unwind the error stack to get each error out.  We do this by scanning
— the error stack string.  Start with the index at the beginning of the
— string.
v_Index := 1;

— Loop through the string, finding each newline.  A newline ends each
— error on the stack.
WHILE v_Index <  LENGTH(v_ErrorStack) LOOP
  — v_End is the position of the newline.
  v_End := INSTR(v_ErrorStack, v_NewLine, v_Index);

  — Thus, the error is between the current index and the newline.
  v_Error := SUBSTR(v_ErrorStack, v_Index, v_End - v_Index);

  — Skip over the current error, for the next iteration.
  v_Index := v_Index + LENGTH(v_Error) + 1;

  — An error looks like 'facility-number: mesg'.  We need to get each
  — piece out for insertion.

  — First, the facility is the first 3 characters of the error.
  v_Facility := SUBSTR(v_Error, 1, 3);

  — Remove the facility and the dash (always 4 characters).
  v_Error := SUBSTR(v_Error, 5);
  — Now we can get the error number.
  v_ErrNum := TO_NUMBER(SUBSTR(v_Error, 1, INSTR(v_Error, ':') - 1));

  — Remove the error number, colon and space (always 7 characters).
  v_Error := SUBSTR(v_Error, 8);

  — What's left is the error message.
  v_ErrMsg := v_Error;

  — Insert the errors, and grab the first error number and message
  — while we're at it.
  INSERT INTO error_stacks
     (module, seq_number, error_order, facility, error_number, error_mesg)
  VALUES
     (p_Module, p_SeqNum, v_ErrorOrder, v_Facility, v_ErrNum, v_ErrMsg);

  IF v_ErrorOrder = 1 THEN
    v_FirstErrNum := v_ErrNum;
```

```
      v_FirstErrMsg := v_Facility || '-' || TO_NUMBER(v_ErrNum) ||
                      ': ' || v_ErrMsg;
  END IF;

  v_ErrorOrder := v_ErrorOrder + 1;
END LOOP;

- Update the errors table with the message and code.
UPDATE errors
  SET error_number = v_FirstErrNum,
      error_mesg = v_FirstErrMsg
  WHERE module = p_Module
  AND seq_number = v_SeqNum;

- Now we need to unwind the call stack, to get each call out.  We do this
- by scanning the call stack string.  Start with the index after the
- first call on the stack.  This will be after the first occurrence of
- 'name' and the newline.
v_Index := INSTR(v_CallStack, 'name') + 5;

- Loop through the string, finding each newline.  A newline ends each
- call on the stack.
WHILE v_Index <  LENGTH(v_CallStack) LOOP
  - v_End is the position of the newline.
  v_End := INSTR(v_CallStack, v_NewLine, v_Index);

  - Thus, the call is between the current index and the newline.
  v_Call := SUBSTR(v_CallStack, v_Index, v_End - v_Index);

  - Skip over the current call, for the next iteration.
  v_Index := v_Index + LENGTH(v_Call) + 1;

  - Within a call, we have the object handle, then the line number, then
  - the object name, separated by spaces.  We need to separate them
  - out for insertion.

  - Trim white space from the call first.
  v_Call := LTRIM(v_Call);

  - First get the object handle.
  v_Handle := SUBSTR(v_Call, 1, INSTR(v_Call, ' '));

   - Now, remove the object handle, then the white space from the call.
  v_Call := SUBSTR(v_Call, LENGTH(v_Handle) + 1);
  v_Call := LTRIM(v_Call);
```

```
      -- Now we can get the line number.
      v_LineNum := TO_NUMBER(SUBSTR(v_Call, 1, INSTR(v_Call, ' ')));

      -- Remove the line number, and white space.
      v_Call := SUBSTR(v_Call, LENGTH(v_LineNum) + 1);
      v_Call := LTRIM(v_Call);

      -- What is left is the object name.
      v_ObjectName := v_Call;

      -- Insert all calls except the call for ErrorPkg.
      IF v_CallOrder > 1 THEN
        INSERT INTO call_stacks
           (module, seq_number, call_order, object_handle, line_num, object_name)
        VALUES
          (p_Module, v_SeqNum, v_CallOrder, v_Handle, v_LineNum, v_ObjectName);
      END IF;

      v_Callorder := v_CallOrder + 1;

    END LOOP;

    IF p_CommitFlag THEN
      commit;
    END IF;
  END StoreStacks;
END ErrorPkg;
```

Now, suppose we put a trigger on **temp_table** to raise the
ZERO_DIVIDE exception, and modify **A**, **B**, and **C** as follows:

-- **Available online as abc2.sql**

```
CREATE OR REPLACE TRIGGER temp_insert
  BEFORE INSERT ON temp_table
BEGIN
  RAISE ZERO_DIVIDE;
END ttt_insert;

CREATE OR REPLACE PROCEDURE C AS
BEGIN
  INSERT INTO temp_table (num_col) VALUES (7);
EXCEPTION
  WHEN OTHERS THEN
    ErrorPkg.HandleAll(FALSE);
    RAISE;
```

```
END C;

CREATE OR REPLACE PROCEDURE B AS
BEGIN
  C;
EXCEPTION
  WHEN OTHERS THEN
    ErrorPkg.HandleAll(FALSE);
    RAISE;
END B;

CREATE OR REPLACE PROCEDURE A AS
  v_ErrorSeq NUMBER;
BEGIN
  B;
EXCEPTION
  WHEN OTHERS THEN
    ErrorPkg.HandleAll(TRUE);
    ErrorPkg.StoreStacks('Error Test', v_ErrorSeq, TRUE);
    ErrorPkg.PrintStacks('Error Test', v_ErrorSeq);
END A;
```

The important thing to note is that, except for the top level (procedure **A**), all of the exception handlers look like

```
WHEN OTHERS THEN
   ErrorPkg.HandleAll(FALSE);
RAISE;
```

This tells **ErrorPkg** to record the call and error stack if necessary, then propagate the error out to the calling procedure. At the lop level, **HandleAll** should be called with TRUE. This tells **ErrorPkg** that it is at the top level, and that no more propagating will occur. **StoreStacks** then stores the call and error stacks in the **errors**, **error_stacks**, and **call_stacks** tables, indexed by a module name. The module should be the name of the package, or other determining identifier. All errors are stored using both the module name, and the error number, which is returned by **StoreStacks**. A call to **PrintStacks** will query the error tables and print the results using DBMS_OUTPUT. For example, if we call **A** from SQL*Plus we see the following:

```
SQL> SET SERVEROUTPUT ON SIZE 1000000 FORMAT TRUNCATED
SQL> EXEC A;
18-JAN-97 22:14:49  Module: Error Test  Error #7:  ORA-1476: divisor is equal to zero
Complete Call Stack:
  Object Handle  Line Number  Object Name
  -------------  -----------  -----------
    16998f0          6         procedure EXAMPLE.C
    1699ca0          3         procedure EXAMPLE.B
    169f918          4         procedure EXAMPLE.A
    16570e0          1         anonymous block
Complete Error Stack:
  ORA-1476: divisor is equal to zero
  ORA-6512: at "EXAMPLE.TEMP_INSERT", line 2
  ORA-4088: error during execution of trigger 'EXAMPLE.TEMP_INSERT'

PL/SQL procedure successfully completed.
```

Summary

This chapter explained how PL/SQL programs can detect and react intelligently to run-time errors. The mechanism provided by PL/SQL to do this includes exceptions and exception handlers. We have seen how exceptions are defined and how they correspond to either user-defined errors or predefined Oracle errors. We have also discussed the rules for exception propagation, including exceptions raised in all parts of a PL/SQL block. The chapter concluded with guidelines on using exceptions.

CHAPTER
11

Objects

bjects are one of the main new features of Oracle8 and PL/SQL 8. In this chapter, we will see how to create and use objects, including methods and constructors, along with object references. We will also discuss the implications of storing objects in the database, including how to manipulate objects in DML statements.

Background

Before we can introduce Oracle's implementation of objects, we need to discuss the fundamentals of object-oriented design and methodology. A full discussion of this paradigm is beyond the scope of this book; however, we can cover the fundamentals here. Once we understand the fundamentals of this design philosophy, we will discuss Oracle's implementation of object types in the following sections.

Basis of Object-Oriented Programming

Why do we write computer applications? One possible answer to this question is to model the real world. A software system is designed to simulate both the objects that exist in the world, and the interactions between them. Once the objects and interactions are modeled, the application can be used to track how they evolve, and automate the processes involved. An order entry system, for example, allows a salesperson to concentrate on making a sale, by providing him or her with all the necessary information and then handling the interactions with other departments, such as accounts receivable and shipping.

Consider a university. What are the entities in this world? We have students, who communicate with the registrar to sign up for classes. The registrar informs professors of students' registrations for their classes. Professors communicate with students during the class and when they assign grades. The people who run the university bookstore need to know from the professors which books they want for their classes, and then they make the books available to the students. This model is illustrated in Figure 11-1. The circles in the figure represent the entities involved (students, registrar, professors, and the bookstore), and the arrows represent interactions between the entities, such as a student purchasing a book from the bookstore.

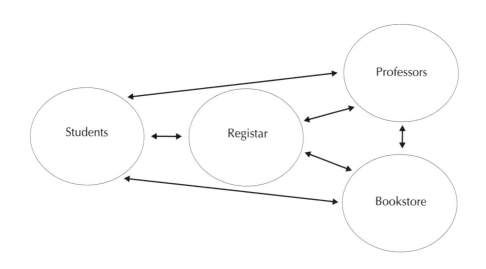

FIGURE 11-1. *A model of a university*

This is a reasonable model. By examining the model, we can determine information about the real world. For example, we can see that the registrar is centrally involved because all of the other entities need to communicate with the registrar.

Object-oriented design essentially turns this model directly into a computer application. Each of the entities is represented by an object in the system. An object represents the attributes of the real-world entity and operations that act on those attributes. Consider the student object represented in Figure 11-2. A student has *attributes*, such as first and last name, major, and current credits. The operations that act on these attributes are also included, such as **ChangeMajor** (which modifies the major) and **UpdateCredits** (which adds credits to the student's record for completed classes). The operations are known as *methods*.

Objects can communicate with each other by invoking methods. For example, the registrar can invoke the **UpdateCredits** method for a particular student after that student has passed a class.

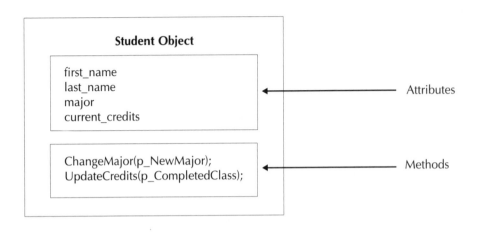

FIGURE 11-2. *A Student Object*

Abstraction

The attributes and methods of an object neatly implement both data and procedural abstraction, as we discussed in Chapter 8 for packages. Ideally, a client using a given object manipulates the attributes only through the methods. By doing this, the client application does not have to know the actual implementation of the methods, and can just call them.

Objects vs. Object Instances

It is important to note the difference between an object type itself, and an *instance* of that type. There can be only one object type in a given environment, but many instances of it. An object instance is similar to a variable—each instance has its own memory, and thus its own copy of the attributes. For example, Figure 11-3 illustrates two instances of the **StudentObj** type. This is analogous to two different PL/SQL records declared of the same type.

Object-Relational Databases

Many object-oriented programming languages are available, including C++ and Java. Programming languages like this allow you to define objects and

Object 1	Object 2
first_name: Scott last_name: Smith major: Computer Science current_credits: 4	first_name: Margaret last_name: Mason major: History current_credits: 8

FIGURE 11-3. *Instances of StudentObj*

manipulate them. What they are lacking, however, is persistence—the ability to store and retrieve objects in a safe, consistent way. This is where object-relational databases such as Oracle8 come in. Oracle8 is designed to store and retrieve object data just as it does relational data, by using SQL as the standard way of communicating with the database. In an object-relational database, SQL (and PL/SQL) can be used to manipulate both relational and object data. Oracle8 also provides the advantages of consistent transactional control, secure backup and recovery, excellent query performance, locking and concurrency, and scalability. By combining objects with the relational model, we have the best of both worlds—the power and reliability of a relational database along with the flexibility and modeling capabilities of objects.

In the rest of this chapter, we will see how Oracle8 implements object storage and retrieval. We will discuss how to create objects and methods, as well as the data structures available for storing them in the database—object tables. We will also see how object views allow relational data to be represented as an object, which is a valuable tool for migrating existing Oracle7 data models.

Object Types

PL/SQL **8.0** ...and HIGHER Objects are created in Oracle8 with *object types*. The object type describes both the attributes and the methods associated with a particular kind of object. In the next few sections, we will see how to create and use object types. Before you can use objects, however, the *objects option* is required. When you connect to an Oracle8 database, you should see a message something like the following:

```
Oracle8 Enterprise Edition Release 8.0.3.0.0 - Production
With the Partitioning and Objects options
PL/SQL Release 8.0.3.0.0 - Production
```

If you don't see the objects option in the version information line, it has not been installed. Consequently, you will not be able to create and use object types. If this is the case, the Oracle executable may have to be relinked with the objects option, by using the Oracle installer. Check the installation and user's guide for your system for more information. In the rest of this chapter, it is assumed that you have the objects option available.

Defining Object Types

An object type is similar to a package—it has both a specification and body. The type specification contains the attributes and forward declarations for the methods. The type body contains the actual code for the methods. The syntax for creating a type specification is below; the syntax for creating the type body is in the section "Methods" later in this chapter.

Object type specifications are defined with the CREATE TYPE ... AS OBJECT statement, the syntax of which is

> CREATE [OR REPLACE] TYPE [*schema.*]*type_name* AS OBJECT (
>   *attribute_name datatype*[, *attribute_name datatype*]...
> | [{MAP | ORDER} MEMBER *function_specification*]
> | [MEMBER {*procedure_specification* | *function_specification*}
>   [, MEMBER {*procedure_specification* | *function_specification*}]...]
> | [PRAGMA RESTRICT_REFERENCES (*method_name, constraints*)
>   [, PRAGMA RESTRICT_REFERENCES (*method_name, constraints*)]...]
>);

where *type_name* is the name of the new object type, and *schema* is the owner. The object type attributes are listed first, with a comma-separated list of pairs like

> *attribute_name datatype*

where *attribute_name* is the name of an attribute, and *datatype* is either a built-in Oracle datatype, an already defined user-defined datatype, or a reference to an object type (see the section "Object Identifiers and Object References" later in this chapter for more information on object references). The methods are specified following the attributes, along with any PRAGMA RESTRICT_REFERENCES statements for them, as described in Chapter 8. We will examine the syntax for creating methods, including the special MAP and ORDER methods, in the "Methods" section.

For example, the following statement creates a type that can represent a student:

```
-- Available online as part of tables8.sql
CREATE OR REPLACE TYPE StudentObj AS OBJECT(
  ID                NUMBER(5),
  first_name        VARCHAR2(20),
  last_name         VARCHAR2(20),
  major             VARCHAR2(30),
  current_credits   NUMBER(3)
  );
```

NOTE
The tables8.sql script (available as part of the online distribution) creates all of the types and their methods described in this chapter. Consequently, the examples given in this and later sections are only part of this file. Tables8.sql redefines many of the example tables in this book (including **students** *and* **classes***). The new tables are used only in the Oracle8 chapters—11, 12, 17, 20, and 21.*

TIP
*When creating a type specification (or type body) using SQL*Plus, you must include a forward slash on the line following the type definition to execute the CREATE TYPE ... AS OBJECT statement, similar to executing a PL/SQL block.*

There are several things to note about object types:

1. The CREATE TYPE statement is a DDL statement. As such, it can't be used directly in a PL/SQL block. You can, however, use the DBMS_SQL package (described in Chapter 15) to execute the CREATE TYPE statement.

2. You must have the CREATE TYPE system privilege (which is part of the RESOURCE role) in order to create an object type.

3. Object types are created as data dictionary objects. Consequently, they are created in the current schema, unless a different schema is specified in the CREATE TYPE ... AS OBJECT statement.

4. The attributes of the newly created type are specified similar to the fields of a PL/SQL record, or the columns of a table in the CREATE TABLE statement.

5. Unlike record fields, the attributes of an object type cannot be constrained to be NOT NULL, nor can they be initialized to a default value.

6. Like a PL/SQL record, you can refer to the attributes within an object using dot notation.

There are also several restrictions on the datatype of object attributes. Object attributes can be any Oracle8 datatype except:

- A LONG or LONG RAW. They can be a LOB type (described in Chapter 21), however.

- Any national language type, such as NCHAR, NVARCHAR2, or NCLOB.

- ROWID.

- Types available only in PL/SQL but not in the database. These include BINARY_INTEGER, BOOLEAN, PLS_INTEGER, RECORD, and REF CURSOR.

■ A type defined with %TYPE or %ROWTYPE.

■ Types defined within a PL/SQL package.

The reason for these restrictions is that an object type, as defined for Oracle Release 8, is a data dictionary object. Thus, only features and types available directly to the database are legal. PL/SQL types and constructs like %TYPE are not allowed. These restrictions will likely be lifted in future releases of Oracle8, when an object type can be declared local to a PL/SQL block as well as in the data dictionary.

Declaring and Initializing Objects

Just like any other PL/SQL variable, an object is declared simply by placing it syntactically after its type in the declarative section of the block, for example:

```
DECLARE
  v_Student StudentObj;
```

The above block declares **v_Student** as an instance of the object type **StudentObj**. In accordance with the rules of PL/SQL, an object instance declared in this manner is initialized to NULL. Note that the entire object is NULL, not necessarily the attributes within it. If an object is NULL in this manner, it is illegal to refer to an attribute within it. NULL issues with objects are described in the next section, "Object NULL vs. Attribute NULL".

Initializing Objects

How then do you initialize objects? This is done with a constructor. A *constructor* is a function that returns an initialized object and takes as arguments the values for the object's attributes. For every object type, Oracle predefines a constructor with the same name as the type. For example, the **StudentObj** constructor would have the following specification:

```
FUNCTION StudentObj(ID IN NUMBER,
                    first_name IN VARCHAR2,
                    last_name IN VARCHAR2,
                    major IN VARCHAR2,
                    current_credits IN NUMBER)
     RETURN StudentObj;
```

NOTE
The constructor is not explicitly defined. However, it can be thought of as having the specification above. The name of the constructor is the same as the name of the object type.

We can therefore create an initialized instance of a **StudentObj**, and refer to its attributes, as follows:

```
-- Available online as objinit.sql
DECLARE
   -- Creates the object instance, with the attributes set.
   v_Student StudentObj :=
     StudentObj(10020, 'Chuck', 'Choltry', NULL, 0);
BEGIN
   -- Modifies the major attribute to 'Music'.  Note the use of
   -- dot notation to refer to the attribute.
   v_Student.major := 'Music';
END;
```

Object NULL vs. Attribute NULL

An object declaration that does not use the constructor creates a NULL object. It is important to note the difference between the NULL-ness of an object and the NULL-ness of its attributes. If an object is NULL (this can be described as *atomically* NULL), it is illegal to refer to the attributes of it. For example, the following block raises the error "ORA-06530: Reference to uninitialized composite":

```
DECLARE
   v_Student StudentObj;
BEGIN
   v_Student.ID := 10020;
END;
```

The IS NULL condition can be applied to objects, to test whether or not they are NULL. For example, the **AssignName** procedure checks the NULL-ness of its argument before assigning to it:

```
-- Available online as aname.sql
CREATE OR REPLACE PROCEDURE AssignName(
  p_Student IN OUT StudentObj,
  p_FirstName IN StudentObj.first_name%TYPE,
  p_LastName IN StudentObj.last_name%TYPE) AS
BEGIN
  IF p_Student IS NULL THEN
    RAISE_APPLICATION_ERROR(-20000, 'Student is NULL');
  ELSE
    p_Student.first_name := p_FirstName;
    p_Student.last_name := p_LastName;
  END IF;
END AssignName;
```

Forward Type Definitions

It is sometimes useful to create a type before you know the attributes and/or methods which it will contain. You can do this with a *forward type declaration*, which is similar to a forward declaration of a procedure or method. The syntax is simply

CREATE TYPE *type_name*;

This is useful for mutually referential types, and also to allow other types to refer to this one before it is fully fleshed out.

Methods

Methods are declared after the attributes in an object type specification, and implemented in the type body. Recall the syntax for an object type specification which we examined earlier in this chapter:

CREATE [OR REPLACE] TYPE [*schema.*]*type_name* AS OBJECT (
   attribute_name datatype[, *attribute_name datatype*]...
  | [{MAP | ORDER} MEMBER *function_specification*]
  | [MEMBER {*procedure_specification* | *function_specification*}
   [, MEMBER {*procedure_specification* | *function_specification*}]...]

```
  | [PRAGMA RESTRICT_REFERENCES (method_name, constraints)
   [, PRAGMA RESTRICT_REFERENCES (method_name, constraints)]... ]
  );
```

The methods are specified in a comma-separated list of method declarations, each of which looks just like a standard PL/SQL stored subprogram specification, except that the keyword MEMBER is necessary before the declaration. For example, we can extend the specification for **StudentObj** as follows:

```
-- Available online as part of tables8.sql
CREATE OR REPLACE TYPE StudentObj AS OBJECT (
  ID               NUMBER(5),
  first_name       VARCHAR2(20),
  last_name        VARCHAR2(20),
  major            VARCHAR2(30),
  current_credits  NUMBER(3),

  -- Returns the first and last names, separated by a space.
  MEMBER FUNCTION FormattedName
    RETURN VARCHAR2,
  PRAGMA RESTRICT_REFERENCES(FormattedName,
    RNDS, WNDS, RNPS, WNPS),

  -- Updates the major to the specified value in p_NewMajor.
  MEMBER PROCEDURE ChangeMajor(p_NewMajor IN VARCHAR2),
  PRAGMA RESTRICT_REFERENCES(ChangeMajor,
    RNDS, WNDS, RNPS, WNPS),

  -- Updates the current_credits by adding the number of
  -- credits in p_CompletedClass to the current value.
  MEMBER PROCEDURE UpdateCredits(p_CompletedClass IN ClassObj),
  PRAGMA RESTRICT_REFERENCES(UpdateCredits,
    RNDS, WNDS, RNPS, WNPS)
);
```

There are several things to note about the method declarations in the type specification:

1. All of the methods must have the keyword MEMBER before the forward declaration.

2. Instead of a semicolon after each declaration (or pragma), there is a comma. This is true for all elements of the type specification, including the attributes, except for the last one.

3. The method declarations must occur after the attribute declarations.

4. The MAP and ORDER functions are used to determine the sort order for this object type. These functions are discussed later in this chapter.

5. The RESTRICT_REFERENCES pragma can be used to enable a method to be called from an SQL statement. The same rules apply when using this pragma for a method as for a subprogram—for more information, see Chapter 8.

Creating a type body is done with the CREATE TYPE BODY command, which is similar to creating a package body. The syntax for creating a type body is

CREATE [OR REPLACE] TYPE [*schema.*]*type_name* BODY {IS | AS}
  [{MAP | ORDER} MEMBER *function_declaration*;]
  | [MEMBER {*procedure_declaration* | *function_declaration*};
    [MEMBER {*procedure_declaration* | *function_declaration* }]...]
END;

For example, we can create the **StudentObj** type body with:

```
-- Available online as part of tables8.sql
CREATE OR REPLACE TYPE BODY StudentObj AS
  MEMBER FUNCTION FormattedName
    RETURN VARCHAR2 IS
  BEGIN
    RETURN SELF.first_name || ' ' || SELF.last_name;
  END FormattedName;

  MEMBER PROCEDURE ChangeMajor(p_NewMajor IN VARCHAR2) IS
  BEGIN
    major := p_NewMajor;
  END ChangeMajor;
```

```
MEMBER PROCEDURE UpdateCredits(p_CompletedClass IN ClassObj)
   IS
BEGIN
   current_credits :=
      current_credits + p_CompletedClass.num_credits;
   END UpdateCredits;
END;
```

NOTE
This type body contains constructs such as the SELF keyword and the **ClassObj** *object type, which are described later in this chapter.*

Object types are similar to packages in many ways. For example:

■ Both promote data abstraction by separating the specification and body into separate data dictionary objects. This separation breaks the dependency chain for object type bodies the same way as it does for package bodies.

■ Both create data dictionary objects.

However, there are some significant differences:

■ A package body can include additional declarations not in the specification. These private declarations are in scope only in the package body. An object type body, on the other hand, can only contain member subprograms.

■ Object types are actual PL/SQL types—variables can be declared of a particular object type. A package is a different type of schema object entirely—it groups together related declarations.

■ Packages can contain an initialization section; objects do not. The initial values of the attributes are set using the constructor, described earlier in this chapter in the section "Declaring and Initializing Objects."

■ An object type body can contain only the implementation for the methods specified in the type specification. Unlike package bodies, an object type body cannot contain additional attributes or private methods. This restriction will likely be lifted in a future release.

■ The END keyword after a type body does not have the name of the type after it.

Calling a Method

Although methods are syntactically like packaged subprograms, they are called differently. A stored subprogram is a stand-alone object, and it is called directly from a PL/SQL block. However, each instantiation of an object has its own state. Since an object's methods are used to modify the object's state, the method needs to reference a particular object instance. So, in order to call a method for a particular instantiation, you use dot notation as follows,

> *object_name.method_name*

where *object_name* is the name of the object variable, and *method_name* is the name of the method. The following block illustrates calling methods on various student objects.

NOTE
If the method has no arguments, it can be called either with no parenthesis (like a normal PL/SQL procedure) or with a set of empty parenthesis. The following block also illustrates this.

 -- Available online as mcall.sql

```
DECLARE
  v_Student1 StudentObj :=
    StudentObj(10020, 'Chuck', 'Choltry', NULL, 0);
  v_Student2 StudentObj :=
    StudentObj(10021, 'Denise', 'Davenport', NULL, 0);
```

```
BEGIN
  -- Change the major of both students.
  v_Student1.ChangeMajor('Economics');
  v_Student2.ChangeMajor('Computer Science');

  -- Print out Student1's name. Note that there are no
  -- parenthesis in this call.
  DBMS_OUTPUT.PUT_LINE(v_Student1.FormattedName);

  -- Print out Student2's name. This call has empty parenthesis.
  DBMS_OUTPUT.PUT_LINE(v_Student2.FormattedName());
END;
```

Like a regular procedure, methods can be called with either positional
or named notation, and the parameters can have default values. They
can also be overloaded on the type and number of arguments. Positional
and named notation, default values, and overloading are discussed in
Chapters 7 and 8.

The SELF Keyword

Consider the **ChangeMajor** method, which is given here:

```
MEMBER PROCEDURE ChangeMajor(p_NewMajor IN VARCHAR2) IS
  BEGIN
    major := p_NewMajor;
  END ChangeMajor;
```

This method modifies the **major** attribute of the **StudentObj** for which it is
called. Inside the method, therefore, the identifier "major" is bound to the
instantiating object. In order to make this clearer, PL/SQL provides a new
keyword—SELF. SELF is automatically bound to the instantiating object
inside a method. So we could rewrite **ChangeMajor** as follows:

```
MEMBER PROCEDURE ChangeMajor(p_NewMajor IN VARCHAR2) IS
  BEGIN
    SELF.major := p_NewMajor;
  END ChangeMajor;
```

In this case, the use of SELF is optional. However, if you want to pass
the current object instance, or a reference to it, as an argument to another
procedure or method, you need to use SELF.

Using %TYPE with Objects

The %TYPE attribute cannot be applied to an attribute of an object type directly. Rather, it must be applied to an attribute of an instantiation of an object type. This restriction also applies to records. This is illustrated in the following example.

```
-- Available online as prcnttyp.sql
DECLARE
  -- First declare a record type, and a variable of the record
  -- and object type.
  TYPE t_Rec IS RECORD (
    f1 NUMBER,
    f2 VARCHAR2(10));
  v_Student StudentObj;
  v_Rec      t_Rec;

  -- This declaration is legal, since %TYPE is applied to a
  -- variable.
  v_ID v_Student.ID%TYPE;
  -- This declaration raises PLS-206, since %TYPE is applied to
  -- an object type.
  v_ID2 StudentObj.ID%TYPE;

  -- This declaration is legal, since %TYPE is applied to a
  -- variable.
  v_F1 v_Rec.f1%TYPE;
  -- This declaration raises PLS-206, since %TYPE is applied to
  -- a record type.
  v_F2 t_Rec.f2%TYPE;
BEGIN
  NULL;
END;
```

Both of the illegal declarations in the preceding example raise the error

```
PLS-206: %TYPE must be applied to a variable, column, field or
          attribute
```

because they don't specify a construct to which values can be assigned.

Exceptions and Object Type Attributes

As we discussed in Chapter 7, the values of OUT and IN OUT parameters are not assigned their values if a stored subprogram does not handle a raised exception. This is also true if an unhandled exception is raised inside a method. In addition, any attribute assignments that the method has done are not completed. Consider the **ErrorObj** object:

```
-- Available online as part of error.sql
CREATE OR REPLACE TYPE ErrorObj AS OBJECT (
  attribute NUMBER,
  MEMBER PROCEDURE RaiseError(p_RaiseIt IN BOOLEAN,
                             p_OutParam IN OUT NUMBER),
  MEMBER PROCEDURE Print(p_Comment IN VARCHAR2 DEFAULT NULL)
);

CREATE OR REPLACE TYPE BODY ErrorObj AS
  MEMBER PROCEDURE RaiseError(p_RaiseIt IN BOOLEAN,
                             p_OutParam IN OUT NUMBER) IS
  BEGIN
    -- Assign the IN value to attribute, and increment it by 1
    -- for the OUT value.
    SELF.attribute := p_outParam;
    p_OutParam := p_OutParam + 1;
    IF p_RaiseIt THEN
      RAISE NO_DATA_FOUND;
    END IF;
  END RaiseError;

  MEMBER PROCEDURE Print (p_Comment IN VARCHAR2 DEFAULT NULL) IS
  BEGIN
    -- Print the comment as well as the attribute value.
    IF p_Comment IS NOT NULL THEN
      DBMS_OUTPUT.PUT(p_Comment || ', ');
    END IF;
    DBMS_OUTPUT.PUT_LINE('attribute = ' || attribute);
  END Print;
END;
```

If we then execute the following block:

```
-- Available online as part of error.sql
DECLARE
  v_Test ErrorObj := ErrorObj(1);
  v_NumVal NUMBER := 10;
BEGIN
  -- First print the attribute and v_NumVal
  v_Test.Print('After initialization, v_NumVal = ' || v_NumVal);
  -- Call RaiseError with FALSE, so the parameter and attribute
```

```
  -- are assigned.
  v_Test.RaiseError(FALSE, v_NumVal);
  v_Test.Print('After call with no exception, v_NumVal = ' ||
          v_NumVal);
  -- Call RaiseError with TRUE, so the parameter and attribute
  -- are not assigned.
  v_Test.RaiseError(TRUE, v_NumVal);
EXCEPTION
  WHEN NO_DATA_FOUND THEN
    v_Test.Print('After call with exception, v_NumVal = ' ||
            v_NumVal);
END;
```

we get the following output:

```
After initialization, v_NumVal = 10, attribute = 1
After call with no exception, v_NumVal = 11, attribute = 10
After call with exception, v_NumVal = 11, attribute = 10
```

Note that both the attribute and OUT value are assigned to if the procedure completes successfully, but if NO_DATA_FOUND is raised they keep their original values.

Altering and Dropping Types

Similar to other kinds of schema objects, you can modify an existing object type using the ALTER TYPE statement. ALTER TYPE can be used to compile the type specification or body, or to add methods to a type. Object types can be dropped using the DROP TYPE statement.

ALTER TYPE ... COMPILE

This format of the ALTER TYPE command has the following structure,

ALTER TYPE *type_name* COMPILE [SPECIFICATION | BODY];

where *type_name* is the type to be altered. This command will compile either the specification or body of the type, using the existing definition as stored in the data dictionary. If neither the SPECIFICATION nor the BODY keywords are present, both the specification and the body are recompiled. For example, the following command will recompile the body of **StudentObj**:

```
ALTER TYPE StudentObj COMPILE BODY;
```

ALTER TYPE ... REPLACE AS OBJECT

An alternate format of ALTER TYPE is used to add methods. The syntax is

> ALTER TYPE *type_name* REPLACE AS OBJECT (
> *object_type_specification*);

where *type_name* is the name of the object type, and *object_type_specification* is a complete type definition as defined for CREATE TYPE. The new definition must be the same as the original definition, except for the addition of new methods. The original attributes and types must be included. If a type body exists, it is invalidated because it does not define the new methods. The following SQL*Plus session illustrates the use of ALTER TYPE ... REPLACE AS OBJECT:

```
-- Available online as alter.sql
SQL> /* Create a simple object type with two attributes and two
        methods. */
SQL> CREATE OR REPLACE TYPE DummyObj AS OBJECT (
  2    f1 NUMBER,
  3    f2 NUMBER,
  4    MEMBER PROCEDURE Method1(x IN VARCHAR2),
  5    MEMBER FUNCTION Method2 RETURN DATE
  6  );
  7  /

Type created.

SQL> /* Create the type body. */
SQL> CREATE OR REPLACE TYPE BODY DummyObj AS
  2    MEMBER PROCEDURE Method1(x IN VARCHAR2) IS
  3    BEGIN
  4      NULL;
  5    END Method1;
  6
  6    MEMBER FUNCTION Method2 RETURN DATE IS
  7    BEGIN
  8      RETURN SYSDATE;
  9    END Method2;
 10  END;
 11  /
```

```
Type body created.

SQL> SELECT object_name, object_type, status
  2    FROM user_objects
  3    WHERE object_name = 'DUMMYOBJ';

OBJECT_NAME              OBJECT_TYPE       STATUS
------------------       ----------------  -------
DUMMYOBJ                 TYPE              VALID
DUMMYOBJ                 TYPE BODY         VALID

SQL> /* Alter the type to add a new method.  This invalidates
        the type body. */
SQL> ALTER TYPE DummyObj REPLACE AS OBJECT (
  2    f1 NUMBER,
  3    f2 NUMBER,
  4    MEMBER PROCEDURE Method1(x IN VARCHAR2),
  5    MEMBER FUNCTION Method2 RETURN DATE,
  6    MEMBER PROCEDURE Method3
  7  );

Type altered.

SQL> SELECT object_name, object_type, status
  2    FROM user_objects
  3    WHERE object_name = 'DUMMYOBJ';

OBJECT_NAME              OBJECT_TYPE       STATUS
------------------       ----------------  -------
DUMMYOBJ                 TYPE              VALID
DUMMYOBJ                 TYPE BODY         INVALID
```

DROP TYPE

The DROP TYPE command is used to drop an object type or type body. The syntax is

DROP TYPE [*schema.*]*type_name* [FORCE];

If the FORCE option is not specified, then the object type will be dropped only if there is no other schema object which depends on it. If FORCE is specified, then the object is dropped, possibly invalidating any dependent objects.

DROP TYPE BODY can be used to drop just the body of an object type, leaving the specification and any dependent objects intact. It is defined with

DROP TYPE BODY [*schema.*]*type_name*;

Object Dependencies

Similar to records, an object type can have another object type embedded within it. Consider the following declarations:

```
-- Available online as odepend.sql
CREATE OR REPLACE TYPE Obj1 AS OBJECT (
  f1 NUMBER,
  f2 VARCHAR2(10),
  f3 DATE
);

CREATE OR REPLACE TYPE Obj2 AS OBJECT (
  f1 DATE,
  f2 CHAR(1)
);

CREATE OR REPLACE TYPE Obj3 AS OBJECT (
  a Obj1,
  b Obj2
);
```

Note that **Obj3** has attributes of type **Obj1** and **Obj2**. As a result of this, **Obj1** depends on both **Obj2** and **Obj3**, in the same way that a procedure can depend on a table. Because of this, it is illegal to drop or alter either **Obj1** or **Obj2** without first dropping **Obj3**. Consider the following SQL*Plus session:

```
SQL> DROP TYPE Obj1;
DROP TYPE Obj1
*
ERROR at line 1:
ORA-02303: cannot drop or replace a type with type or table
            dependents

SQL> DROP TYPE Obj3;
Type dropped.

SQL> DROP TYPE Obj1;
Type dropped.
```

NOTE
If an object has an attribute that is a reference to a different object type, it also depends on that type. Likewise, if an object table is defined for a particular type, the object type depends on the table. Object references and object tables are discussed in the following section.

Objects in the Database

The object methodology we've examined so far is very similar to the features of any object-oriented design language. Issues such as declaring and creating objects and method initialization are common to any object framework. However, Oracle8 allows you to store objects in the database. This capability adds persistence to objects and is the subject of this part of the chapter.

Object Locations

Objects can be found in different places in an Oracle8 application: stored in the database, declared locally in a PL/SQL block, or kept in a client-side cache. An object has different properties, and different operations are allowed on it, depending on where the object is located.

Persistent vs. Transient Objects

A *persistent object* is an object that is stored in the database, as opposed to a *transient object*, which is local to a PL/SQL block. Transient objects, like local PL/SQL variables, are deallocated when they go out of scope. A persistent object, on the other hand, is available until it is explicitly deleted. Persistent objects are stored in database tables, just like the Oracle7 predefined scalar types (NUMBER, VARCHAR2, DATE, and so on). There are two different ways of storing an object in a table—as a row or column object.

ROW OBJECTS   A *row object* takes up an entire database row. The row contains only the object and no other columns. A table defined like this is known as an *object table*. An object table is created using the syntax

> CREATE TABLE *table_name* OF *object_type*;

where *table_name* is the name of the table to be created, and *object_type* is the type of the row object. For example, we can create the **rooms** object table with the following declarations:

```
-- Available online as part of tables8.sql
-- First create the object type specification and body.
CREATE OR REPLACE TYPE RoomObj AS OBJECT (
  ID             NUMBER(5),
  building       VARCHAR2(15),
  room_number    NUMBER(4),
  number_seats   NUMBER(4),
  description    VARCHAR2(50),
  MEMBER PROCEDURE Print
);

CREATE OR REPLACE TYPE BODY RoomObj AS
  MEMBER PROCEDURE Print IS
  BEGIN
    DBMS_OUTPUT.PUT('Room ID:' || ID || ' is located in ');
    DBMS_OUTPUT.PUT(building || ', room ' || room_number);
    DBMS_OUTPUT.PUT(', and has ' || number_seats || ' seats.');
    DBMS_OUTPUT.NEW_LINE;
  END Print;
END;

-- And now create the object table.
CREATE TABLE rooms OF RoomObj;
```

Each row of **rooms** contains an instantiation of a **RoomObj**. Thus, only objects can be inserted. The following example shows some sample INSERT statements. Note the use of the **RoomObj** constructor.

```
-- Available online as part of tables8.sql
INSERT INTO rooms VALUES
  (RoomObj(99999, 'Building 7', 310, 1000,
           'Large Lecture Hall'));
INSERT INTO rooms VALUES
```

```
(RoomObj(99998, 'Building 6', 101, 500,
        'Small Lecture Hall'));
INSERT INTO rooms VALUES
  (RoomObj(99997, 'Building 6', 150, 50,
          'Discussion Room A'));
INSERT INTO rooms VALUES
  (RoomObj(99996, 'Building 6', 160, 50,
          'Discussion Room B'));
```

An object table is very similar to a standard relational table. In fact, all relational operations will work for an object table. We could have inserted into **rooms** with the following INSERT statement as well:

```
INSERT INTO rooms VALUES
  (99999, 'Building 7', 310, 1000, 'Large Lecture Hall');
```

This feature makes it easier to migrate to Oracle8 from Oracle7. Many relational tables can be re-created as object tables, and existing applications can be used against them without change. New applications can be written to use the object constructor and any methods defined for the object. We will see more examples of INSERT statements later in this chapter.

COLUMN OBJECTS   A *column object*, on the other hand, is only one column of a table. To create a table with a column object, simply use the object type for the column type in the table CREATE statement. A table can have a combination of scalar and column object types. For example, the following declarations (assuming the previous definition of **StudentObj**) create the **students** table:

```
-- Available online as part of tables8.sql
CREATE OR REPLACE TYPE AddressObj AS OBJECT (
  line1    VARCHAR2(40),
  line2    VARCHAR2(40),
  city     VARCHAR2(30),
  state    CHAR(2),
  zipcode  NUMBER(5)
);
CREATE TABLE students (
  student  StudentObj,
  address  AddressObj
);
```

The **students** table has two columns—**student** and **address**. We can therefore insert into **students** with the following example. Note that both the **StudentObj** and **AddressObj** constructors are used, and the third row inserted has a NULL value for **address**.

```
-- Available online as part of tables8.sql
INSERT INTO students VALUES
    (StudentObj(student_sequence.NEXTVAL, 'Scott', 'Smith',
            'Computer Science', 0),
     AddressObj('100 Main St', NULL, 'East Brunswick', 'CA',
            91234));
INSERT INTO students VALUES
    (StudentObj(student_sequence.NEXTVAL, 'Margaret', 'Mason',
            'History', 0),
     AddressObj('350 Sorority Row', 'Apt# 2B', 'East Brunswick',
            'CA', 91234));
INSERT INTO students VALUES
    (StudentObj(student_sequence.NEXTVAL, 'Joanne', 'Junebug',
            'Computer Science', 0),
     NULL);
```

Object Identifiers and Object References

An *object identifier* (OID) is a unique locator for certain types of persistent objects. Similar to a ROWID, which uniquely identifies a row, an object identifier uniquely identifies an object. Object identifiers are guaranteed to be unique across the entire Oracle8 universe—it is impossible for two objects to have the same OID. Furthermore, once an OID is created it will not be used again, even if the object it identifies is deleted. An OID is an internally defined structure that has the capacity for 2^{128} different values.

Only row objects and rows in object views (object views are described later in this chapter) have OIDs. Neither column objects nor transient objects (those local to a PL/SQL block) have OIDs. If an object has an OID, then you can construct a reference to it. As we discussed in Chapter 2, PL/SQL provides two kinds of reference types. REF CURSORs, which we examined in Chapter 6, implement references to cursors. As we saw, a REF CURSOR variable is not the same as a CURSOR variable, rather, it is a pointer to a cursor. Object references behave the same way. An object reference is a pointer to an object, and not the object itself. The syntax for declaring an object reference in a declarative section or table definition is

variable_name REF *object_type*;

where *variable_name* is the name of the object reference, and *object_type* is the object type. For example, the **ClassObj** type defined next contains a reference to a **RoomObj**:

```
-- Available online as part of tables8.sql
CREATE OR REPLACE TYPE ClassObj AS OBJECT (
   department        CHAR(3),
   course            NUMBER(3),
   description       VARCHAR2(2000),
   max_students      NUMBER(3),
   current_students  NUMBER(3),
   num_credits       NUMBER(1),
   room              REF RoomObj
);
```

Object references can be used in PL/SQL blocks and in SQL statements by using the VALUE and REF operators, defined in the next section.

Objects in DML Statements

In many ways, objects behave the same as scalars with regard to DML statements. For example, you can select an object from a database table into a variable of the same type, or update an object table using an object in the WHERE clause. All DML operations on tables that contain either row or column objects operate the same as relational DML operations. For example, they operate within a transaction and have the same read-consistency and rollback issues. However, there are some considerations for some DML statements, which we discuss in the following sections.

INSERT

We've already seen some examples of INSERT statements using objects. In this case, you can use the object constructor, or an object PL/SQL variable, which contains the object to be inserted. Objects behave much like scalar types for INSERT statements.

UPDATE

Objects can be used as bind variables in an UPDATE statement, in the WHERE or VALUES clauses. The following block creates a new room and updates the **classes** table to reflect the new value:

```
-- Available online as update.sql
DECLARE
  v_NewRoom RoomObj :=
    RoomObj(99990, 'Building 7', 200, 50, 'Discussion Room F');
  v_RoomRef REF RoomObj;
BEGIN
  -- The RETURNING clause on this statement puts a reference to
  -- the newly inserted room into v_RoomRef.
  INSERT INTO rooms r VALUES (v_NewRoom)
    RETURNING REF(r) INTO  v_RoomRef;

  UPDATE classes
    SET room = v_RoomRef
    WHERE department = 'NUT' and course = 307;
END;
```

DELETE

Similarly, the DELETE statement can reference an object or object attributes in the WHERE clause. For example, the following DELETE statement will remove all history students:

```
DELETE FROM students s
  WHERE s.student.major = 'History';
```

Column Objects in SELECT Statements

If an object is stored as a column object in a table, you can simply retrieve it using a standard SELECT statement, as the following example illustrates.

```
-- Available online as part of colsel.sql
DECLARE
  v_Student StudentObj;
  v_Address AddressObj;

  CURSOR c_Students IS
    SELECT student, address
      FROM students;
BEGIN
  -- Print out the ID's of all students.
  OPEN c_Students;

  LOOP
    FETCH c_Students INTO v_Student, v_Address;
```

```
      EXIT WHEN c_Students%NOTFOUND;

      DBMS_OUTPUT.PUT_LINE('Student ID: ' || v_Student.ID);
   END LOOP;

   CLOSE c_Students;
END;
```

You can also reference a column object in the WHERE clause, as long as you fully qualify the object. For example, the following SELECT statement is legal because of the complete path to the ID attribute:

```
SELECT student
  FROM students
  WHERE students.student.id = 10009;
```

However, you cannot issue the same statement in PL/SQL, because the table is not aliased. The following block will raise the error "PLS-327: students is not in SQL scope here":

```
-- Available online as part of colsel.sql
DECLARE
   v_Student StudentObj;
BEGIN
   -- Raises PLS-327
   SELECT student
     INTO v_Student
     FROM students
     WHERE students.student.ID = 10009;
END;
```

The solution to this is to use a table alias:

```
-- Available online as part of colsel.sql
DECLARE
   v_Student StudentObj;
BEGIN
   -- Succeeds, because of the table alias
   SELECT student
     INTO v_Student
     FROM students s
     WHERE s.student.ID = 10009;
END;
```

TIP
Always use a table alias when selecting from a table which contains either column or row objects. This way, you can be sure that the query will work in both PL/SQL and SQL.

Row Objects in SELECT Statements

A row object behaves differently in queries. Since an object table is described just like a relational table, you can't name the object itself. Consequently, in order to retrieve the object or a reference to the object, you can use the VALUE or REF operator.

VALUE OPERATOR   VALUE returns an object, rather than a list of the attributes. It takes a correlation variable as an argument. In this context, a *correlation variable* is simply a table alias. The following example illustrates VALUE and how it is used.

```
-- Available online as valueop.sql
DECLARE
  v_RoomID        rooms.id%TYPE;
  v_Building      rooms.building%TYPE;
  v_RoomNumber    rooms.room_number%TYPE;
  v_NumberSeats   rooms.number_seats%TYPE;
  v_Description   rooms.description%TYPE;
  v_RoomObj       RoomObj;
BEGIN
  -- SELECT without using VALUE.  This is just like a relational
  -- query.
  SELECT *
    INTO v_RoomID, v_Building, v_RoomNumber, v_NumberSeats,
         v_Description
    FROM rooms r
    WHERE ID = 99993;

  -- SELECT using VALUE.  In this case, we retrieve a RoomObj.
  SELECT VALUE(r)
    INTO v_RoomObj
    FROM rooms r
    WHERE ID = 99993;
END;
```

The result set of a query returning VALUE is a set of objects, not a set of attributes.

REF OPERATOR   The REF operator will return a REF to the requested object, rather than the object itself. Like VALUE, REF takes a correlation variable as an argument. The following example illustrates this.

```
-- Available online as part of refop.sql
DECLARE
  v_RoomRef REF RoomObj;
BEGIN
  -- Select a reference to the room, not the room itself.
  SELECT REF(r)
    INTO v_RoomRef
    FROM rooms r
    WHERE ID = 99993;
END;
```

DEREF OPERATOR   Given a reference, DEREF will return the original object. We can continue the previous example to illustrate this.

```
-- Available online as refop.sql
DECLARE
  v_RoomRef REF RoomObj;
  v_Room    RoomObj;
BEGIN
  -- Select a reference to the room, not the room itself.
  SELECT REF(r)
    INTO v_RoomRef
    FROM rooms r
    WHERE ID = 99993;

  -- Dereference v_RoomRef to get an object, and update it.
  -- This will return a local object, which is not the same
  -- as the object stored in the rooms table.
  SELECT DEREF(v_RoomRef)
    INTO v_Room
    FROM dual;

  -- This updates the local object.
  v_Room.room_number := 201;
END;
```

DANGLING REFS   If the object to which a REF points is deleted, the REF is said to be *dangling*, since it now points to a nonexistent object. It is illegal to dereference a dangling REF. You can check for it, however, using the IS DANGLING predicate, as the following UPDATE statement illustrates.

```
BEGIN
  -- Set all dangling REFs to NULL.
  UPDATE classes
    SET room = NULL
    WHERE room IS DANGLING;
END;
```

> **NOTE**
> *All of these operators (VALUE, REF, DEREF, and IS DANGLING) can be used in SQL statements only. They cannot be used in procedural statements.*

RETURNING Clause

Oracle8 provides a new clause for INSERT and UPDATE statements. RETURNING can be used to retrieve information from the newly inserted or updated row, without requiring an additional query. The syntax of the RETURNING clause is

RETURNING *select_list* INTO *into_list*;

where *select_list* is similar to a select list of a query, and *into_list* is the same as the INTO clause of a query. For example, if you are inserting an object into an object table, you can get a reference to the newly inserted object with the following:

```
-- Available online as return.sql
DECLARE
  v_ClassRef REF ClassObj;
BEGIN
  INSERT INTO CLASSES c VALUES
    (ClassObj('HIS', 101, 'History 101', 30, 0, 4, NULL))
    RETURNING REF(c) INTO v_ClassRef;
END;
```

MAP and ORDER Methods

Predefined scalar types have an implicit ordering associated with them—you can compare two NUMBERs, for example, and determine which is greater. An object type, on the other hand, can only be compared for equality. This would prevent object types from being used in clauses such as ORDER BY or DISTINCT, since they require ordering. There is a solution to this, however—MAP and ORDER methods. These special methods are used to implement ordering of objects.

MAP

A MAP method is a function which returns a scalar type. When the database needs to sort the object, it can call the MAP function to convert the object to a type which can be sorted. The method thus acts like a hash function. The following example illustrates a map method for **RoomObj**:

```
-- Available online as part of tables8.sql
CREATE OR REPLACE TYPE RoomObj AS OBJECT (
  ID NUMBER(5),
  ...
  -- MAP function used to sort rooms.
  MAP MEMBER FUNCTION ReturnID RETURN NUMBER
);

CREATE OR REPLACE TYPE BODY RoomObj AS
  ...
  MAP MEMBER FUNCTION ReturnID RETURN NUMBER IS
  BEGIN
    RETURN SELF.ID;
  END ReturnID;
END RoomObj;
```

A MAP method is identified by the keyword MAP in front of the declaration. This function must take no parameters, and return one of the following scalar types: DATE, NUMBER, VARCHAR2, CHAR, or REAL. The **ReturnID** function returns the room ID number, which is how rooms will be sorted. After this function has been created, we can execute the following SELECT statement, for example:

```
SQL> SELECT VALUE(r)
  2    FROM rooms r
  3    ORDER BY 1;

VALUE(R)(ID, BUILDING, ROOM_NUMBER, NUMBER_SEATS, DESCRIPTION)
--------------------------------------------------------------
ROOMOBJ(99991, 'Building 7', 310, 50, 'Discussion Room E')
ROOMOBJ(99992, 'Building 7', 300, 75, 'Discussion Room D')
ROOMOBJ(99993, 'Music Building', 200, 1000, 'Concert Room')
ROOMOBJ(99994, 'Music Building', 100, 10, 'Music Practice Room')
ROOMOBJ(99995, 'Building 6', 170, 50, 'Discussion Room C')
ROOMOBJ(99996, 'Building 6', 160, 50, 'Discussion Room B')
ROOMOBJ(99997, 'Building 6', 150, 50, 'Discussion Room A')
ROOMOBJ(99998, 'Building 6', 101, 500, 'Small Lecture Hall')
ROOMOBJ(99999, 'Building 7', 310, 1000, 'Large Lecture Hall')
```

ORDER

Alternatively, you can create an ORDER method. ORDER methods take one parameter (of the object type), and return the following values:

- ■ >1 if the parameter is greater than SELF
- ■ <1 if the parameter is less than SELF
- ■ = if the parameter is equal to SELF

An ORDER method is used similar to the MAP method. We can create an ORDER method for students which sorts by name with the following:

```
-- Available online as part of tables8.sql
CREATE OR REPLACE TYPE StudentObj AS OBJECT (
  ID               NUMBER(5),
  first_name       VARCHAR2(20),
  last_name        VARCHAR2(20),
  major            VARCHAR2(30),
  current_credits  NUMBER(3),

  ...
  -- ORDER function used to sort students.
  ORDER MEMBER FUNCTION CompareStudent(p_Student IN StudentObj)
    RETURN NUMBER
);
```

```
CREATE OR REPLACE TYPE BODY StudentObj AS
  ...
  ORDER MEMBER FUNCTION CompareStudent(p_Student IN StudentObj)
    RETURN NUMBER IS
  BEGIN
    IF p_Student.last_name = SELF.last_name THEN
      IF p_Student.first_name < SELF.first_name THEN
        RETURN 1;
      ELSIF p_Student.first_name > SELF.first_name THEN
        RETURN -1;
      ELSE
        RETURN 0;
      END IF;
    ELSE
      IF p_Student.last_name < SELF.last_name THEN
        RETURN 1;
      ELSIF p_Student.last_name > SELF.last_name THEN
        RETURN -1;
      ELSE
        RETURN 0;
      END IF;
    END IF;
  END CompareStudent;
END;
```

After creating this ORDER method, we can issue the following:

```
SQL> SELECT student
  2     FROM students
  3     ORDER BY student DESC;

STUDENT(ID, FIRST_NAME, LAST_NAME, MAJOR, CURRENT_CREDITS)
-----------------------------------------------------------------
STUDENTOBJ(10005, 'Timothy', 'Taller', 'History', 0)
STUDENTOBJ(10000, 'Scott', 'Smith', 'Computer Science', 0)
STUDENTOBJ(10009, 'Rose', 'Riznit', 'Music', 0)
STUDENTOBJ(10010, 'Rita', 'Razmataz', 'Nutrition', 0)
STUDENTOBJ(10004, 'Patrick', 'Poll', 'History', 0)
STUDENTOBJ(10003, 'Manish', 'Murgratroid', 'Economics', 0)
STUDENTOBJ(10001, 'Margaret', 'Mason', 'History', 0)
STUDENTOBJ(10002, 'Joanne', 'Junebug', 'Computer Science', 0)
STUDENTOBJ(10008, 'Ester', 'Elegant', 'Nutrition', 0)
STUDENTOBJ(10007, 'David', 'Dinsmore', 'Music', 0)
STUDENTOBJ(10006, 'Barbara', 'Blues', 'Economics', 0)
```

Guidelines

There are several things to keep in mind about MAP and ORDER methods:

- A given object type can have either a MAP or an ORDER method, but it is an error to define both.

- A MAP method will be more efficient, since it will convert the entire set of objects to a simpler type (operating as a hash function), which is then sorted directly. With the ORDER method, only two objects can be compared at a time, and thus must be called repeatedly.

- Without either a MAP or ORDER method, objects can be compared only for equality and only in SQL statements. The MAP or ORDER method allows the object to be sorted, and also to be compared in procedural statements.

Summary

This chapter began with a general discussion of object-oriented design methodologies and how Oracle implements such a paradigm with object types. We discussed the syntax for defining object types and methods, and how to create database tables with either row or column objects. The chapter concluded with a discussion of object references and how they are used. In the next chapter, we will examine collections, which are a specific type of object.

CHAPTER
12

Collections

I t is often convenient in a PL/SQL program to manipulate many variables at once, as one unit. Datatypes like this are known as *collections*. PL/SQL version 2 provides only one type of collection—a PL/SQL table, as described in Chapter 2. PL/SQL 8.0, however, adds two collection types—nested tables and varrays. Each of these collection types can be thought of as an object type, with attributes and methods. In this chapter, we will discuss the features of these new object types.

Nested Tables

Nested tables are very similar to the PL/SQL tables we saw in Chapter 2, which are known in Oracle8 as *index-by tables*. Nested tables extend the functionality of index-by tables by adding extra collection methods (known as table attributes for index-by tables) and by adding the ability to store nested tables within a database table, which is why they are called *nested* tables. Nested tables can also be manipulated directly using SQL, and have additional predefined exceptions available.

Other than these extra features, the basic functionality of a nested table is the same as a PL/SQL table. A nested table can be thought of as a database table with two columns—key and value, as discussed in Chapter 3. Like index-by tables, nested tables can be sparse, and the keys do not have to be sequential.

Declaring a Nested Table

The syntax for creating a nested table type is

```
TYPE table_name is TABLE OF table_type [NOT NULL];
```

where *table_name* is the name of the new type, and *table_type* is the type of each element in the nested table. *Table_type* can be a built-in type, a user-defined object type, or an expression using %TYPE.

NOTE
*The only syntactic difference
between index-by tables and nested
tables is the presence of the INDEX BY
BINARY_INTEGER clause. If this clause is
not present, then the type is a nested table
type, and the Oracle8 features described in
this chapter are available. If this clause is
present, then the type is an index-by table
type, and only the Oracle7 PL/SQL table
features are available, as described in
Chapter 3.*

The following declarative section of code shows some valid table declarations:

 `-- Available online as part of nested.sql`

```
DECLARE
    -- Define a table type based on an object type
    TYPE t_ClassesTab IS TABLE OF ClassObj;

    -- A type based on %ROWTYPE
    TYPE t_StudentsTab IS TABLE OF students%ROWTYPE;

    -- Variables of the above types
    v_ClassList t_ClassesTab;
    v_StudentList t_StudentsTab;
```

NOTE
*All of the object types and tables referenced
in this example (such as **ClassObj** and
students) are defined in tables8.sql, which
is available online.*

Table Initialization

When a table is declared as in the preceding block, it is initialized to be atomically NULL, like an object type. If you try to assign to a NULL table, the error "ORA-6531: Reference to uninitialized collection," which corresponds to the predefined exception COLLECTION_IS_NULL, is raised. Continuing the previous example, the following execution section will raise this error:

```
-- Available online as part of nested.sql
BEGIN
  -- This assignment will raise COLLECTION_IS_NULL because
  -- v_ClassList is atomically NULL.
  v_ClassList(1) := ClassObj('HIS', 101, 'History 101', 30, 0, 4,
NULL);
END;
```

So how do you initialize a nested table? This can be done by using the constructor. Like an object type constructor, the constructor for a nested table has the same name as the table type itself. However, it takes as an argument a list of elements, each of which should be type compatible with the table element type. The following example illustrates the use of nested table constructors:

```
-- Available online as tconstr.sql
DECLARE
  TYPE t_NumbersTab IS TABLE OF NUMBER;

  -- Create a table with one element.
  v_Tab1 t_NumbersTab := t_NumbersTab(-1);

  -- Create a table with five elements.
  v_Primes t_NumbersTab := t_NumbersTab(1, 2, 3, 5, 7);

  -- Create a table with no elements.
  v_Tab2 t_NumbersTab := t_NumbersTab();
BEGIN
  -- Assign to v_Tab1(1). This will replace the value already
  -- in v_Tab(1), which was initialized to -1.
  v_Tab1(1) := 12345;
END;
```

EMPTY TABLES   Note the declaration of **v_Tab2** in the preceding block:

```
-- Create a table with no elements.
  v_Tab2 t_NumbersTab := t_NumbersTab();
```

v_Tab2 is initialized by calling the constructor with no arguments. This creates a table that has no elements, but is not atomically NULL. The following block illustrates this:

```
-- Available online as nulltab.sql
DECLARE
  TYPE t_WordsTab IS TABLE OF VARCHAR2(50);

  -- Create a NULL table.
  v_Tab1 t_WordsTab;

  -- Create a table with one element, which itself is NULL.
  v_Tab2 t_WordsTab := t_WordsTab();
BEGIN
  IF v_Tab1 IS NULL THEN
    DBMS_OUTPUT.PUT_LINE('v_Tab1 is NULL');
  ELSE
    DBMS_OUTPUT.PUT_LINE('v_Tab1 is not NULL');
  END IF;

  IF v_Tab2 IS NULL THEN
    DBMS_OUTPUT.PUT_LINE('v_Tab2 is NULL');
  ELSE
    DBMS_OUTPUT.PUT_LINE('v_Tab2 is not NULL');
  END IF;
END;
```

If we run this block (with 'set serveroutput on' in SQL*Plus—see Chapter 14 for information about the DBMS_OUTPUT package), we get the following output:

```
v_Tab1 is NULL
v_Tab2 is not NULL
```

KEYS AT INITIALIZATION   When a table is initialized using a constructor, the elements of the table are numbered sequentially, ranging from 1 to the number of elements specified in the constructor call. During later processing, the values stored at some keys may be deleted (using the DELETE method, described later in this chapter). When a nested table is selected from the database (as described in the section "Nested Tables in the Database," later in this chapter) the keys are renumbered if necessary to be sequential, as they are at initialization.

Adding Elements to an Existing Table

Although a table is unconstrained, you cannot assign to an element that does not exist yet, and would thus cause the table to increase in size. If you attempt to do this, PL/SQL will raise the error "ORA-6533: Subscript beyond count," which is equivalent to the SUBSCRIPT_BEYOND_COUNT predefined exception. This is illustrated by the following example:

```
-- Available online as tassign.sql
DECLARE
  TYPE t_NumbersTab IS TABLE OF NUMBER;
  v_Numbers t_NumbersTab := t_NumbersTab(1, 2, 3);
BEGIN
  -- v_Numbers was initialized to have 3 elements. So the
  -- following assignments are all legal.
  v_Numbers(1) := 7;
  v_Numbers(2) := -1;

  -- However, this assignment will raise ORA-6533.
  v_Numbers(4) := 4;
END;
```

TIP
You can increase the size of a nested table by using the EXTEND method, described later in this chapter.

Nested Tables in the Database

A nested table can be stored as a database column. This means that the entire nested table is contained in one row of the database table, and each row of the database table can contain a different nested table. In order to store a nested table in the database, you must use the CREATE TYPE statement to create the nested table type, rather than a TYPE statement in a PL/SQL block. By using CREATE TYPE, the type is stored in the data dictionary and is thus available for use as a column type. The following example illustrates how to create a nested table as a database column:

```
-- Available online as part of tables8.sql
CREATE TYPE BookObj AS OBJECT (
  title          VARCHAR2(40),
  author         VARCHAR2(40),
  catalog_number NUMBER(4)
);

CREATE TYPE BookList AS TABLE OF BookObj;

CREATE TABLE course_material (
  department      CHAR(3),
  course          NUMBER(3),
  required_reading BookList)
  NESTED TABLE required_reading STORE AS required_tab;
```

There are several things to note about the preceding listing and creating nested tables in the database:

- The table type is created with the CREATE TYPE statement so it can be stored in the data dictionary.

- The table type is used in the table definition, just like a column object.

- For each nested table in a given database table, the NESTED TABLE clause is required. This clause indicates the name of the store table.

A *store table* is a system-generated table that is used to store the actual data in the nested table. This data is not stored inline with the rest of the table columns; it is stored separately. The **required_reading** column will actually store a REF into the **required_tab** table, where the list of books will be stored. The storage for **course_material** is illustrated by Figure 12-1. For each row of **course_material**, **required_reading** contains a REF to the corresponding rows in **required_tab**.

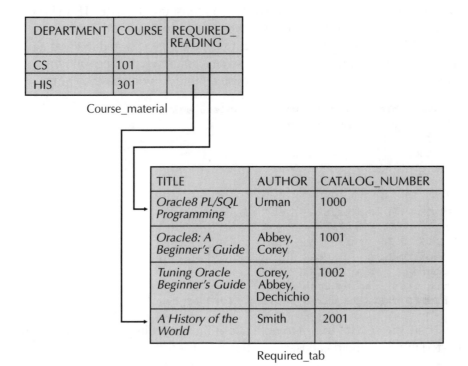

Course_material

Required_tab

FIGURE 12-1. *Nested tables in the database*

NOTE
*The store table (**required_tab** in the above example) can exist in another schema, and can have different storage parameters from the main table. The store table can be described, and exists in **user_tables**, but can not be accessed directly. If you attempt to query or modify the store table directly, you will get the Oracle error "ORA-22812: cannot reference nested table column's storage table". The contents of the store table are manipulated through SQL on the main table.*

Manipulating Entire Tables

You can manipulate a nested table stored in a database table in its entirety, or you can manipulate individual rows. Either way, you can use SQL statements. In the database, a nested table has no ordering—it is essentially just like a regular table. The index can be used only when the table is in PL/SQL.

INSERT In order to insert a table into a database row, you use INSERT, as illustrated by the following example. Note that the table is constructed and initialized in PL/SQL first, then inserted into the database.

```
-- Available online as tinsert.sql
DECLARE
  v_Books Booklist :=
    BookList(BookObj('A History of the World', 'Smith', 2001));
BEGIN
  -- INSERT using a newly constructed nested table of 2 elements.
  INSERT INTO course_material VALUES (
  'CS', 101,
    BookList(BookObj('Oracle8 PL/SQL Programming',
                     'Urman', 1000),
            BookObj('Oracle8: A Beginner''s Guide',
                     'Abbey, Corey', 1001),
            BookObj('Tuning Oracle',
                     'Corey, Abbey, Dechichio', 1002)));

  -- INSERT using a previously initialized nested table of 1
element.
  INSERT INTO course_material VALUES (
    'HIS', 301, v_Books);
END;
```

After running the above example, **course_material** will have the values shown in Figure 12-1.

UPDATE Similarly, UPDATE is used to modify a stored table. The following example adds the required reading for History 301:

```
-- Available online as tupdate.sql
DECLARE
  v_Books Booklist :=
    BookList(BookObj('A History of the World', 'Smith', 2001),
            BookObj('Another World History', 'Jones', 2002));
BEGIN
```

```
    UPDATE course_material
      SET required_reading = v_Books
      WHERE department = 'HIS'
      AND course = 301;
END;
```

DELETE   DELETE can remove a row containing a nested table, as the following example illustrates:

-- **Available online as tdelete.sql**

```
BEGIN
  -- Remove the required reading for all history courses.
  DELETE FROM course_material
    WHERE department = 'HIS';
END;
```

SELECT   When a nested table is retrieved into a PL/SQL variable, it is assigned keys starting at 1, and ranging to the number of elements in the table. The latter can be determined by the COUNT method, which is described later in this chapter. (These are the same keys that are established by the table constructor.) The following example illustrates this:

-- **Available online as tselect.sql**

```
DECLARE
  v_Books course_material.required_reading%TYPE;
  v_Course course_material.course%TYPE;
  v_Department course_material.department%TYPE;

  CURSOR c_AllBooks IS
    SELECT required_reading, course, department
      FROM course_material;
BEGIN
  -- Loop over all the courses, and print out (using DBMS_OUTPUT)
  -- the required book titles.
  OPEN c_AllBooks;

  LOOP
    -- Fetch all the columns in this row, including the entire
    -- nested table stored in required_reading.
    FETCH c_AllBooks INTO v_Books, v_Course, v_Department;
    EXIT WHEN c_AllBooks%NOTFOUND;

    DBMS_OUTPUT.PUT('Required reading for ' || v_Department || '
```

```
');
    DBMS_OUTPUT.PUT_LINE(v_Course || ':');

    -- Loop over the entire selected table, printing out each row.
    FOR v_Index IN 1..v_Books.COUNT LOOP
      DBMS_OUTPUT.PUT_LINE('  ' || v_Books(v_Index).title);
    END LOOP;
  END LOOP;

  CLOSE c_AllBooks;
END;
```

Assuming the INSERT and UPDATE (but not the DELETE) statements in the prior examples have been run, this block produces the following output when run in SQL*Plus:

```
Required reading for CS  101:
   Oracle8 PL/SQL Programming
   Oracle8: A Beginner's Guide
   Tuning Oracle
Required reading for HIS 301:
   A History of the World
   Another World History
```

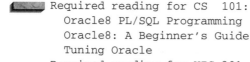

NOTE
You may have noticed that none of the prior examples used the nested table in a WHERE clause. This is a restriction on nested tables. Since there is no predefined MAP or ORDER method, nested tables cannot be compared for equality, which is required for the WHERE clause. This also means that nested tables cannot be used where an implicit comparison is necessary, such as the ORDER BY, GROUP BY, or DISTINCT clause.

Manipulating Individual Rows

The last several examples have modified a stored nested table in PL/SQL, and then changed in the database. Oracle8 also provides an operator that allows a nested table to be manipulated using DML while it is stored in a table, rather than manipulating it in PL/SQL. The operator THE is used to accomplish this. THE takes a subquery as argument, and it returns the nested table, suitable for use in a DML statement. The subquery must return a single nested table column. For example, the following UPDATE statement adds 10 to the catalog numbers for the books required by CS 101:

```
UPDATE THE(SELECT required_reading
            FROM course_material
            WHERE department = 'CS' AND course = 101)
  SET catalog_number = catalog_number + 10;
```

Nested Tables vs. Index-by Tables

Nested tables are similar to the index-by tables found in Oracle7 in many ways. For example:

- Both table datatypes have the same structure.

- Individual elements in both are accessed using subscript notation.

- The methods available for nested tables include all of the 2.3 table attributes for index-by tables.

- Code previously written for index-by tables will still work for nested tables.

- However, there are also several significant differences:

- Nested tables can be manipulated using SQL and can be stored in the database, while index-by tables cannot.

- Nested tables have a legal subscript range of 1..2147483647, while index-by tables have a range of –2147483647.. 2147483647. Thus, index-by tables can have negative subscripts while nested tables cannot.

- Nested tables can be atomically NULL (testable with the IS NULL operator).

- Nested tables have additional methods available, such as EXTEND and TRIM (described in the section "Collection Methods" later in this chapter).

Varrays

A *varray* (variable length array) is a datatype very similar to an array in C or Pascal. Syntactically, a varray is accessed in much the same way as a nested or index-by table. However, a varray is implemented differently. Rather than being a sparse data structure with no upper bound, elements are inserted into a varray starting at index 1, up to the maximum length declared in the varray type.

The storage for a varray is the same as a C or Pascal array, as opposed to the storage for a nested table, which is more like a database table.

Declaring a Varray

A varray type is declared using the syntax

> TYPE *type_name* IS {VARRAY | VARYING ARRAY} (*maximum_size*)
> OF *element_type* [NOT NULL];

where *type_name* is the name of the new varray type, *maximum_size* is an integer specifying the maximum number of elements in the varray, and *element_type* is a PL/SQL scalar, record, or object type. The *element_type* can be specified using %TYPE as well, but cannot be BOOLEAN, NCHAR, NCLOB, NVARCHAR2, REF CURSOR, TABLE, or another VARRAY type. The following example shows some legal varray types:

```
DECLARE
  TYPE t_BookList IS VARRAY(25) OF BookObj;
  TYPE t_Numbers IS VARRAY(10) OF NUMBER(3) NOT NULL;
  TYPE t_Students IS VARRAY(100) OF students%ROWTYPE;
```

Varray Initialization

Similar to tables, varrays are initialized using a constructor. The following block illustrates this:

```
-- Available online as vconstr.sql
DECLARE
  -- Define a VARRAY type.
  TYPE t_Numbers IS VARRAY(20) OF NUMBER(3);

  -- Declare a NULL varray.
```

```
  v_NullList t_Numbers;

  -- This varray has 2 elements.
  v_List1 t_Numbers := t_Numbers(1, 2);

  -- This varray has one element, which itself is NULL.
  v_List2 t_Numbers := t_Numbers(NULL);
BEGIN
  IF v_NullList IS NULL THEN
    DBMS_OUTPUT.PUT_LINE('v_NullList is NULL');
  END IF;

  IF v_List2(1) IS NULL THEN
    DBMS_OUTPUT.PUT_LINE('v_List2(1) is NULL');
  END IF;
END;
```

If we run the above block in SQL*Plus, we get the following output:

```
v_NullList is NULL
v_List2(1) is NULL
```

Manipulating Varray Elements

Like nested tables, the initial size of a varray is set by the number of elements used in the constructor when it is declared. Assignments to elements outside this range will raise the error "ORA-6533: subscript beyond count", just like a nested table. The following example illustrates this.

```
-- Available online as vassign.sql
DECLARE
  TYPE t_Strings IS VARRAY(5) OF VARCHAR2(10);

  -- Declare a varray with three elements. The maximum size of
  -- this type is five elements.
  v_List t_Strings := t_Strings('Scott', 'David', 'Urman');
BEGIN
  -- Subscript between 1 and 3, so this is a legal assignment.
  v_List(2) := 'DAVID';

  -- Subscript out of range, raises ORA-6533.
  v_List(4) := '!!!';
END;
```

TIP
Like nested tables, the size of a varray can be increased using the EXTEND method, described later in this chapter. Unlike a nested table, however, a varray cannot be extended past the maximum size declared for the varray type.

Varrays in the Database

Like nested tables, varrays can be stored in database columns. Unlike nested tables, however, a varray can only be manipulated in its entirety — you can't modify individual elements of a stored varray as you can a stored nested table (using the THE operator). For example, consider the following declarations:

```
-- Available online as part of tables8.sql
CREATE OR REPLACE TYPE BookList2 AS VARRAY(10) OF BookObj;

CREATE TABLE checked_out (
  student_id number(5),
  books BookList2
);
```

The **checked_out** table will contain a list of the books which are checked out of the library for each student. There are several things to note about this example, which are relevant for creating stored varrays:

- The type must be known to the database and stored in the data dictionary, so the CREATE TYPE statement is necessary (the type cannot be local to a PL/SQL block).

- Each row of **checked_out** will contain a varray of up to 10 books. The storage for the varray is the same as the database row, and the varray data is kept inline with the table data.

Manipulating Stored Varrays

To modify a stored varray, you must first select it into a PL/SQL variable. You can then change the variable, and insert it back into the table. The **CheckOut** procedure below illustrates this technique.

```
-- Available online as checkout.sql
CREATE OR REPLACE PROCEDURE CheckOut(
  p_StudentID IN NUMBER,
  p_NewBook IN BookObj) AS

  v_Books BookList2;
  v_Found BOOLEAN := FALSE;
  v_Book BookObj;
BEGIN
  -- First get the current list of books this student has checked
  -- out.
  BEGIN
    SELECT books
      INTO v_Books
      FROM checked_out
      WHERE student_id = p_StudentID;
  EXCEPTION
    WHEN NO_DATA_FOUND THEN
      -- Student has no books checked out.
      v_Books := BookList2(NULL);
  END;

  -- Search the list to see if this student already has this book.
  FOR v_Counter IN 1..v_Books.COUNT LOOP
    v_Book := v_Books(v_Counter);

    IF v_Book.catalog_number = p_NewBook.catalog_number THEN
      RAISE_APPLICATION_ERROR(-20001, 'Book is already checked
                              out');
    END IF;
  END LOOP;

  -- Make sure there is still room.
  IF v_Books.COUNT = v_Books.LIMIT THEN
    RAISE_APPLICATION_ERROR(-20001, 'Cannot check out any more
                            books');
  END IF;

  -- Check out the book by adding it to the list.
  v_Books.EXTEND;
  v_Books(v_Books.COUNT) := p_NewBook;

  -- And put it back in the database.
  UPDATE checked_out
    SET books = v_Books
```

•

```
      WHERE student_id = p_StudentID;
   IF SQL%NOTFOUND THEN
     INSERT INTO checked_out (student_id, books)
       VALUES (p_StudentID, v_Books);
   END IF;
END CheckOut;
```

We can call **CheckOut** from a block similar to the following:

```
-- Available online as co.sql
DECLARE
  v_RequiredBooks BookList;
  v_Book BookObj;

BEGIN
  SELECT required_reading
    INTO v_RequiredBooks
    FROM course_material
    WHERE department = 'CS'
    AND course = 101;

  FOR v_Counter IN 1..v_RequiredBooks.COUNT LOOP
    v_Book := v_RequiredBooks(v_Counter);
    CheckOut(1005, v_Book);
  END LOOP;
END;
```

Varrays vs. Nested Tables

Both varrays and nested tables are collections, and as such they have several similarities:

- Both types allow access to individual elements using subscript notation.

- Both types can be stored in database tables.

However, there are also some differences:

- Varrays have a maximum size, while nested tables do not.

- Varrays are stored inline with the containing table, while nested tables are stored in a separate table, which can have different storage characteristics.

- When stored in the database, varrays retain the ordering and subscript values for the elements, while nested tables do not.

- Individual elements can be deleted from a nested table (using the TRIM method, described in the next section), which causes the size of the table to shrink. A varray is always a constant size, however.

Collection Methods

Collections are object types, and as such they have methods defined on them. These methods include the attributes available for PL/SQL tables (with version 2.3 and higher), which we saw in Chapter 2. Except where noted, the methods can be used for both nested tables and varrays. Collection methods can be called only from procedural statements, and not from SQL statements.

All of the remaining examples assume the following declarations:

```
-- Available online as part of tables8.sql
CREATE OR REPLACE TYPE NumTab AS TABLE OF NUMBER;
CREATE OR REPLACE TYPE NumVar AS VARRAY(25) OF NUMBER;
```

The methods are listed in Table 12-1, and described in the sections that follow.

EXISTS

EXISTS is used to determine whether the referenced element actually exists. The syntax is

EXISTS(*n*)

where *n* is an integer expression. It returns TRUE if the element specified by *n* exists, even if it is NULL. If *n* is out of range, EXISTS returns FALSE, rather than raising the SUBSCRIPT_OUTSIDE_LIMIT exception. EXISTS and DELETE can be used to maintain sparse nested tables. The following example illustrates the use of EXISTS:

```
-- Available online as exists.sql
DECLARE
  v_Table NumTab := NumTab(-7, 14.3, 3.14159, NULL, 0);
  v_Count BINARY_INTEGER := 1;
```

```
BEGIN
  -- Loop over v_Table, and print out the elements, using EXISTS
  -- to indicate the end of the loop.
  LOOP
    IF v_Table.EXISTS(v_Count) THEN
      DBMS_OUTPUT.PUT_LINE('v_Table(' || v_Count || '): ' ||
                            v_Table(v_Count));
      v_Count := v_Count + 1;
    ELSE
      EXIT;
    END IF;
  END LOOP;
END;
```

The above example produces the following output:

```
v_Table(1): -7
v_Table(2): 14.3
v_Table(3): 3.14159
v_Table(4):
v_Table(5): 0
```

Method	Description
EXISTS	Determines whether a collection element exists.
COUNT	Returns the number of elements in a collection.
LIMIT	Returns the maximum number of elements for a collection.
FIRST & LAST	Returns the first (or last) element in a collection.
NEXT & PRIOR	Returns the next (or prior) element, relative to a given element, in a collection.
EXTEND	Adds elements to a collection.
TRIM	Removes elements from the end of a collection.
DELETE	Removes specified elements from a collection.

TABLE 12-1. *Collection Methods*

EXISTS can be applied to an atomically NULL collection, in which case it will always return FALSE.

COUNT

COUNT returns the number of elements currently in a collection, as an integer. It takes no arguments and is valid wherever an integer expression is valid. The following example illustrates the use of COUNT:

```
-- Available online as count.sql
DECLARE
  v_Table NumTab := NumTab(1, 2, 3);
  v_Varray NumVar := NumVar(-1, -2, -3, -4);
BEGIN
  DBMS_OUTPUT.PUT_LINE('Table Count: ' || v_Table.COUNT);
  DBMS_OUTPUT.PUT_LINE('Varray Count: ' || v_Varray.COUNT);
END;
```

The output from the preceding example is

```
Table Count: 3
Varray Count: 4
```

For varrays, COUNT always equals LAST (described later in this section), since elements can't be deleted from a varray. However, elements can be deleted from the middle of a nested table, so COUNT could be different from LAST for a table. COUNT is most useful when selecting a nested table from the database, since the number of elements is unknown at that point. COUNT ignores deleted elements when computing the total.

LIMIT

LIMIT returns the current maximum number of elements for a collection. Since nested tables have no maximum size, LIMIT always returns NULL when applied to a nested table. The following example illustrates the use of LIMIT:

```
-- Available online as limit.sql
DECLARE
  v_Table NumTab := NumTab(1, 2, 3);
  v_Varray NumVar := NumVar(1234, 4321);
BEGIN
  -- Output the limit and count for the collections.
```

```
   DBMS_OUTPUT.PUT_LINE('Varray limit: ' || v_Varray.LIMIT);
   DBMS_OUTPUT.PUT_LINE('Varray count: ' || v_Varray.COUNT);
   IF v_Table.LIMIT IS NULL THEN
     DBMS_OUTPUT.PUT_LINE('Table limit is NULL');
   ELSE
     DBMS_OUTPUT.PUT_LINE('Table limit: ' || v_Table.LIMIT);
   END IF;
   DBMS_OUTPUT.PUT_LINE('Table count: ' || v_Table.COUNT);
END;
```

The output for this example is

```
Varray limit: 25
Varray count: 2
Table limit is NULL
Table count: 3
```

Note that the varray limit is 25, as defined in the CREATE TYPE statement, even though **v_Varray** currently contains only two elements. COUNT returns the current number of elements, as described in the previous section.

FIRST and LAST

FIRST returns the index of the first element of a collection, and LAST returns the index of the last element. For a varray, FIRST always returns 1 and LAST always returns the value of COUNT, since a varray is dense and elements cannot be deleted. FIRST and LAST are used along with NEXT and PRIOR to loop through a collection, as illustrated by the example in the next section.

NEXT and PRIOR

NEXT and PRIOR are used to increment and decrement the key for a collection. The syntax is

NEXT(*n*)
PRIOR(*n*)

where *n* is an integer expression. NEXT(*n*) returns the key of the element immediately prior to element *n*, and PRIOR(*n*) returns the key of the element immediately after element *n*. If there is no next or prior element, NEXT and PRIOR will return NULL. The following example illustrates how to use NEXT and PRIOR, along with FIRST and LAST, to loop through a nested table:

```
-- Available online as loops.sql
DECLARE
  TYPE t_CharTab IS TABLE OF CHAR(1);
  v_Characters t_CharTab := t_CharTab('M', 'a', 'd', 'a', 'm',
                 ',', ' ', 'I', '''', 'm', ' ', 'A', 'd', 'a', 'm');

  v_Index INTEGER;
BEGIN
  -- Loop forwards over the table.
  v_Index := v_Characters.FIRST;
  WHILE v_Index <= v_Characters.LAST LOOP
    DBMS_OUTPUT.PUT(v_Characters(v_Index));
    v_Index := v_Characters.NEXT(v_Index);
  END LOOP;
  DBMS_OUTPUT.NEW_LINE;

  -- Loop backwards over the table.
  v_Index := v_Characters.LAST;
  WHILE v_Index >= v_Characters.FIRST LOOP
    DBMS_OUTPUT.PUT(v_Characters(v_Index));
    v_Index := v_Characters.PRIOR(v_Index);
  END LOOP;
  DBMS_OUTPUT.NEW_LINE;
END;
```

EXTEND

EXTEND is used to add elements to the end of a nested table. EXTEND has three forms:

```
EXTEND
EXTEND(n)
EXTEND(n, i)
```

EXTEND with no arguments simply adds a NULL element to the end of the table, with index LAST+1. EXTEND(n) adds n NULL elements to the end of the table, while EXTEND(n, i) adds n copies of element i to the end of the table. If the table has been created with a NOT NULL constraint, then only

the last form can be used, since it does not add a null element. The
following example illustrates the use of EXTEND:

 `-- Available online as extend.sql`

```
DECLARE
  v_Numbers NumTab := NumTab(1, 2, 3, 4, 5);
BEGIN
  -- This assignment will raise SUBSCRIPT_BEYOND_COUNT, since
  -- v_Numbers has only 5 elements.
  v_Numbers(26) := -7;
EXCEPTION
  WHEN SUBSCRIPT_BEYOND_COUNT THEN
    DBMS_OUTPUT.PUT_LINE('ORA-6533 raised');

    -- We can fix this by adding 30 additional elements to
    -- v_Numbers.
    v_Numbers.EXTEND(30);

    -- And now do the assignment.
    v_Numbers(26) := -7;
END;
```

NOTE
*Since a varray has a fixed maximum size,
EXTEND will have no effect on a VARRAY.
It is not illegal to use it, however.*

EXTEND operates on the internal size of a collection, which includes
any deleted elements. When an element is deleted (using the DELETE
method, described later in this section), the data for that element is
removed, but the key remains. The following example illustrates the
interaction between EXTEND and DELETE.

`-- Available online as extdel.sql`

```
DECLARE
  -- Initialize a table to 5 elements.
  v_Numbers NumTab := NumTab(-2, -1, 0, 1, 2);

  -- Local procedure to print out a table.
  PROCEDURE Print(p_Table IN NumTab) IS
    v_Index INTEGER;
```

```
  BEGIN
    v_Index := p_Table.FIRST;
    WHILE v_Index <= p_Table.LAST LOOP
      DBMS_OUTPUT.PUT('Element ' || v_Index || ': ');
      DBMS_OUTPUT.PUT_LINE(p_Table(v_Index));
      v_Index := p_Table.NEXT(v_Index);
    END LOOP;
  END Print;

BEGIN
  DBMS_OUTPUT.PUT_LINE('At initialization, v_Numbers contains');
  Print(v_Numbers);

  -- Delete element 3. This removes the '0', but keeps a
  -- placeholder where it was.
  v_Numbers.DELETE(3);

  DBMS_OUTPUT.PUT_LINE('After delete, v_Numbers contains');
  Print(v_Numbers);

  -- Add 2 copies of element 1 onto the table. This will add
  -- elements 6 and 7.
  v_Numbers.EXTEND(2, 1);

  DBMS_OUTPUT.PUT_LINE('After extend, v_Numbers contains');
  Print(v_Numbers);

  DBMS_OUTPUT.PUT_LINE('v_Numbers.COUNT = ' || v_Numbers.COUNT);
  DBMS_OUTPUT.PUT_LINE('v_Numbers.LAST = ' || v_Numbers.LAST);
END;
```

This example produces the following output. Note the value of COUNT and LAST after the DELETE and EXTEND operation.

```
At initialization, v_Numbers contains
Element 1: -2
Element 2: -1
Element 3: 0
Element 4: 1
Element 5: 2
After delete, v_Numbers contains
Element 1: -2
Element 2: -1
```

```
Element 4: 1
Element 5: 2
After extend, v_Numbers contains
Element 1: -2
Element 2: -1
Element 4: 1
Element 5: 2
Element 6: -2
Element 7: -2
v_Numbers.COUNT = 6
v_Numbers.LAST = 7
```

TRIM

TRIM is used to remove elements from the end of a nested table. Since a varray is a fixed size, TRIM will have no effect when used on a varray. It has two forms, defined with:

TRIM
TRIM(*n*)

With no arguments, TRIM removes 1 element from the end of the collection. Otherwise, *n* elements are removed. If *n* is greater than COUNT, the SUBSCRIPT_BEYOND_COUNT exception is raised. After the TRIM, COUNT will be smaller, since the elements have been removed.

Similar to EXTEND, TRIM operates on the internal size of a collection, including any elements removed with DELETE. This is illustrated by the following example.

```
-- Available online as trim.sql
DECLARE
  -- Initialize a table to 7 elements.
  v_Numbers NumTab := NumTab(-3, -2, -1, 0, 1, 2, 3);

  -- Local procedure to print out a table.
  PROCEDURE Print(p_Table IN NumTab) IS
    v_Index INTEGER;
  BEGIN
    v_Index := p_Table.FIRST;
    WHILE v_Index <= p_Table.LAST LOOP
      DBMS_OUTPUT.PUT('Element ' || v_Index || ': ');
      DBMS_OUTPUT.PUT_LINE(p_Table(v_Index));
```

```
        v_Index := p_Table.NEXT(v_Index);
      END LOOP;
      DBMS_OUTPUT.PUT_LINE('COUNT = ' || p_Table.COUNT);
      DBMS_OUTPUT.PUT_LINE('LAST = ' || p_Table.LAST);
    END Print;

BEGIN
    DBMS_OUTPUT.PUT_LINE('At initialization, v_Numbers contains');
    Print(v_Numbers);

    -- Delete element 6.
    v_Numbers.DELETE(6);
    DBMS_OUTPUT.PUT_LINE('After delete , v_Numbers contains');
    Print(v_Numbers);

    -- Trim the last 3 elements. This will remove the 2 and 3, but
    -- also remove the (now empty) spot where 1 was.
    v_Numbers.TRIM(3);
    DBMS_OUTPUT.PUT_LINE('After trim, v_Numbers contains');
    Print(v_Numbers);
END;
```

This example produces the following output:

```
At initialization, v_Numbers contains
Element 1: -3
Element 2: -2
Element 3: -1
Element 4: 0
Element 5: 1
Element 6: 2
Element 7: 3
COUNT = 7
LAST = 7
After delete , v_Numbers contains
Element 1: -3
Element 2: -2
Element 3: -1
Element 4: 0
Element 5: 1
Element 7: 3
COUNT = 6
LAST = 7
After trim, v_Numbers contains
```

```
Element 1: -3
Element 2: -2
Element 3: -1
Element 4: 0
COUNT = 4
LAST = 4
```

DELETE

DELETE will remove 1 or more elements from a nested table. Like TRIM, DELETE has no effect on a varray because of its fixed size. DELETE has three forms:

> DELETE
> DELETE(*n*)
> DELETE(*m,n*)

With no arguments, DELETE will remove the entire table. DELETE(*n*) will remove the element at index *n*, and DELETE(*m,n*) will remove all the elements between indexes *m* and *n*. After the DELETE, COUNT will be smaller, reflecting the new size of the nested table. If the element to be deleted does not exist, DELETE will not raise and error, and will simply skip that element. The following example illustrates the use of DELETE.

```
-- Available online as delete.sql
DECLARE
  -- Initialize a table to 10 elements.
  v_Numbers NumTab := NumTab(10, 20, 30, 40, 50, 60, 70, 80,
                             90, 100);

  -- Local procedure to print out a table.
  PROCEDURE Print(p_Table IN NumTab) IS
    v_Index INTEGER;
  BEGIN
    v_Index := p_Table.FIRST;
    WHILE v_Index <= p_Table.LAST LOOP
      DBMS_OUTPUT.PUT('Element ' || v_Index || ': ');
      DBMS_OUTPUT.PUT_LINE(p_Table(v_Index));
      v_Index := p_Table.NEXT(v_Index);
    END LOOP;
    DBMS_OUTPUT.PUT_LINE('COUNT = ' || p_Table.COUNT);
    DBMS_OUTPUT.PUT_LINE('LAST = ' || p_Table.LAST);
  END Print;
```

```
BEGIN
  DBMS_OUTPUT.PUT_LINE('At initialization, v_Numbers contains');
  Print(v_Numbers);

  -- Delete element 6.
  DBMS_OUTPUT.PUT_LINE('After delete(6), v_Numbers contains');
  v_Numbers.DELETE(6);
  Print(v_Numbers);

  -- Delete elements 7 through 9.
  DBMS_OUTPUT.PUT_LINE('After delete(7,9), v_Numbers contains');
  v_Numbers.DELETE(7,9);
  Print(v_Numbers);
END;
```

This example produces the following output:

```
At initialization, v_Numbers contains
Element 1: 10
Element 2: 20
Element 3: 30
Element 4: 40
Element 5: 50
Element 6: 60
Element 7: 70
Element 8: 80
Element 9: 90
Element 10: 100
COUNT = 10
LAST = 10
After delete(6), v_Numbers contains
Element 1: 10
Element 2: 20
Element 3: 30
Element 4: 40
Element 5: 50
Element 7: 70
Element 8: 80
Element 9: 90
Element 10: 100
COUNT = 9
LAST = 10
After delete(7,9), v_Numbers contains
```

```
Element 1: 10
Element 2: 20
Element 3: 30
Element 4: 40
Element 5: 50
Element 10: 100
COUNT = 6
LAST = 10
```

Summary

Collections are a useful construct for any programming language. In this chapter, we have examined nested tables and varrays. Depending on your needs, you can use whichever collection is more appropriate. This chapter completes the discussion of PL/SQL syntax and constructs. Now that we have the building blocks of the language, we move on in the next chapter to PL/SQL execution environments.

CHAPTER
13

PL/SQL Execution
Environments

n Chapters 2 through 12, we have covered the basics of
PL/SQL. In this chapter, we will explore different PL/SQL
run-time environments. In some environments (like Oracle
Forms or Procedure Builder), PL/SQL blocks can be run
entirely on the client, without interacting with the database
server. In other environments (such as the precompilers or SQL-Station),
they can be submitted from a client program to run on the server.
Depending on the environment, different features are available for the
control of the PL/SQL block.

Different PL/SQL Engines

PL/SQL has been available in the database server since version 6 of Oracle.
This means that both SQL statements and PL/SQL blocks can be sent to the
database and processed. As described in Chapter 1, Oracle7 contains
version 2 of PL/SQL, and Oracle8 contains version 8 of PL/SQL. A client
application, written using either Oracle's development tools or tools by
another vendor, can issue both SQL statements and PL/SQL blocks to the
server. SQL*Plus is an example of such a client application in which SQL
statements and PL/SQL blocks entered interactively at the SQL prompt are
sent to the server for execution.

Figure 13-1 illustrates this scenario. The client application issues both a
PL/SQL block (which contains both procedural and SQL statements), and a
separate SQL statement to the server. Both the PL/SQL block and the SQL
statement are sent over the network to the server. Once there, the SQL
statement is sent directly to the SQL statement executor contained in the
server. However, the procedural statements in the block (such as the
assignment) are parsed and executed by the PL/SQL engine. Any SQL
statements inside the block (such as the SELECT statement) are sent to the
same SQL statement executor.

In addition to the PL/SQL engine on the server, several of Oracle's tools
contain a PL/SQL engine. The development tool itself runs on the client, not
the server. The PL/SQL engine also runs on the client. With client-side
PL/SQL, procedural statements within PL/SQL blocks are run on the client
and not sent to the server. As an example, Oracle Forms (bundled as part of
the Developer 2000 suite of Oracle products) contains a separate PL/SQL
engine. Other tools in this suite, such as Oracle Reports or Oracle
Graphics, also contain a PL/SQL engine. This engine is different from the

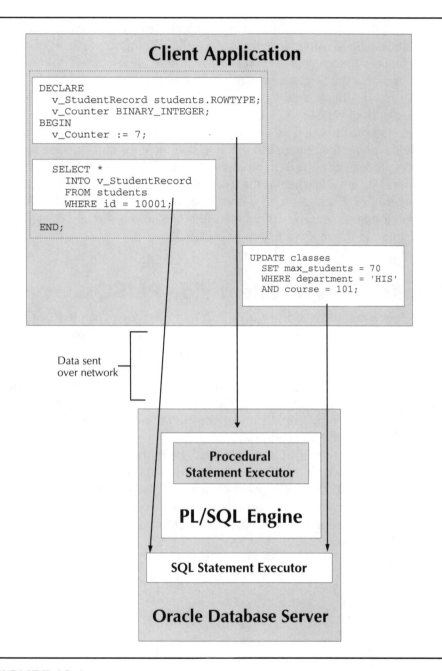

FIGURE 13-1. *PL/SQL engine on the server*

PL/SQL on the server. PL/SQL blocks are contained within a client-side application written using these tools. An Oracle Forms application, for example, contains triggers and procedures. These are executed on the client, and only the SQL statements within them are sent to the server for processing. The local PL/SQL engine on the client processes the procedural statements, as illustrated in Figure 13-2.

SQL statements issued by the application (the UPDATE statement) are sent directly over the network to the SQL statement executor on the server, as before. However, the client processes PL/SQL blocks locally. Any procedural statements (such as the assignment) can be processed without network traffic. SQL statements within PL/SQL blocks (such as SELECT) are also sent to the server. The rationale for this situation is discussed later in this chapter, in the section "Client-side PL/SQL."

Implications of Client-side PL/SQL

In this scenario illustrated in Figure 13-2, there are two separate PL/SQL engines, which communicate between each other. For example, a trigger within a form (running in client-side PL/SQL) can call a stored procedure within the database (running in server-side PL/SQL). Communications such as these take place through remote procedure calls. A similar mechanism is used to communicate between PL/SQL engines in two different servers, through database links. The dependencies between the various PL/SQL objects are discussed in Chapter 7.

In general, the two PL/SQL engines may be different versions. Developer 2000 version 1.2, for example, uses PL/SQL version 1, while the server uses PL/SQL version 2 (or 8 if Oracle8). This implies that features contained in PL/SQL version 2 and higher, such as user-defined tables and records and fixed-length CHAR datatypes, among others, can't be used in client-side PL/SQL.

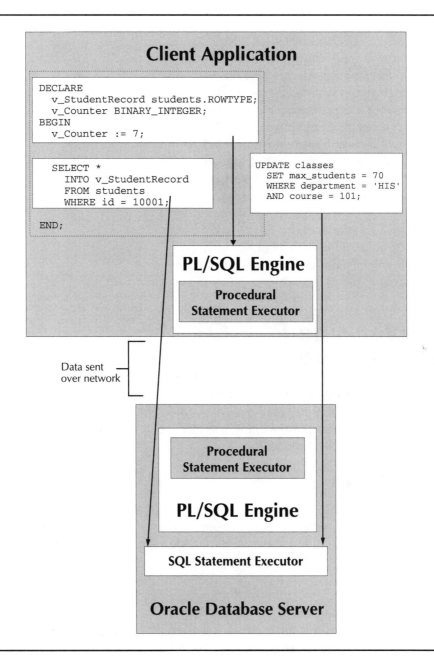

FIGURE 13-2. *PL/SQL engine on the client*

TIP
When PL/SQL 2 becomes available for client-side applications, the PL/SQL blocks contained within these applications will have to be migrated to version 2 syntax and semantics. One of the main differences is the behavior of the CHAR datatype. In version 1 of PL/SQL, both CHAR and VARCHAR2 variables are variable length strings. In version 2, CHAR variables are fixed length, and VARCHAR2 variables are variable length. In order to make migration easier, avoid using CHAR variables in client-side PL/SQL, and use VARCHAR or VARCHAR2 instead. For more information on character comparison semantics, see Chapter 3.

Server-side PL/SQL

This section covers PL/SQL blocks that run on the server. They can be submitted to the server from various client tools, including SQL*Plus, the Oracle precompilers, and the OCI (Oracle Call Interface). They can also be submitted from third-party applications such as SQL-Station. Applications written in tools that contain a PL/SQL engine, such as Oracle Forms, can also make calls to server-side PL/SQL.

SQL*Plus

SQL*Plus allows the user to enter SQL statements and PL/SQL blocks interactively from a prompt. These statements are sent directly to the database, and the results are returned to the screen. Because of its interactive nature, SQL*Plus is perhaps the most convenient way to manipulate PL/SQL on the server. For more information on SQL*Plus and the commands not covered in this section, see the *SQL*Plus User's Guide and Reference*.

SQL*Plus commands are not case sensitive. For example, all of the following commands declare bind variables:

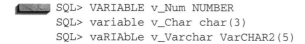

```
SQL> VARIABLE v_Num NUMBER
SQL> variable v_Char char(3)
SQL> vaRIAbLe v_Varchar VarCHAR2(5)
```

Manipulating Blocks in SQL*Plus

When you execute a SQL statement in SQL*Plus, the semicolon terminates the statement. The semicolon is not part of the statement itself—it is the statement terminator. When SQL*Plus reads the semicolon, it knows that the statement is complete and sends it to the database. On the other hand, with a PL/SQL block, the semicolon is a syntactic part of the block itself—it is not a statement terminator. When you enter the DECLARE or BEGIN keyword, SQL*Plus detects this and knows that you are running a PL/SQL block rather than a SQL statement. But SQL*Plus still needs to know when the block has ended. This is done with a forward slash, which is short for the SQL*Plus RUN command.

Note the slash after the PL/SQL block that updates the **registered_students** table in Figure 13-3. The SELECT statement after the block does not need the slash because the semicolon is present.

```
± Oracle SQL*Plus                                          _□X
File Edit Search Options Help
SQL> DECLARE
  2    CURSOR c_Music410Students IS
  3      SELECT *
  4        FROM registered_students
  5        WHERE department = 'MUS' and course = 410
  6        FOR UPDATE OF grade;
  7  BEGIN
  8    FOR v_Student IN c_Music410Students LOOP
  9      UPDATE registered_students
 10        SET grade = 'A'
 11        WHERE CURRENT OF c_Music410Students;
 12    END LOOP;
 13  END;
 14  /

PL/SQL procedure successfully completed.

SQL> SELECT * FROM registered_students
  2    WHERE department = 'MUS' and course = 410;

STUDENT_ID DEP   COURSE G
---------- ---   --------- -
     10009 MUS      410 A
     10006 MUS      410 A

SQL>
```

FIGURE 13-3. *PL/SQL in SQL*Plus*

Substitution Variables

PL/SQL doesn't really have any capabilities for input from the user and output to the screen. There is a built-in package, DBMS_OUTPUT, which allows limited output in SQL*Plus. This package is discussed in detail in Chapter 14. PL/SQL 2.3 also has a built-in package, UTL_FILE (discussed in Chapter 18), which allows input from and output to operating system files. However, SQL*Plus itself has a mechanism for accepting input from the user. Input is accomplished through *substitution variables*. A textual substitution of the variable is done by SQL*Plus before the PL/SQL block or SQL statement is sent to the server, similar to the behavior of C macros. Substitution variables are delineated by the ampersand (&) character.

Figure 13-4 illustrates the use of substitution variables. The same block is run twice, each time initializing **v_StudentID** to a different value. The

```
Oracle SQL*Plus                                          _ □ ×
File  Edit  Search  Options  Help

SQL> DECLARE
  2     v_StudentID students.id%TYPE := &student_id;
  3  BEGIN
  4     Register(v_StudentID, 'CS', 102);
  5  END;
  6  /
Enter value for student_id: 10004
old   2:   v_StudentID students.id%TYPE := &student_id;
new   2:   v_StudentID students.id%TYPE := 10004;

PL/SQL procedure successfully completed.

SQL> DECLARE
  2     v_StudentID students.id%TYPE := &student_id;
  3  BEGIN
  4     Register(v_StudentID, 'CS', 102);
  5  END;
  6  /
Enter value for student_id: 10005
old   2:   v_StudentID students.id%TYPE := &student_id;
new   2:   v_StudentID students.id%TYPE := 10005;

PL/SQL procedure successfully completed.

SQL>
```

FIGURE 13-4. *SQL*Plus substitution variables*

user inputs the values 10004 and 10005, and they are textually replaced in the block for **&student_id**.

It is important to note that no memory is actually allocated for substitution variables. SQL*Plus replaces the substitution variable with the value you input before the block is sent to the database for execution. Because of this, substitution variables can be used for input only. Bind variables, however, can be used for input or output.

Although substitution variables can be used for input only, they can be used anywhere in the SQL statement or PL/SQL block. Figure 13-5 illustrates this. The substitution variables **&columns** and **&where_clause** are used for structural parts of the statements themselves—table and column names, for example. The only way to accomplish this in pure PL/SQL is to use the DBMS_SQL package, explained in Chapter 15.

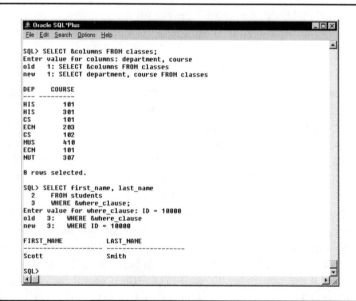

FIGURE 13-5.   *More substitution variables*

TIP
*Suppose you enter the following SQL
statement from the SQL> prompt:*

```
SQL> SELECT *
        FROM students
        WHERE first_name = &first_name;
```

*In this case, when SQL*Plus prompts you for
a value, you must include the single quotes,
such as 'SCOTT'. Compare this to the
following statement*

```
SQL> SELECT *
        FROM students
        WHERE first_name = '&first_name';
```

*Now, you don't enter the quotes, since they
are already part of the statement.*

SQL*Plus Bind Variables

SQL*Plus can also allocate memory. This storage can be used inside
PL/SQL blocks and SQL statements. Because this storage is allocated
outside the block, it can be used for more than one block in succession,
and it can be printed after a block completes. This storage is known as a
bind variable, illustrated in Figure 13-6. The **v_Count** bind variable is
allocated using the SQL*Plus command VARIABLE. Note that this
command is valid only from the SQL prompt, and not inside a PL/SQL
block. Inside the block, the bind variable is delimited by the leading colon
rather than an ampersand. After the block, the PRINT command shows the
value of the variable. The only types valid for SQL*Plus bind variables are
VARCHAR2, CHAR, and NUMBER (or, with SQL*Plus 3.2 and higher,
REFCURSOR). If the length isn't specified for bind variables of type
VARCHAR2 or CHAR, the length defaults to 1. NUMBER bind variables
cannot be constrained by a precision or scale.

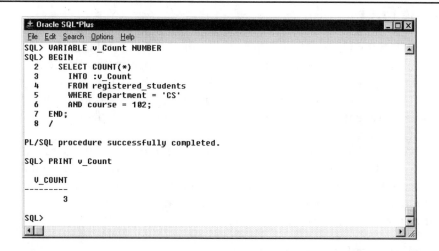

```
± Oracle SQL*Plus                                    _□×
File Edit Search Options Help
SQL> VARIABLE v_Count NUMBER
SQL> BEGIN
  2    SELECT COUNT(*)
  3      INTO :v_Count
  4      FROM registered_students
  5      WHERE department = 'CS'
  6      AND course = 102;
  7  END;
  8  /

PL/SQL procedure successfully completed.

SQL> PRINT v_Count

  V_COUNT
---------
        3

SQL>
```

FIGURE 13-6.   *SQL*Plus bind variables*

Calling Stored Procedures with EXECUTE

A stored procedure call must be made from the executable or exception handling section of a PL/SQL block. SQL*Plus provides a useful shorthand for this syntax—the EXECUTE command. All that EXECUTE does is to take its arguments, put BEGIN before them, and END; after. The resulting block is then submitted to the database. For example, if we enter

```
SQL> EXECUTE Register(10006, 'CS', 102)
```

from the SQL prompt, the PL/SQL block

```
BEGIN Register(10006, 'CS', 102); END;
```

would actually be sent to the database. A semicolon is optional after the EXECUTE command. This is true of all the SQL*Plus commands—if a semicolon is present, it is ignored. Like PRINT or VARIABLE, EXECUTE is a SQL*Plus command and thus is not valid inside a PL/SQL block.

Using Files

SQL*Plus can save the current PL/SQL block or SQL statement to a file, and this file can then be read back in and executed. This useful feature is valuable both during development of a PL/SQL program and later execution of it. For example, you can store a CREATE OR REPLACE command in a file. This way, any modifications to the procedure can be done to the file. In order to save the changes in the database, you can simply read the file into SQL*Plus.

The SQL*Plus GET command reads a file from disk into the local buffer. A forward slash will then run it, as if it had been entered directly from the keyboard. If the file contains a slash at the end, however, it can be read in and run using the at sign (@) shortcut. For example, assume that the file **call_reg.sql** contains the following lines:

```
- Available online as call_reg.sql
VARIABLE v_Count NUMBER

BEGIN
  Register(&student_id, 'CS', 102);
  SELECT COUNT(*)
    INTO :v_Count
    FROM registered_students
    WHERE department = 'CS'
    AND course = 102;
END;
/

PRINT v_Count
```

We can now execute this file from the SQL prompt with

```
SQL> @call_reg
```

The output from this is shown in Figure 13-7. The SET ECHO ON command tells SQL*Plus to echo the contents of the file to the screen as they are read from the file.

Using the SHOW ERRORS Command

As discussed in Chapter 7, when a stored subprogram is created, information about it is stored in the data dictionary. Specifically, any compile errors are stored in the **user_errors** data dictionary view. SQL*Plus

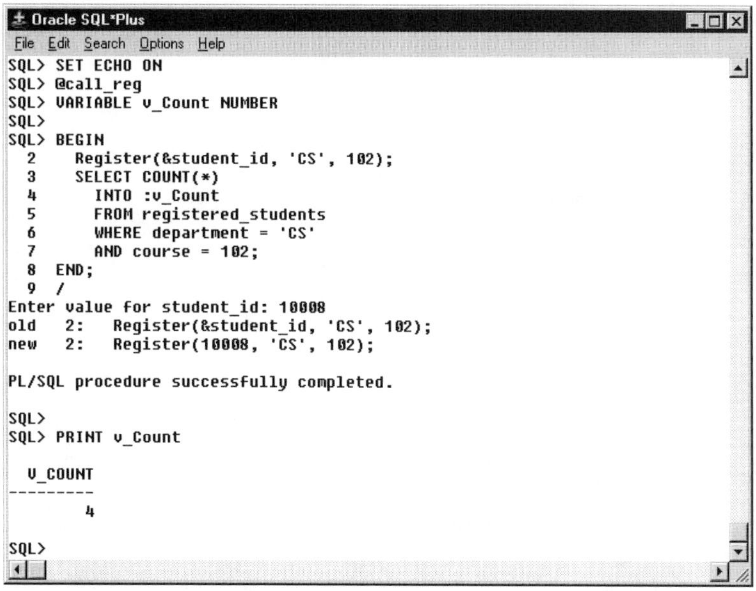

```
Oracle SQL*Plus                                                  _ □ ×
File  Edit  Search  Options  Help
SQL> SET ECHO ON                                                    ▲
SQL> @call_reg
SQL> VARIABLE v_Count NUMBER
SQL>
SQL> BEGIN
  2     Register(&student_id, 'CS', 102);
  3     SELECT COUNT(*)
  4       INTO :v_Count
  5       FROM registered_students
  6       WHERE department = 'CS'
  7       AND course = 102;
  8  END;
  9  /
Enter value for student_id: 10008
old   2:    Register(&student_id, 'CS', 102);
new   2:    Register(10008, 'CS', 102);

PL/SQL procedure successfully completed.

SQL>
SQL> PRINT v_Count

  V_COUNT
---------
        4

SQL>                                                                ▼
```

FIGURE 13-7.   *Using a file in SQL*Plus*

provides a useful command, SHOW ERRORS, which will query this view and report the errors. Figure 13-8 illustrates this. SHOW ERRORS can be used after SQL*Plus reports this message:

```
Warning: Procedure created with compilation errors.
```

Oracle Precompilers

Using the Oracle precompilers, SQL statements and PL/SQL blocks can be contained inside 3GL programs written in C, C++, COBOL, Pascal, FORTRAN, PL/1, and Ada. The precompilers are known as Pro*C, Pro*Cobol, Pro*Pascal, and so on. This form of PL/SQL is known as *embedded PL/SQL*. The language in which PL/SQL is embedded is known as the *host language*. The precompiler will translate the embedded SQL and PL/SQL statements into calls to the precompiler's run-time library. The

```
Oracle SQL*Plus                                             _ □ ☒
File  Edit  Search  Options  Help

SQL> CREATE OR REPLACE PROCEDURE TooManyErrors (
  2    p_ParameterA IN VARCHAR2,
  3    p_ParameterB OUT DATE) AS
  4  BEGIN
  5    INSERT INTO non_existent_table VALUES (p_ParameterA);
  6    RETURN p_ParameterB;
  7  END TooManyErrors;
  8  /

Warning: Procedure created with compilation errors.

SQL> show errors
Errors for PROCEDURE TOOMANYERRORS:

LINE/COL ERROR
-------- ---------------------------------------------------------
5/3      PL/SQL: SQL Statement ignored
5/15     PLS-00201: identifier 'NON_EXISTENT_TABLE' must be declared
6/3      PLS-00372: In a procedure, RETURN statement cannot contain an
         expression

6/3      PL/SQL: Statement ignored
SQL>
```

FIGURE 13-8. *Using SHOW ERRORS*

output of the precompiler must then be compiled and linked with this
library to create an executable. Similar to SQL*Plus, there is no PL/SQL
engine on the client—the SQL statements and PL/SQL blocks are sent to the
server to be executed. The program itself resides on the client.

Communication between the program and the database is done through
host variables. These are variables declared according to the rules of the
host language, except that they are inside a special section of the program
known as the declare section. The declare section is delimited by

```
EXEC SQL BEGIN DECLARE SECTION;
```

and

```
EXEC SQL END DECLARE SECTION;
```

in the source code.

NOTE
With version 2.0 and higher of Pro*C/C++, the declare section is no longer required. Any host variable can be used in an embedded SQL statement or PL/SQL block whether or not it is declared in a declare section.

There are several differences between embedded PL/SQL and PL/SQL entered interactively in SQL*Plus. These include the use of bind variables, statement terminators, and precompiler requirements. For more information on the Oracle precompilers, see the *Programmer's Guide to the Pro*C/C++ Precompiler,* or the *Programmer's Guide to the Oracle Precompilers.*

Bind Variables in the Precompilers
Variables that are declared in the declare section are legal to use inside embedded PL/SQL blocks and embedded SQL statements. Inside of an embedded statement, the bind variables are delimited by a leading colon. For example, the following Pro*C program fragment calls the **Register** stored procedure. For the benefit of readers who may not be familiar with C, this code is more heavily commented than usual.

```
/* Available online as call_reg.pc */
EXEC SQL BEGIN DECLARE SECTION;
  /* Declare C variables. */
  VARCHAR v_Department[4]; /* The VARCHAR pseudo-type is
                              available only in Pro*C, and is
                              converted into a record type with
                              two fields - .arr and .len */
  int v_Course;           /* v_Course is an integer. */
  int v_StudentID;        /* So is v_StudentID. */
EXEC SQL END DECLARE SECTION;

  /* Initialize the host variables. Here we are just assigning
     to them, but they could be read from a file, accepted from
     user input, etc. For the VARCHAR variables, the string is
     copied into the .arr field, and the length of the string
     (3 in this case) is assigned to the .len field. */
  strcpy(v_Department.arr, "ECN");
  v_Department.len = 3;
  v_Course = 101;
```

```
v_StudentID = 10006;

/* Begin the embedded PL/SQL block. Note the EXEC SQL EXECUTE
   and END-EXEC; keywords, which delimit the block for the
   precompiler. */
EXEC SQL EXECUTE
  BEGIN
    Register(:v_Department, :v_Course, :v_StudentID);
  END;
END-EXEC;
```

Inside the embedded block, the host variables **v_Department**, **v_Course**, and **v_StudentID** are prefixed by colons. If they were not, the program would not precompile and would return the error:

```
PLS-201: identifier must be declared
```

Embedding a Block
Note how the PL/SQL block itself is delimited in the preceding program fragment. An embedded PL/SQL block starts with the keywords

```
EXEC SQL EXECUTE
```

and ends with

```
END-EXEC;
```

The semicolon after the END-EXEC is required. Between these two keywords, place an entire PL/SQL block, including the trailing semicolon following the END. The embedded block can have declarative and exception handling sections as well.

Indicator Variables
PL/SQL variables, like database columns, can have either a value or the non-value NULL. However, 3GLs, such as C, have no concept of NULL. C can simulate NULLs for strings with the empty string, but there is no way to have a NULL integer, for example. In order to remedy this, an *indicator variable* is used. An indicator variable is simply a 2-byte integer that is appended to the host variable reference in the embedded block or SQL statement. For example, the following embedded block selects from the

registered_students table. The grade column in this table can have a NULL value, so we need the indicator variable to detect this.

```
/* Available online as part of indicator.pc */
EXEC SQL BEGIN DECLARE SECTION;
  char v_Grade;    /* v_Grade is a single character. */
  short i_Grade;   /* Note that the indicator is declared as a
                      short, which is a 2 byte integer. */
EXEC SQL END DECLARE SECTION;

EXEC SQL EXECUTE
  BEGIN
    SELECT grade
      INTO :v_Grade INDICATOR :i_Grade
      FROM registered_students
      WHERE student_id = 10006
      AND department = 'ECN'
      AND course = 101;
  END;
END-EXEC;

if (i_Grade != 0)
  printf("No grade recorded for this student\n");
else
  printf("The grade recorded is %c\n", v_Grade);
```

Between the host variable and the indicator variable, the keyword INDICATOR can be used, as in the preceding example. This keyword is optional, so we could have written the block with

```
/* Available online as part of indicator.pc */
EXEC SQL EXECUTE
  BEGIN
    SELECT grade
      INTO :v_Grade:i_Grade
      FROM registered_students
      WHERE student_id = 10006
      AND department = 'ECN'
      AND course = 101;
  END;
```

The **v_Grade** variable in the preceding example is an *output variable*—the variable is assigned to by the block. For output variables, the indicator has the meaning as described in the following table:

Value of Indicator Variable	Meaning
0	The host variable was retrieved successfully.
–1	The host variable was assigned a NULL value.
>0	The host variable was not large enough to hold the returned value and was truncated. The indicator variable contains the original length of the result. This value is applicable only for character host variables.
–2	The host variable was not large enough to hold the returned value and was truncated. However, the original length was too large to fit in 2 bytes. This value is applicable only for character host variables.

An *input variable* is read from inside the embedded block. Indicator variables can also be used for input variables. Their meaning is similar to indicators used for output variables and is described as follows:

Value of Indicator Variable	Meaning
0	The associated host variable should be used.
–1	A NULL should be used.

Error Handling

Error handling in a Pro*C program is done with either the sqlca structure or the SQLCODE and/or SQLSTATE status variables. After each executable embedded SQL statement, the status variables will contain the error code from the statement, or zero if the statement is successful. This behavior is the same for embedded PL/SQL blocks. If the block exits with an unhandled exception, the error code is returned to the status variable. If the block handles any exceptions that are raised, then the entire block completes successfully, and the status variable would contain zero, indicating successful completion. The complete rules for exception propagation are described in Chapter 10.

For example, the following Pro*C fragment contains an embedded block that calls the **RecordFullClasses** procedure, defined in Chapter 7. After the block completes, the program checks the **sqlca.sqlcode** status variable to see if the block was successful. If not, the error message is printed.

```
/* Available online as error.pc */
EXEC SQL INCLUDE SQLCA; /* This statement includes the SQLCA
                           structure. This structure contains
                           fields used for error handling. */
EXEC SQL EXECUTE
  BEGIN
    RecordFullClasses;
  END;
END-EXEC;
/* sqlca.sqlcode will be zero if the statement was successful,
   and will contain the error code if the statement completed
   with an error. If an error occurs, sqlca.sqlerrm.sqlerrmc
   will contain the error message text, and sqlca.sqlerrm.sqlerrml
   will contain the length of the message. */
if (sqlca.sqlcode != 0) {
  printf("Error during execution of RecordFullClasses.\n");
  printf("%.70s\n", sqlca.sqlerrm.sqlerrml, sqlca.sqlerrm.sqlerrmc);
  }
else
  printf("Execution successful.\n");
```

Necessary Precompiler Options

In order to precompile a program with an embedded PL/SQL block, the precompiler option SQLCHECK must be set to SEMANTICS. When SQLCHECK=SEMANTICS, the precompiler will attempt to connect to the database during precompile time to verify the syntax and semantics of the database objects referenced by the program. In order to do this, the precompiler needs a user name and password. This is provided through the USERID precompiler option. The same user name and password that the program uses at run time should be used at precompile time. For example, if your program connects to the database as the Oracle user example, with password example, the precompiler options would have to include the following:

```
SQLCHECK=SEMANTICS USERID=example/example
```

The USERID parameter can accept both a user name and a password, as in the preceding example, or just the user name. If the password is not specified, then the precompiler will prompt you for it.

If the USERID option is not specified, you must supply embedded DECLARE TABLE statements to identify the structure of tables referenced. However, there is no DECLARE PROCEDURE statement, so if your program calls stored procedures, USERID is required along with SQLCHECK=SEMANTICS.

NOTE
If USERID is not specified and there are no DECLARE TABLE statements for the tables referenced by the program, the precompiler will return errors such as

```
PLS-201: identifier must be declared
```

which can be confusing. The table does exist and the user does have permission to access it, but the error seems to imply otherwise. This error is a result of the missing USERID parameter, rather than a missing table. As a general rule, whenever SQLCHECK=SEMANTICS, USERID should also be specified to avoid confusion.

OCI

The Oracle Call Interface (OCI) provides another method of accessing the database from a 3GL program. Rather than embedding PL/SQL and SQL statements, however, you call functions defined in the OCI library. The OCI library provides functions to parse SQL statements, bind input variables, define output variables, execute statements, and fetch the results. The source program is written entirely in the third-generation language, and no precompiler is required. For more information on OCI, see the *Programmer's Guide to the Oracle Call Interface*.

Using PL/SQL with OCI is straightforward. Rather than parsing a SQL statement, simply parse an anonymous PL/SQL block. For example, the following program fragment parses an anonymous block:

```
char *plsql_block =
  "BEGIN \
     Register(:v_StudentID, :v_Department, :v_Course); \
  END;";
int return_val;
Cda_Def cda;

return_val = oparse(&cda, plsql_block, -1, 1, 2);
```

> **NOTE**
> *The examples in this section use the OCI as defined for Oracle7. The Oracle8 OCI has a different interface, which can manipulate objects and the client-side object cache as well as issue SQL statements. All of the Oracle7 OCI calls are still included in the Oracle8 OCI library, and are valid against an Oracle8 database.*

Guidelines for PL/SQL Blocks in OCI

The **oparse** call expects a string containing the SQL statement that you want to execute. In order to execute a PL/SQL block, this string should contain the entire block, including the trailing semicolon, as in the preceding example.

> **CAUTION**
> *Beware of comments inside the block. Newlines are not significant inside a string passed to **oparse**, so a --I comment will comment out the entire remaining portion of the block, rather than to the return character. Use the C-style comments /* and */ instead, to ensure the correct behavior.*

OCI Calling Structure

PL/SQL blocks are executed like other DML statements. Notably, it is illegal to fetch from a PL/SQL block. Here are the required steps:

    1. Parse the block using **oparse**.

    2. Bind any placeholders using **obndrv** or **obndra**.

    3. Execute the block with **oexec**.

It is illegal to use **odefin** or **ofetch** for a PL/SQL block; they are valid only for SELECT statements. In addition, all placeholders must be bound by name using **obndrv** or **obndra**—**obndrn** is not allowed.

The following is a complete OCI example that calls the **Register** procedure. It is written for a Unix system, and thus won't necessarily compile on other platforms.

```c
/* Available online as oci.c */
/* Include the standard header files, plus the OCI headers. */
#include <stdio.h>
#include <oratypes.h>
#include <ocidfn.h>
#include <ociapr.h>

/* Declare an LDA, HDA and CDA for use in later statements. */
Lda_Def lda;
ub1 HDA[512];
Cda_Def cda;

/* Declare the variables which will be used for input. */
char v_Department[4] = "ECN";
int v_Course = 101;
int v_StudentID = 10006;

/* String which contains the block calling Register.
   Note that the return characters are escaped with a
   backslash to keep this all in one C string.  The trailing
   semicolon is included in the string, since it is a
   syntactic part of the block. */
char *plsqlBlock =
  "BEGIN \
       Register(:v_StudentID, :v_Department, :v_Course); \
    END;";

/* User name and password to connect the database. */
char *username = "example";
char *password = "example";


/* Error reporting function.  Uses oerhms to get the full
```

```
    error, and prints it to the screen. */
void print_error(Lda_Def *lda, Cda_Def *cda) {
  int v_ReturnChars;
  char v_Buffer[1000];

  v_ReturnChars = oerhms(lda, cda->rc, (text *) v_Buffer,
                         (sword) sizeof(v_Buffer));
  printf("Oracle error occurred!\n");
  printf("%s\n", v_Buffer);
}


main() {
  /* Connect to the database. */
  if (orlon(&lda, HDA, (text *) username, -1,
           (text *) password, -1, 0)) {
    print_error(&lda, &lda);
    exit(-1);
  }
  printf("Connected to Oracle\n");

  /* Open a cursor for later use. */
  if (oopen(&cda, &lda, (text *) 0, -1, -1,
           (text *) 0, -1)) {
    print_error(&lda, &cda);
    exit(-1);
  }

  /* Parse the PL/SQL block. */
  if (oparse(&cda, (text *) plsqlBlock,
           (sb4) -1, 1, (ub4) 2)) {
    print_error(&lda, &cda);
    exit(-1);
  }

  /* Bind the department using type 5, STRING. */
  if (obndrv(&cda, (text *) ":v_Department", -1,
           (ub1 *) v_Department, sizeof(v_Department),
           5, -1, (sb2 *) 0, 0, -1, -1)) {
    print_error(&lda, &cda);
    exit(-1);
  }

  /* Bind the course using type 3, INTEGER. */
  if (obndrv(&cda, (text *) ":v_Course", -1,
```

```
                (ub1 *) &v_Course, sizeof(v_Course),
                3, -1, (sb2 *) 0, 0, -1, -1)) {
    print_error(&lda, &cda);
    exit(-1);
  }

  /* Bind the student ID using type 3, INTEGER. */
  if (obndrv(&cda, (text *) ":v_StudentID", -1,
               (ub1 *) &v_StudentID, sizeof(v_StudentID),
               3, -1, (sb2 *) 0, 0, -1, -1)) {
    print_error(&lda, &cda);
    exit(-1);
  }

  /* Execute the statement. */
  if (oexec(&cda)) {
    print_error(&lda, &cda);
    exit(-1);
  }

  /* Commit our work. */
  if (ocom(&lda)) {
    print_error(&lda, &cda);
    exit(-1);
  }

  /* Close the cursor. */
  if (oclose(&cda)) {
    print_error(&lda, &cda);
    exit(-1);
  }

  /* Log off from the database. */
  if (ologof(&lda)) {
    print_error(&lda, &cda);
    exit(-1);
  }
}
```

SQL-Station

In addition to Oracle products such as Developer 2000 and the precompilers, many third-party tools allow you to issue PL/SQL statements to be executed on the database. Like the precompilers, these tools do not have a local PL/SQL engine. Thus all of the processing must take place on the server.

One such tool is SQL-Station, by Platinum Corporation. SQL-Station has three components: SQL-Station Coder, SQL-Station Debugger, and SQL-Station Plan Analyzer. The Coder is used to create PL/SQL objects and execute SQL scripts. The Debugger allows you to step through PL/SQL code on the server and examine variables as the program is running. The Plan Analyzer allows you to view the execution plan for a statement in order to tune it properly. We will discuss the Coder in this section, the Debugger in Chapter 14, and the Plan Analyzer in Chapter 22.

NOTE
A trial version of SQL-Station is available on the accompanying CD, in the "station" directory. In order to install the product, see the online documentation. For more information on purchasing or using SQL-Station, see Platinum's web site at http://www.platinum.com.

The Coder's General Environment

The Coder's environment is shown in Figure 13-9. The workspace is divided into several windows. On the left is the Catalog Browser. This pane allows you to see all of the database objects, organized by object type. In the figure, the **AddNewStudent** procedure is expanded. Simply double-click on an object name to drill down into the details of an object.

To the right of the Catalog Browser is a workspace for editing windows. Figure 13-9 shows two editing windows—one with the code for **AddNewStudent**, and the other is currently empty. At the bottom of the screen is a message window, and a toolbar is across the top.

CATALOG BROWSER   The Catalog Browser can be used to drill down into database objects. For PL/SQL objects, you can view the code (and modify it) in an editing window. For tables, you can view both the table description and the table data in separate editing windows by double-clicking on the corresponding entries in the browser. Figure 13-10 shows two editing windows for the **classes** table.

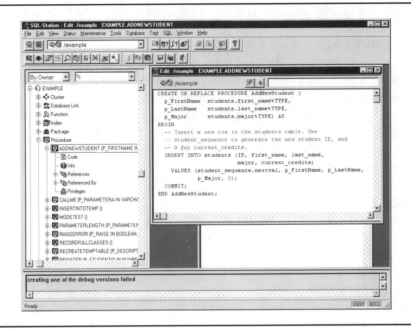

FIGURE 13-9. *SQL-Station Coder*

EDITING WINDOWS   Editing windows can be used for different things. In Figure 13-10, for example, one window contains SQL text and another contains table data. The editing windows are displayed in the right-hand side of the workspace, and they can be tiled or overlapping, as desired.

MESSAGE WINDOW   The message window across the bottom will display SQL-Station and/or Oracle error messages. It cannot be edited.

Calling a Stored Procedure

You can call a stored procedure and interactively enter the procedure parameters using the Procedure Execution tool, available under the Tools menu or by right-clicking on an object in the Catalog Browser. The Execution tool is a fill-in form that allows you to specify the values used for each of the procedure parameters. Figure 13-11 shows the Execution tool for **AddNewStudent**, with parameters entered. Once the parameters are

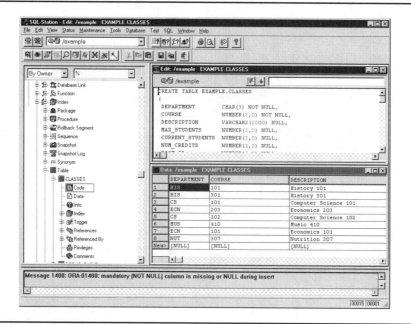

FIGURE 13-10.   *Viewing the* **classes** *table*

entered, you can execute the procedure by clicking on the Execute button in the toolbar, or by selecting Execute from the File menu. The results of executing the window in Figure 13-11 are shown in Figure 13-12. Note the status message in Figure 13-12, which says that the execution was successful.

Executing a SQL Script

To execute a SQL script, simply read it into an editing window and click the Execute button. This will run the script and display the output in a pane of the window. Figure 13-13 shows the result of running a SELECT statement in an editing window that has been maximized.

Client-side PL/SQL

The Oracle tools that contain a PL/SQL engine on the client include the Developer 2000, Designer 2000, and Discoverer 2000 suites. Each suite consists of several development or query tools bundled together.

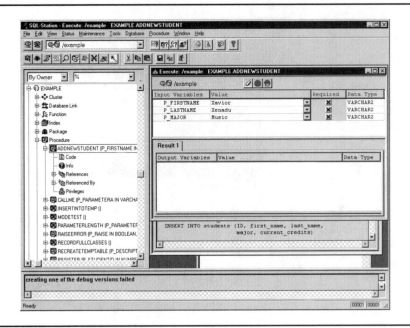

FIGURE 13-11. *Calling* **AddNewStudent**

All of them contain a PL/SQL engine locally on the client. This PL/SQL engine is used to control the processing of the application, as illustrated in Figure 13-2.

If a PL/SQL object is created within client-side PL/SQL, it is accessible only within the object that creates it. For example, a Forms procedure is accessible from only one form. It is not accessible from other database procedures or other forms. Table 13-1 compares stored procedures and client procedures, and Table 13-2 compares database triggers and client triggers. Stored procedures and database triggers are discussed in Chapters 7 and 9, respectively.

Why a Client-side Engine Is Provided

Most of the work in applications developed using the Developer, Designer, and Discoverer 2000 tools is very suitable for PL/SQL. Oracle Forms, especially, uses PL/SQL constructs heavily. Every form trigger is a PL/SQL

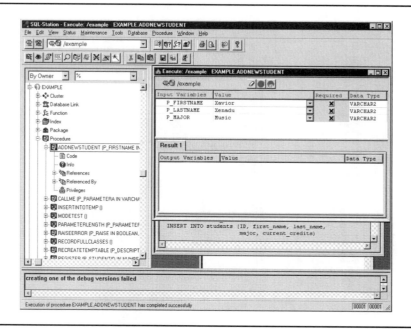

FIGURE 13-12.   *Results of calling* **AddNewStudent**

Stored Procedures	Client Procedures
Stored in the data dictionary as a database object.	Stored as part of the client application; does not exist as a database object.
Can be executed by any session connecting to a user who has EXECUTE privilege on the procedure.	Can only be executed from the application that defines the procedure.
Can call other stored procedures.	Can call client procedures within the same application and stored procedures in the database.
Can manipulate data stored in Oracle tables via SQL statements.	Can manipulate data stored in Oracle tables, as well as variables in the application.

TABLE 13-1.   *Stored Procedures vs. Client Procedures*

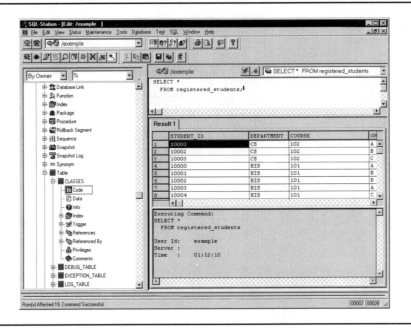

FIGURE 13-13. *Running a SQL statement*

Database Triggers	Form Triggers
Fired when a DML operation is performed on a database table.	Fired when the user presses a key or navigates between fields on the screen.
Can be row level or statement level.	No distinction between row and statement level.
Can manipulate data stored in Oracle tables via SQL.	Can manipulate data in Oracle tables as well as variables in forms.
Can be fired from any session executing the triggering DML statement.	Can be fired only from the form that defines the trigger.
Can cause other database triggers to fire.	Can cause database triggers to fire, but not other form triggers.

TABLE 13-2. *Database Triggers vs. Form Triggers*

block, for example. Fields within the form are treated as bind variables. At first glance, it may seem that having a PL/SQL engine on the client removes the benefit of PL/SQL. After all, one of the purposes of the language is to reduce network traffic, as we saw in Chapter 1. With a client-side PL/SQL engine, the SQL statements go over the network while the procedural statements are processed on the client. This appears to generate more network traffic and thus cause the application to run slower.

However, the majority of the work done in a Forms application is procedural in nature. As the user navigates between fields and blocks in the form, or presses a key, triggers automatically fire, and the form's fields get different values. These are all procedural actions and thus should be done on the client for best performance.

All of these suites of tools behave the same with regard to PL/SQL. In this chapter, we will look at Oracle Forms and Procedure Builder.

Oracle Forms

The Forms Designer is a GUI environment. As such, it has several different windows available to you. The windows that are relevant to PL/SQL are the Object Navigator and the PL/SQL Editor. For more information on Oracle Forms and how it is used, see the *Oracle Forms User's Guide.*

PL/SQL Editor

The PL/SQL Editor can be used to modify procedures and functions both on the client and on the server. The Editor looks different depending on the location of the object being modified. Figure 13-14 shows a PL/SQL Editor with the **Register** procedure. This procedure is stored on the server. The Save button in the Editor is the equivalent of the CREATE OR REPLACE PROCEDURE command; by pressing it, the procedure is created in the data dictionary. The Drop button is the equivalent of the DROP PROCEDURE command; pressing this button drops the object from the data dictionary.

Compare Figure 13-14 with Figure 13-15. Figure 13-15 shows the PL/SQL Editor with a local procedure. The Save button has been replaced by Compile. Compile will save the procedure to the PL/SQL engine on the client, not the server. The data dictionary in the database will not be modified. Likewise, the Delete button will remove the procedure from the local PL/SQL engine. The New button allows creation of a new form procedure, function, or trigger.

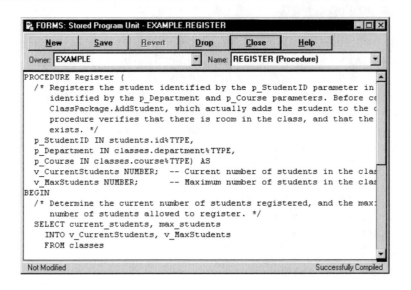

FIGURE 13-14. *PL/SQL Editor with a stored procedure*

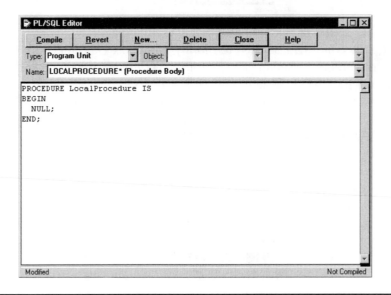

FIGURE 13-15. *PL/SQL Editor with a local procedure*

Object Navigator

The Object Navigator is used to manipulate all of the objects within the form. By clicking on each object icon, the properties of that object can be edited. Objects can also be moved around by dragging and dropping. This includes moving procedures from the client to the server and vice versa. Figure 13-16 illustrates the Object Navigator, along with a Property sheet for the canvas object.

Procedure Builder

Procedure Builder is part of the Developer 2000 toolset, along with Oracle Forms, Oracle Reports, and Oracle Graphics. It extends the PL/SQL manipulation tools of Forms by adding the PL/SQL Interpreter. This window is the main part of Procedure Builder, because it allows you to step through client-side PL/SQL line-by-line, examining the values of local variables as you go. This capability is very similar to the debuggers available for other third-generation languages such as C, and also to SQL-Station Debugger.

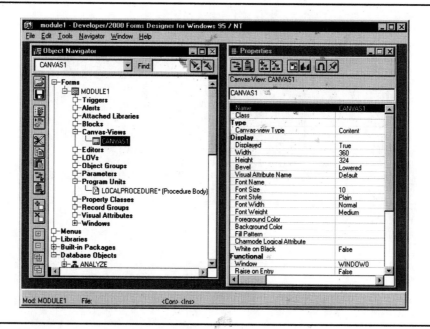

FIGURE 13-16. *Object Navigator*

The Interpreter, illustrated in Figure 13-17, is divided into two panes—the viewer and the command prompt.

The Viewer
The viewer pane of the Interpreter shows the block, procedure, or function that is currently being executed. It shows the entire block, with line numbers. The buttons at the top of the window are used for stepping line-by-line through the code. By double-clicking on a line number, a breakpoint can be set as well. Figure 13-18 shows the same block shown in Figure 13-17, but with a breakpoint set at line 9.

The Command Prompt
The command prompt section of the Interpreter allows execution of individual PL/SQL statements on-the-fly. This prompt is similar to the SQL prompt in SQL*Plus, in that SQL statements can be typed in and executed. However, PL/SQL procedural statements can also be entered, including variable assignments and procedure calls. This is also shown in Figure 13-18.

```
PL/SQL Interpreter

00001  PROCEDURE AddDays(
00002    /* Adds the specified number of days to SYSDATE, and returns the
00003       result as a character string. */
00004    p_NumberDays IN NUMBER,
00005    p_Output OUT VARCHAR2) IS
00006
00007    v_TempVar DATE;
00008  BEGIN
00009    v_TempVar := SYSDATE + p_NumberDays;
00010    p_Output := TO_CHAR(v_TempVar, 'DD-MON-YY HH24:MI:SS');
00011  END;

PL/SQL>
```

FIGURE 13-17. *PL/SQL Interpreter*

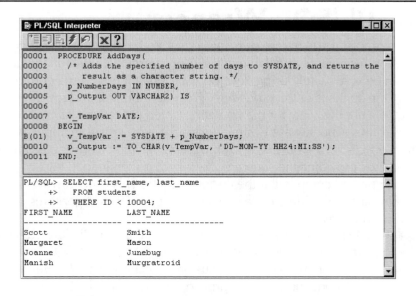

FIGURE 13-18. *Debugging a PL/SQL block*

Interactive PL/SQL Debugging

Because Procedure Builder allows interactive debugging of PL/SQL code, it is invaluable during development. The benefits of this feature are discussed in more detail in Chapter 14, but here are a few of them:

■ Ability to examine the values of local variables while the block is running. Without this ability, the variables would have to be inserted into a database table and queried after the block is finished, or echoed using the DBMS_OUTPUT package.

■ Ability to modify local variables while the block is running. During execution of **AddDays**, for example, we can change **p_NumberDays** to test different results.

■ Ability to run PL/SQL commands and stored procedures on-the-fly from the command prompt in the Interpreter. Although SQL*Plus can do this to a certain extent, Procedure Builder greatly enhances this feature.

The PL/SQL Wrapper

When a procedure, function, or package is stored in the database, the source for this object is available in the **user_source** data dictionary view. This can be very useful during development, since it provides a current view of the contents of the procedure. Procedure Builder and the other client tools use this view for manipulating stored procedures as well. However, this is not always desired. If you are developing an application written in PL/SQL, the only way to ship the application to your customers would be by providing the source code, which is then loaded into the database and compiled at the customer's site. This is not always desirable, since the source code may contain proprietary algorithms and data structures.

PL/SQL 2.2 ...and HIGHER Oracle provides a solution for this, available with PL/SQL 2.2 and higher—the PL/SQL wrapper. This utility encodes PL/SQL source code into a hexadecimal format that customers cannot read. However, the database can decode the wrapped procedure and store it in the database.

Running the Wrapper

The wrapper is an operating system executable. The location and name of the executable is system dependent, but on most systems it is named WRAP. The format for executing the wrapper is

WRAP INAME=*input_file* [ONAME=*output_file*]

where *input_file* is the name of a file containing a CREATE OR REPLACE statement. The filename can have any extension, but by default it is assumed to be .sql. If specified, *output_file* is the name of the output file. If the output file is not specified, it defaults to the name of the input file with extension .plb.

The following listing shows some legal WRAP command lines. All of them take a file called **register.sql** as input and create **register.plb** as output.

```
WRAP INAME=register.sql
WRAP INAME=register
WRAP INAME=register.sql ONAME=register.plb
```

The options INAME and ONAME are not case sensitive, but your operating system may be. In this case, the name of the WRAP executable itself, as well as the filenames, could be case sensitive.

Input and Output Files

The input file for the wrapper can contain only the following SQL commands (in addition to comments):

```
CREATE [OR REPLACE] PROCEDURE
CREATE [OR REPLACE] PACKAGE
CREATE [OR REPLACE] PACKAGE BODY
CREATE [OR REPLACE] FUNCTION
```

Given an input file that looks like this,

```
CREATE OR REPLACE PROCEDURE Register(...) AS
  ...
BEGIN
  ...
END Register;
```

the output of the wrapper could look like this:

```
CREATE OR REPLACE PROCEDURE Register WRAPPED
  012ba779f...
```

All of the source code for the procedure has been converted into hexadecimal digits. The **.plb** file can be loaded from SQL*Plus like any other **.sql** file and the **Register** procedure created. However, the **user_source** view will hold the wrapped version of the code, preventing exposure of the actual algorithm.

The size of the output file is usually significantly longer than the size of the input file. However, the size of the compiled p-code is the same, since it does not change.

Checking Syntax and Semantics

The wrapper will check the syntax of the input file, but it will not check the semantics. This means that if any objects referenced in the file don't exist, the errors won't be reported until run time. For example, if we wrap an input file that looks like this,

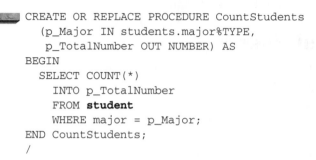

```
CREATE OR REPLACE PROCEDURE CountStudents
    (p_Major IN students.major%TYPE,
     p_TotalNumber OUT NUMBER) AS
BEGIN
  SELECT COUNT(*)
    INTO p_TotalNumber
    FROM student
    WHERE major = p_Major;
END CountStudents;
/
```

we don't get any errors, even though the **student** table doesn't exist (it should be **students**). We will get the following error if we try to run the output **.plb** file, however:

```
PLS-201: identifier 'student' must be declared
```

In this case, the **.plb** file can't be edited to fix the error since the source is not available. The original **.sql** file would have to be modified, then wrapped again.

Guidelines for the Wrapper

Once a procedure, function, or package is wrapped, the output file cannot be edited. The contents are not readable and thus can't be changed. The only way to change a wrapped object is to modify the original source file. So, don't wrap an object until it is completely developed.

The package bodies for Oracle-supplied packages (DBMS_OUTPUT, DBMS_PIPE, and so on) are shipped in wrapped form. (These packages are described in the following chapters and in Appendix B.) However, the package headers are shipped in clear text. This is a good guideline to follow for your own packages as well. The public portions of the package—namely, the package header—should be visible so that users will know the names of the procedures and their parameters. Only the package body needs to be wrapped. This neatly hides the actual implementation while allowing the interface to be visible.

Summary

In this chapter, we have discussed various environments from which PL/SQL can be run. These can be divided into client- and server-side PL/SQL. Server PL/SQL environments include SQL*Plus, the Oracle Precompilers, OCI, and third-party tools such as SQL-Station. Client-side PL/SQL is available through tools such as Oracle Forms and Procedure Builder. Procedure Builder also provides an interactive PL/SQL debugging and testing environment. Finally, the PL/SQL wrapper allows procedures to be packaged into a binary equivalent for shipment to end users. Chapter 14 continues the PL/SQL development process with testing and debugging tips and techniques.

CHAPTER
14

Testing and Debugging

ery few programs perform correctly the first time they are written. Also, the requirements for a program often change during development, and the program must be rewritten. In either case, the program needs to be tested thoroughly to make sure that it is working properly and performing as expected. This chapter describes three techniques for testing and debugging PL/SQL programs: inserting into a test table, using the DBMS_OUTPUT package, and using PL/SQL debuggers such as Procedure Builder and SQL-Station. We will also discuss programming strategies that can help avoid errors in the first place.

Problem Diagnosis

Every bug is different from the last, which is what makes debugging and testing a challenge. You can reduce the occurrences of bugs through testing and QA analysis during development, but if you do program development for a while, you will almost certainly have to find the bugs and errors in your own or somebody else's code.

Debugging Guidelines

Even though every bug is different, and there could be many fixes for any given bug, the process of finding and fixing bugs can be defined. I have developed several guidelines for determining the cause of a problem over the past few years of debugging both my own and other programmers' code. These guidelines can be applied to development in any programming language, not just PL/SQL.

Find the Place Where the Error Occurs

Obvious though it may seem, finding the place where the error occurs is crucial to fixing coding problems. If you have a large, complicated program that simply fails, the first step is to determine exactly where the failure is occurring. This is not necessarily an easy task, depending on the complexity of the code. The easiest way to find the source of an error is to trace the program as it runs, examining the values of the data structures to determine what went wrong.

Define Exactly What Is Wrong

Once you know where the problem happens, you need to define exactly what the problem is. Is an Oracle error returned? Does a calculation return the wrong result? Does the wrong data get inserted into the database? In order to fix a bug, it is necessary to know how the bug manifests itself.

Reduce the Program to a Simple Test Case

A good strategy to follow when you don't know where the error is occurring is to reduce the program to a simple test case. Start cutting out parts of the code, and rerun the program. If the error still occurs, you know that the section you removed did not cause the error. If the error goes away, examine the section that was removed.

Remember that one area of your code may have the bug, but the problem may manifest itself in another part of the code. For example, a procedure may return an incorrect value, but the returned value is not actually used until later in the main program. The problem here is not the main program (where the error appears to be) but in the procedure. Cutting out the procedure call and replacing it with a direct assignment to the returned value would reveal the source of the problem. We will examine this particular case later in this chapter.

Establish a Testing Environment

Ideally, testing and debugging is not done in a production environment. It is a good idea to maintain a testing environment that duplicates production as much as possible—the same database structure but with less data, for example. This way you can develop and test newer versions of your application without affecting the production version that is already running. If a problem occurs in production, try reproducing the problem in test first. This follows the previous principle of reducing the problem to a smaller test case. A test case may involve more than just the code—PL/SQL is very dependent on the database structure and the contents of the data, and these should be reduced as well.

The Debug Package

PL/SQL is designed primarily for manipulation of data stored in an Oracle database. The structure of the language is based on this use, and it performs admirably. For practical purposes, however, we need some additional tools to help write and debug programs.

The rest of this chapter examines in detail several methods of debugging PL/SQL code. Each section focuses on a different problem and uses a different method to isolate the problem following the guidelines just given. Each section will first describe the general debugging method, then give a description of the problem to be solved. In the course of solving each problem, we will develop different versions of a debugging package, Debug, which you can use in your own programs. Depending on your environment and needs, the different capabilities of each package will be useful.

Inserting into a Test Table

The simplest method of debugging is to insert the values of local variables into a temporary table as the program is running. When the program has completed, you can query the table to determine the values of the variables. This method requires the least effort to implement and will work regardless of the execution environment, since it simply involves extra INSERT statements.

Problem I

Suppose we want to write a function that will return the average grade for each class, based on currently registered students. We could write this function as follows:

```
-- Available online as avgrade1.sql
CREATE OR REPLACE FUNCTION AverageGrade (
/* Determines the average grade for the class specified. Grades are
   stored in the registered_students table as single characters
   A through E. This function will return the average grade, again,
   as a single letter. If there are no students registered for
   the class, an error is raised. */
  p_Department IN VARCHAR2,
  p_Course IN NUMBER) RETURN VARCHAR2 AS

  v_AverageGrade VARCHAR2(1);
  v_NumericGrade NUMBER;
  v_NumberStudents NUMBER;
```

```
    CURSOR c_Grades IS
      SELECT grade
        FROM registered_students
        WHERE department = p_Department
        AND course = p_Course;
BEGIN
  /* First we need to see how many students there are for
     this class. If there aren't any, we need to raise an error. */
  SELECT COUNT(*)
    INTO v_NumberStudents
    FROM registered_students
    WHERE department = p_Department
      AND course = p_Course;

  IF v_NumberStudents = 0 THEN
    RAISE_APPLICATION_ERROR(-20001, 'No students registered for ' ||
      p_Department || ' ' || p_Course);
  END IF;

  /* Since grades are stored as letters, we can't use the AVG
     function directly on them. Instead, we can use the DECODE
     function to convert the letter grades to numeric values,
     and take the average of those. */
  SELECT AVG(DECODE(grade, 'A', 5,
                           'B', 4,
                           'C', 3,
                           'D', 2,
                           'E', 1))
    INTO v_NumericGrade
    FROM registered_students
    WHERE department = p_Department
    AND course = p_Course;

  /* v_NumericGrade now contains the average grade, as a number from
     1 to 5. We need to convert this back into a letter. The DECODE
     function can be used here as well. Note that we are selecting
     the result into v_AverageGrade rather than assigning to it,
     because the DECODE function is only legal in a SQL statement. */
  SELECT DECODE(ROUND(v_NumericGrade), 5, 'A',
                                       4, 'B',
                                       3, 'C',
                                       2, 'D',
                                       1, 'E')
    INTO v_AverageGrade
    FROM dual;
```

```
    RETURN v_AverageGrade;
END AverageGrade;
```

Suppose the contents of **registered_students** looks like this:

```
SQL> select * from registered_students;

STUDENT_ID DEP    COURSE G
---------- ---  --------- -
     10000 CS         102 A
     10002 CS         102 B
     10003 CS         102 C
     10000 HIS        101 A
     10001 HIS        101 B
     10002 HIS        101 B
     10003 HIS        101 A
     10004 HIS        101 C
     10005 HIS        101 C
     10006 HIS        101 E
     10007 HIS        101 B
     10008 HIS        101 A
     10009 HIS        101 D
     10010 HIS        101 A
     10008 NUT        307 A
     10010 NUT        307 A
     10009 MUS        410 B
     10006 MUS        410 E

18 rows selected.
```

NOTE

registered_students *is populated with these 18 rows by the tables.sql script, available online. For more information on tables.sql, see Chapter 1.*

Four classes have students registered in them: Computer Science 102, History 101, Nutrition 307, and Music 410. So we can call **AverageGrade** with these four classes. Any other classes should raise the error "No students registered." A sample SQL*Plus output is shown here:

```
SQL> VARIABLE v_AveGrade VARCHAR2(1)
SQL> exec :v_AveGrade := AverageGrade('HIS', 101)
```

```
PL/SQL procedure successfully completed.

SQL> print v_AveGrade

V_AVEGRADE
------------------------------
B

SQL> exec :v_AveGrade := AverageGrade('NUT', 307)

PL/SQL procedure successfully completed.

SQL> print v_AveGrade

V_AVEGRADE
------------------------------
A

SQL> exec :v_AveGrade := AverageGrade('MUS', 410)

PL/SQL procedure successfully completed.

SQL> print v_AveGrade

V_AVEGRADE
------------------------------
C

SQL> exec :v_AveGrade := AverageGrade('CS', 102)
begin :v_AveGrade := AverageGrade('CS', 102); end;

  *
ERROR at line 1:
ORA-20001: No students registered for CS 102
ORA-06512: at "EXAMPLE.AVERAGEGRADE", line 21
```

The last call illustrates the bug. The ORA-20001 error is returned even though students are registered for Computer Science 102.

Problem 1: The Debug Package

The version of Debug that we will use to find this bug is shown next. The **Debug.Debug** procedure is the main procedure in the package. It takes two parameters—a description and a variable. These are concatenated and inserted into the **debug_table** table. The **Debug.Reset** procedure should be called at the start of the program, to initialize the table and the internal line counter. The line counter is necessary to ensure that the rows in **debug_table** will be selected in the order in which they were inserted.

```
-- Available online as debug1.sql
CREATE OR REPLACE PACKAGE Debug AS
  /* First version of the debug package. This package works
     by inserting into the debug_table table. In order to see
     the output, select from debug_table in SQL*Plus with:
  SELECT debug_str FROM debug_table ORDER BY linecount; */

  /* This is the main debug procedure. p_Description will be
     concatenated with p_Value, and inserted into debug_table. */
  PROCEDURE Debug(p_Description IN VARCHAR2, p_Value IN VARCHAR2);

  /* Resets the Debug environment. Reset is called when the
     package is instantiated for the first time, and should be
     called to delete the contents of debug_table for a new
     session. */
  PROCEDURE Reset;
END Debug;

CREATE OR REPLACE PACKAGE BODY Debug AS
  /* v_LineCount is used to order the rows in debug_table. */
  v_LineCount NUMBER;

  PROCEDURE Debug(p_Description IN VARCHAR2, p_Value IN VARCHAR2) IS
  BEGIN
    INSERT INTO debug_table (linecount, debug_str)
      VALUES (v_LineCount, p_Description || ': ' || p_Value);
    COMMIT;
    v_LineCount := v_LineCount + 1;
  END Debug;

  PROCEDURE Reset IS
  BEGIN
    v_LineCount := 1;
    DELETE FROM debug_table;
  END Reset;

BEGIN /* Package initialization code */
  Reset;
END Debug;
```

Problem 1: Using the Debug Package

In order to determine the problem with **AverageGrade**, we need to look at the value of the variables used by the procedure. We do this by adding debugging statements in the code. With this version of Debug, we need to call **Debug.Reset** at the start of **AverageGrade** and **Debug.Debug** whenever we want to look at a variable. The modified version is given next. Some of the comments have been removed for brevity.

```
-- Available online as avgrade2.sql
CREATE OR REPLACE FUNCTION AverageGrade (
  p_Department IN VARCHAR2,
  p_Course IN NUMBER) RETURN VARCHAR2 AS

  v_AverageGrade VARCHAR2(1);
  v_NumericGrade NUMBER;
  v_NumberStudents NUMBER;

  CURSOR c_Grades IS
    SELECT grade
      FROM registered_students
      WHERE department = p_Department
      AND course = p_Course;
BEGIN
  Debug.Reset;
  Debug.Debug('p_Department', p_Department);
  Debug.Debug('p_Course', p_Course);

  /* First we need to see how many students there are for
     this class. If there aren't any, we need to raise an
     error. */
  SELECT COUNT(*)
    INTO v_NumberStudents
    FROM registered_students
    WHERE department = p_Department
    AND course = p_Course;

  Debug.Debug('After select, v_NumberStudents', v_NumberStudents);
  IF v_NumberStudents = 0 THEN
    RAISE_APPLICATION_ERROR(-20001, 'No students registered for ' ||
      p_Department || ' ' || p_Course);
  END IF;
```

```
SELECT AVG(DECODE(grade, 'A', 5,
                         'B', 4,
                         'C', 3,
                         'D', 2,
                         'E', 1))
  INTO v_NumericGrade
  FROM registered_students
  WHERE department = p_Department
    AND course = p_Course;

SELECT DECODE(ROUND(v_NumericGrade), 5, 'A',
                                     4, 'B',
                                     3, 'C',
                                     2, 'D',
                                     1, 'E')
  INTO v_AverageGrade
  FROM dual;

RETURN v_AverageGrade;
END AverageGrade;
```

Now we can call **AverageGrade** again and select from **debug_table** afterwards to see the results:

```
SQL> EXEC :v_AveGrade := AverageGrade('CS', 102)
begin :v_AveGrade := AverageGrade('CS', 102); end;

  *
ERROR at line 1:
ORA-20001: No students registered for CS 102
ORA-06512: at "EXAMPLE.AVERAGEGRADE", line 25
ORA-06512: at line 1


SQL> SELECT debug_str FROM debug_table ORDER BY linecount;

DEBUG_STR
-----------------------------------------------------------
p_Department: CS
p_Course: 102
After select, v_NumberStudents: 0
```

We have verified that **v_NumberStudents** is in fact 0, which explains why we are getting the ORA-20001 error. This narrows the problem down to the SELECT statement, which isn't matching any rows. We therefore need to examine the WHERE clause of this statement in more detail:

```
SELECT COUNT(*)
    INTO v_NumberStudents
    FROM registered_students
    WHERE department = p_Department
    AND course = p_Course;
```

The Debug output seems to show the correct values for **p_Department** and **p_Course**, but SQL*Plus does not indicate where the newline character may be, so this output may be deceiving. Let's change the calls to **Debug.Debug** to put quotes around **p_Department** and **p_Course**. This will reveal any leading or trailing spaces.

```
-- Available online as avgrade3.sql
CREATE OR REPLACE FUNCTION AverageGrade
  ...
BEGIN
  Debug.Reset;
  Debug.Debug('p_Department', '''' || p_Department || '''');
  Debug.Debug('p_Course', '''' || p_Course || '''');

  /* First we need to see how many students there are for
     this class. If there aren't any, we need to raise an error. */
  SELECT COUNT(*)
    INTO v_NumberStudents
    FROM registered_students
    WHERE department = p_Department
      AND course = p_Course;

  Debug.Debug('After select, v_NumberStudents', v_NumberStudents);
  ...
```

Now when we run **AverageGrade** and query **debug_table**, we get the following result:

```
SQL> exec :v_AveGrade := AverageGrade('CS', 102)
begin :v_AveGrade := AverageGrade('CS', 102); end;

 *
ERROR at line 1:
ORA-20001: No students registered for CS 102
```

```
ORA-06512: at "EXAMPLE.AVERAGEGRADE", line 25
ORA-06512: at line 1


SQL> SELECT debug_str FROM debug_table ORDER BY linecount;

DEBUG_STR
------------------------------------------------------------
p_Department: 'CS'
p_Course: '102'
After select, v_NumberStudents: 0
```

We can see that **p_Department** doesn't have a trailing space. This is the problem. The **department** column of **registered_students** is CHAR(3), and **p_Department** is VARCHAR2. This means that the database column contains 'CS ' (with a trailing space), which explains why the SELECT statement doesn't return any rows. Thus **v_NumberStudents** is assigned 0.

TIP
The built-in function DUMP can be used to examine the exact contents of a database column. For example, we can determine the contents of the **department** *column in* **registered_students** *with:*

```
SQL> SELECT DISTINCT DUMP(department)
  2    FROM registered_students
  3    WHERE department = 'CS';

DUMP(DEPARTMENT)
--------------------------------------
Typ=96 Len=3: 67,83,32
```

The type is 96, indicating CHAR, and the last byte in the column is 32, which is the ASCII code for a space. This tells us that the column is blank-padded. For more information on DUMP and other built-in functions, see Chapter 5. The datatype codes are described in the Oracle SQL Reference.

One fix for this problem is to change the type of **p_Department** to CHAR:

```
CREATE OR REPLACE FUNCTION AverageGrade (
    p_Department IN CHAR,
    p_Course IN NUMBER) RETURN VARCHAR2 AS
    ...
BEGIN
    ...
END AverageGrade;
```

After doing this, we get the correct result for **AverageGrade**:

```
SQL> exec :v_AveGrade := AverageGrade('CS', 102)

PL/SQL procedure successfully completed.

SQL> print v_AveGrade

V_AVEGRADE
--------------------------------
B
```

This works because both values in the WHERE clause are now CHAR, and blank-padded character comparison semantics are used, resulting in the match. See Chapter 2 for more information on the semantics of character comparison.

TIP
Had we used the %TYPE attribute in the function declaration, the type of **p_Department** *would have been correct. This is another reason why using %TYPE is advisable. Also, since the return value of* **AverageGrade** *is a character string of length 1, and it will always be 1, we can use the fixed-length type CHAR for the RETURN clause as well. The declaration of* **AverageGrade** *therefore looks like this:*

```
-- Available online as avgrade4.sql
CREATE OR REPLACE FUNCTION AverageGrade (
```

```
    p_Department IN registered_students.department%TYPE,
    p_Course IN registered_students.course%TYPE) RETURN CHAR AS

    v_AverageGrade CHAR(1);
    v_NumericGrade NUMBER;
    v_NumberStudents NUMBER;
...
BEGIN
    ...
END AverageGrade;
```

Problem 1: Comments

This version of Debug is very simple. All it does is insert into **debug_table**. But we were still able to use it to find the bug in **AverageGrade**. There are some advantages to this technique:

- Since Debug doesn't rely on anything but SQL, it can be used from any environment. The SELECT statement that shows the output can be run from SQL*Plus or another tool.

- Debug is simple, so it doesn't add too much overhead to the procedure being debugged.

There are also disadvantages:

- **AverageGrade** raised an exception in the preceding example. This causes any SQL done by the program to be rolled back. Thus the COMMIT in **Debug.Debug** is required to insure that the inserts into **debug_table** are not rolled back as well. This can cause a problem if other work in the procedure being debugged shouldn't be committed. This commit will also invalidate any SELECT FOR UPDATE cursors that may be open.

- As currently written, Debug won't work properly if more than one session is using it simultaneously. The SELECT statement will return the results from both sessions. This can be fixed by modifying both the Debug package and **debug_table** to include a column uniquely identifying the session.

The disadvantages of this version of Debug will be resolved by using the DBMS_OUTPUT package, described in the next section.

DBMS_OUTPUT

The first version of Debug, which we saw in the last section, essentially implemented a limited version of I/O. PL/SQL has no input/output capability built into the language. This was an intentional design decision, since the ability to print out the values of variables and data structures is not required to manipulate data stored in the database. It is, however, a very useful debugging tool. As a result, output capability was added to PL/SQL 2.0 through the built-in package DBMS_OUTPUT. We will use DBMS_OUTPUT in the second version of Debug, described in this section.

PL/SQL still doesn't have input capability built into the language, but SQL*Plus substitution variables (described in Chapter 13) can be used to overcome this. PL/SQL 2.3 has a new package UTL_FILE, which is used to read from and write to operating system files. Chapter 18 will examine UTL_FILE in detail.

The DBMS_OUTPUT Package

Before we discuss the debugging problem for this section, we need to examine DBMS_OUTPUT in some detail. This package, like other DBMS packages, is owned by the Oracle user SYS. The script which creates DBMS_OUTPUT grants the EXECUTE permission on the package to PUBLIC, and creates a public synonym for it. This means that any Oracle user can call the routines in DBMS_OUTPUT without having to prefix the package name with SYS.

How does DBMS_OUTPUT work? Two basic operations, GET and PUT, are implemented through procedures in the package. A PUT operation takes its argument and places it into an internal buffer for storage. A GET operation reads from this buffer and returns the contents as an argument to the procedure. There is also an ENABLE procedure that sets the size of the buffer.

Procedures in DBMS_OUTPUT

The PUT routines in the package are PUT, PUT_LINE, and NEW_LINE. The GET routines are GET_LINE and GET_LINES. ENABLE and DISABLE control the buffer.

PUT and PUT_LINE   The syntax for the PUT and PUT_LINE calls is

```
PROCEDURE PUT(a VARCHAR2);
PROCEDURE PUT(a NUMBER);
PROCEDURE PUT(a DATE);

PROCEDURE PUT_LINE(a VARCHAR2);
PROCEDURE PUT_LINE(a NUMBER);
PROCEDURE PUT_LINE(a DATE);
```

where *a* is the argument to be placed in the buffer. Note that these procedures are overloaded by the type of the parameter (overloading is discussed in Chapter 7). Because of the three different versions of PUT and PUT_LINE, the buffer can contain values of types VARCHAR2, NUMBER, and DATE. They are stored in the buffer in their original format. However, GET_LINE and GET_LINES retrieve from the buffer and return character strings only. When a GET operation is performed, the contents of the buffer will be converted to a character string according to the default datatype conversion rules. If you want to specify a format for the conversion, use an explicit TO_CHAR call on the PUT, rather than the GET.

The buffer is organized into lines, each of which can have a maximum of 255 bytes. PUT_LINE appends a newline character after its argument, signaling the end of a line. PUT does not. PUT_LINE is equivalent to calling PUT and then calling NEW_LINE.

NEW_LINE   The syntax for the NEW_LINE call is

```
PROCEDURE NEW_LINE;
```

NEW_LINE puts a newline character into the buffer, signaling the end of a line. There is no limit to the number of lines in the buffer. The total size of the buffer is limited to the value specified in ENABLE, however.

GET_LINE   The syntax for GET_LINE is

```
PROCEDURE GET_LINE(line OUT VARCHAR2, status OUT INTEGER);
```

where *line* is a character string that will contain one line of the buffer, and *status* indicates whether the line was retrieved successfully. The maximum length of a line is 255 bytes. If the line was retrieved, *status* will be 0; if there are no more lines in the buffer, it will be 1.

NOTE
Although the maximum size of a buffer line is 255 bytes, the output variable line can be more than 255 characters. The buffer line can consist of DATE values, for example. These take up 7 bytes of storage in the buffer but are usually converted to character strings with lengths greater than 7.

GET_LINES   The GET_LINES procedure has an argument that is a PL/SQL table. The table type and the syntax are

```
TYPE CHARARR IS TABLE OF VARCHAR2(255)
   INDEX BY BINARY_INTEGER;
PROCEDURE GET_LINES(lines OUT CHARARR,
                    numlines IN OUT INTEGER);
```

where *lines* is a PL/SQL table that will contain multiple lines from the buffer, and *numlines* indicates how many lines are requested. On input to GET_LINES, *numlines* specifies the requested number of lines. On output, *numlines* will contain the actual number of lines returned, which will be less than or equal to the number requested. GET_LINES is designed to replace multiple calls to GET_LINE.

The CHARARR type is also defined in the DBMS_OUTPUT package. Therefore, if you want to call GET_LINES explicitly in your code, you need to declare a variable of type DBMS_OUTPUT.CHARARR. For example:

```
-- Available online as output.sql
DECLARE
  /* Demonstrates using PUT_LINE and GET_LINE. */
  v_Data       DBMS_OUTPUT.CHARARR;
  v_NumLines   NUMBER;
BEGIN
  -- Enable the buffer first.
  DBMS_OUTPUT.ENABLE(1000000);

  -- Put some data in the buffer first, so GET_LINES will
  -- retrieve something.
  DBMS_OUTPUT.PUT_LINE('Line One');
```

```
   DBMS_OUTPUT.PUT_LINE('Line Two');
   DBMS_OUTPUT.PUT_LINE('Line Three');

   -- Set the maximum number of lines that we want to retrieve.
   v_NumLines := 3;

   /* Get the contents of the buffer back. Note that v_Data is
      declared of type DBMS_OUTPUT.CHARARR, so that it matches
      the declaration of DBMS_OUTPUT.GET_LINES. */
   DBMS_OUTPUT.GET_LINES(v_Data, v_NumLines);

   /* Loop through the returned buffer, and insert the contents
      into temp_table. */
   FOR v_Counter IN 1..v_NumLines LOOP
     INSERT INTO temp_table (char_col)
       VALUES (v_Data(v_Counter));
   END LOOP;
END;
```

ENABLE and DISABLE   The syntax for the ENABLE and DISABLE calls is

> PROCEDURE ENABLE (*buffer_size* IN INTEGER DEFAULT 20000);
>
> PROCEDURE DISABLE;

where *buffer_size* is the initial size of the internal buffer, in bytes. The default size is 20,000 bytes, and the maximum size is 1,000,000 bytes. Later, arguments to PUT or PUT_LINE will be placed in this buffer. They are stored in their internal format, taking up as much space in the buffer as their structure dictates. If DISABLE is called, the contents of the buffer are purged, and subsequent calls to PUT and PUT_LINE have no effect.

Using DBMS_OUTPUT

The DBMS_OUTPUT package itself does not contain any mechanism for printing. Essentially, it simply implements a first in, first out data structure. Having said that, how can we use DBMS_OUTPUT for printing? SQL*Plus, SQL*DBA, and Server Manager all have an option known as SERVEROUTPUT. In addition, some third-party products (SQL-Station included) have an option that allows the display of DBMS_OUTPUT data. With this option on, SQL*Plus will automatically call

DBMS_OUTPUT.GET_LINES when a PL/SQL block concludes and print the results, if any, to the screen. This is illustrated by Figure 14-1.

The SQL*Plus command SET SERVEROUTPUT ON implicitly calls DBMS_OUTPUT.ENABLE, which sets up the internal buffer. Optionally, you can specify a size with

SET SERVEROUTPUT ON SIZE *buffer_size*

where *buffer_size* will be used as the initial size of the buffer (the argument to DBMS_OUTPUT.ENABLE). With SERVEROUTPUT on, SQL*Plus will call DBMS_OUTPUT.GET_LINES *after* the PL/SQL block has completed. This means that the output will be echoed to the screen when the block has finished and *not* during execution of the block. This is normally not a problem when DBMS_OUTPUT is used for debugging.

CAUTION
*DBMS_OUTPUT is designed to be used primarily for debugging. It is not meant for general reporting. If you need to customize the output from your queries, it is better to use tools such as Oracle Reports than DBMS_OUTPUT and SQL*Plus.*

```
± Oracle SQL*Plus                                          _□x
File  Edit  Search  Options  Help
SQL> SET serveroutput on SIZE 1000000
SQL> BEGIN
  2    DBMS_OUTPUT.PUT_LINE('Before loop');
  3    FOR v_Counter IN 1..10 LOOP
  4      DBMS_OUTPUT.PUT_LINE('Inside loop, counter = ' || v_Counter);
  5    END LOOP;
  6    DBMS_OUTPUT.PUT_LINE('After loop');
  7  END;
  8  /
Before loop
Inside loop, counter = 1
Inside loop, counter = 2
Inside loop, counter = 3
Inside loop, counter = 4
Inside loop, counter = 5
Inside loop, counter = 6
Inside loop, counter = 7
Inside loop, counter = 8
Inside loop, counter = 9
Inside loop, counter = 10
After loop

PL/SQL procedure successfully completed.

SQL>
```

FIGURE 14-1. *Using SERVEROUTPUT and PUT_LINE*

The internal buffer does have a maximum size (specified in DBMS_OUTPUT.ENABLE), and each line has a maximum length of 255 bytes. As a result, calls to DBMS_OUTPUT.PUT, DBMS_OUTPUT.PUT_LINE, and DBMS_OUTPUT.NEW_LINE can raise either

```
ORA-20000: ORU-10027: buffer overflow,
           limit of <buf_limit> bytes.
```

or

```
ORA-20000: ORU-10028: line length overflow,
           limit of 255 bytes per line.
```

The message depends on which limit is exceeded.

See Appendix B for more information on DBMS_OUTPUT and the other supplied DBMS packages.

TIP
It is a good idea always to specify a buffer length in the SET SERVEROUTPUT ON command. Although the default value for DBMS_OUTPUT.ENABLE is 20,000 bytes, SQL*Plus will call DBMS_OUTPUT.ENABLE with a size of 2,000 if you don't specify an explicit size in SET SERVEROUTPUT ON.

Problem 2

The **students** table has a column for the current number of credits for which the student is registered. The **Register** procedure does not update this column as it is currently written. To fix this, we can write a function that will count the total credits for which a student is registered. **Register** can then update the **current_credits** column of the **students** table. We could write function **CountCredits** with:

```
-- Available online as cntcred1.sql
CREATE OR REPLACE FUNCTION CountCredits (
   /* Returns the number of credits for which the student
      identified by p_StudentID is currently registered */
   p_StudentID IN students.ID%TYPE)
```

```
      RETURN NUMBER AS

      v_TotalCredits NUMBER;   -- Total number of credits
      v_CourseCredits NUMBER; -- Credits for one course
      CURSOR c_RegisteredCourses IS
        SELECT department, course
          FROM registered_students
          WHERE student_id = p_StudentID;
BEGIN
      FOR v_CourseRec IN c_RegisteredCourses LOOP
        -- Determine the credits for this class.
        SELECT num_credits
          INTO v_CourseCredits
          FROM classes
          WHERE department = v_CourseRec.department
          AND course = v_CourseRec.course;

        -- Add it to the total so far.
        v_TotalCredits := v_TotalCredits + v_CourseCredits;
      END LOOP;

      RETURN v_TotalCredits;
END CountCredits;
```

Since **CountCredits** doesn't modify any database or package state, we can call it directly from a SQL statement (with PL/SQL 2.1 or higher). (Calling functions from SQL statements is discussed in Chapter 8.) We can therefore determine the current number of credits for all students by selecting from the **students** table. We get the following result:

```
SQL> SELECT ID, CountCredits(ID) "Total Credits"
   2    FROM students;

       ID Total Credits
--------- -------------
    10000
    10001
    10002
    10003
    10004
    10005
    10006
    10007
```

```
10008
10009
10010
```

11 rows selected.

There is no output for **CurrentCredits**, which means that the function is returning NULL. This is not the correct result.

Problem 2: The Debug Package

We will use the DBMS_OUTPUT package to find the bug in **CountCredits**. To do this, we can use the following version of Debug. It has the same interface as the first version of Debug, which we saw in the previous section, so we only have to change the package body.

```
-- Available online as debug2.sql
CREATE OR REPLACE PACKAGE BODY Debug AS
  PROCEDURE Debug(p_Description IN VARCHAR2,
                  p_Value IN VARCHAR2) IS
  BEGIN
    DBMS_OUTPUT.PUT_LINE(p_Description || ': ' || p_Value);
  END Debug;

  PROCEDURE Reset IS
  BEGIN
      /* Disable the buffer first, then enable it with the
         maximum size. Since DISABLE purges the buffer, this
         ensures that we will have a fresh buffer whenever
         Reset is called. */
    DBMS_OUTPUT.DISABLE;
    DBMS_OUTPUT.ENABLE(1000000);
  END Reset;
BEGIN /* Package initialization code */
  Reset;
END Debug;
```

We no longer use **debug_table**; instead, we use DBMS_OUTPUT. As a result, the version of Debug will work only in SQL*Plus, SQL*DBA, Server Manager, or SQL-Station because these tools automatically call DBMS_OUTPUT.GET_LINES and print the buffer contents. SERVEROUTPUT also needs to be on before using Debug.

Problem 2: Using the Debug Package

CountCredits is returning a NULL result. Let's verify this, as well as what value we are adding to **v_TotalCredits** in the loop. We do this by adding Debug calls:

```
-- Available online as cntcred2.sql
CREATE OR REPLACE FUNCTION CountCredits (
  /* Returns the number of credits for which the student
     identified by p_StudentID is currently registered */
  p_StudentID IN students.ID%TYPE)
  RETURN NUMBER AS

  v_TotalCredits NUMBER;  -- Total number of credits
  v_CourseCredits NUMBER; -- Credits for one course
  CURSOR c_RegisteredCourses IS
    SELECT department, course
      FROM registered_students
      WHERE student_id = p_StudentID;
BEGIN
  Debug.Reset;
  FOR v_CourseRec IN c_RegisteredCourses LOOP
    -- Determine the credits for this class.
    SELECT num_credits
      INTO v_CourseCredits
      FROM classes
      WHERE department = v_CourseRec.department
      AND course = v_CourseRec.course;

    Debug.Debug('Inside loop, v_CourseCredits', v_CourseCredits);
    -- Add it to the total so far.
    v_TotalCredits := v_TotalCredits + v_CourseCredits;
  END LOOP;

  Debug.Debug('After loop, returning', v_TotalCredits);
  RETURN v_TotalCredits;
END CountCredits;
```

We now get the following output:

```
SQL> VARIABLE v_Total NUMBER
SQL> SET SERVEROUTPUT ON
SQL> exec :v_Total := CountCredits(10006);
Inside loop, v_CourseCredits: 4
```

```
Inside loop, v_CourseCredits: 3
After loop, returning:

PL/SQL procedure successfully completed.

SQL> print v_Total

  V_TOTAL
---------


SQL>
```

NOTE
*We are testing **CountCredits** with a SQL*Plus bind variable rather than selecting the value of the function from the **students** table. This is because **CountCredits** now calls DBMS_OUTPUT, which is not considered to be a pure function. If we were to use **CountCredits** inside a SQL statement, we would get the ORA-6571 error. See Chapter 8 for more information on this error and calling stored functions from SQL statements.*

Based on this Debug output, it looks like the number of credits calculated for each class is correct: the loop was executed twice, with 4 and 3 credits returned each time. But clearly, this isn't being added to the total properly. Let's add some more debugging statements:

```
CREATE OR REPLACE FUNCTION CountCredits (
    /* Returns the number of credits for which the student
       identified by p_StudentID is currently registered */
    p_StudentID IN students.ID%TYPE)
    RETURN NUMBER AS

    v_TotalCredits NUMBER;   -- Total number of credits
    v_CourseCredits NUMBER; -- Credits for one course
    CURSOR c_RegisteredCourses IS
      SELECT department, course
        FROM registered_students
```

```
          WHERE student_id = p_StudentID;
BEGIN
  Debug.Reset;
  Debug.Debug('Before loop, v_TotalCredits', v_TotalCredits);
  FOR v_CourseRec IN c_RegisteredCourses LOOP
    -- Determine the credits for this class.
    SELECT num_credits
      INTO v_CourseCredits
      FROM classes
      WHERE department = v_CourseRec.department
      AND course = v_CourseRec.course;

    Debug.Debug('Inside loop, v_CourseCredits', v_CourseCredits);
    -- Add it to the total so far.
    v_TotalCredits := v_TotalCredits + v_CourseCredits;
    Debug.Debug('Inside loop, v_TotalCredits', v_TotalCredits);
  END LOOP;

  Debug.Debug('After loop, returning', v_TotalCredits);
  RETURN v_TotalCredits;
END CountCredits;
```

The output from this latest version of **CountCredits** is

```
SQL> exec :v_Total := CountCredits(10006);
Before loop, v_TotalCredits:
Inside loop, v_CourseCredits: 4
Inside loop, v_TotalCredits:
Inside loop, v_CourseCredits: 3
Inside loop, v_TotalCredits:
After loop, returning:

PL/SQL procedure successfully completed.
```

We can see the problem from this output. Notice that **v_TotalCredits** is NULL before the loop starts and remains NULL during the loop. This is because we didn't initialize **v_TotalCredits** in the declaration. We can fix this with the final version of **CountCredits**, which also has the debugging statements removed:

```
-- Available online as cntcred4.sql
CREATE OR REPLACE FUNCTION CountCredits (
  /* Returns the number of credits for which the student
     identified by p_StudentID is currently registered */
  p_StudentID IN students.ID%TYPE)
```

```
  RETURN NUMBER AS

  v_TotalCredits NUMBER := 0;   -- Total number of credits
  v_CourseCredits NUMBER;       -- Credits for one course
  CURSOR c_RegisteredCourses IS
    SELECT department, course
      FROM registered_students
      WHERE student_id = p_StudentID;
BEGIN
  FOR v_CourseRec IN c_RegisteredCourses LOOP
    -- Determine the credits for this class.
    SELECT num_credits
      INTO v_CourseCredits
      FROM classes
      WHERE department = v_CourseRec.department
      AND course = v_CourseRec.course;

    -- Add it to the total so far.
    v_TotalCredits := v_TotalCredits + v_CourseCredits;
  END LOOP;

  RETURN v_TotalCredits;
END CountCredits;
```

The output from this is as follows:

```
SQL> exec :v_Total := CountCredits(10006);
PL/SQL procedure successfully completed.
SQL> print v_Total
  V_TOTAL
---------
        7
SQL> SELECT ID, CountCredits(ID) "Total Credits"
  2    FROM students;

       ID Total Credits
--------- -------------
    10000             8
    10001             4
    10002             8
    10003             8
    10004             4
    10005             4
    10006             7
    10007             4
```

```
10008              8
10009              7
10010              8
```

We can see that **CountCredits** is working properly now, both for the single student example and for the entire table. If a variable is not initialized when it is declared, it is assigned the non-value NULL. The NULL value is maintained throughout the addition operation, according to the rules for evaluating NULL expressions, as described in Chapter 2.

Problem 2: Comments

This version of Debug has different features than the first version. Namely, we have eliminated the dependency on **debug_table**. This gives us several advantages:

- There is no worry about multiple database sessions interfering with each other, since each session will have its own DBMS_OUTPUT internal buffer.

- We no longer have to issue a COMMIT inside **Debug.Debug**.

- As long as SERVEROUTPUT is on, no additional SELECT statement is necessary to see the output. Also, we can turn off debugging by simply setting SERVEROUTPUT off.

On the other hand, there are still some things to be aware of with this version:

- If we are not using SQL*Plus, SQL*DBA, or Server Manager, the debugging output will not be printed to the screen automatically. The package can still be used from other PL/SQL execution environments (such as Pro*C or Oracle Forms), but you may have to call DBMS_OUTPUT.GET_LINE or DBMS_OUTPUT.GET_LINES explicitly and display the results yourself.

- The amount of debugging output is limited by the size of the DBMS_OUTPUT buffer. This affects both the size of each line and the total size of the buffer. If you find that there is too much output and the buffer is not large enough, the first version of Debug may be a better option.

PL/SQL Debuggers

As of this writing, there are several PL/SQL development tools available that include an integrated debugger. A tool like this is very valuable, since it allows you to step through PL/SQL code line-by-line to determine where a bug lies. We will examine two of these tools in this section: Oracle Procedure Builder and Platinum's SQL-Station Debugger.

Procedure Builder

Procedure Builder is a PL/SQL development environment that is part of the Developer 2000 series of products. Procedure Builder allows us to step through PL/SQL code line-by-line, examining variables as we go. As with debuggers for other languages, we can also set breakpoints and modify the value of variables while the program is running. We examined Procedure Builder in Chapter 13, but in this section we will focus on the debugging aspects. We won't develop a Debug package in this section because Procedure Builder incorporates the debugging features we need.

NOTE
One important thing to keep in mind about Procedure Builder is that PL/SQL can only be debugged on the client, not on the server. So in order to debug a particular object, you must first transfer the object to the client (using the Object Navigator). The procedure can be edited on the client and then copied back to the server.

Problem 3

Consider the following procedure:

```
-- Available online as crloop1.sql
CREATE OR REPLACE PROCEDURE CreditLoop AS
   /* Inserts the student ID numbers and their current credit
      values into temp_table. */
   v_StudentID students.ID%TYPE;
```

```
    v_Credits    students.current_credits%TYPE;
    CURSOR c_Students IS
      SELECT ID
        FROM students;
BEGIN
  OPEN c_Students;
  LOOP
    FETCH c_Students INTO v_StudentID;
    v_Credits := CountCredits(v_StudentID);
    INSERT INTO temp_table (num_col, char_col)
      VALUES (v_StudentID, 'Credits = ' || TO_CHAR(v_Credits));
    EXIT WHEN c_Students%NOTFOUND;
  END LOOP;
  CLOSE c_Students;
END CreditLoop;
```

CreditLoop simply records the number of credits for each student in
temp_table. When running **CreditLoop** and querying **temp_table** in
SQL*Plus, we get

```
SQL> exec CreditLoop;
PL/SQL procedure successfully completed.
SQL> SELECT * FROM temp_table
  2    ORDER BY num_col;

  NUM_COL CHAR_COL
--------- --------------------
    10000 Credits = 8
    10001 Credits = 4
    10002 Credits = 8
    10003 Credits = 8
    10004 Credits = 4
    10005 Credits = 4
    10006 Credits = 7
    10007 Credits = 4
    10008 Credits = 8
    10009 Credits = 7
    10010 Credits = 8
    10010 Credits = 8

12 rows selected.
```

The problem is that the last two rows are inserted twice—there are two
rows for student ID 10010 and one row for all the others.

Problem 3: Debugging with Procedure Builder

The first step is to copy **CreditLoop** into the client-side PL/SQL engine. (Procedure Builder can call server-side stored procedures, but it can't debug them.) We do this by dragging the procedure from "Stored Program Units" to "Program Units" in the Object Navigator window, as shown in Figure 14-2.

Once **CreditLoop** is on the client side, we can view it in the PL/SQL Interpreter window. This is where we will control the execution of the procedure. First, we should set a breakpoint. When we run the procedure, execution will stop at the breakpoint, and we can look at the values of the local variables in the Object Navigator. One way of setting breakpoints is to double-click on the line number at the desired place. For **CreditLoop**, this is at line 13, which is immediately after the FETCH statement. We want to examine **v_StudentID** to see where the duplicate value is coming from. Figure 14-3 shows the Interpreter with the breakpoint set.

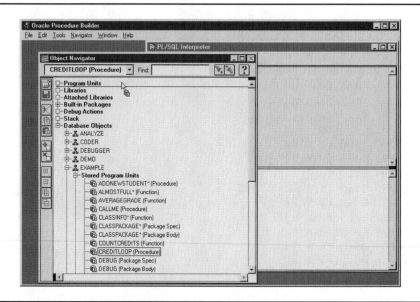

FIGURE 14-2. *Copying* **CreditLoop** *to the client*

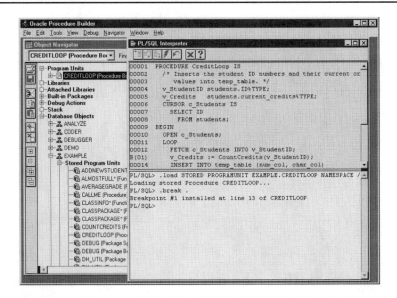

FIGURE 14-3. *Setting a breakpoint*

We are now ready to run **CreditLoop**. We do this by entering

```
CreditLoop;
```

at the PL/SQL prompt in the Interpreter. This will start the procedure and stop at the breakpoint that we set. This situation is shown in Figure 14-4.

At this point, we have several options. We can continue execution of the procedure through the buttons at the top of the Interpreter. These allow us to step through the code in various ways (the first three buttons) or allow the procedure to run until completion (the fourth button, with the lightning bolt). We can also look at the value of local variables. This is done by looking at the "Stack" section in the Object Navigator. Figure 14-5 shows the values of the two local variables visible at the breakpoint: **v_StudentID** and **v_Credits**. We can see that **v_StudentID** contains the first ID, resulting from the FETCH statement, and that **v_Credits** is NULL. This is what we expect.

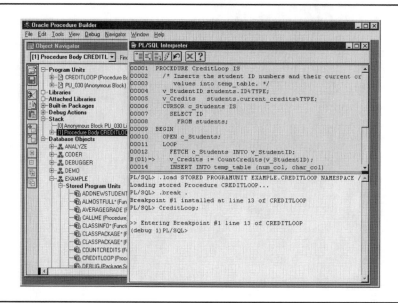

FIGURE 14-4. *Stopped at the breakpoint*

From here, we can step through the code and examine **v_StudentID** after each FETCH. As we do this, we can see **v_StudentID** changing, as it should. This continues until the last FETCH, which happens to return student ID 10010. We insert this value into **temp_table** and then loop again. The next FETCH doesn't change the value of **v_StudentID**—it is still 10010. Thus it gets inserted twice. After the second INSERT, the loop exits because **c_Students%NOTFOUND** becomes TRUE. This points out the problem, which is that the EXIT statement should be immediately after the FETCH. We can modify **CreditLoop** in the Program Unit Editor and then test it. The correct version is shown in Figure 14-6.

Now that we have fixed the problem, we need to copy **CreditLoop** back to the server so it can be called from other sessions as well. Similar to the procedure that we followed to copy it to the client, we simply drag the procedure from the "Program Units" section of the Object Navigator to the

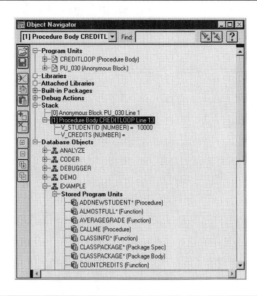

FIGURE 14-5. *Examining local variables in the Object Navigator*

```
Program Unit - CREDITLOOP                                        _ □ ×
┌────────┬────────┬────────┬────────┬────────┬────────┬────────┐
│ Compile│ Apply  │ Revert │ New... │ Delete │ Close  │ Help   │
└────────┴────────┴────────┴────────┴────────┴────────┴────────┘
Name: CREDITLOOP (Procedure Body)                                   ▼

PROCEDURE CreditLoop IS
  /* Inserts the student ID numbers and their current credit
     values into temp_table. */
  v_StudentID students.ID%TYPE;
  v_Credits   students.current_credits%TYPE;
  CURSOR c_Students IS
    SELECT ID
      FROM students;
BEGIN
  OPEN c_Students;
  LOOP
    FETCH c_Students INTO v_StudentID;
    EXIT WHEN c_Students%NOTFOUND;
    v_Credits := CountCredits(v_StudentID);
    INSERT INTO temp_table (num_col, char_col)
      VALUES (v_StudentID, 'Credits = ' || TO_CHAR(v_Credits));
  END LOOP;
  CLOSE c_Students;
END CreditLoop;

Not Modified                                        Successfully Compiled
```

FIGURE 14-6. *Correct version of* **CreditLoop**

"Stored Program Units" section, as shown in Figure 14-7. After doing this, we can test the procedure again from SQL*Plus. The output is shown here:

```
SQL> exec CreditLoop
PL/SQL procedure successfully completed.

SQL> SELECT * FROM temp_table
  2    ORDER BY num_col;

   NUM_COL CHAR_COL
--------- ------------------------------
     10000 Credits = 8
     10001 Credits = 4
     10002 Credits = 8
     10003 Credits = 8
     10004 Credits = 4
     10005 Credits = 4
     10006 Credits = 7
     10007 Credits = 4
     10008 Credits = 8
     10009 Credits = 7
     10010 Credits = 8

11 rows selected.
```

Problem 3: Comments

Using Procedure Builder has several advantages:

■ We don't need to add any debugging code to the procedure; we simply run the procedure in a controlled debugging environment.

■ Since the code doesn't have to be changed, then recompiled, then run to see different variables, it is more convenient to debug.

■ Procedure Builder provides an integrated development environment, including the PL/SQL Editor and the Object Navigator. No other tool is necessary to develop PL/SQL.

However, there are still some concerns. Notably, the current version of Procedure Builder (1.5) can only debug client-side PL/SQL. The version of PL/SQL on the client is still version 1.0, as opposed to PL/SQL 2.0 or higher

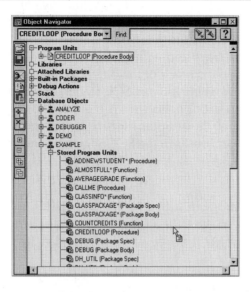

FIGURE 14-7. *Copying* **CreditLoop** *back to the server*

on the server. This means that you can't debug any code that uses version 2 features, such as PL/SQL tables and user-defined records.

SQL-Station

Like Procedure Builder, SQL-Station provides an integrated PL/SQL development environment, with an editor and debugger. However, SQL-Station allows you to debug stored procedures on the server without copying them to the client first. In fact, SQL-Station does not have a client-side PL/SQL engine, so all of the PL/SQL code will be executed on the server.

As we discussed in Chapter 13, SQL-Station consists of three modules: the Coder, the Debugger, and the Plan Analyzer. We will examine the Debugger in this section. In order to debug a PL/SQL subprogram, SQL-Station automatically creates a special debug version of the subprogram. The debug version is a copy of the original subprogram with code added that allows SQL-Station to keep track of the state, and this version is re-created each time you debug a subprogram.

Debug versions always start with the characters X#, followed by a sequence number and the name of the object. If desired, they can be deleted automatically when you exit SQL-Station by setting the "Clear debug objects after session" option in the preferences. Or they can be explicitly deleted using the Maintenance menu. For more information on maintaining debug versions, see the SQL-Station online documentation.

Problem 4

In many cases, the problem with a PL/SQL program is not with the program itself but with the data on which it operates. For example, consider the following SQL script, which copies data from the **source** to **destination** table:

```
-- Available online as copytab1.sql
CREATE OR REPLACE PROCEDURE CopyTables AS
  v_Key    source.key%TYPE;
  v_Value source.value%TYPE;

  CURSOR c_AllData IS
    SELECT *
      FROM source;
BEGIN
  OPEN c_AllData;

  LOOP
    FETCH c_AllData INTO v_Key, v_Value;
    EXIT WHEN c_AllData%NOTFOUND;

    INSERT INTO destination (key, value)
      VALUES (v_Key, TO_NUMBER(v_Value));
  END LOOP;

  CLOSE c_AllData;
END CopyTables;
```

The **source** and **destination** tables are created with:

```
-- Available online as part of tables.sql
CREATE TABLE source (
```

```
  key NUMBER(5),
  value VARCHAR2(50)   );

CREATE TABLE destination (
  key NUMBER(5),
  value NUMBER);
```

Note that the **value** column of **source** is VARCHAR2, but the **value** column of **destination** is NUMBER. Suppose we then populate **source** with the following PL/SQL block, which will insert 500 rows. Of these, 499 have a legal string (which can be converted into a NUMBER). However, one row (chosen at random, using the **Random** package from Chapter 8) has an illegal value.

```
-- Available online as populate.sql
DECLARE
  v_RandomKey source.key%TYPE;
BEGIN
  -- First fill up the source table with legal values.
  FOR v_Key IN 1..500 LOOP
    INSERT INTO source (key, value)
      VALUES (v_Key, TO_CHAR(v_Key));
  END LOOP;

  -- Now, pick a random number between 1 and 500, and update that
  -- row to an illegal value.
  v_RandomKey := Random.RandMax(500);
  UPDATE source
    SET value = 'Oops, not a number!'
    WHERE key = v_RandomKey;

  COMMIT;
END;
```

If we call **CopyTables** now, we will get an ORA-1722 error:

```
SQL> exec CopyTables
begin CopyTables; end;
*
ERROR at line 1:
ORA-01722: invalid number
ORA-06512: at "EXAMPLE.COPYTABLES", line 12
ORA-06512: at line 1
```

Clearly, the error is occurring on the INSERT statement. The question is, which value is bad? We can use the debugger to determine this.

Problem 4: SQL-Station Debugger

The first thing we need to do is add an exception handler to **CopyTables**. This way, we can set a breakpoint in the handler and examine **v_Key** to find the offending row. Figure 14-8 shows this modified version of **CopyTables** in a Coder editing window. We can store this version by clicking on the Execute button, as shown.

Once we have this version stored on the server, we can start a debugging window for **CopyTables** by selecting Debug from the Tools menu or by clicking on the Debug tool on the toolbar. This will cause SQL-Station to create a debug version of **CopyTables** and initialize the environment. This is shown in Figure 14-9. The next step is to set a breakpoint in the exception handler, by clicking on the Set Breakpoint button while the exception handler code is highlighted, as illustrated in Figure 14-10.

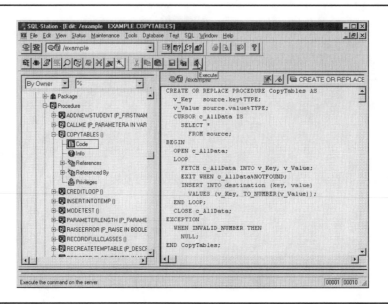

FIGURE 14-8.   *Modifying* **CopyTables**

We can now run the procedure. This will run until it encounters the breakpoint in the exception handler. At this point, the local variables are shown in the bottom pane of the debugging window. We can see that the offending row has key 409. This is illustrated in Figure 14-11.

Problem 4: Comments

Although this is a simple example, data can be invalid in more complicated or subtle ways, depending on your application. In this case, the data was of the wrong type and thus couldn't be converted. It is also possible for the data to be out of range, for example. Note that invalid data may not always raise an exception; depending on your error handling and the nature of the inconsistency, you may get different results.

It is important to note, however, that in this case the PL/SQL code is fine. The problem is not with the code, it is with the data on which the code operates. Thus you may be able to find the incorrect data by querying the tables directly rather than debugging the program.

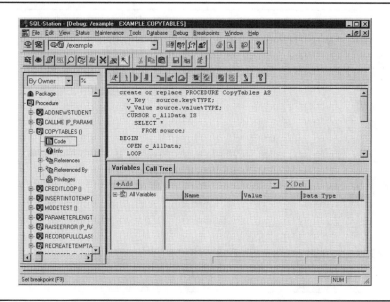

FIGURE 14-9. CopyTables *in a debugging window*

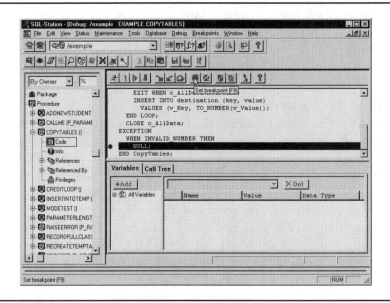

FIGURE 14-10. *Setting a breakpoint*

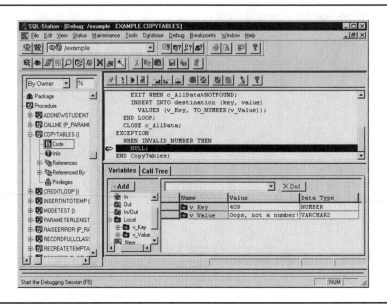

FIGURE 14-11. *Stopped at the breakpoint*

Comparison Between Procedure Builder and SQL-Station

Both Procedure Builder and SQL-Station are powerful and offer a similar set of features. For example, both products

■ Allow both editing and debugging of PL/SQL objects within the same environment

■ Have similar features for the debugger—both allow you to set breakpoints and examine (and modify) the values of local variables

■ Provide an object navigator that allows you to view and modify server (and client, in the case of Procedure Builder) objects of different types

■ Require a windowing environment to run, unlike the Debug package and other simpler debugging methods

However, they also have some differences:

■ Procedure Builder has a client-side PL/SQL engine. In order to debug an object, it must be copied to the client first. SQL-Station allows you to debug server-side objects directly. This has the advantage of allowing you to debug triggers, for example.

■ Procedure Builder can manipulate the PL/SQL code directly, without having to create a separate debug version. SQL-Station has to create this extra version to let you debug.

Each of these products has more features than we discussed here. For more information, see the Procedure Builder and/or SQL-Station online documentation.

Programming Methodologies

We have examined several different methods of debugging PL/SQL programs in this chapter. However, you can minimize the occurrence of bugs in the first place if you practice good programming design and methodologies. These concepts can be applied to other programming languages as well, not just PL/SQL.

Modular Programming

Modular programming simply means separating your program into distinct parts, or modules, each of which performs a specific function. You can then develop and test each module in turn and assemble them into the final program. In addition, the individual modules can be reused for other programs. This concept is best illustrated by example. Suppose we want to write a program that will print student transcripts. We can divide this task into steps, which constitute the algorithm for the program:

1. Determine the student ID whose transcript we want to output.

2. Determine the classes for which this student is registered.

3. For each class, output the department, course, course description, and grade.

4. Determine the grade point average (GPA) for the student and output it.

Each of these steps can be accomplished by a different PL/SQL construct. We then combine all of the constructs to get the final program. For example, we can implement each of the steps as follows:

1. The student ID can be passed to the procedure as a parameter.

2. The classes for this student are determined by selecting from **registered_students**.

3. The information about each class is selected from the **classes** table.

4. Calculating the GPA for the student can be done by another procedure, **CalculateGPA**.

Now that we have decided on the basic design for the procedure, we can sketch the procedure out as follows:

```
CREATE OR REPLACE PROCEDURE PrintTranscript(
    /* Outputs a transcript for the indicated student. The
       transcript will consist of the classes for which the
       student is currently registered and the grade received
```

```
    for each class. At the end of the transcript, the student's
    GPA is output. */
  p_StudentID IN students.ID%TYPE) AS

  v_StudentGPA  NUMBER;  -- Grade point average for this student.
  CURSOR CurrentClasses IS
    SELECT *
      FROM registered_students
      WHERE student_id = p_StudentID;
BEGIN
  -- Output some header information about the student such
  -- as first and last name, major, etc.

  FOR v_ClassesRecord IN CurrentClasses LOOP
    -- Output information about each class.
    NULL;
  END LOOP;

  -- Determine the GPA.
  CalculateGPA(p_StudentID, v_StudentGPA);

  -- Output the GPA.
END PrintTranscript;
```

We now have the basic structure of **PrintTranscript**. We can implement the individual sections of the procedure one by one, ensuring that each is correct before proceeding. We will do this in Chapter 18.

Top-Down Design

Top-down design complements modular programming. This means to develop the basic shell of the program first and then implement the details. By doing this, we can define exactly what each subprogram will have to do before implementing it. PL/SQL allows us to do this through procedure stubs. Consider the **CalculateGPA** procedure. We will need this for **PrintTranscript**. Without having to develop the actual algorithm for **CalculateGPA**, we can still write the stub of the procedure:

```
CREATE OR REPLACE PROCEDURE CalculateGPA(
  /* Returns the grade point average for the student identified
     by p_StudentID in p_GPA. */
  p_StudentID IN students.ID%TYPE,
  p_GPA OUT NUMBER) AS
```

```
BEGIN
  NULL;
END CalculateGPA;
```

This procedure can be compiled, which allows the skeleton of **PrintTranscript** to be compiled as well. The NULL statement by itself serves as a placeholder for the actual code of the procedure. By creating this stub first, we can now continue with the development of **PrintTranscript** without worrying about the details of **CalculateGPA**.

We have worked from the top of the program first, then developed the details. This is the principle of top-down design. If we had chosen *bottom-up design* instead, we would have implemented **CalculateGPA** before **PrintTranscript**. Top-down design allows more flexibility. As we develop **PrintTranscript**, for example, we may determine that **CalculateGPA** works better as a function. Or it might need to take additional parameters. We can simply modify the stub of **CalculateGPA** to continue development of **PrintTranscript** and complete **CalculateGPA** once we are sure of its interface and requirements.

Data Abstraction

Data abstraction is another good programming technique. This means that we can hide some of the implementation details for a particular algorithm and just present the interface to it. **CalculateGPA** is a good example of this. **PrintTranscript** doesn't need to know how the GPA is determined, only that it is determined, and **CalculateGPA** determines it. We are free to change the contents of **CalculateGPA**, as long as we don't change how it is called.

The fact that objects within a package body are private to that package also can be used to implement data abstraction. The package header documents the external interface to the data, and the package body actually does the manipulation. The DBMS_OUTPUT package itself uses this technique. The interface to GET_LINES, for example, is documented with the declaration of the procedure and the CHARARR type in the package header. The body of GET_LINES would have to loop through the buffer in some way and return the contents in the *lines* parameter. But we don't know how this is done, or even how the buffer is implemented. We don't need to know how the buffer is implemented (perhaps it uses a PL/SQL table, perhaps a database table, or some other data structure) to use DBMS_OUTPUT.

PL/SQL 8.0 ...and HIGHER In PL/SQL version 8, PL/SQL object types also implement data abstraction. The methods and attributes in the type specification define the public interface for using the object type, and the type body implements them. Once again, we are free to change the type body without changing the interface to the type. For more information, see Chapter 12.

Summary

In this chapter, we have examined three different methods for debugging PL/SQL code—inserting into an output table, using the DBMS_OUTPUT package, and using a PL/SQL debugger such as Procedure Builder or SQL-Station. Depending on your environment and needs, different methods may be appropriate. As we examined each of these debugging methods, we also discussed four common PL/SQL errors and how to resolve them. These were incorrect character comparison, uninitialized variables, an improper exit condition for a loop, and incorrect data. We also introduced principles of good programming methodology, which can be applied to program development in general, not just PL/SQL.

```
  /* Close the cursor, now that we are finished. */
  DBMS_SQL.CLOSE_CURSOR(v_Cursor);
EXCEPTION
  WHEN OTHERS THEN
    /* Close the cursor first, then reraise the error so it is
       propagated out. */
    DBMS_SQL.CLOSE_CURSOR(v_Cursor);
    RAISE;
END RecreateTempTable;
```

CAUTION

In order to run this example, you must have the CREATE TABLE and DROP TABLE system privileges granted directly, rather than via a role. See the section "Privileges and DBMS_SQL" later in this chapter for more information.

From this example, we can observe several things:

- The string that is parsed can be a constant, such as **v_DropString**, or it can be created dynamically by the program using string functions such as concatenation (**v_CreateString** is done this way).

- Error handling is the same as static SQL—errors are raised, and handled by exceptions, as we saw in Chapter 10. The difference is that we can now get compile errors (such as ORA-942) at run time. With static PL/SQL, these would be caught during compile time, before the block starts to run.

- We have more direct control of cursor processing, including when cursors are opened and closed. It is necessary to close any cursors that we open, even if an error is raised. The call to DBMS_SQL .CLOSE_CURSOR in the second exception handler guarantees this.

The flowchart in Figure 15-1 illustrates the order in which the calls to DBMS_SQL are typically made.

Three different kinds of statements can be processed with DBMS_SQL: DML and DDL statements, queries, and anonymous PL/SQL blocks. Each

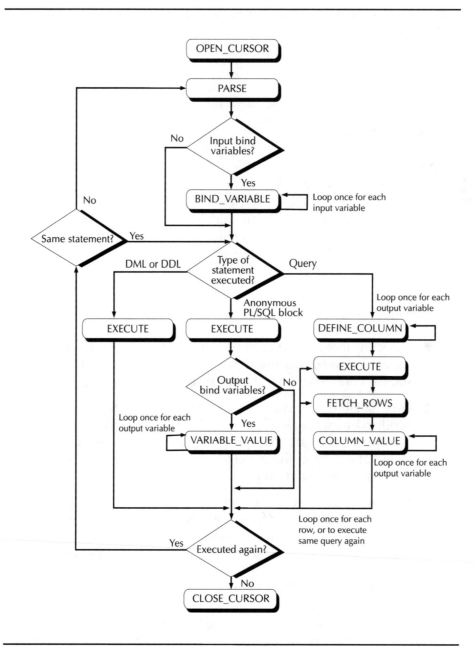

FIGURE 15-1. *The flow of execution in DBMS_SQL*

type is executed with different procedures. Brief descriptions of each of the procedures follow, with more detailed explanations later in this chapter.

OPEN_CURSOR   Like static SQL, every SQL statement is executed within a cursor. For dynamic PL/SQL, you control the cursor processing. OPEN_CURSOR returns a cursor ID number that is used to identify the context area in which the statement will be processed. All subsequent calls will use this cursor ID number.

PARSE   Parsing a statement involves sending it to the server, where the syntax and semantics of the statement are checked and verified. If the statement is a query, the execution plan is also determined at this point.

BIND_VARIABLE   Binding a variable to a placeholder is similar to the binding process PL/SQL uses for static SQL. A placeholder is a special identifier in the statement string. Binding is the act of associating this placeholder with an actual variable and telling DBMS_SQL the type and length of the variable. Binding is done for input variables.

DEFINE_COLUMN   Defining an output variable is similar to binding an input variable. The output variables in this case are the results of a query. DEFINE_COLUMN identifies the type and length of the PL/SQL variables that will receive the data when it is retrieved by FETCH_ROWS. DEFINE_COLUMN is used for output variables (the results of queries) only, while BIND_VARIABLE is used for input variables (placeholders in statements).

EXECUTE   For a non-query, EXECUTE will carry out the statement and return the number of rows processed. For a query, EXECUTE will determine the active set. The data is then fetched with FETCH_ROWS. For all statements, bind variables are examined at EXECUTE time.

FETCH_ROWS   Each call to FETCH_ROWS will return more data from the server. The data will be converted into the datatypes specified by DEFINE_COLUMN. EXECUTE_AND_FETCH combines the execute and fetch operations in one call.

VARIABLE_VALUE   This routine is used to determine the value of a bind variable if it is modified by the statement. This is only used when the statement is a PL/SQL block (perhaps calling a stored procedure).

COLUMN_VALUE   After calling FETCH_ROWS, COLUMN_VALUE is used to actually return the data. It takes variables of the same type specified in DEFINE_COLUMN. COLUMN_VALUE should only be used for queries.

CLOSE_CURSOR   When processing is complete, the cursor is closed. This frees all resources used by the cursor.

Executing Non-Query DML and DDL Statements

NOTE
The discussion in this and the following two sections describes DBMS_SQL for PL/SQL versions 2.1 through 2.3. PL/SQL 8.0 provides enhancements to several of the procedures discussed in these sections. These enhancements are discussed in the section "DBMS_SQL Enhancements for PL/SQL 8.0" later in this chapter.

This section discusses in detail the steps necessary for executing INSERT, UPDATE, DELETE, and DDL statements. Processing for anonymous PL/SQL blocks is described in the "Executing PL/SQL" section, and processing for queries is described in the "Executing Queries" section, both later in this chapter.

The following steps are required for non-query DML and DDL statements:

1. Open the cursor (OPEN_CURSOR).
2. Parse the statement (PARSE).

3. Bind any input variables (BIND_VARIABLE).

4. Execute the statement (EXECUTE).

5. Close the cursor (CLOSE_CURSOR).

Open the Cursor

Every SQL statement or PL/SQL block (static or dynamic) is executed within a cursor. For static SQL, the PL/SQL engine handles the cursor processing for most statements. You can control the processing for queries with the OPEN and CLOSE commands, as discussed in Chapter 6.

Dynamic SQL is no different. Each call to OPEN_CURSOR returns an integer, which is the cursor ID number. This ID is used in subsequent calls. More than one SQL statement can be executed sequentially within the same cursor, or the same statement can be executed multiple times.

Every call to OPEN_CURSOR should be matched by a call to CLOSE_CURSOR, to free the resources used by the cursor. OPEN_CURSOR is defined with

    OPEN_CURSOR RETURN INTEGER;

It takes no parameters.

Parse the Statement

When the statement is parsed, it is sent to the server. The server checks the syntax and semantics of the statement, and returns an error (via a raised exception) if the statement has a parse error. The execution plan for the statement is determined at PARSE time as well. The equivalent call in OCI, **oparse**, optionally allows the parse to be deferred. Deferring the parse reduces network traffic by buffering the statement until execute time. The statement is then parsed, resulting in only one network round-trip. However, DBMS_SQL does not currently support deferred parsing. This is often not an issue, since the entire PL/SQL block can be executed on the server (perhaps in a stored procedure), thus requiring no network round-trips.

PARSE is defined with

PROCEDURE PARSE(*c* IN INTEGER,
                    statement IN VARCHAR2,
                    language_flag IN INTEGER);

The parameters for PARSE are described as follows:

Parameter	Type	Description
c	INTEGER	ID number for a cursor in which to parse the statement. The cursor must already have been opened with OPEN_CURSOR.
statement	VARCHAR2	SQL statement to be parsed. If the statement is a DML or DDL command, it should not include the final semicolon. If the statement is an anonymous PL/SQL block, it should include the semicolon after the final END.
language_flag	INTEGER	Determines how the statement is treated. SQL statements can be executed with version 6 or version 7 behavior. This parameter has three possible values: V6: version 6 behavior V7: Oracle7 behavior NATIVE: behavior for the database to which the program is connected

The *language_flag* parameter specifies version 6 or version 7 behavior with the packaged constant DBMS_SQL.V6, DBMS_SQL.V7, or DBMS_SQL.NATIVE. There is no DBMS_SQL.V8 parameter for Oracle8; Oracle8 behaves the same way as Oracle7 in this respect.

NOTE
The only way to use DBMS_SQL against a version 6 database is if the statement involves a database link. DBMS_SQL itself is contained in PL/SQL 2.1 or higher, which requires at least Oracle7.

Bind Any Input Variables

Binding associates placeholders in the statement with actual PL/SQL variables. A placeholder is identified by a colon in front of the identifier. For example, the statement

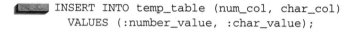

```
INSERT INTO temp_table (num_col, char_col)
    VALUES (:number_value, :char_value);
```

has two placeholders—**:number_value** and **:char_value**. The names of the placeholders are not significant. If the same placeholder name is used more than once in the statement, the same value will be bound for all occurrences. If there are no placeholders in the statement, then no binds are necessary.

The BIND_VARIABLE procedure is used for the bind. It identifies placeholders by name. For example, we could bind the placeholders in the preceding INSERT statement with

```
DBMS_SQL.BIND_VARIABLE(v_CursorID, ':number_value', -7);
DBMS_SQL.BIND_VARIABLE(v_CursorID, ':char_value', 'Hello');
```

NOTE
The colon in the bind variable name is optional. However, for the sake of consistency, all of the examples in this chapter do include the colon.

The length and datatype of the actual variable are also determined by BIND_VARIABLE, through a set of overloaded calls. The following call is used to bind NUMBERs:

```
PROCEDURE BIND_VARIABLE(c IN INTEGER,
                        name IN VARCHAR2,
                        value IN NUMBER);
```

These are used for binding VARCHAR2s:

```
PROCEDURE BIND_VARIABLE(c IN INTEGER,
                        name IN VARCHAR2,
                        value IN VARCHAR2);
PROCEDURE BIND_VARIABLE(c IN INTEGER,
                        name IN VARCHAR2,
                        value IN VARCHAR2,
                        out_value_size IN INTEGER);
```

This call is used for binding DATEs:

```
PROCEDURE BIND_VARIABLE(c IN INTEGER,
                        name IN VARCHAR2,
                        value IN DATE);
```

The following are used for binding CHARs. Their names are different because PL/SQL does not allow overloading on CHAR & VARCHAR2.

```
PROCEDURE BIND_VARIABLE_CHAR(c IN INTEGER,
                             name IN VARCHAR2,
                             value IN CHAR);

PROCEDURE BIND_VARIABLE_CHAR(c IN INTEGER,
                             name IN VARCHAR2,
                             value IN CHAR,
                             out_value_size IN INTEGER);
```

Likewise, these are used for binding RAWs:

```
PROCEDURE BIND_VARIABLE_RAW(c IN INTEGER,
                            name IN VARCHAR2,
                            value IN RAW);
```

```
PROCEDURE BIND_VARIABLE_RAW(c IN INTEGER,
                                name IN VARCHAR2,
                                value IN RAW,
                                out_value_size IN INTEGER);
```

This call is used for binding MLSLABELs:

```
PROCEDURE BIND_VARIABLE (c IN INTEGER,
                            name IN VARCHAR2,
                            value IN MLSLABEL);
```

Finally, this call is used for binding ROWIDs:

```
PROCEDURE BIND_VARIABLE_ROWID(c IN INTEGER,
                                name IN VARCHAR2,
                                value IN ROWID);
```

The various parameters used with these calls are described in the following table:

Parameter	Type	Description
c	INTEGER	ID number for a cursor. This cursor should have been previously opened with OPEN_CURSOR, and should have had a statement parsed with PARSE.
name	VARCHAR	Name of the placeholder for which this variable will be bound. The colon should be included.
value	NUMBER, CHAR, VARCHAR2, DATE, ROWID, RAW	Data that will actually be bound. The type and length of this variable are retrieved as well. The data in this variable will be converted if necessary.

Parameter	Type	Description
out_value_size	INTEGER	Optional parameter for CHAR and ROWID binds only. If specified, this is the maximum expected OUT value size, in bytes. If this parameter is not specified, the size of *value* is used. *Out_value_size* should only be specified when executing an anonymous PL/SQL block, when the bind variable could be written to. For input variables, the size of *value* won't change. For more information, see the example later in this chapter.

Execute the Statement

The EXECUTE function is used to execute the statement. It returns the number of rows processed. The return value of EXECUTE is valid only for DML statements. For queries, DDL statements, and anonymous PL/SQL blocks, this value is undefined and should be ignored. EXECUTE is a function, so it needs to be called from an expression. EXECUTE is defined with

FUNCTION EXECUTE(*c* IN INTEGER) RETURN INTEGER;

The parameters and return value are described here:

Parameter	Type	Description
c	INTEGER	Cursor ID for the cursor containing the statement to be executed. The cursor should have already been opened, a statement parsed in it, and any placeholders bound.
return value	INTEGER	Number of rows processed by the statement. This is analogous to the %ROWCOUNT cursor attribute. Only defined when the statement executed is an INSERT, UPDATE, or DELETE.

Close the Cursor

The cursor should be closed when processing is complete. This frees the resources allocated by the cursor and signals that it will no longer be used. After a cursor is closed, it can no longer be used unless it is reopened. The syntax for CLOSE_CURSOR is

PROCEDURE CLOSE_CURSOR(*c* IN OUT INTEGER);

The value passed into CLOSE_CURSOR should be a valid cursor ID. After the call, the actual parameter is set to NULL, meaning that the cursor is closed.

Example

The **UpdateClasses** procedure updates the number of credits for classes in the specified department. Although this procedure could have been written using static SQL, this example illustrates the necessary steps for processing.

```
-- Available online as updclass.sql
CREATE OR REPLACE PROCEDURE UpdateClasses(
  /* Uses DBMS_SQL to update the classes table, setting the
     number of credits for all classes in the specified
     department to the specified number of credits. */
  p_Department  IN classes.department%TYPE,
  p_NewCredits  IN classes.num_credits%TYPE,
  p_RowsUpdated OUT INTEGER) AS

  v_CursorID   INTEGER;
  v_UpdateStmt VARCHAR2(100);
BEGIN
  -- Open the cursor for processing.
  v_CursorID := DBMS_SQL.OPEN_CURSOR;

  -- Determine the SQL string.
  v_UpdateStmt :=
    'UPDATE classes
       SET num_credits = :nc
       WHERE department = :dept';
```

```
   -- Parse the statement.
   DBMS_SQL.PARSE(v_CursorID, v_UpdateStmt, DBMS_SQL.V7);

   -- Bind p_NewCredits to the placeholder :nc.
   DBMS_SQL.BIND_VARIABLE(v_CursorID, ':nc', p_NewCredits);

   -- Bind p_Department to the placeholder :dept.
   DBMS_SQL.BIND_VARIABLE(v_CursorID, ':dept', p_Department);

   -- Execute the statement.
   p_RowsUpdated := DBMS_SQL.EXECUTE(v_CursorID);

   -- Close the cursor.
   DBMS_SQL.CLOSE_CURSOR(v_CursorID);
EXCEPTION
   WHEN OTHERS THEN
     -- Close the cursor, then raise the error again.
     DBMS_SQL.CLOSE_CURSOR(v_CursorID);
     RAISE;
END UpdateClasses;
```

The following SQL*Plus excerpt shows the results of **UpdateClasses**.

```
SQL> VARIABLE v_RowsUpdated NUMBER
SQL> exec UpdateClasses('MUS', 5, :v_RowsUpdated)

PL/SQL procedure successfully completed.

SQL> print v_RowsUpdated

V_ROWSUPDATED
-------------
            1
```

Executing DDL Statements

The processing for a DDL statement is slightly different from the processing for a DML statement. There are two differences between DDL and DML processing:

■ Since bind variables are illegal in a DDL statement, no call to BIND_VARIABLE is necessary after the parse.

■ DDL statements are actually executed on the PARSE call. The EXECUTE call is not necessary—if it is included, then it has no effect.

Parse the Statement

PARSE behaves the same as for the DML case, but the string for a query needs to meet certain restrictions. It is important that the statement be a single SELECT, and not a SELECT embedded in a PL/SQL block. If the query is inside a block, it is processed according to the rules for PL/SQL blocks, which are described in the next section. In addition, the query should not have an INTO clause. Instead of this clause, we use the DEFINE_COLUMN and COLUMN_VALUE procedures. Finally, as for DML or DDL statements, the trailing semicolon should not be included. For example, all of the following queries are legal strings for use with DBMS_SQL.PARSE:

```
SELECT * FROM students

SELECT COUNT(*) "Number of Students", department || course
  FROM registered_students
  WHERE department IN (:d1, :d2)
  GROUP BY department || course

SELECT FullName(ID), ID
  FROM students
  WHERE ID = :student_id
```

Define the Output Variables

The define process is very similar to the bind, except that input variables need to be bound, while only output variables in a query need to be defined. The DEFINE_COLUMN procedure specifies the type and length for the output variables. Each select list item (see Chapter 4) will be converted into the type of its associated output variable.

Unlike BIND_VARIABLE placeholders, select list items are identified by position, not by name. The first position is number 1, the second is number 2, and so on. For example, if the query

```
SELECT first_name, last_name, num_credits
  FROM students
```

were parsed, the DEFINE_COLUMN calls could look like this:

```
DECLARE
    v_FirstName    students.first_name%TYPE,
    v_LastName     students.last_name%TYPE,
```

```
  v_NumCredits students.num_credits%TYPE,
  v_CursorID   INTEGER;
BEGIN
  ...
  DBMS_SQL.DEFINE_COLUMN(v_CursorID, 1, v_FirstName);
  DBMS_SQL.DEFINE_COLUMN(v_CursorID, 2, v_LastName);
  DBMS_SQL.DEFINE_COLUMN(v_CursorID, 3, v_NumCredits);
  ...
END;
```

Similar to BIND_VARIABLE, DEFINE_COLUMN is overloaded on the type of the output variable. The following call is used for defining NUMBERs:

```
PROCEDURE DEFINE_COLUMN(c IN INTEGER,
                        position IN INTEGER,
                        column IN NUMBER);
```

This call is used for defining VARCHAR2s:

```
PROCEDURE DEFINE_COLUMN(c IN INTEGER,
                        position IN INTEGER,
                        column IN VARCHAR2,
                        column_size IN INTEGER);
```

Here is the call for defining DATEs:

```
PROCEDURE DEFINE_COLUMN(c IN INTEGER,
                        position IN INTEGER,
                        column IN DATE,
                        column_size IN INTEGER);
```

This call is used for defining CHARs:

```
PROCEDURE DEFINE_COLUMN_CHAR(c IN INTEGER,
                             position IN INTEGER,
                             column IN CHAR,
                             column_size IN INTEGER);
```

This is used for defining RAWs:

```
PROCEDURE DEFINE_COLUMN_RAW(c IN INTEGER,
                            position IN INTEGER,
                            column IN RAW,
                            column_size IN INTEGER);
```

The following call is used for defining MLSLABELs:

```
PROCEDURE DEFINE_COLUMN(c IN INTEGER,
                        position IN INTEGER,
                        column IN MLSLABEL);
```

And finally, here is the call used for defining ROWIDs:

```
PROCEDURE DEFINE_COLUMN(c IN INTEGER,
                        position IN INTEGER,
                        column IN ROWID);
```

NOTE
*The DEFINE_COLUMN calls for
VARCHAR2, CHAR, and RAW require the
column_size parameter. This is needed
because the PL/SQL engine needs to know
the maximum length of these variables at
run time. Unlike NUMBER, DATE,
MLSLABEL, and ROWID, these types do not
have a fixed length known to the PL/SQL
compiler.*

The parameters for DEFINE_COLUMN are very similar to those for BIND_VARIABLE, and are listed here:

Parameter	Type	Description
c	INTEGER	Cursor ID number. The cursor should already have a query parsed and any input variables bound.
position	INTEGER	Relative position of the select list item. The first select list item is at position 1.

Parameter	Type	Description
column	NUMBER, VARCHAR2, CHAR, DATE, MLSLABEL, RAW, ROWID	Variable that defines the type and length of the output variable. The variable itself isn't necessarily important, but its type and length are. Usually, however, the same variables are used in DEFINE_COLUMN and COLUMN_VALUE.
column_size	INTEGER	Maximum expected size of the output data. If this isn't specified, the length of *column* is used instead.

Fetch the Rows

The rows that match the WHERE clause of the query are fetched into a buffer by FETCH_ROWS. COLUMN_VALUE is then called to retrieve the actual data from this buffer into PL/SQL variables. FETCH ROWS looks like this:

FUNCTION FETCH_ROWS(*c* IN INTEGER) RETURN INTEGER;

The only parameter is the cursor ID number. FETCH_ROWS returns the number of rows returned. Typically, FETCH_ROWS and COLUMN_VALUE are called repeatedly in a loop until FETCH_ROWS returns zero.

NOTE
The exit condition for the loop is when FETCH_ROWS returns zero, not the NO_DATA_FOUND exception or the %NOTFOUND cursor attribute.

The EXECUTE and the first call to FETCH_ROWS can be combined in one call—EXECUTE_AND_FETCH. When used against a remote database, this can save a network trip and thus improve performance. The syntax for EXECUTE_AND_FETCH is

```
FUNCTION EXECUTE_AND_FETCH(c IN INTEGER,
                                exact IN BOOLEAN DEFAULT FALSE)
                                RETURN INTEGER;
```

The parameters are as follows:

Parameter	Type	Description
c	INTEGER	Cursor ID number. The cursor should already have a query parsed in it, any input variables bound, and the output variables defined.
exact	BOOLEAN	If TRUE, the TOO_MANY_ROWS exception is raised if the query returns more than one row. Even if the exception is raised, the rows are still fetched and can be retrieved.
return value	INTEGER	The number of rows fetched so far. This is similar to FETCH_ROWS.

Return the Results to PL/SQL Variables

Once the data is retrieved into the local buffer by FETCH_ROWS, use COLUMN_VALUE to get the data into PL/SQL variables. Typically, the same variables used in DEFINE_COLUMN are used in COLUMN_VALUE. Each call to DEFINE_COLUMN should be matched by a call to COLUMN_VALUE.

Similar to BIND_VARIABLE and DEFINE_COLUMN, COLUMN_VALUE is overloaded on the type of the output variable. These are the calls used for NUMBERs:

```
PROCEDURE COLUMN_VALUE(c IN INTEGER,
                           position IN INTEGER,
                           value OUT NUMBER);
```

```
PROCEDURE COLUMN_VALUE(c IN INTEGER,
                       position IN INTEGER,
                       value OUT NUMBER,
                       column_error OUT NUMBER,
                       actual_length OUT INTEGER);
```

These are used for VARCHAR2s:

```
PROCEDURE COLUMN_VALUE(c IN INTEGER,
                       position IN INTEGER,
                       value OUT VARCHAR2);
```

```
PROCEDURE COLUMN_VALUE(c IN INTEGER,
                       position IN INTEGER,
                       value OUT VARCHAR2,
                       column_error OUT NUMBER,
                       actual_length OUT INTEGER);
```

The following calls are used for DATEs:

```
PROCEDURE COLUMN_VALUE(c IN INTEGER,
                       position IN INTEGER,
                       value OUT DATE);
```

```
PROCEDURE COLUMN_VALUE(c IN INTEGER,
                       position IN INTEGER,
                       value OUT DATE,
                       column_error OUT NUMBER,
                       actual_length OUT INTEGER);
```

These are used for CHARs:

```
PROCEDURE COLUMN_VALUE_CHAR(c IN INTEGER,
                            position IN INTEGER,
                            value OUT CHAR);
```

```
PROCEDURE COLUMN_VALUE_CHAR(c IN INTEGER,
                           position IN INTEGER,
                           value OUT CHAR,
                           column_error OUT NUMBER,
                           actual_length OUT INTEGER);
```

These are the calls used for RAWs:

```
PROCEDURE COLUMN_VALUE_RAW(c IN INTEGER,
                          position IN INTEGER,
                          value OUT RAW);
```

```
PROCEDURE COLUMN_VALUE_RAW(c IN INTEGER,
                          position IN INTEGER,
                          value OUT RAW,
                          column_error OUT NUMBER,
                          actual_length OUT INTEGER);
```

These are for MLSLABELs:

```
PROCEDURE COLUMN_VALUE(c IN INTEGER,
                      position IN INTEGER,
                      value OUT MLSLABEL);
```

```
PROCEDURE COLUMN_VALUE(c IN INTEGER,
                      position IN INTEGER,
                      value OUT MLSLABEL,
                      column_error OUT NUMBER,
                      actual_length OUT INTEGER);
```

Finally, these calls are used for ROWIDs:

```
PROCEDURE COLUMN_VALUE_ROWID(c IN INTEGER,
                            position IN INTEGER,
                            value OUT ROWID);
```

PROCEDURE COLUMN_VALUE_ROWID(*c* IN INTEGER,
                               position IN INTEGER,
                               value OUT **ROWID**,
                               column_error OUT NUMBER,
                               actual_length OUT INTEGER);

The parameters for these calls are described in the following table:

Parameter	Type	Description
c	INTEGER	Cursor ID number. The cursor should have had a query parsed, any placeholders bound, and have been executed and fetched.
position	INTEGER	Relative position within the select list. Similar to DEFINE_COLUMN, the first select list is position 1.
value	NUMBER, DATE, MLSLABEL, CHAR, VARCHAR2, RAW, ROWID	Output variable. The contents of the buffer for this row and column will be returned in this variable. If the type of *value* differs from the type specified in DEFINE_COLUMN, the error "ORA-6562: type of OUT argument must match type of column or bind variable" is raised, which is equivalent to the exception DBMS_SQL.INCONSISTENT_TYPES.
column_error	NUMBER	Column-level error code. If specified, this variable will return errors such as "ORA-1406: fetched column value is truncated." The code is returned as a negative value, similar to SQLCODE. The error will also be raised as an exception, but *column_error* allows you to determine which column caused the error. If the column was retrieved successfully, *column_error* is zero.

Retrieve the Value of Any Output Variables

After the statement has been executed, the value of any output variables can be retrieved with VARIABLE_VALUE. Similar to a query, the value is stored in a buffer first by EXECUTE, and retrieved from this buffer with VARIABLE_VALUE. Only those bind variables that are used as output variables need to be retrieved. Typically, the same variables used in BIND_VARIABLE are used in VARIABLE_VALUE, but this is not required.

Similar to BIND_VARIABLE and COLUMN_VALUE, VARIABLE_VALUE is overloaded by the type of the output variable. The following call is used for NUMBERs:

```
PROCEDURE VARIABLE_VALUE(c IN NUMBER,
                            name IN VARCHAR2,
                            value OUT NUMBER);
```

This call is used for VARCHAR2s:

```
PROCEDURE VARIABLE_VALUE(c IN NUMBER,
                            name IN VARCHAR2,
                            value OUT VARCHAR2);
```

Here is the call used for DATEs:

```
PROCEDURE VARIABLE_VALUE(c IN NUMBER,
                            name IN VARCHAR2,
                            value OUT DATE);
```

This call is used for CHARs:

```
PROCEDURE VARIABLE_VALUE_CHAR(c IN NUMBER,
                                name IN VARCHAR2,
                                value OUT CHAR);
```

The following is used for RAWs:

```
PROCEDURE VARIABLE_VALUE_RAW(c IN NUMBER,
                            name IN VARCHAR2,
                            value OUT RAW);
```

This is the call used for MLSLABELs:

```
PROCEDURE VARIABLE_VALUE(c IN NUMBER,
                         name IN VARCHAR2,
                         value OUT MLSLABEL);
```

And here is the call used for ROWIDs:

```
PROCEDURE VARIABLE_VALUE_ROWID(c IN NUMBER,
                               name IN VARCHAR2,
                               value OUT ROWID);
```

The parameters for these calls are listed in the following table:

Parameter	Type	Description
c	INTEGER	Cursor ID number. The cursor should already have been opened, have had a PL/SQL block parsed in it, any placeholders bound, and been executed.
name	VARCHAR2	Name of the placeholder (including the colon) whose value is to be retrieved.
value	NUMBER, CHAR, VARCHAR2, DATE, ROWID, MLSLABEL	Output variable to receive the result. If the type of value does not match the type used in BIND_VARIABLE, the error "ORA-6562: type of OUT argument must match type of column or bind variable" is raised, which is equivalent to the exception DBMS_SQL.INCONSISTENT_TYPES. This is similar to the behavior of COLUMN_VALUE.

Example

The **DynamicPLSQL** procedure executes a PL/SQL block that queries students. Note that we have to pass the maximum length for the output placeholders **:first_name** and **:last_name**. They don't have a value before the block is run, and thus the maximum length can't be determined automatically.

```
-- Available online as dynPLSQL.sql
CREATE OR REPLACE PROCEDURE DynamicPLSQL (
   /* Executes a PL/SQL block dynamically. The block
      selects from students, and uses p_StudentID as an
      input placeholder. */
   p_StudentID IN students.ID%TYPE) IS

   v_CursorID  INTEGER;
   v_BlockStr  VARCHAR2(500);
   v_FirstName students.first_name%TYPE;
   v_LastName  students.last_name%TYPE;
   v_Dummy     INTEGER;

BEGIN
   -- Open the cursor for processing.
   v_CursorID := DBMS_SQL.OPEN_CURSOR;

   -- Create the string containing the PL/SQL block.
   -- In this string, the :first_name and :last_name
   -- placeholders are output variables, and :ID is an
   -- input variable.
   v_BlockStr :=
     'BEGIN
        SELECT first_name, last_name
          INTO :first_name, :last_name
          FROM students
          WHERE ID = :ID;
      END;';

   -- Parse the statement.
   DBMS_SQL.PARSE(v_CursorID, v_BlockStr, DBMS_SQL.V7);

   -- Bind the placeholders to the variables. Note that we
   -- do this for both the input and output variables.
   -- We pass the maximum length for :first_name and
   -- :last_name.
```

```
DBMS_SQL.BIND_VARIABLE(v_CursorID, ':first_name', v_FirstName, 20);
DBMS_SQL.BIND_VARIABLE(v_CursorID, ':last_name', v_LastName, 20);
DBMS_SQL.BIND_VARIABLE(v_CursorID, ':ID', p_StudentID);

-- Execute the statement. We don't care about the return
-- value, but we do need to declare a variable for it.
v_Dummy := DBMS_SQL.EXECUTE(v_CursorID);

-- Retrieve the values for the output variables.
DBMS_SQL.VARIABLE_VALUE(v_CursorID, ':first_name', v_FirstName);
DBMS_SQL.VARIABLE_VALUE(v_CursorID, ':last_name', v_LastName);

-- Insert them into temp_table.
INSERT INTO temp_table (num_col, char_col)
   VALUES (p_StudentID, v_FirstName || ' ' || v_LastName);

-- Close the cursor.
DBMS_SQL.CLOSE_CURSOR(v_CursorID);

-- Commit our work.
COMMIT;
EXCEPTION
  WHEN OTHERS THEN
    -- Close the cursor, then raise the error again.
    DBMS_SQL.CLOSE_CURSOR(v_CursorID);
    RAISE;
END DynamicPLSQL;
```

We can run **DynamicPLSQL** from SQL*Plus with

```
SQL> exec DynamicPLSQL(10010)
PL/SQL procedure successfully completed.

SQL> exec DynamicPLSQL(10003)
PL/SQL procedure successfully completed.

SQL> SELECT * FROM temp_table;
  NUM_COL CHAR_COL
--------- -------------------------
    10010 Rita Razmataz
    10003 Manish Murgratroid
```

Using out_value_size

When using BIND_VARIABLE for an output character variable, it is important to provide a value for the **out_value_size** parameter. Suppose we modify the bind calls in **DynamicPLSQL** as follows:

```
-- Bind the placeholders to the variables. Note that we
-- do this for both the input and output variables.
-- Do not pass the maximum length for v_FirstName and
-- v_LastName.
DBMS_SQL.BIND_VARIABLE(v_CursorID, ':first_name', v_FirstName);
DBMS_SQL.BIND_VARIABLE(v_CursorID, ':last_name', v_LastName);
DBMS_SQL.BIND_VARIABLE(v_CursorID, ':ID', p_StudentID);
```

Now when we run **DynamicPLSQL** we receive a numeric or value error:

```
SQL> exec DynamicPLSQL(10010)
begin DynamicPLSQL(10010); end;

*
ERROR at line 1:
ORA-06502: PL/SQL: numeric or value error
ORA-06512: at "EXAMPLE.DYNAMICPLSQL", line 51
ORA-06512: at line 1
```

Why is this? The answer lies in how the Oracle database processes bind variables in general. Bind variables are not examined until the statement is actually executed. At this time, the actual length of the variable is determined, based on the value of the variable. In **DynamicPLSQL**, both **v_FirstName** and **v_LastName** are not initialized by the program. This results in the bind variables being assigned a length of zero. Thus, when the VARIABLE_VALUE call attempts to assign a value back to **v_FirstName**, the error is raised. If the *out_value_size* parameter is passed to BIND_VARIABLE as in the original example, then this length is used instead of the actual length of the variable.

An alternative is to initialize the bind variables to a string with the maximum length, as follows:

```
-- Bind the placeholders to the variables. Note that we
-- do this for both the input and output variables.
-- First initialize both variables to their maximum
-- lengths.
v_FirstName := '12345678901234567890';
```

```
v_LastName := '12345678901234567890';
DBMS_SQL.BIND_VARIABLE(v_CursorID, ':first_name', v_FirstName);
DBMS_SQL.BIND_VARIABLE(v_CursorID, ':last_name', v_LastName);
DBMS_SQL.BIND_VARIABLE(v_CursorID, ':ID', p_StudentID);
```

PL/SQL at Work: Executing Arbitrary Stored Procedures

PL/SQL 2.3 ...and HIGHER DBMS_SQL, when combined with the DBMS_DESCRIBE package, can be a very powerful tool for executing arbitrary stored procedures. This functionality could be used in a dynamic program that accepts input from the user, or as a wrapper around the DBMS_SQL package.

DBMS_DESCRIBE is a package with one procedure—DESCRIBE _PROCEDURE. It will return information about the parameters of a procedure, including their names, modes, and types. The interface is similar to DBMS_SQL.DESCRIBE_COLUMNS, described later in this chapter. See Appendix B for more information.

The code for the **ExecuteAny** package follows. Since it uses a table of records, this package requires PL/SQL 2.3 or higher.

```
-- Available online as execany.sql
CREATE OR REPLACE PACKAGE ExecuteAny AS
  -- Generic parameter for a stored procedure or function
  TYPE t_Parameter IS RECORD (
    actual_type    VARCHAR2(8),    -- One of 'NUMBER', 'VARCHAR2',
                                   -- 'DATE', 'CHAR'
    actual_length INTEGER,
    name           VARCHAR2(50),
    num_param      NUMBER,
    vchar_param    VARCHAR2(500),
    char_param     CHAR(500),
    date_param     DATE);

  -- Generic parameter list
  TYPE t_ParameterList IS TABLE OF t_Parameter
    INDEX BY BINARY_INTEGER;

  -- Runs an arbitrary procedure. All of the IN parameters in
  -- p_Parameters must have at least the _param and actual_type fields
  -- filled in, and all OUT parameters must have the actual_type field
```

```
-- populated. On output, the name field is populated.
PROCEDURE RunProc(p_NumParams IN NUMBER,
                  p_ProcName IN VARCHAR2,
                  p_Parameters IN OUT t_ParameterList);

-- Populates the internal data structures with description about the
-- procedure given by p_ProcName. If p_Print is TRUE, this
-- information is output using DBMS_OUTPUT.
PROCEDURE DescribeProc(p_ProcName IN VARCHAR2,
                       p_Print IN BOOLEAN);

-- Displays, using DBMS_OUTPUT, the parameters in p_Parameters.
PROCEDURE Printparams(p_Parameters IN t_ParameterList,
                      p_NumParams IN NUMBER);
END ExecuteAny;

CREATE OR REPLACE PACKAGE BODY ExecuteAny AS
  -- internal DBMS_DESCRIBE.DESCRIBE_PROCEDURE variables
  v_Overload     DBMS_DESCRIBE.NUMBER_TABLE;
  v_Position     DBMS_DESCRIBE.NUMBER_TABLE;
  v_Level        DBMS_DESCRIBE.NUMBER_TABLE;
  v_ArgumentName DBMS_DESCRIBE.VARCHAR2_TABLE;
  v_Datatype     DBMS_DESCRIBE.NUMBER_TABLE;
  v_DefaultValue DBMS_DESCRIBE.NUMBER_TABLE;
  v_InOut        DBMS_DESCRIBE.NUMBER_TABLE;
  v_Length       DBMS_DESCRIBE.NUMBER_TABLE;
  v_Precision    DBMS_DESCRIBE.NUMBER_TABLE;
  v_Scale        DBMS_DESCRIBE.NUMBER_TABLE;
  v_Radix        DBMS_DESCRIBE.NUMBER_TABLE;
  v_Spare        DBMS_DESCRIBE.NUMBER_TABLE;

  -- Local function to convert datatype codes to strings.
  FUNCTION ConvertDatatype(p_Code IN NUMBER)
    RETURN VARCHAR2 IS
    v_Output VARCHAR2(20);
  BEGIN
    SELECT DECODE(p_Code, 0, ' ',
                          1, 'VARCHAR2',
                          2, 'NUMBER',
                          3, 'BINARY_INTEGER',
                          8, 'LONG',
                          11, 'ROWID',
                          12, 'DATE',
```

```
                          23, 'RAW',
                          24, 'LONG RAW',
                          96, 'CHAR',
                          106, 'MLSLABEL',
                          250, 'RECORD',
                          251, 'TABLE',
                          252, 'BOOLEAN')
  INTO v_Output
  FROM dual;

  RETURN v_Output;
END ConvertDatatype;

-- Local function to convert parameter modes to strings.
FUNCTION ConvertMode(p_Code IN NUMBER)
  RETURN VARCHAR2 IS
  v_Output VARCHAR2(10);
BEGIN
  SELECT DECODE(p_Code, 0, 'IN',
                        1, 'IN OUT',
                        2, 'OUT')
    INTO v_Output
    FROM dual;

  RETURN v_Output;
END ConvertMode;

PROCEDURE DescribeProc(p_ProcName IN VARCHAR2,
                       p_Print IN BOOLEAN) IS
  v_ArgCounter NUMBER := 1;
BEGIN
  -- First call DESCRIBE_PROCEDURE to populate the internal variables
  -- about the procedure.
  DBMS_DESCRIBE.DESCRIBE_PROCEDURE(
    p_ProcName,
    null,
    null,
    v_Overload,
    v_Position,
    v_Level,
    v_ArgumentName,
    v_Datatype,
    v_DefaultValue,
    v_InOut,
```

```
      v_Length,
      v_Precision,
      v_Scale,
      v_Radix,
      v_Spare);

   IF NOT p_Print THEN
     RETURN;
   END IF;

   -- Output titles.
   DBMS_OUTPUT.PUT_LINE('Description of ' || p_ProcName || ':');
   DBMS_OUTPUT.PUT('Overload Position Argument Name Level ');
   DBMS_OUTPUT.PUT('Datatype        Mode    Length Precision Scale');
   DBMS_OUTPUT.NEW_LINE;
   DBMS_OUTPUT.PUT('-------- ------- ------------- -----
   DBMS_OUTPUT.PUT('-------------- ------ ------ --------- -----');
   DBMS_OUTPUT.NEW_LINE;

   -- Output information about the parameters.
   LOOP
     BEGIN
       DBMS_OUTPUT.PUT(RPAD(TO_CHAR(v_Overload(v_ArgCounter)), 9));
       DBMS_OUTPUT.PUT(RPAD(TO_CHAR(v_Position(v_ArgCounter)), 9));
       DBMS_OUTPUT.PUT(RPAD(v_ArgumentName(v_ArgCounter), 14));
       DBMS_OUTPUT.PUT(RPAD(TO_CHAR(v_Level(v_ArgCounter)), 6));
       DBMS_OUTPUT.PUT(RPAD(ConvertDatatype(v_Datatype
                                     (v_ArgCounter)), 15));
       DBMS_OUTPUT.PUT(RPAD(ConvertMode(v_InOut(v_ArgCounter)), 7));
       DBMS_OUTPUT.PUT(RPAD(TO_CHAR(v_Length(v_ArgCounter)), 7));
       DBMS_OUTPUT.PUT(RPAD(TO_CHAR(v_Precision(v_ArgCounter)), 10));
       DBMS_OUTPUT.PUT(RPAD(TO_CHAR(v_Scale(v_ArgCounter)), 5));
       DBMS_OUTPUT.NEW_LINE;
       v_ArgCounter := v_ArgCounter + 1;
     EXCEPTION
       WHEN NO_DATA_FOUND THEN
         EXIT;
     END;
   END LOOP;

END DescribeProc;

PROCEDURE RunProc(p_NumParams IN NUMBER,
                  p_ProcName IN VARCHAR2,
                  p_Parameters IN OUT t_ParameterList) IS
```

```
  -- DBMS_SQL variables
  v_Cursor  NUMBER;
  v_NumRows NUMBER;

  v_ProcCall VARCHAR2(500);
  v_FirstParam BOOLEAN := TRUE;
BEGIN

  -- First describe the procedure.
  DescribeProc(p_ProcName, TRUE);

  -- Now we need to create the procedure call string. This consists
  -- of 'BEGIN <procedure_name>(:p1, :p2, ...); END;'
  v_ProcCall := 'BEGIN ' || p_ProcName || '(';

  FOR v_Counter IN 1..p_NumParams LOOP
    IF v_FirstParam THEN
      v_ProcCall := v_ProcCall || ':' || v_ArgumentName(v_Counter);
      v_FirstParam := FALSE;
    ELSE
      v_ProcCall := v_ProcCall || ', :' || v_ArgumentName(v_Counter);
    END IF;
  END LOOP;

  v_ProcCall := v_ProcCall || '); END;';

  -- Open the cursor and parse the statement.
  v_Cursor := DBMS_SQL.OPEN_CURSOR;
  DBMS_SQL.PARSE(v_Cursor, v_ProcCall, DBMS_SQL.V7);

  -- Bind the procedure parameters.
  FOR v_Counter IN 1..p_NumParams LOOP

    -- First set the parameter name.
    p_Parameters(v_Counter).name := v_ArgumentName(v_Counter);

    -- Bind based on the parameter type.
    IF p_Parameters(v_Counter).actual_type = 'NUMBER' THEN
      DBMS_SQL.BIND_VARIABLE(v_Cursor, p_Parameters(v_Counter).name,
                             p_Parameters(v_Counter).num_param);
    ELSIF p_Parameters(v_Counter).actual_type = 'VARCHAR2' THEN
      DBMS_SQL.BIND_VARIABLE(v_Cursor, p_Parameters(v_Counter).name,
```

```
                                   p_Parameters(v_Counter).vchar_param, 500);
          ELSIF p_Parameters(v_Counter).actual_type = 'DATE' THEN
            DBMS_SQL.BIND_VARIABLE(v_Cursor, p_Parameters(v_Counter).name,
                              p_Parameters(v_Counter).date_param);
          ELSIF p_Parameters(v_Counter).actual_type = 'CHAR' THEN
            DBMS_SQL.BIND_VARIABLE_CHAR(v_Cursor,p_Parameters(v_Counter).name,
                              p_Parameters(v_Counter).char_param,
500);
        ELSE
          RAISE_APPLICATION_ERROR(-20001, 'Invalid type');
        END IF;
      END LOOP;

      -- Execute the procedure.
      v_NumRows := DBMS_SQL.EXECUTE(v_Cursor);

      -- Call VARIABLE_VALUE for any OUT or IN OUT parameters.
      FOR v_Counter IN 1..p_NumParams LOOP
        IF v_InOut(v_Counter) = 1 OR v_InOut(v_Counter) = 2 THEN
          IF p_Parameters(v_Counter).actual_type = 'NUMBER' THEN
            DBMS_SQL.VARIABLE_VALUE(v_Cursor, ':' ||
                              p_Parameters(v_Counter).name,
                              p_Parameters(v_Counter).num_param);
          ELSIF p_Parameters(v_Counter).actual_type = 'VARCHAR2' THEN
            DBMS_SQL.VARIABLE_VALUE(v_Cursor, ':' ||
                              p_Parameters(v_Counter).name,

p_Parameters(v_Counter).vchar_param);
          ELSIF p_Parameters(v_Counter).actual_type = 'DATE' THEN
            DBMS_SQL.VARIABLE_VALUE(v_Cursor, ':' ||
                              p_Parameters(v_Counter).name,
                              p_Parameters(v_Counter).date_param);
          ELSIF p_Parameters(v_Counter).actual_type = 'CHAR' THEN
            DBMS_SQL.VARIABLE_VALUE_CHAR(v_Cursor, ':' ||
                              p_Parameters(v_Counter).name,
                              p_Parameters(v_Counter).char_param);
          ELSE
            RAISE_APPLICATION_ERROR(-20001, 'Invalid type');
          END IF;
        END IF;
      END LOOP;

    END RunProc;
```

```
PROCEDURE Printparams(p_Parameters IN t_ParameterList,
                      p_NumParams IN NUMBER) IS
BEGIN
  -- Loop over the parameters, and print the name, type, and value.
  FOR v_Counter IN 1..p_NumParams LOOP
    DBMS_OUTPUT.PUT('Parameter ' || v_Counter || ': Name = ');
    DBMS_OUTPUT.PUT(p_Parameters(v_Counter).name || ', Type = ');
    DBMS_OUTPUT.PUT(p_Parameters(v_Counter).actual_type ||
                    ', Value = ');
    IF p_Parameters(v_Counter).actual_type = 'NUMBER' THEN
      DBMS_OUTPUT.PUT_LINE(p_Parameters(v_Counter).num_param);
    ELSIF p_Parameters(v_Counter).actual_type = 'VARCHAR2' THEN
      DBMS_OUTPUT.PUT_LINE(p_Parameters(v_Counter).vchar_param);
    ELSIF p_Parameters(v_Counter).actual_type = 'DATE' THEN
      DBMS_OUTPUT.PUT_LINE(p_Parameters(v_Counter).date_param);
    ELSE
      DBMS_OUTPUT.PUT_LINE(p_Parameters(v_Counter).char_param);
    END IF;
  END LOOP;
END PrintParams;

END ExecuteAny;
```

The following example illustrates how to use **ExecuteAny**. Suppose we create **TestPkg** as follows:

```
-- Available online as testpkg.sql
CREATE OR REPLACE PACKAGE TestPkg AS
  -- This is a very simple package, with procedures that take
  -- different types of arguments, to better illustrate ExecuteAny.
  PROCEDURE P1(p_Num IN NUMBER, p_Date OUT DATE);
  PROCEDURE P2(p_String OUT VARCHAR2);
  PROCEDURE P3(p_Num IN OUT NUMBER, p_String OUT VARCHAR2);
END TestPkg;

CREATE OR REPLACE PACKAGE BODY TestPkg AS
  PROCEDURE P1(p_Num IN NUMBER, p_Date OUT DATE) IS
  BEGIN
    p_Date := SYSDATE;
  END P1;

  PROCEDURE P2(p_String OUT VARCHAR2) IS
  BEGIN
    p_String := 'Hello World!';
  END P2;
```

```
PROCEDURE P3(p_Num IN OUT NUMBER, p_String OUT VARCHAR2) IS
BEGIN
  p_String := 'Original value was ' || TO_NUMBER(p_Num);
  p_Num := p_Num + 25;
END P3;
END TestPkg;
```

We can use **ExecuteAny** to call the procedures in **TestPkg** with the following block. The output is shown in Figure 15-2.

-- **Available online as `anyexamp.sql`**

```
DECLARE
  -- v_Params will hold the parameter list for the procedures we call.
  v_Params ExecuteAny.t_ParameterList;
BEGIN
  -- Fill in v_Params with the info for TestPkg.P1. Note that since the
  -- first parameter is IN and the second is OUT, we only fill in a
  -- _param value for parameter 1. ExecuteAny.RunProc will fill in any
  -- OUT parameters. We do, however, have to fill in the type
  -- information for both parameters.
  v_Params(1).actual_type := 'NUMBER';
  v_Params(1).num_param := 7;
  v_Params(2).actual_type := 'DATE';
  ExecuteAny.RunProc(2, 'TestPkg.P1', v_Params);
  DBMS_OUTPUT.PUT_LINE('After call to RunProc for P1:');
  ExecuteAny.PrintParams(v_Params, 2);
  DBMS_OUTPUT.NEW_LINE;

  -- Fill in v_Params for TestPkg.P2. Since P2 has only one OUT
  -- parameter, we only need to fill in the type.
  v_Params(1).actual_type := 'VARCHAR2';
  ExecuteAny.RunProc(1, 'TestPkg.P2', v_Params);
  DBMS_OUTPUT.PUT_LINE('After call to RunProc for P2:');
  ExecuteAny.PrintParams(v_Params, 1);
  DBMS_OUTPUT.NEW_LINE;

  -- Fill in v_Params for TestPkg.P3.
  v_Params(1).actual_type := 'NUMBER';
  v_Params(1).num_param := -34;
  v_Params(2).actual_type := 'VARCHAR2';
  ExecuteAny.RunProc(2, 'TestPkg.P3', v_Params);
  DBMS_OUTPUT.PUT_LINE('After call to RunProc for P3:');
  ExecuteAny.PrintParams(v_Params, 2);
  DBMS_OUTPUT.NEW_LINE;
END;
```

```
Oracle SQL*Plus                                                    _ □ X
File  Edit  Search  Options  Help
SQL> @ch15\anyexamp
Description of TestPkg.P1:
Overload Position Argument Name Level Datatype    Mode    Length Precision Scale
-------- -------- ------------- ----- --------    ----    ------ --------- -----
0        1        P_NUM         0     NUMBER      IN      0      0         0
0        2        P_DATE        0     DATE        IN OUT  0      0         0
After call to RunProc for P1:
Parameter 1: Name = P_NUM, Type = NUMBER, Value = 7
Parameter 2: Name = P_DATE, Type = DATE, Value = 03-APR-97

Description of TestPkg.P2:
Overload Position Argument Name Level Datatype    Mode    Length Precision Scale
-------- -------- ------------- ----- --------    ----    ------ --------- -----
0        1        P_STRING      0     VARCHAR2    IN OUT  0      0         0
After call to RunProc for P2:
Parameter 1: Name = P_STRING, Type = VARCHAR2, Value = Hello World!

Description of TestPkg.P3:
Overload Position Argument Name Level Datatype    Mode    Length Precision Scale
-------- -------- ------------- ----- --------    ----    ------ --------- -----
0        1        P_NUM         0     NUMBER      OUT     0      0         0
0        2        P_STRING      0     VARCHAR2    IN OUT  0      0         0
After call to RunProc for P3:
Parameter 1: Name = P_NUM, Type = NUMBER, Value = -9
Parameter 2: Name = P_STRING, Type = VARCHAR2, Value = Original value was -34


PL/SQL procedure successfully completed.

SQL>
```

FIGURE 15-2.   *Output of **ExecuteAny** example*

DBMS_SQL Enhancements for PL/SQL 8.0

PL/SQL 8.0 ...and HIGHER There are several enhancements to the DBMS_SQL package for Oracle8 and PL/SQL 8.0. These include the ability to parse large SQL strings, use of array processing, the ability to bind and define Oracle8 types such as objects and LOBs, and use of the DESCRIBE_COLUMNS procedure. All of the examples in this section require Oracle8.

Parsing Large SQL Strings

Because the maximum length of a VARCHAR is 32,767 bytes and the *statement* parameter of the PARSE call is a VARCHAR, the maximum size of a SQL statement that can be executed using DBMS_SQL is limited. This restriction is lifted with the following alternative to the PARSE call:

```
PROCEDURE DBMS_SQL.PARSE(c IN INTEGER,
                         statement IN VARCHAR2S,
                         lb IN INTEGER,
                         ub IN INTEGER,
                         lfflg IN BOOLEAN,
                         language_flag IN INTEGER);
```

The VARCHAR2S type is defined as

```
TYPE VARCHAR2S IS TABLE OF VARCHAR2(256)
   INDEX BY BINARY_INTEGER;
```

Because the SQL statement is now passed in a PL/SQL table, statements of arbitrary length (up to the maximum size limit of the server) can be parsed. The parameters to this version of PARSE are described in the following table.

Parameter	Type	Description
c	INTEGER	Cursor number.
statement	DBMS_SQL.VARCHAR2S	String to be parsed. The string should be broken up into pieces, each of which has a maximum length of 256 characters.
lb	INTEGER	Lower bound in the statement table.
ub	INTEGER	Upper bound in the statement table.
lfflg	BOOLEAN	If TRUE, insert a linefeed after each element in the statement table.
language_flag	INTEGER	Determines how Oracle handles the statement. Behaves the same as before.

In order to use this version of PARSE, copy the statement into the *statement* table, putting each section of the statement into consecutive elements of the table, from element *lb* to element *ub*. The DBMS_SQL package will then combine these into a full statement that would look like this:

```
statement(lb) || statement(lb + 1) || ... || statement(ub)
```

For example, we could rewrite the parse section of **DynamicPLSQL** as follows:

```
CREATE OR REPLACE PROCEDURE DynamicPLSQL (
  p_StudentID IN students.ID%TYPE) IS

  v_CursorID  INTEGER;
  v_BlockStr  DBMS_SQL.VARCHAR2S;
  ...
BEGIN
  -- Open the cursor for processing.
  v_CursorID := DBMS_SQL.OPEN_CURSOR;

  -- Create the string containing the PL/SQL block.
  -- In this string, the :first_name and :last_name
  -- placeholders are output variables, and :ID is an
  -- input variable.
  v_BlockStr(1) := 'BEGIN';
  v_BlockStr(2) := 'SELECT first_name, last_name';
  v_BlockStr(3) := '  INTO :first_name, :last_name';
  v_BlockStr(4) := '    FROM students';
  v_BlockStr(5) := '    WHERE ID = :ID;';
  v_BlockStr(6) := 'END;';

  -- Parse the statement.
  DBMS_SQL.PARSE(v_CursorID, v_BlockStr, 1, 6, TRUE, DBMS_SQL.V7);
  ...
END DynamicPLSQL;
```

DBMS_SQL Array Processing

Array processing adds the ability to process large amounts of data with a single SQL statement. For example, you could insert 100 rows into the database with a single round-trip from the client to the server. Without array processing, the same operation would take 100 round-trips.

Array processing is done in DBMS_SQL with the BIND_ARRAY (used for batch inserts, updates, and deletes) and DEFINE_ARRAY (used for batch queries) procedures.

BIND_ARRAY

The BIND_ARRAY procedure operates much like the BIND_VARIABLE procedure, and takes similar arguments. The variable to be bound, however, is a PL/SQL table rather than a scalar variable. The allowed types are:

```
TYPE NUMBER_TABLE IS TABLE OF NUMBER
  INDEX BY BINARY_INTEGER;
TYPE VARCHAR2_TABLE IS TABLE OF VARCHAR2(2000)
  INDEX BY BINARY_INTEGER;
TYPE DATE_TABLE IS TABLE OF DATE
  INDEX BY BINARY_INTEGER;
TYPE BLOB_TABLE IS TABLE OF BLOB
  INDEX BY BINARY_INTEGER;
TYPE CLOB_TABLE IS TABLE OF CLOB
  INDEX BY BINARY_INTEGER;
TYPE BFILE_TABLE IS TABLE OF BFILE
  INDEX BY BINARY_INTEGER;
```

The other difference between BIND_ARRAY and BIND_VARIABLE is that BIND_ARRAY can take the range of values in the PL/SQL table to bind. Thus BIND_ARRAY is overloaded on the type of the table, and also on the table indices:

```
PROCEDURE BIND_ARRAY(c IN INTEGER,
                name IN VARCHAR2,
                table_variable IN table_datatype);

PROCEDURE BIND_ARRAY(c IN INTEGER,
                name IN VARCHAR2,
                table_variable IN table_datatype,
                index1 IN INTEGER,
                index2 IN INTEGER);
```

The parameters for BIND_VARIABLE are described in the following table.

Parameter	Datatype	Description
c	INTEGER	Cursor number
name	VARCHAR2	Name of the placeholder in the statement
table_variable	One of NUMBER_TABLE, VARCHAR2_TABLE, DATE_TABLE, BLOB_TABLE, CLOB_TABLE, BFILE_TABLE	PL/SQL table which contains the data to be bound
index1	INTEGER	Index of the table element which is the low bound of the range to be bound
index2	INTEGER	Index of the table element which is the upper bound of the range to be bound

If *index1* and *index2* are not specified, then the entire PL/SQL table will be used. If more than one PL/SQL table is bound to the same statement (for different placeholders) with different sizes, then the size of the smallest array will be used. An example using both BIND_ARRAY and DEFINE_ARRAY can be found after the next section.

DEFINE_ARRAY

Similar to BIND_ARRAY, the DEFINE_ARRAY procedure operates like DEFINE_COLUMN, except that it takes PL/SQL table arguments. The table types are the same as those used by BIND_VARIABLE. The syntax is

```
PROCEDURE DEFINE_ARRAY(c IN INTEGER,
                       position IN INTEGER,
                       table_variable IN table_datatype,
                       cnt IN INTEGER,
                       indx IN INTEGER);
```

The parameters are described in the following table.

Parameter	Datatype	Description
c	INTEGER	Cursor number.
position	INTEGER	Position within the select list of this column. The first column has position 1.
table_variable	One of NUMBER_TABLE, VARCHAR2_TABLE, DATE_TABLE, BLOB_TABLE, CLOB_TABLE, BFILE_TABLE	PL/SQL table variable in which the data will be placed by a subsequent FETCH_ROWS statement.
cnt	INTEGER	Maximum number of rows which will be retreived by each call to FETCH_ROWS.
indx	INTEGER	Starting index of the result set. At most *cnt* rows will be written into *table_variable*, starting with index *indx*.

See the next section for an example using both BIND_ARRAY and DEFINE_ARRAY.

Array Processing Example

The **CopyRegisteredStudents** procedure will make a copy of the **registered_students** table. Although this could be done without using DBMS_SQL, it illustrates the concepts of array processing.

-- **Available online as copyRS.sql**

```
CREATE OR REPLACE PROCEDURE CopyRegisteredStudents(
  p_NewName IN VARCHAR2) AS
  /* Creates a new table, with a name given by p_NewName, with the
     same structure as registered_students. The contents of
     registered_students are then read into PL/SQL tables, and inserted
     into the new table. */
```

```
    v_BatchSize CONSTANT INTEGER := 5;
    v_IDs DBMS_SQL.NUMBER_TABLE;
    v_Departments DBMS_SQL.VARCHAR2_TABLE;
    v_Courses DBMS_SQL.NUMBER_TABLE;
    v_Grades DBMS_SQL.VARCHAR2_TABLE;

    v_Cursor1 INTEGER;
    v_Cursor2 INTEGER;
    v_ReturnCode INTEGER;
    v_NumRows INTEGER;
    v_SQLStatement VARCHAR2(200);
    v_SelectStmt VARCHAR2(200);
    v_InsertStmt VARCHAR2(200);

BEGIN
  v_Cursor1 := DBMS_SQL.OPEN_CURSOR;
  v_Cursor2 := DBMS_SQL.OPEN_CURSOR;

  -- First drop the new table. Ignore ORA-942 (table or view does not
  -- exist) error.
  BEGIN
    v_SQLStatement := 'DROP TABLE ' || p_NewName;
    DBMS_SQL.PARSE(v_Cursor1, v_SQLStatement, DBMS_SQL.V7);
    v_ReturnCode := DBMS_SQL.EXECUTE(v_Cursor1);
  EXCEPTION
    WHEN OTHERS THEN
      IF SQLCODE != -942 THEN
        RAISE;
      END IF;
  END;

  -- Create the new table.
  v_SQLStatement := 'CREATE TABLE ' || p_NewName || '(';
  v_SQLStatement := v_SQLStatement || 'student_id NUMBER(5),';
  v_SQLStatement := v_SQLStatement || 'department CHAR(3),';
  v_SQLStatement := v_SQLStatement || 'course NUMBER(3),';
  v_SQLStatement := v_SQLStatement || 'grade CHAR(1))';
  DBMS_SQL.PARSE(v_Cursor1, v_SQLStatement, DBMS_SQL.V7);
  v_ReturnCode := DBMS_SQL.EXECUTE(v_Cursor1);

  -- Parse both the select and insert statements.
  v_SelectStmt := 'SELECT * FROM registered_students';
  v_InsertStmt := 'INSERT INTO ' || p_NewName || ' VALUES ';
  v_InsertStmt := v_InsertStmt || '(:ID, :department, :course,
                                    :grade)';
```

```
DBMS_SQL.PARSE(v_Cursor1, v_SelectStmt, DBMS_SQL.V7);
DBMS_SQL.PARSE(v_Cursor2, v_InsertStmt, DBMS_SQL.V7);

-- Use DEFINE_ARRAY to specify the output variables for the select.
DBMS_SQL.DEFINE_ARRAY(v_Cursor1, 1, v_IDs, v_BatchSize, 1);
DBMS_SQL.DEFINE_ARRAY(v_Cursor1, 2, v_Departments, v_BatchSize, 1);
DBMS_SQL.DEFINE_ARRAY(v_Cursor1, 3, v_Courses, v_BatchSize, 1);
DBMS_SQL.DEFINE_ARRAY(v_Cursor1, 4, v_Grades, v_BatchSize, 1);

-- Execute the select statment.
v_ReturnCode := DBMS_SQL.EXECUTE(v_Cursor1);

-- This is the fetch loop. Each call to FETCH_ROWS will retreive
-- v_BatchSize rows of data. The loop is over when FETCH_ROWS
-- returns a value < v_BatchSize.
LOOP
  v_NumRows := DBMS_SQL.FETCH_ROWS(v_Cursor1);
  DBMS_SQL.COLUMN_VALUE(v_Cursor1, 1, v_IDs);
  DBMS_SQL.COLUMN_VALUE(v_Cursor1, 2, v_Departments);
  DBMS_SQL.COLUMN_VALUE(v_Cursor1, 3, v_Courses);
  DBMS_SQL.COLUMN_VALUE(v_Cursor1, 4, v_Grades);

  -- If this is the last fetch, then FETCH_ROWS will return less than
  -- v_BatchSize rows. However, there could still be rows returned,
  -- and there are exactly v_NumRows number of them. Thus we need to
  -- use v_NumRows instead of v_BatchSize in these binds.

  -- The special case of v_NumRows = 0 needs to be checked here. This
  -- means that the previous fetch returned all the remaining rows
  -- and therefore we are done with the loop.
  IF v_NumRows = 0 THEN
    EXIT;
  END IF;

  -- Use BIND_ARRAY to specify the input variables for the insert.
  -- Only elements 1..v_NumRows will be used.
  DBMS_SQL.BIND_ARRAY(v_Cursor2, ':ID', v_IDs, 1, v_NumRows);
  DBMS_SQL.BIND_ARRAY(v_Cursor2, ':department', v_Departments, 1,
                      v_NumRows);
  DBMS_SQL.BIND_ARRAY(v_Cursor2, ':course', v_Courses, 1, v_NumRows);
  DBMS_SQL.BIND_ARRAY(v_Cursor2, ':grade', v_Grades, 1, v_NumRows);

  -- Execute the insert statement.
  v_ReturnCode := DBMS_SQL.EXECUTE(v_Cursor2);
```

```
      -- Exit condition for the loop. Note that the loop processing
has
      -- been done before we check this.
      EXIT WHEN v_NumRows < v_BatchSize;
    END LOOP;

    COMMIT;

    DBMS_SQL.CLOSE_CURSOR(v_Cursor1);
    DBMS_SQL.CLOSE_CURSOR(v_Cursor2);
END CopyRegisteredStudents;
```

NOTE
*The semantics of FETCH_ROWS change slightly when doing an array fetch. The EXIT WHEN statement of the fetch loop is done only after the rows have been inserted into the new table, not immediately after the FETCH_ROWS statement. (Compare this fetch loop to the one in **DynamicQuery** earlier in this chapter.) This is necessary because there may still be rows left to process after FETCH_ROWS returns less than the requested amount of rows. This condition indicates that all rows have been fetched from the database, but they may not all have been processed yet.*

Describing the Select List

If a SELECT statement is completely dynamic, the program may not know anything about the columns it will return at compile time. The DESCRIBE_COLUMNS procedure can provide this information. DESCRIBE_COLUMNS can be called any time after a query is parsed. The syntax of the procedure and its types are as follows:

```
TYPE DESC_REC IS RECORD (
  col_type    BINARY_INTEGER := 0;
  col_max_len  BINARY_INTEGER := 0;
  col_name      VARCHAR2(32) := '';
```

Code	Description
1	VARCHAR2
2	NUMBER
8	LONG
12	DATE
23	RAW
24	LONG RAW
69	ROWID
96	CHAR
106	MLSLABEL
112	CLOB
113	BLOB
114	BFILE

TABLE 15-1. *Internal Datatype Codes*

```
col_name_len  BINARY_INTEGER := 0;
col_schema_name  VARCHAR2(32) := '';
col_schema_name_len  BINARY_INTEGER := 0;
col_precision  BINARY_INTEGER := 0;
col_scale  BINARY_INTEGER := 0;
col_charsetid  BINARY_INTEGER := 0;
col_charsetform  BINARY_INTEGER := 0;
col_null_ok  BOOLEAN := TRUE);

TYPE DESC_TAB IS TABLE OF DESC_REC
  INDEX BY BINARY_INTEGER;

PROCEDURE DBMS_SQL.DESCRIBE_COLUMNS(c IN INTEGER,
                              col_cnt OUT INTEGER,
                              dest_t OUT DESC_TYPE);
```

The parameters for DESCRIBE_COLUMNS are described in the following table.

Parameter	Type	Description
c	INTEGER	Cursor number.
col_cnt	INTEGER	Number of columns in the select list.
desc_t	DESC_TYPE	PL/SQL table containing column description information.

The fields in the DESC_REC type have the following meanings:

Field	Type	Description
col_type	BINARY_INTEGER	Type code for the column being described. The codes are listed in Table 15-1.
col_max_len	BINARY_INTEGER	Maximum length of the column.
col_name	VARCHAR2(32)	Name of the column.
col_name_len	BINARY_INTEGER	Length of the column name.
col_schema_name	VARCHAR2(32)	Name of the schema in which the column type was defined (valid for object types only).
col_schema_name_len	BINARY_INTEGER	Length of the schema name.
col_precision	BINARY_INTEGER	Precision of the column. Valid only for NUMBER columns.
col_scale	BINARY_INTEGER	Scale of the column. Valid only for NUMBER columns.
col_charsetid	BINARY_INTEGER	Character set ID of the column.

Field	Type	Description
col_charsetform	BINARY_INTEGER	Character set form of the column.
col_null_ok	BOOLEAN	TRUE if the column allows NULLs, FALSE otherwise.

As an example of DESCRIBE_COLUMNS, the following **DescribeTable** procedure will take a table name as input, and then output (using DBMS_OUTPUT) a description of the table to the screen.

-- **Available online as descrtab.sql**

```
CREATE OR REPLACE PROCEDURE DescribeTable(p_Table IN VARCHAR2) AS
  v_Cursor        INTEGER;
  v_SQLStatement  VARCHAR2(100);
  v_DescribeInfo  DBMS_SQL.DESC_TAB;
  v_DRec          DBMS_SQL.DESC_REC;
  v_ReturnCode    INTEGER;
  v_NumColumns    INTEGER;

  FUNCTION ConvertDatatype (v_Datatype IN NUMBER)
    RETURN VARCHAR2 IS
    v_Output VARCHAR2(20);
  BEGIN
    SELECT DECODE(v_Datatype, 1,  'VARCHAR2',
                              2,  'NUMBER',
                              8,  'LONG',
                              12, 'DATE',
                              23, 'RAW',
                              24, 'LONG RAW',
                              69, 'ROWID',
                              96, 'CHAR',
                              106, 'MLSLABEL',
                              112, 'CLOB',
                              113, 'BLOB',
                              114, 'BFILE')
      INTO v_Output
      FROM dual;

    RETURN v_Output;
  END ConvertDatatype;

BEGIN
```

```
      v_Cursor := DBMS_SQL.OPEN_CURSOR;

      -- Parse a select statement for the table.
      -- We don't need to execute it.
      v_SQLStatement := 'SELECT * FROM ' || p_Table;
      DBMS_SQL.PARSE(v_Cursor, v_SQLStatement, DBMS_SQL.V7);

      -- Describe the statement, which will give us a table description.
      DBMS_SQL.DESCRIBE_COLUMNS(v_Cursor,  v_NumColumns, v_DescribeInfo);

      -- Output header info.
      DBMS_OUTPUT.PUT_LINE('Description of ' || p_Table || ':');
      DBMS_OUTPUT.PUT('Column Name     Datatype Length Precision Scale ');
      DBMS_OUTPUT.PUT_LINE('Null?');
      DBMS_OUTPUT.PUT('------------- -------- ------ ------- ----- ');
      DBMS_OUTPUT.PUT_LINE('-----');

      -- Loop over the columns, outputting the describe info for each.
      FOR v_Col IN 1..v_NumColumns LOOP
        v_DRec := v_DescribeInfo(v_Col);
        DBMS_OUTPUT.PUT(RPAD(v_DRec.col_name, 16));
        DBMS_OUTPUT.PUT(RPAD(ConvertDatatype(v_DRec.col_type), 9));
        DBMS_OUTPUT.PUT(RPAD(v_DRec.col_max_len, 7));
        DBMS_OUTPUT.PUT(RPAD(v_DRec.col_precision, 10));
        DBMS_OUTPUT.PUT(RPAD(v_DRec.col_scale, 6));
        IF v_DescribeInfo(v_Col).col_null_ok THEN
          DBMS_OUTPUT.NEW_LINE;
        ELSE
          DBMS_OUTPUT.PUT_LINE('NOT NULL');
        END IF;
      END LOOP;

    END DescribeTable;
```

Miscellaneous Procedures

There are additional procedures in DBMS_SQL that are used for fetching
LONG data, and for additional error handling.

Fetching LONG Data

PL/SQL 2.2 ...and HIGHER   Since a LONG column can hold up to 2 gigabytes of data, and a
PL/SQL LONG can hold only 32K, DBMS_SQL has the ability to
fetch LONG data in more manageable pieces. This is done through two

procedures: DEFINE_COLUMN_LONG and COLUMN_VALUE_LONG. These procedures are available starting with PL/SQL 2.2.

They are used in the same way as DEFINE_COLUMN and COLUMN_VALUE, except that COLUMN_VALUE_LONG is typically called in a loop to fetch all of the pieces.

DEFINE_COLUMN_LONG

The syntax for DEFINE_COLUMN_LONG is

```
PROCEDURE DEFINE_COLUMN_LONG(c IN INTEGER,
                                    position IN INTEGER);
```

The parameters are described here:

Parameter	Type	Description
c	INTEGER	Cursor ID number. The cursor should have been opened and parsed with a query that contains a LONG column. Any placeholders should have been bound as well.
position	INTEGER	Relative position within the select list of the LONG item. The first select list item is at position 1.

COLUMN_VALUE_LONG

The syntax for COLUMN_VALUE_LONG is

```
PROCEDURE COLUMN_VALUE_LONG(c IN INTEGER,
                                 position IN INTEGER,
                                 length IN INTEGER,
                                 offset IN INTEGER,
                                 value OUT VARCHAR2,
                                 value_length OUT INTEGER);
```

with the following parameters:

Parameter	Type	Description
c	INTEGER	Cursor ID number. The cursor should have been opened, a query parsed, input placeholders bound, the long column defined with DEFINE_COLUMN_LONG and other columns with DEFINE_COLUMN, executed, and fetched.
position	INTEGER	Relative position within the select list of the LONG item. The first select list item is at position 1.
length	INTEGER	Length in bytes of this segment.
offset	INTEGER	Byte offset within the data at which the piece starts. The piece will be length bytes long. A zero offset indicates the first piece.
value	VARCHAR2	Output variable to receive this piece.
value_length	INTEGER	Actual returned length of the piece. When value_length < length, the total column value has been retrieved.

It is most efficient to start at the beginning of the LONG value and fetch from there, rather than starting in the middle or the end. Each call to COLUMN_VALUE_LONG will return a piece of the LONG value, starting at *offset*, that is *length* bytes long. The piece is returned in *value*, and the length of the piece in *value_length*. If *value_length* is less than *length*, the end of the data has been reached. See the 'PL/SQL At Work' example later in this chapter for an example using COLUMN_VALUE_LONG.

Additional Error Functions

These functions can be used for additional error reporting and management of DBMS_SQL cursors. Some of the calls are only valid in certain places, and these are noted in the descriptions.

```
   dbms_sql.close_cursor(mycursor);
   utl_file.fclose(file_handle);
   return('Success');
EXCEPTION
   WHEN OTHERS THEN
     utl_file.fclose(file_handle);
     return('Failure');
END dump_doc;
```

Privileges and DBMS_SQL

Several issues arise with privileges when using DBMS_SQL. These include the privilege to execute DBMS_SQL itself, and the way roles interact with DBMS_SQL.

Privileges Required for DBMS_SQL

In order to use DBMS_SQL, you need the EXECUTE privilege on the package. Like the other DBMS packages, DBMS_SQL is owned by SYS. The install script that creates the package typically grants EXECUTE on the package to PUBLIC, so all users will have access to the package. You may want to revoke this privilege from PUBLIC and grant it only to select users.

Typically, procedures run under the privilege set of their owners. In this case, DBMS_SQL is owned by SYS, which would mean that any commands executed using DBMS_SQL would be run as SYS. Needless to say, this would be a serious security breach. To prevent this, the procedures and functions in DBMS_SQL run under the privilege set of their caller, not SYS. If you connect as **UserA** and call **RecreateTempTable**, for example, **temp_table** would be created under **UserA**'s schema, even though DBMS_SQL is owned by SYS.

Roles and DBMS_SQL

As we discussed in Chapter 7, all roles are disabled inside stored procedures. This applies to DBMS_SQL as well. However, since we can execute arbitrary commands using DBMS_SQL, the user calling DBMS_SQL needs the privileges to execute the dynamic command, as well as EXECUTE on DBMS_SQL itself. Furthermore, the privilege to execute the dynamic command needs to be granted explicitly, and not through a role.

The role is disabled inside DBMS_SQL, so the privilege would not be available.

For example, the RESOURCE role is commonly granted to users. This role contains the system privilege CREATE TABLE. Suppose **UserA** has been granted RESOURCE. Then **UserA** can issue commands such as

```
DROP TABLE temp_table;
CREATE TABLE temp_table (num_col NUMBER, char_col VARCHAR2(50));
```

from SQL, since the role is enabled. However, when these same commands are executed using DBMS_SQL (the **RecreateTempTable** procedure, for example), the role is disabled and the error

```
ORA-1031: insufficient privileges
```

is returned. The solution for this is to grant CREATE TABLE directly to **UserA**.

TIP
Whenever you receive the ORA-1031 error when using DBMS_SQL, check the SQL statement or PL/SQL block being executed by DBMS_SQL. Make sure that the user executing this has the appropriate system and object privileges granted directly, not via a role. This is most likely the cause of the problem.

Comparison Between DBMS_SQL and Other Dynamic Methods

Three different tools can perform dynamic SQL and PL/SQL for Oracle: the DBMS_SQL package, OCI, and the Oracle precompilers. The steps required for each are the same—opening cursors, parsing statements, binding input variables, defining output variables, executing and fetching, and closing the cursors at the end. However, each interface has different features with regard to dynamic SQL.

The main differences between these interfaces are listed in Table 15-2 and described in detail in the following sections.

Feature	Present in DBMS_SQL?	Present in the Precompilers?	Present in OCI?
Describing the select list	Available with 8.0 and higher	Yes, all versions	Yes, all versions
Array processing	Available with 8.0 and higher	Yes, all versions	Yes, all versions
Fetch longs piecewise	Available with 2.2 and higher	Not available	Yes, all versions
Insert/update of longs piecewise	Not available	Not available	Yes, with version 7.3 and higher

TABLE 15-2. *Comparison of Features Among Dynamic Methods*

Describing the Select List

Describing the select list of a query allows you to determine at run time what kinds of items will be returned—their lengths and datatypes. This feature is available in the precompilers and OCI, but is only available with DBMS_SQL with 8.0 or higher (the DESCRIBE_COLUMNS procedure).

Even with DESCRIBE_COLUMNS, this feature is less useful in DBMS_SQL. The reason for this has to do with the fact that PL/SQL does not currently allow the user to dynamically allocate and deallocate memory (in the sense of C's **malloc** and **free** functions). In the precompilers or OCI, after the statement is described, the output variables are often dynamically allocated to fit the size of the expected data. A PL/SQL program would have to simulate this with PL/SQL tables or varrays.

Column information can still be determined from PL/SQL without using DESCRIBE_COLUMNS, however. The **user_tab_columns** data dictionary view contains information about the type and length of database table columns, so a PL/SQL program can query this table to determine the select list structure.

Array Processing

Both OCI and the precompilers can use the Oracle Array Interface. This method allows data to be inserted into the database directly from C arrays, or fetched from the database directly into C arrays. This is a very useful feature, which can significantly reduce network traffic. This feature is available with the PL/SQL 8.0 BIND_ARRAY and DEFINE_ARRAY procedures.

Piecewise Operations on LONG Data

The precompilers cannot currently operate on LONG data piecewise. However, OCI can. Many of the calls in DBMS_SQL are implemented by calling the OCI equivalents, which includes the **oflng** procedure. This procedure provides the ability to fetch LONG data piecewise and is implemented in DBMS_SQL with the DEFINE_COLUMN_LONG and FETCH_COLUMN_LONG procedures.

Piecewise insertion and update of LONG data is more complicated in OCI and is not currently implemented in DBMS_SQL.

NOTE
Although you cannot insert or update LONG data piecewise in DBMS_SQL (or the precompilers, for that matter), you can manipulate LOB data easily with the DBMS_LOB package. See Chapter 21 for more information.

Interface Differences

Because PL/SQL does not yet (as of 8.0) provide a user-accessible interface for pointer variables, all fetch operations have to be put into a local buffer and then retrieved with COLUMN_VALUE or VARIABLE_VALUE. These extra calls are not necessary with either OCI or the precompilers, since both of these other methods can pass the addresses of program variables directly to the server. When the statement is executed, the database writes directly into the program variables. No buffer is needed.

Tips and Techniques

In this section I suggest several tips for using DBMS_SQL. DBMS_SQL is a powerful feature, but it is also fairly complicated. I recommend using DBMS_SQL when your application demands it. If, however, the application can be implemented using other means (such as cursor variables), those may be a better option.

Reusing Cursors

Whenever possible, cursors should be reused. Avoid unnecessary calls to OPEN_CURSOR and CLOSE_CURSOR. Since different SQL statements can be processed in the same cursor, you can avoid the extra overhead associated with repeatedly opening and closing the cursor. If you are executing the same statement repeatedly, there is no need to rePARSE the statement either—simply reEXECUTE it.

Permissions

Roles are disabled inside packaged procedures, including DBMS_SQL. This can cause strange errors, such as ORA-1031. For more information, see the earlier section, "Privileges and DBMS_SQL."

DDL Operations and Hanging

If you are not careful, using DBMS_SQL to dynamically execute DDL statements can cause hanging. For example, a call to a packaged procedure places a lock on the procedure until the call completes. If you try to dynamically drop the package while another user is executing a procedure in that package, the EXECUTE call will hang. The maximum length of the time-out is five minutes.

Summary

In this chapter, we have examined the DBMS_SQL package, which allows dynamic processing of SQL and PL/SQL from a PL/SQL program. Depending on the type of statement being processed (query, DDL or DML, PL/SQL block), different procedures in DBMS_SQL are used. We also compared DBMS_SQL to the dynamic methods available with the precompilers and OCI, and discussed tips and techniques for using dynamic SQL in your programs.

CHAPTER
16

Intersession
Communication

n addition to reading and writing into database tables, PL/SQL provides two built-in packages for intersession communication. These packages are DBMS_PIPE and DBMS_ALERT. They can be used to send messages between sessions connected to the same database instance. As such, they provide an extremely useful facility that has many applications. In this chapter, we will examine DBMS_PIPE and DBMS_ALERT in detail and compare their behavior so you can choose the appropriate package for your needs.

PL/SQL 8.0 ...and HIGHER The Oracle8 Advanced Queuing package, described in Chapter 17, can also be used for intersession communication. Oracle/AQ has features similar to both DBMS_PIPE and DBMS_ALERT, although it is a much more powerful and complex communication system.

DBMS_PIPE

The DBMS_PIPE package implements *database pipes*. A database pipe is similar to a Unix pipe, but is implemented entirely in Oracle. Thus, a database pipe is independent of operating systems and will work on any platform on which Oracle runs. Different sessions connected to the same Oracle instance can send and receive messages over a pipe. Pipes can have multiple *readers* (sessions that receive the message) and *writers* (sessions that send the message). Readers and writers can be on different machines and can be using different PL/SQL execution environments. All that is required is that they connect to the same Oracle instance, and that they both have the ability to execute PL/SQL blocks.

Pipes are *asynchronous*—they operate independent of transactions. Once a message is sent along a pipe, there is no way of retrieving it, even if the transaction that sent it issues a ROLLBACK.

The writer packs a series of data items into a local message buffer. This buffer is then sent over the pipe into the message buffer of the reader process. The reader then unpacks its buffer into the data. For example, the **LogRSInserts** trigger records the inserts into **registered_students**. The changes are sent over a pipe, so the trigger is the writer in this case.

```
-- Available online as logRSins.sql
CREATE OR REPLACE TRIGGER LogRSInserts
  BEFORE INSERT ON registered_students
  FOR EACH ROW
DECLARE
```

```
    v_Status      INTEGER;
BEGIN

  /* Pack the description into the buffer first. */
  DBMS_PIPE.PACK_MESSAGE('I');

  /* Pack the current user and the timestamp. */
  DBMS_PIPE.PACK_MESSAGE(user);
  DBMS_PIPE.PACK_MESSAGE(sysdate);

  /* Pack the new values. */
  DBMS_PIPE.PACK_MESSAGE(:new.student_ID);
  DBMS_PIPE.PACK_MESSAGE(:new.department);
  DBMS_PIPE.PACK_MESSAGE(:new.course);
  DBMS_PIPE.PACK_MESSAGE(:new.grade);

  /* Send the message over the 'RSInserts' pipe. */
  v_Status := DBMS_PIPE.SEND_MESSAGE('RSInserts');

  /* If the send is unsuccessful, raise an error so the change
     doesn't go through. */
  IF v_Status != 0 THEN
    RAISE_APPLICATION_ERROR(-20010, 'LogRSInserts trigger ' ||
      'couldn''t send the message, status = ' || v_Status);
  END IF;

END LogRSInserts;
```

The trigger is only one component of a logging system, however. It is the writer on the **RSInserts** pipe. We still need a reader. This can be done by the following Pro*C program, which reads from the pipe and writes the changes to an operating system file.

```
/* Available online as RSinsert.pc */
/* This program receives messages from the RSInserts pipe, and
   logs them to a file. */

/* C and SQL header files */
#include <stdio.h>
EXEC SQL INCLUDE sqlca;

EXEC SQL BEGIN DECLARE SECTION;
  /* Username and password to connect to the database */
  char *v_Connect = "example/example";
```

```
  /* Status variables used in the calls to DBMS_PIPE */
  int v_Status;
  VARCHAR v_Code[5];

  /* Variables sent over the pipe - these will be logged. */
  VARCHAR v_Userid[9];
  VARCHAR v_Changedate[10];
  int v_StudentID;
  VARCHAR v_Department[4];
  int v_Course;
  VARCHAR v_Grade[2];
  short v_Grade_ind;
EXEC SQL END DECLARE SECTION;

/* File pointer to log file */
FILE *outfile;

void sqlerror();

int main() {

  /* Set up the error handling. */
  EXEC SQL WHENEVER SQLERROR DO sqlerror();

  /* Connect to the database. */
  EXEC SQL CONNECT :v_Connect;

  /* Open the log file. */
  outfile = fopen("rs.log", "w");

  /* Main loop. The only way we'll break out of the loop is if we
     receive the 'STOP' message or if an error occurs. */
  for (;;) {
    /* Sleep until a message is received over the 'RSInserts'
       pipe. The timeout is not specified, so the default will
       be used. */
    EXEC SQL EXECUTE
      BEGIN
        :v_Status := DBMS_PIPE.RECEIVE_MESSAGE('RSInserts');
      END;
    END-EXEC;

    if (v_Status == 0) {
      /* Successful retrieval of the message. We now need to get
         the first data element, to decide what to do with it. */
```

```
v_Code.len = 5;
EXEC SQL EXECUTE
  BEGIN
    DBMS_PIPE.UNPACK_MESSAGE(:v_Code);
  END;
END-EXEC;
v_Code.arr[v_Code.len] = '\0';

if (!strcmp(v_Code.arr, "STOP")) {
  /* Stop message received. Break out of the loop. */
  break;
}

/* Retrieve the rest of the message, which consists of the
   userid, date, and new values. */
v_Userid.len = 9;
v_Changedate.len = 10;
v_Department.len = 4;
v_Grade.len = 2;
EXEC SQL EXECUTE
  DECLARE
    v_ChangeDate DATE;
  BEGIN
    DBMS_PIPE.UNPACK_MESSAGE(:v_Userid);
    DBMS_PIPE.UNPACK_MESSAGE(v_ChangeDate);
    :v_Changedate := TO_CHAR(v_ChangeDate, 'DD-MON-YY');
    DBMS_PIPE.UNPACK_MESSAGE(:v_StudentID);
    DBMS_PIPE.UNPACK_MESSAGE(:v_Department);
    DBMS_PIPE.UNPACK_MESSAGE(:v_Course);
    DBMS_PIPE.UNPACK_MESSAGE(:v_Grade:v_Grade_ind);
  END;
END-EXEC;

/* Null terminate the character strings */
v_Userid.arr[v_Userid.len] = '\0';
v_Changedate.arr[v_Changedate.len] = '\0';
v_Department.arr[v_Department.len] = '\0';

if (v_Grade_ind == -1)
  v_Grade.arr[0] = '\0';
else
  v_Grade.arr[v_Grade.len] = '\0';

/* Print the data to the log file. */
fprintf(outfile, "User: %s Timestamp: %s",
```

```
        v_Userid.arr, v_Changedate.arr);
      fprintf(outfile, " ID: %d Course: %s %d Grade: %s\n",
        v_StudentID, v_Department.arr, v_Course, v_Grade.arr);

  }
  else if (v_Status == 1) {
    /* The RECEIVE_MESSAGE call timed out.
       Loop back to wait again. */
    continue;
  }
  else {
    /* The RECEIVE_MESSAGE call exited with an error. Print it,
       and exit. */
    printf("RECEIVE_MESSAGE Error!  Status = %d\n", v_Status);
    EXEC SQL ROLLBACK WORK RELEASE;
    exit(1);
  }

}  /* End of main loop */

/* Close the file */
fclose(outfile);

/* Disconnect from the database. */
EXEC SQL COMMIT WORK RELEASE;
}


/* Error handling function. Print the error to the screen,
   and exit. */
void sqlerror() {

  printf("SQL Error!\n");
  printf("%.*s\n", sqlca.sqlerrm.sqlerrml,
sqlca.sqlerrm.sqlerrmc);

  EXEC SQL WHENEVER SQLERROR CONTINUE;

  EXEC SQL ROLLBACK RELEASE;
}
```

Since the write to the pipe is asynchronous, the insert into **registered_ students** will be logged, even if the transaction rolls back. This trigger will thus log both attempted and actual changes to the database.

Sending a Message

Messages are sent in two steps. First the data is packed into the local message buffer, and then the buffer is sent along the pipe. Data is packed using the PACK_MESSAGE procedure, and the SEND_MESSAGE function sends the buffer along the pipe.

PACK_MESSAGE

The PACK_MESSAGE procedure is overloaded to accept different types of data items. On the receiving end of the pipe, the UNPACK_MESSAGE procedure is similarly overloaded to retrieve the different types. The procedure is defined with

```
PROCEDURE PACK_MESSAGE(item IN VARCHAR2);
PROCEDURE PACK_MESSAGE(item IN NUMBER);
PROCEDURE PACK_MESSAGE(item IN DATE);
PROCEDURE PACK_MESSAGE_RAW(item IN RAW);
PROCEDURE PACK_MESSAGE_ROWID(item IN ROWID);
```

The size of the buffer is 4,096 bytes. If the total size of the packed data exceeds this value, ORA-6558 is generated. Each item in the buffer takes 1 byte to represent the datatype, 2 bytes to represent the length, and the size of the data itself. One additional byte is needed to terminate the message. Because the buffer size is limited, there is no way to send LONG or LONG RAW data along a pipe.

SEND_MESSAGE

Once the local message buffer is filled with one or more calls to PACK_MESSAGE, the contents of the buffer are sent along the pipe with SEND_MESSAGE:

```
FUNCTION SEND_MESSAGE(pipename IN VARCHAR2,
                      timeout IN INTEGER DEFAULT MAXWAIT,
                      maxpipesize IN INTEGER DEFAULT 8192)
    RETURN INTEGER;
```

If the pipe does not yet exist, SEND_MESSAGE will create it. Pipes can also be created with the CREATE_PIPE procedure, which is available in

PL/SQL 2.2 and higher and described in the "Creating and Managing Pipes" section later in this chapter. The parameters for SEND_MESSAGE are described in the following table:

Parameter	Type	Description
pipename	VARCHAR2	Name of the pipe. Pipe names are limited to 30 characters and are not case sensitive. Names beginning with ORA$ are reserved for use by the database.
timeout	INTEGER	Time-out in seconds. If the message can't be sent for some reason (indicated by the return code), then the call will return after *timeout* seconds. The default value is DBMS_PIPE.MAXWAIT, which is defined as 86,400,000 seconds (1,000 days).
maxpipesize	INTEGER	Total size of the pipe, in bytes. Defaults to 8,192 bytes (two messages of the maximum size). The sum of the sizes of all the messages in the pipe cannot exceed this value. (As a message is retrieved with RECEIVE_MESSAGE, it is removed from the pipe.) Once the pipe is created, its maximum size is part of the pipe definition, and it persists as long as the pipe itself persists. Different calls to SEND_MESSAGE can provide different *maxpipesize* values. If the new value provided is larger than the existing size, the pipe size is increased. If the new value provided is smaller, the existing larger value is kept.

The return values for SEND_MESSAGE are described here:

Return Value	Meaning
0	The message was sent successfully. A call to RECEIVE_MESSAGE will retrieve it.
1	The call timed out. This can happen if the pipe is too full for the message, or if a lock on the pipe could not be obtained.
3	The call was interrupted because of an internal error.

Receiving a Message

Three calls in DBMS_PIPE can be used to receive messages sent along a pipe and to unpack the messages into the original data items. They are RECEIVE_MESSAGE, NEXT_ITEM_TYPE, and UNPACK_MESSAGE.

RECEIVE_MESSAGE

RECEIVE_MESSAGE is the counterpart to SEND_MESSAGE. It retrieves a message from a pipe and places it into the local message buffer. UNPACK_MESSAGE is then used to retrieve the data from the buffer. RECEIVE_MESSAGE is defined as

FUNCTION RECEIVE_MESSAGE(*pipename* IN VARCHAR2,
                                    timeout IN INTEGER DEFAULT MAXWAIT)
    RETURN INTEGER;

Typically, the receiving program issues a RECEIVE_MESSAGE call. If there is no message waiting, RECEIVE_MESSAGE will block until a message is retrieved. This causes the receiving session to sleep until the message is sent along the pipe. The receiving program is very similar to a Unix daemon, in that it sleeps until a message is received along the pipe to wake it up. The parameters to RECEIVE_MESSAGE are described here:

Parameter	Type	Description
pipename	VARCHAR2	Name of the pipe. This should be the same pipe name as used in SEND_MESSAGE, subject to the same restrictions (less than 30 characters, case insensitive).

Parameter	Type	Description
timeout	INTEGER	Maximum time, in seconds, to wait for a message. Similar to SEND_MESSAGE, the time-out defaults to MAXWAIT (1000 days). If *timeout* is 0, RECEIVE_MESSAGE returns immediately with a status of 0 (message retrieved) or 1 (time-out).

The return codes for RECEIVE_MESSAGE are described here:

Return Value	Meaning
0	Success. The message was retrieved into the local buffer and can be unpacked with UNPACK_MESSAGE.
1	Time-out. No message was sent along the pipe during the time that RECEIVE_MESSAGE was waiting.
2	The message in the pipe was too large for the buffer. This is an internal error, which should not normally occur.
3	The call was interrupted because of an internal error.

NEXT_ITEM_TYPE

The NEXT_ITEM_TYPE function returns the datatype of the next item in the buffer. Based on this value, you can determine which variable should receive the data. If you know this in advance, you don't have to use NEXT_ITEM_TYPE. For more information on how this can be set up, see the section "Establishing a Communications Protocol" later in this chapter. NEXT_ITEM_TYPE is defined with

    FUNCTION NEXT_ITEM_TYPE RETURN INTEGER;

The return codes are as follows:

Return Value	Meaning
0	No more items
6	NUMBER
9	VARCHAR2
11	ROWID
12	DATE
23	RAW

NOTE
These are the only types available that can be sent along a database pipe. Specifically, user-defined types such as PL/SQL tables or records (or Oracle8 object types) cannot be sent.

UNPACK_MESSAGE
UNPACK_MESSAGE is the counterpart to PACK_MESSAGE. Like PACK_MESSAGE, it is overloaded on the type of the item to retrieve. It is defined with

```
PROCEDURE UNPACK_MESSAGE(item OUT VARCHAR2);
PROCEDURE UNPACK_MESSAGE(item OUT NUMBER);
PROCEDURE UNPACK_MESSAGE(item OUT DATE);
PROCEDURE UNPACK_MESSAGE_RAW(item OUT RAW);
PROCEDURE UNPACK_MESSAGE_ROWID(item OUT ROWID);
```

The *item* parameter will receive the data item in the buffer. If there are no more items in the buffer, or if the next item in the buffer is not of the same type as requested, the Oracle errors ORA-6556 or ORA-6559 are raised. Before raising the error, PL/SQL will try to convert the next item to the requested type using the default conversion format as described in Chapter 2.

Creating and Managing Pipes
The first time a pipe name is referenced in a SEND_MESSAGE call, the pipe is created implicitly, if it does not already exist. With PL/SQL 2.2 and higher, pipes can be created and dropped explicitly with the CREATE_PIPE and REMOTE_PIPE procedures.

Pipes and the Shared Pool
A pipe itself consists of a data structure in the shared pool area of the SGA (system global area). As such, it does take up space that could be used by other database objects as they are read from disk. Because of this, pipes are automatically purged from the shared pool when the space is required. A pipe will only be purged if it has no waiting messages. The algorithm for

doing this is the LRU (least recently used) algorithm: at any given point, the pipe that will be purged is the one that hasn't been used for the longest amount of time. For more information on the shared pool and how it affects performance, see Chapter 22.

The maximum size of a pipe, and hence the size of the data structure in the shared pool, is given by the *maxpipesize* parameter in SEND_MESSAGE and CREATE_PIPE.

Public vs. Private Pipes

Pipes created implicitly with SEND_MESSAGE are known as *public* pipes. Any user with EXECUTE permission on the DBMS_PIPE package, and who knows the pipe name, can read and write to a public pipe. *Private* pipes, on the other hand, have restricted access. Access to a private pipe is restricted to the user who created the pipe, to stored procedures running under the privilege set of the pipe owner, or to users connected as SYSDBA or INTERNAL.

PL/SQL **2.2** PL/SQL 2.0 and 2.1 have only public pipes, created implicitly.
...and HIGHER With PL/SQL 2.2 and higher, private pipes can be created explicitly with the CREATE_PIPE function. This function is the only way to create a private pipe. It can also be used to create a public pipe, if desired. Pipes created with CREATE_PIPE remain in the shared pool until they are explicitly dropped with REMOVE_PIPE, or until the instance is shut down. They are never purged automatically from the SGA. The syntax for CREATE_PIPE is

```
FUNCTION CREATE_PIPE(pipename IN VARCHAR2,
                     maxpipesize IN INTEGER DEFAULT 8192,
                     private IN BOOLEAN DEFAULT TRUE)
    RETURN INTEGER;
```

CREATE_PIPE will return zero if the pipe was successfully created. If the pipe already exists, and the current user has privileges to access it, a zero is returned and any data already in the pipe remains. If a public pipe exists with the same name, or a private pipe exists with the same name owned by another user, the error "ORA-23322: insufficient privilege to access pipe" is raised and the function does not succeed. The parameters are described here:

Parameter	Type	Description
pipename	VARCHAR2	Name of the pipe to be created. Pipe names are restricted to 30 characters or less. Names beginning with ORA$ are reserved for internal use.
maxpipesize	INTEGER	Maximum pipe size in bytes. This is the same parameter as in SEND_MESSAGE for implicitly created pipes. The default value is 8,192 bytes. If SEND_MESSAGE is called with a higher value for *maxpipesize*, the pipe size is increased to the new larger value. If SEND_MESSAGE is called with a lower value, the existing higher value is retained.
private	BOOLEAN	TRUE if the pipe should be private, FALSE otherwise. The default is TRUE. Since public pipes are created implicitly by CREATE_MESSAGE, there is normally little reason to set *private* to FALSE.

Pipes created explicitly with CREATE_PIPE are dropped with the REMOVE_PIPE function. If any messages still exist in the pipe when it is removed, they are deleted. This is the only way to drop pipes created explicitly other than shutting down the instance. The syntax for REMOVE_PIPE is

```
FUNCTION REMOVE_PIPE(pipename IN VARCHAR)
  RETURN INTEGER;
```

The only parameter is the name of the pipe to be removed. If the pipe exists and the current user has privileges on the pipe, the pipe is removed and the function returns zero. If the pipe does not exist, zero is also returned. If the pipe exists but the current user does not have privileges to access it, ORA-23322 is raised (similar to CREATE_PIPE).

The PURGE Procedure

PURGE will remove the contents of a pipe. The pipe itself will still exist. If it is an implicitly created pipe, since it is now empty, it is eligible to be aged out of the shared pool according to the LRU algorithm. PURGE calls RECEIVE_MESSAGE repeatedly, so the contents of the local message buffer may be overwritten. PURGE is defined with

PROCEDURE PURGE(*pipename* IN VARCHAR2);

Privileges and Security

Three different levels of security are implemented with the DBMS_PIPE package. The first is the EXECUTE privilege on the package itself. By default, when the package is created, the privilege is not granted to any user. Therefore, only users with the EXECUTE ANY PROCEDURE system privilege will be able to access the DBMS_PIPE package. In order to allow other database users to utilize the package, use GRANT to assign them EXECUTE privileges on the package.

NOTE
The DBA role includes the EXECUTE ANY PROCEDURE system privilege. Consequently, users with the DBA role granted to them (such as SYSTEM) will be able to access DBMS_PIPE from anonymous PL/SQL blocks by default. Since this privilege is granted via a role, they will not be able to access DBMS_PIPE from stored procedures and triggers, since roles are disabled there. For more information on roles and their interaction with stored subprograms, see Chapter 7.

A good method for using this security is to grant the EXECUTE privilege on DBMS_PIPE only to certain database users. Then you can design your own package to control access to the underlying pipes. The EXECUTE privilege on this package can then be granted to other users.

The second security method is the pipe name itself. Unless users know the name of a pipe, they cannot send or receive messages along it. You can take advantage of this situation by using randomly generated pipe names, or by making the pipe names specific to the two sessions communicating over the pipe. The latter method can be accomplished with the UNIQUE_SESSION_NAME function and is described in the upcoming section, "Establishing a Communications Protocol."

Private Pipes

PL/SQL 2.2 ...and HIGHER The most reliable security method to use, however, is the private pipes available with PL/SQL 2.2. Since a private pipe is available only to the user who created it and users connected as SYSDBA or INTERNAL, access is significantly limited. Even if another user has EXECUTE privileges on the DBMS_PIPE package and knows the name of the pipe, he or she will receive the Oracle error:

```
ORA-23322: Insufficient privilege to access pipe
```

This error is raised in the situations identified in Table 16-1. Note that the error is raised only when creating or dropping a pipe or trying to send or receive a message. The other calls in DBMS_PIPE do not actually access pipes themselves.

Procedure or Function	When ORA-23322 Is Raised
CREATE_PIPE	A private pipe with the same name already exists, and the current user does not have privileges to access it. If the current user does have privileges, CREATE_PIPE returns 0 and the pipe ownership is not changed.
SEND_MESSAGE	The current user does not have privileges to access the pipe.
RECEIVE_MESSAGE	The current user does not have privileges to access the pipe.
REMOVE_PIPE	The current user does not have privileges to access the pipe. The pipe will still exist, including any messages currently in it.

TABLE 16-1. *Situations in Which ORA-23322 Is Raised*

Again, the best way to use private pipes is to create stored procedures or packages that in turn call DBMS_PIPE. Since stored subprograms run under the privilege set of the user who owns them, private pipes can be accessed from stored subprograms.

Establishing a Communications Protocol

Using pipes is similar to using other low-level communications packages, such as TCP/IP. You have the flexibility of deciding how the data will be formatted and how it will be sent. In addition, you can decide who will receive the message. In order to use this flexibility properly, however, you should keep in mind the suggestions in the following sections.

Data Formatting

Each message sent over a pipe consists of one or more data items. The data items are inserted into the message buffer using PACK_MESSAGE, and the entire buffer is then sent with SEND_MESSAGE. At the receiving end, the buffer is received with RECEIVE_MESSAGE and the data items retrieved with NEXT_ITEM_TYPE and UNPACK_MESSAGE.

Typically, the receiving program can do different things based on the contents of the message received. For example, the Pro*C program that implements the back end of the **LogRSInserts** trigger (described earlier in this chapter) uses the first data item to format the message logged to the data file. Essentially, the first data item is an opcode, or instruction, which tells the receiving program how to interpret the remainder of the data. Depending on the type of information, there may be different datatypes in the message, or different numbers of data elements.

TIP
It is a good idea to include a STOP instruction in addition to other instructions that you may need. You can use STOP to cause the waiting program to disconnect from the database and exit cleanly. Without a message such as this, the waiting program would have to be killed from the operating system and/or database level, which is not as clean. We will see an example of this in the following section.

Data Addressing

There can be multiple readers and writers for the same pipe. Only one reader will receive the message, however. Furthermore, it is not defined which reader will actually get it. Because of this, it is best to address your messages to a specific reader program. This can be accomplished by generating a unique pipe name that will be used only by the two sessions involved—one reader and one writer. The UNIQUE_SESSION_NAME function can be used for this. It is defined with

FUNCTION UNIQUE_SESSION_NAME RETURN VARCHAR2;

Each call to UNIQUE_SESSION_NAME will return a string with a maximum length of 30 characters. Every call from the same database session will return the same string. This string will be unique among all sessions currently connected to the database. If a session disconnects, however, its name can be used by another session at a later point.

UNIQUE_SESSION_NAME can be used as the pipe name, which ensures that the message will go to only one recipient. One method of setting this up is to send the initial message over a pipe with a predefined name. Part of the initial message is the name of the pipe over which to send the response. The receiving program then decodes the initial message and sends the response over this new pipe, which will be used only by these two sessions. Since there is only one reader and one writer, there is no ambiguity about which session will receive the information. We will see an example of this technique in the following section.

Example

This is another version of the Debug package, which we first examined in Chapter 14. Similar to the example at the beginning of this chapter, one of the two sessions communicating is a Pro*C program. The Debug package itself communicates with this program.

Debug.pc

The program (debug.pc) is given here:

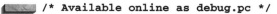

```
/* Available online as debug.pc */
/* This program is the back end of the DBMS_PIPE version of the
   Debug package. It should be running in another window from
```

```
      the PL/SQL session which you are trying to debug. */

/* C and SQL header files */
#include <stdio.h>
EXEC SQL INCLUDE sqlca;

EXEC SQL BEGIN DECLARE SECTION;
  /* Username and password to connect to the database */
  char *v_Connect = "example/example";

  /* Status variables used in the calls to DBMS_PIPE */
  int v_Status;
  VARCHAR v_Code[6];

  /* Variables send and received along pipes. */
  VARCHAR v_ReturnPipeName[31];
  VARCHAR v_Description[100];
  VARCHAR v_Value[100];
EXEC SQL END DECLARE SECTION;

/* Error handling function. */
void sqlerror();

int main() {

  /* Set up the error handling. */
  EXEC SQL WHENEVER SQLERROR DO sqlerror();

  /* Connect to the database. */
  EXEC SQL CONNECT :v_Connect;

  printf("Debug ready for input.\n");

  /* Main loop. The only way we'll break out of the loop is if
     we receive the 'STOP' message or if an error occurs. */
  for (;;) {
    /* Sleep until a message is received over the 'Debug' pipe.
       The timeout is not specified, so the default will be
       used. */
    EXEC SQL EXECUTE
      BEGIN
        :v_Status := DBMS_PIPE.RECEIVE_MESSAGE('DebugPipe');
      END;
    END-EXEC;
    if (v_Status == 0) {
```

```
/* Successful retrieval of the message. We now need to get
   the first data element, to decide what to do with it. */
v_Code.len = 6;
EXEC SQL EXECUTE
  BEGIN
    DBMS_PIPE.UNPACK_MESSAGE(:v_Code);
  END;
END-EXEC;
v_Code.arr[v_Code.len] = '\0';

if (!strcmp(v_Code.arr, "STOP")) {
  /* STOP message received. Break out of the loop. */
  break;
} /* End of STOP processing */

else if (!strcmp(v_Code.arr, "TEST")) {
  /* TEST message received. Send back a handshake over the
     same pipe. */
  EXEC SQL EXECUTE
    BEGIN
      DBMS_PIPE.PACK_MESSAGE('Handshake');
      :v_Status := DBMS_PIPE.SEND_MESSAGE('DebugPipe');
    END;
  END-EXEC;

  if (v_Status != 0) {
    /* Error message. Print it out. */
    printf("Error %d while responding to TEST message\n",
           v_Status);
  }
} /* End of TEST processing */

else if (!strcmp(v_Code.arr, "DEBUG")) {
  /* DEBUG message received. Unpack the return pipe,
     description, and output value. */
  v_ReturnPipeName.len = 30;
  v_Description.len = 100;
  v_Value.len = 100;
  EXEC SQL EXECUTE
    BEGIN
      DBMS_PIPE.UNPACK_MESSAGE(:v_ReturnPipeName);
      DBMS_PIPE.UNPACK_MESSAGE(:v_Description);
      DBMS_PIPE.UNPACK_MESSAGE(:v_Value);
    END;
  END-EXEC;
```

```
          /* Null-terminate the output variables. */
          v_Description.arr[v_Description.len] = '\0';
          v_Value.arr[v_Value.len] = '\0';

          /* Echo the debugging info to the screen. */
          printf("%s: %s\n", v_Description.arr, v_Value.arr);

          /* Send the handshake message back. */
          EXEC SQL EXECUTE
            BEGIN
              DBMS_PIPE.PACK_MESSAGE('Processed');
              :v_Status := DBMS_PIPE.SEND_MESSAGE(:v_ReturnPipeName);
            END;
          END-EXEC;

          if (v_Status != 0) {
            /* Error message. Print it out. */
            printf("Error %d while sending handshake message\n",
                   v_Status);
          }
        } /* End of DEBUG processing */
      } /* End of successful retrieve of a message */

      else if (v_Status == 1) {
        /* The RECEIVE_MESSAGE call timed out. Loop back to
           wait again. */
        continue;
      }

      else {
        /* The RECEIVE_MESSAGE call exited with an error.
           Print it, and exit. */
        printf("Main loop RECEIVE_MESSAGE Error. Status = %d\n",
               v_Status);
        EXEC SQL ROLLBACK WORK RELEASE;
        exit(1);
      }

    }  /* End of main loop */

  /* Disconnect from the database. */
  EXEC SQL COMMIT WORK RELEASE;
}
```

```
/* Error handling function. Print the error to the screen,
   and exit. */
void sqlerror() {

  printf("SQL Error!\n");
  printf("%.*s\n", sqlca.sqlerrm.sqlerrml,
                   sqlca.sqlerrm.sqlerrmc);

  EXEC SQL WHENEVER SQLERROR CONTINUE;

  EXEC SQL ROLLBACK RELEASE;
}
```

Debug Package

The Debug package itself is defined with:

-- Available online as debug.sql
```
CREATE OR REPLACE PACKAGE Debug AS
  -- Maximum number of seconds to wait for a handshake message.
  v_TimeOut NUMBER := 10;

  -- Main Debug procedure.
  PROCEDURE Debug(p_Description IN VARCHAR2,
                  p_Value IN VARCHAR2);

  -- Sets up the Debug environment.
  PROCEDURE Reset;

  -- Causes the daemon to exit.
  PROCEDURE Exit;
END Debug;

CREATE OR REPLACE PACKAGE BODY Debug as
  v_CurrentPipeName VARCHAR2(30);

  PROCEDURE Debug(p_Description IN VARCHAR2,
                  p_Value IN VARCHAR2) IS
    v_ReturnCode NUMBER;
    v_Handshake  VARCHAR2(10);
  BEGIN
    /* If we don't already have a pipe name, determine one. */
    IF v_CurrentPipeName IS NULL THEN
```

```
      v_CurrentPipeName := DBMS_PIPE.UNIQUE_SESSION_NAME;
   END IF;

   /* Send the 'DEBUG' message, along with:
         - pipe name for the handshake
         - description
         - value
   */
   DBMS_PIPE.PACK_MESSAGE('DEBUG');
   DBMS_PIPE.PACK_MESSAGE(v_CurrentPipeName);
   DBMS_PIPE.PACK_MESSAGE(p_Description);
   DBMS_PIPE.PACK_MESSAGE(p_Value);
   v_ReturnCode := DBMS_PIPE.SEND_MESSAGE('DebugPipe');

   IF v_ReturnCode != 0 THEN
     RAISE_APPLICATION_ERROR(-20210,
       'Debug.Debug: SEND_MESSAGE failed with ' || v_ReturnCode);
   END IF;

   /* Wait for the handshake message on the return pipe. */
   v_ReturnCode := DBMS_PIPE.RECEIVE_MESSAGE(v_CurrentPipeName);

   IF v_ReturnCode = 1 THEN
      -- Timeout
     RAISE_APPLICATION_ERROR(-20211,
       'Debug.Debug: No handshake message received');
   ELSIF v_ReturnCode != 0 THEN
     -- Other error
     RAISE_APPLICATION_ERROR(-20212,
       'Debug.Debug: RECEIVE_MESSAGE failed with ' ||
       v_ReturnCode);
   ELSE
     -- Check for the handshake message.
     DBMS_PIPE.UNPACK_MESSAGE(v_Handshake);
     IF v_Handshake = 'Processed' THEN
       -- Output processed.
       NULL;
     ELSE
       -- No handshake
       RAISE_APPLICATION_ERROR(-20213,
         'Debug.Debug: Incorrect handshake message received');
     END IF;
   END IF;
END Debug;
PROCEDURE Reset IS
```

```
     /* Check to make sure the daemon is running by sending the test
        message over the pipe. If not, raise an error. */
     v_ReturnCode NUMBER;
   BEGIN
     DBMS_PIPE.PACK_MESSAGE('TEST');
     v_ReturnCode := DBMS_PIPE.SEND_MESSAGE('DebugPipe');

     IF v_ReturnCode != 0 THEN
       RAISE_APPLICATION_ERROR(-20200,
         'Debug.Reset: SEND_MESSAGE failed with ' || v_ReturnCode);
     END IF;

     /* The daemon will respond over the same pipe. If this call
        times out, then the daemon isn't ready and we should raise
        an error. */
     v_ReturnCode :=
       DBMS_PIPE.RECEIVE_MESSAGE('DebugPipe', v_TimeOut);
     IF v_ReturnCode = 1 THEN
       -- Timeout
       RAISE_APPLICATION_ERROR(-20201,
         'Debug.Reset: Daemon not ready');
     ELSIF v_ReturnCode != 0 THEN
       -- Other error
       RAISE_APPLICATION_ERROR(-20202,
         'Debug.Reset: RECEIVE_MESSAGE failed with ' ||
         v_ReturnCode);
     ELSE
       -- Daemon is ready.
       NULL;
     END IF;
   END Reset;

   PROCEDURE Exit IS
     v_ReturnCode NUMBER;
   BEGIN
     -- Send the 'STOP' message.
     DBMS_PIPE.PACK_MESSAGE('STOP');
     v_ReturnCode := DBMS_PIPE.SEND_MESSAGE('DebugPipe');

     IF v_ReturnCode != 0 THEN
       RAISE_APPLICATION_ERROR(-20230,
         'Debug.Exit: SEND_MESSAGE failed with ' || v_ReturnCode);
     END IF;
   END Exit;

END Debug;
```

Comments

There are several things to note about this version of Debug. First of all, the Pro*C program is necessary for the output. When you call **Debug.Debug**, the output will be printed to the screen by the Pro*C program, not by the PL/SQL session. Thus, you should run the program in a separate window from your PL/SQL session. The program is essentially functioning as a daemon—it spends most of its time sleeping, waiting for a message to be sent along the pipe.

OPCODES　　The first message sent along **DebugPipe** is the opcode for the daemon. This can be either "STOP", "TEST", or "DEBUG". Depending on this opcode, the daemon will respond differently, allowing it to function as a dispatcher. In a more complicated scenario, the daemon could then spawn other processes depending on the opcode, which would then process the data. The daemon itself would then wait for another message.

COMMUNICATIONS PROTOCOL　　**Debug.Debug** passes a pipe name as part of the initial message. This pipe name is generated uniquely by UNIQUE_SESSION_NAME. After **Debug.Debug** sends the message, it then listens on this new pipe. This is a very useful technique, since it allows multiple daemons to be running at the same time. The first message will be received by a waiting daemon. The return pipe name will be used by only one session, so it uniquely identifies the session that sent the message. This neatly solves the problem of multiple readers on the same pipe. Once the unique pipe name is established, both sessions can send and receive messages along this new pipe, with the assurance that no other session will be listening.

HANDSHAKE MESSAGES　　Both the PL/SQL package and the Pro*C daemon are readers and writers. Consider the "TEST" message as an example, which **Debug.Debug** sends. The Debug package sends a message, then waits for a reply. If the reply times out, we know that the initial message was not received properly. Using handshake messages is a valuable part of a good communications protocol.

DBMS_ALERT

The DBMS_ALERT package implements database alerts. An *alert* is a message that is sent when a transaction commits. Unlike pipes, which are asynchronous, alerts are synchronized with transactions. Alerts are generally used for one-way communication, while a pipe is used for two-way communication.

The sending session issues a SIGNAL call for a particular alert. This call records the fact that the alert has been signaled in the data dictionary, but does not actually send it. When the transaction containing the SIGNAL call commits, the alert is actually sent. If the transaction rolls back, the alert is not sent. The receiving session first registers interest in particular alerts using the REGISTER procedure. Only alerts that have been registered will be received. The receiving session then waits for alerts to be signaled using the WAITONE or WAITANY procedure.

Sending an Alert

Alerts are sent with the SIGNAL procedure, which records the alert information in the data dictionary. The syntax for SIGNAL is

```
PROCEDURE SIGNAL(name IN VARCHAR2,
                 message IN VARCHAR2);
```

SIGNAL takes only two parameters—the name of the alert to be signaled and a message. Alert names have a maximum length of 30 characters and are not case sensitive. Similar to pipes, alert names beginning with ORA$ are reserved for use by Oracle and should not be used for user applications. The maximum message length is 1,800 bytes.

A given alert can only be in one of two states—signaled or not signaled. The SIGNAL call changes the state of the alert to signaled. This change is recorded in the **dbms_alert_info** data dictionary table, described in the "Alerts and the Data Dictionary" section later in this chapter. Because of this, only one session can signal an alert at a time. Multiple sessions can signal the same alert. However, the first session will cause the later sessions to block.

When the alert is sent, all sessions currently waiting for that alert will receive the message. If no sessions are currently waiting, the next session to wait for it will receive it immediately.

Receiving an Alert

Receiving an alert involves two steps—registering interest in an alert and then waiting for it. A receiving session will only receive the alerts for which it has registered.

Registering

The REGISTER procedure is used to register interest in a particular alert. A database session can register for as many alerts as desired. The session will remain registered until it disconnects from the database, or until it calls the REMOVE procedure (described later in this chapter) to indicate that it is no longer interested. The REGISTER procedure is defined with

```
PROCEDURE REGISTER(name IN VARCHAR2);
```

The only parameter is the name of the alert. Registering for an alert does not cause the session to block; it only records that this session is interested.

Waiting for One Alert

The WAITONE procedure is used to wait for a particular alert to occur. If this alert has already been signaled, WAITONE returns immediately with a status of 0, indicating that the alert has been received. If the alert is not signaled, then WAITONE will block until either the alert is signaled or it times out. WAITONE is defined with

```
PROCEDURE WAITONE(name IN VARCHAR2,
                  message OUT VARCHAR2,
                  status OUT INTEGER,
                  timeout IN NUMBER DEFAULT MAXWAIT);
```

Similar to RECEIVE_MESSAGE, WAITONE will cause the receiving session to sleep until the alert is signaled.

The same session can signal an alert and then wait for it. In this case, be sure to issue a commit between the SIGNAL and the WAITONE call. Otherwise, the WAITONE call will always time out, since the alert would never have been sent. The parameters for WAITONE are described here:

Parameter	Type	Description
name	VARCHAR2	Name of the alert for which to wait. The session should have registered interest in this alert with REGISTER prior to calling WAITONE.
message	VARCHAR2	Message text included in the SIGNAL call by the sending session. If there were multiple SIGNAL calls for the same alert before the alert was received, only the latest message is retrieved. Earlier messages are discarded.
status	INTEGER	Returns an indicator as to whether the alert was received. A value of zero indicates that the alert was received, and a value of one indicates that the call timed out.
timeout	NUMBER	Maximum time to wait before returning, in seconds. If *timeout* is not specified, it defaults to DBMS_ALERT.MAXWAIT, which is defined as 1,000 days. If the alert is not received within *timeout* seconds, the call returns with status one.

Waiting for Any Alert

A session can also wait for any alerts for which it has registered interest to be signaled. This is done with the WAITANY procedure. Unlike WAITONE,

WAITANY will return successfully if any of the alerts is signaled, rather than just one. WAITANY is defined with

```
PROCEDURE WAITANY(name OUT VARCHAR2,
                  message OUT VARCHAR2,
                  status OUT INTEGER,
                  timeout IN NUMBER DEFAULT MAXWAIT);
```

The parameters are the same as for WAITONE, with the same meanings. The only difference is that *name* is an OUT parameter and will indicate which alert has actually been signaled.

Again, the same session can both signal an alert and then wait for it with WAITANY. If a COMMIT is not issued between the time the alert is signaled and the WAITANY call, WAITANY will always time out, since the alert will never have been actually sent. The parameters for WAITANY are described in the following table:

Parameter	Type	Description
name	VARCHAR2	Name of the alert that was signaled. The session will only receive alerts for which it has registered interest prior to WAITONE.
message	VARCHAR2	Message text included in the SIGNAL call by the sending session. If there were multiple SIGNAL calls for the same alert before the alert was received, only the latest message is retrieved. Earlier messages are discarded.
status	INTEGER	Returns an indicator as to whether the alert was received. A value of zero indicates that the alert was received, and a value of one indicates that the call timed out.
timeout	NUMBER	Maximum time to wait before returning, in seconds. If *timeout* is not specified, it defaults to DBMS_ALERT.MAXWAIT, which is defined as 1,000 days. If the alert is not received within *timeout* seconds, the call returns with status one.

Other Procedures

Two additional procedures are used to manage alerts: REMOVE and
SET_DEFAULTS.

"Unregistering" for an Alert

When a session is no longer interested in an alert, it should unregister for it.
This helps free the resources used to signal and receive the alert.
Unregistering is accomplished with the REMOVE procedure:

    PROCEDURE REMOVE(*name* IN VARCHAR2);

The only parameter is the name of the alert. REMOVE is the counterpart
to REGISTER.

Polling Intervals

In most cases, Oracle is event driven. This means that a session waiting for
something will be notified when that event occurs, rather than having to
check in a loop for the event. If a loop is required, it is known as a *polling
loop*. The amount of time between each check is known as the *polling
interval*. There are two cases in which polling is required for the
implementation of alerts:

1. If the database is running in shared mode, polling is required to
   check for alerts signaled by another instance. The polling interval
   for this loop can be set by the SET_DEFAULTS procedure.

2. If no registered alerts have been signaled for the WAITANY call, a
   polling loop is required to check for the signaled alerts. The polling
   interval starts at 1 second and exponentially increases to a
   maximum of 30 seconds. This interval is not user configurable.

The SET_DEFAULTS procedure is defined with

    PROCEDURE SET_DEFAULTS(*polling_interval* IN NUMBER);

The only parameter is the polling interval, in seconds. The default is 5 seconds.

Alerts and the Data Dictionary

Alerts are implemented using a data dictionary view, **dbms_alert_info**. A row gets inserted into this table for each alert that a session registers interest in. If more than one session registers interest in the same alert, a row is inserted for each session. The **dbms_alert_info** view has four columns, with the structure indicated by the following table:

Column	Datatype	Null?	Description
name	VARCHAR2(30)	NOT NULL	Name of the alert that was registered
SID	VARCHAR2(30)	NOT NULL	Session identifier for the session that registered interest
changed	VARCHAR2(1)		Y if the alert is signaled, N if not
message	VARCHAR2(1800)		Message passed with the signal call

We can see how this view works, and the implications it has, by examining the scenario illustrated in Figure 16-1. This figure shows three database sessions and the commands they issue over time. The contents of **dbms_ alert_info** are shown at each time as well. Here is a description of events:

Time T1: Session B registers interest in the alert. At this point, a row is inserted into **dbms_alert_info**, recording this. Note that the Changed field reads N, indicating that the alert has not yet been signaled.

Time T2: Session A signals the alert, with message 'Message A'. Since session A hasn't issued a commit, **dbms_alert_info** is unchanged.

Time T3: Session C signals the same alert, with message 'Message C'. Session A hasn't yet committed. Only one session can signal an alert at a time, so the SIGNAL call issued by session C will block.

Time T4: Session A commits. Two things happen now. The SIGNAL issued by session C returns, and A's message is put into **dbms_alert_info**. The Changed field is set to Y, indicating that the alert has been signaled.

Time T5: Session C commits. This *replaces* the message in **dbms_alert_info**. Session A's message is lost.

Time T6: Session B finally decides to wait for the alert. The WAITONE call returns immediately, with 'Message C'. The Changed field is reset to N, indicating that the alert is not signaled anymore.

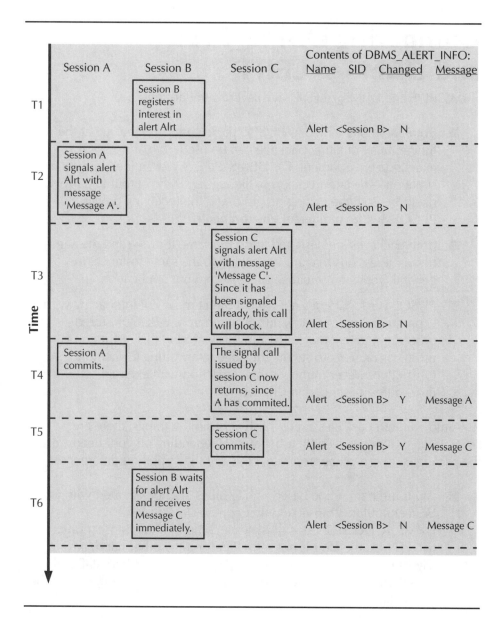

FIGURE 16-1. *Signaling and receiving an alert*

Comparing DBMS_PIPE and DBMS_ALERT

DBMS_PIPE and DBMS_ALERT have several similarities:

- Both are implemented as PL/SQL packages. This means that the functionality of either package can be used from any PL/SQL execution environment. For DBMS_PIPE, we examined one such situation—the latest version of Debug sends the output to a Pro*C daemon. Both the calling program and the receiving program use PL/SQL, but from different environments.

- Both packages are designed to do the same thing—send messages between sessions that are connected to the same instance. In general, you can use either package for your application.

- PL/SQL version 2 does not have a direct means of interfacing with a C program. You can't call a C program from a PL/SQL stored procedure, for example. The only way around this restriction is to use pipes or alerts to send a message to a waiting C daemon. Oracle8, however, removes this restriction with external procedures, described in Chapter 20.

Although both packages accomplish very similar things, there are several differences between their behavior. Depending on your needs, use the package that is most appropriate. Here are the important differences:

- Alerts are transaction based, while pipes are not. An alert will not be sent until the transaction that contains the DBMS_ALERT.SIGNAL call issues a commit. If the transaction is rolled back, the alert is not sent. Pipes, on the other hand, are asynchronous. As soon as the DBMS_PIPE.SEND_MESSAGE call is issued, the message is sent. There is no way to retrieve it, even if the transaction is rolled back.

- When an alert is signaled, all sessions that have registered interest in the alert, and are waiting, will receive the message. If there is more than one session waiting on the alert, all of them will receive it. This is different behavior from pipes, where exactly one of the waiting sessions will receive the message. It is not defined which session will receive the message if there is more than one waiting.

■ The methods of sending the information differ as well. Alerts do not have the ability to pass more than a single character string in the message. When a message is sent along a pipe, however, the entire contents of the message buffer are sent. This can include several differing pieces of information, of different types.

■ Because the messages that can be sent with pipes are more complex than alerts, pipes can be easily used for two-way communication. A communications protocol is thus important for good pipe usage. Alerts, on the other hand, are generally used for a single one-way message.

Summary

We have discussed two different mechanisms for intersession communication in this chapter. Database pipes, implemented with the DBMS_PIPE package, allow two-way communication with complex messages. Database alerts, implemented with the DBMS_ALERT package, allow one-way, transaction-based messages. The packages behave differently and are used for different types of applications. In the next chapter, we will examine the Advanced Queuing option available with Oracle8.

CHAPTER
17

Oracle
Advanced Queuing

n the last chapter we examined the intersession communication features available with Oracle7: pipes and alerts. These allow you to implement basic messaging capabilities. Oracle8 provides a more comprehensive messaging system, however, known as Oracle Advanced Queuing. We will examine this system in this chapter, including detailed examples.

Introduction

In general, an application can be thought of as a set of programs or modules that communicate with each other. The communication consists of messages passed between the modules. In order for such a system to work reliably, the message system must have certain properties:

- **Reliability** A given message should be guaranteed to be delivered to the desired recipient or recipients, and the message should be delivered only once.

- **Scalability** The system should not lose performance as the number of modules and/or messages increases.

- **Restorability** No messages should be lost as a result of a system failure. In case of a failure, all messages that were sent and committed should be recoverable.

PL/SQL 8.0 ...and HIGHER Oracle Advanced Queuing provides all of these properties. This system consists of a set of PL/SQL packages and background processes that implement a queuing system. Such systems are often found in third-party products such as TP monitors, but Oracle Advanced Queuing is implemented as part of Oracle8. Because it is implemented using SQL and Oracle tables, it provides the same benefits as other database objects, namely:

- Queues are stored in database tables, so they are part of the standard backup and recovery mechanism supported by Oracle. They can also be exported and imported.

- All queue operations take place using SQL, so they have full transactional control.

■ Messages are object types, so they can have varying attributes within them. One message can consist of several attributes, all sent as a unit.

Because of this implementation, Oracle Advanced Queuing satisfies the reliability, scalability, and restorability requirements. The messaging features available with Oracle7 (pipes and alerts) are not nearly as full featured, and thus Advanced Queuing is a better mechanism for implementing new applications.

Components of Advanced Queuing

The basic component of any queuing system is a queue. In general, a *queue* is essentially an ordered list of items. The *enqueue* operation inserts new items into the queue, and the *dequeue* operation removes items from the queue. For Oracle Advanced Queuing, the items in a queue are messages, which in turn consist of both the data and routing information. Queues are not separate data dictionary objects; they are stored in *queue tables*. The following sections describe the components of Oracle Advanced Queuing.

ENQUEUE Operation

ENQUEUE inserts a message into a given queue. Along with the message data itself (which can be either an object type or RAW data) is the routing information, which specifies how the message is to be inserted and who the intended recipients are. The routing information can optionally include the following:

■ **Correlation identifier** This is a user-specified identifier to specify individual messages. The correlation identifier can be used to dequeue this message later.

■ **Subscription and recipient lists** A queue can have a recipient list that specifies which readers will get an enqueued message. A message can specify a subscription list, which can override the queue's recipient list.

■ **Priority** Messages can have a priority. The higher priority messages will be inserted into the queue ahead of lower priority messages.

- **Grouping**   Messages can be grouped. A message group will be retrieved by a given process as a unit, and this process can successively dequeue from the queue, eventually getting all the messages in the group. Other dequeue operations by other processes will receive the following messages, and not the messages contained in the group.

- **Time specification**   A message can be set to expire if it is not dequeued by a certain time. If it expires, it is moved to an exception queue. A minimum time can also be specified, before which the message will not be dequeued.

- **Transaction protection**   The ENQUEUE operation can be part of the current transaction, or it can be a separate transaction that is immediately committed on its own, thus making the message immediately available for a subsequent DEQUEUE.

DEQUEUE Operation

DEQUEUE retrieves a message from a specified queue. If there are no messages, then DEQUEUE will block until a message is retrieved, or until the operation times out. DEQUEUE has the following options:

- **Dequeue mode**   You can specify that the message remains in the queue after you retrieve it (BROWSE mode), or that it be deleted from the queue after you retrieve it.

- **Time-out**   If there are no waiting messages, the DEQUEUE operation can specify how long to wait.

- **Transaction protection**   The DEQUEUE operation can be part of the current transaction, or it can be a separate transaction that is immediately committed on its own.

- **Message specification**   DEQUEUE can retrieve the first waiting message, or the next message after a given message, or it can select based on a correlation identifier.

- **Retries with delays**   If the DEQUEUE fails and the transaction is rolled back, the message can be made available for reprocessing after a user-specified delay, for a user-specified number of retries.

exception_queue VARCHAR2(51) DEFAULT NULL,
enqueue_time DATE,
state BINARY_INTEGER);

The fields of this type are described in Table 17-3.

Field	Datatype	Description
priority	BINARY_INTEGER	Priority of the accompanying message. A smaller number indicates a higher priority. Priorities can be any integer value, including negative values.
delay	BINARY_INTEGER	Delay for the accompanying message. *delay* can be either NO_DELAY, indicating that the message is available for immediate dequeuing, or the number of seconds to wait. A dequeue that specifies the message identifier will override the delay. A message that is delayed is enqueued in the WAITING state and then moves to the READY state after *delay* seconds.
expiration	BINARY_INTEGER	Time in seconds after which the message will expire if it is not dequeued. If *expiration* is set to NEVER, the message will not expire. The expiration time is counted after the delay time, if it is specified. After the expiration, the message is moved to the exception queue in the EXPIRED state.

TABLE 17-3. *MESSAGE_PROPERTIES_T*

Field	Datatype	Description
correlation	VARCHAR2(128)	Correlation identifier. Messages can be retrieved by correlation identifier if desired.
attempts	BINARY_INTEGER	Number of attempts made to dequeue this message. This parameter is set at DEQUEUE time only.
recipient_list	AQ$_RECIPIENT_LIST_T	List of recipients for this message. This parameter is read at ENQUEUE time and is not returned by the DEQUEUE operation.
exception_queue	VARCHAR2(51)	Exception queue for this message. If the message expires or the number of dequeue attempts exceeds *max_retries*, then the message is moved to the exception queue in the EXPIRED state. If *exception_queue* is not specified, then the message is moved to the default exception queue for the queue table. If *exception_queue* is specified but this queue is not valid at the time of the move, the message is moved to the default exception queue for the queue table and a message is written to the alert log.

TABLE 17-3.   *MESSAGE_PROPERTIES_T (continued)*

Field	Datatype	Description
enqueue_time	DATE	Time when the message was enqueued. This parameter is returned by DEQUEUE and is set automatically by the system at ENQUEUE time.
state	BINARY_INTEGER	State of the message at the time of the DEQUEUE. This parameter cannot be set by ENQUEUE, and is updated automatically by the system as appropriate. The values are WAITING (the message delay has not yet been reached), READY (the message is ready to be processed), PROCESSED (the message has been processed but was retained in the queue), and EXPIRED (the message has been moved to the exception queue).

TABLE 17-3. *MESSAGE_PROPERTIES_T (continued)*

ENQUEUE_OPTIONS_T

This type is used to specify the options for the ENQUEUE operation, other than those of the message itself. It is defined as a PL/SQL record:

```
TYPE ENQUEUE_OPTIONS_T IS RECORD (
  visibility BINARY_INTEGER DEFAULT ON_COMMIT,
  relative_msgid RAW(16)  DEFAULT NULL,
  sequence_deviation BINARY_INTEGER DEFAULT NULL);
```

The fields within the type are described in Table 17-4.

Field	Datatype	Description
visibility	BINARY_INTEGER	Specifies the transactional behavior. If *visibility* is ON_COMMIT (the default), then the enqueue will be complete when the current transaction commits. If *visibility* is IMMEDIATE, then the enqueue constitutes a separate transaction that is immediately committed. Even if the current transaction is rolled back, the enqueue will be performed.
relative_msgid	RAW	If BEFORE is specified in *sequence_deviation*, then the accompanying message will be inserted before the message identified by *relative_msgid*. If *sequence_deviation* is not specified, then *relative_msgid* is ignored.
sequence_deviation	BINARY_INTEGER	Specifies the location of the accompanying message in the queue. Valid values are BEFORE (the message is to be enqueued ahead of the message specified by *relative_msgid*), TOP (the message is to be enqueued ahead of any other messages), and NULL (the priority of the message specifies its position in the queue). The default is NULL.

TABLE 17-4. *ENQUEUE_OPTIONS_T*

DEQUEUE_OPTIONS_T

This record is used to specify the options for the DEQUEUE operation, as opposed to the options in the message itself. It is defined with

```
TYPE DEQUEUE_OPTIONS_T IS RECORD (
consumer_name VARCHAR2(30) DEFAULT NULL,
dequeue_mode BINARY_INTEGER DEFAULT REMOVE,
navigation BINARY_INTEGER DEFAULT NEXT_MESSAGE,
visibility BINARY_INTEGER DEFAULT ON_COMMIT,
wait BINARY_INTEGER DEFAULT FOREVER,
msgid RAW(16) DEFAULT NULL,
correlation VARCHAR2(30) DEFAULT NULL);
```

The fields of DEQUEUE_OPTIONS_T are described in Table 17-5.

Field	Datatype	Description
consumer_ name	VARCHAR2(30)	Name of the consumer to receive the message. If specified, only those messages which match this consumer are eligible for the dequeue. If the queue is not set up for multiple consumers, consumer_name should be NULL.
dequeue_ mode	BINARY_INTEGER	Specifies the locking behavior of the dequeue. Valid values are BROWSE (read the message without locking or dequeuing, similar to a SELECT), LOCKED (read and obtain a write lock on the message, similar to a SELECT FOR UPDATE), and REMOVE (read and then update or delete the message, depending on the retention properties of the queue). REMOVE is the default.

TABLE 17-5. *DEQUEUE_OPTIONS_T*

Field	Datatype	Description
navigation	BINARY_INTEGER	Specifies the position of the message to be retrieved. After the position is determined, the search criterion (consisting of *consumer_name*, *msgid* and *correlation*) is applied. Valid values are NEXT_MESSAGE (retrieve the next available message matching the search criterion), NEXT_TRANSACTION (skip the remainder of the current message group, if any, and retrieve the first available message in the next message group), and FIRST_MESSAGE (retrieve the first available message matching the search criterion, searching from the start of the queue). NEXT_MESSAGE is the default.
visibility	BINARY_INTEGER	Specifies whether the DEQUEUE is part of the current transaction. If ON_COMMIT (the default), the dequeue operation is part of the current transaction. If IMMEDIATE, the dequeue is a transaction of its own, that is committed immediately.
wait	BINARY_INTEGER	Number of seconds to wait if there is currently no message available which matches the search criterion. This is ignored if messages in the same group are being dequeued. Valid values are FOREVER (no timeout, this is the default), NO_WAIT (do not wait, return immediately if no message is available), or the number of seconds to wait.
msgid	RAW(16)	Specifies a message identifier for the message to be dequeued.
correlation	VARCHAR2(30)	Specifies a correlation identifier for the message to be dequeued.

TABLE 17-5. *DEQUEUE_OPTIONS_T* (continued)

Enumerated Constants

Many of the fields for the supporting types in DBMS_AQ are enumerated constants. The fields are defined as BINARY_INTEGER, and DBMS_AQ defines the appropriate values. When setting these options, they need to be prefixed with the package name—DBMS_AQ.IMMEDIATE, for example. The following table lists all of the enumerated constants, their values, and where they are used.

Field	Values	Where Used
sequence_deviation	BEFORE, TOP	ENQUEUE_OPTIONS_T
visibility	IMMEDIATE, ON_COMMIT	ENQUEUE_OPTIONS_T
dequeue_mode	BROWSE, LOCKED, REMOVE	DEQUEUE_OPTIONS_T
navigation	FIRST_MESSAGE, NEXT_MESSAGE, NEXT_TRANSACTION	DEQUEUE_OPTIONS_T
wait	FOREVER, NO_WAIT	DEQUEUE_OPTIONS_T
state	WAITING, READY, PROCESSED, EXPIRED	MESSAGE_PROPERTIES_T
delay	NO_DELAY	MESSAGE_PROPERTIES_T
expiration	NEVER	MESSAGE_PROPERTIES_T

ENQUEUE

DBMS_AQ.ENQUEUE can accept a message payload that is either an object type or RAW. It is defined as follows:

```
PROCEDURE ENQUEUE (
  queue_name IN VARCHAR2,
  enqueue_options IN ENQUEUE_OPTIONS_T,
  message_properties IN MESSAGE_PROPERTIES_T,
  payload IN message_type,
  msgid OUT RAW);
```

The parameters are described in the following table:

Parameter	Datatype	Description
queue_name	VARCHAR2	Queue into which the message should be inserted.
enqueue_ options	ENQUEUE_OPTIONS_T	Options for the enqueue. The fields in this type are described in Table 17-4.
message_ properties	MESSAGE_PROPERTIES_T	Properties for the message. The properties are returned on a subsequent DEQUEUE operation. The fields in this type are described in Table 17-3.
payload	message_type	Message data. This can be either a RAW or object type. If it is an object type, it must match the type specified for the queue when it was created.
msgid	RAW	Message ID returned. This ID can be used to dequeue this particular message, regardless of priority or delay.

The *sequence_deviation* field in the enqueue options specifies a relationship between two messages. If this is specified, then there are two restrictions for the delay and priority of the enqueued message:

■ The delay of the newly enqueued message must be less than or equal to the delay of the message before which this message is to be enqueued.

■ The priority of the newly enqueued message must be greater than or equal to the priority of the message before which this message is to be enqueued.

DEQUEUE

DBMS_AQ.DEQUEUE is also overloaded to accept either a RAW or object type message. It is defined with

```
PROCEDURE DEQUEUE (
  queue_name IN VARCHAR2,
  dequeue_options IN DEQUEUE_OPTIONS_T,
  message_properties OUT MESSAGE_PROPERTIES_T,
  payload OUT message_type,
  msgid OUT RAW);
```

The parameters are described in the following table.

Parameter	Datatype	Description
queue_name	VARCHAR2	Name of the queue to query for messages.
dequeue_options	DEQUEUE_OPTIONS_T	Options for the dequeue. The fields in this type are described in Table 17-5.
message_properties	MESSAGE_PROPERTIES_T	Properties of the retrieved message. The fields in this type are described in Table 17-3.
payload	message_type	Either the RAW or object type message.
msgid	RAW	Message ID for this message.

The search criterion for the dequeue is determined by the *consumer_name*, *msgid*, and/or *correlation* fields in *dequeue_options*. Only messages in the READY state are dequeued unless *msgid* is specified.

Queue Administration

In this section, we will examine the DBMS_AQADM packages, and the privileges required to use queues. We will also examine the data dictionary views relevant to queues.

DBMS_AQADM Subprograms

The DBMS_AQADM package defines subprograms to administer queues and queue tables. Each of the subprograms is described in this section.

CREATE_QUEUE_TABLE

CREATE_QUEUE_TABLE is used to create a queue table, and to specify the default properties for any queues created in this table later, including the sort ordering for the queues. CREATE_QUEUE_TABLE creates the following objects, where *queue_table* is the name of the newly created table:

- A default exception queue associated with this queue table, called **aq$_*queue_table*_e**.

- A read-only view which can be used to query the queue, called **aq$_*queue_table***.

- An index for the time manager, called **aq$_*queue_table*_t**.

- An index (or index organized table) for multiple consumer queues, called **aq$_*queue_table*_i**.

The syntax for CREATE_QUEUE_TABLE follows, and the parameters are described in the following table.

```
PROCEDURE CREATE_QUEUE_TABLE(
    queue_table IN VARCHAR2,
    queue_payload_type IN VARCHAR2,
    storage_clause IN VARCHAR2 DEFAULT NULL,
    sort_list IN VARCHAR2 DEFAULT NULL,
    multiple_consumers IN BOOLEAN DEFAULT FALSE,
    message_grouping IN BINARY_INTEGER DEFAULT NONE,
    comment IN VARCHAR2 DEFAULT NULL,
    auto_commit IN BOOLEAN  DEFAULT TRUE);
```

Parameter	Datatype	Description
queue_table	VARCHAR2	Name of the queue table to be created.
queue_payload_type	VARCHAR2	Type of the user data in this queue. This should be either RAW or an object type.
storage_clause	VARCHAR2	Storage parameter to be used for the CREATE TABLE statement. This can include the specification of clauses such as TABLESPACE, PCTFREE, PCTUSED, LOB, INITTRANS, and MAXTRANS. See the *SQL Reference Guide* for a full description of the storage clause.
sort_list	VARCHAR2	Defines the columns to be used as the sort key, and thus the sort behavior of queues created in this table. See the description following this table for more details.
multiple_consumers	BOOLEAN	If TRUE, queues created in this table can have multiple consumers per message. The user must have been granted type access using GRANT_TYPE_ACCESS first. If FALSE (the default), queues created in this table can have only one consumer per message.

Parameter	Datatype	Description
message_grouping	BINARY_INTEGER	If NONE (the default), then each message in queues created in this queue table is treated individually. If TRANSACTIONAL, then all messages enqueued as part of one transaction are considered part of the same message group, and thus are dequeued together.
comment	VARCHAR2	Comment for the newly created table. This will be recorded in the queue catalog.
auto_commit	BOOLEAN	If TRUE (the default), the current transaction is committed before the queue table is created, and the operation is persistent when CREATE_QUEUE_TABLE returns. If FALSE, then the create is part of the current transaction, and will become persistent when the current transaction commits.

SORT_LIST   The *sort_list* parameter of CREATE_QUEUE_TABLE specifies the sorting properties of the queue table, and hence the properties of any queues created in this table. It is a comma-separated list of sort columns. The allowable sort columns are 'priority' and 'enq_time'. If both are specified, the first column defines the most significant order. If *sort_list* is not specified, then the default is to sort by enqueue time, which implements a FIFO queue.

Individual messages can still be dequeued regardless of the sort order by specifying a correlation or message identifier at dequeue time.

DROP_QUEUE_TABLE
This procedure drops the specified queue table. All the queues in the table must be stopped and then dropped before the table can be dropped. The syntax is

```
PROCEDURE DROP_QUEUE_TABLE(
  queue_table IN VARCHAR2,
  force IN BOOLEAN DEFAULT FALSE,
  auto_commit IN BOOLEAN DEFAULT TRUE);
```

The parameters for DROP_QUEUE_TABLE are described in the following table.

Parameter	Datatype	Description
queue_table	VARCHAR2	Queue table to be dropped.
force	BOOLEAN	If TRUE, all queues in the table are stopped and dropped automatically. If FALSE (the default), an error is returned if there are still queues in the table.
auto_commit	BOOLEAN	If TRUE (the default), the current transaction is committed before the queue table is dropped, and the operation is persistent when the procedure returns. If FALSE, the operation will become persistent when the current transaction commits.

CREATE_QUEUE

CREATE_QUEUE creates a queue in the specified queue table. The queue name must be unique within the current schema, and both enqueue and dequeue operations on the queue are disabled by default. After the queue is created, it must be enabled using START_QUEUE. The syntax for CREATE_QUEUE is

```
PROCEDURE CREATE_QUEUE(
  queue_name IN VARCHAR2,
  queue_table IN VARCHAR2,
  queue_type IN BINARY_INTEGER DEFAULT NORMAL_QUEUE,
  max_retries IN NUMBER DEFAULT 0,
  retry_delay IN NUMBER DEFAULT 0,
  retention_time IN NUMBER DEFAULT 0,
  dependency_tracking IN BOOLEAN DEFAULT FALSE,
  comment IN VARCHAR2 DEFAULT NULL,
  auto_commit IN BOOLEAN DEFAULT TRUE);
```

and the parameters are described in the following table.

Parameter	Datatype	Description
queue_name	VARCHAR2	Name of the queue to be created.
queue_table	VARCHAR2	Queue table which will contain the newly created queue. The new queue will assume the properties of the queue table, such as sort order and payload type.
queue_type	BINARY_INTEGER	Type of queue. Valid values are NORMAL_QUEUE (creates a normal queue) or EXCEPTION_QUEUE (creates an exception queue). The default is NORMAL_QUEUE.
max_retries	NUMBER	Maximum number of dequeue attempts with REMOVE specified. If an agent dequeues a message, but then rolls back, the count is incremented. When it reaches *max_retries*, the message is moved to the exception queue. The default is 0, indicating no retries.
retry_delay	NUMBER	Delay in seconds between retries. If *max_retries* is 0, then *retry_delay* has no effect. If the queue has multiple consumers, then *retry_delay* cannot be specified.

Parameter	Datatype	Description
retention_time	NUMBER	Number of seconds for which a message will be retained in the queue table after being dequeued. Valid values are INFINITE (the message will be retained forever) or the number of seconds. The default is 0.
dependency_tracking	BOOLEAN	This parameter is reserved for future use. The default is FALSE, and it is currently an error to specify TRUE.
comment	VARCHAR2	Description for the newly created queue. This comment will be added to the queue catalog.
auto_commit	BOOLEAN	If TRUE (the default), the current transaction is committed before the queue is created, and the operation is persistent when CREATE_QUEUE returns. If FALSE, the operation will become persistent when the current transaction commits.

DROP_QUEUE

DROP_QUEUE drops an existing queue from its containing queue table. The queue must have been stopped with STOP_QUEUE prior to being dropped. All of the queue data is deleted as part of the drop operation. DROP_QUEUE is defined with

```
PROCEDURE DROP_QUEUE(
  queue_name IN VARCHAR2,
  auto_commit IN BOOLEAN DEFAULT TRUE);
```

where *queue_name* is the name of the queue to be dropped, and *auto_commit* specifies the transactional behavior of this operation. If *auto_commit* is TRUE (the default), the current transaction is committed first. If *auto_commit* is FALSE, the queue will be dropped when the current transaction commits.

ALTER_QUEUE

This procedure is used to modify certain properties of a queue. Only the *max_retries*, *retry_delay*, and *retention_time* properties can be modified. To change other properties, the queue must be dropped and recreated. The syntax for ALTER_QUEUE follows, and the parameters are described in the following table.

```
PROCEDURE ALTER_QUEUE(
  queue_name IN VARCHAR2,
  max_retries IN NUMBER DEFAULT NULL,
  retry_delay IN NUMBER DEFAULT NULL,
  retention_time IN NUMBER DEFAULTNULL,
  auto_commit IN BOOLEAN DEFAULT TRUE);
```

Parameter	Datatype	Description
queue_name	VARCHAR2	Name of the queue to be modified.
max_retries	NUMBER	Maximum number of dequeue attempts with REMOVE specified. If an agent dequeues a message, but then rolls back, the count is incremented. When it reaches *max_retries*, the message is moved to the exception queue.
retry_delay	NUMBER	Delay in seconds between retries. If *max_retries* is 0, then *retry_delay* has no effect. If the queue has multiple consumers, then *retry_delay* cannot be specified.

Parameter	Datatype	Description
retention_time	NUMBER	Number of seconds for which a message will be retained in the queue table after being dequeued. Valid values are INFINITE (the message will be retained forever) or the number of seconds. The default is 0.
auto_commit	BOOLEAN	If TRUE, the current transaction is committed before the queue is created, and the operation is persistent when ALTER_QUEUE returns. If FALSE, the operation will become persistent when the current transaction commits.

START_QUEUE

START_QUEUE is used to enable a queue for enqueue and/or dequeue operations. A queue must be started after it is created. Only dequeues are allowed on an exception queue, so enabling an exception queue for enqueue has no effect. The queue is started when this procedure returns, even if the transaction is rolled back. START_QUEUE is defined with

```
PROCEDURE START_QUEUE(
  queue_name IN VARCHAR2,
  enqueue IN BOOLEAN DEFAULT TRUE,
  dequeue IN BOOLEAN DEFAULT TRUE);
```

where *queue_name* is the name of the queue to be started, and *enqueue* and *dequeue* specify that the queue should be enabled for enqueue and dequeue operations, respectively.

STOP_QUEUE

STOP_QUEUE is used to disable enqueue and/or dequeue operations for the specified queue. A queue cannot be stopped if there are outstanding transactions against it. The queue is stopped when this procedure returns, even if the current transaction is rolled back. STOP_QUEUE is defined with

```
PROCEDURE STOP_QUEUE(
  queue_name IN VARCHAR2,
```

```
enqueue IN BOOLEAN DEFAULT TRUE,
dequeue IN BOOLEAN DEFAULT TRUE,
wait IN BOOLEAN DEFAULT TRUE);
```

where *queue_name* is the name of the queue to be stopped, and *enqueue* and *dequeue* specify that the queue should be disabled for enqueue and dequeue operations, respectively. If *wait* is TRUE, then this call will block until all outstanding transactions against *queue_name* are committed or rolled back. If *wait* is FALSE, then STOP_QUEUE returns immediately with success or failure.

ADD_SUBSCRIBER

ADD_SUBSCRIBER will add a default subscriber to a queue. This is only valid on queues which can have multiple consumers. ADD_SUBSCRIBER takes effect immediately, and the current transaction is committed. The user must have been granted access to this queue with GRANT_TYPE_ACCESS. The syntax is

```
PROCEDURE ADD_SUBSCRIBER(
  queue_name IN VARCHAR2,
  subscriber IN SYS.AQ$_AGENT);
```

where *queue_name* is the queue to be modified, and *subscriber* is the new subscriber.

REMOVE_SUBSCRIBER

This procedure will remove the specified subscriber from the specified queue. It takes effect immediately, and the current transaction is committed. As part of the remove, all references to the subscriber are deleted from existing messages. The user must have been granted access to this queue with GRANT_TYPE_ACCESS. The syntax is

```
PROCEDURE REMOVE_SUBSCRIBER(
  queue_name IN VARCHAR2,
  subscriber IN SYS.AQ$_AGENT);
```

where *queue_name* is the queue to be modified, and *subscriber* is the subscriber to be removed.

QUEUE_SUBSCRIBERS

This function will return a PL/SQL table of the subscribers for a given queue. The syntax is

```
FUNCTION QUEUE_SUBSCRIBERS(
queue_name IN VARCHAR2)
RETURN AQ$_SUBSCRIBER_LIST_T;
```

GRANT_TYPE_ACCESS

GRANT_TYPE_ACCESS is used to enable a given user to perform queue administrative operations. Unless this is done, the user cannot execute CREATE_QUEUE_TABLE, CREATE_QUEUE, ADD_SUBSCRIBER, and REMOVE_SUBSCRIBER. It is defined with

```
PROCEDURE GRANT_TYPE_ACCESS(
user_name IN VARCHAR2);
```

where *user_name* is the database user to be granted the permission.

START_TIME_MANAGER

This procedure enables the time manager process. The AQ_TM_PROCESS init.ora parameter must have been set to 1 first, which starts the process at database startup time. The time manager is started when this call returns, even if the current transaction is rolled back. START_TIME_MANAGER takes no arguments and is defined with

```
PROCEDURE START_TIME_MANAGER;
```

STOP_TIME_MANAGER

STOP_TIME_MANAGER disables the time manager. It does not kill the process, however. Rather, it causes the process to stop its operations. The time manager is stopped when this call returns, even if the current transaction is rolled back. STOP_TIME_MANAGER takes no arguments and is defined with

```
PROCEDURE STOP_TIME_MANAGER;
```

Queue Privileges

In order to use the DBMS_AQ or DBMS_AQADM package, there are certain steps which must be performed by the system administrator. There are two roles which must be granted, followed by access to the AQ object types.

AQ_ADMINISTRATOR_ROLE

The role AQ_ADMINISTRATOR_ROLE is predefined by Oracle. It contains all the necessary GRANTs to allow the grantee EXECUTE permission on DBMS_AQ and DBMS_AQADM. This role should be granted to users who will need to administer queues.

AQ_USER_ROLE

The AQ_USER_ROLE role, on the other hand, just grants EXECUTE on DBMS_AQ. This role should be granted to users who will need to enqueue and dequeue messages, but not administer queues.

Access to AQ Object Types

Finally, the queue administrator needs access to the object types used in queues. This is done with the DBMS_AQADM.GRANT_TYPE_ACCESS procedure, which should be called by SYS. This enables the grantee to run the CREATE_QUEUE_TABLE, CREATE_QUEUE, ADD_SUBSCRIBER, and REMOVE_SUBSCRIBER routines.

Queues and the Data Dictionary

There are several data dictionary views which enable you to find out information about the queues in the system. These include a view for every queue table, as well as views for all queues and all queue tables.

Queue Table View

Every time you create a queue table (with DBMS_AQADM.CREATE_QUEUE_TABLE), a view is created in the current schema which contains information about the messages in that table. Each row provides data about one message. The name of this view is **aq$*queue_table_name***, and has the structure defined in the following table:

Column	Datatype	Description
queue	VARCHAR2(30)	Name of the queue containing this message
msg_id	RAW(16)	Message identifier
corr_id	VARCHAR2(30)	Correlation identifier
msg_priority	NUMBER	Priority of this message
msg_state	VARCHAR2(9)	State of this message—one of READY, DELAYED, PROCESSED, or EXPIRED
delay	DATE	Delay specified at enqueue time
expiration	NUMBER	Expiration specified at enqueue time
enq_time	DATE	Time this message was enqueued
enq_user_id	NUMBER	User ID of the user who issued the enqueue
enq_txn_id	VARCHAR2(30)	Transaction ID of the enqueue
deq_time	DATE	Time this message was dequeued
deq_user_id	NUMBER	User ID of the user who issued the dequeue
deq_txn_id	VARCHAR2(30)	Transaction ID of the dequeue
retry_count	NUMBER	Number of dequeue attempts for this message
exception_queue_owner	VARCHAR2(30)	Owner of the exception queue specified at enqueue time, if any
exception_queue	VARCHAR2(30)	Exception queue specified at enqueue time, if any
user_data	*object_type* or RAW	Data that was enqueued

DBA_QUEUE_TABLES/USER_QUEUE_TABLES

The **dba_queue_tables** view contains information about all the queue tables in the database, and **user_queue_tables** contains information about the current user's queue tables. They both have the following structure:

Column	Datatype	Description
owner	VARCHAR2(30)	Owner of the queue table (dba_queue_tables only)
queue_table	VARCHAR2(30)	Name of the queue table
type	VARCHAR2(7)	Payload type—OBJECT or RAW
sort_order	VARCHAR2(22)	Sort order specified at queue table creation time
recipients	VARCHAR2(8)	Either SINGLE or MULTIPLE
message_grouping	VARCHAR2(13)	Either NONE or TRANSACTIONAL
user_comment	VARCHAR2(50)	Comment specified at queue table creation time

DBA_QUEUES/USER_QUEUES

The **dba_queues** view contains information about all the queues in the database, and **user_queues** information about the current user's queues. They have the following structure:

Column	Datatype	Description
owner	VARCHAR2(30)	Owner of the queue (**dba_queues** only)
name	VARCHAR2(30)	Queue name
queue_table	VARCHAR2(30)	Queue table in which this queue resides
qid	NUMBER	Unique queue identifier, generated when the queue was created
queue_type	VARCHAR2(15)	One of NORMAL_QUEUE or EXCEPTION_QUEUE

Column	Datatype	Description
max_retries	NUMBER	Number of dequeue attempts allowed
retry_delay	NUMBER	Delay between retries
enqueue_enabled	VARCHAR2(7)	Either YES or NO
dequeue_enabled	VARCHAR2(7)	Either YES or NO
retention	VARCHAR2(40)	Number of seconds a message is retained after a dequeue
user_comment	VARCHAR2(50)	Comment specified at queue creation

Extended Examples

In this section, we will examine many of the features of Advanced Queuing through a series of examples. The examples illustrate the following features:

- Creating queues and queue tables

- Simple enqueue and dequeue

- Clearing a queue

- Enqueue and dequeue by priority

- Enqueue and dequeue by correlation or message identifier

- Browsing a queue

- Using exception queues

- Dropping queues

Creating Queues and Queue Tables

The first step is to grant the necessary permissions to the queue owner. Suppose we are want to create queues under the **example** schema. In order to do this, we must grant the AQ_ADMINISTRATOR_ROLE role first, and then grant type access to **example**. So, we could execute the following statements while connected as **system** or another DBA account:

```
GRANT AQ_ADMINISTRATOR_ROLE TO example;
BEGIN DBMS_AQADM.GRANT_TYPE_ACCESS('example'); END;
```

Once this is done, we can proceed to create queue tables and queues. The following script will create and start all of the queues used in these examples.

```
-- Available online as createq.sql
CREATE OR REPLACE TYPE MessageObj AS OBJECT (
  title   VARCHAR2(30),
  data1   NUMBER,
  data2   VARCHAR2(100),
  data3   DATE,

  MEMBER PROCEDURE Print(v_Message IN VARCHAR2)
);

CREATE OR REPLACE TYPE BODY MessageObj AS
  MEMBER PROCEDURE Print(v_Message IN VARCHAR2) IS
  BEGIN
    DBMS_OUTPUT.PUT_LINE(v_Message || ': ' || title);
    DBMS_OUTPUT.PUT('Data 1: ' || data1);
    DBMS_OUTPUT.PUT(' Data 2: ' || data2);
    DBMS_OUTPUT.PUT_LINE(' Data 3: ' || data3);
  END Print;
END;

BEGIN
  -- Create a simple table, with all of the defaults. This will allow
  -- FIFO queues, with no message grouping or multiple consumers.
  DBMS_AQADM.CREATE_QUEUE_TABLE(
    queue_table => 'SimpleQTab',
    queue_payload_type => 'MessageObj',
    comment => 'Simple Queue Table');

  -- Create a simple queue contained within SimpleQTab. Again, use
  -- the default parameters.
  DBMS_AQADM.CREATE_QUEUE(
    queue_name => 'SimpleQ',
    queue_table => 'SimpleQTab',
    comment => 'Simple Queue');

  -- Enable enqueue and dequeue operations for SimpleQ.
  DBMS_AQADM.START_QUEUE('SimpleQ');
```

```
   -- Create an exception queue within SimpleQTab.
   DBMS_AQADM.CREATE_QUEUE(
     queue_name => 'ExceptionQ',
     queue_table => 'SimpleQTab',
     queue_type => DBMS_AQADM.EXCEPTION_QUEUE,
     comment => 'Exception Queue');

   -- Enable dequeue operations for ExceptionQ.
   DBMS_AQADM.START_QUEUE('ExceptionQ', FALSE, TRUE);
END;

BEGIN
   -- Create a priority queue table, by specifying the sort order.
   -- This queue has no message grouping or multiple consumers.
   DBMS_AQADM.CREATE_QUEUE_TABLE(
     queue_table => 'PriorityQTab',
     queue_payload_type => 'MessageObj',
     sort_list => 'priority,enq_time',
     comment => 'Priority Queue Table');

   -- Create a priority queue contained within PriorityQTab. Again,
   -- use the default parameters.

   DBMS_AQADM.CREATE_QUEUE(
     queue_name => 'PriorityQ',
     queue_table => 'PriorityQTab',
     comment => 'Priority Queue');

   -- Enable enqueue and dequeue operations for PriorityQ.
   DBMS_AQADM.START_QUEUE('PriorityQ');
END;
```

Simple Enqueue and Dequeue

The following example illustrates a series of enqueue and dequeue
operations on **SimpleQ**.

```
-- Available online as simple.sql
DECLARE
   v_Message MessageObj;
   v_EnqueueOptions DBMS_AQ.ENQUEUE_OPTIONS_T;
   v_DequeueOptions DBMS_AQ.DEQUEUE_OPTIONS_T;
   v_MessageProperties DBMS_AQ.MESSAGE_PROPERTIES_T;
   v_MsgID RAW(16);
```

```
  c_NumMessages CONSTANT INTEGER := 10;

  e_QTimeOut EXCEPTION;
  PRAGMA EXCEPTION_INIT(e_QTimeOut, -25228);
BEGIN
  FOR v_Counter IN 1..c_NumMessages LOOP
    -- Create a message to enqueue.
    v_Message :=
      MessageObj('Message ' || v_Counter, v_Counter * 10,
                 'abcdefghijklmnopqrstuvwxyz', SYSDATE + v_Counter);

    -- Enqueue it with the default options.
    DBMS_AQ.ENQUEUE(
      queue_name => 'SimpleQ',
      enqueue_options => v_EnqueueOptions,
      message_properties => v_MessageProperties,
      payload => v_Message,
      msgid => v_MsgID);
  END LOOP;

  -- Commit all the enqueues.
  COMMIT;

  -- Loop until there are no more messages to dequeue.
  BEGIN
    LOOP
      -- Dequeue the first message into v_Message, waiting a maximum
      -- of 1 second.
      v_DequeueOptions.wait := 1;
      DBMS_AQ.DEQUEUE(
        queue_name => 'SimpleQ',
        dequeue_options => v_DequeueOptions,
        message_properties => v_MessageProperties,
        payload => v_Message,
        msgid => v_MsgID);

      -- And print it.
      v_Message.Print('After dequeue');
    END LOOP;
  EXCEPTION
    WHEN e_QTimeOut THEN
      -- End of the queue reached.
      NULL;
  END;
```

```
  -- Commit all the dequeues.
  COMMIT;
END;
```

When run in SQL*Plus, this script produces the following output:

```
After dequeue: Message 1
Data 1: 10 Data 2: abcdefghijklmnopqrstuvwxyz Data 3: 15-AUG-97
After dequeue: Message 2
Data 1: 20 Data 2: abcdefghijklmnopqrstuvwxyz Data 3: 16-AUG-97
After dequeue: Message 3
Data 1: 30 Data 2: abcdefghijklmnopqrstuvwxyz Data 3: 17-AUG-97
After dequeue: Message 4
Data 1: 40 Data 2: abcdefghijklmnopqrstuvwxyz Data 3: 18-AUG-97
After dequeue: Message 5
Data 1: 50 Data 2: abcdefghijklmnopqrstuvwxyz Data 3: 19-AUG-97
After dequeue: Message 6
Data 1: 60 Data 2: abcdefghijklmnopqrstuvwxyz Data 3: 20-AUG-97
After dequeue: Message 7
Data 1: 70 Data 2: abcdefghijklmnopqrstuvwxyz Data 3: 21-AUG-97
After dequeue: Message 8
Data 1: 80 Data 2: abcdefghijklmnopqrstuvwxyz Data 3: 22-AUG-97
After dequeue: Message 9
Data 1: 90 Data 2: abcdefghijklmnopqrstuvwxyz Data 3: 23-AUG-97
After dequeue: Message 10
Data 1: 100 Data 2: abcdefghijklmnopqrstuvwxyz Data 3: 24-AUG-97
```

The messages have been dequeued in the same order in which they were enqueued, because this is a FIFO queue.

Clearing a Queue

We can adapt the second portion of the above example into a procedure that will delete all the messages in a queue, by simply dequeuing until there are none left:

```
-- Available online as clearq.sql
CREATE OR REPLACE PROCEDURE ClearQueue(p_QueueName IN VARCHAR2) AS
  v_Message MessageObj;
  v_DequeueOptions DBMS_AQ.DEQUEUE_OPTIONS_T;
  v_MessageProperties DBMS_AQ.MESSAGE_PROPERTIES_T;
  v_MsgID RAW(16);
```

```
  e_QTimeOut EXCEPTION;
  PRAGMA EXCEPTION_INIT(e_QTimeOut, -25228);
BEGIN
  -- Loop until there are no more messages to dequeue.
  BEGIN
    LOOP
      -- Dequeue the first message into v_Message, waiting a maximum
      -- of 1 second.
      v_DequeueOptions.wait := 1;
      DBMS_AQ.DEQUEUE(
        queue_name => 'SimpleQ',
        dequeue_options => v_DequeueOptions,
        message_properties => v_MessageProperties,
        payload => v_Message,
        msgid => v_MsgID);
    END LOOP;
  EXCEPTION
    WHEN e_QTimeOut THEN
      -- End of the queue reached.
      NULL;
  END;

  -- Commit all the dequeues.
  COMMIT;
END;
```

Enqueue and Dequeue by Priority

The following example illustrates a series of enqueues and dequeues on a priority queue.

-- **Available online as priority.sql**

```
DECLARE
  v_Message MessageObj;
  v_EnqueueOptions DBMS_AQ.ENQUEUE_OPTIONS_T;
  v_DequeueOptions DBMS_AQ.DEQUEUE_OPTIONS_T;
  v_MessageProperties DBMS_AQ.MESSAGE_PROPERTIES_T;
  v_MsgID RAW(16);

  c_NumMessages CONSTANT INTEGER := 10;

  e_QTimeOut EXCEPTION;
  PRAGMA EXCEPTION_INIT(e_QTimeOut, -25228);
BEGIN
  FOR v_Counter IN 1..c_NumMessages LOOP
```

```
  v_Message MessageObj;
  v_EnqueueOptions DBMS_AQ.ENQUEUE_OPTIONS_T;
  v_DequeueOptions DBMS_AQ.DEQUEUE_OPTIONS_T;
  v_MessageProperties DBMS_AQ.MESSAGE_PROPERTIES_T;
  v_MsgID RAW(16);
  v_TigerMsgID RAW(16);

  c_NumMessages CONSTANT INTEGER := 10;

  TYPE t_Correlations IS TABLE OF VARCHAR2(30)
    INDEX BY BINARY_INTEGER;
  v_Correlations t_Correlations;

  e_QTimeOut EXCEPTION;
  PRAGMA EXCEPTION_INIT(e_QTimeOut, -25228);
BEGIN
  -- Initialize the array of correlation identifiers.
  -- There will be a total of 5 different correlation IDs, with two
  -- messages getting each one.
  FOR v_Counter IN 1..c_NumMessages LOOP
    IF MOD(v_Counter, 5) = 1 THEN
      v_Correlations(v_Counter) := 'Lion';
    ELSIF MOD(v_Counter, 5) = 2 THEN
      v_Correlations(v_Counter) := 'Tiger';
    ELSIF MOD(v_Counter, 5) = 3 THEN
      v_Correlations(v_Counter) := 'Bear';
    ELSIF MOD(v_Counter, 5) = 4 THEN
      v_Correlations(v_Counter) := 'Fish';
    ELSE
      v_Correlations(v_Counter) := 'Horse';
    END IF;
  END LOOP;

  FOR v_Counter IN 1..c_NumMessages LOOP
    -- Create a message to enqueue.
    v_Message :=
      MessageObj('Message ' || v_Counter, v_Counter * 10,
                 'abcdefghijklmnopqrstuvwxyz', SYSDATE + v_Counter);

    v_MessageProperties.correlation := v_Correlations(v_Counter);
    DBMS_OUTPUT.PUT_LINE('Enqueing message ' || v_Counter ||
      ' with correlation ID ' || v_Correlations(v_Counter));
    DBMS_AQ.ENQUEUE(
      queue_name => 'SimpleQ',
      enqueue_options => v_EnqueueOptions,
```

```
      message_properties => v_MessageProperties,
      payload => v_Message,
      msgid => v_MsgID);

    -- Save one of the tiger message ID's.
    IF v_Correlations(v_Counter) = 'Tiger' THEN
      v_TigerMsgID := v_MsgID;
    END IF;
END LOOP;

-- Commit all the enqueues.
COMMIT;

-- Dequeue only the messages with correlation ID 'Fish'.
BEGIN
  LOOP
    -- Dequeue the first message into v_Message, waiting a maximum
    -- of 1 second.
    v_DequeueOptions.wait := 1;
    v_DequeueOptions.correlation := 'Fish';
    DBMS_AQ.DEQUEUE(
      queue_name => 'SimpleQ',
      dequeue_options => v_DequeueOptions,
      message_properties => v_MessageProperties,
      payload => v_Message,
      msgid => v_MsgID);

    -- And print it.
    v_Message.Print('After dequeue with correlation ID Fish');
  END LOOP;
EXCEPTION
  WHEN e_QTimeOut THEN
    -- End of the queue reached.
    NULL;
END;

-- Dequeue only the message with the saved message ID.
v_DequeueOptions.correlation := NULL;
v_DequeueOptions.msgid := v_TigerMsgID;
DBMS_AQ.DEQUEUE(
  queue_name => 'SimpleQ',
  dequeue_options => v_DequeueOptions,
  message_properties => v_MessageProperties,
  payload => v_Message,
  msgid => v_MsgID);
```

```
-- And print it.
v_Message.Print('After dequeue with saved message ID');

-- Clear all the remaining messages.
ClearQueue('SimpleQ');

-- Commit all the dequeues.
COMMIT;
END;
```

This script produces the following output when run:

```
Enqueing message 1 with correlation ID Lion
Enqueing message 2 with correlation ID Tiger
Enqueing message 3 with correlation ID Bear
Enqueing message 4 with correlation ID Fish
Enqueing message 5 with correlation ID Horse
Enqueing message 6 with correlation ID Lion
Enqueing message 7 with correlation ID Tiger
Enqueing message 8 with correlation ID Bear
Enqueing message 9 with correlation ID Fish
Enqueing message 10 with correlation ID Horse
After dequeue with correlation ID Fish: Message 4
Data 1: 40 Data 2: abcdefghijklmnopqrstuvwxyz Data 3: 18-AUG-97
After dequeue with correlation ID Fish: Message 9
Data 1: 90 Data 2: abcdefghijklmnopqrstuvwxyz Data 3: 23-AUG-97
After dequeue with saved message ID: Message 7
Data 1: 70 Data 2: abcdefghijklmnopqrstuvwxyz Data 3: 21-AUG-97
```

Browsing a Queue

By setting the dequeue_mode in the dequeue options to BROWSE, you can
examine the contents of a queue without actually removing the elements.
This technique can be used to search a queue for a particular message, for
example. The **SearchQueue** function does exactly that:

```
-- Available online as part of searchq.sql
CREATE OR REPLACE FUNCTION SearchQueue(
  /* Searches the queue for the first occurrence of a message with
     title p_MessageTitle, and returns the message ID for that
     occurrence. If there is no match, returns NULL. */
  p_QueueName IN VARCHAR2,
  p_MessageTitle IN VARCHAR2)
  RETURN RAW AS
```

```
   v_Message MessageObj;
   v_DequeueOptions DBMS_AQ.DEQUEUE_OPTIONS_T;
   v_MessageProperties DBMS_AQ.MESSAGE_PROPERTIES_T;
   v_MsgID RAW(16);

   e_QTimeOut EXCEPTION;
   PRAGMA EXCEPTION_INIT(e_QTimeOut, -25228);
BEGIN
   -- Loop until there are no more messages to dequeue, or we have
   -- found the desired message.
   BEGIN
     LOOP
       -- Dequeue (in browse mode) the first message into v_Message,
       -- waiting a maximum of 1 second. Since we are browsing, the
       -- message will not be removed from the queue.
       v_DequeueOptions.wait := 1;
       v_DequeueOptions.dequeue_mode := DBMS_AQ.BROWSE;
       DBMS_AQ.DEQUEUE(
         queue_name => p_QueueName,
         dequeue_options => v_DequeueOptions,
         message_properties => v_MessageProperties,
         payload => v_Message,
         msgid => v_MsgID);

       -- Check the message titles.
       IF v_Message.title = p_MessageTitle THEN
         -- Found a match, return the message ID.
         COMMIT;
         RETURN v_MsgID;
       END IF;
     END LOOP;
   EXCEPTION
     WHEN e_QTimeOut THEN
       -- End of the queue reached.
       NULL;
   END;

   -- Commit all the dequeues and return NULL, indicating no match.
   COMMIT;
   RETURN NULL;
END;
```

The following block illustrates how to call **SearchQueue**:

```
-- Available online as part of searchq.sql
DECLARE
  v_Message MessageObj;
  v_EnqueueOptions DBMS_AQ.ENQUEUE_OPTIONS_T;
  v_DequeueOptions DBMS_AQ.DEQUEUE_OPTIONS_T;
  v_MessageProperties DBMS_AQ.MESSAGE_PROPERTIES_T;
  v_MsgID RAW(16);

  c_NumMessages CONSTANT INTEGER := 10;

  e_QTimeOut EXCEPTION;
  PRAGMA EXCEPTION_INIT(e_QTimeOut, -25228);
BEGIN
  FOR v_Counter IN 1..c_NumMessages LOOP
    -- Create a message to enqueue.
    v_Message :=
      MessageObj('Message ' || v_Counter, v_Counter * 10,
                 'abcdefghijklmnopqrstuvwxyz', SYSDATE + v_Counter);

    -- Enqueue it with the default options.
    DBMS_AQ.ENQUEUE(
      queue_name => 'SimpleQ',
      enqueue_options => v_EnqueueOptions,
      message_properties => v_MessageProperties,
      payload => v_Message,
      msgid => v_MsgID);
  END LOOP;

  -- Commit all the enqueues.
  COMMIT;

  -- Search for message 4
  v_MsgID := SearchQueue('SimpleQ', 'Message 4');

  -- If found, dequeue and print.
  IF v_MsgID IS NOT NULL THEN
    v_DequeueOptions.wait := 1;
    v_DequeueOptions.msgid := v_MsgID;
    DBMS_AQ.DEQUEUE(
      queue_name => 'SimpleQ',
      dequeue_options => v_DequeueOptions,
      message_properties => v_MessageProperties,
      payload => v_Message,
```

```
      msgid => v_MsgID);
    v_Message.Print('After search');
  ELSE
    DBMS_OUTPUT.PUT_LINE('Message 4 not found');
  END IF;

  -- Clear the queue.
  ClearQueue('SimpleQ');
END;
```

Using Exception Queues

Messages are automatically moved to exception queues if either of the following conditions is true:

1. An expiration is specified as part of the message properties at enqueue time, and the message is not dequeued before it expires.

2. The number of dequeue attempts exceeds the *max_retries* specified for the queue.

The following block illustrates the latter case.

```
-- Available online as except.sql
DECLARE
  v_Message MessageObj;
  v_EnqueueOptions DBMS_AQ.ENQUEUE_OPTIONS_T;
  v_DequeueOptions DBMS_AQ.DEQUEUE_OPTIONS_T;
  v_MessageProperties DBMS_AQ.MESSAGE_PROPERTIES_T;
  v_MsgID RAW(16);
  v_NormalCount INTEGER;
  v_ExceptionCount INTEGER;

  c_NumMessages CONSTANT INTEGER := 3;

  e_QTimeOut EXCEPTION;
  PRAGMA EXCEPTION_INIT(e_QTimeOut, -25228);
BEGIN
  -- Enqueue 3 messages with the exception queue set.
  FOR v_Counter IN 1..c_NumMessages LOOP
    -- Create a message to enqueue.
    v_Message :=
      MessageObj('Message ' || v_Counter, v_Counter * 10,
                 'abcdefghijklmnopqrstuvwxyz', SYSDATE + v_Counter);
```

```
  -- Enqueue it.
  v_MessageProperties.exception_queue := 'ExceptionQ';
  DBMS_AQ.ENQUEUE(
    queue_name => 'SimpleQ',
    enqueue_options => v_EnqueueOptions,
    message_properties => v_MessageProperties,
    payload => v_Message,
    msgid => v_MsgID);
END LOOP;

-- Commit all the enqueues.
COMMIT;

-- Verify that there are three messages in the normal queue, and
-- none in the exception queue.
SELECT COUNT(*)
  INTO v_NormalCount
  FROM aq$SimpleQTab
  WHERE queue = UPPER('Simpleq');
SELECT COUNT(*)
  INTO v_ExceptionCount
  FROM aq$SimpleQTab
  WHERE queue = UPPER('ExceptionQ');
DBMS_OUTPUT.PUT('After initial enqueues, count(simple) = ' ||
                v_NormalCount);
DBMS_OUTPUT.PUT_LINE(', count(exception) = ' || v_ExceptionCount);

-- Dequeue the first message, then rollback. This will rollback the
-- dequeue, and increase the attempts field in the message
-- properties. Since the max_retries for SimpleQ is 0, this will
-- move the message to the exception queue.
v_DequeueOptions.wait := 1;
DBMS_AQ.DEQUEUE(
  queue_name => 'SimpleQ',
  dequeue_options => v_DequeueOptions,
  message_properties => v_MessageProperties,
  payload => v_Message,
  msgid => v_MsgID);

ROLLBACK;

-- Verify that there are two messages in the normal queue, and one
-- in the exception queue.
SELECT COUNT(*)
  INTO v_NormalCount
```

```
    FROM aq$SimpleQTab
    WHERE queue = UPPER('Simpleq');
  SELECT COUNT(*)
    INTO v_ExceptionCount
    FROM aq$SimpleQTab
    WHERE queue = UPPER('ExceptionQ');
  DBMS_OUTPUT.PUT('After dequeue and rollback, count(simple) = ' ||
                  v_NormalCount);
  DBMS_OUTPUT.PUT_LINE(', count(exception) = ' || v_ExceptionCount);

  -- Now we can get the message from the exception queue. Note that
  -- we have to use the message ID, since the state of this message is
  -- EXPIRED, and the dequeue will not normally return any messages
  -- with a state other than READY.
  v_DequeueOptions.msgid := v_MsgID;
  DBMS_AQ.DEQUEUE(
    queue_name => 'ExceptionQ',
    dequeue_options => v_DequeueOptions,
    message_properties => v_MessageProperties,
    payload => v_Message,
    msgid => v_MsgID);
  v_Message.Print('After exception dequeuing');

  -- Verify that there are two messages in the normal queue, and none
  -- in the exception queue.
  SELECT COUNT(*)
    INTO v_NormalCount
    FROM aq$SimpleQTab
    WHERE queue = UPPER('Simpleq');
  SELECT COUNT(*)
    INTO v_ExceptionCount
    FROM aq$SimpleQTab
    WHERE queue = UPPER('ExceptionQ');
  DBMS_OUTPUT.PUT('After exception dequeue, count(simple) = ' ||
                  v_NormalCount);
  DBMS_OUTPUT.PUT_LINE(', count(exception) = ' ||
v_ExceptionCount);

  -- Clear the queue, and commit.
  ClearQueue('SimpleQ');
  COMMIT;
END;
```

Dropping Queues

The following script will stop all of the queues, drop them, and drop their containing queue tables.

```
-- Available online as dropq.sql
BEGIN
  DBMS_AQADM.STOP_QUEUE('SimpleQ');
  DBMS_AQADM.DROP_QUEUE('SimpleQ');
  DBMS_AQADM.STOP_QUEUE('ExceptionQ');
  DBMS_AQADM.DROP_QUEUE('ExceptionQ');
  DBMS_AQADM.DROP_QUEUE_TABLE('SimpleQTab');
END;

BEGIN
  DBMS_AQADM.STOP_QUEUE('PriorityQ');
  DBMS_AQADM.DROP_QUEUE('PriorityQ');
  DBMS_AQADM.DROP_QUEUE_TABLE('PriorityQTab');
END;

DROP TYPE MessageObj;
```

Summary

In this chapter, we have examined the Oracle Advanced Queuing system. This robust implementation provides a queuing system built into the database, rather than with a separate product. Thus, all of the advantages of Oracle are supplied for Advanced Queuing. We have discussed the operations necessary for the use and administration of queues, with their supporting PL/SQL packages. In the next chapter, we will examine additional DBMS packages available with Oracle: DBMS_JOB and UTL_FILE.

CHAPTER
18

Database Jobs
and File I/O

long with the other DBMS packages that we've seen so far, PL/SQL provides DBMS_JOB and UTL_FILE. The DBMS_JOB package, available with PL/SQL 2.2 and higher, allows stored procedures to be run periodically by the system, without user intervention. The UTL_FILE package, available with PL/SQL 2.3 and higher, adds the ability to read and write to operating system files. These packages extend PL/SQL and provide functions that are available with other third-generation languages.

Database Jobs

With PL/SQL 2.2 and higher, you can schedule PL/SQL routines to run at specified times. This is done with the DBMS_JOB package, which implements *job queues*. A job is run by submitting it to a job queue, along with parameters specifying how often the job should be run. Information about currently executing jobs, and the success or failure of previously submitted jobs, is available in the data dictionary. For more information about database jobs, see the *Server Administrator's Guide*, release 7.2 or later.

Oracle Advanced Queuing, available with PL/SQL 8.0 and described in Chapter 17, enhances the queuing capabilities of PL/SQL well beyond what DBMS_JOB provides.

Background Processes

An Oracle instance is made up of various processes running on the system. Different processes are in charge of running different aspects of the database, such as reading database blocks into memory, writing blocks back to disk, and archiving data to offline storage. These processes are described in Chapter 22. In addition to the processes that manage the database, there are processes known as the SNP processes. SNP processes implement database snapshots, and also job queues.

SNP processes run in the background, like other database processes. Unlike other database processes, however, if an SNP process fails, Oracle restarts it without affecting the rest of the database. If other database processes fail, this generally brings down the database. Periodically, an SNP process will wake up and check for a job. If a job is due to be run, the SNP process will execute it and then go back to sleep. A given process can be running only one job at a time. In Oracle7, there can be a maximum of ten SNP processes (numbered SNP0 through SNP9), so a maximum of ten database jobs can be running simultaneously. In Oracle8, this limit has been increased to 36 SNP processes, SNP0 through SNP9 and SNPA through SNPZ.

Three parameters in the INIT.ORA initialization file control the behavior of the SNP processes. They are described in Table 18-1. Note that if JOB_QUEUE_PROCESSES is set to zero, no jobs will be executed. Since each process will sleep for JOB_QUEUE_INTERVAL seconds before checking for new jobs, JOB_QUEUE_INTERVAL specifies the minimum amount of time between job executions.

Parameter	Default Value	Range of Values	Description
JOB_QUEUE_PROCESSES	0	0..10	How many processes to start.
JOB_QUEUE_INTERVAL	60	1..3600	Interval between wake-ups of the process. The process will sleep for the specified number of seconds before checking for a new job.
JOB_QUEUE_KEEP_ CONNECTIONS	FALSE	TRUE, FALSE	Controls whether an SNP process closes any remote database connections it makes. If TRUE, then all connections will be kept until the process is shut down. If FALSE, then the connections are kept only as long as there are jobs to execute.

TABLE 18-1.   *Job Initialization Parameters*

Running a Job

There are two ways of running a job—submitting it to a job queue, or forcing it to run immediately. When a job is submitted to a job queue, an SNP process will run it when it is scheduled. If specified, this job can then be run automatically thereafter. If a job is run immediately, it is run only once.

SUBMIT

A job is submitted to the job queue with the SUBMIT procedure. SUBMIT is defined as

```
PROCEDURE SUBMIT(job OUT BINARY_INTEGER,
                 what IN VARCHAR2,
                 next_date IN DATE DEFAULT SYSDATE,
                 interval IN VARCHAR2 DEFAULT NULL,
                 no_parse IN BOOLEAN DEFAULT FALSE);
```

The parameters for SUBMIT are described in the following table:

Parameter	Type	Description
job	BINARY_INTEGER	Job number. When the job is created, a number is assigned to it. As long as the job exists, its job number will remain the same. Job numbers are unique across an instance.
what	VARCHAR2	PL/SQL code that makes up the job. Typically, this is a call to a stored procedure.
next_date	DATE	Date when the job will next run.
interval	VARCHAR2	Function that calculates the time at which the job will run again.
no_parse	BOOLEAN	If TRUE, the job code will not be parsed until the first time it is executed. If FALSE (the default), the job code is parsed when it is submitted. This is useful if the database objects referenced by the job do not yet exist, but you still want to submit it.

For example, suppose we create a procedure **TempInsert** with:

```
-- Available online as tmpins.sql
CREATE SEQUENCE temp_seq
  START WITH 1
  INCREMENT BY 1;

CREATE OR REPLACE PROCEDURE TempInsert AS
BEGIN
  INSERT INTO temp_table (num_col, char_col)
    VALUES (temp_seq.nextval, TO_CHAR(SYSDATE,
            'DD-MON-YY HH24:MI:SS'));
  COMMIT;
END TempInsert;
```

We can have **TempInsert** run every 10 seconds with the following SQL*Plus script:

```
-- Available online as part of tmpins.sql
SQL> VARIABLE v_JobNum NUMBER
SQL> BEGIN
  2     DBMS_JOB.SUBMIT(:v_JobNum, 'TempInsert;', SYSDATE,
  3                     'sysdate + (10/(24*60*60))');
  4  END;
  5  /

PL/SQL procedure successfully completed.
SQL> print v_JobNum


  V_JOBNUM
---------
        2
```

JOB NUMBERS   The job number is assigned to the job when it is first submitted. Job numbers are generated from the sequence SYS.JOBSEQ. Once a job number is assigned to a job, it will never change unless the job is removed and then resubmitted.

CAUTION
Jobs can be exported and imported, like other database objects. This does not change the job number. If you try to import a job whose number already exists, you will receive an error and the job cannot be imported. In this case, simply resubmit the job, which will generate a new job number.

JOB DEFINITIONS The *what* parameter specifies the code for the job. Jobs generally consist of stored procedures, and *what* should be a string that calls the procedure. This procedure can have any number of parameters. All parameters should be IN parameters, since there aren't any actual parameters that could receive the value of an OUT or IN OUT formal parameter. The only exceptions to this rule are the special identifiers *next_date* and *broken*, described next.

CAUTION
Once the job is submitted, it will be run by one of the SNP processes in the background. In order to see the results, be sure to code a COMMIT at the end of the job procedure.

There are three special identifiers that are valid in a job definition, listed in Table 18-2. *job* is an IN parameter, so the job can only read this value. *next_date* and *broken* are IN OUT parameters, so the job itself can modify them. If we modify **TempInsert** as follows

```
-- Available online as tmpins1.sql
CREATE OR REPLACE PROCEDURE TempInsert
  (p_NextDate IN OUT DATE) AS
  v_SeqNum    NUMBER;
  v_StartNum NUMBER;
  v_SQLCode NUMBER;
  v_Errmsg  VARCHAR2(60);
BEGIN
  SELECT temp_seq.nextval
    INTO v_SeqNum
    FROM dual;
  -- See if this is the first time we're called
  BEGIN
    SELECT num_col
      INTO v_StartNum
      FROM temp_table
      WHERE char_col = 'TempInsert Start';

    -- We've been called before, so insert a new value
    INSERT INTO temp_table (num_col, char_col)
      VALUES (v_SeqNum, TO_CHAR(SYSDATE, 'DD-MON-YY HH24:MI:SS'));
  EXCEPTION
```

```
    WHEN NO_DATA_FOUND THEN
      -- First time we're called, so insert
      INSERT INTO temp_table (num_col, char_col)
        VALUES (v_SeqNum, 'TempInsert Start');
  END;

  -- If we've been called more than 15 times, exit.
  IF v_SeqNum - V_StartNum > 15 THEN
    p_NextDate := NULL;
  END IF;

  COMMIT;
END TempInsert;
```

and submit it with

```
BEGIN
  DBMS_JOB.SUBMIT(:v_JobNum, 'TempInsert(next_date);', sysdate,
              'sysdate + (5/(24*60*60))');
END;
```

then the job will automatically remove itself from the job queue (by setting **p_NextDate** to NULL) when the sequence number is greater than 15. Because the job can return the value of *next_date* and *broken*, a job can remove itself from the queue when desired.

The *what* parameter is a VARCHAR2 character string. As a result, any character literals that should be used in the call to the job procedure should be delimited by two single quotes. The procedure call should also be

Identifier	Type	Description
job	BINARY_INTEGER	Evaluates to the number of the current job.
next_date	DATE	Evaluates to the date when the job will next run.
broken	BOOLEAN	Evaluates to the job status—TRUE if the job is broken, FALSE otherwise.

TABLE 18-2. *Job Control Identifiers*

terminated with a semicolon. For example, we could call **Register** with the following *what* string:

```
'Register(10006, ''MUS'', 410);'
```

EXECUTION INTERVALS   The first time the job will be run after the SUBMIT call is given by the *next_date* parameter. Just before the job itself is executed, the function given by *interval* is evaluated. If the job is successful, the result returned by *interval* becomes the new *next_date*. If the job is successful and *interval* evaluates to NULL, the job is deleted from the queue. The expression given by *interval* is passed as a character string, but should evaluate to a date. Some common expressions and their effects are described here:

Interval Value	Result
'SYSDATE + 7'	Exactly seven days from the last execution. If the job is initially submitted on Tuesday, then the next run will be the following Tuesday. If the second run fails, and it then runs successfully on Wednesday, subsequent runs will be on Wednesdays.
'NEXT_DAY(TRUNC(SYSDATE), ''FRIDAY'') + 12	Every Friday at noon. Note the use of the two single quotes around the literal 'FRIDAY' within the string.
SYSDATE + 1/24	Every hour.

RUN
The DBMS_JOB.RUN procedure will run a job immediately. It is defined with

```
RUN(job IN BINARY_INTEGER);
```

The job must already have been created by calling SUBMIT. Regardless of the current status of the job, it is run immediately by the current process. Note that the job is *not* run by an SNP background process.

Broken Jobs

Oracle will automatically attempt to run a job again if it fails. The job will be run again starting one minute after the first failure. If that attempt also fails, the next attempt is two minutes later. The interval doubles each time, to four minutes, then to eight, and so on. If the retry interval exceeds the execution interval specified for the job, the execution interval is used. Once the job fails 16 times, it is marked as broken. Broken jobs will not be run again automatically.

You can run a broken job with RUN, however. If that call succeeds, then the failure count is reset to zero and the job is marked as not broken. The BROKEN procedure can also be used to change the status of a job. It is defined with

```
BROKEN(job IN BINARY_INTEGER,
       broken IN BOOLEAN,
       next_date IN DATE DEFAULT SYSDATE);
```

The parameters are described here:

Parameter	Type	Description
job	BINARY_INTEGER	Job number of the job whose status will be changed.
broken	BOOLEAN	New status of the job. If TRUE, the job is marked as broken. If FALSE, the job is marked as not broken and will be run next at the time specified by **next_date**.
next_date	DATE	Date at which the job will be run next. Defaults to SYSDATE.

Removing a Job

A job can be removed from a job queue explicitly with the REMOVE procedure,

```
REMOVE(job IN BINARY_INTEGER);
```

where the only parameter is the job number. If the *next_date* for a job evaluates to NULL (either because the job has set it or *interval* evaluates to NULL), then the job will be removed after it has finished executing. If the job is currently running when REMOVE is called, it will be removed from the queue after it has finished.

Altering a Job

The parameters for a job can be altered after the job has been submitted. This is done using one of the following procedures:

```
PROCEDURE CHANGE(job IN  BINARY_INTEGER,
                 what IN  VARCHAR2,
                 next_date IN  DATE,
                 interval  IN  VARCHAR2);
PROCEDURE WHAT(job IN  BINARY_INTEGER,
              what IN  VARCHAR2);
PROCEDURE NEXT_DATE(job IN  BINARY_INTEGER,
                   next_date IN  DATE);
PROCEDURE INTERVAL(job IN  BINARY_INTEGER,
                  interval  IN  VARCHAR2);
```

The CHANGE procedure is used to alter more than one job characteristic at once, and the WHAT, NEXT_DATE, and INTERVAL procedures are used to change the characteristic identified by their respective arguments.

All the arguments behave the same as they do in the SUBMIT procedure. If you change *what* using CHANGE or WHAT, then the current environment becomes the new execution environment for the job. For more information on job environments, see the section "Job Execution Environments," which follows shortly.

Viewing Jobs in the Data Dictionary

Several data dictionary views record information about jobs. **dba_jobs** and **user_jobs** return information about a job, such as *what*, *next_date*, and *interval*. Information about the execution environment is also included. The **dba_jobs_running** view describes the jobs that are currently running. These views are described in Appendix D.

Job Execution Environments

When you submit a job to a queue, the current environment is recorded. This includes the settings of NLS parameters such as NLS_DATE_FORMAT. The settings recorded at job creation will be used whenever the job is run. These settings will be changed if the *what* characteristic is changed using CHANGE or WHAT.

> **NOTE**
> *A job can change its environment by issuing the ALTER SESSION command through the DBMS_SQL package. If this is done, it will only affect the current execution of the job, not future executions. The DBMS_SQL package is described in Chapter 15.*

File I/O

PL/SQL 2.3 ...and HIGHER As we have seen, PL/SQL does not have input and output capability built into the language itself, but does have this functionality through supplied packages. I/O to the screen has been implemented with the DBMS_OUTPUT package, described in Chapter 14. PL/SQL 2.3 extends I/O to text files, with the UTL_FILE package. There is no way to output directly to a binary file with this version of UTL_FILE. This restriction will likely be lifted in future versions of PL/SQL.

PL/SQL 8.0 ...and HIGHER Oracle8 allows binary files to be read by using BFILEs, which are a special form of external LOBs. BFILEs are discussed, along with the other LOB types, in Chapter 21.

This section describes how UTL_FILE works. Three complete examples at the end of the section demonstrate the package.

Security

Client-side PL/SQL has a package similar to UTL_FILE, known as TEXT_IO. There are different security issues on the client than on the server, however. Files created with the client-side TEXT_IO package can be placed anywhere on the client, subject to operating system privileges. There are no privileges associated with PL/SQL or the database itself for client-side file I/O.

Database Security

On the server, a more rigorous security mechanism is needed. This is implemented by restricting the directories into which the package can write. *Accessible directories* are the directories into which UTL_FILE can write. They are defined by the UTL_FILE_DIR parameter in the INIT.ORA initialization file. Each accessible directory is indicated by a line such as

    UTL_FILE_DIR = *directory_name*

in the initialization file. The specification of *directory_name* will vary, depending on the operating system. If the operating system is case sensitive, then *directory_name* is case sensitive. For example, the following entries in INIT.ORA are legal for a Unix system, assuming that the directories specified actually exist:

```
UTL_FILE_DIR = /tmp
UTL_FILE_DIR = /home/oracle/output_files
```

In order to access a file with UTL_FILE, the directory name and the filename are passed as separate parameters to the FOPEN function. The directory name is compared against the accessible files list. If it is found, then the operation is allowed. If the directory name specified by FOPEN is not accessible, an error is returned. Subdirectories of accessible directories are not allowed, unless the subdirectory is also listed explicitly as accessible. Given the preceding accessible directories, Table 18-3 describes legal and illegal directory/filename pairs.

NOTE
Even if the operating system is not case sensitive, the comparison between the specified directory and the accessible directories is always case sensitive.

If the INIT.ORA file contains

```
UTL_FILE_DIR = *
```

then database permissions are disabled. This makes all directories accessible to UTL_FILE.

Directory Name	Filename	Comment
/tmp	myfile.out	Legal
/home/oracle/output_files	students.list	Legal
/tmp/1995	january.results	Illegal—subdirectory /tmp/1995 is not accessible
/home/oracle	output_files/classes.list	Illegal—subdirectory passed as part of the filename
/TMP	myfile.out	Illegal—case different

TABLE 18-3. *Legal and Illegal File Specifications*

CAUTION
Turning off database permissions should be used very carefully. Oracle does not recommend that you use this option in production systems, since it can circumvent operating system permissions. In addition, do not use "." (the current directory on Unix systems) as part of the accessible directories list. Always use explicit directory paths.

Operating System Security

The file I/O operations that are performed by UTL_FILE will be done as the Oracle user. (The Oracle user is the owner of the files that are used to run the database, and also the owner of the processes that make up a database instance.) Consequently, the Oracle user has to have operating system privileges to read from and write to all of the accessible directories. If the Oracle user does not have privileges for an accessible directory, then any operations in that directory will be prohibited by the operating system.

Any files created by UTL_FILE will be owned by the Oracle user and created with the default operating system privileges for the Oracle user. If it is necessary for other users to access these files outside of UTL_FILE, then the system administrator should change the permissions on the files.

WARNING
It is also good security practice to prohibit write operations on directories in the accessible directory list. The only user who should be given write permission on accessible directories should be the Oracle user. If users are allowed write permission, they can create symbolic links to other directories, and thus circumvent operating system privilege checking.

Exceptions Raised by UTL_FILE

If a procedure or function in UTL_FILE encounters an error, it will raise an exception. The possible exceptions are listed in Table 18-4. Note that these exceptions include seven that are defined in UTL_FILE, and two predefined exceptions (NO_DATA_FOUND and VALUE_ERROR). The UTL_FILE exceptions can be caught by name or by an OTHERS exception handler. The predefined exceptions can be identified by their SQLCODE values as well.

Opening and Closing Files

All of the operations in UTL_FILE use a file handle. The *file handle* is a value that you use in PL/SQL to identify the file, similar to the cursor ID in DBMS_SQL. All file handles have the type UTL_FILE.FILE_TYPE. FILE_TYPE is defined in the specification of UTL_FILE. File handles are returned by FOPEN.

FOPEN

FOPEN opens a file for input or output. A given file can be opened for input only or output only at any time. A file can't be used for both input and output simultaneously. FOPEN is defined with

```
FUNCTION FOPEN(location IN VARCHAR2,
              filename IN VARCHAR2,
              open_mode IN VARCHAR2)
    RETURN FILE_TYPE;
```

Exception	Raised When	Raised By
INVALID_PATH	Directory or filename is invalid or not accessible.	FOPEN
INVALID_MODE	Invalid string specified for file mode.	FOPEN
INVALID_FILEHANDLE	File handle does not specify an open file.	FCLOSE, GET_LINE, PUT, PUT_LINE, NEW_LINE, PUTF, FFLUSH
INVALID_OPERATION	File could not be opened as requested, perhaps because of operating system permissions. Also raised when attempting a write operation on a file opened for read, or a read operation on a file opened for write.	GET_LINE, PUT, PUT_LINE, NEW_LINE, PUTF, FFLUSH
READ_ERROR	Operating system error occurred during a read operation.	GET_LINE
WRITE_ERROR	Operating system error occurred during a write operation.	PUT, PUT_LINE, NEW_LINE, FFLUSH, FCLOSE, FCLOSE_ALL
INTERNAL_ERROR	Unspecified internal error.	All functions
NO_DATA_FOUND	End of file reached during a read.	GET_LINE
VALUE_ERROR	Input line too large for buffer specified in GET_LINE.	GET_LINE

TABLE 18-4.   *Exceptions Raised by UTL_FILE*

The directory path specified must already exist—FOPEN will not create it. It will, however, overwrite an existing file if the mode is 'w'. The parameters and return value for FOPEN are described in the following table. FOPEN can raise any of the following exceptions:

- UTL_FILE.INVALID_PATH

- UTL_FILE.INVALID_MODE

- UTL_FILE.INVALID_OPERATION

- UTL_FILE.INTERNAL_ERROR

Parameter	Type	Description
location	VARCHAR2	Directory path where the file is located. If this directory is not in the accessible directories list, UTL_FILE.INVALID_PATH is raised.
filename	VARCHAR2	Name of the file to be opened. If the mode is 'w', any existing file is overwritten.
open_mode	VARCHAR2	Mode to be used. Valid values are 'r' : Read text 'w': Write text 'a': Append text This parameter is not case sensitive. If 'a' is specified and the file does not exist, it is created with 'w' mode.
return value	UTL_FILE.FILE_TYPE	File handle to be used in subsequent functions.

FCLOSE

When you are finished reading from or writing to a file, it should be closed with FCLOSE. This frees the resources used by UTL_FILE to operate on the file. FLCOSE is defined with

PROCEDURE FCLOSE(*file_handle* IN OUT FILE_TYPE);

where the only parameter is the file handle. Any pending changes that have yet to be written to the file are done before the file is closed. If there is an error while writing, UTL_FILE.WRITE_ERROR is raised. If the file handle does not point to a valid open file, UTL_FILE.INVALID_FILEHANDLE is raised.

IS_OPEN

This boolean function returns TRUE if the specified file is open, FALSE if not. IS_OPEN is defined as

FUNCTION IS_OPEN(*file_handle* IN FILE_TYPE)
  RETURN BOOLEAN;

There could still be operating system errors if the file is used, even if IS_OPEN returns TRUE.

FCLOSE_ALL

FCLOSE_ALL will close all open files. It is meant to be used for cleanup, especially in an error handler. The procedure is defined as

PROCEDURE FCLOSE_ALL;

and does not take any parameters. Any pending changes will be flushed before the files are closed. Because of this, FCLOSE_ALL can raise UTL_FILE.WRITE_ERROR if an error occurs during the write operation.

CAUTION
FCLOSE_ALL will close the files and free the resources used by UTL_FILE. However, it does not mark the files as closed—IS_OPEN will still return TRUE after an FCLOSE_ALL. Any read or write operations on files after FCLOSE_ALL will fail unless the file is reopened with FOPEN.

File Output

Five procedures are used to output data to a file: PUT, PUT_LINE, NEW_LINE, PUTF, and FFLUSH. PUT, PUT_LINE, and NEW_LINE behave very much like their counterparts in the DBMS_OUTPUT package, discussed in Chapter 14. The maximum size for an output record is 1,023 bytes.

PUT

PUT will output the specified string to the specified file. The file should have been opened for write operations. PUT is defined with

```
PROCEDURE PUT(file_handle IN FILE_TYPE,
             buffer IN VARCHAR2);
```

PUT will not append a newline character in the file. You must use PUT_LINE or NEW_LINE to include the line terminator in the file. If there is an operating system error during the write operation, UTL_FILE.WRITE_ERROR is raised. The parameters for PUT are described here:

Parameter	Type	Description
file_handle	UTL_FILE.FILE_TYPE	File handle returned by FOPEN. If this is not a valid handle, then UTL_FILE.INVALID_FILEHANDLE is raised.
buffer	VARCHAR2	Text string to be output to the file. If the file was not opened in 'w' or 'a' mode, UTL_FILE.INVALID_OPERATION is raised.

NEW_LINE

NEW_LINE writes one or more line terminators to the specified file. It is defined with

```
PROCEDURE NEW_LINE(file_handle IN FILE_TYPE,
                  lines IN NATURAL := 1);
```

The line terminator is system dependent—different operating systems will use different terminators. If there is an operating system error during the write, UTL_FILE.WRITE_ERROR is raised. The parameters for NEW_LINE are described here:

Parameter	Type	Description
file_handle	UTL_FILE.FILE_TYPE	File handle returned by FOPEN. If this is not valid, UTL_FILE.INVALID_ FILEHANDLE is raised.
lines	NATURAL	Number of line terminators to output. The default value is 1, which outputs a single newline. If the file was not opened in 'w' or 'a' mode, UTL_FILE.INVALID_OPERATION is raised.

PUT_LINE

PUT_LINE outputs the specified string to the specified file, which must have been opened for write operations. After the string is output, the platform-specific newline character is output. PUT_LINE is defined with

PROCEDURE PUT_LINE(*file_handle* IN FILE_TYPE,
                   buffer IN VARCHAR2);

The parameters for PUT_LINE are described in the following table. Calling PUT_LINE is equivalent to calling PUT followed by NEW_LINE to output the newline. If there is an operating system error during the write, UTL_FILE.WRITE_ERROR is raised.

Parameter	Type	Description
file_handle	UTL_FILE.FILE_TYPE	File handle returned by FOPEN. If this is not a valid handle, UTL_FILE.INVALID_FILEHANDLE is raised.
buffer	VARCHAR2	Text string to be output to the file. If the file was not opened in 'w' or 'a' mode, UTL_FILE.INVALID_ OPERATION is raised.

PUTF

PUTF is similar to PUT, but it allows the output string to be formatted.
PUTF is a limited version of the C function *printf()* and has syntax similar to
printf(). PUTF is defined with

```
PROCEDURE PUTF(file_handle IN FILE_TYPE,
              format IN VARCHAR2,
              arg1 IN VARCHAR2 DEFAULT NULL,
              arg2 IN VARCHAR2 DEFAULT NULL,
              arg3 IN VARCHAR2 DEFAULT NULL,
              arg4 IN VARCHAR2 DEFAULT NULL,
              arg5 IN VARCHAR2 DEFAULT NULL);
```

The format string contains regular text, along with two special
characters %s and \n. Each occurrence of %s in the format string is
replaced with one of the optional arguments. Each occurrence of \n is
replaced by a newline character. The parameters are described in the table
after the example. As with PUT and PUT_LINE, if there is an operating
system error during the write, UTL_FILE.WRITE_ERROR is raised.

For example, if we were to execute the block

```
DECLARE
   v_OutputFile UTL_FILE.FILE_TYPE;
   v_Name VARCHAR2(10) := 'Scott';
BEGIN
   v_OutputFile := UTL_FILE.FOPEN(...);
   UTL_FILE.PUTF(v_OutputFile,
      'Hi there!\nMy name is %s, and I am a %s major.\n',
      v_Name, 'Computer Science');
   FCLOSE(v_OutputFile);
END;
```

the output file would contain the lines

```
Hi There!
My name is Scott, and I am a Computer Science major.
```

Parameter	Type	Description
file_handle	UTL_FILE.FILE_TYPE	File handle returned by FOPEN. If this is not a valid handle, UTL_FILE.INVALID_FILEHANDLE is raised.

```
END Debug;

CREATE OR REPLACE PACKAGE BODY Debug AS
  v_DebugHandle UTL_FILE.FILE_TYPE;

  PROCEDURE Debug(p_Description IN VARCHAR2,
                  p_Value IN VARCHAR2) IS
  BEGIN
    /* Output the info, and flush the file. */
    UTL_FILE.PUTF(v_DebugHandle, '%s: %s\n',
                  p_Description, p_Value);
    UTL_FILE.FFLUSH(v_DebugHandle);
  EXCEPTION
    WHEN UTL_FILE.INVALID_OPERATION THEN
      RAISE_APPLICATION_ERROR(-20102,
                              'Debug: Invalid Operation');
    WHEN UTL_FILE.INVALID_FILEHANDLE THEN
      RAISE_APPLICATION_ERROR(-20103,
                              'Debug: Invalid File Handle');
    WHEN UTL_FILE.WRITE_ERROR THEN
      RAISE_APPLICATION_ERROR(-20104,
                              'Debug: Write Error');
  END Debug;

  PROCEDURE Reset(p_NewFile IN VARCHAR2 := v_DebugFile,
                  p_NewDir IN VARCHAR2 := v_DebugDir) IS
  BEGIN

    /* Make sure the file is closed first. */
    IF UTL_FILE.IS_OPEN(v_DebugHandle) THEN
      UTL_FILE.FCLOSE(v_DebugHandle);
    END IF;

    /* Open the file for writing. */
    v_DebugHandle := UTL_FILE.FOPEN(p_NewDir, p_NewFile, 'w');

    /* Set the packaged variables to the values just passed in. */
    v_DebugFile := p_NewFile;
    v_DebugDir := p_NewDir;
  EXCEPTION
    WHEN UTL_FILE.INVALID_PATH THEN
      RAISE_APPLICATION_ERROR(-20100, 'Reset: Invalid Path');
    WHEN UTL_FILE.INVALID_MODE THEN
      RAISE_APPLICATION_ERROR(-20101, 'Reset: Invalid Mode');
    WHEN UTL_FILE.INVALID_OPERATION THEN
```

```
      RAISE_APPLICATION_ERROR(-20101, 'Reset: Invalid Operation');
   END Reset;

   PROCEDURE Close IS
   BEGIN
     UTL_FILE.FCLOSE(v_DebugHandle);
   END Close;

BEGIN
  v_DebugDir := '/tmp';
  v_DebugFile := 'debug.out';
  Reset;
END Debug;
```

This version of Debug behaves the same as the other versions we have examined in Chapters 13 and 14, with some minor changes. **Debug.Reset** takes the name and location of the debug file as parameters—if they are not specified, the output file defaults to /tmp/debug.out. All debugging statements will add a line to this file. We've also added a new procedure, **Debug.Close**. This procedure should be called to close the debugging file. Although **Debug.Debug** flushes the output file, the file should still be closed to free the resources associated with it.

TIP
Note the exception handlers for the various routines. They identify which errors were actually raised, and by which procedures. This is a good technique to follow when using UTL_FILE. Otherwise, you would have to trap errors with a WHEN OTHERS handler.

Student Loader

The **LoadStudents** procedure will insert into **students** based on the contents of the file that is passed to it. The file is comma delimited, which means that each record is contained on one line, with commas used to separate the fields. This is a common format for text files. **LoadStudents** is created with:

 -- Available online as loadstud.sql
```
CREATE OR REPLACE PROCEDURE LoadStudents (
```

```
/* Loads the students table by reading a comma-delimited file.
   The file should have lines that look like:

   first_name,last_name,major

   The student ID is generated from student_sequence.
   The total number of rows inserted is returned by
   p_TotalInserted. */
p_FileDir  IN VARCHAR2,
p_FileName IN VARCHAR2,
p_TotalInserted IN OUT NUMBER) AS

v_FileHandle UTL_FILE.FILE_TYPE;
v_NewLine  VARCHAR2(100);  -- Input line
v_FirstName students.first_name%TYPE;
v_LastName students.last_name%TYPE;
v_Major students.major%TYPE;
/* Positions of commas within input line. */
v_FirstComma NUMBER;
v_SecondComma NUMBER;

BEGIN
  -- Open the specified file for reading.
  v_FileHandle := UTL_FILE.FOPEN(p_FileDir, p_FileName, 'r');

  -- Initialize the output number of students.
  p_TotalInserted := 0;

  -- Loop over the file, reading in each line. GET_LINE will
  -- raise NO_DATA_FOUND when it is done, so we use that as the
  -- exit condition for the loop.
  LOOP
    BEGIN
      UTL_FILE.GET_LINE(v_FileHandle, v_NewLine);
    EXCEPTION
      WHEN NO_DATA_FOUND THEN
        EXIT;
    END;

    -- Each field in the input record is delimited by commas. We
    -- need to find the locations of the two commas in the line
    -- and use these locations to get the fields from v_NewLine.
    -- Use INSTR to find the locations of the commas.
    v_FirstComma := INSTR(v_NewLine, ',', 1, 1);
    v_SecondComma := INSTR(v_NewLine, ',', 1, 2);
```

```
      -- Now we can use SUBSTR to extract the fields.
      v_FirstName := SUBSTR(v_NewLine, 1, v_FirstComma - 1);
      v_LastName := SUBSTR(v_NewLine, v_FirstComma + 1,
                          v_SecondComma - v_FirstComma - 1);
      v_Major := SUBSTR(v_NewLine, v_SecondComma + 1);

      -- Insert the new record into students.
      INSERT INTO students (ID, first_name, last_name, major)
        VALUES (student_sequence.nextval, v_FirstName,
                v_LastName, v_Major);

      p_TotalInserted := p_TotalInserted + 1;
   END LOOP;

   -- Close the file.
   UTL_FILE.FCLOSE(v_FileHandle);

   COMMIT;
EXCEPTION
   -- Handle the UTL_FILE exceptions meaningfully, and make sure
   -- that the file is properly closed.
   WHEN UTL_FILE.INVALID_OPERATION THEN
     UTL_FILE.FCLOSE(v_FileHandle);
     RAISE_APPLICATION_ERROR(-20051,
                             'LoadStudents: Invalid Operation');
   WHEN UTL_FILE.INVALID_FILEHANDLE THEN
     UTL_FILE.FCLOSE(v_FileHandle);
     RAISE_APPLICATION_ERROR(-20052,
                             'LoadStudents: Invalid File Handle');
   WHEN UTL_FILE.READ_ERROR THEN
     UTL_FILE.FCLOSE(v_FileHandle);
     RAISE_APPLICATION_ERROR(-20053,
                             'LoadStudents: Read Error');
   WHEN OTHERS THEN
     UTL_FILE.FCLOSE(v_FileHandle);
     RAISE;
END LoadStudents;
```

A sample input file for **LoadStudents** could look like:

```
Scott,Smith,Computer Science
Margaret,Mason,History
Joanne,Junebug,Computer Science
Manish,Murgratroid,Economics
```

```
Patrick,Poll,History
Timothy,Taller,History
Barbara,Blues,Economics
David,Dinsmore,Music
Ester,Elegant,Nutrition
Rose,Riznit,Music
Rita,Razmataz,Nutrition
```

NOTE

LoadStudents uses the **student_sequence** sequence number to determine the student ID. If this sequence has not been initialized, it could return a value which is already in **students**. In this case, the primary key constraint for **students** would be violated.

Printing Transcripts

We first saw **PrintTranscript** in Chapter 13. Now that we know how to use UTL_FILE, we can complete the procedure. We first need the **Calculate GPA** procedure:

```
-- Available online as calcGPA.sql
CREATE OR REPLACE PROCEDURE CalculateGPA (
  /* Returns the grade point average for the student identified
     by p_StudentID in p_GPA. */
  p_StudentID IN students.ID%TYPE,
  p_GPA OUT NUMBER) AS

  CURSOR c_ClassDetails IS
    SELECT classes.num_credits, rs.grade
      FROM classes, registered_students rs
      WHERE classes.department = rs.department
      AND classes.course = rs.course
      AND rs.student_id = p_StudentID;

  v_NumericGrade NUMBER;
  v_TotalCredits NUMBER := 0;
  v_TotalGrade NUMBER := 0;

BEGIN
  FOR v_ClassRecord in c_ClassDetails LOOP
    -- Determine the numeric value for the grade.
```

```
     SELECT DECODE(v_ClassRecord.grade, 'A', 4,
                                         'B', 3,
                                         'C', 2,
                                         'D', 1,
                                         'E', 0)
       INTO v_NumericGrade
       FROM dual;

     v_TotalCredits := v_TotalCredits + v_ClassRecord.num_credits;
     v_TotalGrade := v_TotalGrade +
                     (v_ClassRecord.num_credits * v_NumericGrade);
   END LOOP;

   p_GPA := v_TotalGrade / v_TotalCredits;
END CalculateGPA;
```

PrintTranscript is created with:

```
-- Available online as printran.sql
CREATE OR REPLACE PROCEDURE PrintTranscript (
  /* Outputs a transcript for the indicated student. The
     transcript will consist of the classes for which the
     student is currently registered and the grade received
     for each class. At the end of the transcript, the student's
     GPA is output. */
  p_StudentID IN students.ID%TYPE,
  p_FileDir IN VARCHAR2,
  p_FileName IN VARCHAR2) AS

  v_StudentGPA NUMBER;
  v_StudentRecord  students%ROWTYPE;
  v_FileHandle UTL_FILE.FILE_TYPE;
  v_NumCredits NUMBER;

  CURSOR c_CurrentClasses IS
    SELECT *
      FROM registered_students
      WHERE student_id = p_StudentID;

BEGIN
  -- Open the output file in append mode.
  v_FileHandle := UTL_FILE.FOPEN(p_FileDir, p_FileName, 'w');

  SELECT *
    INTO v_StudentRecord
```

```
    FROM students
    WHERE ID = p_StudentID;

  -- Output header information. This consists of the current
  -- date and time, and information about this student.

  UTL_FILE.PUTF(v_FileHandle, 'Student ID: %s\n',
    v_StudentRecord.ID);
  UTL_FILE.PUTF(v_FileHandle, 'Student Name: %s %s\n',
    v_StudentRecord.first_name, v_StudentRecord.last_name);
  UTL_FILE.PUTF(v_FileHandle, 'Major: %s\n',
    v_StudentRecord.major);
  UTL_FILE.PUTF(v_FileHandle, 'Transcript Printed on: %s\n\n\n',
    TO_CHAR(SYSDATE, 'Mon DD,YYYY HH24:MI:SS'));

  UTL_FILE.PUT_LINE(v_FileHandle, 'Class    Credits Grade');
  UTL_FILE.PUT_LINE(v_FileHandle, '------- ------- -----');
  FOR v_ClassesRecord in c_CurrentClasses LOOP
    -- Determine the number of credits for this class.
    SELECT num_credits
      INTO v_NumCredits
      FROM classes
      WHERE course = v_ClassesRecord.course
      AND department = v_ClassesRecord.department;

    -- Output the info for this class.
    UTL_FILE.PUTF(v_FileHandle, '%s %s %s\n',
      RPAD(v_ClassesRecord.department || ' '   ||
          v_ClassesRecord.course, 7),
      LPAD(v_NumCredits, 7),
      LPAD(v_ClassesRecord.grade, 5));
  END LOOP;
  -- Determine the GPA.
  CalculateGPA(p_StudentID, v_StudentGPA);

  -- Output the GPA.
  UTL_FILE.PUTF(v_FileHandle, '\n\nCurrent GPA: %s\n',
    TO_CHAR(v_StudentGPA, '9.99'));

  -- Close the file.
  UTL_FILE.FCLOSE(v_FileHandle);

EXCEPTION
  -- Handle the UTL_FILE exceptions meaningfully, and make sure
  -- that the file is properly closed.
```

```
    WHEN UTL_FILE.INVALID_OPERATION THEN
      UTL_FILE.FCLOSE(v_FileHandle);
      RAISE_APPLICATION_ERROR(-20061,
                                 'PrintTranscript: Invalid Operation');
    WHEN UTL_FILE.INVALID_FILEHANDLE THEN
      UTL_FILE.FCLOSE(v_FileHandle);
      RAISE_APPLICATION_ERROR(-20062,
                                 'PrintTranscript: Invalid File
Handle');
    WHEN UTL_FILE.WRITE_ERROR THEN
      UTL_FILE.FCLOSE(v_FileHandle);
      RAISE_APPLICATION_ERROR(-20063,
                                 'PrintTranscript: Write Error');
    WHEN OTHERS THEN
      UTL_FILE.FCLOSE(v_FileHandle);
      RAISE;
END PrintTranscript;
```

If the **registered_students** table looks like:

```
SQL> select * from registered_students;
STUDENT_ID DEP     COURSE G
---------- --- ---------- -
     10002 CS         102 B
     10002 HIS        101 B
     10002 ECN        203 A
     10002 CS         101 A
     10009 HIS        101 D
     10009 MUS        410 B
     10009 HIS        301 C
     10009 MUS        410 B

8 rows selected.
```

and we call **PrintTranscript** for students 10002 and 10009, we get the following two output files:

```
Student ID: 10002
Student Name: Joanne Junebug
Major: Computer Science
Transcript Printed on: Jan 27,1996 17:37:43


Class    Credits Grade
```

```
------- ------- -----
CS   102      4      B

IS 101        4      B
ECN 203       3      A
CS   101      4      A


Current GPA:  3.47

Student ID: 10009
Student Name: Rose Riznit
Major: Music
Transcript Printed on: Jan 27,1996 17:38:56


Class   Credits Grade
------- ------- -----
HIS 101       4      D
MUS 410       3      B
HIS 301       4      C
MUS 410       3      B


Current GPA:  2.14
```

Summary

We have examined two more utility packages in this chapter: DBMS_JOB and UTL_FILE. Database jobs allow procedures to be automatically run by the database at predefined times. UTL_FILE adds file I/O capability to PL/SQL, subject to security issues on the server. Each of these utilities provides useful functionality that is not inherent in the language.

CHAPTER
19

Oracle's
WebServer Program

racle's WebServer software provides more functionality than a traditional web server. Integrated with the Oracle database, it allows a PL/SQL stored procedure to generate HTML pages. Thus you can create dynamic web pages based on both user input and database information. In this chapter, we will examine the structure of the Oracle web server and how PL/SQL works with it, and we will look at the PL/SQL data structures required. We will also discuss how SQL-Station Coder can be used to execute PL/SQL over the web.

The WebServer Environment

NOTE
All of the discussion in this chapter, including the examples, is written for and is tested with version 2.1 of the Oracle web server. A trial version of the web server for Solaris and Windows NT systems is available for download from http://www.oracle.com and is also on the CD accompanying this book. As of this writing, version 3.0 of the Oracle web server (known as the web application server) is also available. The discussion in this chapter is also applicable for version 3.0.

The Oracle web server is more complicated than traditional web servers and also more powerful. Here, we will examine the components of the web server and how they interact with each other and the Oracle database. A full discussion of the web server and the interfaces to it is beyond the scope of this book. For more information on administering the web server and more details, see the online documentation available when you install the server.

The components of Oracle's WebServer program are illustrated in Figure 19-1. The server consists of the following components, which are listed below and described in the following sections:

- Web listener
- CGI (Common Gateway Interface)

■ Web Request Broker (WRB) interface

■ WRB dispatcher

■ PL/SQL Agent

WEB LISTENER   The web listener is responsible for receiving a URL (Uniform Resource Locator) from the client browser and sending back the appropriate output. It does this by processing the requested URL to determine which additional component of the web server is best suited to creating the desired output. For example, the output could be a text file stored on the operating system, or it could be the output from a program. Or, the output could be retrieved from the WRB interface.

COMMON GATEWAY INTERFACE   The purpose of a web server is to service requests from a client browser. The responses typically are HTML pages. The CGI (Common Gateway Interface) provides an interface for a program running on the server to generate the HTML as output, rather than

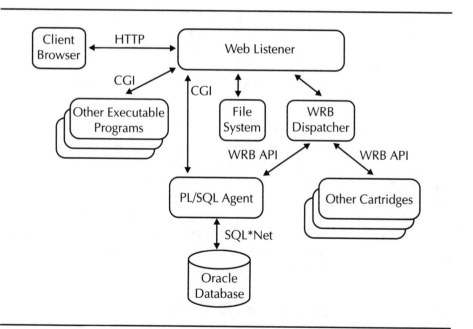

FIGURE 19-1.   *The components of Oracle's WebServer*

simply reading a static text file on the operating system. With CGI, the web pages can be created dynamically. The CGI is often used to implement HTML forms.

WEB REQUEST BROKER INTERFACE   The web request broker (WRB) interface is an additional interface that enables the web listener to call an executable program. When the listener detects that the WRB interface is needed, it hands processing to the WRB dispatcher and returns to processing incoming requests. The WRB interface is specific to Oracle's WebServer, while the CGI is a component of all web servers.

WRB DISPATCHER   The WRB dispatcher routes an incoming WRB request with the aid of a set of processes known as *WRB executable engines* (WRBX). A WRBX communicates with a back-end application known as a *cartridge*. A cartridge is a specialized application to implement a desired task, which communicates with the WRBX (and thus eventually to the client through the WRBX and listener), using an open WRB API. The dispatcher is also specific to WebServer.

PL/SQL AGENT   The PL/SQL agent is the final link in the process between a client browser and the Oracle server. The agent executes a call to an Oracle stored procedure. This procedure creates a dynamic HTML page as output, and the agent passes the output back to the client through the listener. The agent can use either the CGI or WRB interface.

The PL/SQL Agent

The PL/SQL agent serves as the primary means of accessing an Oracle database. When the web listener receives a URL specifying that the PL/SQL agent should be called, the agent will establish a connection to the database and call a PL/SQL stored procedure. Information can be passed to the procedure through its parameters, and it can include information specified in the URL or information generated from an HTML form. The procedure in turn generates HTML output through a set of specialized packages that are provided as part of the web server distribution.

The Database Connection Descriptor

In order to call the stored procedure, the PL/SQL agent must establish a connection to the database. In order to do this, it must know information such as the user name and password, along with the database SID or SQL*Net connect string. This information is stored in a *database connection descriptor* (DCD). The fields contained in a DCD are described in Table 19-1.

You can administer DCDs from the web server Administration page created when you install the web server. This allows you to create and modify DCDs online. Or you can directly modify the fields in a DCD by

Field	Description
username	Oracle user to which to connect. Any stored procedures called with this DCD must be owned by this user.
password	Password for this user.
ORACLE_HOME	Root for the Oracle software on the server's operating system.
ORACLE_SID	Database SID, if the DCD specifies a local database.
SQL*Net V2 connect string	SQL*Net version 2 connect string if the DCD specifies a remote database.
owa_error_page	Absolute path to an HTML page, which the web agent can return in case of an operating system or database error. Note that this is not a virtual path for the web server—it is a direct operating system path.
owa_valid_ports	List of valid ports on which the listener will respond. Different ports can be specified in the URL.
owa_log_dir	Log directory where the PL/SQL agent will write a log file. This file can be used to diagnose errors, as well as log activities.
owa_nls_lang	NLS_LANG environment for the Oracle session. This is specified in the same format as it would be for a standard Oracle connection, such as AMERICAN_ AMERICA.US7ASCII. For more information on NLS_LANG, see the *Oracle Server Reference*.

TABLE 19-1.   *Database Connection Descriptor Fields*

editing the configuration file on the server file system. For more information on DCDs and these files, see Oracle's WebServer documentation.

CGI vs. WRB

The PL/SQL agent can be called with either the CGI or WRB interface. Either way, the DCD is used to indicate the database connection information. Which interface is better? With the WRB interface, the WRBX establishes the connection in two stages:

1. The connection itself is established. The WRBX does this as soon as it is created.

2. For each request, the WRBX will log on to the database. When the request is complete, the WRBX logs off. The connection remains active.

With the CGI interface, however, the PL/SQL agent must complete both stages of the connection for each request. This is necessary because each CGI request will spawn a new process, which must begin anew. But the WRBX process remains alive, which means that only stage 2 is required.

Since stage 1 is the most time consuming, using the WRB interface is significantly faster and is thus recommended.

Specifying Procedure Parameters

A PL/SQL procedure can be called through the web agent using either the GET or the POST method. With the GET method, the parameters are passed directly in the URL. The POST method is used when the procedure is the target of an HTML form. The web agent will automatically determine which method is used and call the procedure appropriately. We will see an example of the GET method in this section. The POST method is used automatically with HTML forms, and is described later in this chapter. Consider the following stored procedure:

```
-- Available online as hello.sql
CREATE OR REPLACE PROCEDURE hello(p_Greeting IN VARCHAR2) AS
BEGIN
  HTP.htmlOpen;
  HTP.headOpen;
  HTP.Title('Hello World!');
```

```
    HTP.headClose;
    HTP.bodyOpen;
    HTP.print(p_Greeting);
    HTP.bodyClose;
    HTP.htmlClose;
END hello;
```

The calls to the HTP package will generate the actual HTML code, as described in the next section, "PL/SQL Web Toolkit." In order to call this procedure from a URL, the following steps have to be done:

1. Create the procedure in a particular schema. Suppose that the database user is **example** in this case.

2. Create a DCD for the web listener that specifies **example** as the user ID. Suppose that is also called **example**.

3. Create a WRB that specifies the virtual path /example/owa as a call to the Oracle web agent.

We can now call **hello** by using a URL similar to the following,

```
http://host:port/example/owa/hello?p_Greeting=Welcome!
```

where *host* and *port* are the machine and port on which the listener is running. The listener will parse the URL given to it and will direct further processing based on the components of the URL, each of which can be retrieved with the appropriate CGI environment variable. This is described in the following table:

URL Component	CGI Environment Variable	Explanation
/example/owa	SCRIPT_NAME	This tells the listener that the DCD example should be used. Because the WRB specified /example/owa as a virtual path, the web agent will process the remainder of the URL.

URL Component	CGI Environment Variable	Explanation
hello	PATH_INFO	This identifies the procedure to be called. The web agent will expect this procedure to produce HTML output using the web toolkit packages.
p_Greeting= Welcome!	QUERY_STRING	This identifies the procedure parameters, if specified. Note that the name of the parameter is specified along with the value. If there is more than one parameter, they should be separated by question marks.

When we call **hello** from this URL in a web browser, the output is displayed in Netscape Navigator 3.0 as shown in Figure 19-2. The HTML that **hello** generates is as follows:

```
<HTML>
<HEAD>
<TITLE>Hello World!</TITLE>
</HEAD>
<BODY>
Welcome!
</BODY>
</HTML>
```

NOTE
Generated HTML pages, like any HTML page, can be viewed in a variety of different browsers. Figure 19-2, for example, uses Netscape Navigator version 3.0. Other figures in this chapter show different browsers.

FIGURE 19-2. *Output from **hello** in Netscape Navigator*

PL/SQL Web Toolkit

The PL/SQL web toolkit is a set of packages that enable a PL/SQL procedure to generate HTML output. The packages in the toolkit are described in Table 19-2. In the following sections, we will see examples of many of these packages. For more information on the packages, including definitions of the subprograms, see the PL/SQL Web Toolkit Reference, which is available online when you install WebServer.

NOTE
The purpose of the web toolkit is to generate HTML. We will examine the toolkit and the HTML it generates. We will not, however, discuss the meaning of the HTML code itself. For more information on HTML, see the Oracle WebServer documentation.

Package	Description
HTP	Hypertext procedures. This package contains procedures that generate many common HTML tags.
HTF	Hypertext functions. This package contains the same functionality as HTP, but the subprograms are implemented as functions rather than procedures.
OWA*	This package contains internal procedures that are called by the PL/SQL agent itself. They are not meant to be called externally.
OWA_UTIL	Useful utility functions for manipulating dates and dynamic SQL, as well as getting the value of CGI environment variables.
OWA_OPT_LOCK*	Allows you to impose optimistic locking strategies to prevent lost updates.
OWA_PATTERN*	Functions that implement regular expression pattern matching.
OWA_TEXT*	Procedures, functions, and datatypes that allow you to manipulate large text strings. OWA_PATTERN uses OWA_TEXT internally.
OWA_IMAGE	Utilities for manipulating server-side image maps.
OWA_COOKIE	Utilities for manipulating HTML cookies.

TABLE 19-2. *Supplied Packages in the PL/SQL Web Toolkit*

* These packages are not described in detail in the following sections; see the online documentation for more information and examples.

HTP and HTF

These two packages form the basics of HTML output. The HTP package consists only of procedures. Each call to an HTP procedure will produce one HTML tag. When the procedure is called via the PL/SQL agent, this tag will be returned as part of the generated page. The HTF package, on the other hand, contains only functions. The functions are the equivalent of the

```
  HTP.header(2, 'Formats');
  HTP.print(HTF.centerOpen || 'These lines are centered, using ');
  HTP.br;
  HTP.print('the HTF.centerOpen and HTF.centerClose functions.');
  HTP.centerClose;

  HTP.strike('Here''s some strikethrough text.');
  OWA_UTIL.signature('BodyDemo')
  HTP.bodyClose;
  HTP.htmlClose;
END BodyDemo;
```

The HTML that **BodyDemo** generates is given next, and the page itself (in Netscape Navigator 4.0) is shown in Figure 19-3.

```
<HTML>
<HEAD>
<TITLE>Body tags demo</TITLE>
</HEAD>
<BODY>
This page demonstrates several of the tags
available for formatting the text in the body
of a web page, and for inserting additional
tags.<P>
<H2>Links</H2>
Here are some links to check out.  These are
generated using the HTP.anchor procedure.
<P>
<A HREF="//www.oracle.com/">Oracle Corporation</A>
<P>
<A HREF="//www.osborne.com/oracle/index.htm">Oracle Press</A>
<P>
<A HREF="//www.platinum.com/">Platinum Corporation</A>
<P>
<H2>Formats</H2>
<CENTER>These lines are centered, using
<BR>
the HTF.centerOpen and HTF.centerClose functions.
</CENTER>
<STRIKE>Here's some strikethrough text.</STRIKE>
</BODY>
</HTML>
```

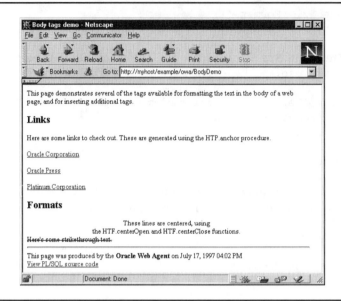

FIGURE 19-3. *Output from* **BodyDemo** *in Netscape Navigator*

List

There are several different kinds of lists available in HTML. Each list consists of a set of items, usually one per line, with a formatting tag (such as a bullet or number) in front of each one. The available lists are described here:

- An *ordered list* has numbered items.

- An *unordered list* has bullets.

- A *menu list* is similar to an unordered list, but is usually presented in a more compact form.

- A *definition list* includes an item, followed by a definition.

- A *directory list* is usually arranged in columns, typically 24 characters wide. Each list element should have a maximum of 20 characters.

Lists typically start with a list open tag, followed by the list items (delimited by a list item tag), then a list close tag. The **ListDemo** package illustrates different types of lists. The package is below, and Figure 19-4 shows the output of an ordered list in Microsoft Internet Explorer 3.0.

```
-- Available online as listdemo.sql
CREATE OR REPLACE PACKAGE ListDemo AS
  PROCEDURE Go;
  PROCEDURE ShowList(p_ListType IN CHAR);
END ListDemo;

CREATE OR REPLACE PACKAGE BODY ListDemo AS
  -- Set c_OWAPath to the virtual path (including the DCD) where
  -- the Oracle Web Agent is installed.
  c_OWAPath CONSTANT VARCHAR2(50) := '/example/owa/';

  -- Presents the user with the available list types.
  PROCEDURE ShowChoices IS
    c_ListPath VARCHAR2(100) :=
      c_OWAPATH || 'ListDemo.ShowList?p_ListType=';
  BEGIN
    HTP.line;
    HTP.p('Click on any of the following links to see the ');
    HTP.p('students in the specified list type.' || HTF.para);

    HTP.anchor(c_ListPath || 'U', 'Unordered');
    HTP.anchor(c_ListPath || 'O', 'Ordered');
    HTP.anchor(c_ListPath || 'M', 'Menu');
    HTP.anchor(c_ListPath || 'D', 'Directory');
  END ShowChoices;

  -- Presents the first and last names of the students in the
  -- specified list type.
  PROCEDURE ShowList(p_ListType IN CHAR) IS
    v_Title VARCHAR2(20);
    v_ListOpen VARCHAR2(10);
    v_ListClose VARCHAR2(10);
    CURSOR c_Names IS
      SELECT first_name || ' ' || last_name name
        FROM students
        ORDER BY last_name;
  BEGIN
    IF p_ListType = 'U' THEN
      v_Title := 'Unordered List';
      v_ListOpen := HTF.ulistOpen;
      v_ListClose := HTF.ulistClose;
    ELSIF p_ListType = 'O' THEN
      v_Title := 'Ordered List';
```

```
      v_ListOpen := HTF.olistOpen;
      v_ListClose := HTF.olistClose;
   ELSIF p_ListType = 'M' THEN
      v_Title := 'Menu List';
      v_ListOpen := HTF.menulistOpen;
      v_ListClose := HTF.menulistClose;
   ELSIF p_ListType = 'D' THEN
      v_Title := 'Directory List';
      v_ListOpen := HTF.dirlistOpen;
      v_ListClose := HTF.dirlistClose;
   END IF;
   HTP.htmlOpen;
   HTP.headOpen;
   HTP.title(v_Title);
   HTP.headClose;

   HTP.bodyOpen;
   -- Output the list itself.
   HTP.p(v_ListOpen);
   FOR v_NamesRec IN c_Names LOOP
      HTP.listItem(v_NamesRec.name);
   END LOOP;
   HTP.p(v_ListClose);

   -- Output the choices.
   ShowChoices;

   OWA_UTIL.signature('ListDemo.ShowList');
   HTP.bodyClose;
END ShowList;

PROCEDURE Go IS
BEGIN
   HTP.htmlOpen;
   HTP.headOpen;
   HTP.title('List Demo');
   HTP.headClose;

   HTP.bodyOpen;
   HTP.header(2, 'Welcome to the list demo');
   ShowChoices;
   OWA_UTIL.signature('ListDemo.Go');
   HTP.bodyClose;
   HTP.htmlClose;
END Go;
END ListDemo;
```

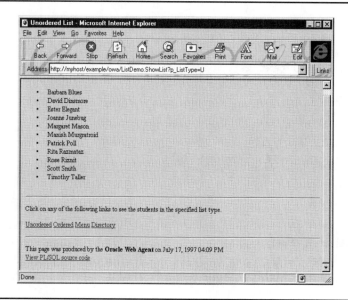

FIGURE 19-4. *Output of **ListDemo** in Internet Explorer*

Character Format

The character format tags specify how characters should be formatted. They do not specify exact characteristics, however. Rather, each browser is free to render the style how it chooses. For example, the STRONG tag is usually rendered as bold text, but some browsers could choose to have the text blink. Specific formatting tags are described in the next section, "Physical Format." The following example illustrates some character format tags. The output from **CharDemo** in NCSA Mosaic 3.0 is shown in Figure 19-5.

```
CREATE OR REPLACE PROCEDURE CharDemo AS
BEGIN
  HTP.htmlOpen;
  HTP.headOpen;
  HTP.title('Character Formatting Tags');
  HTP.headClose;

  HTP.bodyOpen;
  HTP.header(2, 'This page demonstrates character formatting
             tags.');
```

```
  HTP.para;
  HTP.cite('This text is a citation, usually rendered as
           italics.');
  HTP.para;
  HTP.code('This text is code, usually rendered as a monospace
           font.');
  HTP.para;
  HTP.strong('This text is strong, usually rendered as bold.');
  HTP.para;

  OWA_UTIL.signature('CharDemo');
  HTP.bodyClose;
  HTP.htmlClose;
END CharDemo;
```

Physical Format

The physical format tags specify the physical attributes of the text. There are three subprograms in this category: BOLD, ITALIC, and TELETYPE. BOLD

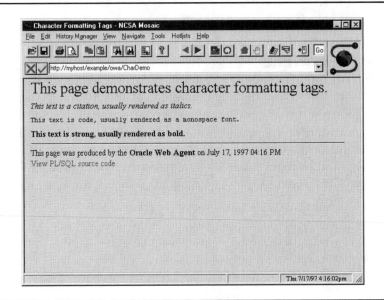

FIGURE 19-5. *Output of* **CharDemo** *in NCSA Mosaic*

specifies that its argument should be rendered in bold, ITALIC specifies italics, and TELETYPE specifies a typewriter font, such as Courier.

Form

The form tags are used to implement *HTML forms*. A form can accept input from the user, in the form of GUI elements such as text entry fields, and check boxes. This input is passed to the server using the POST method. The Web agent automatically detects this protocol and passes the entered data to a PL/SQL procedure. As an example, consider the **FormDemo** package:

```
-- Available online as formdemo.sql
CREATE OR REPLACE PACKAGE FormDemo AS
  PROCEDURE Go;
  PROCEDURE Process(p_Checkbox IN VARCHAR2 DEFAULT 'off',
                    p_Password IN VARCHAR2 DEFAULT NULL,
                    p_Radio IN VARCHAR2 DEFAULT NULL);
END FormDemo;

CREATE OR REPLACE PACKAGE BODY FormDemo AS
  -- Set c_OWAPath to the virtual path (including the DCD) where
  -- the Oracle Web Agent is installed.
  c_OWAPath CONSTANT VARCHAR2(50) := '/example/owa/';

  PROCEDURE ShowForm IS
  BEGIN
    HTP.line;
    -- First open the form, specifying the Process procedure as the
    -- target URL.
    HTP.formOpen(curl => c_OWAPath || 'FormDemo.Process');

    -- Now print some text, followed by input devices.
    HTP.p('Welcome to a HTML form.  Fill out some information'):
    HTP.p('below, and press the ''Submit'' button to process it.');
    HTP.p('Press ''Reset'' to clear your entries.');
    HTP.para;

    HTP.p('Here is a checkbox: ');
    HTP.formCheckbox(cname => 'p_CheckBox');
    HTP.para;
    HTP.p('Here is a password entry: ');
    HTP.formPassword(cname => 'p_Password',
```

```
                           csize => 10);
     HTP.para;
     HTP.p('Select one of the following radio buttons:');
     HTP.nl;
     HTP.formRadio(cname => 'p_Radio', cvalue => 'One');
     HTP.p('One');
     HTP.formRadio(cname => 'p_Radio', cvalue => 'Two');
     HTP.p('Two');
     HTP.formRadio(cname => 'p_Radio', cvalue => 'Three');
     HTP.p('Three' || HTF.nl);
     HTP.formRadio(cname => 'p_Radio', cvalue => 'Four');
     HTP.p('Four');
     HTP.formRadio(cname => 'p_Radio', cvalue => 'Five');
     HTP.p('Five' || HTF.para);
     HTP.formSubmit;
     HTP.formReset;
     HTP.formClose;
   END ShowForm;

   PROCEDURE Process(p_Checkbox IN VARCHAR2 DEFAULT 'off',
                     p_Password IN VARCHAR2 DEFAULT NULL,
                     p_Radio IN VARCHAR2 DEFAULT NULL) IS
   BEGIN
     HTP.htmlOpen;
     HTP.headOpen;
     HTP.title('Form Results');
     HTP.headClose;

     HTP.bodyOpen;
     HTP.header(2, 'Form Results:');
     HTP.p('p_Checkbox = ' || p_Checkbox || HTF.nl);
     HTP.p('p_Password = ' || p_Password || HTF.nl);
     HTP.p('p_Radio = ' || p_Radio || HTF.para);
     ShowForm;
     OWA_UTIL.signature('FormDemo.Process');
     HTP.bodyClose;
     HTP.htmlClose;
   END Process;

   PROCEDURE Go IS
   BEGIN
     HTP.htmlOpen;
     HTP.headOpen;
     HTP.title('Forms Demo');
     HTP.headClose;
```

```
      HTP.bodyOpen;
      ShowForm;
      OWA_UTIL.signature('FormDemo.Go');
      HTP.bodyClose;
      HTP.htmlClose;
   END Go;
END FormDemo;
```

The main procedure for setting up a form is HTP.FORMOPEN. The syntax is below, and the parameters are described in the Table 19-4. Figure 19-6 shows the output of **FormDemo.60** in Internet Explorer.

```
PROCEDURE FORMOPEN(curl IN VARCHAR2,
                   cmethod IN VARCHAR2 DEFAULT 'POST',
                   ctarget IN VARCHAR2 DEFAULT NULL,
                   cenctype IN VARCHAR2 DEFAULT NULL,
                   cattributes IN VARCHAR2 DEFAULT NULL);
```

Parameter	Datatype	Description
curl	VARCHAR2	URL which will process the form. This is typically another PL/SQL stored procedure, called through the Web Agent.
cmethod	VARCHAR2	HTTP method to use—either 'GET' or 'POST'.
ctarget	VARCHAR2	TARGET attribute—if set, the curl will be opened in a new window.
cenctype	VARCHAR2	Encoding type to use when sending the data. If not specified, the cmethod will usually dictate the protocol.
cattributes	VARCHAR2	Any additional attributes desired.

TABLE 19-4.   *Parameters for FORMOPEN*

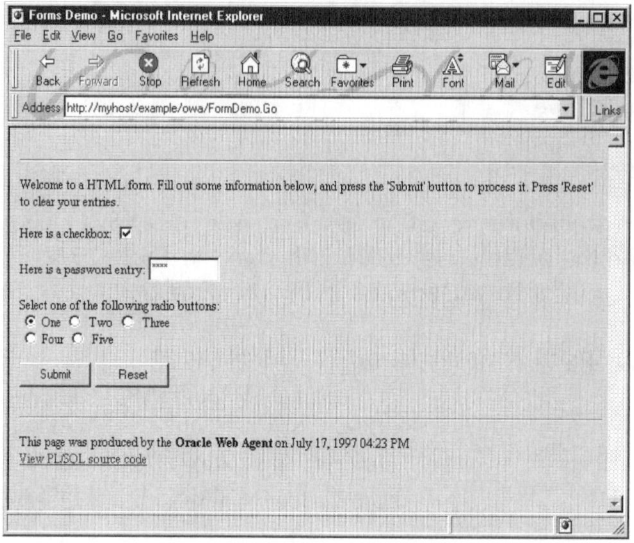

FIGURE 19-6. *Output of* **FormDemo.60** *in Internet Explorer*

FORMOPEN will generate HTML code similar to

```
<FORM ACTION="curl" METHOD="cmethod" TARGET="ctarget"
    ENCTYPE="cenctype" cattributes>
```

The procedure specified in *curl* should have parameters which match the names of the entries in the form. In the above example, **FormDemo. Process** accepts three parameters: **p_Checkbox**, **p_Password**, and **p_Radio**. These are the names of the entries used in **FormDemo.ShowForm**.

Either the GET or POST method can be used. With the GET method, the client browser will assemble a URL to call the procedure specified by *curl*, as if it had been called directly. All of the parameters will be included in the URL. On some systems, the maximum length of a URL will limit the number of parameters. Thus the POST method is default. When using POST, the parameters are sent by the browser after the URL. The Web Agent will read them and call the procedure appropriately.

TIP

It is a good idea to have defaults for all of the parameters accepted by an action procedure. If the user does not enter a value for a form entry, then that parameter will not be passed. If there is no default, then an error will be raised and the procedure call will not be successful.

Table

The table formatting subprograms are used to create HTML tables. Tables consist of rows and columns, each of which can contain any formatted HTML. The **TableDemo** procedure demonstrates the use of some of the table formatting procedures. The listing follows, and Figure 19-7 shows the output in Netscape 4.0.

```
-- Available online as tabldemo.sql
CREATE OR REPLACE PROCEDURE TableDemo AS
  CURSOR c_Students IS
    SELECT *
      FROM students
      ORDER BY ID;
BEGIN
  HTP.htmlOpen;
  HTP.headOpen;
  HTP.title('Table Demo');
  HTP.headClose;

  HTP.bodyOpen;
  HTP.tableOpen(cborder => 'BORDER=1');

  -- Loop over the students, and for each one output two table
  -- rows, which look something like:
  -- +-------------------------------+
  -- |    | first_name last_name     |
  -- | ID +---------+----------------+
  -- |    | major   | current_credits|
  -- +----+---------+----------------+
  FOR v_StudentRec in c_Students LOOP
    HTP.tableRowOpen;
    HTP.tableData(crowspan => 2,
                  cvalue => HTF.bold(v_StudentRec.ID));
    HTP.tableData(ccolspan => 2,
```

```
                calign => 'CENTER',
                cvalue => v_StudentRec.first_name || ' ' ||
                          v_StudentRec.last_name);
    HTP.tableRowClose;
    HTP.tableRowOpen;
    HTP.tableData(cvalue => 'Major: ' || v_StudentRec.major);
    HTP.tableData(cvalue => 'Credits: ' ||
                          v_StudentRec.current_credits);
    HTP.tableRowClose;
  END LOOP;

  HTP.tableClose;
  OWA_UTIL.signature('TableDemo');
  HTP.bodyClose;
  HTP.htmlClose;
END TableDemo;
```

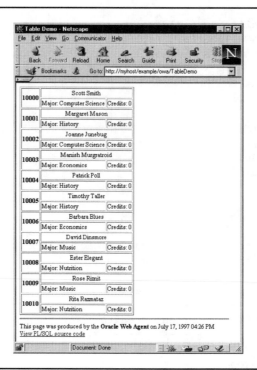

FIGURE 19-7. *Output of* **TableDemo** *in Netscape 4.0*

OWA_UTIL

The OWA_UTIL package adds additional functionality. It is written using the HTP and HTF packages. There are three different sets of subprograms in OWA_UTIL, which are described in the following sections:

- HTML Utilities
- Dynamic SQL Utilities
- Date Utilities

TIP
In order to use the OWA_UTIL package, the Protect_OWA_Pkg parameter must be set to FALSE in the OWA configuration for the Web Request Broker. For more information, see the online documentation.

HTML Utilities

The following table lists the subprograms available in this category. The functionality ranges from outputting a signature to displaying an Oracle table as an HTML table. These subprograms are described in Table 19-5,

Subprogram	Description
signature	Outputs a horizontal line, followed by a line similar to "This page was produced by the **Oracle PL/SQL Agent** on August 9, 1995 09:30." A link to show the PL/SQL source can also be included.
showsource	Outputs the source of the supplied package or procedure. If a packaged procedure is specified, then the entire package is output.

TABLE 19-5.   *OWA_UTIL HTML Utilities*

Subprogram	Description
showpage	Outputs (using DBMS_OUTPUT) the last page which was generated using the Web Toolkit. This is useful to test the output of procedures in SQL*Plus or SQL-Station. For more information, see the section "Development Environments for OWA Procedures" at the end of this chapter.
get_cgi_env	Returns the value of the specified CGI environment variable. If this variable is not set, then this function returns NULL.
print_cgi_env	Outputs the values of all the CGI environment variables. This is useful for debugging.
mime_header	Used to change the default MIME header which the Agent returns. This procedure must be called before any HTP.PRINT or HTP.PRN calls; otherwise, the Web Agent will return the default header.
redirect_url	Specifies that WebServer visit a different URL. As the generated code is part of the header, this must be called before any HTP.PRINT or HTP.PRN calls.
status_line	Sends a standard HTTP status code to the client. As the generated code is part of the header, this must be called before any HTP.PRINT or HTP.PRN calls.
header_close	Explicitly closes the header. This must be called before any HTP.PRINT or HTP.PRN calls if MIME_HEADER, REDIRECT_URL, or STATUS_LINE has not been called with the *bclose_header* parameter set to TRUE.
get_owa_ service_path	Returns the full service path (including the DCD) for the currently executing procedure.
tableprint	Prints the contents of a database table as either an HTML table or preformatted text.
who_called_me	Returns information about the PL/SQL object which is executing, including the name and type of object.

TABLE 19-5. *OWA_UTIL HTML Utilities* (Continued)

```
   OWA_UTIL.signature('DynamicDemo.Process');
    HTP.bodyClose;
    HTP.htmlClose;
  END Process;

  /* Processes the form containing the picklist. */
  PROCEDURE ListProcess(p_Value IN VARCHAR2 DEFAULT NULL) IS
  BEGIN
    HTP.htmlOpen;
    HTP.headOpen;
    HTP.title('List Results');
    HTP.headClose;

    HTP.bodyOpen;
    HTP.p('You picked ' || p_Value || '.');
    ShowForm;
    OWA_UTIL.signature('DynamicDemo.ListProcess');
    HTP.bodyClose;
    HTP.htmlClose;
  END ListProcess;
END DynamicDemo;
```

Date Utilities

The date utilities in OWA_UTIL implement two different features to help you manage date values in Web pages. The CALENDARPRINT procedure will output a calendar (as an HTML table) based on the results of a query, while the CHOOSE_DATE procedure will generate code to accept a date as a day, month, and year.

CALENDARPRINT   CALENDARPRINT takes as input either a string containing a query, or a cursor prepared with OWA_UTIL.BIND_VARIABLES, and generates a calendar based on the results of the query. The query can have either two or three columns:

- Column 1: DATE value used to correlate the returned data with the displayed calendar.

- Column 2: Text, if any, to be printed for this date.

- Column 3: If this column is present, then the second column will be displayed as a link, with destination indicated by column 3. If there are only two columns, then the values will be displayed as text only.

CHOOSE_DATE   CHOOSE_DATE will output three fields, to be used to input the year, month, and day. The target of these fields should be a procedure with parameter type OWA_UTIL.DATETYPE. OWA_UTIL.TO_DATE can convert DATETYPE values to a standard Oracle DATE.

The **DateDemo** package demonstrates the use of these utilities, and Figure 19-8 shows the output of **DateDemo.Go** in Internet Explorer. In order to create the package, the **calendar** table is first created with:

```
-- Available online as part of datedemo.sql
CREATE TABLE calendar (
  today        DATE,
  description  VARCHAR2(25),
  link         VARCHAR2(20)
);

INSERT INTO calendar (today, description, link)
  VALUES (SYSDATE - 5, 'Hello!', '//www.oracle.com');
INSERT INTO calendar (today, description, link)
  VALUES (SYSDATE - 4, 'Getting there...', '//www.oracle.com');
INSERT INTO calendar (today, description, link)
  VALUES (SYSDATE - 3, 'How''s it going?', '//www.oracle.com');
INSERT INTO calendar (today, description, link)
  VALUES (SYSDATE - 2, 'Soon...', '//www.oracle.com');
INSERT INTO calendar (today, description, link)
  VALUES (SYSDATE - 1, 'Tomorrow, tomorrow', '//www.oracle.com');
INSERT INTO calendar (today, description, link)
  VALUES (SYSDATE, 'Made it!', '//www.oracle.com');
INSERT INTO calendar (today, description, link)
  VALUES (SYSDATE + 1, 'Did you miss it?', '//www.oracle.com');
INSERT INTO calendar (today, description, link)
  VALUES (SYSDATE + 2, 'Sure hope not...', '//www.oracle.com');
INSERT INTO calendar (today, description, link)
  VALUES (SYSDATE + 3, 'It was pretty cool', '//www.oracle.com');
INSERT INTO calendar (today, description, link)
  VALUES (SYSDATE + 4, 'Better luck next year',
          '//www.oracle.com');
INSERT INTO calendar (today, description, link)
  VALUES (SYSDATE + 5, 'Goodbye!', '//www.oracle.com');
```

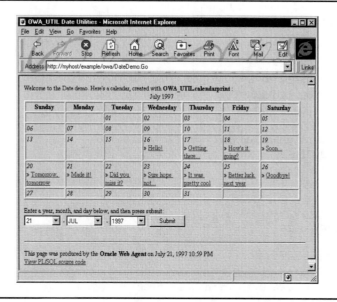

FIGURE 19-8. *Output of* **DateDemo** *in Internet Explorer*

The package itself is defined below.

```
-- Available online as datedemo.sql
CREATE OR REPLACE PACKAGE DateDemo AS
  PROCEDURE Go;
  PROCEDURE Process(p_DateVal IN OWA_UTIL.dateType);
END DateDemo;

CREATE OR REPLACE PACKAGE BODY DateDemo AS
  -- Set c_OWAPath to the virtual path (including the DCD)
  -- where the Oracle Web Agent is installed.
  c_OWAPath CONSTANT VARCHAR2(50) := '/example/owa/';

  -- Receives the date selected.
  PROCEDURE Process(p_DateVal IN OWA_UTIL.dateType) IS
```

```
BEGIN
  HTP.htmlOpen;
  HTP.headOpen;
  HTP.title('Results');
  HTP.headClose;
  HTP.bodyOpen;
  HTP.p('You picked ');
  HTP.p(TO_CHAR(OWA_UTIL.todate(p_DateVal)));
  HTP.nl;
  OWA_UTIL.signature('DateDemo.Process');
  HTP.bodyClose;
  HTP.htmlClose;
END Process;

-- Main entry procedure.
PROCEDURE Go IS
BEGIN
  HTP.htmlOpen;
  HTP.headOpen;
  HTP.title('OWA_UTIL Date Utilities');
  HTP.headClose;

  HTP.bodyOpen;
  HTP.p('Welcome to the Date demo.  Here''s a calendar, ');
  HTP.p('created with ' || HTF.bold('OWA_UTIL.calendarprint'));
  HTP.p(':' || HTF.nl);
  OWA_UTIL.calendarprint(
     'SELECT * FROM calendar ORDER BY today');

  HTP.para;
  HTP.p('Enter a year, month, and day below, and then press');
  HTP.p(' submit:' || HTF.nl);
  HTP.formOpen(curl => c_OWAPath || 'DateDemo.Process');
  OWA_UTIL.choose_date(p_name => 'p_DateVal');
  HTP.formSubmit;
  HTP.formClose;
  OWA_UTIL.signature('DateDemo.Go');
  HTP.bodyClose;
  HTP.htmlClose;
  END Go;
END DateDemo;
```

OWA_IMAGE

The OWA_IMAGE package provides a way to handle image maps. An *image map* is a graphic on a web page. Any graphic can be used as an anchor for a link, but an image map is sensitive to the location within the graphic where you click. Based on the x and y coordinates within the graphic, the web server can return different URLs. Unlike other web servers, which process image maps by using a separate CGI program, the Oracle web server can handle them internally. A procedure that references the OWA_IMAGE package is used as the target of an image map to handle the x and y coordinates. OWA_IMAGE defines one datatype, POINT, which contains the x and y values. Two functions are provided to retrieve these values, defined with

FUNCTION GET_X(*p* IN POINT) RETURN INTEGER;
FUNCTION GET_Y(*p* IN POINT) RETURN INTEGER;

where *p* is a point selected with an image map. The **Imagemap** package illustrates one way of using OWA_IMAGE:

```
-- Available online as imagemap.sql
CREATE OR REPLACE PACKAGE Imagemap AS
  PROCEDURE Go;
  PROCEDURE Process(p_Img IN OWA_IMAGE.POINT);
END Imagemap;

CREATE OR REPLACE PACKAGE BODY Imagemap AS
  -- Set c_ImagePath to the virtual path on your server where the
  -- boxes.gif file has been stored.
  c_ImagePath CONSTANT VARCHAR2(50) := '/ows-img/boxes.gif';

  -- Set c_OWAPath to the virtual path (including the DCD) where
  -- the Oracle Web Agent is installed.
  c_OWAPath CONSTANT VARCHAR2(50) := '/example/owa/';

  PROCEDURE ShowBoxes IS
  BEGIN
    HTP.p('Click anywhere on the image below.' || HTF.para);
```

```
    -- Set up a form with one clickable image.  The target of this
    -- image is the Process procedure.  Since the type of this form
    -- field is an image, the p_Img parameter will be passed a
    -- value of type OWA_IMAGE.POINT.
    HTP.formOpen(curl => c_OWAPath || 'Imagemap.Process');
    HTP.formImage(cname => 'p_Img',
                  csrc => c_ImagePath,
                  cattributes => 'BORDER=0');
    HTP.formClose;
END ShowBoxes;

PROCEDURE Go IS
BEGIN
  HTP.htmlOpen;
  HTP.headOpen;
  HTP.title('Imagemap test');
  HTP.headClose;

  HTP.bodyOpen;
  ShowBoxes;
  HTP.bodyClose;
  HTP.htmlClose;
END Go;

PROCEDURE Process(p_Img IN OWA_IMAGE.POINT) IS
  v_x INTEGER := OWA_IMAGE.GET_X(p_Img);
  v_y INTEGER := OWA_IMAGE.GET_Y(p_Img);
  v_Color VARCHAR2(5);
BEGIN
  IF v_x < 200 THEN
    IF v_y < 100 THEN
      v_Color := 'Blue';
    ELSE
      v_Color := 'Red';
    END IF;
  ELSE
    IF v_y < 100 THEN
      v_Color := 'Green';
    ELSE
      v_Color := 'Black';
    END IF;
  END IF;
```

```
      HTP.htmlOpen;
      HTP.headOpen;
      HTP.title('Imagemap results');
      HTP.headClose;

      HTP.bodyOpen;
      HTP.print('Processed.  X = ' || v_x || ' and Y = ' || v_y);
      HTP.print('.  This means that you selected the ' || v_Color);
      HTP.print(' box.' || HTF.para);

      ShowBoxes;
      HTP.bodyClose;
      HTP.htmlClose;
   END Process;

END Imagemap;
```

NOTE
*In order to set this up on your system, copy
the boxes.gif file (found on the CD) to an
image directory on your web server and
specify the path in* **c_ImagePath**.

In order to set up the image map, you create a form with one clickable image. The target of this image is **ImageMap.Process**. The form is created by the **ShowBoxes** procedure. The boxes.gif image is simply four boxes of different colors. The results of calling **ImageMap.Go** and clicking on the blue box (in Netscape Navigator 4.0) are shown in Figure 19-9.

OWA_COOKIE

OWA_COOKIE allows you to manage HTML cookies. A *cookie* is a piece of data stored on the client, rather than the server. Cookies can be used to maintain state between calls to the server. In normal processing, the client is not aware that the cookie exists. However, many browsers do have a setting that enables the user to be notified of cookie transmissions and, optionally, to refuse them.

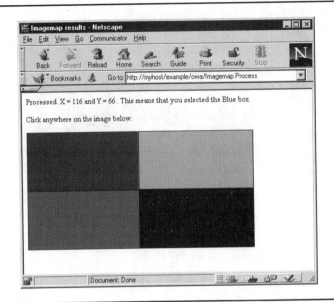

FIGURE 19-9. *Results of clicking on an image map*

Datatypes

The HTTP specification for cookies stipulates that a cookie is a name-value pair. The value can be set or retrieved for a given name. The name and value are limited to 4,096 bytes, and multiple values can be stored with one name. To implement this, the OWA_COOKIE package defines the following datatypes:

```
TYPE VC_ARR IS TABLE OF VARCHAR2(4096)
  INDEX BY BINARY_INTEGER;
TYPE COOKIE IS RECORD (
  name     VARCHAR2(4096),
  vals       VC_ARR,
  num_vals INTEGER);
```

The OWA_COOKIE.COOKIE datatype is implemented as a record with a PL/SQL table so that it can contain multiple values.

SEND

The SEND procedure is used to pass a cookie to the client for storage. It is defined with

```
PROCEDURE SEND(name IN VARCHAR2,
              value IN VARCHAR2,
              expires IN DATE DEFAULT NULL,
              path IN VARCHAR2 DEFAULT NULL,
              domain IN VARCHAR2 DEFAULT NULL,
              secure IN VARCHAR2 DEFAULT NULL);
```

SEND must be called from the HTTP header of a page, as illustrated by the example at the end of this section. SEND will generate an HTTP header line that looks like:

```
Set-Cookie: name=value expires=expires path=path
            domain=domain [secure]
```

The only required parameters are *name* and *value*. If the others are not specified, the appropriate clause is not generated. *expires* specifies the time when the cookie will expire. It cannot be retrieved after this time. If it is not specified, the cookie expires when the client session is ended (that is, when the browser is closed).

GET

The GET function returns a cookie with the specified name. If there is no data on the client for the requested name, *num_vals* in the returned cookie will be zero. It is defined with

```
FUNCTION GET(name IN VARCHAR2) RETURN COOKIE;
```

where *name* is the name of the desired cookie.

GET_ALL

GET_ALL will return all the name-value pairs of the cookies retrieved from the browser, in the order in which they were sent. It is defined with

```
PROCEDURE GET_ALL(names OUT VC_ARR,
                  vals OUT VC_ARR,
                  num_vals OUT INTEGER);
```

REMOVE

REMOVE forces the expiration of an existing cookie. Like SEND, it must be called from the HTTP header. It is defined with

```
PROCEDURE REMOVE(name IN VARCHAR2,
                 val IN VARCHAR2,
                 path IN VARCHAR2 DEFAULT NULL);
```

It generates a line similar to

```
Set-Cookie: name=value path=path expires=01-JAN-1990
```

If the *path* parameter isn't specified, then the path clause is omitted. Expiration is caused by setting the date to one that has already passed (January 1, 1990).

Example

The CookieDemo procedure demonstrates the use of OWA_COOKIE.

```
-- Available online as cookie.sql
CREATE OR REPLACE PROCEDURE CookieDemo(
  p_NewVal IN NUMBER DEFAULT NULL) AS
  -- Set c_OWAPath to the virtual path (including the DCD) where
  -- the Oracle Web Agent is installed.
  c_OWAPath CONSTANT VARCHAR2(50) := '/example/owa/';

  v_Cookie OWA_COOKIE.COOKIE;
BEGIN
  -- Retrieve the current value of the cookie, and send the new
  -- value based on the parameters.
  v_Cookie := OWA_COOKIE.GET('Count');
  OWA_UTIL.MIME_HEADER('text/html', FALSE);
  IF p_NewVal IS NOT NULL THEN
    OWA_COOKIE.SEND('Count', p_NewVal + 1);
```

```
<CENTER>These lines are centered, using
<BR>
the HTF.centerOpen and HTF.centerClose functions.
</CENTER>
<STRIKE>Here's some strikethrough text.</STRIKE>
</BODY>
</HTML>

PL/SQL procedure successfully completed.
```

   SHOWPAGE enables you to see the HTML output from a procedure to
verify its accuracy.

SQL-Station Coder

You can also execute OWA procedures from SQL-Station Coder. The
procedure execution window has three execute buttons. The first will
execute the procedure normally. The next two buttons, however, are used
to call a procedure with the Web Agent, as shown in Figure 19-10. The
"Web execute" button will call a browser on the client and pass it the

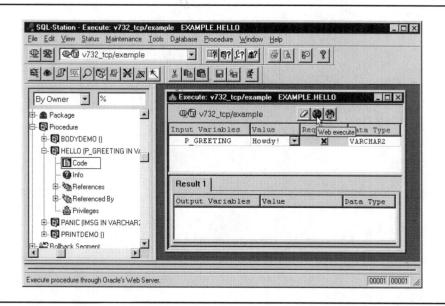

FIGURE 19-10.   *Web executing stored procedures in SQL-Station Coder*

correct URL to execute the procedure with the supplied parameters, using the GET method. The "Generate URL" button will allow you to see (and optionally edit) the generated URL and copy it to the clipboard. By using SQL-Station Coder in this manner, you can create web-enabled procedures the same way you create normal procedures. For more information on SQL-Station Coder, see Chapter 13 and the SQL-Station online documentation.

Summary

In this chapter, we have discussed Oracle's WebServer program and examined how PL/SQL is an integral part of it. Through the PL/SQL web agent, a PL/SQL stored procedure can generate HTML output. This allows you to create dynamic web pages, based on data in the database. We have discussed the packages in the web toolkit that aid in this, including the OWA_UTIL package. The chapter concluded with a discussion of development environments useful for web agent procedures.

CHAPTER
20

External Procedures

L/SQL is a very powerful language with many features, but there are some things for which it is not suited, such as interaction with the file system and other system devices, or complex numerical calculations. In these cases, another 3GL such as C is more appropriate. Oracle8 provides the ability to call a C procedure directly from PL/SQL as an external procedure, which allows these additional features to be integrated with the PL/SQL environment. In this chapter, we will discuss how external procedures work, including the necessary requirements to make them work.

What Is an External Procedure?

PL/SQL 8.0 ...and HIGHER An *external procedure* is a procedure written in a language other than PL/SQL but callable from a PL/SQL program. External procedures are a new feature of Oracle8. As of Oracle8 version 8.0.3, the only supported language for external procedures is C. Future versions of Oracle8, however, will have support for additional languages (such as Java or C++). Consequently, the syntax for declaring and calling external procedures is more generic than it needs to be for the current version, to accommodate future languages.

How do external procedure calls work? Figure 20-1 illustrates the communication between a client process and the Oracle8 server. The client process communicates with the shadow process, which in turn communicates with the rest of the database. The client process sends SQL statements and PL/SQL blocks to the shadow process, which executes them and sends back the results. For more information on client and shadow processes, including how they interact with other Oracle processes, see Chapter 22.

In order to execute an external procedure, some additional processes and libraries are required. These are illustrated in Figure 20-2. When the initial call to an external procedure is made by a shadow, the SQL*Net listener spawns a special process known as *extproc*. This process will dynamically load a shared library (or more than one shared library) that contains the C procedure and then execute it, sending the results back to the shadow process and, in turn, back to the client. Once extproc is spawned, it will persist for the life of the session. In order to execute additional procedures, the shadow process and extproc can communicate directly, without going through the listener.

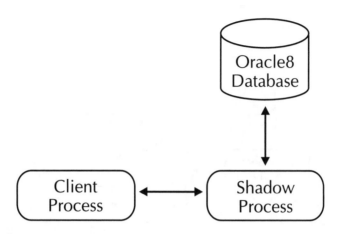

FIGURE 20-1. *Client and shadow processes*

There are several things to note about this environment, which illustrate some requirements for using external procedures:

■ The external procedure must be in a shared library. Extproc will dynamically load the library when the procedure is called. If external procedures are called later in the session that are in a different library, extproc will also load that library. Thus, external procedures are only supported if the underlying operating system supports shared libraries. For example, on Windows NT the external procedure would be compiled into a DLL, and on Solaris the external procedure would be compiled into a shared object (.so).

■ Each session that calls an external procedure will have its own extproc process spawned by the SQL*Net listener.

■ The listener and extproc must be on the same machine as the database. As we will see in the next sections, the syntax for creating a library data dictionary object has no means for specifying a host name.

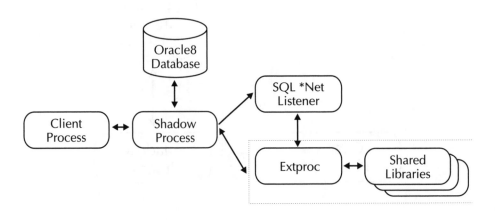

FIGURE 20-2. *SQL*Net listener and extproc processes*

■ The external procedure can in turn make callbacks to the database to execute additional SQL statements or PL/SQL blocks. Callbacks are done using the Oracle8 Call Interface (OCI). They are discussed in the section "Callbacks to the Database" later in this chapter.

Required Steps

In order to call an external procedure, you must complete the following steps:

1. Code the procedure in C and compile it into a shared library.

2. Configure the SQL*Net parameter files and start the listener.

3. Create a library data dictionary object to represent the operating system library.

4. Create a wrapper procedure in PL/SQL that maps PL/SQL parameters to C parameters.

Let's examine these steps in detail.

Code the Procedure

The first step is to write the procedure itself. Suppose we want to create an operating system file and write a string to it. We can do this with the **OutputString** procedure defined here:

```
/* Available online as part of outstr.c */
#include <stdio.h>

/* Outputs the string contained in message to a file specified by
   path. The file will be created if it doesn't exist. */
void OutputString(path, message)
char *path;
char *message;   {

  FILE *file_handle;

  /* Open the file for writing. */
  file_handle = fopen(path, "w");

  /* Output the string followed by a newline. */
  fprintf(file_handle, "%s\n", message);

  /* Close the file. */
  fclose(file_handle);
}
```

Once this file is created, we need to compile it into a shared library. On a Solaris Unix system, we can do this with the command

```
cc -G -o /home/utils/stringlib.so outstr.c
```

which will create the shared library /home/utils/stringlib.so. The command for doing this on other operating systems will likely vary—consult your operating system and/or compiler documentation for more information.

TIP
On Unix systems, the makefile
$ORACLE_HOME/rdbms/demo/demo_rdbms
.mk *contains targets for linking shared
libraries. The* **extproc_nocallback** *target will
build a library that doesn't make callbacks
to the database, and the* **extproc_callback**
*target will build a library that does make
callbacks. (Callbacks are discussed later in
this chapter, in the section "Callbacks to the
Database.") See this makefile for
instructions and examples.*

Configure the SQL*Net Listener

The listener needs to be configured only once. Once it is set up and
running, the extproc process will be automatically spawned as needed.
Configuring the listener requires two files—listener.ora and tnsnames.ora.
Once these files are created, the listener can be started.

The default location for SQL*Net configuration files will vary depending
on your operating system. On Unix, for example, the default location is
$ORACLE_HOME/network/admin. This can be overridden by specifying the
TNS_ADMIN environment variable.

listener.ora   This file specifies the parameters for the listener. It should
look something like the following:

```
#Available online as listener.ora
#Sample listener.ora for external procedures.
#Replace <<ORACLE_HOME>> with the $ORACLE_HOME directory,
#replace <<LISTENER_KEY>> with an IPC key, and
#replace <<EXTPROC_SID>> with an identifier for extproc.

listener =
  (ADDRESS_LIST =
    (ADDRESS =
      (PROTOCOL = ipc)
      (KEY = <<LISTENER_KEY>>)
    )
  )
```

```
Start Date              12-AUG-97 01:04:00
Uptime                  0 days 0 hr. 0 min. 1 sec
Trace Level             off
Security                OFF
SNMP                    OFF
Listener Parameter File
  /oracle/app/oracle/product/8.0.3/network/admin/listener.ora
Listener Log File
  /oracle/app/oracle/product/8.0.3/network/log/listener.log
Services Summary...
  V803            has 1 service handler(s)
The command completed successfully
```

For more information on using lsnrctl, see the *Net8 Administrator's Guide*.

Create the Library

A *library* is a data dictionary object that contains information about the operating system location of the shared library on disk. Since the shared library is outside the database, PL/SQL needs something in the database to represent it. Libraries are created using the DDL command CREATE LIBRARY, which has the following syntax,

> CREATE LIBRARY *library_name* {IS | AS}
> '*operating_system_path*';

where *library_name* is the name of the new library, and *operating_system_path* is the complete path (including directory) of the shared library on the file system. For example, we can create the library **stringlib** using the following statement:

```
CREATE LIBRARY stringlib AS
  '/home/utils/stringlib.so';
```

The database does not verify that the operating system shared library actually exists at this point. However, if it does not, you will receive an error when trying to call a procedure declared to use the library.

A library can be dropped using the DROP LIBRARY command, which has the syntax

DROP LIBRARY *library_name*;

where *library_name* is the name of the library to be dropped.

Privileges on Libraries   In order to create a library, you need the CREATE LIBRARY system privilege, similar to the privileges required for other DDL commands. Once you have created a library, you can allow other users to access it by granting the EXECUTE privilege on it to other users.

Libraries in the Data Dictionary   Like other database objects, information about libraries is stored in the data dictionary. Library information is stored in the **user_libraries**, **all_libraries**, and **dba_libraries** tables. The main columns in these tables are described here:

Column	Datatype	Description
library_name	VARCHAR2(30)	Name of the library.
file_spec	VARCHAR2(2000)	Operating system path of the shared library as specified in the CREATE LIBRARY statement.
dynamic	VARCHAR2(1)	If Y, the library is dynamic. If N, it is not. With Oracle8 version 8.0, only dynamic libraries can be created.
status	VARCHAR2(7)	VALID or INVALID, similar to the *status* column in other dictionary views.

The following query shows the information about **stringlib**:

```
SQL> SELECT * FROM user_libraries
  2    WHERE library_name = 'STRINGLIB';
```

```
LIBRARY_NAME    FILE_SPEC                        D STATUS
--------------  -------------------------------  - -------
STRINGLIB       /home/utils/stringlib.so         Y VALID
```

For more information on the data dictionary and other information stored there, see Appendix D.

Create the Wrapper Procedure

In order to call an external procedure, you need to create a *wrapper procedure*. This procedure serves several purposes: it maps the PL/SQL parameters to C parameters, it serves as a placeholder so that calling procedures can determine dependencies, and it tells PL/SQL the name of the external library. A wrapper procedure consists of a procedure specification (including the parameters, if any), followed by the EXTERNAL clause. The syntax is as follows:

```
CREATE [OR REPLACE] PROCEDURE procedure_name [parameter_list]
  AS EXTERNAL
  LIBRARY library_name
  [NAME external_name]
  [LANGUAGE language_name]
  [CALLING STANDARD {C | PASCAL}]
  [WITH CONTEXT]
  [PARAMETERS (external_parameter_list)];
```

Each of the clauses is described in the following sections.

LIBRARY   This is the only required clause, and it is used to specify the library that represents the operating system shared library containing the C procedure. This library must either be in the current schema, or you must have EXECUTE privileges on it.

NAME   This clause specifies the name of the C procedure. If it is not specified, it defaults to the name of the PL/SQL wrapper procedure. Note, however, that PL/SQL names are stored in all uppercase, so if the C procedure is lowercase or mixed case, a double-quoted identifier is necessary here.

LANGUAGE   The LANGUAGE clause is used to specify the language in which the external procedure is written. If not specified, it defaults to C, which as of version 8.0.3 is the only supported language for external procedures.

CALLING STANDARD   The calling standard can be either C or PASCAL. This determines the order in which parameters are placed on the stack. The default is C, which should normally be used for external procedures written in C. With the PASCAL calling standard, the external procedure is responsible for explicitly popping the stack to retrieve the parameters, and the parameters themselves are in reverse order.

WITH CONTEXT   This clause will add a parameter to the C procedure, which can be used to get OCI handles used for calling back to the database. This clause is discussed in detail in the section "Callbacks to the Database" later in this chapter.

PARAMETERS   The PARAMETERS clause specifies how the PL/SQL parameters of the wrapper procedure are mapped into C parameters for the external procedure. If it is not specified, then the default mappings are used. This clause is discussed in detail in the next section, "Parameter Mappings."

The following example is a wrapper procedure for **OutputString**:

```
-- Available online as part of outstr.sql
CREATE OR REPLACE PROCEDURE OutputString(
  p_Path IN VARCHAR2,
  p_Message IN VARCHAR2) AS EXTERNAL

  LIBRARY stringlib
  NAME "OutputString"
  PARAMETERS (p_Path STRING,
              p_Message STRING);
```

After creating this, we can call **OutputString** directly from a PL/SQL block. For example, the following block will create a file called output.txt in the /tmp directory, which contains the single line "Hello World!" This is illustrated by the sample SQL*Plus and host session that follows.

```
SQL> BEGIN
  2    OutputString('/tmp/output.txt', 'Hello World!');
```

```
3  END;
4  /
PL/SQL procedure successfully completed.

SQL> exit
Disconnected from Oracle8 Server Release 8.0.3.0.0 - Production
With the Partitioning and Objects options
PL/SQL Release 8.0.3.0.0 - Production
$ cat /tmp/output.txt
Hello World!
```

Parameter Mappings

One of the main issues when communicating between two languages is
how to convert between datatypes. This is true with external procedures as
well: you need to specify how the PL/SQL datatypes used for the
parameters in the wrapper procedure map to the C datatypes used for the
parameters in the external procedure. Besides the datatypes themselves,
there are other issues that need to be resolved:

- In PL/SQL, any variable can be NULL. C has no concept of NULL,
  and so an additional variable known as an *indicator* can be passed
  to indicate whether the parameter is NULL or not.

- PL/SQL includes datatypes that are not in C, and C includes
  datatypes that are not in PL/SQL. For example, C has no DATE or
  BOOLEAN type, while PL/SQL does not distinguish between a one-,
  two- or four-byte integer.

- PL/SQL version 8 can accommodate character variables in different
  character sets. These character sets need to be communicated to C.

- C needs to know the current and/or maximum length for character
  strings passed from PL/SQL.

- PL/SQL needs to know the current and/or maximum length for
  character strings passed from C.

The PARAMETERS clause is used to resolve all of these concerns, as we
will see in this section. It has the following structure:

PARAMETERS (*external_parameter_list*);

The *external_parameter_list* is a list of parameters, each of which has the structure

{*parameter_name* | RETURN} *property* [BY REF] [*external_datatype*]

where *parameter_name* is the name of the parameter, *external_datatype* is the C datatype to be assigned to this parameter, and *property* is one or more of INDICATOR, LENGTH, MAXLEN, CHARSETID, and CHARSETFORM. We will examine these clauses in the next sections.

PL/SQL vs. C Datatypes

Since PL/SQL and C do not have the same set of datatypes, Oracle8 provides a default C datatype for each PL/SQL datatype. You can override this default if desired. To facilitate this process, Oracle defines a set of *external datatypes*, which are defined in Table 20-1. An external datatype is a mnemonic for a commonly used C type. External datatypes are also used in Pro*C and OCI programs. Oracle also defines additional external datatypes which are not standard to C, such as OCILOBLOCATOR. Table 20-2 describes the available external datatypes for each PL/SQL datatype.

External Datatype	Description	C Datatype
CHAR[1]	One-byte quantity, used to store either a character or integer ranging from −128 to +127.	char
UNSIGNED CHAR[1]	One-byte quantity, used to store integers ranging from 0 to 255.	unsigned char
SHORT[1,2]	Usually a two-byte quantity, used to store an integer ranging from -2^{15} to $+2^{15}-1$.	short
UNSIGNED SHORT[1,2]	Usually an unsigned two-byte quantity, used to store an integer ranging from 0 to $+2^{16}$.	unsigned short

TABLE 20-1.   *External Datatypes*

External Datatype	Description	C Datatype
INT[1, 2]	Usually a four-byte quantity, used to store an integer ranging from -2^{31} to $+2^{31} -1$.	int
UNSIGNED INT[1, 2]	Usually an unsigned four-byte quantity, used to store an integer ranging from 0 to 2^{32}.	unsigned int
LONG[1, 2]	Usually a four-byte quantity, used to store an integer ranging from -2^{31} to $+2^{31} -1$.	long
UNSIGNED LONG[1, 2]	Usually an unsigned four-byte quantity, used to store an integer ranging from 0 to 2^{32}.	unsigned long
SIZE_T[1, 2]	Number of bytes as specified by the operating system and compiler.	size_t
SB1[3]	Signed one-byte quantity.	sb1
UB1[3]	Unsigned one-byte quantity.	ub1
SB2[3]	Signed two-byte quantity.	sb2
UB2[3]	Unsigned two-byte quantity.	ub2
SB4[3]	Signed four-byte quantity.	sb4
UB4	Unsigned four-byte quantity.	ub4
FLOAT[1, 2]	Usually a four-byte quantity, used to store floating point numbers.	float
DOUBLE[1, 2]	Usually a four-byte quantity, used to store floating point numbers.	double
STRING[1]	Used to store variable length null-terminated character strings.	char *

TABLE 20-1. *External Datatypes* (continued)

External Datatype	Description	C Datatype
RAW[1]	Used to store variable length byte strings.	unsigned char *
OCILOBLOCATOR[4]	Used in OCI functions to manipulate LOBs in the database.	OCILobLocater *

TABLE 20-1. *External Datatypes* (continued)

[1] A standard C datatype.

[2] The size of this type can vary, depending on the operating system and compiler. Thus it is not always portable.

[3] An Oracle-defined datatype that is defined in the header file oratypes.h. Each platform defines this type such that it meets its definition, ensuring that it is portable.

[4] An Oracle-defined datatype that is defined in the header file oci.h. This type is used only in the OCI functions that manipulate LOBs in the database.

PL/SQL Type	Supported External Datatypes
CHAR, CHARACTER, LONG, ROWID, VARCHAR, VARCHAR2	STRING*
BINARY_INTEGER, BOOLEAN, PLS_INTEGER	INT*, CHAR, UNSIGNED CHAR, SHORT, UNSIGNED SHORT, UNSIGNED INT, LONG, UNSIGNED LONG, SB1, UB1, SB2, UB2, SB4, UB4, SIZE_T
NATURAL, NATURALN, POSITIVE, POSITIVEN, SIGNTYPE	UNSIGNED INT*, CHAR, UNSIGNED CHAR, SHORT, UNSIGNED SHORT, INT, LONG, UNSIGNED LONG, SB1, UB1, SB2, UB2, SB4, UB4, SIZE_T

TABLE 20-2. *PL/SQL and External Datatype Mappings*

PL/SQL Type	Supported External Datatypes
FLOAT, REAL	FLOAT*
DOUBLE PRECISION	DOUBLE*
LONG RAW, RAW	RAW*
BFILE, BLOB, CLOB	OCILOBLOCATOR*

TABLE 20-2. *PL/SQL and External Datatype Mappings*

*Default external datatype

Each entry in the PARAMETERS clause represents a parameter to the C external function. For example, consider the **OutputString** function that we examined earlier. The wrapper function has a PARAMETERS clause like

```
CREATE OR REPLACE PROCEDURE OutputString(
   p_Path IN VARCHAR2,
   p_Message IN VARCHAR2) AS EXTERNAL
   ...
   PARAMETERS (p_Path STRING,
               p_Message STRING);
```

and the C function is defined with

```
void OutputString(path, message)
char *path;
char *message;  {
  ...
```

This clause specifies that **p_Path** and **p_Message** are to be passed to C as null-terminated strings of type **char ***. Since the default external datatype for VARCHAR2 is STRING, the PARAMETERS clause could have been omitted in this case.

Alternatively, consider **OutputString2**, which takes an **int** parameter. This parameter indicates the number of times the message should be repeated. The C function is defined with:

```
-- Available online as part of outstr.c
/* Outputs the string contained in message to a file specified by
```

path. The message is repeated num_times times. The file will be
created if it doesn't exist. */

```
void OutputString2(path, message, num_times)
char *path;
char *message;
int    num_times;  {

  FILE *file_handle;
  int counter;

  /* Open the file for writing. */
  file_handle = fopen(path, "w");

  for (counter = 0; counter < num_times; counter++)
    /* Output the string followed by a newline. */
    fprintf(file_handle, "%s\n", message);

  /* Close the file. */
  fclose(file_handle);
}
```

and the wrapper procedure is defined with

```
-- Available online as part of outstr.sql
CREATE OR REPLACE PROCEDURE OutputString2(
  p_Path IN VARCHAR2,
  p_Message IN VARCHAR2,
  p_NumLines IN BINARY_INTEGER) AS EXTERNAL

  LIBRARY stringlib
  NAME "OutputString2"
  PARAMETERS (p_Path STRING,
              p_Message STRING,
              p_NumLines INT);
```

Note that **p_NumLines** specifies INT as the external datatype.

Parameter Modes

The parameters for the wrapper procedure (and hence for the external
procedure) can be of any PL/SQL mode—IN, OUT, or IN OUT. If the
parameter is OUT or IN OUT, then the associated C parameter must be
passed by reference rather than by value, regardless of the datatype. The
only exception to this rule is external datatype STRING, which is passed by
reference regardless of the associated parameter mode. **OutputString3**

illustrates this. Note that **p_NumLinesWritten** is OUT, and thus the associated C parameter is passed as **int ***, rather than **int**. The code for the wrapper and external procedures follows.

/* **Available online as part of outstr.c** */

```c
/* Outputs the string contained in message to a file specified by
   path. The message is repeated num_times times. The file will be
   created if it doesn't exist. The number of lines actually
written
   is returned in num_lines_written. */
void OutputString3(path, message, num_times, num_lines_written)
char *path;
char *message;
int  num_times;
ub2 *num_lines_written;  {

  FILE *file_handle;
  int counter;

  /* Open the file for writing. */
  file_handle = fopen(path, "w");

  for (counter = 0; counter < num_times; counter++)  {
    /* Output the string followed by a newline. */
    fprintf(file_handle, "%s\n", message);
    (*num_lines_written)++;
  }

  /* Close the file. */
  fclose(file_handle);
}
```

-- **Available online as part of outstr.sql**

```sql
CREATE OR REPLACE PROCEDURE OutputString3(
  p_Path IN VARCHAR2,
  p_Message IN VARCHAR2,
  p_NumLines IN BINARY_INTEGER,
  p_NumLinesWritten OUT NATURAL) AS EXTERNAL

  LIBRARY stringlib
  NAME "OutputString3"
  PARAMETERS (p_Path STRING,
              p_Message STRING,
              p_NumLines INT,
              p_NumLinesWritten UB2);
```

Parameter Properties

Along with the datatype, the PARAMETERS clause is used to specify additional information, known as *properties*, for each parameter. Each property maps to another parameter in the external procedure, but not the wrapper procedure. The available properties are described below, and their supported datatypes in Table 20-3.

INDICATOR   An indicator is used to specify if the associated parameter is NULL. PL/SQL variables can be NULL, while C variables cannot. Thus the indicator is required, since the external procedure may need to know if a parameter is NULL, or the RDBMS may need to know if a returned parameter is NULL. The external procedure can check the value of the indicator—if it is OCI_IND_NULL, then the parameter is NULL, if it is OCI_IND_NOTNULL, the parameter is not NULL. These values can also be set for output parameters.

LENGTH and MAXLEN   LENGTH is used to store the current length, and MAXLEN the maximum length, of a character or RAW parameter. If a

Property	Supported External Datatypes
INDICATOR	SHORT*, INT, LONG
LENGTH	INT*, SHORT, UNSIGNED SHORT, UNSIGNED INT, LONG, UNSIGNED LONG
MAXLEN	INT*, SHORT, UNSIGNED SHORT, UNSIGNED INT, LONG, UNSIGNED LONG
CHARSETID, CHARSETFORM	UNSIGNED INT*, UNSIGNED SHORT, UNSIGNED LONG

TABLE 20-3.   *Parameter Properties*

*Default external datatype

parameter is OUT or IN OUT, then its return value must not exceed
MAXLEN.

CHARSETID and CHARSETFORM These properties are used to
specify the character set ID and form, respectively. They are used in NLS
environments for CHAR, CLOB, and VARCHAR2 parameters. The
equivalent OCI attributes are OCI_ATTR_CHARSET_ID and
OCI_ATTR_CHARSET_FORM.

OutputString4 illustrates the use of properties. The code for the external
procedure and wrapper procedure follows. Note that an indicator is not
necessary for **num_lines_written** since it will always return a value, and
will thus never be NULL.

```
/* Available online as part of outstr.c */
/* Outputs the string contained in message to a file specified by
   path. The message is repeated num_times times. The file will be
   created if it doesn't exist. The number of lines actually written
   is returned in num_lines_written. The NULL-ness of each
   parameter is checked. */
void OutputString4(path, path_ind,
                   message, message_ind,
                   num_times, num_times_ind,
                   num_lines_written)
char *path;
short path_ind;
char *message;
short message_ind;
int   num_times;
short num_times_ind;
ub2  *num_lines_written;  {

  FILE *file_handle;
  int counter;

  /* If any of the input parameters are NULL, return zero and
     don't output anything. */
  if (path_ind == OCI_IND_NULL || message_ind == OCI_IND_NULL ||
      num_times_ind == OCI_IND_NULL) {
    *num_lines_written = 0;
    return;
  }
```

```
   /* Open the file for writing. */
   file_handle = fopen(path, "w");

   for (counter = 0; counter < num_times; counter++)  {
     /* Output the string followed by a newline. */
     fprintf(file_handle, "%s\n", message);
     (*num_lines_written)++;
   }

   /* Close the file. */
   fclose(file_handle);
}
```

-- Available online as part of **outstr.sql**
```
CREATE OR REPLACE PROCEDURE OutputString4(
   p_Path IN VARCHAR2,
   p_Message IN VARCHAR2,
   p_NumLines IN BINARY_INTEGER,
   p_NumLinesWritten OUT NATURAL) AS EXTERNAL

   LIBRARY stringlib
   NAME "OutputString4"
   PARAMETERS (p_Path STRING,
               p_Path INDICATOR,
               p_Message STRING,
               p_Message INDICATOR,
               p_NumLines INT,
               p_NumLines INDICATOR,
               p_NumLinesWritten UB2);
```

External Functions and Packaged Procedures

In addition to external procedures, you can create external functions. External procedures and functions can be contained in packages, and thus take advantage of packages features such as overloading.

Function Return Values

An external function is created just like a procedure. The return value of the function is specified using the keyword RETURN in the PARAMETERS clause. Properties can be associated with the return value as well, as **OutputString5** shows:

```
/* Available online as part of outstr.c */
/* Outputs the string contained in message to a file specified by
   path. The message is repeated num_times times. The file will be
   created if it doesn't exist. The number of lines actually
   written is returned. The NULL-ness of each parameter
   is checked. */
ub2 OutputString5(path, path_ind,
                  message, message_ind,
                  num_times, num_times_ind,
                  retval_ind)
char  *path;
short  path_ind;
char  *message;
short  message_ind;
int    num_times;
short  num_times_ind;
short  *retval_ind;  {

  FILE *file_handle;
  ub2 counter;

  /* If any of the input parameters are NULL, return NULL and
     don't output anything. */
  if (path_ind == OCI_IND_NULL || message_ind == OCI_IND_NULL ||
      num_times_ind == OCI_IND_NULL) {
    *retval_ind = OCI_IND_NULL;
    return 0;
  }

  /* Open the file for writing. */
  file_handle = fopen(path, "w");

  for (counter = 0; counter < num_times; counter++)  {
    /* Output the string followed by a newline. */
    fprintf(file_handle, "%s\n", message);
  }

  /* Close the file. */
  fclose(file_handle);

  /* Set up return values. */
  *retval_ind = OCI_IND_NOTNULL;
  return counter;
}
```

`-- Available online as part of outstr.sql`

```
CREATE OR REPLACE FUNCTION OutputString5(
  p_Path IN VARCHAR2,
  p_Message IN VARCHAR2,
  p_NumLines IN BINARY_INTEGER)
  RETURN NATURAL AS EXTERNAL

  LIBRARY stringlib
  NAME "OutputString5"
  PARAMETERS (p_Path STRING,
              p_Path INDICATOR,
              p_Message STRING,
              p_Message INDICATOR,
              p_NumLines INT,
              p_NumLines INDICATOR,
              RETURN INDICATOR,
              RETURN UB2);
```

Overloading

Wrapper procedures (or functions) can be in packages, as well as standalone. In this case, the wrapper procedure should be in the package body, with a forward declaration in the package header, as normal. The **debug_extproc** package later in this chapter illustrates this technique.

RESTRICT_REFERENCES

If an external function is in a package, you can assert the RESTRICT_REFERENCES pragma to allow it to be used in a SQL statement. However, the PL/SQL compiler has no way of verifying that the external function does not violate the pragma, since it is not written in PL/SQL. It is your responsibility to insure this. If the external function violates the pragma, internal errors can result.

Callbacks to the Database

An external procedure can make callbacks to the database, to raise errors or issue SQL commands. These are done using the Oracle8 OCI interface. All SQL statements executed from an external procedure use the existing connection and transaction established in the PL/SQL wrapper procedure.

Service Routines

Service routines are used to raise exceptions in the database, allocate memory, and retrieve OCI handles to execute SQL statements. All of the service routines take a context as one of their parameters. In C, the context is of type **OCIExtProcContext**, and is indicated by the CONTEXT keyword in the parameter list. The WITH CONTEXT clause is also required.

OCIExtProcRaiseExcp

This service routine raises a predefined exception, similar to the RAISE statement. The C prototype is defined with

```
int OCIExtProcRaiseExcp(with_context, error_number)
  OCIExtProcContext *with_context;
  size_t error_number;
```

Like RAISE, when you call OCIExtProcRaiseExcp, no values are assigned to OUT or IN OUT parameters, and the procedure must return immediately. **OutputString6** illustrates this service routine by raising ORA-6502 if a NULL value is passed. Note the use of WITH CONTEXT in the PARAMETERS clause.

```
/* Available online as part of outstr.c */
/* Outputs the string contained in message to a file specified by
   path. The message is repeated num_times times. The file will be
   created if it doesn't exist. The number of lines actually
   written is returned. The NULL-ness of each parameter is
   checked, and ORA-6502 is raised if any input parameter is
   NULL. */
ub2 OutputString6(context, path, path_ind,
                  message, message_ind,
                  num_times, num_times_ind,
                  retval_ind)
OCIExtProcContext *context;
char              *path;
short              path_ind;
char              *message;
short              message_ind;
int                num_times;
short              num_times_ind;
short             *retval_ind;  {

  FILE *file_handle;
```

```
  ub2 counter;

  /* If any of the input parameters are NULL, raise ORA-6502 and
     return immediately. */
  if (path_ind == OCI_IND_NULL || message_ind == OCI_IND_NULL ||
      num_times_ind == OCI_IND_NULL) {
    OCIExtProcRaiseExcp(context, 6502);
    return 0;
  }

  /* Open the file for writing. */
  file_handle = fopen(path, "w");

  for (counter = 0; counter < num_times; counter++)  {
    /* Output the string followed by a newline. */
    fprintf(file_handle, "%s\n", message);
  }

  /* Close the file. */
  fclose(file_handle);

  /* Set up return values. */
  *retval_ind = OCI_IND_NOTNULL;
  return counter;
}
```

-- **Available online as part of outstr.sql**

```
CREATE OR REPLACE FUNCTION OutputString6(
  p_Path IN VARCHAR2,
  p_Message IN VARCHAR2,
  p_NumLines IN BINARY_INTEGER)
RETURN NATURAL AS EXTERNAL

  LIBRARY stringlib
  NAME "OutputString6"
  WITH CONTEXT
  PARAMETERS (CONTEXT,
              p_Path STRING,
              p_Path INDICATOR,
              p_Message STRING,
              p_Message INDICATOR,
              p_NumLines INT,
              p_NumLines INDICATOR,
              RETURN INDICATOR,
              RETURN UB2);
```

OCIExtProcRaiseExcpWithMsg

This service routine is similar to RAISE_APPLICATION_ERROR. Unlike OCIExtProcRaiseExcp, it allows you to pass a user-defined message along with the error. The error number should be between 20,000 and 20,999, just like RAISE_APPLICATION_ERROR. The prototype is

```
int OCIExtProcRaiseExcpWithMsg(
   with_context, error_number, error_message, len)
OCIExtProcContext *with_context;
size_t            error_number;
text              *error_message;
size_t            len;
```

If **error_message** is a null-terminated string, then **len** should be zero. Otherwise, **len** should be the length of the string. **OutputString7** (in the next section) illustrates this technique.

OCIExtprocAllocCallMemory

If you need to allocate memory in your external procedure, you can use OCIExtprocAllocCallMemory. This routine will allocate memory that will last for the duration of the call, and will be freed automatically by PL/SQL when the external procedure returns. The prototype is

```
dvoid *OCIExtprocAllocCallMemory(with_context, amount);
OCIExtProcContext *with_memory;
size_t            amount;
```

where **amount** is the number of bytes to allocate. **OutputString7** uses this routine to allocate memory for the error message text.

```
/* Available online as part of outstr.c */
/* Outputs the string contained in message to a file specified by
   path. The message is repeated num_times times. The file will be
   created if it doesn't exist. The number of lines actually
   written is returned. The NULL-ness of each parameter is
   checked, and ORA-6502 is raised if any input parameter is
   NULL. If the file  cannot be opened, a user-defined error is
   returned. */
ub2 OutputString7(context, path, path_ind,
                  message, message_ind,
                  num_times, num_times_ind,
                  retval_ind)
```

```
OCIExtProcContext *context;
char              *path;
short              path_ind;
char              *message;
short              message_ind;
int               num_times;
short             num_times_ind;
short             *retval_ind;  {

  FILE *file_handle;
  ub2 counter;

  /* If any of the input parameters are NULL, raise ORA-6502 and
     return immediately. */
  if (path_ind == OCI_IND_NULL || message_ind == OCI_IND_NULL ||
      num_times_ind == OCI_IND_NULL) {
    OCIExtProcRaiseExcp(context, 6502);
    return 0;
  }

  /* Open the file for writing. */
  file_handle = fopen(path, "w");

  /* Check for success. If not, raise an error. */
  if (!file_handle) {
    text *initial_msg = (text *)"Cannot open file ";
    text *error_msg;

    /* Allocate space for the error message text, and set it up.
       We do not have to free this memory - PL/SQL will do that
       automatically. */
    error_msg = OCIExtProcAllocCallMemory(context,
                   strlen(path) + strlen(initial_msg) + 1);
    strcpy((char *)error_msg, (char *)initial_msg);
    strcat((char *)error_msg, path);

    OCIExtProcRaiseExcpWithMsg(context, 20001, error_msg, 0);
    return 0;
  }

  for (counter = 0; counter < num_times; counter++)  {
    /* Output the string followed by a newline. */
    fprintf(file_handle, "%s\n", message);
  }
```

```
/* Close the file. */
fclose(file_handle);

/* Set up return values. */

*retval_ind = OCI_IND_NOTNULL;
return counter;
}
```

Executing SQL in an External Procedure

The Oracle8 OCI is used to execute SQL statements from an external procedure. In order to use the OCI, you need to set up several OCI handles. The OciExtProcGetEnv routine is used to do this.

OciExtProcGetEnv

This service routine is defined with

```
sword OciExtProcGetEnv(with_context, envh, svch, errh)
OCIExtProcContext *with_context;
OCIEnv           **envh;
OCISvcCtx        **svch;
OCIError         **errh;
```

You can use the returned environment, service context, and error handles in subsequent OCI calls that execute SQL statements. These handles can be used only for callbacks—they cannot be used for standard OCI calls. For more information on the OCI handles and their use, see the *Programmer's Guide to the Oracle Call Interface*.

Restrictions

There are several restrictions to keep in mind when issuing SQL statements within an external procedure. The following kinds of statements are not allowed:

- Transaction control commands like COMMIT or ROLLBACK
- DDL commands which would cause an implicit COMMIT
- Calls to other external procedures

In addition, there are certain OCI calls which are not allowed in an external procedure. See the *Oracle8 PL/SQL User's Guide and Reference* for a complete list.

Tips, Guidelines, and Restrictions

In this last part of the chapter, we will discuss some debugging tips and explore guidelines and restrictions for external procedures.

Debugging External Procedures

As we have seen, external procedures are a very useful and powerful feature. However, because we are dealing with two different languages (PL/SQL and C) and the interface between them, debugging external procedures can be tricky. Here, we will look at some different methods for debugging external procedures.

Call from C Directly

Perhaps the simplest method of debugging is to call the external procedure directly from C, without any PL/SQL at all. You can call the procedure from either a statically or dynamically linked program and use the standard C debugger provided on your system (or other means) to debug the program. While this method won't uncover problems relating to the PL/SQL-to-C interface, it can uncover coding errors in the external procedure itself. This method is only available if the external procedure does not make any database callbacks.

Attaching to extproc with a Debugger

In order to step through a C procedure with a debugger, the program is typically started under control of the debugger. With external procedures, however, extproc is started automatically by the SQL*Net listener. This precludes you from starting it under control of a debugger. The solution to this is to start extproc first (by calling a dummy external procedure) and then attach to the running process with the debugger.

NOTE
In order to use this method, your operating system must support a debugger that allows you to attach to a running process. For example, on many Unix systems you can use the gdb debugger.

To facilitate this process, Oracle provides a package called **debug_extproc**. The script to create this package can be found in the PL/SQL demo directory under $ORACLE_HOME and also on the CD accompanying this book. The code for **debug_extproc** is as follows:

```
-- Available online as dbgextp.sql
CREATE OR REPLACE PACKAGE debug_extproc IS
  -- Start up the extproc agent process in the session
  --   Executing this procedure starts up the extproc agent process
  --   in the session allowing one to be able get the PID of the
  --   executing process. This PID is needed to be able to attach
  --   to the running process using a debugger.
  PROCEDURE startup_extproc_agent;
END debug_extproc;

CREATE OR REPLACE LIBRARY debug_extproc_library IS STATIC;

CREATE OR REPLACE PACKAGE BODY debug_extproc IS
  extproc_lib_error EXCEPTION;
  PRAGMA EXCEPTION_INIT (extproc_lib_error, -6520);

  extproc_func_error EXCEPTION;
  PRAGMA EXCEPTION_INIT (extproc_func_error, -6521);

  PROCEDURE local_startup_extproc_agent IS EXTERNAL
    LIBRARY debug_extproc_library;

  PROCEDURE startup_extproc_agent is
  BEGIN
    -- call a dummy procedure and trap all errors.
    local_startup_extproc_agent;
  EXCEPTION
    -- Ignore any errors if the function or library is not found.
    WHEN extproc_func_error then NULL;
    WHEN extproc_lib_error then NULL;
```

```
    END startup_extproc_agent;
END debug_extproc;
```

The steps for using this package are as follows:

1. Make sure that your C program is compiled and linked into the shared library with debug symbols. On Unix systems, this is usually done by passing the -g flag to the compiler.

2. In a SQL*Plus or other connection to the database, call **debug_extproc.startup_extproc_agent**. Although there is no actual C procedure associated with this wrapper procedure, extproc is started. No errors are signaled because of the exception handlers in **startup_extproc_agent**.

3. Determine the operating system process ID of extproc. On Unix, this can be done with a ps command.

4. Start the debugger, and attach to the running process determined in step 3.

5. Set a breakpoint in the function "pextproc," and allow the debugger to continue.

6. In the original session, call the wrapper procedure. This will in turn call extproc, which will then stop in pextproc.

7. At this point, the external procedure has been resolved by extproc, so you can set a breakpoint for it. As the symbol will have been dynamically loaded, some debuggers may not immediately recognize it, and you may have to tell the debugger to load the symbols again. (This is done with the share command in gdb.)

8. Continue in the debugger, which will then break in your procedure. You can now step through the external procedure code and debug.

Guidelines

There are several things to keep in mind when using external procedures:

■ Calling an external procedure does involve some overhead, especially the first time in a session. A request has to be made to the listener, and extproc needs to be spawned. Therefore, use external procedures when the efficiency gained by coding in C outweighs the cost of spawning the process.

■ extproc will assume the operating system privileges of the listener that spawned it. Consequently, it is a good idea to start a separate listener for external procedures from an account with restricted access. If the listener is running as the Oracle user, for example, then any user with permission to create a library can potentially write a C program that could modify the files under $ORACLE_HOME, possibly corrupting the database.

■ Be sure to write a value to any OUT or IN OUT parameters, as well as the function return value. PL/SQL has no means of checking this, and internal errors can result if these parameters are not assigned.

■ Likewise, do not write to IN parameters or overflow the capacity (as specified by the MAXLEN property) of OUT parameters.

■ Use the LENGTH and INDICATOR properties to handle all cases of character parameters. If you are returning a NULL value, then set the LENGTH parameter to zero.

■ If there is a PRAGMA RESTRICT_REFERENCES statement for the wrapper function, the external function cannot violate the pragma. PL/SQL has no way of checking this, and internal errors can result if the external function modifies the database in violation of the pragma.

Restrictions

Currently (as of Oracle8 version 8.0) external procedures have the following restrictions:

■ If the underlying platform does not support dynamic linking and shared libraries, then external procedures are not available.

■ The SQL*Net listener and extproc must run on the same machine as the database. Similarly, you cannot use a database link in the LIBRARY clause to specify a library on a remote database.

■ The only language currently supported is C. If you want to call another language, however, you can write a C external procedure to serve as an intermediary. PL/SQL would then call your C procedure, and your procedure could then call a procedure written in still another language, as long as that procedure is accessible from the shared library.

■ Parameters cannot be PL/SQL cursor variables, records, collections, or object type instances. However, you can retrieve these objects by using a callback to the database in the external procedure.

■ The Oracle server cannot be running MTS. extproc needs a dedicated server process with which to communicate.

■ The maximum number of parameters that can be passed to a C external procedure is 128. This includes parameters used to retrieve properties such as INDICATOR or LENGTH. However, if float or double parameters are passed by reference, then the maximum is less than 128. Each parameter passed like this takes up approximately the space of two parameters passed by value.

Summary

In this chapter, we have discussed external procedures, which allow a PL/SQL program to directly call a C procedure. We discussed the issues involved with doing this, including mapping PL/SQL datatypes to C datatypes and the use of properties. We also reviewed several methods for debugging external procedures. In the next chapter, we will examine another new Oracle8 feature, LOBs (large objects).

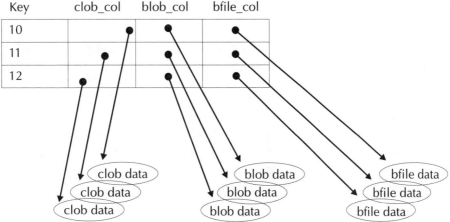

FIGURE 21-1. *LOB storage in the database*

Initializing a LOB Column

A LOB column can be set to NULL, as in the following INSERT statement:

```
INSERT INTO lobdemo(key, clob_col, blob_col, bfile_col)
   VALUES (10, NULL, NULL, NULL);
```

In this case, a NULL value is inserted in the column, rather than a LOB locator. There is no actual storage allocated for the lob data, since there is no locator to point to it. Because of this, you cannot use DBMS_LOB on a NULL value. The row must be updated to a valid locator first.

One way of doing this is with the EMPTY_BLOB() and EMPTY_CLOB() functions. These functions take no arguments, and return a valid LOB locator. DBMS_LOB can then be used to populate the LOB data. For example, consider the following INSERT statement:

```
INSERT INTO lobdemo(key, clob_col, blob_col, bfile_col)
   VALUES (11, empty_clob(), empty_blob(), NULL);
```

NOTE
*The empty parenthesis are required for
EMPTY_BLOB() and EMPTY_CLOB().*

After executing the above two statements, the **lobdemo** table will look
like Figure 21-2. After the column has been initialized, you can SELECT the
lob locator into a PL/SQL variable and use it with DBMS_LOB.
Alternatively, you could use the RETURNING clause on the INSERT to
retrieve the locator directly.

BFILEs are not initialized with EMPTY_CLOB() or EMPTY_BLOB();
rather, the BFILENAME function is used instead. This is described in the
following section, "Manipulating BFILEs".

Example
The following example illustrates some DML statements which manipulate
LOBs. Note that without DBMS_LOB, only the entire LOB can be

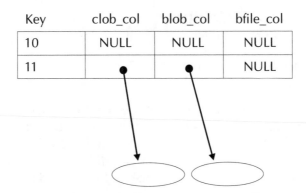

lobdemo

Key	clob_col	blob_col	bfile_col
10	NULL	NULL	NULL
11	•	•	NULL

FIGURE 21-2. *lobdemo table after inserts*

referenced. Also, a SELECT from a LOB column will return the locator, not the data itself.

```
-- Available online as lobdml.sql
DECLARE
  v_CLOBlocator CLOB;
  v_BLOBlocator BLOB;
BEGIN
  -- Initializes the clob_col to the specified string, and returns
  -- the locator into v_LOBlocator.
  INSERT INTO lobdemo (key, clob_col)
    VALUES (20, 'abcdefghijklmnopqrstuvwxyz')
    RETURNING clob_col INTO v_CLOBlocator;

  -- Modifies blob_col for the same row.
  UPDATE lobdemo
    SET blob_col = HEXTORAW('00FF00FF00FF')
    WHERE key = 20;

  -- Retrieves the locator for the newly updated value, not the
  -- value itself.
  SELECT blob_col
    INTO v_BLOBlocator
    FROM lobdemo
    WHERE key = 20;
END;
```

Manipulating BFILEs

The main characteristic of BFILEs is that they are stored outside the database. Like other kinds of LOBs, you use a locator to manipulate the file. However, there are several things to note about BFILEs:

- Because the file is maintained outside of Oracle, there is no transactional control for BFILE manipulations. Oracle does not provide support for integrity or durability of these external files, so this must be supplied by the underlying operating system.

- BFILEs are read-only. Both the DBMS_LOB package and the Oracle8 OCI can be used to read the files, but they cannot modify them.

■ As of Oracle8 Release 8.0, session migration in MTS (multi-threaded server) mode is not supported for BFILEs. Thus open BFILEs cannot persist beyond the end of a call to an MTS server, so the session needs to be bound to one shared server to process them.

Directories

In order to access an external file, the Oracle server needs to know the location of the file on the operating system. This is done through a new type of data dictionary object called a *directory*. The directory is a logical alias for an actual file system path. A directory is created with the CREATE DIRECTORY statement:

CREATE DIRECTORY *dir_name* AS *os_path*;

where *dir_name* is the name of the new directory, and *os_path* specifies a complete path of a directory on the operating system. For example, the following statement creates a directory which points to the operating system directory "/home/utils":

```
CREATE DIRECTORY utils AS '/home/utils';
```

Privileges Required for Directories

In order to issue the CREATE DIRECTORY command, you must have the CREATE DIRECTORY system privilege. This privilege is granted by default to the DBA role, but can be granted to other users by the database administrator. Once you have created a directory, you can GRANT the READ privilege on it to another user. This privilege is checked by both the DBMS_LOB and the OCI interfaces.

Furthermore, the operating system directory specified must exist, and be readable by the Oracle user. It is the system administrator's responsibility to insure this.

Directories in the Data Dictionary

The **dba_directories** and **all_directories** data dictionary views describe the directories that have been created on the system. **Dba_directories** contains information about all directories in the database, and **all_directories**

INSTR
READ
SUBSTR

In addition, DBMS_LOB contains six subprograms that write to LOB values. These are

APPEND
COPY
ERASE
LOADFROMFILE
TRIM
WRITE

Finally, the following six routines can be used for manipulating BFILEs:

FILECLOSE
FILECLOSEALL
FILEEXISTS
FILEGETNAME
FILEISOPEN
FILEOPEN

All of the DBMS_LOB routines are described in the following sections, in alphabetical order. Following the descriptions is a list of the exceptions which can be raised by these routines. The examples assume the **lobdemo** table has been created and populated with the following script:

```
-- Available online as lobtest.sql
INSERT INTO lobdemo (key, clob_col, blob_col, bfile_col)
  VALUES (-1, EMPTY_CLOB(), EMPTY_BLOB(), NULL);
INSERT INTO lobdemo (key, clob_col, blob_col, bfile_col)
  VALUES (1, 'abcdefghijklmnopqrstuvwxyz',
            HEXTORAW('000102030405060708090A0B0C0D0E0F'),
            NULL);
INSERT INTO lobdemo (key, clob_col, blob_col, bfile_col)
  VALUES (2, 'A Quick Brown Fox Jumps Over the Lazy Dog',
            HEXTORAW('FFFEFDFCFBFAF9F8F7F6F5F4F3F2F1F0'),
            NULL);
COMMIT;
```

For more information on the DBMS_LOB package, see the *Oracle8 Server Application Developer's Guide.*

APPEND

Use this routine to append the contents of a source LOB to the destination LOB. The source LOB is unchanged. APPEND is overloaded to accept binary or character LOBs with the following definitions:

```
PROCEDURE APPEND(
  dest_lob IN OUT BLOB,
  src_lob IN BLOB);

PROCEDURE APPEND(
  dest_lob IN OUT CLOB CHARACTER SET ANY_CS;
  src_lob IN CLOB CHARACTER SET dest_lob%CHARSET);
```

Here, *dest_lob* is the destination LOB, and *src_lob* is the source LOB. Note that APPEND cannot be used for BFILEs, since they are read-only. The VALUE_ERROR exception is raised if either *src_lob* or *dest_lob* is NULL. (The complete list of exceptions raised by DBMS_LOB routines can be found at the end of this section.)

NOTE
APPEND, along with many of the other DBMS_LOB routines, uses the syntax CHARACTER SET ANY_CS to specify that either a CLOB or NCLOB can be used. The %CHARSET attribute returns the character set of its argument, and insures that both src_lob *and* dest_lob *are in the same character set.*

COMPARE

This function is used to compare two entire LOB values or parts of two LOB values. It will return zero if the LOB values are identical or non-zero if they are not. COMPARE is overloaded to accept all four types of LOBs with the following definitions:

```
FUNCTION COMPARE(
lob_1   IN BLOB,
lob_2   IN BLOB,
amount   IN INTEGER := 4294967295,
offset_1 IN INTEGER := 1,
offset_2 IN INTEGER := 1)
 RETURN INTEGER;
PRAGMA RESTRICT_REFERENCES(compare, WNDS, RNDS, WNPS, RNPS);


FUNCTION COMPARE(
lob_1   IN CLOB CHARACTER SET ANY_CS,
lob_2   IN CLOB CHARACTER SET lob_1%CHARSET,
amount   IN INTEGER := 4294967295,
offset_1 IN INTEGER := 1,
offset_2 IN INTEGER := 1)
 RETURN INTEGER;
PRAGMA RESTRICT_REFERENCES(compare, WNDS, RNDS, WNPS, RNPS);


FUNCTION COMPARE(
file_1   IN BFILE,
file_2   IN BFILE,
amount   IN INTEGER,
offset_1 IN INTEGER := 1,
offset_2 IN INTEGER := 1)
 RETURN INTEGER;
PRAGMA RESTRICT_REFERENCES(compare, WNDS, RNDS, WNPS, RNPS);
```

Note that COMPARE can only be used to compare to LOB values of the same type, such as two BLOBs, two BFILEs, and so on. The parameters and return value for COMPARE are described in the following table:

Parameter	Datatype	Description
lob_1, file_1	BLOB, CLOB, NCLOB, BFILE	LOB locator for the first LOB to be compared.
lob_2, file_2	BLOB, CLOB, NCLOB, BFILE	LOB locator for the second LOB to be compared.

Parameter	Datatype	Description
amount	INTEGER	Maximum number of characters (CLOB, NCLOB) or bytes (BLOB, BFILE) to compare.
offset_1	INTEGER	Offset in characters (CLOB, NCLOB) or bytes (BLOB, BFILE) into the first LOB before starting comparison. The first byte or character has offset 1.
offset_2	INTEGER	Offset in characters (CLOB, NCLOB) or bytes (BLOB, BFILE) into the second LOB before starting comparison. The first byte or character has offset 1.
return value	INTEGER	Zero if the two LOB values are identical, non-zero if not. A NULL value is returned if *amount, offset_1,* or *offset_2* is < 1 or > LOBMAXSIZE.

COPY

COPY is used to copy all or part of a source LOB to a destination LOB. If the specified offset for the destination LOB is beyond the end of the data currently in this LOB, zero-byte characters (for BLOBs) or spaces (for CLOBs and NCLOBs) are inserted. If the destination offset is less than the current length of the destination LOB, the current data is overwritten. If the specified amount is greater than the length of the source LOB, then the entire source LOB is copied and no error is raised. COPY can be used to copy data between like LOBs only. It is defined with

```
PROCEDURE COPY (
   dest_lob IN OUT BLOB,
   src_lob IN BLOB,
   amount IN INTEGER,
   dest_offset IN INTEGER := 1,
   src_offset IN INTEGER := 1);
```

```
FUNCTION FILEISOPEN(file_loc IN BFILE)
  RETURN INTEGER;
PRAGMA RESTRICT_REFERENCES(fileisopen,
  WNDS, RNDS, WNPS, RNPS);
```

where *file_loc* is the BFILE locator for the desired file. If the file has been opened with this locator, the function returns 1, otherwise it returns 0. FILEISOPEN just checks the status of the given locator passed to it; if it returns 0 another locator could have the same external file open.

FILEOPEN

This function is used to open a BFILE for processing. It is defined with

```
PROCEDURE FILEOPEN(
  file_loc IN OUT BFILE,
  open_mode IN BINARY_INTEGER := FILE_READONLY);
```

where *file_loc* is the locator for the desired file. The *open_mode* is used to indicate the desired mode for the BFILE, similar to UTL_FILE. As of Oracle8 Release 8.0, however, the only available mode is read-only. This is indicated by passing the constant DBMS_LOB.FILE_READONLY for *open_mode*. Future versions of Oracle8 will likely include additional modes and additional constants in DBMS_LOB for specifying them. INVALID_ARGVAL is raised if you pass a value other than DBMS_LOB.FILE_READONLY for *open_mode*.

The **FileExec** procedure in the section "LOADFROMFILE" later in this chapter demonstrates FILEOPEN.

GETLENGTH

The GETLENGTH function returns the current length of the specified LOB, in bytes (BLOB, BFILE) or characters (CLOB, NCLOB). Any spaces or null bytes in the LOB (perhaps by previous ERASE or WRITE operations) are included in the length. The length of an empty LOB is zero. GETLENGTH is overloaded to accept all four types of LOBs with

```
FUNCTION GETLENGTH(lob_loc IN BLOB)
  RETURN INTEGER;
  PRAGMA RESTRICT_REFERENCES(getlength,
    WNDS, RNDS, WNPS, RNPS);

FUNCTION GETLENGTH(lob_loc IN CLOB CHARACTER SET ANY_CS)
  RETURN INTEGER;
  PRAGMA RESTRICT_REFERENCES(getlength,
    WNDS, RNDS, WNPS, RNPS);

FUNCTION GETLENGTH(file_loc IN BFILE)
  RETURN INTEGER;
  PRAGMA RESTRICT_REFERENCES(getlength,
    WNDS, RNDS, WNPS, RNPS);
```

Here, *lob_loc* or *file_loc* specifies the LOB locator whose length is to be returned. A NULL is returned if any of the following conditions is TRUE:

- The input LOB is NULL

- *file_loc* is not a valid open file

- *file_loc* doesn't have the necessary directory and operating system privileges

- *file_loc* cannot be read because of an operating system error

Note that an exception is not raised in these cases.

The **FileExec** procedure in the section "LOADFROMFILE" later in this chapter demonstrates GETLENGTH.

INSTR

The DBMS_LOB.INSTR function is similar to the INSTR function defined in package STANDARD for CHAR and VARCHAR2 character strings. It is used to find the position of the *n*th occurrence of a pattern in a given LOB. INSTR is overloaded to accept all four types of LOBs:

```
FUNCTION INSTR(
  lob_loc IN BLOB,
  pattern IN RAW,
  offset IN INTEGER := 1,
  nth IN INTEGER := 1);
PRAGMA RESTRICT_REFERENCES(instr,
  WNDS, RNDS, WNPS, RNPS);

FUNCTION INSTR(
  lob_loc IN BFILE,
  pattern IN RAW,
  offset IN INTEGER := 1,
  nth IN INTEGER := 1);
PRAGMA RESTRICT_REFERENCES(instr,
  WNDS, RNDS, WNPS, RNPS);

FUNCTION INSTR(
  lob_loc IN CLOB CHARACTER SET ANY_CS,
  pattern IN VARCHAR2 CHARACTER SET lob_loc%CHARSET,
  offset IN INTEGER := 1,
  nth IN INTEGER := 1);
PRAGMA RESTRICT_REFERENCES(instr,
  WNDS, RNDS, WNPS, RNPS);
```

The parameters and return value for INSTR are described in the following table:

Parameter	Datatype	Description
lob_loc, file_loc	BLOB, BFILE, CLOB, NCLOB	Locator for the LOB to be examined.
pattern	VARCHAR2, RAW	String of bytes (BLOB, BFILE) or characters (CLOB, NCLOB) for which to search. For NCLOBs, pattern must have the same character set as lob_loc.

Parameter	Datatype	Description
offset	INTEGER	1-based offset in bytes (BLOB, BFILE) or characters (CLOB, NCLOB) into lob_loc or file_loc at which the pattern matching should start.
nth	INTEGER	Occurrence number to return, starting with 1.
return value	INTEGER	Position in bytes (BLOB, BFILE) or characters (CLOB, NCLOB) within the LOB where the nth occurrence of pattern starts, or 0 if it cannot be found.

The **FileExec** procedure in the next section "LOADFROMFILE" demonstrates INSTR.

LOADFROMFILE

This procedure can be used to populate a binary or character LOB from an operating system file. You can specify which portion of the source LOB is to be read, and an offset into the destination LOB for the write. It is overloaded to accept BLOB, CLOB, and NCLOB destinations with:

```
PROCEDURE LOADFROMFILE(
   dest_lob IN OUT BLOB,
   src_lob IN BFILE,
   amount IN INTEGER,
   dest_offset IN INTEGER := 1;
   src_offset IN INTEGER := 1);

PROCEDURE LOADFROMFILE(
   dest_lob IN OUT NCLOB CHARACTER SET ANY_CS,
   src_lob IN BFILE,
   amount IN INTEGER,
   dest_offset IN INTEGER := 1;
   src_offset IN INTEGER := 1);
```

The parameters are described in the following table:

Parameter	Datatype	Description
dest_lob	BLOB, CLOB, NCLOB	LOB into which to write the data.
src_lob	BFILE	File which should be read. *src_lob* must have already been opened and initialized (using FILEOPEN) prior to calling LOADFROMFILE.
amount	INTEGER	Number of bytes to read from the source file.
dest_offset	INTEGER	Offset (in bytes for BLOBs and characters for CLOBS and NCBLOBS) starting from 1 into *dest_lob* to start the write.
src_offset	INTEGER	Offset (in bytes, starting from 1) into the source file to start the read.

There are several things to note about LOADFROMFILE:

- If *dest_offset* is beyond the current length of *dest_lob*, then null bytes or spaces are inserted to fill the gap, similar to COPY.

- The destination LOB must be locked prior to calling LOADFROMFILE. This implies that you have to SELECT a lob from a table FOR UPDATE. Furthermore, the destination LOB cannot be NULL.

- If you are loading a CLOB, the operating system file should be in the same character set as the database. No checking is done to verify this.

The **FileExec** procedure illustrates LOADFROMFILE, along with several other BFILE manipulation functions. It can be used to read in and execute a file of SQL statements.

-- Available online as fileexec.sql
```
CREATE OR REPLACE PROCEDURE FileExec(
```

```
      -- Executes the SQL statements in the file identified by
      -- p_Directory and p_FileName.  Each statement should not
      -- contain the trailing semicolon (unless it is a PL/SQL
      -- block) and should be separated by p_SeparationChar.
      p_Directory IN VARCHAR2,
      p_FileName IN VARCHAR2,
      p_SeparationChar IN CHAR) AS

      v_FileLocator BFILE;
      v_CLOBLocator CLOB;
      v_SQLCursor INTEGER;
      v_StartPoint INTEGER := 1;
      v_EndPoint INTEGER;
      v_SQLStatement VARCHAR2(32000);
      v_StatementLength INTEGER;
      v_RC INTEGER;
    BEGIN
      -- Initialize the character locator for writing.  Note that we
      -- have to select a CLOB from a table FOR UPDATE.  This locks
      -- the row, and is a requirement for LOADFROMFILE.
      SELECT clob_col
        INTO v_CLOBLocator
        FROM lobdemo
        WHERE key = -1
        FOR UPDATE;

      -- Initialize the BFILE locator for reading.
      v_FileLocator := BFILENAME(p_Directory, p_FileName);
      DBMS_LOB.FILEOPEN(v_FileLocator, DBMS_LOB.FILE_READONLY);

      -- Set up the cursor.
      v_SQLCursor := DBMS_SQL.OPEN_CURSOR;

      -- Load the entire file into the character LOB.
      -- This is necessary so that we have the data in
      -- character rather than RAW variables.
      DBMS_LOB.LOADFROMFILE(v_CLOBLocator, v_FileLocator,
                        DBMS_LOB.GETLENGTH(v_FileLocator));

      -- Loop over the LOB, searching for each occurrence of
      -- the separation character.
      LOOP
        v_EndPoint := DBMS_LOB.INSTR(v_CLOBLocator,
                                  p_SeparationChar,
                                  v_StartPoint, 1);
```

```
        EXIT WHEN v_EndPoint = 0;

        -- Extract the contents between the starting and ending
        -- points.  This is the SQL statement to be executed.
        v_StatementLength := v_EndPoint - v_StartPoint;
        v_SQLStatement := DBMS_LOB.SUBSTR(v_CLOBLocator,
            v_StatementLength, v_StartPoint);

        -- Echo the statement to the screen, and then execute it
        -- using DBMS_SQL.
        DBMS_OUTPUT.PUT_LINE(v_SQLStatement);
        DBMS_SQL.PARSE(v_SQLCursor, v_SQLStatement, DBMS_SQL.V7);
        v_RC := DBMS_SQL.EXECUTE(v_SQLCursor);

        -- Increment the statement pointer for the next statement.
        v_StartPoint := v_EndPoint + 1;
    END LOOP;

    -- Clean up.
    DBMS_LOB.FILECLOSE(v_FileLocator);
    DBMS_SQL.CLOSE_CURSOR(v_SQLCursor);
EXCEPTION
    WHEN OTHERS THEN
        -- Close the cursor and file, and reraise.
        DBMS_LOB.FILECLOSE(v_FileLocator);
        DBMS_SQL.CLOSE_CURSOR(v_SQLCursor);
        RAISE;
END FileExec;
```

Assuming that you have created a directory **statements** which contains the following file:

```
-- Available online as inserts.sql
INSERT INTO temp_table (num_col, char_col)
  VALUES (1, 'hello')
/
INSERT INTO temp_table (num_col, char_col)
  VALUES (2, 'hello')
/
INSERT INTO temp_table (num_col, char_col)
  VALUES (3, 'hello')
/
INSERT INTO temp_table (num_col, char_col)
  VALUES (4, 'hello')
/
```

```
INSERT INTO temp_table (num_col, char_col)
  VALUES (5, 'hello')
/
INSERT INTO temp_table (num_col, char_col)
  VALUES (6, 'hello')
/
INSERT INTO temp_table (num_col, char_col)
  VALUES (7, 'hello')
/
```

we can call **FileExec** to insert 7 rows into **temp_table** with the following PL/SQL block:

```
BEGIN
  FileExec('STATEMENTS', 'inserts.sql', '/');
END;
```

READ

READ is used to return a portion of a LOB, starting from a given offset. If the end of the LOB is reached during the read, *amount* is returned as zero, and NO_DATA_FOUND is raised. READ is overloaded to accept all four LOB types with:

```
PROCEDURE READ(lob_loc IN BLOB,
               amount IN OUT BINARY_INTEGER,
               offset IN INTEGER,
               buffer OUT RAW);


PROCEDURE READ(lob_loc IN CLOB CHARACTER SET ANY_CS,
               amount IN OUT BINARY_INTEGER,
               offset IN INTEGER,
               buffer OUT VARCHAR2);


PROCEDURE READ(lob_loc IN BFILE,
               amount IN OUT BINARY_INTEGER,
               offset IN INTEGER,
               buffer OUT RAW);
```

The parameters are described in the following table.

Parameter	Datatype	Description
lob_loc	BLOB, CLOB, NCLOB, BFILE	LOB from which to read the data.
amount	BINARY_INTEGER	Number of bytes (BLOB, BFILE) or characters (CLOB, NCLOB) to read. The actual number of bytes or characters read is returned.
offset	INTEGER	Offset in bytes (BLOB, BFILE) or characters (CLOB, NCLOB) into *lob_loc* to start the read, starting at 1.
buffer	VARCHAR2, RAW	Output buffer to receive the data.

The **LOBPrint** procedure demonstrates how to use READ to scan an entire LOB. It will echo the contents of a CLOB to the screen using DBMS_OUTPUT, with 80 characters per line.

```
-- Available online as lobprint.sql
CREATE OR REPLACE PROCEDURE LOBPrint(p_CLOB IN CLOB) AS
  v_Buffer VARCHAR2(80);
  v_Offset INTEGER := 1;
  v_Amount INTEGER := 80;
BEGIN
  LOOP
    -- Read and output the next 80 characters.
    DBMS_LOB.READ(p_CLOB, v_Amount, v_Offset, v_Buffer);
    DBMS_OUTPUT.PUT_LINE(v_Buffer);

    v_Offset := v_Offset + v_Amount;
  END LOOP;
EXCEPTION
  WHEN NO_DATA_FOUND THEN
    -- End of loop, just return.
    NULL;
END LOBPrint;
```

SUBSTR

DBMS_LOB.SUBSTR behaves just like the SUBSTR defined in package STANDARD. It is used to return a portion of a LOB, similar to READ. SUBSTR is overloaded to accept all four kinds of LOBs with:

```
FUNCTION SUBSTR(lob_loc IN BLOB,
                amount IN INTEGER := 32767,
                offset IN INTEGER := 1)
  RETURN RAW;
PRAGMA RESTRICT_REFERENCES(substr,
  WNDS, WNPS, RNDS, RNPS);

FUNCTION SUBSTR(lob_loc IN CLOB CHARACTER SET ANY_CS,
                amount IN INTEGER := 32767,
                offset IN INTEGER := 1)
  RETURN VARCHAR2;
PRAGMA RESTRICT_REFERENCES(substr,
  WNDS, WNPS, RNDS, RNPS);

FUNCTION SUBSTR(lob_loc IN BFILE,
                amount IN INTEGER := 32767,
                offset IN INTEGER := 1)
  RETURN RAW;
PRAGMA RESTRICT_REFERENCES(substr,
  WNDS, WNPS, RNDS, RNPS);
```

The parameters are described below.

Parameter	Datatype	Description
lob_loc	BLOB, CLOB, NCLOB, BFILE	LOB from which to read the data.
amount	INTEGER	Number of bytes (BLOB, BFILE) or characters (CLOB, NCLOB) to read.
offset	INTEGER	Offset in bytes (BLOB, BFILE) or characters (CLOB, NCLOB) into lob_loc to start the read, starting at 1.
return value	VARCHAR2, RAW	Selected portion of the LOB.

The **FileExec** procedure in the section "LOADFROMFILE" earlier in this chapter demonstrates SUBSTR.

TRIM

TRIM is used to remove data from the end of a LOB. Unlike ERASE, which replaces portions of a LOB with spaces or NULLs, TRIM deletes the data, and shortens the internal length. It is overloaded to accept both BLOBs and CLOBs with

> PROCEDURE TRIM(*lob_loc* IN **CLOB**,
> *newlen* IN INTEGER);

> PROCEDURE TRIM(*lob_loc* IN **BLOB**,
> *newlen* IN INTEGER);

where *lob_loc* is a locator for the LOB to be trimmed, and *newlen* is the new length of the LOB. Any data past *newlen* will be deleted. If *newlen* is greater than the size of the LOB, the error " ORA-22926: specified trim length is greater than current LOB value's length" is raised. If *lob_loc* is NULL, then VALUE_ERROR is raised. However, if you call TRIM on an empty LOB, no error is raised and the LOB is unchanged. The following example illustrates the behavior of TRIM.

```
-- Available online as lobtrim.sql
DECLARE
  v_BLOB BLOB;
BEGIN
  SELECT blob_col
    INTO v_BLOB
    FROM lobdemo
    WHERE key = 1
    FOR UPDATE;

  DBMS_OUTPUT.PUT_LINE('Before trim, length = ' ||
                    DBMS_LOB.GETLENGTH(v_BLOB));
  DBMS_LOB.TRIM(v_BLOB, 5);
  DBMS_OUTPUT.PUT_LINE('After trim, length = ' ||
                    DBMS_LOB.GETLENGTH(v_BLOB));

  -- Raises ORA-22926, since the length is now 5.
  DBMS_LOB.TRIM(v_BLOB, 10);
END;
```

WRITE

DBMS_LOB.WRITE is used to write data into a section of a LOB. It will overwrite any existing data in the range specified. If the offset is beyond the length of the destination LOB, then spaces or zero bytes are inserted as filler. WRITE is overloaded to accept both CLOBs and NCLOBs with

```
PROCEDURE WRITE(lob_loc IN OUT BLOB,
                amount IN BINARY_INTEGER,
                offset IN INTEGER,
                buffer IN RAW);

PROCEDURE WRITE(lob_loc IN OUT CLOB CHARACTER SET ANY_CS,
                amount IN BINARY_INTEGER,
                offset IN INTEGER,
                buffer IN VARCHAR2);
```

The parameters for WRITE are described in the following table.

Parameter	Datatype	Description
lob_loc	BLOB, CLOB, NCLOB	LOB into which the data should be written.
amount	BINARY_INTEGER	Number of characters (CLOB, NCLOB) or bytes (BLOB) to write. amount should be <= the length of buffer.
offset	INTEGER	Offset in bytes (BLOB) or characters (CLOB< NCLOB) starting from 1 into lob_loc.
buffer	RAW, VARCHAR2	Data to be written into the destination LOB.

Exception	Error Code	Error Message
ACCESS_ERROR	22925	Operation would exceed maximum size allowed for a LOB
INVALID_ARGVAL	21560	Argument is NULL, invalid, or out of range
INVALID_DIRECTORY	22287	Invalid or modified directory
NO_DATA_FOUND*	1403	No data found
NOEXIST_DIRECTORY	22285	Directory does not exist
NOPRIV_DIRECTORY	22286	Insufficient privileges on directory
OPEN_TOOMANY	22290	Maximum limit reached on number of open files
OPERATION_FAILED	22288	File operation failed
UNOPENED_FILE	22289	Cannot perform operation on unopened file
VALUE_ERROR*	6502	Numeric or value error

TABLE 21-2. *Exceptions Raised by the DBMS_LOB BFILE Routines*

* This exception is defined in package STANDARD, rather than DBMS_LOB.

Exceptions Raised by DBMS_LOB Routines

Table 21-2 describes the exceptions that can be raised by the DBMS_LOB routines. For more information, see the descriptions of the individual routines in the previous sections. Except where noted, all these exceptions are defined in DBMS_LOB.

DBMS_LOB vs. OCI

Besides the DBMS_LOB package, LOB values can be manipulated using the Oracle8 OCI. A full discussion of the OCI LOB functions is beyond the scope of the book. For more information see the *Programmer's Guide to the*

OCI Function	DBMS_LOB Equivalent Function	Description
OCILobAppend()	APPEND	Appends the contents of one LOB value to another LOB
OCILobAssign()	N/A	Assigns one LOB locator to another
OCILobCharSetForm()	N/A	Returns the character set form for a given LOB
OCILobCharSetId()	N/A	Returns the character set ID for a given LOB
OCILobCopy()	COPY	Copies a portion of a source LOB into a destination LOB
OCILobErase()	ERASE	Erases part of a LOB from a specified offset
OCILobGetLength()	GETLENGTH	Returns the length of a LOB or BFILE
OCILobIsEqual()	N/A	Checks if two LOB locators point to the same LOB value
OCILobLocatorIsInit()	N/A	Checks if a given LOB locator is initialized
OCILobLocatorSize()	N/A	Returns the size of a LOB locator
OCILobRead()	READ	Reads a specified portion of a source LOB or BFILE into a supplied buffer
OCILobTrim()	TRIM	Truncates a LOB
OCILobWrite()	WRITE	Writes data from a buffer into a LOB starting at a given offset, overwriting existing data
OCILobFileOpen()	FILEOPEN	Opens a BFILE
OCILobFileIsOpen()	FILEISOPEN	Returns TRUE if a BFILE is open

TABLE 21-3. *OCI LOB Manipulation Functions*

OCI Function	DBMS_LOB Equivalent Function	Description
OCILobFileExists()	FILEEXISTS	Checks whether a BFILE exists
OCILobFileClose()	FILECLOSE	Closes a BFILE
OCILobFileCloseAll()	FILECLOSEALL	Closes all BFILEs currently open
OCILobFileSetName()	N/A	Sets the name of a BFILE in a locator
OCILobFileGetName()	FILEGETNAME	Returns the name of a BFILE
N/A	COMPARE	Compares portions of two LOB values
N/A	INSTR	Used to pattern match within a character LOB
N/A	SUBSTR	Returns a specified portion of a LOB value
N/A	LOADFROMFILE	Copies a BFILE into a CLOB or BLOB

TABLE 21-3.   *OCI LOB Manipulation Functions (continued)*

Oracle8 Call Interface, Volume 1: OCI Concepts. For reference, however, Table 21-3 lists the DBMS_LOB functions and their OCI equivalents. Note that there are several functions available only in OCI and several available only in DBMS_LOB.

PL/SQL at Work: Copying LONG Data into a LOB

As we have seen in this chapter, LOBs offer many advantages over Oracle7 LONG and LONG RAW types. As a result of these, you may want to convert existing data in LONG columns to an equivalent LOB. The **Long2Lob** procedure is designed to do exactly that, entirely in PL/SQL.

Long2Lob uses DBMS_SQL to fetch the LONG data piecewise, and then DBMS_LOB to insert it piecewise into the LOB. (See Chapter 15 for information on DBMS_SQL.) The procedure is defined as follows:

```
-- Available online as long2lob.sql
CREATE OR REPLACE PROCEDURE Long2Lob(
  -- Uses DBMS_SQL to select a LONG column identified by
  -- p_LongQuery, and returns it in p_CLob.
  p_LongQuery IN VARCHAR2,
  p_CLob IN OUT CLOB) AS

  c_ChunkSize CONSTANT INTEGER := 100;

  v_CursorID INTEGER;
  v_RC INTEGER;
  v_Chunk VARCHAR2(100);
  v_ChunkLength INTEGER;
  v_Offset INTEGER := 0;
BEGIN
  -- Open the cursor, define, execute, and fetch.
  v_CursorID := DBMS_SQL.OPEN_CURSOR;
  DBMS_SQL.PARSE(v_CursorID, p_LongQuery, DBMS_SQL.V7);
  DBMS_SQL.DEFINE_COLUMN_LONG(v_CursorID, 1);
  v_RC := DBMS_SQL.EXECUTE_AND_FETCH(v_CursorID);

  -- Loop over the LONG, fetching c_ChunkSize characters at a
  -- time from the LONG and adding them to the LOB.
  LOOP
    DBMS_SQL.COLUMN_VALUE_LONG(v_CursorID, 1, c_ChunkSize,
      v_Offset, v_Chunk, v_ChunkLength);
    DBMS_LOB.WRITE(p_CLob, v_ChunkLength, v_Offset + 1,
      v_Chunk);
    IF v_ChunkLength < c_ChunkSize THEN
      EXIT;
    ELSE
      v_Offset := v_Offset + v_ChunkLength;
    END IF;
  END LOOP;

  DBMS_SQL.CLOSE_CURSOR(v_CursorID);
```

```
EXCEPTION
  WHEN OTHERS THEN
    -- Clean up, and reraise the error.
    DBMS_SQL.CLOSE_CURSOR(v_CursorID);
    RAISE;
END Long2Lob;
```

Suppose we have a table containing a LONG, created and populated with:

-- Available online as part of 121test.sql
```
CREATE TABLE long_tab (
  key NUMBER,
  long_col LONG
);
INSERT INTO long_tab (key, long_col)
  VALUES (100,
'abcdefghijklmnopqrstuvwxyzABCDEFGHIJKLMNOPQRSTUVWZYZabcdefghijklmn
opqrstuvwxyzABCDEFGHIJKLMNOPQRSTUVWZYZabcdefghijklmnopqrstuvwxyzABC
DEFGHIJKLMNOPQRSTUVWZYZabcdefghijklmnopqrstuvwxyzABCDEFGHIJKLMNOPQR
STUVWZYZabcdefghijklmnopqrstuvwxyzABCDEFGHIJKLMNOPQRSTUVWZYZabcdefg
hijklmnopqrstuvwxyzABCDEFGHIJKLMNOPQRSTUVWZYZabcdefghijklmnopqrstuv
wxyzABCDEFGHIJKLMNOPQRSTUVWZYZabcdefghijklmnopqrstuvwxyzABCDEFGHIJK
LMNOPQRSTUVWZYZabcdefghijklmnopqrstuvwxyzABCDEFGHIJKLMNOPQRSTUVWZYZ
abcdefghijklmnopqrstuvwxyzABCDEFGHIJKLMNOPQRSTUVWZYZabcdefghijklmno
pqrstuvwxyzABCDEFGHIJKLMNOPQRSTUVWZYZabcdefghijklmnopqrstuvwxyzABCD
EFGHIJKLMNOPQRSTUVWZYZabcdefghijklmnopqrstuvwxyzABCDEFGHIJKLMNOPQRS
TUVWZYZabcdefghijklmnopqrstuvwxyzABCDEFGHIJKLMNOPQRSTUVWZYZabcdefgh
ijklmnopqrstuvwxyzABCDEFGHIJKLMNOPQRSTUVWZYZabcdefghijklmnopqrstuvwxy
zABCDEFGHIJKLMNOPQRSTUVWZYZabcdefghijklmnopqrstuvwxyzABCDEFGHIJKLMNOP
QRSTUVWZYZabcdefghijklmnopqrstuvwxyzABCDEFGHIJKLMNOPQRSTUVWZYZ');
```

We can move the data from **long_col** into **lobdemo** by calling **Long2Lob** with the following:

-- Available online as part of 121test.sql
```
DECLARE
  v_Query VARCHAR2(200);
  v_NewLOB CLOB;
BEGIN
  v_Query := 'SELECT long_col FROM long_tab where key = 100';
  INSERT INTO lobdemo (key, clob_col)
```

```
    VALUES (100, EMPTY_CLOB())
    RETURNING clob_col INTO v_NewLOB;

  Long2Lob(v_Query, v_NewLOB);
  LOBPrint(v_NewLOB);
  COMMIT;
END;
```

There are several things to note about the usage of **Long2Lob**:

- **p_LongQuery** must be a SELECT statement which matches 1 row and returns 1 column, which is the LONG.

- If you select an existing LOB locator from a table, rather than inserting a new one, be sure to SELECT FOR UPDATE to lock the row, since **Long2Lob** will update it.

- The technique used on **Long2Lob** can be adapted to convert an entire table, by using DBMS_SQL to select the LONG column from every row, and then looping over each returned row to write the data into the LOB.

Summary

In this chapter, we have examined the Oracle8 implementation of LOBs (large objects). The four different types of LOBs—CLOBs, NCLOBs, BLOBs, and BFILEs—are used to store different types of data, which can be up to 4 gigabytes in length. Data can be stored internal to Oracle, and thus be managed by the database, or it can be stored external to Oracle, and thus be managed by the underlying operating system. We also examined the DBMS_LOB package, which is the PL/SQL interface to manipulate LOB data. In the next (and final) chapter, we will look at improving the performance of your PL/SQL applications.

CHAPTER
22

Performance and Tuning

t is important that your application do what it is expected to do. It is equally important that it do the necessary processing as fast and efficiently as possible. Developing a properly tuned PL/SQL application is not difficult, as long as you keep in mind a few concepts. These are the shared pool, properly designed SQL statements, and an understanding of network issues. We will discuss all of these in this chapter and see how you can use them in your own applications. We will also discuss the third and final component of SQL-Station, the Plan Analyzer.

The Shared Pool

The shared pool is an area of memory in which Oracle stores information about SQL statements and stored subprograms. Setting the size of the shared pool and using it properly are key components of a properly tuned PL/SQL application.

Structure of an Oracle Instance

In order to discuss how the shared pool works and its implications for PL/SQL programming, we first need to examine the structure of a running Oracle *instance*. An instance consists of processes, memory, and operating system files, all running on the server. Additional client processes can connect to the database as well. Figure 22-1 illustrates the structure of an instance.

NOTE
On some systems (such as Windows 3.1) an Oracle instance consists of a single process only. This process is responsible for all database administration, in addition to serving as a shadow process. The shared pool behaves the same, however.

Processes

When an instance is started, a number of Oracle background processes are started. These processes communicate with each other via shared memory, known as the SGA (system global area). All of the Oracle processes can

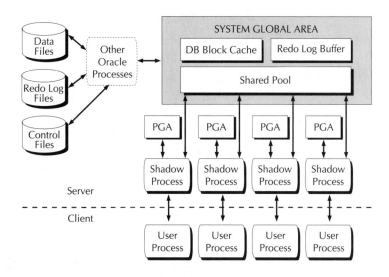

FIGURE 22-1. *An Oracle instance*

read and write to various data structures in the SGA. Each process is in charge of a different aspect of running the database. Some of these processes are described in Table 22-1. A full discussion of how these processes work is beyond the scope of this book; for more information, see *Oracle Server Concepts.* Here, we will examine user and shadow processes.

USER PROCESSES   A user process is an application that sends SQL and PL/SQL to the server to be processed. These applications can be developed using any of Oracle's development tools, such as the precompilers, OCI, SQL*Plus, and the Developer 2000 suite, or a third-party application development tool, such as SQL-Station. The user process communicates with the shadow process over the network using SQL*Net. This communication and its implications are discussed later in this chapter, in the "Network Issues" section.

SHADOW PROCESSES   The shadow process is responsible for passing information back and forth between a user process and the rest of the instance. Without the multithreaded server, there is one shadow process

Process	Description
Database Writer (DBWR)	Writes changed information from the buffer cache in the SGA to the database files.
Process Monitor (PMON)	Cleans up after failed user processes, such as releasing locks and rolling back any uncommitted SQL statements.
System Monitor (SMON)	Performs instance recovery (if necessary) when the instance is started. Also responsible for freeing temporary segments and coalescing free space in the SGA.
Recover (RECO)	Resolves failures with distributed transactions. RECO is only present when the Distributed Option is used.
Log Writer (LGWR)	Writes the redo log buffer to the redo log on disk. LGWR and DBWR work together to ensure that all committed information is properly written before the commit is successful.
Archiver (ARCH)	Copies full redo logs to an offline storage device, such as a tape drive. ARCH is only running when the database is in ARCHIVELOG mode.
Snapshot Refresh (SNP)	Refreshes table snapshots and runs database jobs (see Chapter 18).
Shadow Process	Manages the information transfer between the user process and other database resources.
User Process	Runs a user application, sending SQL statements and PL/SQL blocks to the database.
Dispatcher Process	Allows multiple user processes to share a single shadow process, as part of the multithreaded server. The user processes connect to the dispatcher, which in turn passes information on to the shadow process. The connections between the user and dispatcher process must use SQL*Net version 2.

TABLE 22-1. *Database Processes*

per user process. With the multithreaded server, a single shadow process can manage multiple user processes, with the help of the dispatcher processes. For more information on the multithreaded server and how to configure it, see *Oracle Server Concepts*.

Memory

The memory used by the instance is partitioned into different areas, which are used by different processes. There are four different kinds of memory: the shared pool, DB block cache, redo log buffer, and the process global area (PGA). All but the PGA are allocated as part of the SGA and are thus available to all processes. The SGA is completely allocated when the instance starts up. Its size is determined by various INIT.ORA parameters, including SHARED_POOL_SIZE, LOG_BUFFER, and DB_BLOCK_BUFFERS. For more information on these and other INIT.ORA parameters, see the *Oracle Server Reference*.

SHARED POOL   The shared pool is the memory structure that most affects the performance of PL/SQL. The shared pool contains the text of SQL statements and PL/SQL blocks sent to the database, along with the parsed representation of them. Items in the shared pool do not necessarily remain there forever; they are aged out of the pool when they are no longer necessary. We will see how this works and examine the shared pool in detail shortly.

DB BLOCK CACHE   Data is read from and written to database files in *blocks*. For maximum efficiency, the size of data blocks is usually a multiple of the operating system block size and is specified by the INIT.ORA parameter DB_BLOCK_SIZE. Typical values for DB_BLOCK_SIZE are 2048 or 4096, since operating system blocks are often 1024 bytes. The shadow processes read data blocks from the data files. These are stored in the DB block cache and manipulated there. If the contents of a block are changed, DBWR will write the block back to the file.

REDO LOG BUFFER   The redo log buffer behaves the same as the DB block cache except that it contains redo blocks rather than data blocks. Redo information is generated by SQL statements and PL/SQL blocks as they are processed. This redo information is used in case of instance failure and for read-consistency. LGWR is responsible for writing the blocks in the redo log buffer to the online redo logs.

PGA   Each shadow process allocates memory for its own use. This memory is known as the *process global area* (PGA). Information in the PGA includes the active sets for any currently open cursors, pointers to the parsed SQL statements and PL/SQL blocks in the shared pool, and memory used to execute PL/SQL. The PGA is allocated when the shadow process is started and remains as long as the connection does. When running in MTS mode (using the multithreaded server), some of the information in the PGA is kept in the SGA. This is necessary because a session can migrate between shadow processes with MTS.

Files

The database uses three different kinds of operating system files, each of which stores different kinds of information. Different processes are in charge of maintaining different files. The three kinds of files are database files, redo log files, and control files. These files are different from external files used by the UTL_FILE package (see Chapter 18) and external files used to store BFILEs (see Chapter 21) in Oracle8.

DATABASE FILES   These files store the actual data found in the database. This includes table and index data, code for stored subprograms, view definitions, and sequence information, along with the data dictionary itself. DBWR is responsible for writing to database files, and the shadow processes can read from them.

REDO LOG FILES   The redo log records all of the changes made to database objects. This information is used to generate a read-consistent view of the data for queries and to perform rollbacks. LGWR is responsible for writing to the redo log. If archiving is enabled (the database is running in ARCHIVELOG mode), then the ARCH process is responsible for reading the redo logs and copying them to offline storage.

CONTROL FILES   The current state of the database is stored in one or more control files. If there is more than one file, all of them are kept in the same state (they are *mirrored*) to aid recovery in case one is lost. The database state includes the number of data and redo files and how much information has been written to each. LGWR also modifies the control files, and ARCH is responsible for recording these changes in the offline storage.

How the Shared Pool Works

Whenever a SQL statement is received by the database, it is parsed and the execution plan determined. This information is then stored in the shared pool. If the same SQL statement is received by the database at a later point (issued by the same user process or a different user process), the database does not have to reparse the statement. The parsed form is already there in the shared pool. This performance enhancement can significantly reduce the amount of work done by the server, especially in environments with a large number of users running the same application.

When the database receives a SQL statement from a client application, it first checks to see if the statement is in the shared pool. If it is already there, the parsed form and execution plan are immediately available. If the statement is not in the shared pool, it will be placed there after it is parsed. The important thing to note about this process is that the database has to receive the statement before it can be compared. Even if the statement is found in the shared pool, the statement does travel over the network each time. Although the database may not have to do any work with the statement once it gets it (since it's in the pool already), it does have to receive the entire statement first. For long SQL statements, this can be significant. Because a pointer to the parsed statement is returned to the client the first time the statement is issued, the client application can be written to avoid subsequent parse calls altogether. See the section "Avoiding Unnecessary Reparsing" later in this chapter for more information.

Besides the parsed form of SQL statements, the shared pool also holds the compiled p-code for stored subprograms and the contents of database pipes. When a stored subprogram is called for the first time, the p-code is retrieved from disk and kept in the shared pool. The next time the same object is referenced, the disk access can be avoided since the p-code is already in memory.

When the shared pool fills up, objects within it are aged out according to an LRU (least recently used) algorithm. The object that hasn't been accessed for the longest time is removed from the pool, and the space it took up is used for a new object. Only those objects that are not currently being used are eligible for aging. If a subprogram is still being executed, for example, it will not be aged out. Since all objects are not the same size, this can result in shared pool fragmentation—the space for a new object may be available, but it is not contiguous. When there is not enough memory in the shared pool for a new object, the following Oracle error is returned:

```
ORA-4031: unable to allocate X bytes of shared memory
```

This can happen either because the shared pool is not big enough, or the space in it has become fragmented.

Flushing the Shared Pool

If you receive the ORA-4031 error, one solution is to flush the shared pool. This will remove all eligible objects (those that are not currently being used). The command to do this is

```
ALTER SYSTEM FLUSH SHARED POOL;
```

You can issue this command from any account with the ALTER SYSTEM system privilege. The shared pool can be flushed while the database is still running without affecting current applications. This ALTER SYSTEM command is not usually issued from an application; rather, it is issued from a DBA session when necessary.

The shared pool is also flushed when the instance is brought down. When an instance is brought up, the shared pool is empty because no SQL has been executed yet.

Triggers and the Shared Pool

P-code is only cached if the subprogram is stored. Prior to Oracle7 Release 7.3, this does not include triggers. In releases earlier than 7.3, the compiled p-code for triggers is not stored in the data dictionary—only the source is. Consequently, when a trigger is fired for the first time, it must be compiled. The compiled code is then stored in the shared pool for subsequent trigger firings. However, if the trigger gets aged out of the shared pool, it must be recompiled before it can be executed again.

It is a good idea to keep your trigger code as small as possible, to minimize the time spent compiling it. This can be accomplished by moving the work done in a trigger into a packaged subprogram and then calling the

Objects with a size greater than *minsize* will be returned. SIZES uses DBMS_OUTPUT to return the data, so be sure to use "set serveroutput on" in SQL*Plus or Server Manager before calling the procedure. For more information on DBMS_OUTPUT, see Chapter 13.

SQL Statement Tuning

In order to execute a SQL statement, the database must determine the *execution plan*. An execution plan is the method by which the database will actually process the statement—what tables and indexes it needs to access, whether or not a sort operation needs to be done, and so on. The execution plan can have a large impact on the length of time it takes to execute a SQL statement. This section describes how to tune SQL statements in general, whether or not they are inside a PL/SQL block.

Determining the Execution Plan

There are several different methods for determining the execution plan. The EXPLAIN PLAN statement is a good method for querying the plan quickly and easily. The TKPROF utility will also give you the execution plan, along with additional statistics about the SQL processing. SQL-Station Plan Analyzer can also be used to determine the plan.

EXPLAIN PLAN
The EXPLAIN PLAN SQL statement will determine an execution plan for a given statement and insert it into another database table. The format for EXPLAIN PLAN is

```
EXPLAIN PLAN [SET STATEMENT_ID = 'statement_info']
   [INTO plan_table] FOR sql_statement;
```

where *sql_statement* is the statement you want to explain. The plan will be inserted into *plan_table*. If *plan_table* isn't specified, then it defaults to PLAN_TABLE. This table can be created with:

```
CREATE TABLE plan_table (
   statement_id     VARCHAR2(30),
   timestamp        DATE,
```

```
remarks          VARCHAR2(80),
operation        VARCHAR2(30),
options          VARCHAR2(30),
object_node      VARCHAR2(30),
object_owner     VARCHAR2(30),
object_name      VARCHAR2(30),
object_instance  NUMBER,
object_type      VARCHAR2(30),
search_columns   NUMBER,
id               NUMBER,
parent_id        NUMBER,
position         NUMBER,
other            LONG);
```

In order to use EXPLAIN PLAN, you should either have **plan_table** in your own schema, or you should specify another plan table (with the preceding definition) in the EXPLAIN PLAN statement. The *statement_id*, if specified in EXPLAIN PLAN, will be inserted into the **statement_id** column of **plan_table**. This is used to store multiple plans in the same table—the statement ID is the key for each statement. If the statement ID already exists in the plan table, its plan is replaced.

TIP
The **utlxplan.sql** *file will create a plan_table for you. The location of this file is operating-system specific. On Unix systems, it is located with the other data dictionary scripts in $ORACLE_HOME/rdbms/admin.*

For example, we can determine an execution plan for a query against **registered_students** and **classes** with

```
EXPLAIN PLAN
  SET STATEMENT_ID = 'Query 1' FOR
    SELECT rs.course, rs.department, students.ID
      FROM registered_students rs, students
      WHERE rs.student_id = students.id
      AND students.last_name = 'Razmataz';
```

Once we issue this statement, we can query the plan table with the following SQL statement:

```
SELECT LPAD(' ', 2 * (LEVEL - 1)) || operation ||
        ' ' || options || ' ' || object_name || ' ' ||
        DECODE(id, 0, 'Cost = ' || position) "Execution Plan"
    FROM plan_table
    START WITH id = 0
      AND statement_id = 'Query 1'
    CONNECT BY PRIOR id = parent_id
      AND statement_id = 'Query 1';
```

Note that the same statement ID is used both in the EXPLAIN PLAN statement and the query of the plan table. The previous query returns the following output:

```
Execution Plan
-------------------------------------------
SELECT STATEMENT    Cost =
  NESTED LOOPS
    TABLE ACCESS FULL REGISTERED_STUDENTS
    TABLE ACCESS BY ROWID STUDENTS
      INDEX UNIQUE SCAN SYS_C00859
```

We will discuss how to interpret the execution plan later in this chapter, in the section "Using the Plan."

TKPROF Utility

The EXPLAIN PLAN statement is useful for determining the execution plan, as we saw in the previous section. The TKPROF utility, however, can give us the execution plan as well as statistics about how well the SQL statement actually performed. In order to use TKPROF, first you need to get a SQL trace file for your session. TKPROF is then used to format the trace file and make it readable. In order to generate a trace file, issue the SQL command

```
ALTER SESSION SET SQL_TRACE = TRUE;
```

before any SQL statements you want to examine. This will start a trace file, which will contain information about any subsequent SQL statements or PL/SQL blocks submitted to the database. Information will be dumped to the trace file until the session ends or tracing is turned off with

```
ALTER SESSION SET SQL_TRACE = FALSE;
```

The location of the trace file is determined by the USER_DUMP_DEST parameter in INIT.ORA. The name of the trace file is system specific but will usually start with "ora" and contain the process identifier of the shadow process. For example, a trace filename could be "ora_12345.trc". The easiest way to determine the correct trace file is to look in USER_DUMP_DEST for the newest file immediately after issuing the trace.

CAUTION
ALTER SESSION is not allowed in a PL/SQL block, since it is not a DML statement. You can issue the ALTER SESSION before issuing the block, however. Alternatively, you can trace SQL statements outside of a block.

For example, we can issue the following statements from SQL*Plus:

```
SQL> ALTER SESSION SET SQL_TRACE = TRUE;
Session altered.
SQL> SELECT rs.course, rs.department, students.ID
        FROM registered_students rs, students
        WHERE rs.student_id = students.id
        AND students.last_name = 'Razmataz';

    COURSE DEP          ID
---------- --- ----------
       101 HIS       10010
       307 NUT       10010
SQL> ALTER SESSION SET SQL_TRACE = FALSE;
Session altered.
```

This produced a file "ora_29338.trc" in USER_DUMP_DEST. We now need to format this trace file to produce a readable output. We use TKPROF to do this. TKPROF is a utility that is run from the operating system. Its location is system dependent, but it is usually found in the same directory as other Oracle executables such as SQL*Plus itself. The format for TKPROF is

TKPROF *input_file output_file* [SORT = *sort_options*] [PRINT = *num_print*]
[EXPLAIN = *user/password*]

where *input_file* is the name of the generated trace file (ora_29338.trc in this case), and *output_file* will contain the formatted trace file. If SORT is not specified, the SQL statements will appear in the order they were submitted. Otherwise, you can sort based on one or more of the options listed in Table 22-2. To specify more than one sort option, use the syntax

SORT = (*option1, option2, ...*)

To include an execution plan in the trace file, specify a user name and password in the EXPLAIN option. TKPROF will create a plan table, run EXPLAIN PLAN into this table, select the output into the file, and drop the table. If specified, only *num_print* statements will be included in the file, after sorting.

We can format our trace file with

TKPROF ora_29338.trc trace.out EXPLAIN=example/example

which produces an output file "trace.out". A portion of this file follows:

```
SELECT rs.course, rs.department, students.ID
      FROM registered_students rs, students
      WHERE rs.student_id = students.id
      AND students.last_name = 'Razmataz'

call       count  cpu   elapsed  disk  query  current  rows
--------   -----  ----  -------  ----  -----  -------  ----
Parse          1  0.00  0.00        0      0        0     0
Execute        1  0.00  0.00        0      0        0     0
Fetch          1  0.00  0.00        0     55        3     2
--------   -----  ----  -------  ----  -----  ------   ----
total          3  0.00  0.00        0     55        3     2

Misses in library cache during parse: 1
Optimizer hint: CHOOSE
Parsing user id: 9   (EXAMPLE)
Rows       Execution Plan
-------    -------------------------------------------------------
0   SELECT STATEMENT    OPTIMIZER HINT: CHOOSE
      2       NESTED LOOPS
     18         TABLE ACCESS (FULL) OF 'REGISTERED_STUDENTS'
     18         TABLE ACCESS (BY ROWID) OF 'STUDENTS'
     18           INDEX (UNIQUE SCAN) OF 'SYS_C00859' (UNIQUE)


********************************************************************
```

Sort Option	Description
PRSCNT	Parse count
PRSCPU	Amount of CPU time spent parsing
PRSELA	Elapsed time during the parse
PRSDSK	Number of disk reads during the parse
PRSQRY	Number of consistent block reads during the parse
PRSCU	Number of current block reads during the parse
PRSMIS	Number of library cache misses during the parse
EXECNT	Number of executes
EXECPU	Amount of CPU time spent during the execute
EXEELA	Elapsed time during the execute
EXEDSK	Number of physical disk reads during the execute
EXEQRY	Number of consistent block reads during the execute
EXECU	Number of current block reads during the execute
EXEROW	Number of rows processed during the execute
EXEMIS	Number of library cache misses during the execute
FCHCNT	Number of fetches
FCHCPU	Amount of CPU time spent during the fetch
FCHELA	Elapsed time during the fetch
FCHDSK	Number of physical disk reads during the fetch
FCHQRY	Number of consistent block reads during the fetch
FCHCU	Number of current block reads during the fetch
FCHROW	Number of rows fetched

TABLE 22-2. *TKPROF Sort Options*

The statement itself, statistics about the execution of the statement, and the execution plan are all included in the output. In this case, no CPU time was necessary for the parse, since this statement had been executed already and thus was already in the shared pool. (The **v$sql** and **v$sqlarea** data dictionary views can be used to see which statements are currently in the shared pool.) Note, however, that the parse count is still 1, because a parse call was issued to the database.

NOTE
The trace file will also show the recursive SQL statements generated automatically by your SQL. For any given statement, Oracle can issue up to six recursive statements, which do such things as check the NLS settings and verify object privileges. Because the trace file shows all of the SQL statements, recursive and otherwise, it can be a useful debugging technique.

SQL-Station Plan Analyzer

The Plan Analyzer component of SQL-Station provides the functionality of both the EXPLAIN PLAN statement and TKPROF. When you first start Plan Analyzer and connect to the database, you are presented with two windows. The upper window allows you to enter a SQL statement, and the lower window will show the execution plan for the statement. Above the SQL window is a toolbar that allows you to select different optimizer modes. The Analyzer with the SQL statement entered is shown in Figure 22-2.

TIP
When you enter the statement, do not enter the trailing semicolon. If it is there, it will be sent to the database as part of the statement. The database will then return "ORA-911: invalid character."

In order to view a plan, simply click on the toolbar button for the desired plan, or select from the Plan menu. You can choose from three default optimizer modes or supply your own with optimizer hints. The default plans include the Rule-based optimizer and the First Row and All Rows cost-based optimizer modes. Figure 22-3 shows the Rule-based optimizer plan for the SQL statement.

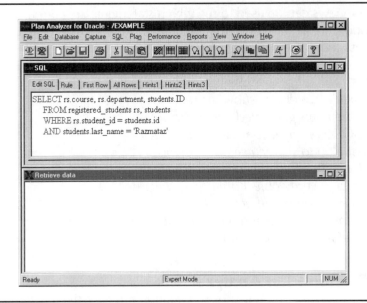

FIGURE 22-2. *Plan Analyzer with a SQL statement entered*

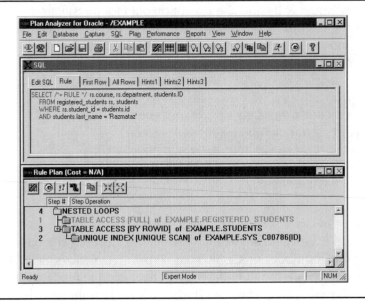

FIGURE 22-3. *The Rule-based execution plan*

In order to look at the execution statistics for the statement, select the Statistics option from the Performance menu. This allows you to view the statistics for different optimizer modes and compare the results in either a graphical or textual format. Figure 22-4 shows the Statistics window with results from the Rule-based optimizer. Results from the other optimizer modes can be viewed by clicking on the appropriate tabs in the window, and the Compare button will allow you to view side-by-side comparisons for the different modes.

The Plan Analyzer has many more features than those shown here. Other features include the ability to analyze database objects used in a given statement and step through each step of a given plan, with an explanation for each one. For more information about Plan Analyzer and its features, see the online SQL-Station documentation.

Using the Plan

The execution plan is the same for a given SQL statement and optimizer mode regardless of how it is determined. A plan is composed of individual

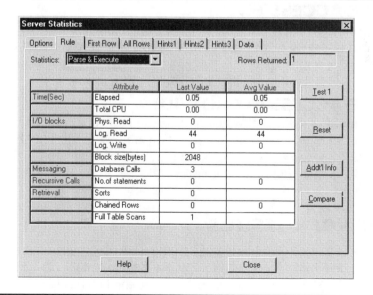

FIGURE 22-4.   *Execution statistics*

operations. Operations (such as a full table scan or an index scan) are executed individually. Each operation will produce as output a set of rows. The operation can determine this set by querying a table or index or by accepting the output of another operation. The results of the final operation are the result set of the query. Each operation does some of the work for the entire query. A full discussion of the operations and their efficiency is beyond the scope of this chapter. We will briefly discuss some of the main operations, however. For more information, see *Oracle Server Tuning*.

The execution plan in the prior two sections has three operations: a NESTED LOOP operation and two different kinds of TABLE ACCESS operations.

NESTED LOOP

A NESTED LOOP operation combines the result sets from two other operations **a** and **b**. Rows in **a** and **b** are compared according to a condition, and those that match are kept. In this case, the condition is the join condition "rs.student_id = students.id" given in the statement. Whenever a join is used, a NESTED LOOP operation is required for execution.

TABLE ACCESS(FULL)

A full table scan simply retrieves all rows from a table. In this case, a full table scan is necessary for **registered_students** since there are no indexes created on this table.

TABLE ACCESS (BY ROWID)

This operation is the fastest way to retrieve an individual row. In this case, the results from the INDEX SCAN operation are sent to the TABLE ACCESS BY ROWID operation. The index scan is available since there is an index defined for the **ID** column of **students**.

Network Issues

Once the SQL statement has made it to the database, the structure of the statement determines the execution plan and the resultant performance. However, the SQL statement has to be sent to the database first, from the user process to the shadow process. Even if the user and shadow processes are running on the same machine, the SQL statement or PL/SQL block still needs to be passed between them. In most applications, the majority of the processing time is spent in network transmission. Thus, reducing network traffic is a prime component for application tuning. There are three techniques available for reducing network traffic: using client-side PL/SQL, avoiding unnecessary reparsing, and using the Oracle array interface. Although the latter two methods are primarily applicable when using OCI or the Oracle precompilers, they are still relevant to PL/SQL.

Using Client-side PL/SQL

If the application is written using the Developer or Designer 2000 suite of tools, then there is a PL/SQL engine on the client. This execution environment is discussed in more detail in Chapter 13. Any work that can be done on the client reduces the load on the server. In addition, if many users are running the application simultaneously, they can process on their individual client machines in parallel without bogging down the server.

This PL/SQL engine should be used as much as possible. For example, validation of input data can be done before the data is sent to the server.

Avoiding Unnecessary Reparsing

When a SQL statement or PL/SQL block is sent from the client to the server, the client can keep a reference to the parsed statement. This reference is the cursor data area when using OCI or the cursor cache entry when using the precompilers. If your application issues the same statement more than once, it only needs to parse the statement the first time. For all subsequent executions, the original parsed statement can be used, possibly with different values for the bind variables.

This technique is available primarily with OCI or the precompilers, since they give you more control over cursor processing. In the OCI, cursors are controlled directly with a cursor data area. You make explicit calls to parse (**oparse**) and execute (**oexec**) the statement. With the precompilers, the HOLD_CURSOR and RELEASE_CURSOR options control the behavior.

The most obvious place for this technique directly in PL/SQL is with the DBMS_SQL package, where the interface is similar to OCI. Once a statement is parsed with DBMS_SQL.PARSE, it can be executed multiple times. For more information, see Chapter 15.

Array Processing

The precompilers and OCI can send and retrieve data using host arrays. This technique is known as the Oracle array interface. This is a very useful method, since it allows large amounts of data to be sent over the network as one unit, rather than in several trips. For example, if you are retrieving 100 rows, you can do it in one fetch, which brings back all 100 rows, rather than in 100 fetches, each of which returns one row. This approach is used in SQL*Plus.

PL/SQL does not directly use the Oracle array interface, since it does not store arrays the same way as a host array. PL/SQL tables are implemented differently, as discussed in Chapter 3. However, the array interface should be used whenever possible. If you are issuing PL/SQL commands from OCI or the precompilers, use the array interface for the other SQL statements in your application. For more information on how to use host arrays, consult the precompiler and/or OCI documentation.

Summary

A good application is designed for performance. In this chapter we have examined several different aspects of performance and tuning. We first discussed the structure of an Oracle instance and the process of executing SQL statements. Once the statement gets to the server, it is processed according to its execution plan, which is determined with EXPLAIN PLAN or the TKPROF utility. We also discussed how to minimize network traffic by using client-side PL/SQL, avoiding unnecessary reparsing, and using the Oracle array interface.

PROCEDURE SET_MODULE(*module_name* IN VARCHAR2,
                     action_name IN VARCHAR2);

where *module_name* is the name of the currently running module, and *action_name* is the name of the current action. The module is limited to 48 bytes, and the action to 32 bytes—longer values will be truncated.

READ_MODULE
This procedure is used to read the values of **module** and **action** for the current session. This information can also be determined by querying **v$session**, but by default only users with the DBA privilege can directly read the table. READ_MODULE is defined with

PROCEDURE READ_MODULE(*module_name* OUT VARCHAR2,
                      action_name OUT VARCHAR2);

where *module_name* is the last value set for **module** using SET_MODULE, and *action_name* is the last value set for **action** using SET_MODULE or SET_ACTION.

SET_ACTION
SET_ACTION is used to just set the value of the **action** field for the current session. It should be used before entering a section of your program, and is defined with

PROCEDURE SET_ACTION(*action_name* IN VARCHAR2);

where *action_name* is the name of the current action. *action_name* is limited to 32 bytes—longer values will be truncated. When your program is finished with this section, it is a good idea to set the **action** to NULL.

SET_CLIENT_INFO
This procedure is used to record the value of **client_info** in **v$session** for the current session. Oracle does not use this value, but it can be queried by the DBA. One possible use is the name of the current user, or their machine name as identified by the client program. It is defined with

PROCEDURE SET_CLIENT_INFO(*client_info* IN VARCHAR2);

where *client_info* is the new value for the field. It is limited to 64 bytes, and longer values will be truncated.

READ_CLIENT_INFO
READ_CLIENT_INFO will return the value last set with SET_CLIENT_INFO. It is defined with

PROCEDURE READ_CLIENT_INFO(*client_info* OUT VARCHAR2);

where *client_info* is the last value set using SET_CLIENT_INFO.

DBMS_AQ and DBMS_AQADM

PL/SQL 8.0 ...and HIGHER These packages are used to administer the Oracle Advanced Queuing system. DBMS_AQ implements the enqueue and dequeue operations for queues, and DBMS_AQADM allows you to administer queues and queue tables. For more information, see Chapter 17.

DBMS_DEFER, DBMS_DEFER_SYS and DBMS_DEFER_QUERY

PL/SQL 8.0 ...and HIGHER These packages allow you to build and administer deferred remote procedure calls. A full discussion of these packages is beyond the scope of this book. For more information, see *Oracle8 Server Replication*.

DBMS_DDL

The DBMS_DDL package provides PL/SQL equivalents of some useful DDL commands which cannot be used directly in PL/SQL. Although the DBMS_SQL package can be used to execute these commands as well, DBMS_DDL provides a simpler syntax.

ALTER_COMPILE
This procedure is equivalent to the SQL commands ALTER PROCEDURE COMPILE, ALTER PACKAGE COMPILE, ALTER PACKAGE BODY COMPILE, and ALTER FUNCTION COMPILE. The syntax is

```
PROCEDURE ALTER_COMPILE(
    type VARCHAR2,
    schema VARCHAR2,
    name VARCHAR2);
```

The parameters are described in the following table. ALTER_COMPILE can raise any of the following errors:

- ORA-20000: Insufficient privileges or object does not exist.

- ORA-20001: Remote object, cannot compile.

- ORA-20002: Bad value for object type.

Parameter	Type	Description
type	VARCHAR2	Type of object to compile. Must be one of 'PROCEDURE', 'FUNCTION', 'PACKAGE', or 'PACKAGE BODY'.
schema	VARCHAR2	Schema that owns the object. This is case sensitive.
name	VARCHAR2	Name of the object to compile. Also case sensitive.

ANALYZE_OBJECT

This procedure is equivalent to the SQL commands ANALYZE TABLE, ANALYZE CLUSTER, or ANALYZE INDEX. The syntax is

```
PROCEDURE ANALYZE_OBJECT (
    type VARCHAR2,
    schema VARCHAR2,
    name VARCHAR2,
    method VARCHAR2,
    estimate_rows NUMBER DEFAULT NULL,
    estimate_percent NUMBER DEFAULT NULL);
```

The parameters for ANALYZE_OBJECT are described in the following table.

Parameter	Type	Description
type	VARCHAR2	Type of object to analyze. Should be one of 'TABLE', 'CLUSTER', or 'INDEX'.
schema	VARCHAR2	Schema that owns the object. This parameter is case sensitive.
name	VARCHAR2	Name of the object to analyze. This parameter is also case sensitive.
method	VARCHAR2	Analyze method—NULL or 'ESTIMATE'. If 'ESTIMATE', then one of *estimate_rows* or *estimate_percent* must be non-zero.
estimate_rows	NUMBER	Number of rows to estimate.
estimate_percent	NUMBER	Percentage of rows to estimate. If *estimate_rows* is non-zero, this parameter is ignored.

DBMS_DESCRIBE

The DBMS_DESCRIBE package has only one procedure—DESCRIBE_PROCEDURE. Given the name of a stored procedure or function, it will return information about the parameters that the subprogram takes. If the subprogram is overloaded as part of a package, information about all the overloaded versions is returned. Two table types are used in the procedure specification:

```
TYPE varchar2_table IS TABLE OF VARCHAR2(30)
   INDEX BY BINARY_INTEGER;
TYPE number_table   IS TABLE OF NUMBER
   INDEX BY BINARY_INTEGER;
```

DESCRIBE_PROCEDURE

```
PROCEDURE DESCRIBE_PROCEDURE (
  object_name IN VARCHAR2,
  reserved1 IN VARCHAR2,
```

Datatype Value	Meaning
1	VARCHAR2
2	NUMBER
3	BINARY_INTEGER
8	LONG
11	ROWID
12	DATE
23	RAW
24	LONG RAW
96	CHAR
106	MLSLABEL
250	PL/SQL Record
251	PL/SQL Table
252	BOOLEAN

TABLE B-2.   *Datatype Codes Used for DBMS_DESCRIBE
.DESCRIBE_PROCEDURE*

DBMS_LOB

PL/SQL 8.0 ...and HIGHER DBMS_LOB is used to manage the four types of Oracle8 large objects - CLOBs, BLOBs, NCLOBs, and BFILEs. There are also Oracle8 OCI functions which are equivalent to the functionality in the DBMS_LOB package. For more information, see Chapter 21.

DBMS_LOCK

The DBMS_LOCK package is used to create your own user-defined locks. These locks are managed the same way as other Oracle locks. This means that they can be viewed in the fixed views in the data dictionary. User locks are prefixed with 'UL' so they do not conflict with Oracle locks. For more information on the DBMS_LOCK package, see the *Oracle Server Application Developer's Guide* and the *Oracle Server Reference*.

Several of these procedures use lock modes, which are specified by number. These numbers and their meanings are listed in Table B-3.

ALLOCATE_UNIQUE

This procedure will generate a unique lock ID from a lock name. The syntax is

```
PROCEDURE ALLOCATE_UNIQUE(
    lockname IN VARCHAR2,
    lockhandle OUT VARCHAR2,
    expiration_secs IN INTEGER DEFAULT 864000);
```

A handle to the lock ID is returned in *lockhandle*, which can be up to 128 bytes. Lock IDs are numbers ranging from 0 to 1073741823. Either lock IDs or lock handles are used in subsequent calls. This procedure always issues a COMMIT. *expiration_secs* specifies the minimum time before the lock is subject to cleanup, in seconds.

CAUTION
Lock names beginning with ORA$ are reserved for use by Oracle. The lock name has a maximum length of 128 bytes and is case sensitive.

Identifier	Meaning
1	Null mode
2	Row Share mode (ULRS)
3	Row Share Exclusive mode (ULRX)
4	Share mode (ULS)
5	Share Row Exclusive mode (ULRSX)
6	Exclusive mode (ULX)

TABLE B-3. *Lock Mode Identifiers*

REQUEST

```
FUNCTION  REQUEST(id IN INTEGER,
    lockmode IN INTEGER DEFAULT X_MODE,
    timeout IN INTEGER DEFAULT MAXWAIT,
    release_on_commit IN BOOLEAN DEFAULT FALSE)
  RETURN INTEGER;
FUNCTION  REQUEST(lockhandle IN VARCHAR2,
    lockmode IN INTEGER DEFAULT X_MODE,
    timeout IN INTEGER DEFAULT MAXWAIT,
    release_on_commit IN BOOLEAN DEFAULT FALSE)
  RETURN INTEGER;
```

This function is used to request a lock with a particular mode. It is overloaded on the first parameter—the lock handle or lock ID. The parameters and return values are described in the following tables.

Parameter	Type	Description
id	INTEGER	Lock ID of the lock to request. Ranges from 0 to 1073741823.
lockhandle	VARCHAR	Lock handle, as returned by ALLOCATE_UNIQUE. Either lockhandle or id should be specified, but not both.
lockmode	INTEGER	Lock mode to request. Valid values are listed in Table B-3.
timeout	INTEGER	Maximum time (in seconds) to wait for the lock to be granted. If the lock can't be granted within this period, REQUEST returns 1.
release_on_commit	BOOLEAN	If TRUE, the lock will be released when the transaction issues a COMMIT. If FALSE, the lock is held until it is explicitly released.

REQUEST Return Value	Meaning
0	Success
1	Timeout
2	Deadlock detected
3	Parameter error
4	Already own the lock
5	Illegal lock handle

CONVERT

```
FUNCTION CONVERT(id IN INTEGER,
    lockmode IN INTEGER,
    timeout IN NUMBER DEFAULT MAXWAIT)
  RETURN INTEGER;
FUNCTION CONVERT(lockhandle IN VARCHAR2,
    lockmode IN INTEGER,
    timeout IN NUMBER DEFAULT MAXWAIT)
  RETURN INTEGER;
```

CONVERT is used to change a lock from one mode to another. The arguments and return values are similar to REQUEST, and are described in the following table. Like REQUEST, CONVERT is overloaded on the first parameter.

Parameter	Type	Description
id	INTEGER	User assigned lock identifier, from 0 to 1073741823.
lockhandle	VARCHAR2	Lock handle, as returned by ALLOCATE_UNIQUE. Either id or lockhandle can be specified, but not both.
lockmode	INTEGER	Lock mode requested, as defined in Table B-3.
timeout	NUMBER	Maximum number of seconds to wait before timing out.

CONVERT Return Value	Meaning
0	Success
1	Time-out
2	Deadlock detected
3	Parameter error
4	Don't own the lock specified
5	Illegal lock handle

RELEASE

FUNCTION RELEASE(*id* IN INTEGER) RETURN INTEGER;
FUNCTION RELEASE(*lockhandle* IN VARCHAR2) RETURN INTEGER;

This function releases a lock that was acquired by REQUEST. It is overloaded on the type of its argument—the lock can be specified either by ID or by a lock handle. The return values are listed here:

RELEASE Return Value	Meaning
0	Success
3	Parameter error
4	Don't own the specified lock
5	Invalid lock handle

SLEEP

PROCEDURE SLEEP(*seconds* IN NUMBER);

SLEEP suspends the current session for the specified number of seconds. The maximum resolution is hundredths of a second, so *seconds* can be fractional.

DBMS_OUTPUT

The DBMS_OUTPUT package provides limited output capability to PL/SQL, when used in conjunction with SQL*Plus or Server Manager. It is useful for debugging and testing your PL/SQL code. For more information, see Chapter 14.

DBMS_PIPE

The DBMS_PIPE package is similar to DBMS_ALERT, in that it allows communication between different sessions connected to the same database. Messages sent over pipes, however, are asynchronous. Once a message is sent, it will go through even if the transaction that sent it rolls back. For more information, see Chapter 16.

DBMS_REFRESH & DBMS_SNAPSHOT

These packages are used to manage snapshots and snapshot groups, both of which require the distributed option. DBMS_REFRESH is used to create groups of snapshots which can be refreshed together, and DBMS_SNAPSHOT allows you to refresh a snapshot which is not necessarily part of a snapshot group. For more information, see the Oracle documentation.

DBMS_REPCAT, DBMS_REPCAT_AUTH and DBMS_REPCAT_ADMIN

These packages are used to manage Oracle's symmetric replication facility, which requires the replication option. DBMS_REPCAT allows you to use the facility, while DBMS_REPCAT_AUTH and DBMS_REPCAT_ADMIN allow you to administer the facility. For more information, see the Oracle documentation.

DBMS_ROWID

The DBMS_ROWID package is used to convert between the Oracle7 and Oracle8 ROWID formats. For more information, see the *Oracle8 Server SQL Reference*.

DBMS_SESSION

The ALTER SESSION command is DDL, and thus is not allowed directly in PL/SQL. The DBMS_SESSION package provides an interface to some of the options available with ALTER SESSION, callable from PL/SQL blocks. The DBMS_SQL package can be used as an alternative to DBMS_SESSION, since it allows execution of arbitrary statements, including ALTER SESSION.

SET_ROLE

PROCEDURE SET_ROLE(*role_cmd* VARCHAR2);

SET_ROLE is equivalent to the SQL command SET ROLE. The text of *role_cmd* is appended to 'SET ROLE', and then the string is executed. Since roles are disabled inside stored procedures, calling SET_ROLE in a stored subprogram or trigger will have no effect. If the role requires a password, you include it in the call. For example, the following code enables the role **Administrator** with the password 'admin':

```
DBMS_SESSION.SET_ROLE('Administrator IDENTIFIED BY admin');
```

SET_SQL_TRACE

PROCEDURE SET_SQL_TRACE(*sql_trace* BOOLEAN);

This procedure is used to turn SQL tracing on or off. It is equivalent to ALTER SESSION SET SQL_TRACE = *sql_trace*. For more information on tracing, see Chapter 22.

SET_NLS

PROCEDURE SET_NLS(*param* VARCHAR2, *value* VARCHAR2);

This command is equivalent to ALTER SESSION SET *param* = *value*, where *param* is a valid NLS parameter, and *value* is the value to which it should be set. This procedure is not valid in triggers. *param* and *value* will be used directly in the resulting ALTER SESSION command, so if *value* is a text literal it must contain the embedded single quotes. For example, we can change the date format with

```
DBMS_SESSION.SET_NLS('nls_date_format',
                '''DD-MON-YY HH24:MI:SS''');
```

Note the embedded single quotes in the specification of the format string.

CLOSE_DATABASE_LINK

PROCEDURE CLOSE_DATABASE_LINK(*dblink* VARCHAR2);

This procedure is equivalent to ALTER SESSION CLOSE DATABASE LINK *dblink*. It closes an implicit connection to a remote database.

SET_LABEL

PROCEDURE SET_LABEL(*lbl* VARCHAR2);

This procedure is valid in Trusted Oracle and is equivalent to ALTER SESSION SET LABEL = *lbl*. *lbl* can be 'DBHIGH', 'DBLOW', or another text label.

SET_MLS_LABEL_FORMAT

PROCEDURE SET_MLS_LABEL_FORMAT(*fmt* VARCHAR2);

Also valid in Trusted Oracle, SET_MLS_LABEL_FORMAT is equivalent to ALTER SESSION SET MLS_LABEL_FORMAT = *fmt*. It changes the default label format for the current session.

RESET_PACKAGE

PROCEDURE RESET_PACKAGE;

There is no SQL equivalent for RESET_PACKAGE. It will free the memory used to store the package state and deinstantiate all packages for the session. This is the situation at the beginning of a session.

UNIQUE_SESSION_ID

FUNCTION UNIQUE_SESSION_ID RETURN VARCHAR2;

This function returns a string with a maximum length of 24 bytes, which is unique among all sessions currently connected to the database. Multiple calls to UNIQUE_SESSION_ID from the same session always return the same result. There is no SQL equivalent.

IS_ROLE_ENABLED

```
FUNCTION IS_ROLE_ENABLED(rolename VARCHAR2)
  RETURN BOOLEAN;
```

This function returns TRUE if *rolename* is enabled for this session and FALSE otherwise. If IS_ROLE_ENABLED is called from a stored subprogram or trigger, it will always return FALSE since all roles are disabled there.

DBMS_SHARED_POOL

The DBMS_SHARED_POOL package is used to manage the shared pool. You can pin packages and procedures in the shared pool, so they won't get aged out. This is a key component of a properly tuned PL/SQL environment. For more information, see Chapter 22.

DBMS_SQL

PL/SQL 2.1 ...and HIGHER DBMS_SQL implements dynamic PL/SQL. Using this package, your program can construct SQL statements and PL/SQL blocks at run time and execute them. DBMS_SQL can also be used to execute DDL statements from PL/SQL, which are not permitted otherwise. For more information, see Chapter 15.

DBMS_TRANSACTION

The DBMS_TRANSACTION package provides procedures for transaction management. Many of the commands available here are also available in their SQL equivalents directly in PL/SQL. They are included for completeness.

SET TRANSACTION Commands

```
PROCEDURE READ_ONLY;
PROCEDURE READ_WRITE;
PROCEDURE USE_ROLLBACK_SEGMENT(rb_name VARCHAR2);
```

These procedures are equivalent to the SQL commands SET TRANSACTION READ ONLY, SET TRANSACTION READ WRITE, and SET TRANSACTION USE ROLLBACK SEGMENT *rb_name*. Each must be executed as the first statement in a transaction.

ALTER SESSION ADVISE Commands

```
PROCEDURE ADVISE_COMMIT;
PROCEDURE ADVISE_ROLLBACK;
PROCEDURE ADVISE_NOTHING;
```

These procedures are equivalent to ALTER SESSION ADVISE COMMIT, ALTER SESSION ADVISE ROLLBACK, and ALTER SESSION ADVISE NOTHING. They are used to send advice for a distributed transaction. This advice will be in the **advice** column of the **dba_2pc-pending** data dictionary view in the remote database in case the transaction is in doubt.

COMMIT Commands

```
PROCEDURE COMMIT;
PROCEDURE COMMIT_COMMENT(cmnt VARCHAR2);
PROCEDURE COMMIT_FORCE(
    xid VARCHAR2,
    scn VARCHAR2 DEFAULT NULL);
```

These commands are equivalent to the SQL commands COMMIT, COMMIT COMMENT *cmnt*, and COMMIT FORCE *xid, scn*. COMMIT COMMENT and COMMIT FORCE are typically used in distributed transactions.

ROLLBACK and SAVEPOINT Commands

```
PROCEDURE SAVEPOINT(savept VARCHAR2);
PROCEDURE ROLLBACK;
PROCEDURE ROLLBACK_SAVEPOINT(savept VARCHAR2);
PROCEDURE ROLLBACK_FORCE(xid VARCHAR2);
```

These procedures are equivalent to the SQL commands SAVEPOINT *savept*, ROLLBACK, ROLLBACK TO SAVEPOINT *savept*, and ROLLBACK FORCE *xid*. *xid* is the local or global transaction ID. ROLLBACK_FORCE is typically used in distributed transactions.

BEGIN_DISCRETE_TRANSACTION

PROCEDURE BEGIN_DISCRETE_TRANSACTION;

This procedure is used to mark the current transaction as discrete. A discrete transaction can run faster than a regular transaction, because no undo information is written. All changes to the database are buffered and actually applied at COMMIT time. There are a number of restrictions on discrete transactions, and they should be used with care. For more information, see the *Oracle Server Application Developer's Guide*.

PURGE_MIXED

PROCEDURE PURGE_MIXED(*xid* VARCHAR2);

This procedure can be used to purge mixed transactions, which are distributed transactions in which some sites have committed and others rolled back. It should be used with care by the DBA or application. *xid* should be set to the transaction ID as stored in the **local_tran_id** column in **dba_2pc_pending**.

LOCAL_TRANSACTION_ID

FUNCTION LOCAL_TRANSACTION_ID(
    create_transaction BOOLEAN DEFAULT FALSE)
    RETURN VARCHAR2;

This function returns a unique identifier for the current transaction or NULL if there is no current transaction. The identifier is unique to the local instance. If *create_transaction* is TRUE, a transaction is created if it does not already exist.

STEP_ID

FUNCTION *step_id* RETURN NUMBER;

This function returns a unique positive integer that orders the DML operations of the current transaction. The value returned is unique with respect to the current transaction only.

DBMS_UTILITY

The DBMS_UTILITY package provides additional functionality for managing procedures, reporting errors, and other information.

COMPILE_SCHEMA

PROCEDURE COMPILE_SCHEMA(*schema* VARCHAR2);

This procedure will compile all procedures, functions, and packages in the specified schema, equivalent to the SQL commands ALTER PROCEDURE COMPILE, ALTER FUNCTION COMPILE, or ALTER PACKAGE COMPILE. If you don't have ALTER privileges for one or more objects in *schema*, an ORA-20000 error is raised.

ANALYZE_SCHEMA

PROCEDURE ANALYZE_SCHEMA(
    schema VARCHAR2,
    method VARCHAR2,
    estimate_rows NUMBER DEFAULT NULL,
    estimate_percent NUMBER DEFAULT NULL);

This procedure will analyze all the tables, clusters, and indexes in the schema. The parameters are defined by the following table.

Parameter	Type	Description
schema	VARCHAR2	Schema whose objects should be analyzed.
method	VARCHAR2	Analyze method—either NULL or ESTIMATE. If ESTIMATE, then one of estimate_rows or estimate_percent should be non-zero.
estimate_rows	NUMBER	Number of rows to estimate.
estimate_percent	NUMBER	Percentage of rows to estimate. If estimate_rows is specified, this parameter is ignored.

FORMAT_ERROR_STACK

FUNCTION FORMAT_ERROR_STACK RETURN VARCHAR2;

This function will return the entire error stack, with a maximum length of 2000 bytes. It is useful in exception handlers.

FORMAT_CALL_STACK

FUNCTION FORMAT_CALL_STACK RETURN VARCHAR2;

This function returns a string consisting of the current call stack—all of the procedures that are currently executing. The maximum length is 2000 bytes.

IS_PARALLEL_SERVER

FUNCTION IS_PARALLEL_SERVER RETURN BOOLEAN;

This function returns TRUE if the instance is running in parallel server mode and FALSE otherwise.

GET_TIME

FUNCTION GET_TIME RETURN NUMBER;

Returns elapsed time in hundredths of a second. This is useful for timing a procedure. For example:

```
DECLARE
  v_Start NUMBER;
  v_End NUMBER;
BEGIN
  v_Start := DBMS_UTILITY.GET_TIME;
  /* Do some work here */
  v_End := DBMS_UTILITY.GET_TIME;
  /* The work took (v_Start - v_End) * 100 seconds to execute. */
END;
```

NAME_RESOLVE

```
PROCEDURE NAME_RESOLVE(
  name IN VARCHAR2,
  context IN NUMBER,
  schema OUT VARCHAR2,
  part1 OUT VARCHAR2,
  part2 OUT VARCHAR2,
  dblink OUT VARCHAR2,
  part1_type OUT NUMBER,
  object_number OUT NUMBER);
```

NAME_RESOLVE is used to resolve a given reference into its components. Given input of "example.Debug.Reset@dblink", for example, the output will be separated into 'example', 'Debug', 'Reset', and 'dblink', and returned in *schema*, *part1*, *part2*, and *dblink*, respectively. The parameters are described in the following table.

Parameter	Datatype	Description
name	VARCHAR2	Name of the object to resolve.
context	NUMBER	Reserved for future use—must be passed as 1.

Parameter	Datatype	Description
schema	VARCHAR2	Schema of the object, if specified as part of *name*.
part1	VARCHAR2	First part of the name. This would be the package name if the object is a packaged procedure. If it is not a packaged procedure, this is the entire name. This is also determined by *part1_type*.
part2	VARCHAR2	Second part of the name, if applicable.
dblink	VARCHAR2	Database link name, if applicable.
part1_type	NUMBER	Determines the meaning of part1. Valid values are 5 - synonym 7 - procedure 8 - function 9 - package
object_number	NUMBER	If the object was successfully resolved, this is the object number as recorded in the data dictionary.

PORT_STRING

FUNCTION PORT_STRING RETURN VARCHAR2;

This function returns a string that uniquely identifies both the version of Oracle and the operating system. The maximum length is dependent on the operating system.

UTL_FILE

PL/SQL 2.3 ...and HIGHER The UTL_FILE procedure implements file I/O in PL/SQL. Using this package, PL/SQL programs can read from and write to operating system files located on the server. The accessible files and directories are limited by parameters in the INIT.ORA database initialization file, for security. For more information, see Chapter 18.

comments: single line and multiline or C-style. Single-line comments start with two dashes (--) and continue to the end of the line (delimited by a newline character). Multiline comments start with /* and end with */. See Chapter 2 for more information. For example:

```
-- This is a single line comment.
/* This is a multiline
   comment, continued over two lines. */
```

COMMIT Statement   The COMMIT SQL statement is used to end a transaction and make all changes permanent. Until a transaction is committed, other users cannot see the changes made to the database by the transaction. COMMIT also releases any locks acquired by the transaction. The syntax is

COMMIT [WORK];

where the WORK keyword is optional. For more information, see Chapter 4.

Conditions   A condition is an expression which evaluates to a BOOLEAN value. Conditions are used in IF..THEN, EXIT..WHEN, WHILE..LOOP, and the WHERE clause of SQL statements. Conditions can be combined using the logical operators AND, OR, and NOT. They can be constructed using logical operators such as =, >=, LIKE, IN, and BETWEEN. For more information, see Chapter 2.

CURSOR_ALREADY_OPEN Exception   This predefined exception corresponds to "ORA-6511: PL/SQL: cursor already open." It is raised when you try to open a cursor that is already open. You can determine the open status of a cursor with the %ISOPEN attribute. For more information about cursors, see Chapter 6.

Cursors   Cursors are used to control the processing for queries that return more than one row. A cursor is declared using the CURSOR..IS syntax, then processed with OPEN, FETCH, and CLOSE. Cursor attributes are used to determine the current status of a cursor, with information about how many rows the cursor has returned, whether the cursor is open, and whether the last fetch was successful. For more information, see Chapter 6.

PL/SQL 2.2 ...and HIGHER **Cursor Variables**   Cursor variables are dynamic cursors. A given cursor variable can be opened for different queries using the OPEN.. FOR syntax. Typically, a cursor variable is opened on the server and fetched from and then closed on the client. Cursor variables are available in PL/SQL 2.2 and higher. With release 2.2, you must use a client program such as SQL*Plus, or one written using the precompilers or OCI, to access cursor variables. PL/SQL 2.3 can process cursor variables entirely on the server. A cursor variable is declared with type REF CURSOR and is the only pointer type available in PL/SQL up to release 2.3. For more information, see the section "Cursor Variables" in Chapter 6.

Datatypes   PL/SQL supports all of the datatypes provided by the Oracle server, plus a number of additional ones. The types are described in detail in Chapter 2, and listed below by category and family. Entries in the table with a * are available only in PL/SQL 8.0 and higher.

Category	Family	Types
Reference Types	N/A	REF CURSOR, REF object type*
Composite Types	N/A	RECORD, TABLE, VARRAY*
LOB Types*		BFILE, LOB, CLOB, NLOB
Scalar Types	Numeric	BINARY_INTEGER, DEC, DECIMAL, DOUBLE PRECISION, FLOAT, INT, INTEGER, NATURAL, NATURALN*, NUMBER, NUMERIC, PLS_INTEGER, POSITIVE, POSITIVEN*, REAL, SIGNTYPE*, SMALLINT
	Boolean	BOOLEAN
	Trusted	MLSLABEL
	Character	CHAR, CHARACTER, LONG, NCHAR*, NVARCHAR2*, STRING, VARCHAR, VARCHAR2
	Raw	RAW, LONG RAW
	Date	DATE
	Rowid	ROWID

DDL (Data Definition Language) DDL statements modify data dictionary objects, rather than the data contained in them. They include CREATE TABLE and DROP PROCEDURE, for example. PL/SQL does not allow DDL statements to be used directly, because the compiler is implemented using early binding. PL/SQL 2.1, however, allows the use of DDL statements with the DBMS_SQL package. This package allows statements to be constructed at runtime, rather than compile time. For more information, see Chapter 15.

DELETE Statement The DELETE SQL statement is used to remove rows from a table. It is defined with

> DELETE [FROM] *table* [*alias*]
>   WHERE *where_clause* | CURRENT OF *cursor*;

Table specifies the table from which the rows should be deleted. An alias for the table name can also be specified if desired. The *where_clause* determines which rows will be deleted. If the CURRENT OF *cursor* clause is used, then the last row fetched from *cursor* will be deleted. After a delete that removes one or more rows, SQL%NOTFOUND is FALSE, SQL%FOUND is TRUE, and SQL%ROWCOUNT contains the number of rows deleted. If the *where_clause* does not match any rows, no rows are deleted and SQL%NOTFOUND is TRUE, SQL%FOUND is FALSE, and SQL%ROWCOUNT equals 0. For more information, see Chapter 4.

DML (Data Manipulation Language) DML statements (SELECT, UPDATE, DELETE, INSERT, EXPLAIN PLAN) modify the data in Oracle objects, rather than the objects themselves. DML statements can be included directly in PL/SQL. For more information, see Chapter 4.

DUP_VAL_ON_INDEX Exception This predefined exception corresponds to the Oracle error "ORA-1: unique constraint violated". It is raised when you try to insert a row into a table with a unique index defined for a particular field, and the value for the field you are trying to insert already exists in the table.

EXCEPTION_INIT Pragma   Pragma EXCEPTION_INIT is used to associate a named exception with an Oracle error. This provides named exceptions in addition to the predefined ones. The syntax is

PRAGMA EXCEPTION_INIT(*exception_name, error_number*);

where *exception_name* is an exception currently in scope, and *error_number* is the SQLCODE value corresponding to an Oracle error. For example, the following code will raise **e_NonExistentTable** whenever the error "ORA-942: table or view does not exist" is returned:

```
DECLARE
  e_NonExistentTable  EXCEPTION;
  PRAGMA EXCEPTION_INIT(e_NonExistentTable, -942);
  ...
```

For more information, see Chapter 10.

Exceptions   Exceptions are used to trap runtime errors. When an error occurs, an exception is raised, and control immediately passes to the exception-handling section of the block. If there is no exception-handling section in the current block, the exception is propagated out to the enclosing block. Predefined exceptions are defined in the STANDARD package, and you can define your own exceptions as well. For more information, see Chapter 10.

EXIT Statement   EXIT is used to pass control out of a currently executing loop. It is defined with

EXIT [*loop_name*] [WHEN *condition*];

where *condition* is a boolean expression. If there is no WHEN clause, the loop is exited immediately. If there is a WHEN clause, the loop is exited only if *condition* evaluates to TRUE. If specified, *loop_name* should match a label at the beginning of a loop. For more information, see Chapter 2.

Expressions   An expression is a combination of variables, constants, literals, operators, other expressions, and function calls. An expression evaluates to an rvalue. Expressions can be used in a variety of PL/SQL statements, including the WHERE clause of SELECT, UPDATE, and DELETE statements. Expressions are combined using operators such as +, -, NOT, OR, ||, and -. If an expression is composed of items that have different types, they are converted to the same type first, and then the operators are applied. For more information, see Chapter 2.

PL/SQL 8.0 ...and HIGHER **External Procedures**   External procedures are a new Oracle8 feature which allows you to write a procedure or function in C, and call it directly from PL/SQL. Doing this requires a wrapper function in PL/SQL, which is created with the CREATE [OR REPLACE] PROCEDURE ... AS EXTERNAL statement. You must also specify the mapping between the PL/SQL and C datatypes in the CREATE statement. For more information, see Chapter 20.

PL/SQL 8.0 ...and HIGHER **extproc**   External procedures are called by a special Oracle process known as extproc. Extproc is started the first time a session makes a call to an external procedure, and remains active for the duration of that session. Extproc loads the shared library containing the external procedure, and then calls it. It communicates with the original shadow process with SQL*Net. For more information, see Chapter 20.

FETCH Statement   FETCH is used to retrieve rows from a cursor or cursor variable into PL/SQL variables or a PL/SQL record. It is defined with

    FETCH cursor | cursor_variable
       INTO record | list_of_variables;

where *cursor* is the name of a previously opened cursor, or *cursor_variable* is the name of a previously opened cursor variable (PL/SQL 2.2 and higher). The *list_of_variables* or the fields in *record* should match the select list of the query. Typically, FETCH is called in a loop whose exit condition is determined by the %NOTFOUND attribute. Each call to FETCH will retrieve one more row and increment *cursor* %ROWCOUNT by one. For more information, see Chapter 6.

%FOUND Attribute This boolean cursor attribute is used to determine whether the last FETCH for a cursor or cursor variable (PL/SQL 2.2 and higher) returned a row. It is defined with

> *cursor* %FOUND | *cursor_variable*%FOUND

where *cursor* is the name of a cursor, and *cursor_variable* is the name of a cursor variable. If the last FETCH returned a row, then %FOUND evaluates to TRUE. After a cursor is opened, but before the first FETCH, %FOUND evaluates to NULL. %FOUND is the opposite of the %NOTFOUND cursor attribute. For more information, see Chapter 6.

Functions Functions are named PL/SQL blocks that return a value and can be called with arguments. They can be used as part of an expression. They are legal in procedural statements, and certain functions can be used in SQL statements in PL/SQL 2.1 and higher. Functions can be stored in the database with the CREATE [OR REPLACE] FUNCTION command, or they can be located in the declarative section of another block. For more information, see Chapter 7.

GOTO Statement GOTO passes control to a statement identified by a label. The syntax is

> GOTO *label*;

where *label* is delimited by double angle brackets << and >>. It is illegal to branch into or out of an exception handler, or into an IF statement, loop, or sub-block. For more information, see Chapter 2.

I/O PL/SQL does not have support for input/output directly in the language. The DBMS_OUTPUT package, when used with SQL*Plus, Server Manager, or SQL*DBA, provides output capability. SQL*Plus provides input capability via substitution variables. PL/SQL 2.3 remedies this situation with the UTL_FILE package, which provides file I/O. DBMS_OUTPUT is discussed in Chapter 14, and UTL_FILE in Chapter 18.

Identifiers The name of any PL/SQL object is an identifier. Identifiers are not case-sensitive, and consist of up to 30 characters in the PL/SQL character set. Identifiers must begin with a letter. For more information, see Chapter 2.

IF Statement   The IF statement is used to conditionally execute a sequence of statements. It is defined with

```
IF condition1 THEN
  sequence_of_statements1;
[ELSIF condition2 THEN
  sequence_of_statements2;]
...
[ELSE
  sequence_of_statements3;]
END IF;
```

The *sequence_of_statements* under the first *condition* that evaluates to TRUE is executed. At most, one *sequence_of_statements* will be executed. For more information, see Chapter 2.

INSERT Statement   INSERT is used to add a row to a table. It is defined with

```
INSERT INTO table [(column_list)]
  VALUES (expression_list);
```

where *table* is a reference to the table into which the rows will be inserted, and *expression_list* is a comma-separated list of expressions that make up the fields of the new row. If *column_list* is specified, then it determines the columns that will have values. Columns that are not specified will have a value of NULL. If *column_list* is not specified, then *expression_list* should correspond to all the columns in table. For more information, see Chapter 4.

INVALID_CURSOR Exception   This predefined exception corresponds to the Oracle error "ORA-1001: invalid cursor". It is raised when a cursor is invalid but you try to use it regardless. This can occur if you try to fetch from a cursor before it has been opened, or if you fetch from a cursor declared for update after a commit. For more information on cursor processing, see Chapter 6.

INVALID_NUMBER Exception   This predefined exception corresponds to the Oracle error "ORA-1722: invalid number". It is raised when an attempted conversion to a NUMBER value failed. For example, the string 'Nineteen Hundred and Ninety Five' cannot be converted into a NUMBER since it does not contain only digits, a decimal point, or an optional sign. For more information on number conversions, see Chapters 2 and 4.

ISOPEN   The %ISOPEN cursor attribute is used to determine whether a cursor or cursor variable (PL/SQL 2.2 and higher) is open. It is defined with

   cursor %ISOPEN | *cursor_variable*%ISOPEN

where *cursor* is the name of an explicit cursor, or *cursor_variable* is the name of a cursor variable. If the cursor or cursor variable has been opened with the OPEN or OPEN..FOR statement, and has not yet been closed, %ISOPEN will return TRUE. SQL%ISOPEN always returns FALSE, since the implicit cursor is always closed after execution of the SQL statement. For more information, see Chapter 6.

Literals   Literals can be classified as either numeric or character. A numeric literal is composed of the digits 0 through 9, with an optional sign and/or decimal point. Numeric literals can also be specified in scientific notation. All numeric literals have datatype NUMBER. A character literal is any sequence of characters enclosed in single quotes. A double-quoted string is not treated as a literal, but as a case-sensitive identifier. Character literals have datatype CHAR, not VARCHAR2. For more information, see Chapter 2.

PL/SQL 8.0 ...and HIGHER **LOBs**   Available with Oracle8, LOBs (Large OBjects) provide an enhancement to the LONG and LONG RAW datatypes They can be manipulated using either the PL/SQL DBMS_LOB package, or an OCI interface. A LOB can store up to 4 gigabytes of character or binary data. For more information, see Chapter 21.

LOCK TABLE Statement   LOCK TABLE is a DML statement that can be used to lock an entire table. The SELECT..FOR UPDATE statement is used to lock selected rows within a table. The syntax for LOCK TABLE is

```
LOCK TABLE table IN lock_mode [NOWAIT];
```

where *table* is a reference to the desired table, and *lock_mode* specifies the mode. Available modes include ROW EXCLUSIVE, ROW SHARE, SHARE UPDATE, SHARE, SHARE ROW EXCLUSIVE, and EXCLUSIVE. If NOWAIT is specified, the statement will return immediately either with the lock acquired or with TIMEOUT_ON_RESOURCE raised if the lock cannot be acquired. If NOWAIT is not specified, then the LOCK TABLE will wait until the lock can be acquired. For more information, see the *Oracle Server SQL Reference.*

Loops   There are four different kinds of looping structures in PL/SQL. Basic loops are delimited with the LOOP and END LOOP keywords. WHILE loops start with the WHILE..LOOP keywords and end with END LOOP. Numeric and cursor FOR loops use the FOR *index* IN..LOOP and END LOOP keywords. All loops can optionally begin with a label, which can be used in the EXIT statement within the loop, if desired. For more information on simple, WHILE, and numeric FOR loops, see Chapter 2. For more information on cursor FOR loops, see Chapter 6.

LOGIN_DENIED Exception   This predefined exception corresponds to the Oracle error "ORA-1017: invalid username/password; logon denied". It is raised when an incorrect user name/password combination is specified.

MAP and ORDER Methods *(PL/SQL 8.0 ...and HIGHER)*   MAP and ORDER methods are special methods for object types, which are used to determine how to sort instances of an object type. A given object type can have either a MAP or an ORDER method, but not both. For more information, see Chapter12.

NOT_LOGGED_ON Exception   This predefined exception corresponds to the Oracle error "ORA-1012: not connected to Oracle". It is raised if an SQL statement is issued before a valid connection has been established.

%NOTFOUND   The %NOTFOUND cursor attribute is used to determine whether the last FETCH from a cursor or cursor variable (PL/SQL 2.2 and higher) did not return a row. It is defined with *cursor*%NOTFOUND | *cursor_variable*%NOTFOUND

where *cursor* is an identifier for a cursor, or *cursor_variable* is an identifier for a cursor variable (PL/SQL 2.2 and higher). If the prior FETCH did not return a row because the end of the active set has been reached, then %NOTFOUND will return TRUE. %NOTFOUND is the opposite of %FOUND. For more information, see Chapter 6.

PL/SQL 8.0 ...and HIGHER **Nested Tables**   Nested tables extend the PL/SQL table functions available in version 2. Unlike version 2 PL/SQL tables, a nested table can be stored in the database in a database table. Individual rows in a nested table can be manipulated using SQL statements, or the entire table can be manipulated. The collection methods such as FIRST, LAST, NEXT, and PRIOR can also be used. For more information, see Chapter 12.

NO_DATA_FOUND Exception   This predefined exception corresponds to the Oracle error "ORA-1403: no data found". It is raised if a SELECT.. INTO statement matches no rows, or if you reference a row in a PL/SQL table that has not yet been assigned. For more information on SELECT..INTO, see Chapter 4. For more information on PL/SQL tables, see Chapter 3.

NULL Value   All PL/SQL expressions can evaluate to NULL, unless they are constrained not to when a variable is declared. A NULL means "missing or unknown value." Many expressions will evaluate to NULL if one of the operands evaluates to NULL. This includes BOOLEAN expressions—the logical operators in PL/SQL implement a three-valued logic, not a two-valued logic. For more information on NULL and its implications, see Chapter 2.

NULL Statement   The NULL statement, specified with

    NULL;

performs no work. It is useful for indicating that no action is to be taken at a point where PL/SQL syntax demands a statement. For more information, see Chapter 2.

OPEN Statement The OPEN statement is used to open a cursor (or cursor variable, in release 2.2 and higher). When a cursor is opened, any bind variables in the WHERE clause are evaluated, and the active set is determined. The bind variables will not be examined, nor will the active set change unless the cursor is closed and then reopened. The syntax for OPEN is

  OPEN *cursor_name*; | OPEN *cursor_variable* FOR *select_statement*;

where *cursor_name* specifies a previously defined static cursor, and *cursor_ variable* specifies a previously defined cursor variable. For a cursor variable, the query is specified with *select_statement*. For more information, see Chapter 6.

Packages Packages are defined as two separate data dictionary objects— the package header (or specification) and the package body. The header is created with the CREATE OR REPLACE PACKAGE command, the body with the CREATE OR REPLACE PACKAGE BODY command. Packages must be stored in the database; they cannot be placed in a declarative section like procedures and functions. Packages themselves can contain procedures, functions, variables, types, cursors, and exceptions. Items declared in the package header will be visible outside the package, while items defined only in the package body will be private to the package. Packages also break the dependency chain because the package body can be recompiled without affecting the package specification. For more information, see Chapter 8.

Procedural Statements Procedural statements, as opposed to SQL statements, control the processing of a PL/SQL block. They are processed by the PL/SQL engine and are not sent to the SQL statement executor in the database. Procedural statements include calls to procedures, assignments, conditional control statements such as IF..THEN, and loops. For more information, see Chapter 2.

Procedures Procedures can be stored in the database with the CREATE OR REPLACE PROCEDURE statement, or they can be declared in the declarative section of a block. A procedure is a named block that can be called with parameters. The parameters can either accept a value from the calling environment (IN), return a value to the calling environment (OUT), or both (IN OUT). For more information, see Chapter 7.

PROGRAM_ERROR Exception   This predefined exception corresponds to the Oracle error " PL/SQL: internal error *mmm*, arguments [*mmm*], [*mmm*], [*mmm*], [*mmm*], [*mmm*], [*mmm*]", where *mmm* represents the code and arguments associated with this particular internal error. This error is raised when an internal PL/SQL error has occurred, which should not normally occur.

RAISE Statement   RAISE is used to signal that an error has occurred by raising an exception. The exception can be user defined or predefined. The syntax for RAISE is

    RAISE [*exception_name*];

where *exception_name* specifies the exception to be raised. The only place where it is legal to issue a RAISE statement without a named exception is in an exception handler. In this case, the current exception is raised again. For more information, see Chapter 10.

Records   PL/SQL records are used to group logically related information of different types. Like PL/SQL tables, you must first define a record type and then declare a variable of that type. For example, the following declarative section declares a record to hold some of the student information:

```
DECLARE
  TYPE t_StudentType IS RECORD (
    FirstName students.first_name%TYPE;
    LastName  students.last_name%TYPE;
    ID        students.ID%TYPE);
  v_StudentInfo t_StudentType;
```

The %ROWTYPE attribute returns a PL/SQL record as well. For more information, see Chapter 3.

 RESTRICT_REFERENCES Pragma   The RESTRICT_REFERENCES pragma is used to assert the purity level for user-defined functions and methods. In order to be used in SQL statements, you must guarantee to the PL/SQL engine that the function does not modify any database or package state. The pragma is specified with

PRAGMA RESTRICT_REFERENCES(*function_name*,
    [RNDS] [,WNDS] [,RNPS] [,WNPS]);

where *function_name* is the function whose purity you are asserting. The purity levels, defined in the following table, can be specified in any order. For more information, see Chapter 8.

Purity Level	Meaning
RNDS	Reads no database state
WNDS	Writes no database state
RNPS	Reads no package state
WNPS	Writes no package state

RETURN Statement   RETURN can be used in two ways: to return from a function or from a procedure. It is specified with

RETURN [*return_value*];

RETURN causes control to pass from a function or procedure back to the calling environment. The *return_value* must be specified for a function, and not for a procedure. RETURN is optional for procedures, but it is required for functions, since a function must pass a value back to the calling environment. For more information, see Chapter 7.

ROLLBACK Statement   The ROLLBACK statement is used to end a transaction and undo the work done by that transaction. It is as if the transaction was never begun. The syntax is

ROLLBACK [WORK] [TO SAVEPOINT *savepoint*];

The WORK keyword is optional. Like COMMIT, ROLLBACK also releases any locks acquired by the transaction. If a savepoint is specified, only the work done after *savepoint* is rolled back. For more information, see Chapter 4.

%ROWCOUNT Attribute   This cursor attribute returns the number of rows fetched so far for an explicit cursor, and the number of rows affected by the last statement for the implicit SQL cursor. Each explicit FETCH for a cursor will increment its %ROWCOUNT value by one. For more information, see Chapter 6.

%ROWTYPE Attribute   The %ROWTYPE attribute can be applied to a database table. It will return the type of a PL/SQL record consisting of all the columns in the table, in the order in which they were specified at table creation. For example, the following declare section declares a record that can hold a row in the **classes** table:

```
DECLARE
    v_ClassInfo classes%ROWTYPE;
```

For more information, see Chapter 2.

ROWTYPE_MISMATCH Exception   This predefined exception corresponds to the Oracle error "ORA-6504: PL/SQL: return types of result set variables or query do not match". This error is raised when you open a cursor variable for a different type of query than it was defined for, using the OPEN..FOR syntax. For more information, see Chapter 6.

SAVEPOINT Statement   SAVEPOINT is used to mark the place in a transaction. The syntax is

SAVEPOINT *savepoint_name*;

where *savepoint_name* is the name of the savepoint to be defined. Once the savepoint is defined, you can roll back to it using the ROLLBACK TO SAVEPOINT command. For more information, see Chapter 4.

SELECT..INTO Statement   SELECT..INTO is used to retrieve one row from the database. The syntax is

```
SELECT select_list
  INTO variable_list | record
  FROM table
  [WHERE where_clause]
  [GROUP BY group_clause]
  [ORDER BY order_clause]
  [HAVING having_clause];
```

The variables in *variable_list* should match the items in *select_list*, or the fields in the *record* should match. The row will be retrieved from the table identified by *table*. The rest of the clauses determine which row will be retrieved. If the query returns more than one row, use an explicit cursor. If the query does not return any rows, the NO_DATA_FOUND exception is raised. For more information, see Chapter 4.

SET TRANSACTION Statement   SET TRANSACTION is used to determine the properties of the transaction. It must be called as the first statement in the transaction. The syntax for SET TRANSACTION is

```
SET TRANSACTION
  USE ROLLBACK SEGMENT segment | READ ONLY;
```

SET TRANSACTION can be used both to assign a particular rollback segment to the transaction and to allow only read operations (queries and LOCK TABLE statements). All queries in a read-only transaction will be read consistently from the beginning of the transaction, rather than for each statement. For more information, see the *Oracle Server SQL Reference*.

PL/SQL 8.0 ...and HIGHER   **SUBSCRIPT_BEYOND_COUNT Exception**   This predefined exception corresponds to the Oracle error "ORA-6533: subscript beyond count". It is raised when you reference a collection with a subscript value that greater than the count for a varray, or too large for a nested table. For more information, see Chapter 12.

PL/SQL 8.0 ...and HIGHER   **SUBSCRIPT_OUTSIDE_LIMIT Exception**   This predefined exception corresponds to the Oracle error "ORA-6532: subscript outside of limit". It is raised when you reference a collection with a subscript value greater than the limit for a varray, or non-positive for a varray or nested table. For more information, see Chapter 12.

SQL Cursor   All SQL statements are processed in a cursor. Explicit cursors are used for multirow queries, and they are processed using the OPEN, FETCH, and CLOSE commands. For other SQL statements, an implicit cursor is used. This cursor is known as the SQL cursor. The four cursor attributes are available, and are referenced with SQL%FOUND, SQL%NOTFOUND, SQL%ROWCOUNT, and SQL%ISOPEN. SQL%ISOPEN will always return FALSE since the implicit cursor is opened, the statement is executed within it, and the cursor is closed before %ISOPEN can be checked. For more information, see Chapter 6.

SQL Statements   SQL statements, as opposed to procedural statements, are used to issue commands to the database. Only DML (data manipulation language) and transaction control statements are allowed directly in PL/SQL. The DBMS_SQL package, available with PL/SQL 2.1 and higher, can be used to issue DDL statements from PL/SQL. For more information, see Chapter 4.

SQLCODE Function   SQLCODE is used to return the error code associated with the current error. It is typically used in a WHEN OTHERS handler to determine which Oracle error raised the exception. SQLCODE returns an INTEGER value. For more information, see Chapter 10.

SQLERRM Function   SQLERRM returns the error message text associated with an Oracle error code. If no error code is specified, SQLERRM returns the error message text for the current error. Typically, SQLERRM is used along with SQLCODE in a WHEN OTHERS handler to determine the text of the error that raised the exception. The maximum length of an error message is 512 characters. For more information, see Chapter 10.

STANDARD Package   The predefined exceptions (such as NO_DATA_FOUND or INVALID_CURSOR), types (such as NUMBER or DATE), and functions (such as TO_CHAR or ADD_MONTHS) are all defined in a PL/SQL package known as STANDARD. It is owned by the database user SYS and is created when the data dictionary is created by the **catproc.sql** script. EXECUTE permission on STANDARD is granted to

PUBLIC by **catproc.sql** as well. Unlike other PL/SQL packages, you can refer to objects within STANDARD without prefixing them with the package name.

Statements   There are two kinds of statements: procedural and SQL. Procedural statements consist of assignments, procedure calls, loops, or IF statements, for example. SQL statements can be divided into DML (data manipulation language), DDL (data definition language), transaction control, session control, and system control statements. For more information, see Chapters 2 and 4.

STORAGE_ERROR Exception   This predefined exception corresponds to the Oracle error "ORA-6500: PL/SQL: storage error". This error is raised when PL/SQL cannot allocate enough memory to continue. It is an internal error, which should not normally occur.

Tables   PL/SQL tables are syntactically treated much like arrays in other third-generation languages. To declare a PL/SQL table, first you define a new table type and then a variable of that type. For example, the following declarative section defines a table of DATEs:

```
DECLARE
  TYPE t_DateTable IS TABLE OF DATE
    INDEX BY BINARY_INTEGER;
  v_Dates t_DateTable;
```

Although a table is treated syntactically like an array, it is not implemented like an array. For more information, see Chapter 3.

TIMEOUT_ON_RESOURCE Exception   This predefined exception corresponds to the Oracle error "ORA-51: timeout occurred while waiting for resource". It can be raised if you specify the NOWAIT clause in a SELECT..FOR UPDATE statement, and another session already has a lock on the requested rows.

TOO_MANY_ROWS Exception   This predefined exception corresponds to the Oracle error "Oracle 1422: exact fetch returns more than requested number of rows". It is raised if a SELECT..INTO statement matches more than one row. In this case, a cursor should be used to retrieve the entire active set. For more information, see Chapter 6.

TRANSACTION_BACKED_OUT Exception   This predefined exception corresponds to the Oracle error "ORA-61: another instance has a different DML_LOCKS setting". This exception is predefined only in PL/SQL 2.0 and 2.1, not in 2.2 or higher. It is raised if a transaction has to be rolled back by the database due to a deadlock situation.

Triggers   A trigger is similar to a procedure in that it is a named, callable block that is stored in the database. However, a trigger is not called explicitly. Rather, it is called (or fired) implicitly whenever the triggering event occurs. The triggering event is a DML operation on a database table. There are 12 different kinds of triggers, based on the type of statement (INSERT, UPDATE, DELETE), the type of trigger (ROW, STATEMENT), and the triggering time (BEFORE, AFTER). Oracle8 allows an additional trigger type—INSTEAD OF. For more information, see Chapter 9.

%TYPE Attribute   The %TYPE attribute can be applied to a variable or a table column. It returns the type of the object and is used to make your program more flexible. For example, in the following block, **v_FirstName** is declared with type VARCHAR2(20), and **v_CurrentCredits** is defined with type NUMBER(3), since these are the type of **students.first_name** and **students.current_credits**, respectively.

```
DECLARE
   v_FirstName       students.first_name%TYPE;
   v_CurrentCredits students.current_credits%TYPE;
```

Only the length or precision/scale constraint is taken from the column definition. Even if the column is constrained to be NOT NULL, the variable can contain NULLs (unless it is also constrained). For more information, see Chapter 2.

UPDATE Statement   The UPDATE statement is used to modify existing rows in a database table. The syntax is

UPDATE *table* SET *column1* = *value1*, *column2* = *value2*, ...
   [WHERE *where_clause*];

where *table* is a reference to the table to be modified, and *where_clause* specifies the rows to change. The columns specified by *column1*, *column2*, and so on, will be set to their corresponding *value*s. If an

UPDATE statement affects one or more rows, SQL%FOUND will be TRUE, SQL%NOTFOUND will be FALSE, and SQL%ROWCOUNT will contain the number of rows modified after the statement executes. If the statement does not match any rows, SQL%FOUND will be FALSE, SQL%NOTFOUND will be TRUE, and SQL%ROWCOUNT will be zero. For more information, see Chapter 4.

VALUE_ERROR Exception   This predefined exception corresponds to the Oracle error "ORA-6502: numeric or value error". It is raised if an attempted conversion of a character value to a NUMBER fails. VALUE_ERROR is generally raised for a procedural statement; for a SQL statement, an error such as INVALID_NUMBER is raised instead. For more information on datatype conversion, see Chapters 2 and 4.

Variables and Constants   Variables and constants are defined in the declarative section of a PL/SQL block. A declaration looks like

variable_name type [CONSTANT] [NOT NULL] [:= initial_value];

where variable_name is the name of the new variable or constant, and type is its type. type can be either a predefined type, such as DATE or ROWID, or a user-defined type. If CONSTANT is specified, the value of the variable cannot be changed; it is a constant. The variable or constant will be assigned initial_value if it is specified or NULL if no initial value is specified. For more information, see Chapter 2.

PL/SQL 8.0 ...and HIGHER   **Varrays**   Varrays implement an ordered collection of objects with a maximum size. They can be manipulated with collection methods such as DELETE, COUNT, NEXT, and PRIOR. The following declare section defines a varray type which can hold DATEs:

```
DECLARE
   TYPE t_Dates IS VARRAY(25) OF DATE;
```

For more information, see Chapter 12.

ZERO_DIVIDE Exception   This predefined exception corresponds to the Oracle error "ORA-1476: divisor is equal to zero". It is raised whenever an attempt to divide by zero is performed.

APPENDIX
D

The Data Dictionary

his appendix describes some of the views in the data dictionary that are relevant to PL/SQL programmers. It does not include all of the views, just the more commonly used ones. A brief description of the data dictionary and how it works is also included.

What Is the Data Dictionary?

The data dictionary is where Oracle stores information about the structure of the database. The data itself is located in other areas—the data dictionary describes how the actual data is organized. The dictionary consists of tables and views that you can query, like any other database table or view. The views are owned by the Oracle user SYS.

The data dictionary is typically created when the database is created and installed for the first time. Without the dictionary, no PL/SQL work can be done. On most systems, there is a script called **catproc.sql** that creates the dictionary views. This script should be run while connected as SYS, or connected as internal in SQL*DBA or Server Manager.

In addition to creating the data dictionary itself, **catproc.sql** creates the standard PL/SQL and DBMS packages, which are stored in the data dictionary. For more information on the data dictionary views (including views not discussed here and the v$ performance views), see the *Oracle7 Server Reference*. For more information on the built in packages, see Appendix B.

Naming Conventions

Many of the views have three different instantiations. These are known as **user_***, **all_***, and **dba_***. For example, there are three instantiations of the information about the source for stored objects. The views that represent this are **user_source**, **all_source**, and **dba_source**. In general, the **user_*** views contain information about objects owned by the current user, the **all_*** views contain information about all objects accessible to the current user (not necessarily owned by them), and the **dba_*** views contain information about all objects in the database.

SQL and PL/SQL are not case sensitive. In order to implement this, all objects are converted into uppercase before they are stored. Therefore, you should use uppercase when querying the data dictionary. For example, the **user_objects** view has a column **object_name** that contains the name of the

object. These names are always stored in uppercase. You could query
user_objects with:

```
SQL> SELECT object_type, status
  2     FROM user_objects
  3     WHERE object_name = UPPER('ClassPackage');

OBJECT_TYPE    STATUS
-------------  -------
PACKAGE        VALID
PACKAGE BODY   VALID
```

Note the use of the UPPER function so that the query will return the desired
rows. (**ClassPackage** is described in Chapter 8.)

Permissions

The data dictionary views are owned by SYS. By default, only SYS and
users with the DBA system privilege can see all of the views. Users without
the DBA privilege can see the **user_*** and **all_*** views, in addition to some
others. They cannot see the **dba_*** views unless they have been granted
specific SELECT privileges on them.

   The data dictionary views should *never* be updated, even by SYS. They
are updated automatically by the database as their relevant information
changes. Oracle also provides scripts to modify the data dictionary tables
when a database is upgraded or downgraded (such as **cat7302.sql**, which
upgrades from a 7.3.1 database to a 7.3.2 database). These scripts can be
found in the same directory as **catproc.sql**.

All/User/DBA Dictionary Views

This section describes the data dictionary views that have the **user_***, **dba_***
and **all_*** instantiations. Since the three instantiations have many columns
in common, they are listed together. Each category is listed in Table D-1
for reference and described in detail in the following sections.

Dependencies

The **all_dependencies**, **dba_dependencies**, and **user_dependencies** views
document the dependency relationship between stored objects.

Category	Views
Dependencies	all_dependencies, dba_dependencies, user_dependencies
Collections*	all_coll_types, dba_coll_types, user_coll_types
Compile Errors	all_errors, dba_errors, user_errors
Directories*	all_directories, dba_directories, user_directories
Jobs	all_jobs, dba_jobs, user_jobs
LOBs*	all_lobs, dba_lobs, user_lobs
Libraries*	all_libraries, dba_libraries, user_libraries
Object Method Parameters*	all_method_params, dba_method_params, user_method_params
Object Method Results (return values)*	all_method_results, dba_method_results, user_method_results
Object Methods*	all_type_methods, dba_type_methods, user_type_methods
Object References*	all_refs, dba_refs, user_refs
Object Type Attributes*	all_type_attrs, dba_type_attrs, user_type_attrs
Object Types*	all_types, dba_types, user_types
Schema Objects	all_objects, dba_objects, user_objects
Source Code	all_source, dba_source, user_source
Table Columns	all_tab_columns, dba_tab_columns, user_tab_columns
Tables	all_tables, dba_tables, user_tables, all_catalog, dba_catalog, user_catalog
Triggers	all_triggers, dba_triggers, user_triggers
Trigger Columns	all_trigger_cols, dba_trigger_cols, user_trigger_cols

TABLE D-1.   *Data Dictionary Views in this Appendix*

* Available in Oracle8 and higher

Column	Null?	Type	Description
OWNER	NOT NULL	VARCHAR2(30)	Schema that owns the object (**all_dependencies** and **dba_dependencies** only).
NAME	NOT NULL	VARCHAR2(30)	Name of the object (in uppercase).
TYPE		VARCHAR2(12)	Type of the object—one of PROCEDURE, FUNCTION, PACKAGE, PACKAGE BODY.
REFERENCED_OWNER		VARCHAR2(30)	Schema that owns the referenced object.
REFERENCED_NAME		VARCHAR2(30)	Name of the referenced object.
REFERENCED_TYPE		VARCHAR2(12)	Type of the referenced object—one of PROCEDURE, FUNCTION, PACKAGE, PACKAGE BODY.
REFERENCED_LINK_ NAME		VARCHAR2(128)	Name of the database link to the referenced object (if the referenced object is in a remote database).

Collections

PL/SQL 8.0 ...and HIGHER The **all_coll_types**, **dba_coll_types**, and **user_coll_types** views contain information about the collections accessible to the user. Only collection types which are defined with the CREATE TYPE statement (as opposed to those local to a PL/SQL block) are stored in the data dictionary.

Column	Null?	Type	Description
OWNER	NOT NULL	VARCHAR2(30)	Schema which owns the collection (**all_coll_types** and **dba_coll_types** only)
TYPE_NAME	NOT NULL	VARCHAR2(30)	Name of the collection
COLL_TYPE	NOT NULL	VARCHAR2(30)	Collection type—either TABLE or VARYING ARRAY
UPPER_BOUND		NUMBER	Maximum number of elements for varray types
ELEM_TYPE_MOD		VARCHAR2(7)	Element type modifier (such as REF)
ELEM_TYPE_OWNER		VARCHAR2(30)	Owner of the element type (if different from the owner of the collection itself)
ELEM_TYPE_NAME		VARCHAR2(30)	Name of the element type
LENGTH		NUMBER	If the element type is CHAR or VARCHAR2, its length
PRECISION		NUMBER	If the element type is NUMBER, the specified precision
SCALE		NUMBER	If the element type is NUMBER, the specified scale
CHARACTER_SET_NAME		VARCHAR2(44)	Character set name if specified—CHAR_CS or NCHAR_CS

Compile Errors

The **all_errors**, **dba_errors**, and **user_errors** views contain the text of compile errors for stored objects and views. If there is an entry in one of the _errors views, then the object is necessarily invalid (indicated in **all_objects**, **dba_objects**, and **user_objects**).

A typical query of **user_errors** might look like this:

```
SELECT line, position, text
  FROM user_errors
  WHERE name = object_name
  ORDER BY sequence;
```

Column	Null?	Type	Description
OWNER	NOT NULL	VARCHAR2(30)	Schema that owns the object (**all_errors** and **dba_errors** only).
NAME	NOT NULL	VARCHAR2(30)	Name of the object (in uppercase).
TYPE		VARCHAR2(12)	Type of the object—one of VIEW, PROCEDURE, FUNCTION, PACKAGE, PACKAGE BODY.
SEQUENCE	NOT NULL	NUMBER	Sequence number, used to order the errors.
LINE	NOT NULL	NUMBER	Line number at which the error occurs.
POSITION	NOT NULL	NUMBER	Zero-based offset within the line at which the error occurs.
TEXT	NOT NULL	VARCHAR2(2000)	Text of the error, including both the error code and the error message.

Directories

PL/SQL 8.0 ...and HIGHER The **all_directories**, **dba_directories**, and **user_directories** views contain information about directories, used to specify the location of directories (for BFILEs) on the operating system. For more information, see Chapter 21.

Column	Null?	Type	Description
OWNER	NOT NULL	VARCHAR2(30)	Schema which owns the directory (**all_directories** and **user_directories** only)
DIRECTORY_NAME	NOT NULL	VARCHAR2(30)	Name of the directory
DIRECTORY_PATH	NOT NULL	VARCHAR2(4000)	Operating system path of the directory on the file system

Jobs

PL/SQL 8.0 ...and HIGHER The **all_jobs**, **dba_jobs**, and **user_jobs** views contain information about database jobs.

Column	Null?	Type	Description
JOB	NOT NULL	NUMBER	Job ID number. As long as the job exists, this ID will remain the same.
LOG_USER	NOT NULL	VARCHAR2(30)	User who submitted the job.
PRIV_USER	NOT NULL	VARCHAR2(30)	User whose default privileges apply for this job.
SCHEMA_USER	NOT NULL	VARCHAR2(30)	Default schema for the job.
LAST_DATE		DATE	Date when the job last successfully executed.
LAST_SEC		VARCHAR2(8)	Same as **last_date**, in HH24:MI:SS format.
THIS_DATE		DATE	Date the job started executing. NULL if the job is not currently running.
THIS_SEC		VARCHAR2(8)	Same as **this_date**, in HH24:MI:SS format.
NEXT_DATE	NOT NULL	DATE	Date when the job will next be executed.
NEXT_SEC		VARCHAR2(8)	Same as **next_date**, in HH24:MI:SS format.
TOTAL_TIME		NUMBER	Total time in seconds spent by the system on this job.
BROKEN		VARCHAR2(1)	Y if the job is broken, N if not.
INTERVAL	NOT NULL	VARCHAR2(200)	Date function which is used to calculate the next value of **next_date**.
FAILURES		NUMBER	Number of failures since the last successful run of this job.
WHAT		VARCHAR2(2000)	Body of the anonymous PL/SQL block making up the job.
CURRENT_SESSION _LABEL		RAW MLSLABEL	Trusted Oracle7 Server label of the current job session.

Column	Null?	Type	Description
CLEARANCE_HI		RAW MLSLABEL	Highest clearance level available for the job (Trusted Oracle7 only).
CLEARANCE_LO		RAW MLSLABEL	Lowest clearance level available for the job (Trusted Oracle7 only).
NLS_ENV		VARCHAR2(2000)	NLS environment for the job (as specified by ALTER SESSION).
MISC_ENV		RAW(32)	Other session parameters for the job.

Libraries

PL/SQL 8.0 ...and HIGHER The **all_libraries**, **dba_libraries**, and **user_libraries** views specify the operating system location for shared libraries, used for external procedures. For more information, see Chapter 20.

Column	Null?	Datatype	Description
OWNER	NOT NULL	VARCHAR2(30)	Schema which owns the library (**all_libraries** and **dba_libraries** only)
LIBRARY_NAME	NOT NULL	VARCHAR2(30)	Name of the library
FILE_SPEC		VARCHAR2(2000)	Operating system patch of the library on the file system
DYNAMIC		VARCHAR2(1)	Y if the library is dynamic, N if not
STATUS		VARCHAR2(7)	Library status—VALID or INVALID

LOBs

PL/SQL 8.0 ...and HIGHER The **all_lobs**, **dba_lobs**, and **user_lobs** contain information about LOBs contained in tables accessible by the current user.

Column	Null?	Datatype	Description
OWNER	NOT NULL	VARCHAR2(30)	Schema of the table which contains the LOB (**all_lobs** and **dba_lobs** only)
TABLE_NAME	NOT NULL	VARCHAR2(30)	Name of the table containing the LOB
COLUMN_NAME		VARCHAR2(4000)	Name of the LOB column or attribute
SEGMENT_NAME	NOT NULL	VARCHAR2(30)	Name of the LOB segment
INDEX_NAME	NOT NULL	VARCHAR2(30)	Name of the LOB index
CHUNK		NUMBER	Size of the LOB chunk as a unit of allocation or manipulation, in bytes
PCTVERSION	NOT NULL	NUMBER	Maximum percentage of the LOB storage used for versioning
CACHE		VARCHAR2(3)	YES if the LOB is accessed through the buffer cache, NO otherwise
LOGGING		VARCHAR2(3)	YES if LOB changes are logged, NO otherwise
IN_ROW		VARCHAR2(3)	YES if some of the LOB is stored with the base row, NO otherwise

Object Methods

PL/SQL 8.0 ...and HIGHER The **all_type_methods**, **dba_type_methods**, and **user_type_methods** views contain information about the methods in the object types accessible to the current user.

Column	Null?	Datatype	Description
OWNER	NOT NULL	VARCHAR2(30)	Owner of the object type (**all_type_methods** and **dba_type_methods** only)
TYPE_NAME	NOT NULL	VARCHAR2(30)	Name of the object type

Column	Null?	Datatype	Description
METHOD_NAME	NOT NULL	VARCHAR2(30)	Name of the method
METHOD_NO	NOT NULL	NUMBER	Method number (used for distinguishing between overloaded methods)
METHOD_TYPE		VARCHAR2(6)	Type of the method—one of MAP, ORDER, or PUBLIC
PARAMETERS	NOT NULL	NUMBER	Number of parameters for the method
RESULTS	NOT NULL	NUMBER	Number of results returned by the method

Object Method Parameters

PL/SQL 8.0 ...and HIGHER The views **all_method_params**, **dba_method_params**, and **user_method_params** describe the parameters of the methods for the accessible object types. The ***_method_params**, ***_method_results**, and ***_type_methods** views together completely describe the methods available.

Column	Null?	Datatype	Description
OWNER	NOT NULL	VARCHAR2(30)	Schema which owns the object type (**all_method_params** and **dba_method_params** only)
TYPE_NAME	NOT NULL	VARCHAR2(30)	Name of the object type
METHOD_NAME	NOT NULL	VARCHAR2(30)	Name of the method
METHOD_NO	NOT NULL	NUMBER	Method number (used for distinguishing between overloaded methods)
PARAM_NAME	NOT NULL	VARCHAR2(30)	Parameter name
PARAM_NO	NOT NULL	NUMBER	Parameter number or position
PARAM_MODE		VARCHAR2(6)	Parameter mode (IN, OUT, or IN OUT)

Column	Null?	Datatype	Description
PARAM_TYPE_MOD		VARCHAR2(7)	Parameter type modifier (such as REF)
PARAM_TYPE_OWNER		VARCHAR2(30)	Owner of the type of the parameter (if a user-defined type)
PARAM_TYPE_NAME		VARCHAR2(30)	Parameter type name
CHARACTER_SET_NAME		VARCHAR2(44)	Character set of the parameter, if specified

Object Method Results

PL/SQL 8.0 ...and HIGHER Like the *_method_param views, the **all_method_results**, **dba_method_results**, and **user_method_results** views contain information about the methods in the object types accessible to the user. However, the *_method_results views contain information about the return values of those methods which are functions.

Column	Null?	Datatype	Description
OWNER	NOT NULL	VARCHAR2(30)	Schema which owns the type (**all_method_results** and **dba_method_results** only)
TYPE_NAME	NOT NULL	VARCHAR2(30)	Name of the object type
METHOD_NAME	NOT NULL	VARCHAR2(30)	Method name
METHOD_NO	NOT NULL	NUMBER	Method number (used for distinguishing between overloaded methods)
RESULT_TYPE_MOD		VARCHAR2(7)	Type modifier (such as REF) for the return value
RESULT_TYPE_OWNER		VARCHAR2(30)	Owner of the type of the return value, if a user-defined type
RESULT_TYPE_NAME		VARCHAR2(30)	Name of the type of the return value, if a user-defined type

Column	Null?	Datatype	Description
CHARACTER_SET_NAME		VARCHAR2(44)	Character set of the return value, if specified

Object References

PL/SQL **8.0** ...and HIGHER The **all_refs**, **dba_refs**, and **user_refs** views contain information about the columns in the tables accessible to the user which are REF types.

Column	Null?	Datatype	Description
OWNER	NOT NULL	VARCHAR2(30)	Owner of the table (**all_refs** and **dba_refs** only)
TABLE_NAME	NOT NULL	VARCHAR2(30)	Name of the table containing the REF column
COLUMN_NAME		VARCHAR2(4000)	Name of the column which contains the REF type
WITH_ROWID		VARCHAR2(3)	YES if the REF column is stored with the ROWID, NO otherwise
IS_SCOPED		VARCHAR2(3)	YES if the REF column is scoped, NO otherwise
SCOPE_TABLE_OWNER		VARCHAR2(30)	If the REF column is scoped, the schema of the scope table
SCOPE_TABLE_NAME		VARCHAR2(30)	If the REF column is scoped, the name of the scope table

Object Type Attributes

PL/SQL **8.0** ...and HIGHER The **all_type_attrs**, **dba_type_attrs**, and **user_type_attrs** views contain information about the attributes of the object types accessible to the user.

Column	Null?	Datatype	Description
OWNER		VARCHAR2(30)	Schema which owns the object type (**all_type_attrs** and **dba_type_attrs** only)
TYPE_NAME	NOT NULL	VARCHAR2(30)	Name of the object type
ATTR_NAME	NOT NULL	VARCHAR2(30)	Name of the attribute
ATTR_TYPE_MOD		VARCHAR2(7)	Type modifier (such as REF) of the attribute
ATTR_TYPE_OWNER		VARCHAR2(30)	Owner of the type of the attribute, if it is a user-defined type
LENGTH		NUMBER	Length of a CHAR or VARCHAR2 attribute
PRECISION		NUMBER	Precision of a NUMBER attribute
SCALE		NUMBER	Scale of a NUMBER attribute
CHARACTER_SET_NAME		VARCHAR2(44)	Character set of the attribute, if specified

Schema Objects

The **all_objects**, **dba_objects**, and **user_objects** views contain information about all types of schema objects, including tables, stored subprograms, views, sequences, and indexes. Object types are described in the *_type_methods, *_method_params, *_method_results, *_type_attrs, and *_types views.

Column	Null?	Type	Description
OWNER	NOT NULL	VARCHAR2(30)	Schema that owns the object (**all_objects** and **dba_objects** only).
OBJECT_NAME	NOT NULL	VARCHAR2(30)	Name of the object (in uppercase).
OBJECT_ID	NOT NULL	NUMBER	Object number. Every database object is assigned a unique ID.

Column	Null?	Type	Description
OBJECT_TYPE		VARCHAR2(12)	Type of the object (TABLE, PACKAGE BODY, SEQUENCE, PROCEDURE, etc.).
CREATED	NOT NULL	DATE	Timestamp when the object was created.
LAST_DDL_TIME	NOT NULL	DATE	Timestamp when the last DDL operation (such as an ALTER) was performed on the object. GRANTs and REVOKEs also modify this timestamp.
TIMESTAMP		VARCHAR2(75)	Creation timestamp, in YYYY-MM-DD:HH24:MI:SS format.
STATUS		VARCHAR2(7)	Object status—VALID, INVALID, or N/A.

Source Code

The **all_source**, **dba_source**, and **user_source** views contain the source code for stored procedures, functions, packages, and package bodies. Trigger source code is in the **all_triggers**, **dba_triggers**, and **user_triggers** views. If the stored object is wrapped, these views contain the encoded source rather than clear text.

A typical query of the **user_source** table might look like this:

```
SELECT text
  FROM user_source
  WHERE NAME = object_name
  ORDER BY LINE;
```

Column	Null?	Type	Description
OWNER	NOT NULL	VARCHAR2(30)	Schema that owns the object (**all_source** and **dba_source** only).
NAME	NOT NULL	VARCHAR2(30)	Name of the stored object.

Column	Null?	Type	Description
TYPE		VARCHAR2(12)	Type of the object. Valid values are PACKAGE, PACKAGE BODY, PROCEDURE, and FUNCTION.
LINE	NOT NULL	NUMBER	Line number for this line of source code.
TEXT		VARCHAR2(2000)	Text source at this line.

Tables

The **all_tables**, **dba_tables**, and **user_tables** views contain information about database tables. This information is for the table itself. Column information is stored in **all_tab_columns**, **dba_tab_columns**, and **user_tab_columns**.

Column	Null?	Type	Description
OWNER	NOT NULL	VARCHAR2(30)	Schema that owns the table (**all_tables** and **dba_tables** only).
TABLE_NAME	NOT NULL	VARCHAR2(30)	Name of the table (in uppercase).
TABLESPACE_NAME	NOT NULL	VARCHAR2(30)	Name of the tablespace containing the table.
CLUSTER_NAME		VARCHAR2(30)	Name of the cluster to which the table belongs. NULL if the table is not clustered.
PCT_FREE	NOT NULL	NUMBER	Minimum percentage of free space in a block, specified at table creation, or when the table was last ALTERed.
PCT_USED	NOT NULL	NUMBER	Minimum percentage of used space in a block, specified at table creation, or when the table was last ALTERed.

Column	Null?	Type	Description
INI_TRANS	NOT NULL	NUMBER	Initial number of transactions, specified at table creation, or when the table was last ALTERed.
MAX_TRANS	NOT NULL	NUMBER	Maximum number of transactions, specified at table creation, or when the table was last ALTERed.
INITIAL_EXTENT		NUMBER	Size of the initial extent in bytes, if specified.
NEXT_EXTENT		NUMBER	Size of the next extent in bytes, if specified.
MIN_EXTENTS		NUMBER	Minimum number of extents allowed in the segment, if specified.
MAX_EXTENTS		NUMBER	Maximum number of extents, if specified.
PCT_INCREASE		NUMBER	Percentage increase allowed in extent size, if specified.
FREELISTS		NUMBER	Number of process freelists allocated to the segment, if specified.
FREELIST_GROUPS		NUMBER	Number of freelist groups allocated to the segment, if specified.
BACKED_UP		VARCHAR2(1)	Y if the table has been backed up since the last change, N if not.
NUM_ROWS		NUMBER	Number of rows in the table.
BLOCKS		NUMBER	Number of data blocks allocated to the table.
EMPTY_BLOCKS		NUMBER	Number of data blocks allocated that contain no data. (**empty_blocks / blocks**) * 100 is the percentage used.
AVG_SPACE		NUMBER	Average amount of free space in an allocated data block, in bytes.

Column	Null?	Type	Description
CHAIN_CNT		NUMBER	Number of rows in the table that are chained over more than one block.
AVG_ROW_LEN		NUMBER	Average row length, in bytes.
DEGREE		VARCHAR2(10)	Number of threads per instance for scanning the table (parallel server only).
INSTANCES		VARCHAR2(10)	Number of instances across which the table will be scanned (parallel server only).
CACHE		VARCHAR2(5)	Y if the table is cached in the buffer cache, N if not.
TABLE_LOCK		VARCHAR2(8)	ENABLED if table locking is enabled, DISABLED if not.

The **all_catalog**, **dba_catalog**, and **user_catalog** views provide a subset of the information in **all_tables**, **dba_tables**, and **user_tables**.

Column	Null?	Type	Description
OWNER	NOT NULL	VARCHAR2(30)	Schema that owns the object (**all_catalog** and **dba_catalog** only)
TABLE_NAME	NOT NULL	VARCHAR2(30)	Name of the object (in uppercase)
TABLE_TYPE		VARCHAR2(11)	Type of the object (TABLE, VIEW, SYNONYM, SEQUENCE)

Table Columns

The **all_tab_columns**, **dba_tab_columns**, and **user_tab_columns** views contain information about columns in database tables, views, and clusters. When an object is described, this table is queried.

Column	Null?	Type	Description
OWNER	NOT NULL	VARCHAR2(30)	Schema that owns the object (**all_tab_columns** and **dba_tab_columns** only).
TABLE_NAME	NOT NULL	VARCHAR2(30)	Name of the table, view, or cluster.
COLUMN_NAME	NOT NULL	VARCHAR2(30)	Name of the column.
DATA_TYPE		VARCHAR2(9)	Datatype of the column (NUMBER, CHAR, DATE, etc.).
DATA_LENGTH	NOT NULL	NUMBER	Maximum length of the column in bytes.
DATA_PRECISION		NUMBER	Decimal precision for NUMBER columns, binary precision for FLOAT columns. NULL for other datatypes or when the precision is not specified.
DATA_SCALE		NUMBER	Scale for NUMBER columns. NULL for other datatypes or when the scale is not specified.
NULLABLE		VARCHAR2(1)	'Y' if the column allows NULLs, 'N' if not.
COLUMN_ID	NOT NULL	NUMBER	Unique value assigned to the column. All columns have an ID associated with them.
DEFAULT_LENGTH		NUMBER	Length of the default value for the column, if specified.
DATA_DEFAULT		LONG	Default value for the column, if specified.
NUM_DISTINCT		NUMBER	Number of distinct values in the column.

Column	Null?	Type	Description
LOW_VALUE		RAW(32)	Second lowest value in the table (4 rows or more), or lowest value in the table (3 rows or less). Stored as the internal representation of the first 32 bytes of the column.
HIGH_VALUE		RAW(32)	Second highest value in the table (4 rows or more), or highest value in the table (3 rows or less). Stored as the internal representation of the first 32 bytes of the column.
DENSITY		NUMBER	Density of the column.
NUM_NULLS		NUMBER	Number of rows which contain NULL values.
NUM_BUCKETS		NUMBER	Number of buckets used when ANALYZing the table.
LAST_ANALYZED		DATE	Timestamp when the table was last ANALYZEd.
SAMPLE_SIZE		NUMBER	Sample size used during the last ANALYZE.

Triggers

The **all_triggers**, **dba_triggers**, and **user_triggers** views describe the database triggers accessible to the user. All of the different components in the CREATE TRIGGER statement are columns in these views.

Column	Null?	Type	Description
OWNER	NOT NULL	VARCHAR2(30)	Schema that owns the trigger (**all_triggers** and **dba_triggers** only).
TRIGGER_NAME	NOT NULL	VARCHAR2(30)	Name of the trigger (in uppercase).

Column	Null?	Type	Description
TRIGGER_TYPE		VARCHAR2(16)	Trigger type—BEFORE ROW, BEFORE STATEMENT, AFTER ROW, AFTER STATEMENT.
TRIGGERING_EVENT		VARCHAR2(26)	DML statement that fires the trigger—one or more of INSERT, UPDATE, DELETE.
TABLE_OWNER	NOT NULL	VARCHAR2(30)	Owner of the table on which the trigger is defined.
TABLE_NAME	NOT NULL	VARCHAR2(30)	Name of the table on which the trigger is defined.
REFERENCING_NAMES		VARCHAR2(87)	If specified, names used for referencing **:old** and **:new** in row-level triggers.
WHEN_CLAUSE		VARCHAR2(2000)	WHEN clause of the trigger, if specified.
STATUS		VARCHAR2(8)	ENABLED if the trigger is enabled, DISABLED if not.
DESCRIPTION		VARCHAR2(2000)	Character string containing the trigger name, trigger type, WHEN clause, and referencing clause, as specified in the CREATE TRIGGER statement. Useful for re-creating the statement if the source file is lost.
TRIGGER BODY		LONG	PL/SQL block making up the body of the trigger.

Trigger Columns

The **all_trigger_cols**, **dba_trigger_cols**, and **user_trigger_cols** views show the usage of columns in database triggers. These views complement the **all_triggers**, **dba_triggers**, and **user_triggers** views.

Column	Null?	Type	Description
TRIGGER_OWNER	NOT NULL	VARCHAR2(30)	Schema that owns the trigger.
TRIGGER_NAME	NOT NULL	VARCHAR2(30)	Name of the trigger (in uppercase).
TABLE_OWNER	NOT NULL	VARCHAR2(30)	Schema that owns the table on which the trigger is defined.
TABLE_NAME	NOT NULL	VARCHAR2(30)	Name of the table on which the trigger is defined (in uppercase).
COLUMN_NAME	NOT NULL	VARCHAR2(30)	Name of the column used in the trigger
COLUMN_LIST		VARCHAR2(3)	YES if the column is specified in the UPDATE clause, NO if not.
COLUMN_USAGE		VARCHAR2(17)	Specifies how the column is referenced in the trigger. All applicable combinations of NEW, OLD, IN, OUT, and IN OUT.

Views

The **all_views**, **dba_views**, and **user_views** views describe the views in the database.

Column	Null?	Type	Description
OWNER	NOT NULL	VARCHAR2(30)	Schema that owns the view (**all_views** and **dba_views** only).
VIEW_NAME	NOT NULL	VARCHAR2(30)	Name of the view (in uppercase).

Column	Null?	Type	Description
TEXT_LENGTH		NUMBER	Length of the view text.
TEXT		LONG	Text of the view—the body of the CREATE VIEW statement.

Other Dictionary Views

In addition to the views described in the previous section, there are two other data dictionary views that are useful to the PL/SQL programmer. They are described in this section, listed alphabetically.

dbms_alert_info

The **dbms_alert_info** view contains information about sessions that have registered interest in alerts.

Column	Null?	Type	Description
NAME	NOT NULL	VARCHAR2(30)	Name of the alert for which the session has registered interest.
SID	NOT NULL	VARCHAR2(30)	Session identifier.
CHANGED		VARCHAR2(30)	Y if the alert has been signaled, N if not.
MESSAGE		VARCHAR2(1800)	Message that is included in the SIGNAL call, if any.

dict_columns

The **dict_columns** view describes all of the columns in the data dictionary.

Column	Null?	Type	Description
TABLE_NAME		VARCHAR2(30)	Name of the data dictionary view.
COLUMN_NAME		VARCHAR2(30)	Column in the view.
COMMENTS		VARCHAR2(2000)	Description of the column.

INDEX

3GLs (third-generation languages), 2
4GLs (fourth-generation languages),
  2, 3
"" (double quotation marks), 33
-- (double-dash character), 38

A

ABS function, 147-148
Access restrictions. *See* Privileges;
  Security
Accessible directories, 710
ACCESS_INTO_NULL exception, 915
ACOS function, 148
Active set, 204
Actual parameters, 244-245
Ada programming language, 6
ADD_MONTHS function, 158-159
ADD_SUBSCRIBER procedure,
  DBMS_AQADM package, 676
Advanced Queuing. *See* Oracle
  Advanced Queuing
After update triggers, 347
Agents, producing vs. consuming, 655
Alerts
    data dictionary view, 646-647
    explained, 641
    polling intervals, 645
    receiving, 642-644
    sending, 641-642
    unregistering for, 645
    See also DBMS_ALERT package
all_* views, data dictionary, 939-958
AllObjs procedure, 304
ALLOCATE_UNIQUE procedure,
  DBMS_LOCK package, 898
Allocating storage, for cursor
  variables, 230-231
AlmostFull function, 258

dependencies of, 270
ALTER FUNCTION privilege, 275
ALTER SESSION ADVISE commands,
  DBMS_TRANSACTION package,
  906
ALTER SESSION command, 709, 870,
  902
ALTER SYSTEM privilege, 274, 275,
  862
ALTER TRIGGER statement, 325
ALTER TYPE...COMPILE command,
  413-414
ALTER TYPE...REPLACE AS OBJECT
  command, 414-415
ALTER_COMPILE procedure,
  DBMS_DDL package, 892-893
Altering
    database jobs, 708
    object types, 413-415
    queues, 674-675
ALTER_QUEUE procedure,
  DBMS_AQADM package, 674-675
ANALYZE_OBJECT procedure,
  DBMS_DDL package, 893-894
ANALYZE_SCHEMA procedure,
  DBMS_UTILITY package, 908-909
Anonymous blocks, 24
    example of, 25-28
    executing with DBMS_SQL,
      577-584
ANSI standard, 4-5
APPEND routine, DBMS_LOB
  package, 828
aq$queue_table_name view, 678-679
AQ$_RECIPIENT_LIST_T type,
  DBMS_AQ package, 656-658
AQ_ADMINISTRATOR_ROLE, 678,
  681
AQ_USER_ROLE, 678

Arbitrary stored procedures,
    executing with DBMS_SQL,
      584-592
Archiver (ARCH) process, 858
Array processing, 594-600
    BIND_ARRAY procedure,
      595-596
    comparison of dynamic methods
      for, 613, 614
    DEFINE_ARRAY procedure,
      596-597
    example of, 597-600
    network performance and
      tuning, 878
Arrays
    fetching, 600
    tables compared to, 87-89
AS keyword, 248
ASCII character set, 31
ASCII function, 143-144
ASIN function, 148-149
Assignment operator, 58-59
Assignment statements, 915-916
ATAN function, 149
ATAN2 function, 149-150
Attributes
    cursor, 210-214
    object type, 411-413
    table, 90-94
autocommit option, 124
AVG function, 178

B

Background processes, DBMS_JOB
  package, 700-701
Before update triggers, 347
BEGIN keyword, 29, 30
    procedures and, 248

BEGIN_DISCRETE_TRANSACTION
procedure, DBMS_TRANSACTION
package, 907
BETWEEN operator, 62
BFILENAME function, 183
BFILEs, 817, 821-826
characteristics of, 821-822
copy vs. reference semantics,
824-825
DBMS_LOB routines for
manipulating, 827
deleting locators, 825
directories, 822-823
in DML statements, 824-826
initializing columns, 824
opening and closing, 823
See also LOBs
BINARY_INTEGER datatype, 44-45
PL/SQL tables and, 87, 88, 90
Bind variables
cursors and, 207-208
DML statements, 102, 559-562
in precompilers, 477-478
SQL*Plus, 472-473
BIND_ARRAY procedure, 595-596
example of, 597-600
Binding variables
explained, 99
input variables, 559
to placeholders, 555
privileges and, 280
BIND_VARIABLES subprogram, 760
BIND_VARIABLE procedure, 555,
559-561
parameters for, 141-142, 176
using out_value_size parameter
with, 583-584
Blank-padded semantics, 110-111
BLOB datatypes, 817
See also LOBs
Blocks, 24-30, 916
embedding, 478
error handling, 6-7
example of DynamicPLSQL
procedure, 581-582
executing with DBMS_SQL,
577-584
packages as, 284
retrieving the value of output
variables, 579-581
SQL*Plus, 469
structure of, 5-7, 28-30
syntax, 916
transactions compared to,
126-127
types of, 24-25
using out_value_size parameter,
583-584
See also Execution environments;
Procedures
Body
HTML tags, 744-746
package, 286-288

procedure, 248
BodyDemo procedure, 744-746
BOLD HTML tag, 750-751
BOOLEAN datatype, 50
Boolean expressions, 60-62
Boolean family, 50
Boolean literals, 37-38
Bottom-up design, 546
boxes.gif file, 769
Breakpoints
Procedure Builder, 533, 534
SQL-Station, 540-541, 542
BROKEN procedure, DBMS_JOB
package, 707
Browsing queues, 691-694
Buffer parameter, 719
Buffers, maximum size of, 519, 522
Bugs. *See* Debugging; Testing and
debugging
Built-in packages, 888-911
creating, 888
DBMS_ALERT, 888
DBMS_APPLICATION_INFO,
890-892
DBMS_AQ and DBMS_AQADM,
892
DBMS_DDL, 892-894
DBMS_DEFER,
DBMS_DEFER_SYS, and
DBMS_DEFER_QUERY, 892
DBMS_DESCRIBE, 894-896, 897
DBMS_JOB, 896
DBMS_LOB, 897
DBMS_LOCK, 897-901
DBMS_OUTPUT, 901
DBMS_PIPE, 902
DBMS_REFRESH and
DBMS_SNAPSHOT, 902
DBMS_REPCAT,
DBMS_REPCAT_AUTH, and
DBMS_REPCAT_ADMIN, 902
DBMS_ROWID, 902
DBMS_SESSION, 902-905
DBMS_SHARED_POOL, 905
DBMS_SQL, 905
DBMS_TRANSACTION, 905-908
DBMS_UTILITY, 908-911
list of, 889-890
purity levels, 303
UTL_FILE, 911
See also Packages
Built-in SQL functions, 130-201
character functions returning
character values, 131-143
character functions returning
numeric values, 143-147
conversion functions, 165-177
date functions, 158-165
explained, 130-131
group functions, 177-182
miscellaneous functions, 183-192
numeric functions, 147-158
See also Functions

C

C programming language, 780
calling external procedures
directly from, 808
debugging external procedures
and, 808-810
parameter mappings and,
791-800
PL/SQL vs. C datatypes, 792-796
Calculate GPA procedure, 725-729
CALENDARPRINT procedure, 763
Callbacks to the database, 802-808
executing SQL statements,
807-808
service routines, 803-807
CALLING STANDARD clause,
wrapper procedure, 790
Calling structure, OCI (Oracle Call
Interface), 483-486
Capitalization style, 78
Cartridge application, 734
Cascades
delete cascade utility, 340
update cascade utility, 340-351
Case-sensitivity, 32, 78, 710
Catalog Browser, SQL-Station Coder,
487
catproc.sql script, 888, 938
CD-ROM companion disc
contents of, 12-13
Imagemap package, 769
Oracle web server on, 732
README file on, 26
CEIL function, 150
CELLSPRINT subprogram, 760
CGI (Common Gateway Interface),
733-734
WRB interface compared to, 736
CHANGE procedure, DBMS_JOB
package, 708
CHAR datatype, 46-47
Character compositions, WHERE
clauses, 110-112
Character expressions, 60
Character family, 45-48
CHAR datatype, 46-47
LONG datatype, 47
NCHAR and NVARCHAR2
datatypes, 47-48
VARCHAR2 datatype, 45-46
Character format tags, HTML, 749-750
Character functions returning
character values, 131-143
CHR function, 131
CONCAT function, 132
INITCAP function, 132
LOWER function, 133
LPAD function, 133-134
LTRIM function, 134-135
NLS_INITCAP function, 135-136
NLS_LOWER function, 136
NLS_UPPER function, 136-137

REPLACE function, 137
RPAD function, 138
RTRIM function, 138-139
SOUNDEX function, 139-140
SUBSTR function, 140-141
SUBSTRB function, 141-142
TRANSLATE function, 142
UPPER function, 143
Character functions returning numeric
 values, 143-147
 ASCII function, 143-144
 INSTR function, 144-145
 INSTRB function, 145
 LENGTH function, 146
 LENGTHB function, 146
 NLSSORT function, 147
Character literals, 36
CHARACTER SET ANY_CS syntax, 828
Character set for PL/SQL, 30-31
CharDemo package, 749-750
CHARSETFORM property, parameter
 mappings, 799-800
CHARSETID property, parameter
 mappings, 799-800
CHARTOROWID function, 54, 166
CHECK_PROTECT function, 193
CHOOSE_DATE procedure, 764
CHR function, 131
classes table, 17-18
 cursor variable examples, 232-236
 tables8.sql script and, 401
Classic modulus function, 154
Clearing queues, 685-686
Client procedures
 debugging objects, 530
 stored procedures vs., 491
Client-server model, 4
Client-side PL/SQL, 489-497
 database triggers vs. form
  triggers, 492
 implications of, 466-468
 network performance and
  tuning, 877
 Oracle Forms, 493-495
 Procedure Builder, 495-497
 reasons for, 490, 493
 stored procedures vs. client
  procedures, 491
 tools, 489-490
 See also Server-side PL/SQL
CLOB datatypes, 817
 See also LOBs
CLOSE_CURSOR procedure, 556
CLOSE_DATABASE_LINK procedure,
 DBMS_SESSION package, 904
Closing
 cursor variables, 232
 cursors, 209-210, 563
 files, 712-715
code directory, 13
Coder tool (SQL-Station), 487-488,
 775-776
Collection methods, 450-461

COUNT, 452
DELETE, 459-461
EXISTS, 450-452
EXTEND, 454-457
FIRST and LAST, 453
LIMIT, 452-453
NEXT and PRIOR, 453-454
TRIM, 457-459
COLLECTION_IS_NULL exception,
 436, 916
Collections, 434-461, 916
 data dictionary information on,
  941-942
 methods, 450-461
 nested tables, 434-444
 varrays, 445-450
Column objects, 419-420
 in SELECT statements, 422-424
COLUMN_VALUE_LONG
 procedure, 605-606
 parameters, 606
COLUMN_VALUE procedure, 556,
 571-574
 parameters, 574-575
Command prompt, Procedure
 Builder, 496
Comments, 38-39, 916-917
 multiline, 39
 recommended style for, 76-77
 single-line, 38
COMMIT commands,
 DBMS_TRANSACTION package,
 906
COMMIT statements, 917
 cursor fetch loops, 225-227
 ROLLBACK statements vs.,
  123-124
Common Gateway Interface (CGI),
 733-734, 736
Communications protocols, 632-633,
 640
 data addressing, 633
 data formatting, 632
COMPARE routine, DBMS_LOB
 package, 828-830
Comparison operators, 61
Compile errors
 compile-time errors, 355
 data dictionary information on,
  942-943
COMPILE_SCHEMA procedure,
 DBMS_UTILITY package, 908
Composite types, 50, 82-95
 records, 82-86
 tables, 86-95
CONCAT function, 132
Concatenation expression, 60
Conditions, 917
Configuring the SQL*Net listener,
 784-787
Constants, 40-41, 935
 HTML, 743
Constrained cursor variables, 229

Constrained subtypes, 45
Constraining tables, 334
Constraints on formal parameters,
 249-256
Constructors, 403-404
Consuming agents, 655
Context area, 204
Control files, 860-861
Control structures, 62-75
 GOTO statements, 72-74
 IF-THEN-ELSE statements, 63-72
 labels, 72-74
 NULL statements, 74-75
 pragmas, 75
Conversion functions, 165-177
 CHARTOROWID function, 166
 CONVERT function, 166-167
 HEXTORAW function, 167-168
 RAWTOHEX function, 168
 ROWIDTOCHAR function,
  168-169
 TO_CHAR (dates) function,
  169-171
 TO_CHAR (labels) function,
  171-172
 TO_CHAR (numbers) function,
  172-174
 TO_DATE function, 175
 TO_LABEL function, 175
 TO_MULTI_BYTE function, 176
 TO_NUMBER function, 176
 TO_SINGLE_BYTE function, 177
Conversions
 explicit, 53-54
 implicit, 54-55
CONVERT function, 166-167
 DBMS_LOCK package, 900-901
CookieDemo procedure, 772-773
COPY routine, DBMS_LOB package,
 830-832
Copy semantics, 84, 825
CopyTables procedure, 538-540, 541
Correlation identifier, 688-691
COS function, 150-151
COSH function, 151
COUNT collection method, 452
COUNT function, 178-179
COUNT table attribute, 90-91
CountCredits function, 522-529
CREATE DIRECTORY statement, 822
CREATE LIBRARY command, 787
CREATE OR REPLACE command
 syntax for creating functions,
  258-259
 syntax for creating procedures,
  243-244
CREATE TABLE privilege, 612
CREATE TYPE...AS OBJECT
 statement, 400
CREATE TYPE BODY command, 407
CREATE TYPE statement, nested
 tables, 439
CREATE_PIPE function, 627, 628-629

CREATE_QUEUE_TABLE procedure, DBMS_AQADM package, 668-670
CREATE_QUEUE procedure, DBMS_AQADM package, 671-673
Creating
    DH_UTIL package, 193-201
    functions, 257-261
    packages, 888
    procedures, 243-256
    queues and queue tables, 668-673, 681-683
    triggers, 318-332
CreditLoop procedure, 530-536
CURRENT OF cursor, 107
CURRVAL pseudocolumn, 115-116
Cursor variables, 227-237, 918
    allocating storage for, 230-231
    automatic allocation of, 231
    closing, 232
    constrained, 229
    declaring, 228-230
    examples, 232-236
    explained, 227-228
    opening for queries, 231-232
    restrictions on, 237
    unconstrained, 229
CURSOR_ALREADY_OPEN exception, 917
Cursors, 204-238, 917
    attributes, 210-214
    attributes comparison table, 214
    bind variables and, 207-208
    closing, 209-210, 563
    COMMIT statements, 225-227
    declaring, 205-206
    explained, 204-205
    explicit, 205-215
    fetch loops, 204-205, 217-227
    fetching from, 208-209
    FOR loops, 221-222
    FOR UPDATE clauses, 223-224
    implicit, 215-217
    opening, 207-208, 557
    overview, 9-10
    parameterized, 214-215
    reusing, 615
    SELECT FOR UPDATE statements, 223-227
    simple loops, 217-219
    WHERE CURRENT OF clauses, 224-225
    WHILE loops, 219-221
    See also Cursor variables

D

Dangling REF operator, 426
Data
    inputting from a file, 719-720
    outputting to a file, 716-719
Data abstraction, 546-547

Data addressing, DBMS_PIPE package, 633
Data definition language (DDL) statements. *See* DDL statements
Data dictionary, 938-959
    all_* views, 939-958
    collection information, 941-942
    compile error information, 942-943
    dba_* views, 939-958
    dbms_alert_info view, 641, 646-647, 959
    dependency information, 939, 941
    dict_columns view, 959
    directory information, 943
    job information, 943-945
    library information, 945
    LOB information, 945-946
    naming conventions, 938-939
    object method information, 946-947
    object method parameter information, 947-948
    object method results information, 948-949
    object references information, 949
    object type attributes information, 949-950
    permissions, 939
    queues and, 678-681
    schema object information, 950-951
    source code, 951-952
    stored subprograms and, 263-266
    table column information, 954-956
    table information, 952-954
    trigger column information, 958
    trigger information, 956-957
    triggers and, 324-326
    user_* views, 939-958
    view information, 958-959
    views, 939, 940, 959
Data formatting, DBMS_PIPE package, 632
Data manipulation language (DML) statements. *See* DML statements
Database
    objects in, 417-421
    security, 710-711
    storing nested tables in, 438-444
    storing varrays in, 447-449
Database alerts, 641
    See also DBMS_ALERT package
Database connector descriptor (DCD), 734-736
Database files, 860
Database jobs, 700-709
    altering, 708
    background processes, 700-702
    broken, 707
    data dictionary information on, 943-945

job execution environments, 709
removing, 707-708
running, 702-706
viewing in the data dictionary, 708
    See also DBMS_JOB package
Database links, DML statements, 113
Database permissions, 710-711
Database pipes, 618
    See also DBMS_PIPE package
Database processes, 858
Database security, 710-711
Database triggers
    form triggers vs., 492
    See also Triggers
Database Writer (DBWR) process, 858
Datatypes. *See* Types
Date arithmetic, 164-165
Date conversions, 169-171
DATE datatype, 49
Date family, 49
Date format elements, 170-171
Date functions, 158-165
    ADD_MONTHS function, 158-159
    LAST_DAY function, 159
    MONTHS_BETWEEN function, 160
    NEW_TIME function, 160-161
    NEXT_DAY function, 161-162
    ROUND function, 162
    SYSDATE function, 162-163
    TRUNC function, 163-165
Date utilities, OWA_UTIL package, 763-766
DateDemo package, 764-766
DB block cache, 859
dba_* views, data dictionary, 939-958
dba_jobs_running view, 708
dba_jobs view, 708
dba_object_size view, 864
dba_queues view, 680-681
dba_queue_tables view, 680
dbms_alert_info view, 641, 646-647, 959
DBMS_ALERT package, 641-647, 888
    data dictionary, 646-647
    DBMS_PIPE package compared to, 648-649
    overview, 641
    polling intervals, 645
    receiving alerts, 642-644
    REGISTER procedure, 642
    REMOVE procedure, 645
    sending an alert, 641-642
    SET_DEFAULTS procedure, 645
    SIGNAL procedure, 641-642
    unregistering for alerts, 645
    WAITANY procedure, 643-644
    WAITONE procedure, 642-643
DBMS_APPLICATION_INFO package, 890-892
    READ_CLIENT_INFO procedure, 892

READ_MODULE procedure, 891
SET_ACTION procedure, 891
SET_CLIENT_INFO procedure, 891-892
SET_MODULE procedure, 890-891
DBMS_AQADM package, 667-681, 892
    ADD_SUBSCRIBER procedure, 676
    ALTER_QUEUE procedure, 674-675
    CREATE_QUEUE_TABLE procedure, 668-670
    CREATE_QUEUE procedure, 671-673
    data dictionary views, 678-681
    DROP_QUEUE_TABLE procedure, 670-671
    DROP_QUEUE procedure, 673-674
    examples of using, 681-697
    GRANT_TYPE_ACCESS procedure, 677
    queue privileges, 678
    QUEUE_SUBSCRIBER function, 677
    REMOVE_SUBSCRIBER procedure, 676
    START_QUEUE procedure, 675
    START_TIME_MANAGER procedure, 677
    STOP_QUEUE procedure, 675-676
    STOP_TIME_MANAGER procedure, 677
    subprograms, 657, 668-677
    See also Oracle Advanced Queuing
DBMS_AQ package, 656-667, 892
    AQ$_RECIPIENT_LIST_T type, 656-658
    DEQUEUE operation, 666-667
    DEQUEUE_OPTIONS_T type, 663-664
    ENQUEUE operation, 665-666
    ENQUEUE_OPTIONS_T type, 661-662
    enumerated constants, 665
    examples of using, 681-697
    MESSAGE_PROPERTIES_T type, 658-661
    queue privileges, 678
    subprograms, 657, 665-667
    supporting types, 656-665
    SYS.AQ$_AGENT type, 656
    See also Oracle Advanced Queuing
DBMS_DDL package, 892-894
    ALTER_COMPILE procedure, 892-893
    ANALYZE_OBJECT procedure, 893-894

DBMS_DEFER_QUERY package, 892
DBMS_DEFER_SYS package, 892
DBMS_DEFER package, 892
DBMS_DESCRIBE package, 584, 894-896, 897
    DESCRIBE_PROCEDURE, 894-896, 897
DBMS_JOB package, 700-709, 896
    altering jobs, 708
    background processes, 700-701
    broken jobs, 707
    execution intervals, 706
    job definitions, 704-706
    job execution environments, 709
    job initialization parameters, 701
    job numbers, 703
    removing jobs, 707-708
    RUN procedure, 706
    running a job, 702-706
    SNP processes, 700-701
    SUBMIT procedure, 702-706
    viewing jobs, 708
    See also Database jobs
DBMS_LOB package, 51, 826-849, 897
    APPEND routine, 828
    COMPARE routine, 828-830
    COPY routine, 830-832
    DBMS_LOB routines, 826-846
    ERASE routine, 832-833
    exceptions raised by DBMS_LOB routines, 846-847
    FILECLOSE routine, 833
    FILECLOSEALL routine, 833-834
    FILEEXISTS routine, 834
    FILEGETNAME routine, 834
    FILEISOPEN routine, 834-835
    FILEOPEN routine, 835
    GETLENGTH routine, 835-836
    INSTR routine, 836-838
    LOADFROMFILE routine, 838-842
    OCI LOB functions and, 847-849
    READ routine, 842-843
    SUBSTR routine, 843-844
    TRIM routine, 845
    WRITE routine, 846
    See also LOBs
DBMS_LOCK package, 897-901
    ALLOCATE_UNIQUE procedure, 898
    CONVERT function, 900-901
    RELEASE function, 901
    REQUEST function, 899-900
    SLEEP procedure, 901
DBMS_OUTPUT.PUT_LINE procedure, 89
DBMS_OUTPUT package, 192, 517-529, 901
    debugging code with, 524, 525-529
    ENABLE and DISABLE procedures, 520

GET_LINES procedure, 519-520
GET_LINE procedure, 518
NEW_LINE procedure, 518
printing data from, 520-521
procedures in, 517-520
PUT and PUT_LINE procedures, 517-518
Register procedure, 522-524
SERVEROUTPUT option, 520-522
SET SERVEROUTPUT ON command, 521
using, 520-522
DBMS_PIPE package, 618-640, 902
    communications protocols, 632-633, 640
    creating and managing pipes, 627-630
    data addressing, 633
    data formatting, 632
    DBMS_ALERT package compared to, 648-649
    Debug package, 637-640
    debug.pc program, 633-637
    handshake messages, 640
    opcodes, 640
    ORA-23322 error, 631
    overview, 618-622
    pipes and shared pools, 627-628
    private pipes, 631-632
    privileges and security, 630-632
    public vs. private pipes, 628-629
    PURGE procedure, 630
    readers, 618, 619-622
    receiving messages, 625-627
    registered_students table, 618-619, 622
    sending messages, 623-625
    STOP instructions, 632
    writers, 618, 619-622
DBMS_REFRESH package, 902
DBMS_REPCAT_ADMIN package, 902
DBMS_REPCAT_AUTH package, 902
DBMS_REPCAT package, 902
DBMS_ROWID package, 902
DBMS_SESSION package, 902-905
    CLOSE_DATABASE_LINK procedure, 904
    IS_ROLE_ENABLED function, 905
    RESET_PACKAGE procedure, 904
    SET_LABEL procedure, 904
    SET_MLS_LABEL_FORMAT procedure, 904
    SET_NLS procedure, 903
    SET_ROLE procedure, 903
    SET_SQL_TRACE procedure, 903
    UNIQUE_SESSION_ID function, 904-905
DBMS_SHARED_POOL package, 905
    See also Shared pools
DBMS_SNAPSHOT package, 902
DBMS_SQL package, 100, 550-615, 905

array processing, 594-600
changing job execution
    environments, 709
compared to other dynamic
    methods, 612-614
enhancements for PL/SQL 8.0,
    592-604
error functions, 553, 606-608
executing arbitrary stored
    procedures, 584-592
executing non-query DML and
    DDL statements, 556-566
executing PL/SQL blocks, 577-584
executing queries, 566-577
fetching LONG data, 604-606
HTML utilities, 760-763
overview of, 551-556
privileges required for using, 611
roles and, 611-612
tips and techniques, 615
writing LONG datatypes to files,
    608-611
See also Dynamic PL/SQL
DBMS_TRANSACTION package,
    905-908
    ALTER SESSION ADVISE
        commands, 906
    BEGIN_DISCRETE_TRANSACTION
        procedure, 907
    COMMIT commands, 906
    LOCAL_TRANSACTION_ID
        function, 907
    PURGE_MIXED procedure, 907
    ROLLBACK commands, 906-907
    SAVEPOINT commands, 906-907
    SET TRANSACTION commands,
        905-906
    STEP_ID function, 908
    See also Transactions
DBMS_UTILITY package, 908-911
    ANALYZE_SCHEMA procedure,
        908-909
    COMPILE_SCHEMA procedure,
        908
    FORMAT_CALL_STACK
        function, 384-393, 909
    FORMAT_ERROR_STACK
        function, 365, 384, 909
    GET_TIME function, 910
    IS_PARALLEL_SERVER function,
        909
    NAME_RESOLVE procedure,
        910-911
    PORT_STRING function, 911
DDL statements, 98, 556-577, 919
    binding input variables for,
        559-562
    closing the cursor for, 563
    executing, 564-566
    hanging caused by, 615
    opening the cursor for, 557
    parsing, 557-559
    privileges, 118

synonyms, 113-114
    See also DBMS_DDL package;
        DBMS_SQL package
Debug.Close procedure, 722
Debug.Debug procedure
    DBMS_PIPE package, 640
    test tables, 509-516
    UTL_FILE package, 722
Debug package, 505-506
    DBMS_OUTPUT package,
        517-529
    DBMS_PIPE package, 637-640
    explained, 509-511, 524
    initialization section in, 294
    using, 511-516, 525-529
    UTL_FILE package, 720-722
Debug.pc program, DBMS_PIPE
    package, 633-637
Debug.Reset procedure, 509, 511, 722
Debug versions, 537-538
debug_extproc package, 809-810
    code for, 809-810
    steps for using, 810
Debugging
    external procedures, 808-810
    guidelines for, 504-505
    interactive PL/SQL, 497
    Procedure Builder for, 530-537
    SQL-Station for, 537-542
    See also Testing and debugging
debug_table table, 21, 509, 510, 512,
    529
Declarations
    forward, 267-269
    forward type, 405
    variable, 39-41
Declarative sections
    of blocks, 29
    exceptions raised in, 376-377
    of nested tables, 435
    See also Packages
DECLARE keyword, 29, 30
    procedures and, 248
Declaring
    cursor variables, 228-230
    cursors, 205-206
    exceptions, 356-360
    nested tables, 434-438
    objects, 403-405
DECODE function, 183-184
DEFAULT keyword, 41
DEFINE_ARRAY procedure, 596-597
    example of, 597-600
    parameters for, 597
DEFINE_COLUMN_LONG
    procedure, 605
DEFINE_COLUMN procedure, 555,
    567-569
    parameters, 569-570
Definition lists, 746
Delete cascade utility, 340
DELETE collection method, 459-461
DELETE statements, 107-108, 919

nested tables, 442
objects, 422
:old and :new pseudorecords, 330
triggers, 321-322
DELETE table attribute, 91-92
Delimiters, 34, 35
demobld.sql script, 343-345
Dependencies
    data dictionary information on,
        939, 941
    determining, 272-275
    object, 416
    packages and, 294-297
    subprogram, 269-275
DEQUEUE operation, 654
    DBMS_AQ package, 666-667
    example, 683-685
    message identification, 688-691
    priority queue, 686-688
DEQUEUE_OPTIONS_T type,
    DBMS_AQ package, 663-664
DEREF operator, 425
DESC_REC datatype, field
    descriptions, 602-603
DESCRIBE_COLUMNS procedure,
    600-604
    datatype codes for, 601
    parameters for, 602
    syntax for, 600-601
DESCRIBE_PROCEDURE,
    DBMS_DESCRIBE package, 584,
    894-896, 897
DescribeTable procedure, 603
Destination tables, 538-539
DH_UTIL.CHECK_PROTECT
    function, 195
DH_UTIL.SPELL function, 194
DH_UTIL package
    creating, 193-201
    public functions in, 192-193
dict_columns view, 959
Directories
    accessible, 710
    creating, 822
    data dictionary information on,
        822-823, 943
    dropping, 823
    privileges required for, 822
Directory lists, 746
DISABLE procedure, 520
Disabling triggers, 324-325
Dispatcher process, 858
Distributed transactions, 113
DML statements, 98, 100-114,
    556-577, 919
    BFILEs in, 824-826
    binding input variables for,
        559-562
    closing the cursor for, 563
    database links, 113
    DELETE statements, 107-108
    executing, 562
    INSERT statements, 105-106

LOBs in, 818-821, 824-826
nested tables, 443-444
objects in, 421-426
opening the cursor for, 557
parsing, 557-559
SELECT statements, 102-104
synonyms, 113-114
table references, 112
UPDATE statements, 106-107
WHERE clauses, 108-112
See also DBMS_SQL package
Dot notation, 83
for calling a method, 409
DROP DIRECTORY command, 823
DROP FUNCTION command, 263
DROP LIBRARY command, 788
DROP PROCEDURE command, 244,
263
DROP TYPE BODY command, 416
DROP TYPE command, 415-416
Dropping
directories, 823
libraries, 788
object types, 415-416
procedures and functions, 262-263
queues and queue tables,
670-671, 673-674, 697
triggers, 324-325
DROP_QUEUE_TABLE procedure,
DBMS_AQADM package, 670-671
DROP_QUEUE procedure,
DBMS_AQADM package, 673-674
DUMP function, 184-186, 514
Dump_doc function, code for, 609-611
DUP_VAL_ON_INDEX exception,
361, 919
Dynamic PL/SQL
algorithm for executing
statements with, 551-556
comparison of interfaces using,
612-614
executing arbitrary stored
procedures, 584-592
executing non-query DML and
DDL statements, 556-577
executing PL/SQL blocks, 577-584
executing queries, 566-577
HTML utilities, 760-763
static SQL vs., 550-551
See also DBMS_SQL package
Dynamic SQL utilities, OWA_UTIL
package, 760-763
DynamicDemo package, 761-763
DynamicPLSQL procedure, 581-582
rewriting parse section of, 594
DynamicQuery procedure, 575-577

E

Early binding, 99
Editing windows, SQL-Station Coder,
487

Elements, package, 285-286
ELSE clause, 63
ELSIF clause, 63, 65
Embedded blocks, 478
Embedded PL/SQL, 475-482
Embedded SQL commands, 98
Empty nested tables, 437
EMPTY_BLOB() function, 186, 819,
820
EMPTY_CLOB() function, 186, 819,
820
ENABLE procedure, 520
END keyword, 29, 30
procedures and, 248
Engines, execution environment,
464-468
ENQUEUE operation, 653-654
DBMS_AQ package, 665-666
example, 683-685
message identification, 688-691
priority queue, 686-688
ENQUEUE_OPTIONS_T type,
DBMS_AQ package, 661-662
Enumerated constants, DBMS_AQ
package, 665
Environments, execution, 464-501
ERASE routine, DBMS_LOB package,
832-833
Error handling
blocks, 6-7
mutating table errors, 337-340
precompilers, 480-481
See also Exceptions
Error message creation,
RAISE_APPLICATION_ERROR
function, 369-372
ErrorObj object, 412-413
ErrorPkg package, 385-392
Errors
coding problems, 504-505
creating procedures, 244, 249,
250
DBMS_SQL package, 553,
606-608
equivalent exceptions, 357-358
inside subprograms, 261-262
masking location of, 382-383
shared pool, 862
SHOW ERRORS command, 264
stored subprograms, 264-266
types of, 355
See also Exceptions
Exception handlers, 362-368
log_table table, 368
OTHERS handler, 363-368
WHEN clauses, 363
EXCEPTION keyword, 29, 30
procedures and, 248
Exception propagation, 372-380
declarative sections, 376-377
exception sections, 378-380
executable sections, 373-376
Exception queues, 655

using, 694-696
Exception sections, 29
exceptions raised in, 378-380
in procedures, 248
syntax, 362-363
EXCEPTION_INIT pragma, 368-369,
920
Exceptions, 354-393, 920
ACCESS_INTO_NULL, 915
avoiding unhandled, 382
COLLECTION_IS_NULL, 436,
916
CURSOR_ALREADY_OPEN, 917
DBMS_UTILITY.FORMAT_CALL_S
TACK function, 384-393
declaring, 356-360
DUP_VAL_ON_INDEX, 361, 919
EXCEPTION_INIT pragma,
368-369, 920
explained, 354-356
FFLUSH procedure, 719
guidelines, 380-383
handling, 362-368
INVALID_CURSOR, 359, 923
INVALID_NUMBER, 359, 924
locating source of, 384-393
LOGIN_DENIED, 925
masking location of errors,
382-383
NO_DATA_FOUND, 222, 359,
371-372, 926
NOT_LOGGED_ON, 925
object type attributes and,
411-413
predefined, 357-360
PROGRAM_ERROR, 359, 928
propagation, 372-380
RAISE_APPLICATION_ERROR
function, 369-372
raised by DBMS_LOB routines,
846-847
raised by UTL_FILE package,
712, 713, 722
raised inside subprograms,
261-262
raising, 360-361
ROWTYPE_MISMATCH, 360,
930
scope of, 380-382
STORAGE_ERROR, 359, 933
SUBSCRIPT_BEYOND_COUNT,
931
SUBSCRIPT_OUTSIDE_LIMIT,
931-932
TIMEOUT_ON_RESOURCE, 933
TOO_MANY_ROWS, 933
TRANSACTION_BACKED_OUT,
934
types of, 355
user-defined, 356-357
VALUE_ERROR, 359-360, 935
ZERO_DIVIDE, 391, 935
See also Errors

EXEC SQL ALLOCATE command, 230-231
Executable sections, 29
    exceptions raised in, 373-376
    in procedures, 248
EXECUTE ANY PROCEDURE system privilege, 630
EXECUTE command, SQL*Plus, 473
EXECUTE function, 555
    parameters, 562
EXECUTE privilege, 276-278
    DBMS_PIPE package, 630
ExecuteAny package
    code for, 584-590
    example of using, 590-592
Executing statements with DBMS_SQL
    arbitrary stored procedures, 584-592
    DDL statements, 564-566
    DML statements, 562
    PL/SQL blocks, 577-584
    queries, 566-577
    SQL statements, 551-556
Execution environments, 464-501
    client-side PL/SQL, 466-468, 489-497
    DBMS_JOB package, 709
    PL/SQL engines, 464-468
    PL/SQL wrapper, 498-500
    server-side PL/SQL, 468-489
    See also Blocks; Procedures
Execution intervals, DBMS_JOB package, 706
Execution plans (SQL statements), 867-876
    EXPLAIN PLAN statements, 867-869
    NESTED LOOP operations, 876
    plan_table table, 868
    shared pools and, 861
    SQL-Station Plan Analyzer, 873-875
    TABLE ACCESS operations, 876
    TKPROF utility, 869-873
    using, 875-876
EXISTS collection method, 450-452
EXISTS table attribute, 92
EXIT statement, 920
EXP function, 151-152
EXPLAIN PLAN statements, 99, 867-869
Explicit cursors, 205-215
    attributes, 210-214
    closing, 209-210
    declaring, 205-206
    fetching from, 208-209
    opening, 207-208
    parameterized, 214-215
Explicit datatype conversion, 53-54
Export package, 303-314
    code for, 304-312
    example, 313-314
    procedures, 304

Expressions, 58, 59-62, 920-921
    boolean, 60-62
    character, 60
    See also Operators
EXTEND collection method, 454-457
External datatypes, parameter mappings, 792-796
External functions
    function return values, 800-802
    overloading, 802
    packaged procedures and, 800-802
    RESTRICT_REFERENCES pragma and, 802
External LOBs, 816
External procedures, 780-812, 921
    callbacks to the database, 802-808
    coding, 783-784
    configuring the SQL*Net listener, 784-787
    creating libraries, 787-789
    debugging, 808-810
    executing SQL in, 807-808
    external functions and, 800-802
    guidelines, 810-811
    overview, 780-782
    packaged procedures and, 800-802
    parameter mappings, 791-800
    requirements for using, 812
    restrictions on, 811-812
    service routines, 803-807
    steps for calling, 782-791
    wrapper procedure, 789-791
extproc process, 780, 782, 921
    attaching a debugger to, 808-810

F

Families, numeric, 43-45
FCLOSE function, UTL_FILE package, 714-715
FCLOSE_ALL function, UTL_FILE package, 715
Fetch loops for cursors, 217-227
    COMMIT statements, 225-227
    example, 204-205
    FOR loops, 221-222
    SELECT FOR UPDATE statements, 223-227
    simple loops, 217-219
    WHILE loops, 219-221
FETCH statements, 208, 921
Fetching
    arrays, 600
    from cursors, 208
    LONG data, 604-606
    rows, 570-571
FETCH_ROWS procedure, 555, 570-571
    array fetch with, 600

parameters, 571
FFLUSH procedure, UTL_FILE package, 719
File handles, 712
File I/O, 709-729, 922
    examples, 720-729
    exceptions raised by, 712
    file input, 719-720
    file output, 716-719
    opening and closing files, 712-715
    security, 709-712
    See also UTL_FILE package
FILECLOSE routine, DBMS_LOB package, 833
FILECLOSEALL routine, DBMS_LOB package, 833-834
FileExec procedure, 839-842
FILEEXISTS routine, DBMS_LOB package, 834
FILEGETNAME routine, DBMS_LOB package, 834
FILEISOPEN routine, DBMS_LOB package, 834-835
FILEOPEN routine, DBMS_LOB package, 835
Files
    instance structure, 860-861
    manipulating with SQL*Plus, 474
    opening and closing, 712-715
    writing LONG datatypes to, 608-611
Firing triggers, 318, 326-328
FIRST collection method, 453
FIRST table attribute, 92-93
Fixed-length values, 111
FLOOR function, 152
Flushing shared pools, 862
FOPEN function, UTL_FILE package, 712, 714
FOR loops, 9, 70-71
    cursor fetch loops, 221-222
    loop ranges, 71
FOR UPDATE clause, 223-224
FORCE option, 415
Form tags, HTML, 751-755
Form triggers
    database triggers vs., 492
    See also Triggers
Formal parameters, 244
    constraints on, 249-251
    default values for, 255-256
    modes for, 245-248
Format elements, for dates, 169-170
FORMAT_CALL_STACK function, DBMS_UTILITY package, 384-393, 909
FORMAT_ERROR_STACK function, DBMS_UTILITY package, 365, 384, 909
FormDemo package, 751-753, 754
FORMOPEN procedure, 753-754
Forward declarations, 267-269
Forward type declarations, 405

%FOUND cursor attribute, 210-212, 922
Fourth-generation languages (4GLs), 2, 3
Function return values, 800-802
Functions, 922
    creating, 257-261
    default parameters, 303
    dropping, 262-263
    explained, 242-243
    external, 800-802
    purity levels, 297-303
    RETURN statement in, 259-260
    style guidelines, 260-261
    syntax for creating, 258-259
    See also Procedures; SQL built-in functions; Subprograms; *and names of specific functions*

G

generate.sql script, 346
GET command, SQL*Plus, 474
GET function, OWA_COOKIE package, 771
GET method, web agent, 736, 754
GET_ALL procedure, OWA_COOKIE package, 771-772
GETLENGTH routine, DBMS_LOB package, 835-836
GET_LINES procedure, 519-520
GET_LINE procedure
    DBMS_OUTPUT package, 518
    UTL_FILE package, 719-720
GET_TIME function, DBMS_UTILITY package, 910
GLB function, 179
Glossary of PL/SQL features, 914-935
GOTO statements, 72-74, 922
    guidelines for, 74
    restrictions on, 72-73
GRANT statements, 118-120
    EXECUTE privilege and, 276-277
    roles and, 279, 280
GRANT_TYPE_ACCESS procedure, DBMS_AQADM package, 677
GREATEST function, 186-187
GREATEST_LB function, 187
GROUP BY clause, 104
Group functions, 130, 177-182
    AVG function, 178
    COUNT function, 178-179
    GLB function, 179
    LUB function, 179-180
    MAX function, 180
    MIN function, 180-181
    STDDEV function, 181
    SUM function, 181-182
    VARIANCE function, 182

H

Handlers, exception, 362-368
Handshake messages, DBMS_PIPE package, 640
Hanging, caused by DDL operations, 615
Headers
    HTML tags, 744
    package, 284-286
HEXTORAW function, 54, 167-168
Host language, 475
Host variables, 476-477
HTF package. *See* HTP and HTF packages
HTML code
    cookie management, 769-773
    generating with web toolkit, 739-740
    image map handling, 767-769
    procedures and functions for generating, 740-756
    specifying procedure parameters for, 736-738
    utilities for generating, 757-766
HTML utilities subprograms, 757-760
HTP and HTF packages, 740-756
    body tags, 744-746
    character format tags, 749-750
    constants, 743
    form tags, 751-755
    header tags, 744
    lists, 746-749
    physical format tags, 750-751
    printing procedures, 741, 743
    subprograms in, 742
    table formatting procedures, 755-756

I

I/O. *See* File I/O; UTL_FILE package
Identifiers, 31-34, 922-923
    case-sensitivity, 32
    delimiters, 34, 35
    legal vs. illegal, 31-32
    literals, 34-38
    quoted, 33
    reserved words, 32
IF statement, 923
IF-THEN-ELSE statements, 63-72
    loops in, 67-71
    null conditions, 65-67
    syntax, 63-65
Image maps, 767
Imagemap package, 767-769
Implicit cursors, 215-217, 932
Implicit datatype conversion, 54-55
IN mode, 246
IN operator, 62
IN OUT mode, 246
Indentation style, 78-79

INDEX BY BINARY_INTEGER clause, 86-87, 435
Index-by tables, nested tables compared to, 435, 444
INDICATOR property, parameter mappings, 798
Indicator variables, 478-480
    parameter mappings, 791, 798
Indirect dependencies, 271
INIT.ORA file, 274
    BFILE parameters, 823
    job initialization parameters, 701
INITCAP function, 132
Initialization
    BFILE column, 824
    nested table, 436-438
    object, 403-405
    package, 292-294, 302
    variable, 41
    varray, 445-446
Input files, wrapper, 499
Input variables
    binding, 559
    indicator variables, 480
Inputting data, 719-720
INSERT statements, 105-106, 923
    mutating tables and, 335
    nested tables, 441
    objects, 421
    :old and :new pseudorecords, 330
    RETURNING clause, 426
    triggers, 321-322
Instances, 856-861
    files, 860-861
    memory, 859-860
    object, 398
    processes, 856-859
    structure of, 857
Instantiation, package, 292
Instead-of triggers, 322-323
INSTR function, 144-145
    DBMS_LOB package, 836-838
INSTRB function, 145
INTEGER_TRANSLATION function, 197
Internal LOBs, 816
Intersession communication, 618-649
    Advanced Queuing package, 618
    comparison of built-in packages for, 648-649
    DBMS_ALERT package, 641-647
    DBMS_PIPE package, 618-640
INTERVAL procedure, DBMS_JOB package, 708
INVALID_CURSOR exception, 359, 923
INVALID_NUMBER exception, 359, 924
IS DANGLING predicate, 426
IS keyword, 248
IS NULL operator, 62
%ISOPEN attribute, 213, 924

IS_OPEN function, 608
    UTL_FILE package, 715
IS_PARALLEL_SERVER function,
    DBMS_UTILITY package, 909
IS_ROLE_ENABLED function,
    DBMS_SESSION package, 905
ITALIC HTML tag, 750-751

J

Job identifiers, 704-706
Job numbers, 703
Job queues, 700
Jobs. *See* Database jobs; DBMS_JOB
    package

K

KEEP procedure, 865-866
Keywords. *See* Reserved words

L

Label conversions, 171-172
Labels, 72-74
    for loops, 74
LANGUAGE clause, wrapper
    procedure, 790
Language_flag parameter, 558
Large objects. *See* LOBs
LAST collection method, 453
LAST table attribute, 92-93
LAST_DAY function, 159
LAST_ERROR_POSITION function,
    607
LAST_ROW_COUNT function, 607
LAST_ROW_ID function, 607
LAST_SQL_FUNCTION_CODE
    function, 607-608
Late binding, 99
LEAST function, 187
LEAST_UB function, 188
LENGTH function, 146
LENGTH property, parameter
    mappings, 798-799
LENGTHB function, 146
LEVEL pseudocolumn, 116
Lexical units, 30-39
    comments, 38-39
    delimiters, 34
    identifiers, 31-34
    literals, 34-38
    PL/SQL character set, 30-31
Libraries
    creating, 787-789
    data dictionary information on,
        788-789, 945
    dropping, 788
    external procedures and, 781,
        783

privileges on, 788
LIBRARY clause, wrapper procedure,
    789
LIKE operator, 62
LIMIT collection method, 452-453
ListDemo package, 746-749
listener.ora file, 784-785
Listeners. *See* SQL*Net listener
LISTPRINT subprogram, 760
Lists, HTML, 746-749
Literals, 34-38, 924
    boolean, 37-38
    character, 36
    numeric, 36-37
LN function, 152-153
LOADFROMFILE routine,
    DBMS_LOB package, 838-842
LoadStudents procedure, 722-725
LOB storage clause, 817-818
lobdemo table, 818
LOBPrint procedure, 832, 843
LOBs (large objects), 51, 816-852,
    924
    BFILEs, 817, 821-826
    BLOBs, 817
    characteristics of, 816-817
    CLOBs, 817
    copying LONG data into,
        849-852
    data dictionary information on,
        945-946
    DBMS_LOB package, 826-849
    directories, 822-823
    in DML statements, 818-821,
        824-826
    initializing LOB columns,
        819-821
    internal vs. external, 816
    kinds of, 817
    Long2Lob procedure, 849-852
    NCLOBs, 817
    overview, 816-817
    storage, 817-818, 819
    See also DBMS_LOB package
Local procedures
    PL/SQL Editor with, 494
    See also Procedures; Stored
        procedures
Local subprograms, 266-269
    forward declarations, 267-269
    stored subprograms vs., 269, 270
LOCAL_TRANSACTION_ID function,
    DBMS_TRANSACTION package,
    907
Locations, object, 417-420
LOCK TABLE statement, 924-925
Locks. *See* DBMS_LOCK package
LOG function, 153
Log Writer (LGWR) process, 858
LOGIN_DENIED exception, 925
LogRSChanges trigger, 332-333
LogRSInserts trigger, 618, 632
log_table table, 21

Long2Lob procedure, 849-852
LONG datatypes, 47
    copying into LOBs, 849-852
    fetching, 604-606
    piecewise operations on, 614
    restrictions on, 816
    writing to files, 608-611
LONG RAW datatypes, 48
    copying into LOBs, 849-852
    restrictions on, 816
Loops, 67-71, 925
    cursors and, 9-10
    FOR, 9, 70-71
    labeling, 74
    overview, 8-10
    simple, 67-69
    WHILE, 69-70
LOWER function, 133
LPAD function, 133-134
lsnrctl utility, 786-787
LTRIM function, 134-135
LUB function, 179-180
Lvalues, 58

M

major_stats table, 16
MAP function, 407
MAP method, 427-428, 925
    guidelines, 430
MAX function, 180
MAXLEN property, parameter
    mappings, 798-799
MEMBER keyword, 406
Memory
    allocating for cursor variables,
        230-231
    instance structure, 859-860
    session usage, 864-865
    shared pool, 859, 862
Menu lists, 746
Message identifier, 688-691
Message window, SQL-Station Coder,
    487
MESSAGE_PROPERTIES_T type,
    DBMS_AQ package, 658-661
Messages
    receiving via DBMS_PIPE
        package, 625-627
    sending via DBMS_PIPE
        package, 623-625
Methods
    calling, 409-410
    collection, 450-461
    object type, 405-413
    operations as, 397
MIN function, 180-181
MLSLABEL datatype, 50
MOD function, 153-154
Modes
    formal parameters, 245-248
    parameter, 796-797

Modular programming, 544-545
MONTHS_BETWEEN function, 160
Multiline comments, 39, 917
Multithreaded servers, 863
Mutating tables, 334-340
    example, 336-337
    INSERT statements and, 335
    workaround for errors, 337-340

N

NAME clause, wrapper procedure, 789
Named blocks, 24
Named notation
    compared to positional notation, 254
    in procedures, 251-254
NAME_RESOLVE procedure, DBMS_UTILITY package, 910-911
Names
    triggers, 320-321
    variables, 77
Namespace, 320
Naming conventions, data dictionary, 938-939
NCHAR datatype, 47-48
NCLOB datatypes, 817
    See also LOBs
NESTED LOOP operations, 876
Nested tables, 434-444, 926
    adding elements to, 438
    collection methods, 450-461
    declaring, 434-438
    index-by tables compared to, 435, 444
    initializing, 436-438
    manipulating, 441-444
    storing in the database, 438-444
    varrays compared to, 449-450
Netscape Navigator, 738
Networks, performance and tuning, 876-878
:new and :old pseudorecords, 328-332
NEW_LINE procedure
    DBMS_OUTPUT package, 518
    UTL_FILE package, 716-717
NEW_TIME function, 160-161
NEXT collection method, 453-454
NEXT table attribute, 93-94
NEXT_DATE procedure, DBMS_JOB package, 708
NEXT_DAY function, 161-162
NEXT_ITEM_TYPE function, 626
NEXTVAL pseudocolumn, 115-116
NLS_INITCAP function, 135-136
NLS_LOWER function, 136
NLSSORT function, 147
NLS_UPPER function, 136-137
NO_DATA_FOUND exception, 222, 359, 371-372, 926

Non-blank-padded semantics, 110-111
Non-query DML and DDL statements
    executing, 556-566
    See also DDL statements; DML statements
Notation, positional vs. named, 251-254
%NOTFOUND cursor attribute, 212, 222, 925-926
NOT_LOGGED_ON exception, 925
NULL
    boolean expressions as, 61, 62
    LOB columns as, 819
    object vs. attribute, 404-405
    parameter mappings and, 791, 798
    uninitialized variables as, 41
NULL conditions, IF-THEN-ELSE statements, 65-67
NULL statements, 74-75, 926
NULL values, 926
NUMBER datatype, 43-44
Number format elements, 173-174
Numbers, printing as text strings, 192-201
Numeric conversions, 172-174
Numeric family, 43-45
    BINARY_INTEGER datatype, 44-45
    NUMBER datatype, 43-44
    PLS_INTEGER datatype, 45
Numeric FOR loops, 9
    See also FOR loops
Numeric functions, 147-158
    ABS function, 147-148
    ACOS function, 148
    ASIN function, 148-149
    ATAN function, 149
    ATAN2 function, 149-150
    CEIL function, 150
    COS function, 150-151
    COSH function, 151
    EXP function, 151-152
    FLOOR function, 152
    LN function, 152-153
    LOG function, 153
    MOD function, 153-154
    POWER function, 154
    ROUND function, 154-155
    SIGN function, 155
    SIN function, 155-156
    SINH function, 156
    SQRT function, 156-157
    TAN function, 157
    TANH function, 157-158
    TRUNC function, 158
Numeric literals, 36-37
NVARCHAR2 datatype, 47-48
NVL function, 188

O

Object identifiers (OIDs), 420
Object instances, 398
Object method parameters information, data dictionary, 947-948
Object method results information, data dictionary, 948-949
Object methods, 405-413
    calling, 409-410
    data dictionary information on, 946-947
    MAP method, 427-428, 430
    ORDER method, 428-429, 430
    SELF keyword, 410
    %TYPE attribute, 411
Object Navigator
    examining local variables, 535
    Oracle Forms, 495
Object privileges, 119
    system privileges vs., 118
Object references, 420-421
    data dictionary information on, 949
Object type attributes, 400-401
    data dictionary information on, 949-950
    exceptions and, 411-413
Object types, 399-417
    altering, 413-415
    declaring and initializing, 403-405
    defining, 400-403
    dependencies, 416-417
    dropping, 415-416
    exceptions and, 411-413
    forward type declarations, 405
    MAP method, 427-428
    methods, 405-413
    ORDER method, 428-429
    packages compared to, 408-409
    queue access to, 678
    restrictions, 402-403
    SELF keyword, 410
    %TYPE attribute, 411
Object-oriented programming, 396-398
Object-relational databases, 398-399
Objects, 396-430
    column, 419-420, 422-424
    in the database, 417-421
    declaring, 403
    DELETE statements, 422
    dependencies, 416-417
    in DML statements, 421-426
    identifiers and references, 420-421
    initializing, 403-404
    INSERT statements, 421
    locations, 417-421
    MAP method, 427-428, 430
    NULL, 404-405

object instances vs., 398
ORDER method, 428-429, 430
overview, 396-399
persistent vs. transient, 417-420
RETURNING clause, 426
row, 418, 424-426
SELECT statements, 422-426
types, 399-417
UPDATE statements, 421-422
Objects option, 400
OCI (Oracle Call Interface), 482-486
    calling structure, 483-486
    guidelines for PL/SQL blocks in,
      483
    LOB functions, 847-849
OCIExtprocAllocCallMemory service
    routine, 805-807
OCIExtProcGetEnv service routine,
    807
OCIExtProcRaiseExcp service routine,
    803-804
OCIExtProcRaiseExcpWithMsg
    service routine, 805
odessp procedure, 895
Oflng procedure, 614
:old and :new pseudorecords,
    328-332
OneObj procedure, 304
oparse call, 483
opcodes, DBMS_PIPE package, 640
OPEN..FOR statements, 231-232
OPEN statements, 927
OPEN_CURSOR procedure, 555
Opening
    cursor variables, 231-232
    cursors, 207-208, 557
    files, 712-715
Operand, 59
Operating system security, 711-712
Operations, execution plan, 876
Operators, 58
    assignment, 58-59
    See also Expressions
Oracle Advanced Queuing, 652-697
    administration, 667-681
    browsing queues, 691-694
    clearing queues, 685-686
    components of, 653-655
    creating queues and queue
      tables, 681-683
    data dictionary views, 678-681
    DEQUEUE operation, 654,
      666-667, 683-685
    dropping queues, 697
    ENQUEUE operation, 653-654,
      665-666, 683-685
    enumerated constants, 665
    examples, 681-697
    exception queues, 655, 694-696
    implementation of, 655-656
    intersession communication
      with, 618
    message identification, 688-691

object type access, 678
operations, 656-667
overview, 652-653
priority queues, 686-688
privileges, 678
supporting types, 656-665
user queues, 655
See also DBMS_AQADM
    package; DBMS_AQ package;
    Queues
Oracle Call Interface. *See* OCI
Oracle Forms, 464, 466, 493-495
    Object Navigator, 495
    PL/SQL Editor, 493-494
Oracle Government Products group,
    340
Oracle Graphics, 464
Oracle PL/SQL
    block structure, 5-7
    built-in packages, 888-911
    built-in SQL functions, 130-201
    client-server model, 4
    cursors, 204-238
    data dictionary, 938-959
    DBMS_SQL enhancements for,
      592-604
    DML statements, 100-114
    documentation, 12
    dynamic PL/SQL, 550-615
    embedded, 475-482
    engines, 464-468
    error handling, 354-393
    example tables, 13-21
    execution environments, 464-501
    external procedures, 780-812
    features, 5-10
    glossary, 914-935
    intersession communication,
      618-649
    LOBs, 816-852
    loops, 8-10
    objects, 396-430
    online code, 12-13
    operators, 58-59
    overview, 2-21
    performance and tuning, 856-878
    precompilers, 475-482
    procedural constructs, 3-4
    reserved words, 882-884
    shared pools, 856-867
    SQL overview, 2-4
    SQL statements, 98-100
    SQL within, 98-127
    standards, 4-5
    style guide, 75-79
    testing and debugging, 504-547
    variables and types, 7-8
    versions of, 10-12
    wrapper, 498-500
Oracle Reports, 464
Oracle WebServer, 732-776
    components, 732-734

database connector descriptor,
    734-736
development environments for
    OWA procedures, 774-776
HTP and HTF packages, 740-756
OWA_COOKIE package,
    769-773
OWA_IMAGE package, 767-769
OWA_UTIL.SHOWPAGE
    procedure, 774-775
OWA_UTIL package, 757-766
PL/SQL agent, 734-736
procedure parameters, 736-738
SQL-Station Coder, 775-776
web toolkit, 739-773
ORDER BY clause, 104, 117
ORDER function, 407
ORDER method, 428-429, 925
    guidelines, 430
Ordered lists, 746
OTHERS exception handler, 363-368
    SQLCODE and SQLERRM
      functions, 364-368
OUT mode, 246
Output files, wrapper, 499
Output variables
    defining, 567-570
    indicator variables, 479-480
    line length for, 519
    retrieving value of, 579-580
OutputString procedure, 783, 790
Outputting data, 716-719
Out_value_size parameter, 583-584
Overloaded packages, 289-292
    external functions and, 802
    restrictions on, 291, 302-303
OWA_COOKIE package, 769-773
    datatypes, 770
    demo package, 772-773
    functions and procedures,
      771-772
OWA_IMAGE package, 767-769
    demo package, 767-769
    functions and procedures, 767
OWA_UTIL package, 757-766
    date utilities, 763-766
    dynamic SQL utilities, 760-763
    HTML utilities, 757-760
    SHOWPAGE procedure, 774-775

P

Package body, 286-288
Package elements, 285-286
Package header, 284-286
Package specification, 284-286
Packages, 284-314, 927
    body of, 286-288
    built-in, 303
    dependencies and, 294-297
    explained, 284
    export procedures, 303-314

external functions and
procedures in, 800-802
header for, 284-286
initialization of, 292-294
object types compared to,
408-409
overloading, 289-292
scope and, 288-289
using in SQL statements, 297-303
See also Built-in packages; *and
names of specific packages*
PACK_MESSAGE procedure, 623
Parameter mappings, 791-800
external datatypes, 792-796
modes, 796-797
properties, 798-800
Parameterized cursors, 214-215
Parameters
actual vs. formal, 244-248
constraints on formal, 249-251
default values for, 255-256
PARAMETERS clause
parameter mappings, 791-792
parameter properties, 798-800
wrapper procedure, 790
PARSE procedure, 555
parameters, 558, 593
Parsing, 555
avoiding unnecessary reparsing,
877
DDL and DML statements,
557-559
large SQL strings, 592-594
PL/SQL blocks, 578
queries, 567
P-code
shared pools, 861
subprograms, 263
triggers, 325-326
Performance and tuning, 856-878
networks, 876-878
shared pools, 856-867
SQL statements, 867-876
Permissions
data dictionary, 939
database, 710-711
DBMS_SQL package, 615
write, 712
See also Privileges; Security
Persistent objects, 417-420
PGA (process global area), 860
Physical format tags, HTML, 750-751
Piecewise operations, on LONG data,
614
Pinning objects
KEEP procedure, 865-866
SIZES procedure, 866-867
UNKEEP procedure, 866
Pipes, database
creating and managing, 627-630
explained, 618
private, 631-632
public vs. private, 628-629

shared pools and, 627-628
See also DBMS_PIPE package
PL/SQL. *See* Oracle PL/SQL
PL/SQL agent, 734-736
PL/SQL character set, 30-31
PL/SQL debugging, Procedure
Builder, 497, 530-537
PL/SQL Editor, Oracle Forms, 493-494
PL/SQL engines, 464-468
PL/SQL errors, 355
PL/SQL features, 914-935
PL/SQL Interpreter, 495-496
PL/SQL variables, 571-575
See also Variables
PL/SQL vs. C datatypes, 792-796
PL/SQL web toolkit. *See* Web toolkit
PL/SQL wrapper, 498-500
Plan Analyzer (SQL-Station), 873-875
plan_table table, 868
PLS_INTEGER datatype, 45
POINT datatype, 767
Polling intervals, 645
Polling loops, 645
PORT_STRING function,
DBMS_UTILITY package, 911
Positional notation
compared to named notation,
254
in procedures, 251-254
POST method, web agent, 736, 754
POWER function, 154
Pragmas
control structures, 75
EXCEPTION_INIT, 368-369, 920
RESTRICT_REFERENCES, 75,
300-302, 928-929
Precedence, operator, 59
Precompilers, 475-482
bind variables in, 477-478
embedding blocks, 478
error handling, 480-481
host language, 475
host variables, 476-477
indicator variables, 478-480
necessary options, 481-482
Register procedure, 477-478
SQLCHECK option, 481-482
Predefined exceptions, 357-360
Predicates, trigger, 332-333
PRINT procedure, 741
PrintDemo procedure, 741, 743
Printing procedures, HTML code,
741, 743
PrintTranscript procedure, 725-729
PRIOR collection method, 453-454
PRIOR table attribute, 93-94
Priority queues, 686-688
Private pipes, 631-632
public pipes vs., 628-629
Privileges, 118-122
DBMS_PIPE package, 630-632
DBMS_SQL package, 611
for directories, 822

EXECUTE, 276-278
GRANT statements, 118-120
on libraries, 788
object vs. system, 118
queue, 678
REVOKE statements, 120-121
roles and, 121-122, 278-280
stored subprograms and, 275-278
See also Permissions; Security
Pro*C programs, error handling,
480-481
Problem diagnosis
debugging guidelines, 504-505
See also Testing and debugging
Procedural errors, 355
Procedural statements, 24, 927
collection methods called from,
450
Procedure Builder, 495-497
breakpoints, 533, 534
command prompt, 496
debugging with, 530-537
interactive PL/SQL debugging,
497
Object Navigator, 533, 535
PL/SQL Interpreter, 495-496
SQL-Station compared to, 543
viewer pane, 496
Procedure Execution tool,
SQL-Station, 488-489
Procedures, 927-928
body of, 248
constraints on formal parameters
in, 249-251
creating, 243-256
DBMS_OUTPUT package,
517-520
dropping, 262-263
exceptions raised in, 261-262
EXECUTE command, 473
explained, 242-243
packaged, 800-802
parameter default values for,
255-256
parameters and modes for,
244-248
positional and named notation
in, 251-254
register, 477-478
remote calling of, 273
syntax for creating, 243-244
See also Blocks; External
procedures; Functions;
Subprograms; *and names of
specific procedures*
Process global area (PGA), 860
Process Monitor (PMON) process, 858
Processes, 856-859
database, 858
instance structure, 857
shadow, 857, 858, 859
user, 857, 858
Processing cursors

explicit cursors, 205-215
implicit cursors, 215-217
Producing agents, 655
PROGRAM_ERROR exception, 359,
928
Programming methodologies, 543-547
data abstraction, 546-547
modular programming, 544-545
top-down design, 545-546
Propagation. *See* Exception
propagation
Properties, parameter, 798-800
Protect_OWA_Pkg parameter, 757
Pseudocolumns, 114-117
CURRVAL, 115-116
LEVEL, 116
NEXTVAL, 115-116
ROWID, 116
ROWNUM, 117
Pseudorecords, triggers, 328-332
Public pipes, 628-629
PURGE procedure, DBMS_PIPE
package, 630
PURGE_MIXED procedure,
DBMS_TRANSACTION package,
907
Purity levels
for built-in packages, 303
for functions, 297-303, 928-929
PUT procedure
DBMS_OUTPUT package,
517-518
UTL_FILE package, 716
PUTF procedure, UTL_FILE package,
718-719
PUT_LINE procedure
DBMS_OUTPUT package,
517-518
UTL_FILE package, 717

Q

Queries
defining output variables for,
567-570
example of DynamicQuery
procedure, 575-577
executing with DBMS_SQL,
566-577
fetching the rows for, 570-571
opening cursor variables for,
231-232
parsing the statement, 567
returning results to PL/SQL
variables, 571-575
Queue tables, 655
creating, 668-670, 681-683
data dictionary views, 678-680
dropping, 670-671, 697
Queues
administration, 667-681
browsing, 691-694

clearing, 685-686
creating, 671-673, 681-683
data dictionary and, 678-681
defined, 653
dropping, 673-674, 697
exception, 655, 694-696
message identification, 688-691
modifying, 674-675
operations, 656-667
priority, 686-688
privileges, 678
starting, 675
stopping, 675-676
subscribers, 676-677
user, 655
See also DBMS_AQADM
package; DBMS_AQ package;
Oracle Advanced Queuing
QUEUE_SUBSCRIBER function,
DBMS_AQADM package, 677
Quoted identifiers, 33

R

RAISE statement, 928
RAISE_APPLICATION_ERROR
function, 369-372
mutating tables and, 337
Register procedure, 370-372
Raising exceptions, 355, 360-361
Ranges, loop, 71
RAW datatype, 48
Raw family, 48
RAWTOHEX function, 54, 168
READ routine, DBMS_LOB package,
842-843
READ_CLIENT_INFO procedure,
DBMS_APPLICATION_INFO
package, 892
Read-consistency, 208
Readers, DBMS_PIPE package, 618,
619-622
README file, 26
READ_MODULE procedure,
DBMS_APPLICATION_INFO
package, 891
RECEIVE_MESSAGE function, 625-626
Receiving
alerts, 642-644
messages, 625-627
RecordFullClasses procedure, 271
Records, 82-86, 928
assigning, 84-85
syntax for defining, 83-84
using %ROWTYPE operator,
85-86
See also Tables
Recover (RECO) process, 858
Redo log buffer, 859-860
Redo log files, 860
REF CURSOR datatype, 50
REF INTO clause, 106

REF object type, 51
REF operator, 425
Reference semantics, 825
Reference types, 50-51
Register procedure
bind variables in precompilers,
477-478
DBMS_ALERT package, 642
DBMS_OUTPUT package,
522-524
OCI calling structure example,
484-486
RAISE_APPLICATION_ERROR
function, 370-372
registered_students table, 18-20
DBMS_PIPE package, 618-619,
622
Relational operators, 61
RELEASE function, DBMS_LOCK
package, 901
REMOTE_DEPENDENCIES_MODE
parameter, 274
REMOVE procedure
DBMS_ALERT package, 642, 645
DBMS_JOB package, 707-708
OWA_COOKIE package, 772
REMOVE_PIPE function, 627, 628-629
REMOVE_SUBSCRIBER procedure,
DBMS_AQADM package, 676
Reparsing, avoiding unnecessary, 877
REPLACE function, 137
REQUEST function, DBMS_LOCK
package, 899-900
Reserved words, 32, 882-884
RESET_PACKAGE procedure,
DBMS_SESSION package, 904
RESOURCE role, 612
Restrictions
on cursor variables, 237
on external procedures, 811-812
on GOTO statements, 72-73
on issuing SQL statements within
external procedures, 807-808
on LONG and LONG RAW
datatypes, 816
on object types, 402-403
on overloaded packages, 291,
302-303
on triggers, 323-324
on update cascade package,
341-342
RESTRICT_REFERENCES pragma, 75,
300-302, 928-929
external functions and, 802
object type specification, 407
rationale for, 302
RETURN statements, 259-260, 929
RETURNING clause, 426
Reusing cursors, 615
REVERSE keyword, 71
REVOKE statements, 120-121
roles and, 280
Roles

DBMS_SQL package and,
611-612, 615
privileges and, 121-122
stored subprograms and, 278-280
ROLLBACK commands,
DBMS_TRANSACTION package,
906-907
ROLLBACK statements, 565-566
COMMIT statements vs., 123-124
SAVEPOINT command and,
125-126
rooms table, 16-17
cursor variable examples,
232-236
ROUND function
as date function, 162, 164
as numeric function, 154-155
Row objects, 418
in SELECT statements, 424-426
%ROWCOUNT cursor attribute, 213,
930
ROWID datatype, 49
Rowid family, 49
ROWID pseudocolumn, 116
ROWIDTOCHAR function, 54,
168-169
Row-level triggers, 328-332
ROWNUM pseudocolumn, 117
Rows, fetching, 570-571
%ROWTYPE attribute, 930
%ROWTYPE operator, 85-86
ROWTYPE_MISMATCH exception,
360, 930
RPAD function, 138
RS_audit table, 20
triggers, 332
RTRIM function, 138-139
Rule-based optimizer, 873, 874, 875
RUN procedure, DBMS_JOB
package, 706
Running
broken jobs, 707
database jobs, 702-706
PL/SQL wrapper, 498-499
Run-time errors, 355
Rvalues, 59

S

SAVEPOINT commands, 125-126,
930
DBMS_TRANSACTION package,
906-907
Scalar types, 43-50
boolean family, 50
character family, 45-48
date family, 49
numeric family, 43-45
raw family, 48
rowid family, 49
trusted family, 50
Schema exporter, 303-314

Schema object information, data
dictionary, 950-951
Scope
exceptions, 380-382
packages and, 288-289
variable, 56-58
Scoping rules, FOR loops, 70-71
Security
database, 710-711
DBMS_PIPE package, 630-632
operating system, 711-712
UTL_FILE package, 709-712
See also Permissions; Privileges
SELECT..INTO statement, 930-931
SELECT FOR UPDATE cursors,
223-227
Select list description
comparison of dynamic methods
for, 613
with DBMS_SQL, 600-604
SELECT privilege, 278
SELECT statements, 102-104
column objects in, 422-424
components of, 103
DESCRIBE_COLUMNS
procedure and, 600
nested tables, 442-443
record assignment with, 85
row objects in, 424-426
testing and debugging, 513-514
SELF keyword, 408, 410
SEND procedure, OWA_COOKIE
package, 771
Sending
alerts, 641-642
messages, 623-625
SEND_MESSAGE function, 623-625
Sequences, 115
Server Manager, SERVEROUTPUT
option, 520
SERVEROUTPUT option, 520-522
Server-side PL/SQL, 468-489
OCI (Oracle Call Interface),
482-486
Oracle precompilers, 475-482
SQL*Plus, 468-475
SQL-Station, 486-489
See also Client-side PL/SQL
Service routines, 803-807
OCIExtprocAllocCallMemory,
805-807
OCIExtProcGetEnv, 807
OCIExtProcRaiseExcp, 803-804
OCIExtProcRaiseExcpWithMsg,
805
Session control statements, 98
Session memory usage, 864-865
SESSION_MAX_OPEN_FILES
parameter, 823
SET SERVEROUTPUT ON command,
521

SET TRANSACTION commands,
DBMS_TRANSACTION package,
905-906
SET TRANSACTION statement, 931
SET_ACTION procedure,
DBMS_APPLICATION_INFO
package, 891
SET_CLIENT_INFO procedure,
DBMS_APPLICATION_INFO
package, 891-892
SET_DEFAULTS procedure,
DBMS_ALERT package, 645
SET_LABEL procedure,
DBMS_SESSION package, 904
SET_MLS_LABEL_FORMAT
procedure, DBMS_SESSION
package, 904
SET_MODULE procedure,
DBMS_APPLICATION_INFO
package, 890-891
SET_NLS procedure, DBMS_SESSION
package, 903
SET_ROLE procedure,
DBMS_SESSION package, 903
SET_SQL_TRACE procedure,
DBMS_SESSION package, 903
SGA (system global area), 856-857
Shadow process, 857, 858, 859
Shared libraries
creating, 787-789
data dictionary information on,
788-789, 945
dropping, 788
external procedures and, 781,
783
privileges on, 788
Shared pools, 856-867
DBMS_PIPE package, 627-628
DBMS_SHARED_POOL
package, 905
errors, 862
estimating size of, 863-865
flushing, 862
function of, 861-862
KEEP procedure, 865-866
multithreaded servers and, 863
Oracle instance structure,
856-861
p-code, 861
pinning objects, 865-867
session memory usage, 864-865
SIZES procedure, 866-867
triggers and, 862-863
UNKEEP procedure, 866
SHARED_POOL_SIZE parameter, 863
SHOW ERRORS command, 264
SQL*Plus, 474-475
SHOWPAGE procedure, OWA_UTIL
package, 774-775
SIGN function, 155
SIGNAL procedure, DBMS_ALERT
package, 641-642
Signature model, 274-275

Signature subprogram, OWA_UTIL package, 743, 757
Simple loops, 8, 67-69
   cursor fetch loops, 217-219
SIN function, 155-156
Single-line comments, 38, 917
Single-row functions, 130
SINH function, 156
SIZES procedure, 866-867
SLEEP procedure, DBMS_LOCK package, 901
Snapshot Refresh (SNP) process, 858
SNP processes, DBMS_JOB package, 700-701
SORT_LIST parameter, CREATE_QUEUE_TABLE procedure, 670
SOUNDEX function, 139-140
Source code, data dictionary views, 951-952
Source tables, 538-539
Spaghetti code, 74
SPELCHEK.SQL file, 193
SPELL function, 192-193
SQL%ISOPEN statement, 217
SQL%NOTFOUND statement, 216-217
SQL%ROWCOUNT statement, 215-216
SQL*DBA, SERVEROUTPUT option, 520
SQL*Net listener, 781
   configuring, 784-787
   extproc processes and, 782
   starting, 786-787
SQL*Plus, 468-475
   bind variables, 472-473
   block manipulation, 469
   EXECUTE command, 473
   file manipulation, 474
   SERVEROUTPUT option, 520-521
   SHOW ERRORS command, 474-475
   substitution variables, 470-472
SQL built-in functions, 130-201
   character functions returning character values, 131-143
   character functions returning numeric values, 143-147
   conversion functions, 165-177
   date functions, 158-165
   explained, 130-131
   group functions, 177-182
   miscellaneous functions, 183-192
   numeric functions, 147-158
   See also Functions
SQL cursors (implicit cursors), 215-217, 932
SQL scripts
   executing with SQL-Station, 489
   update cascade utility, 342-346
SQL statements, 24, 98-100, 932

categories of, 98, 99
executing in external procedures, 807-808
executing using DBMS_SQL, 551-556
execution plans for, 867-876
parsing, 592-594, 861
performance and tuning, 867-876
shared pools and, 861
static vs. dynamic, 550-551
using stored functions in, 297-303
SQL within Oracle PL/SQL, 98-127
   categories of statements, 98, 99
   DML statements, 98, 99, 100-114
   privileges, 118-122
   pseudocolumns, 114-117
   SQL statements, 98-100
   transaction controls, 122-127
sqlca.sqlcode status variable, 481
SQLCODE function, 932
   OTHERS exception handler, 364-368
SQLERRM function, 932
   OTHERS exception handler, 364-368
SQL-Station, 486-489
   breakpoints, 540-541, 542
   calling a stored procedure, 488-489
   Coder tool, 487-488, 775-776
   components in, 487
   debugging with, 537-542
   executing SQL scripts, 489
   Plan Analyzer component, 873-875
   Procedure Builder compared to, 543
SQRT function, 156-157
STANDARD package, 42, 82, 932-933
START_QUEUE procedure, DBMS_AQADM package, 675
START_TIME_MANAGER procedure, DBMS_AQADM package, 677
Statements, 933
   See also names of specific statements
Static cursors, 227
Static vs. dynamic SQL, 550-551
STDDEV function, 181
STEP_ID function, DBMS_TRANSACTION package, 908
STOP instructions, 632
STOP_QUEUE procedure, DBMS_AQADM package, 675-676
STOP_TIME_MANAGER procedure, DBMS_AQADM package, 677
Storage
   allocating for cursor variables, 230-231
   LOB data, 817-818, 819

See also Memory
STORAGE_ERROR exception, 359, 933
Store tables, 439-440
Stored functions
   using in SQL statements, 297-303
   See also Functions
Stored procedures
   calling with SQL-Station, 488-489
   client procedures vs., 491
   EXECUTE command, 473
   PL/SQL Editor with, 494
   See also Procedures
Stored subprograms, 263-266
   local subprograms vs., 269, 270
   privileges and, 275-278
   roles and, 278-280
   See also Subprograms
Stored varrays, 447-449
STRING datatype, 796-797
String literals, 36
STRONG tag, 749
Structured Query Language (SQL), 2
StudentObj type, 398, 399, 407
students table, 14-15
   tables8.sql script and, 401
student_sequence sequence, 14, 725
Style guidelines, 75-79
   for capitalization, 78
   for comments, 76-77
   for functions, 260-261
   for indentation, 78-79
   for variable names, 77
SUBMIT procedure, DBMS_JOB package, 702-706
Subprograms, 24, 242-281
   data dictionary and, 263-266
   in DBMS_AQADM package, 657
   DBMS_AQADM package, 657, 668-677
   DBMS_AQ package, 657, 665-667
   debug versions of, 538
   dependencies of, 269-275
   exceptions raised in, 261-262
   functions as, 257-261
   in HTP and HTF packages, 742
   local, 266-269, 270
   overloading packaged, 289-292
   privileges and, 275-278
   procedures as, 243-256
   roles and, 278-280
   stored, 263-266, 270
   See also Functions; Procedures
Subscribers, queue, 676-677
SUBSCRIPT_BEYOND_COUNT exception, 931
SUBSCRIPT_OUTSIDE_LIMIT exception, 931-932
Substitution variables, SQL*Plus, 470-472
SUBSTR function, 140-141
   DBMS_LOB package, 843-844

SUBSTRB function, 141-142
Subtypes, 43
    BINARY_INTEGER, 45
    constrained, 45
    NUMBER, 43-44
    user-defined, 52-53
    See also Types
SUM function, 181-182
Supplied packages. *See* Built-in
    packages
Supporting types, DBMS_AQ
    package, 656-665
Synonyms, DML statements, 113-114
Syntax
    for blocks, 916
    checking with the wrapper,
        499-500
    for creating functions, 258-259
    for creating procedures, 243-244
    for creating triggers, 319-320
    for defining record types, 83
    for defining table types, 86-87
    for dropping procedures and
        functions, 262-263
    for IF-THEN-ELSE statements,
        63-65
    for variable declarations, 40-41
SYS.AQ$_AGENT type, DBMS_AQ
    package, 656
SYSDATE function, 162-163
System control statements, 98
System Monitor (SMON) process, 858
System privileges
    object privileges vs., 118
    predefined, 122

T

TABLE ACCESS operations, 876
Table attributes, 90-94
    COUNT, 90-91
    DELETE, 91-92
    EXISTS, 92
    FIRST and LAST, 92-93
    NEXT and PRIOR, 93-94
Table column information, data
    dictionary, 954-956
Table references, DML statements,
    112
TableDemo procedure, 755-756
tables8.sql script, 401, 435
Tables, 86-95, 933
    arrays compared to, 87-89
    attributes of, 90-94
    data dictionary information on,
        952-954
    formatting for HTML, 755-756
    guidelines for using, 94-95
    nested, 434-444, 926
    source and destination, 538-539
    store, 439-440
    syntax for defining, 86-87

test, 506-516
    See also Records
tables.sql script, 4, 14, 26
TAN function, 157
TANH function, 157-158
TELETYPE HTML tag, 750-751
TempInsert procedure, 704-705
Temporary table, 506
temp_table table, 21
Testing and debugging, 504-547
    DBMS_OUTPUT package,
        517-529
    inserting into test tables, 506-516
    problem diagnosis, 504-506
    Procedure Builder for, 530-537,
        543
    programming methodologies,
        543-547
    SQL-Station for, 537-542, 543
Text strings, printing numbers as,
    192-201
TEXT_IO package, 709
THE operator, nested tables, 444
Third-generation languages (3GLs), 2
Time manager, 655
    starting and stopping, 677
TIMEOUT_ON_RESOURCE
    exception, 933
Timestamp model, 273-274
TKPROF utility, 869-873
    sort options, 872
tnsnames.ora file, 785
TO_CHAR conversion function, 54
    for date conversions, 169-171
    for label conversions, 171-172
    for numeric conversions, 172-174
TO_DATE function, 54, 175
TO_LABEL function, 175
TO_MULTI_BYTE function, 176
TO_NUMBER function, 54, 176
TOO_MANY_ROWS exception, 933
Top-down design, 545-546
TO_SINGLE_BYTE function, 177
Transaction control statements, 98
TRANSACTION_BACKED_OUT
    exception, 934
Transactions, 122-127
    blocks compared to, 126-127
    COMMIT vs. ROLLBACK,
        123-124
    distributed, 113
    SAVEPOINT commands, 125-126
    See also DBMS_TRANSACTION
        package
Transient objects, 417-420
TRANSLATE function, 142
Trigger column information, data
    dictionary, 958
Triggers, 25, 318-351, 934
    components of, 320-324
    creating, 318-332
    data dictionary views and,
        324-326, 956-957

    disabling of roles in, 280
    dropping and disabling, 324-325
    firing, 318, 326
    instead-of, 322-323
    mutating tables, 334-340
    naming, 320-321
    :old and :new pseudorecords,
        328-332
    order of firing, 326-328
    p-code, 325-326
    predicates, 332-333
    restrictions on, 323-324
    row-level, 328-332
    shared pools and, 862-863
    syntax for creating, 319-320
    types of, 321-322
    update cascade utility, 340-351
    views, 324
    WHEN clause and, 331-332
TRIM collection method, 457-459
TRIM routine, DBMS_LOB package,
    845
TRUNC function
    as date function, 163-165
    as numeric function, 158
Trusted family, 50
Tuning performance. *See*
    Performance and tuning
%TYPE attribute, 51-52, 934
    object types and, 411
    procedure parameters and,
        250-251
Types, 42-58, 918
    composite, 50
    converting between, 53-55, 165
    LOB, 51, 816-852, 924
    object, 399-417
    overview, 7-8
    PL/SQL vs. C, 792-796
    reference, 50-51
    scalar, 43-50
    %TYPE attribute, 51-52
    user-defined subtypes, 52-53
    variable scope and visibility,
        56-58
    See also Subtypes

U

uc.sql script, 342-343
UID function, 188-189
Unconstrained cursor variables, 229
Unhandled exceptions, 382
unindex.sql script, 345-346
Uninitialized variables, 41
UNIQUE_SESSION_ID function,
    DBMS_SESSION package, 904-905
UNIQUE_SESSION_NAME function,
    631
Unix systems, 783, 784
UNKEEP procedure, 866
Unordered lists, 746

UNPACK_MESSAGE procedure, 627
Unregistering for alerts, 645
Update cascade utility, 340-351
    contents of, 342-346
    features supported by, 341
    how it works, 347-351
    restrictions on, 341-342
UPDATE statements, 106-107,
  934-935
    nested tables, 441-442
    objects, 421-422
    :old and :new pseudorecords,
      330
    RETURNING clause, 426
    triggers, 321-322
UpdateClasses procedure, 563-564
UpdateMajorStats trigger, 321
UPPER function, 143
user_* views, data dictionary, 939-958
USER function, 189-190
User process, 857, 858
User queues, 655
User-defined exceptions, 356-357
User-defined functions, purity levels
  for, 297-303
User-defined subtypes, 52-53
USER_DUMP_DEST parameter, 870
USERENV function, 190, 191
USERID precompiler option, 481-482
user_jobs view, 708
user_queues view, 680-681
user_queue_tables view, 680
user_source data dictionary view, 498
user_triggers view, 324
UtilDemo procedure, 759-760
UTL_FILE package, 709-729, 911
    database security, 710-711
    Debug package, 720-722
    examples, 720-729
    exceptions raised by, 712, 713
    FCLOSE function, 714-715
    FCLOSE_ALL function, 715
    FFLUSH procedure, 719
    file input, 719-720
    file output, 716-719
    FOPEN function, 712, 714
    GET_LINE procedure, 719-720
    IS_OPEN function, 715
    LoadStudents procedure, 722-725
    NEW_LINE procedure, 716-717
    opening and closing files,
      712-715
    operating system security,
      711-712
    PrintTranscript procedure, 725
    PUT procedure, 716
    PUTF procedure, 718-719
    PUT_LINE procedure, 717
    security, 709-712
    used by Export package, 303-304
    writing LONG datatypes to files
      with, 609

utlxplan.sql file, 868

v$sesstat view, 864
v$statname view, 864
VALUE operator, 424-425
VALUE_ERROR exception, 359-360,
  935
VARCHAR2 datatype, 45-46
Variable declarations, 39-41
    declaration syntax, 40-41
    variable initialization, 41
Variable names
    recommended style for, 77
    WHERE clauses, 108-109
Variable-length values, 111
Variables, 935
    bind, 472-473, 555, 559
    cursor, 227-237, 918
    defined, 39
    host, 476-477
    indicator, 478-480
    naming, 77
    overview, 7-8
    scope and visibility of, 56-58
    substitution, 470-472
    syntax for declaring, 40-41
    uninitialized, 41
    See also Input variables; Output
      variables
VARIABLE_VALUE procedure, 556,
  579-580
    parameters, 580
VARIANCE function, 182
Varrays, 445-450, 935
    collection methods, 450-461
    declaring, 445-447
    initializing, 445-446
    manipulating elements in,
      446-447
    nested tables compared to,
      449-450
    storing in the database, 447-449
View information, data dictionary,
  958-959
Views
    data dictionary, 939, 940, 959
    data dictionary subprogram,
      263-266
    data dictionary triggers, 324-326
    DBMS_JOB package, 708
    queue table, 678-680
    session memory usage, 864-865
Visibility, variable, 56-58
VSIZE function, 190, 192

WAITANY procedure, DBMS_ALERT
  package, 643-644
WAITONE procedure, DBMS_ALERT
  package, 642-643
Web application server. *See* Oracle
  WebServer
Web listener, 733
Web request broker (WRB) interface,
  734, 736
Web toolkit, 739-773
    HTP and HTF packages, 740-756
    OWA_COOKIE package,
      769-773
    OWA_IMAGE package, 767-769
    OWA_UTIL package, 757-766
    supplied packages in, 740
    See also Oracle WebServer
WHAT procedure, DBMS_JOB
  package, 708
WHEN clauses
    exception handlers, 363
    triggers, 331-332
WHERE clauses, 108-112
    character compositions, 110-112
    nested tables and, 443
    testing and debugging, 513
    variable names, 108-109
WHERE CURRENT OF clause,
  224-225
WHILE loops, 69-70
    cursor fetch loops, 219-221
WITH CONTEXT clause, wrapper
  procedure, 790
WORK keyword, 123-124
Wrapper, 498-500
    checking syntax with, 499-500
    guidelines for, 500
    input and output files, 499
    running, 498-499
Wrapper procedures
    creating, 789-791
    in packages, 802
WRB dispatcher, 734
WRB executable engines (WRBX), 734
WRB (web request broker) interface,
  734
    CGI interface compared to, 736
WRITE routine, DBMS_LOB package,
  846
Writers, DBMS_PIPE package, 618,
  619-622
Writing
    granting permission for, 712
    LONG datatypes to files, 608-611

ZERO_DIVIDE exception, 391, 935

Oracle Education[SM]
Is Your Source...

...for the most comprehensive selection of quality training available for Oracle products and related IT technologies.

Media-Based Training: A variety of structured, self-paced courses deliverable to any desktop in your organization

Instructor-Led Training: In-depth knowledge, hands-on experience and personal guidance from expert instructors

Oracle Learning Architecture: Internet-based training providing immediate access to interactive, hands-on training straight from the Web

The Oracle Channel: Live, interactive training broadcast via satellite, ideal for expert-level technical drilldowns or broad overviews

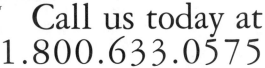

Organizational Change Management: Maximizing your technology investment with organizational assessment, change management plans and total learning solutions

Oracle Education works closely with Oracle software developers to provide you with the most **up-to-date and cost-effective training options** as new products are released. For more information, call **1.800.633.0575** for your copy of the *Oracle Education Americas Schedule and Catalog.*

Call us today at
1.800.633.0575
or 301.657.7819 from outside the U.S.

You can also learn more about our offerings by visiting Oracle Education on the Web at **http://www.oracle.com** or by calling EASI InfoFax at **1.800.405.6336.**

ORACLE®
Enabling the Information Age™

Get Your FREE Subscription to Oracle Magazine

Stay informed and increase your productivity with every issue of *Oracle Magazine*. Inside each FREE, bimonthly issue, you'll get:

- Up-to-date information on the Oracle RDBMS and software tools
- Third-party software and hardware products
- Technical articles on Oracle platforms and operating environments
- Software tuning tips
- Oracle client application stories

Three easy ways to subscribe:

1 **MAIL:** Cut out this page, complete the questionnaire on the back, and mail to: *Oracle Magazine,* 500 Oracle Parkway, Box 659952, Redwood Shores, CA 94065.

2 **FAX:** Cut out this page, complete the questionnaire on the back, and and fax the questionnaire to **+ 415.633.2424.**

3 **WEB:** Visit our Web site at **www.oramag.com.** You'll find a subscription form there, plus much more!

If there are other Oracle users at your location who would like to receive their own copy of *Oracle Magazine,* please photocopy the form on the back, and pass it along.

☐ YES! Please send me a FREE subscription to <u>Oracle Magazine</u>. ☐ NO, I am not interested at this time.

If you wish to receive your free bimonthly subscription to *Oracle Magazine*, you must fill out the entire form, sign it, and date it (incomplete forms cannot be processed or acknowledged). You can also subscribe at our Web Site at **http://www.oramag.com/html/subform.html** or fax your application to *Oracle Magazine* at **+415.633.2424.**

SIGNATURE (REQUIRED) ✓   **DATE**

NAME _____ TITLE _____

COMPANY _____

STREET/P.O. BOX _____

CITY/STATE/ZIP _____

COUNTRY _____ TELEPHONE _____

You must answer all eight of the questions below.

1 What is the primary business activity of your firm at this location?
(circle only one)
01. Agriculture, Mining, Natural Resources
02. Communications Services, Utilities
03. Computer Consulting, Training
04. Computer, Data Processing Service
05. Computer Hardware, Software, Systems
06. Education—Primary, Secondary, College, University
07. Engineering, Architecture, Construction
08. Financial, Banking, Real Estate, Insurance
09. Government—Federal/Military
10. Government—Federal/Nonmilitary
11. Government—Local, State, Other
12. Health Services, Health Institutions
13. Manufacturing—Aerospace, Defense
14. Manufacturing—Noncomputer Products, Goods
15. Public Utilities (Electric, Gas, Sanitation)
16. Pure and Applied Research & Development
17. Retailing, Wholesaling, Distribution
18. Systems Integrator, VAR, VAD, OEM
19. Transportation
20. Other Business and Services ____

2 Which of the following best describes your job function? *(circle only one)*
CORPORATE MANAGEMENT/STAFF
01. Executive Management (President, Chair, CEO, CFO, Owner, Partner, Principal, Managing Director)
02. Finance/Administrative Management (VP/Director/Manager/Controller of Finance, Purchasing, Administration)
03. Other Finance/Administration Staff
04. Sales/Marketing Management (VP/Director/Manager of Sales/Marketing)
05. Other Sales/Marketing Staff ____
TECHNICAL MANAGEMENT/STAFF
06. Computer/Communications Systems Development/Programming Management

07. Computer/Communications Systems Development/Programming Staff
08. Computer Systems/Operations Management (CIO/VP/Director/Manager MIS, Operations, etc.)
09. Consulting
10 DBA/Systems Administrator
11. Education/Training
12. Engineering/R&D/Science Management
13. Engineering/R&D/Science Staff
14. Technical Support Director/Manager
15. Other Technical Management/Staff
_____

3 What is your current primary operating system environment?
(circle all that apply)
01. AIX
02. HP-UX
03. Macintosh OS
04. MPE-ix
05. MS-DOS
06. MVS
07. NetWare
08. OpenVMS
09. OS/2
10. OS/400
11. SCO
12. Solaris/Sun OS
13. SVR4
14. Ultrix
15. UnixWare
16. Other UNIX
17. VAX VMS
18. VM
19. Windows
20. Windows NT
21. Other ____

4 What is your current primary hardware environment? *(circle all that apply)*
01. Macintosh
02. Mainframe
03. Massively Parallel Processing
04. Minicomputer
05. PC (IBM-Compatible)
06. Supercomputer
07. Symmetric Multiprocessing
08. Workstation
09. Other ____

5 In your job, do you use or plan to purchase any of the following products or services
(check all that apply)
SOFTWARE

	Use	Plan to buy
01. Accounting/Finance	☐	☐
02. Business Graphics	☐	☐
03. CAD/CAE/CAM	☐	☐
04. CASE	☐	☐
05. CIM	☐	☐
06. Communications/Networking	☐	☐
07. Database Management	☐	☐
08. Education	☐	☐
09. File Management	☐	☐
10. GIS	☐	☐
11. Image Processing	☐	☐
12. Laboratory Control	☐	☐
13. Materials Resource Planning (MRP, MRP II)	☐	☐
14. Multimedia Authoring Tools	☐	☐
15. Office Automation	☐	☐
16. Order Entry/Inventory Control	☐	☐
17. Programming/Systems Development	☐	☐
18. Project Management	☐	☐
19. Scientific and Engineering	☐	☐
20. Spreadsheets/Financial Planning	☐	☐
21. Systems Management Products	☐	☐
22. Workflow	☐	☐

HARDWARE

	Use	Plan to buy
23. Macintosh	☐	☐
24. Mainframe	☐	☐
25. Massively Parallel Processing	☐	☐
26. Minicomputer	☐	☐
27. PC (IBM-Compatible)	☐	☐
28. Supercomputer	☐	☐
29. Symmetric Multiprocessing	☐	☐
30. Workstation	☐	☐

PERIPHERALS

	Use	Plan to buy
31. Bridges/Routers/Hubs/Gateways	☐	☐
32. CD-ROM Drives	☐	☐
33. Disk Drives/Subsystems	☐	☐
34. Tape Drives/Subsystems	☐	☐
35. Video Boards/Other Multimedia Peripherals	☐	☐

NETWORK/COMMUNICATIONS

	Use	Plan to buy
36. Communications Controllers	☐	☐
37. Local Area Networks	☐	☐
38. Modems	☐	☐
39. Wide Area Networks	☐	☐

SERVICES

	Use	Plan to buy
40. Computer-Based Training	☐	☐
41. Education/Training	☐	☐
42. Maintenance	☐	☐
43. Online Database Services	☐	☐
44. Support	☐	☐
45. **None of the above**	☐	☐

6 What Oracle products are in use at your site? *(circle all that apply)*
SERVERS
01. Oracle7
02. Oracle Media Server
03. Oracle7 Workgroup Server
04. Personal Oracle7
05. Oracle Rdb
TOOLS
06. Designer/2000 (CASE)
07. Developer/2000 (CDE, Forms, Reports, Graphics)
08. Oracle Media Objects
09. Oracle Power Objects
APPLICATIONS
10. Oracle Financials
11. Oracle Human Resources
12. Oracle Manufacturing
13. Other ____
14. **None of the above**

7 What other database products are in use at your site? *(circle all that apply)*
01. CA-Ingres
02. DB2
03. DB2/2
04. DB2/6000
05. dbase
06. Gupta
07. IMS
08. Informix
09. Microsoft Access
10. Microsoft SQL Server
11. Progress
12. Sybase System 10
13. Sybase System 11
14. Sybase SQL Server
15. VSAM
16. Other ____
17. SAP
18. Peoplesoft
19. BAAN
20. **None of the above**

8 During the next 12 months, how much do you anticipate your organization will spend on computer hardware, software, peripherals, and services for your location? *(circle only one)*
01. Less than $10,000
02. $10,000 to $49,999
03. $50,000 to $99,999
04. $100,000 to $499,999
05. $500,000 to $999,999
06. $1,000,000 and over

OMG

License Terms
for Oracle Software

Global License Terms

Enabling the Information Age™

العربية/المملكة العربية السعودية

تنبيه: بمجرد فتح هذا المغلف أو استعمال البرامج الموجودة داخله، فإن الشروط التالية سوف تخضع للتطبيق تلقائيا. وإذا وجدت أن البرامج أو هذه الشروط غير مقبولة لـك، أعد البرامج خـلال ثلاثـون (٣٠) يوما إلى الشركة التي استلمت البرامج منها لاسترداد نقودك.

إن شركة أوراكل السعودية (أوراكل) تمنحك (بصفتك العميل) ترخيصا لاستعمال البرامج المرفقة والوثائق (البرامج) المشار إليها أدناه.

الترخيص: للعميل الحق في إستعمال البرامج ضمن حدود المنطقة في إطار بيئة التشغيل المعرفة من قبل أوراكل. أما (أ) إلى المدى المحدد في وثيقة الطلبية أو شهادة إستخدام الـبرامج التي يحصل العميل عليها مـن أوراكل أو موزعيها أو (ب) إذا ـ يحدد هذا المدى فتستخدم لمستعمل واحد على جهاز كمبيوتر واحد. ويجوز للعميل أن يستخدم البرامج حصريا لعملياته الداخلية في معالجة البيانات ويمكن للعميل أن يستنسـخ نسخة واحدة من كل برنامج مرخص على سبيل الاحتياط. ويمكن تضمين ما يفيد حقوق عمل نسخ إضافية في وثيقة الطلبية أو شهادة إستخدام البرامج. لن يتم عمل أية نسخ أخرى إلا بموافقة أوراكل الخطية المسبقة. يلتزم العميل بعدم (أ) إزالة أي تعريف للمنتج أو ملصقات حقوق الطبع أو أية ملاحظات أخرى و قيود ملكية على البرامج أو (ب) إستعمال البرامج لأغراض المشاركة التجارية أو الإيجار أو لاستعمالات مكتب خدمات أو (ج) نقل ملكية أو بيع أو التنازل أو خلاف ذلك إحالة البرامج إلى طرف آخر بدون موافقة أوراكل الخطية المسبقة أو (د) التسبب أو السماح بعمليات الهندسة الإرتجاعية أو العكسية أو حل البرامج أو (هـ) الكشف عن نتائج أية اختبارات لأي برنامج لأي طرف آخر بدون الموافقة الخطية المسبقة لشركة أوراكل. تخضع كافة عمليات نقل البرامج لأنظمة النقل ورسوم النقل المعتمدة من قبل أوراكل. ويحق للعميل أن يستعمل من البرامج الموجودة في هذا المغلف فقط البرامج المحددة في وثيقة الطلبية أو شهادة إستخدام البرامج.

حقوق الطبع/ ملكية البرامج: تعتبر هذه البرامج ملكية خاصة لشركة أوراكل وفي فهي محمية بقانون حقوق الطبع وحقوق الملكية الفكرية الأخرى. يكتسب العميل فقط حق إستعمال البرامج ولا يعطي ذلك أية حقوق، صريحة كانت أو ضمنية، في البرامج أو البيانات التي تشكل البرامج بخلاف ما هو محدد في هذا الترخيص. وتحتفظ أوراكل أو حامل ترخيصها في كافة الأوقات بكل الحقوق والملكية والمصالح، بما في ذلك حقوق الملكية الفكرية في البرامج والبيانات.

ضمانات محدودة/العلاجات الحصرية: تضمن أوراكل لمدة تسعين (٩٠) يوماً من تاريخ التسليم إلى العميل (أ) خلو البيانات الموجودة في العميل من عيوب المواد والمصنعية تحت الإستخدام الإعتيادي و (ب) تأدية البـرامج غير المعدلة بصورة جوهرية للوظائف الموصوفة في الوثائق المزودة من قبل أوراكل عند تشغيل هذه البرامج على الكمبيوتر ونظام التشغيل المخصصين. بالمقابل، لا تضمن أوراكل أن البرامج سوف تفي بمتطلبـات العميل أو أن البرامج سوف تعمل في التوليفات أو التشكيلات التي قد يختارها العميل أو تشغيل البرامج لن يتعطل و يعمل بدون أخطاء أو أن كافة أخطاء البرامج سوف يتم إصلاحها. إن هـذه الضمانات هـي ضمانات حصرية وتحل محل كافة الضمانات والشروط الأخرى، سواء كانت صريحة أو ضمنية، بموجب القانون أو خلاف، بما في ذلك الضمانات الضمنية لقابلية التسويقية أو ملاءمتها لغرض محدد. وإذا أبلغ العميل عن أي خطأ في برنامج ما خلال فترة التسعين (٩٠) يوم، فسوف تقوم أوراكل حسب خيارها، إما بإصلاح الخطأ أو إعطاء العميل طريقة معقولة لحصر الخطأ أو إعادة رسوم الترخيص مقابل تسلمها للبرامج من العميل. أما فيما يخص أي بيانات معيبة، فإن أوراكل تلتزم باستبدالها بدون مقابل إذا أعيد ذلك إلى أوراكل خلال فترة التسعين (٩٠) يوم. إن العلاجات أعلاه تشكل العلاجات الحصرية والوحيدة التي يحصل عليها العميل لأي خرق للضمان. وبموجب هذا الضمان المحدود، فإن العميل يحصل على حقوق قانونية محددة.

تحديد المسئولية: لن تكون أوراكل مسئولة عن أية أضرار غير مباشرة أو عرضية أو خاصة أو إستتباعية أو أية أضرار عن خسارة الإنتاج أو الإيرادات أو البيانات أو إستعمالات البيانات التي يتكبدها العميل أو أي طرف آخر سواء في إجراء تعاقدي أو شخصي، حتى وإن إبلاغ أوراكل عن أي شخص آخر باحتمالية هذه الأضرار. إن مسئولية أوراكل عن الأضرار تزيد بأي حال من الأحوال عن الرسوم التي يدفعها العميل نظير هذا الترخيص.

المنطقة: تعني المنطقة المملكة العربية السعودية ما ـ يحدد خلاف ذلك في وثيقة الطلبية أو شهادة إستخدام البرامج.

على العميل أن يتقيد تماما بكافة قوانين وأنظمة الولايات المتحدة الأمريكية والمملكة العربية السعودية (قوانين التصدير) بما يكفل له أن البرامج وأية منتجات مباشرة لها (١) لا يتم تصديرها بطريقة مباشرة أو غير مباشرة بصورة تشكل إنتهاكا لقوانين التصدير أو (٢) لا تستعمل في أي غرض محظور بموجب قوانين التصدير، بما يشمل و لا يقتصر على إنتشار الأسلحة الذرية أو الكيماوية أو الجرثومية. تخضع هـذه الإتفاقية وكافة الإجراءات المتعلقة بها لقوانين المملكة العربية السعودية. ويجوز لشركة أوراكل أن تتحرى وتدقق في إستعمالات العميل للبرامج. إن هذا الترخيص ينسخ كافة شروط أية طلبية شراء للعميل أو أية طلبية أخرى للعميل.

تعريفات شهادة إستخدام البرامج:
الوسائل المعاصرة/الدخوليات المعاصرة: أقصى عدد من وسائل الإدخال التي ستدخل على البرامج في أية نقطة زمنية. وفي حالة إستعمال تجمع من البرامج أو الأجهزة (على سبيل المثال شاشة تي يه) فإن هذا العدد يجب أن يحتسب في طرف مقدمة التجمع.

العميل: جهاز كمبيوتر واحد (١) يستخدم من قبل شخص واحد في ذات الوقت (و (٢) يطبق برامج أوراكل في ذاكرة علية أو يخزن البرامج على جهاز تخزين علي.

المستعمل: فرد مصرح له من قبل العميل باستخدام البرامج بصرف النظر عما إذا كان هذا المستعمل يستخدم هذه البرامج بصورة فعالة في أي زمن بعد.

صندوق البريد: النقطة التي يرسل منها أو يستقبل فيها البريد الإلكتروني. ويتم تأسيس صندوق البريد بمجرد فتح حساب أو إنشاء تطبيق للعميل في مكتب أوراكل.

中文 / 中国

ORACLE 公司程序使用许可条款

注意: 如果您打开这个软件包或使用包内的软件, 下列条款将适用于您. 如果本软件或下列条款令您无法接受, 敬请于三十日内将本软件退回于所出售之公司, 以得到退款.

ORACLE公司或其分支机构(简称"ORACLE")基于下述条件授予您(简称"用户")使用本软件及相关资料(简称"程序")之许可证.

许可证: 用户有权在ORACLE认可的操作环境下使用本程序. 该环境包括: (A) 已在 ORACLE或其分销商发给用户的订购文件或程序使用证中特别指定; 或 (B) 如果不存在前述指定, 则适用于单机之单个用户. 用户只能为自己的内部数据处理系统而使用该程序. 对每个获得使用许可的程序, 用户可以复制一个备份; 如需更多复制件, 则应在订购文件或程序使用证中载明. 未获 ORACLE 事先书面许可, 不能制作第二份以上复制品. 用户不得: (A)去掉程序上的产品识别标识、版权告示或 其它告示及 专用权限制说明等; (B) 为商业性计时使用、租赁或服务机构而使用本程序; (C)未经 ORACLE 事先书面许可将程序转让、出售、分配或以其它方式转移给第三人; (D)放任或允许对本程序的转换加工、拆装或 反编译; 或 (E)未经ORACLE事先书面批准将程序的对比测验结果披露于第三人. 所有的程序转让都必须遵循ORACLE 的转让政策和费用. 用户只被授权在订购文件或程序使用证中表明的条件下使用包内的程序.

程序的著作权 / 所有权: 本程序是ORACLE拥有产权之产品, 受著作权法及其它知识产权法的保护. 用户只获得了使用本程序之权利, 而没用对程序或包含程序之媒体通过明示或默示方式获得超出上述许可证表明权利之外的任何其它权利. ORACLE或其许可人将永远保有对程序和媒体的各种权利、所有权和利益, 包括知识产权.

有限保证 / 单一补偿: 从程序送至用户之日起 90 天内, ORACLE保证: (A)所提供之媒体在正常使用状态下没有材料和工艺方面的缺陷, 和 (B) 未经改动的程序在指定的计算机和操作系统内, 将完全按照ORACLE说明文件中描述的功能执行.

ORACLE将不保证: 本程序将完全满足客户的各种要求. 本程序将在客户选择使用的组合系统内顺利运行, 程序的运行将不出现中断、错误或者所有程序错误都被纠正. 这些保证是唯一的、排他的, 将取代所有其他明示或默示

保证，包括销售商的默示保证或适于特定目的之保证．如果用户在90天内指出了程序中的错误，ORACLE将根据实际情况或者帮助用户纠正错误，或者向用户提供一个可以克服错误的合理程序，或者允许用户退货，由公司退款．如果用户在90天内将有问题的软件媒体退还，ORACLE将负责免费更换．上述措施是ORACLE不能履行前述保证义务时的唯一的和排他的补偿方式．这个有限保证赋予用户某些特定法律权利，用户可能享有其他权利，但将因国家而异．

责任限制：ORACLE将不对用户或任何第三人所遭受的任何间接的、突发的、特别的或持续的损害，或者因利润、收入、数据或数据使用损失所引起之损害负责，无论该损害属于违反合同性质还是侵权性质，即使事先向ORACLE咨询过发生该种损害之可能性亦不例外．ORACLE对所有损害之赔偿责任将不超过用户所支付之使用许可费．

权利限制：用户应全面遵守美国和其他国家的所有法律、法规 (简称"出口法")，确保本程序及其直接产品：(1)在出口过程中不直接或间接违反出口法；或(2)不被用于任何出口法所禁止之目的，包括但不限于原子、化学或生物武器等扩散．本许可证及其相关活动将适用美国加利福尼亚州法例．ORACLE有权检查、监督用户对程序的使用．用户订购单或其它用户订购文件中列明的各种条款将全部被本许可证取代．

程序使用证之定义：

并行设备 / 并行访问：在特定时刻运行该程序的输入设备的最大数目．如果使用复合软件或者硬件 (例如TP监视器)，该输入设备的最大数目必须在其终端前测定．

客户机：一台计算机：(1)在特定时刻只被一人使用；和 (2)在本地存储系统中运行ORACLE公司的软件或在本地存储器中储存该软件．

使用人：由用户授权使用程序的人，无论该人在特定时间是否积极使用该程序．

邮件信箱：收发电子邮件的节点，该信箱通过使用人在ORACLE中心网络的开户或开户申请所创建．

中文／台灣

Ｏｒａｃｌｅ程式授權條款

注意：如果你打開這個包裝或使用包裝內的軟體，以下條款
　　　將予適用。如果軟體或這些條款不能為您所接受，
　　　請於３０日內將本軟體退還本公司，您將獲得退款。

Ｏｒａｃｌｅ公司或其子公司（`Ｏｒａｃｌｅ´）授權您（`顧客´）使
用包裝內軟體及文件（`程式´）之權利，詳述如下。

授權：顧客擁有在由Ｏｒａｃｌｅ如下所認定的操作環境中使用程
式的權利，（ａ）於訂貨文件或由Ｏｒａｃｌｅ或其經銷商給予顧客
的「程式使用證」之記載範圍內，或（ｂ）如果未記載，其使用
範圍以在單一電腦上為單一使用者所使用為限。顧客僅能為
其自身內部資料進行操作而使用本程式。顧客可以就每一個
經授權之程式做一份拷貝為備份，或按訂貨文件或程式使用
證之記載而為另外的拷貝。若無Ｏｒａｃｌｅ事先書面同意，顧客
不得為其他拷貝。顧客並不得：（ａ）自程式除去任何產品之辨
認型號、著作權之通知、其他通知、或與使用權利有關之限
制；（ｂ）將程式按時間分配由多人為商業性使用、出租，或做
為服務站使用；（ｃ）無Ｏｒａｃｌｅ事先書面同意，而將程式轉讓
或出賣給任何他人；（ｄ）致使或允許程式的反工程、分解或解
碼；或（ｅ）在未得Ｏｒａｃｌｅ事先書面核准而洩露任何程式的任
何基準測試結果給第三人。所有程式的轉讓應依Ｏｒａｃｌｅ的轉
讓政策及其所訂費用辦理，顧客僅有依訂貨文件或程式使用
證之記載使用本包裝內軟體之權利。

程式著作權／所有權：程式係Ｏｒａｃｌｅ之專屬產品且為著作
權及其他智慧財產權法律所保護。顧客僅取得使用程式的權
利，且除了記載於本授權之權利外，無論明示或暗示，並不
取得程式中或含程式的媒介中之任何其他權利。Ｏｒａｃｌｅ或其
授權人在任何時間均保留所有權利及利益，包括程式中或其
媒介中的智慧財產權。

限制保證／惟一救濟：Ｏｒａｃｌｅ保證自交付顧客日起算９０日
內：（ａ）在正常使用下，內含的媒介在材質及手工並無瑕疵；
且（ｂ）如使用在指定的電腦及操作系統時，未修改的程式將執
行由Ｏｒａｃｌｅ提供之文件中所記載的功能。Ｏｒａｃｌｅ並不保證
：程式將符合顧客的要求，程式會與顧客所選擇使用之其他
程式合併執行，程式的執行是不中斷的或無錯誤的，或所有
程式錯誤將被更正。本授權所載保證是排他的且應取代所有
無論明示的或暗示的其他保證，包括一定商品品質之暗示保
證或為適合特定目的之暗示保證。若顧客在９０日內通知程式
中的錯誤，Ｏｒａｃｌｅ將依其選擇，改正錯誤，提供顧客一個合
理的程序以克服錯誤，或於顧客退還程式給Ｏｒａｃｌｅ後由其返
還授權費用。如顧客於９０日內歸還Ｏｒａｃｌｅ之任何有瑕疵之

媒介，Oracle將免費更換。上述保證係惟一且排他的救濟。本限制保證將給與您特別的法律權利，但您可能隨各州規定而有其他的權利。

責任限制：Oracle對顧客或任何第三人所生任何間接的、零星的、特別的或衍生的損害，或因利潤、收入、資料或資料使用損失所生之損害，無論係以契約訴訟或侵權訴訟方式為之，即使Oracle已經被告知此種損害的可能性，Oracle在本條款下之損害責任不得超過顧客為本授權所付的費用。

權利限制：送往美國國防部的程式係受限制的權利並適用下列規定，權利限制標示：政府使用、重製或公開係受目前技術資料及電腦軟體權利相關法令之規範，DFARS 252-227-7013(C)(1)(ii)(October 1988)。Oracle Corp. 500 Oracle Pkway., Redwood City, CA 94065。送往國防部以外的美國政府機關之一般資料權利見FAR 52.227-14之規定，包括依Alternate III(1987年6月版)定義而交付之〝限制權利〞。

顧客應遵守美國及其它國家的法律及規定（〝出口法律〞），以確保無論本程式或任何直接產品皆不會 出口時直接或間接地違反出口法律，或 為出口法律所禁止之任何目的所使用，包括（但不限於）為核子的、化學的或生化武器擴散之目的而使用之。本授權及所有相關行為應適用加州法律。Oracle可以稽核顧客對程式的使用。任何顧客的購買文件或其訂貨文件所載條款應為本授權所取代。

程式使用證之定義：

> 同步裝置／同步使用：在一定時間內使用程式，輸入設備的最大數量。如果使用多用途軟體或硬體（如：TP螢幕），這個數量必須在多數前端末點測量。

> 客戶：電腦一次僅由一個人使用，且在當地記憶體執行Oracle軟體或儲存軟於當地之儲存裝置。

> 使用者：由顧客授權使用程式的個人，不論此人是否於一定的時間內使用。

> 電子郵箱：電子信件發生或收受之點；當使用者之檔案或有關之申請業已建立於Oracle辦公室而產生。

Česky/Česka

PODMÍNKY LICENCE NA PROGRAM ORACLE

UPOZORNĚNÍ: PO OTEVŘENÍ BALENÍ NEBO POUŽITÍ PŘILOŽENÉHO SOFTWARU SE UPLATŇUJÍ NÁSLEDUJÍCÍ PODMÍNKY. POKUD NEBUDOU TYTO PODMÍNKY NEBO SOFTWARE PRO VÁS PŘIJATELNÉ, VRAŤTE SOFTWARE DO 30 DNŮ SPOLEČNOSTI, KTERÁ VÁM SOFTWARE DODALA. ČÁSTKA UHRAZENÁ ZA SOFTWARE VÁM BUDE NAVRÁCENA.

SPOLEČNOST ORACLE CZECH S.R.O. ("ORACLE") VÁM ("ZÁKAZNÍK") UDĚLUJE LICENCI NA POUŽITÍ PŘILOŽENÉHO SOFTWARU A DOKUMENTACE ("PROGRAMY") PODLE DÁLE UVEDENÝCH PODMÍNEK.

LICENCE: Zákazník je oprávněn používat program Oracle na Území pro operační prostředí definované společností Oracle, v rozsahu stanoveném v objednacím dokumentu Oracle nebo potvrzení o právu užívat program ("Povolení užívat"), které budou distribuovány zákazníkovi společností Oracle nebo jejím distributorem. Pokud nejsou v Povolení identifikována práva na použití, tato licence se uděluje jednomu uživateli pro jeden počítač. Zákazník smí používat programy výhradně pro interní zpracování dat. Zákazník má právo pořídit si jednu záložní kopii každého licencovaného programu; případná práva na další kopie musí být uvedena v každé objednávce nebo v Povolení užívat. Bez předchozího písemného souhlasu společnosti Oracle nemohou být pořizovány další kopie. Zákazník nesmí: 1. odstranit z programů žádné informace týkající se identifikace výrobku, autorských práv a omezení vlastnických práv anebo jiné informace; 2. používat Programy v obchodním provozu na počítači sdíleném s jinými subjekty, půjčovat programy nebo je používat v servisní kanceláři; 3. předávat, prodávat, postupovat nebo jiným způsobem převádět programy jiné straně bez předchozího písemného souhlasu společnosti Oracle; 4. zapříčinit nebo dovolit provedení technických změn na Programech, jejich demontáž nebo dekompilaci; 5. bez předchozího písemného souhlasu společnosti Oracle informovat o výsledcích výkonnostních testů jakéhokoliv Programu třetí stranu. Zákazník je oprávněn užívat pouze programy, které jsou v tomto balení a které jsou specifikovány v objednávacím dokumentu Oracle nebo v Povolení užívat.

Autorská práva/Vlastnictví programů: Programy jsou majetkem firmy Oracle a jsou chráněny zákonem o autorských právech a ostatními relevantními zákony. Zákazník nabývá pouze právo na použití Programů specifikovaných v této licenci, a nenabývá žádná vlastnická práva, explicitně ani implicitně, k Programům nebo nosičům Programů. Společnost Oracle nebo její zástupce udělující licenci si po celý čas podrží veškerá práva včetně autorských práv, vlastnictví a zájmy týkající se programů a příslušných médií.

Záruky/nároky z vad zboží: Společnost se zaručuje, že po dobu 90 dnů od data dodání Zákazníkovi: 1. se při běžném použití neprojeví na přiložených nosičích žádné závady z hlediska materiálu a provedené práce; a 2. Programy, na kterých nebudou provedeny žádné změny, budou v podstatě fungovat podle popisu v dokumentaci poskytnuté společností Oracle, pokud budou používány na určeném počítači a s určeným operačním systémem.

Společnost Oracle nezaručuje: - že programy budou splňovat požadavky Zákazníka; - že Programy budou fungovat v kombinaci s jinými programy podle výběru zákazníka; - že provoz Programu bude bez chyb a přerušení; - že veškeré chyby v programech budou opraveny. Tyto záruky jsou výhradní a nahrazují veškeré jiné záruky, ať už vyslovené nebo implicitní, včetně implicitních záruk prodejnosti nebo vhodnosti pro konkrétní použití. Jestliže Zákazník oznámí do devadesáti dnů závadu v Programech, společnost Oracle podle svého uvážení závadu opraví, nebo poskytne Zákazníkovi informaci o přiměřeném způsobu, jak závadu odstranit, anebo po vrácení Programů společností Oracle Zákazníkem mu refunduje poplatky za licenci. Společnost Oracle vymění bezplatně jakékoliv vadné nosiče, pokud jí budou vráceny do devadesáti dnů. Toto jsou jediné a výhradní nároky z vad zboží, které může Zákazník uplatňovat při jakémkoliv porušení záruky. Tato limitovaná záruka poskytuje Zákazníkovi určitá zákonná práva.

OMEZENÍ ODPOVĚDNOSTI: SPOLEČNOST ORACLE NENESE ODPOVĚDNOST ZA ŽÁDNÉ NEPŘÍMÉ NAHODILÉ SPECIÁLNÍ NEBO NÁSLEDNÉ ŠKODY NEBO ZA ŽÁDNÉ ŠKODY SPOJENÉ SE ZTRÁTOU ZISKU, PŘÍJMU, DAT NEBO Z POUŽITÍ DAT, KTERÉ VZNIKNOU ZÁKAZNÍKOVI NEBO JAKÉKOLIV TŘETÍ STRANĚ, AŤ JAKO VÝSLEDEK ČINNOSTI NA ZÁKLADĚ SMLOUVY NEBO JAKO DŮSLEDEK PORUŠENÍ ZÁKONA A TO ANI V PŘÍPADĚ, ŽE ORACLE NEBO JINÁ OSOBA BYLI INFORMOVÁNI O MOŽNOSTI VZNIKU TAKOVÉ ŠKODY. V ŽÁDNÉM PŘÍPADĚ NEPŘESÁHNE ODPOVĚDNOST ZA ŠKODY ZE STRANY SPOLEČNOSTI ORACLE ČÁSTKU, KTEROU ZÁKAZNÍK UHRADIL ZA UDĚLENÍ LICENCE.

Území: "Územím" se rozumí Česká republika, pokud nebude uvedeno jinak v objednávce nebo v Povolení užívat.

Zákazník se zavazuje, že: 1. bude plně dodržovat veškeré zákonné předpisy a opatření k zajištění toho, aby ani programy ani jakýkoliv jiný přímý produkt těchto Programů, nebyl přímo nebo nepřímo nezákonně exportován. 2. programy nebudou použity pro účely zakázané exportními zákony USA včetně použití k vývoji jaderných, chemických a biologických zbraní. Tato dohoda se řídí českými zákony. Veškeré podmínky uvedené v Zákazníkově objednávce jsou nahrazeny touto licencí.

Definice pojmů v Povolení užívat:
Současný přístup: maximální počet vstupních zařízení pracujících s Programem Oracle, v kterémkoliv časovém okamžiku. Je-li použito multiplexní zařízení, toto číslo je zjišťováno na vstupu multiplexního zařízení (ať už programového nebo fyzického).

Klient: počítač, který je používán pouze jednou osobou v daném čase a vykonává Program Oracle v místní paměti nebo ho ukládá na místním paměťovém médiu.

Uživatel: osoba autorizovaná zákazníkem k použití Programu Oracle bez ohledu na to, zda v daném čase program aktivně používá.

Poštovní schránka: místo, odkud je odesílána a kde je přijímána elektronická pošta. Poštovní schránka je vytvářena při definici uživatele nebo uživatelské aplikace v programu Oracle Office.

Dansk/Danmark

ORACLE PROGRAMMELLICENS

ADVARSEL - HVIS DE ÅBNER DENNE PAKKE ELLER ANVENDER DET HERI INDEHOLDTE PROGRAMMEL, FINDER NEDENSTÅENDE BETINGELSER ANVENDELSE. SÅFREMT DE IKKE KAN ACCEPTERE PROGRAMMELLET ELLER NEDENSTÅENDE BETINGELSER, BEDES DE RETURNERE PROGRAMMELLET INDEN 30 DAGE TIL DET FIRMA, HVORFRA PROGRAMMELLET ER BLEVET LEVERET, HVOREFTER DEN ERLAGTE BETALING VIL BLIVE RETURNERET.

ORACLE DANMARK A/S ("Oracle") GIVER DEM ("Kunden") LICENS TIL AT ANVENDE INDEHOLDTE PROGRAMMEL OG DOKUMENTATION ("Programmel") I HENHOLD TIL NEDENSTÅENDE BETINGELSER.

LICENS: Kunden har ret til at anvende Programmellet i det driftsmiljø, der er defineret af Oracle enten (a) i henhold til de relevante ordre-dokumenter eller et Bruger-Certifikat, som Kunden modtager fra Oracle eller Oracles distributør, eller (b) såfremt det ikke er specificeret for én enkelt bruger på én computer. Kunden må kun anvende Programmellet til intern databehandling. Kunden har ret til at kopiere Programmellet til back-up. Såfremt Kunden har erhvervet ret til at tage yderligere kopier, er dette angivet i ordre-dokumentet eller Bruger-Certifikatet. Kunden har ikke ret til at tage andre kopier uden Oracles forudgående skriftlige godkendelse. Kunden må ikke: (a) fjerne produktidentifikation, copyright-notater, eller andre notater eller immaterialretlige angivelser fra Programmellet; (b) anvende Programmellet til time-sharing, udlejningsformål eller i forbindelse med servicebureau virksomhed; (c) overdrage, videresælge eller på anden måde videregive Programmellet til tredjemand uden Oracles forudgående skriftlige godkendelse; (d) foretage eller tillade reverse engineering, rekonstruktion eller dekompilering af Programmellet, medmindre Kunden inden for rimelig tid efter Kundens skriftlige anmodning herom til Oracle ikke har modtaget fra Oracle den information, som Oracle er i besiddelse af og som er nødvendig for at producere edb-programmer, som kan fungere sammen med Programmellet, men som ikke krænker Oracles immaterielle rettigheder, samt (e) meddele resultater af benchmark tests for Programmellet til tredjemand uden Oracles forudgående skriftlige godkendelse. Overflytning af Programmel til et andet driftsmiljø er underlagt Oracles regler og afgifter for overflytning af Programmel. Kunden har kun ret til at anvende Programmellet i denne pakke i det omfang, det er angivet i ordre-dokumentet eller Bruger-Certifikatet.

IMMATERIELLE RETTIGHEDER/EJENDOMSRET: Oracle er indehaver af ophavsretten og andre immaterielle rettigheder til Programmellet, og Programmellet er beskyttet af den gældende ophavsretlige lovgivning. Kunden erhverver kun ret til at anvende Programmellet, og erhverver således ingen udtrykkelige eller underforståede rettigheder til Programmellet eller det medie, som indeholder Programmel, der ikke er specificeret under nærværende licens. Ejendomsretten og alle immaterielle rettigheder til Programmellet og medie forbliver i alle henseender Oracles eller Oracles underleverandør.

BEGRÆNSNINGER AF GARANTIER/MISLIGHOLDELSESBEFØJELSER: Oracle garanterer i en periode på 90 dage fra leveringstidspunktet til Kunden, at (a) det leverede medie ved normal brug og uden fabrikationsfejl, og at (b) Programmellet, medmindre det er modificeret af Kunden, i al sin væsentlighed kan opfylde den funktionalitet, der er beskrevet i dokumentationen ved drift på den relevante computer med tilhørende operativsystem. Oracle yder ingen garanti for, at Programmellet svarer til Kundens behov, at Programmellet kan anvendes i specifikke kombinationer, som Kunden måtte vælge, at driften vil være uden afbrydelser og fejlfri, eller at alle fejl i Programmellet vil blive rettet. Kun de ovenfor udtrykkeligt angivne garantier er gældende for Programmellet. Andre garantier, som måtte følge af deklaratorisk lovgivning eller af sædvane og kotume, er hermed tilsidesat. Såfremt Kunden rapporterer en fejl i Programmellet inden udløbet af den ovenfor angivne 90 dages garantiperiode for Programmellet, kan Oracle vælge enten at udbedre fejlen, eller at anvise Kunden en rimelig måde, hvorpå fejlen kan omgås, eller såfremt Kunden returnerer Programmellet til Oracle, at tilbagebetale Kunden licensafgiften for Programmellet. Oracle vil ombytte defekte media uden omkostninger for Kunden, såfremt de returneres til Oracle inden udløbet af den ovenfor angivne periode på 90 dage. Ovenstående er de eneste misligholdelsesbeføjelser, som Kunden kan påberåbe sig i forbindelse med Oracles misligholdelse af Oracles garantiforpligtelser.

ANSVARSBEGRÆNSNING: I INTET TILFÆLDE ER ORACLE ANSVARLIG FOR INDIREKTE TAB, FØLGESKADER, TABT AVANCE, DRIFTTAB, TABTE DATA ELLER LIGNENDE TAB, SOM KUNDEN ELLER TREDJEMAND PÅDRAGER SIG, UANSET OM ORACLE AF KUNDEN ELLER AF TREDJEMAND MÅTTE VÆRE BLEVET INFORMERET OM MULIGHEDEN FOR AT SÅDANNE TAB KUNNE OPSTÅ. ORACLES ERSTATNINGSANSVAR SKAL I INTET TILFÆLDE OVERSTIGE DE LICENSBETALINGER, SOM ORACLE HAR MODTAGET FRA KUNDEN FOR PROGRAMMELLET.

Kunden accepterer at overholde alle relevante love og offentlige foreskrifter i Danmark og USA eller andre lande i forbindelse med, at Kunden måtte (1) gøre Programmellet, et direkte produkt heraf eller tekniske data om Programmellet til genstand for direkte eller indirekte eksport, eller (2) måtte anvende Programmellet til formål i forbindelse med spredning af nukleare, kemiske eller biologiske våben i strid med eksportlovgiv-ningen. Nærværende aftale samt aspekter herunder er undergivet dansk ret og alle uoverensstemmelser herunder henvises til Sø- og Handelsretten i København. Oracle har ret til at kontrollere Kundens brug af Programmellet. Nærværende aftale har forrang for alle betingelser i Kundens indkøbsrekvisition eller andet dokument.

BRUGER-CERTIFIKAT DEFINITIONER:
Samtidige Brugere: Det maksimale antal indlæsningsenheder, som på ethvert tidspunkt anvender Programmellet samtidigt. Såfremt multiplexer-software eller -hardware (f.eks. en TP-monitor) anvendes, opgøres antallet af Samtidige Brugere ved multiplexer-indgangen.

Klient: En computer, (1) der kun anvendes af én bruger ad gangen, og (2) som afvikler Programmellet i en lokal hukommelse eller gemmer Programmellet i et lokalt fast lager.

Bruger: En individuel person som af Kunden har fået tilladelse til at bruge Programmellet uanset om en sådan faktisk anvender Programmellet på et givent tidspunkt.

Mailbox: Et punkt hvorfra elektronisk post sendes og modtages. En mailbox opstår, når et bruger-id eller en applikation bliver oprettet i Oracle*Office.

Nederlands/België, Luxemburg, Nederland

ORACLE SOFTWARE GEBRUIKSRECHT VOORWAARDEN

ATTENTIE: DOOR HET OPENEN VAN DEZE VERPAKKING OF HET GEBRUIK VAN DE INGESLOTEN SOFTWARE GAAT U ERMEE ACCOORD GEHOUDEN TE ZIJN AAN DE NAVOLGENDE VOORWAARDEN. INDIEN U NIET ACCOORD GAAT MET DE GELEVERDE SOFTWARE DAN WEL DE VOORWAARDEN, DIENT U DE VERPAKKING EN DE SOFTWARE BINNEN 30 DAGEN TE RETOURNEREN AAN HET BEDRIJF VAN WIE U DIT ONTVANGEN HEEFT WILT U IN AANMERKING KOMEN VOOR TERUGBETALING VAN DE BETAALDE VERGOEDING.

ORACLE CORPORATION DAN WEL HAAR DOCHTERONDERNEMING ("ORACLE") VERLEENT U ("CLIËNT") HET RECHT DE INGESLOTEN SOFTWARE EN DE DOCUMENTATIE ("PROGRAMMA'S") TE GEBRUIKEN ONDER DE VOLGENDE VOORWAARDEN:

GEBRUIKSRECHT: Cliënt heeft het recht de Programma's te gebruiken op a) de door Oracle aangegeven hardware/besturingssysteem combinatie als aangegeven in een order document of het 'Program Use Certificaat' verstrekt aan Cliënt door Oracle of haar distributeurs of b) indien de gebruiksrechten niet nader zijn gespecificeerd voor een enkele gebruiker op een enkele computer. Cliënt mag de Programma's uitsluitend gebruiken voor het verwerken van zijn eigen interne data. Cliënt mag één kopie van ieder gelicentiëerd Programma maken ten behoeve van back-up doeleinden; het recht om meerdere kopiëen te maken kan evenwel op de order of op het Program Use Certificaat zijn vermeld. Additionele kopiëen zullen slechts kunnen worden gemaakt na voorafgaande schriftelijke toestemming van Oracle. Het is Cliënt niet toegestaan: (a) aanduidingen van produkt identificatie, eigendom, titel, handelsmerken en overige rechten van intellectuele eigendom van de Programma's te verwijderen; (b) de Programma's te gebruiken voor commerciële time-sharing, verhuur of als service bureau; (c) de Programma's te verkopen, vervreemden, in zekerheid overdragen of op welke wijze dan ook ter beschikking van enige derde te stellen zonder voorafgaande schriftelijke toestemming van Oracle; (d) de Programma's te "reverse engineeren", decompileren of te disassembleren, behoudens in die gevallen, waarin Cliënt, na een schriftelijk verzoek daartoe, niet binnen een redelijke termijn van Oracle de beschikbare informatie heeft ontvangen die benodigd is om software te ontwikkelen die kan werken in samenhang met het Programma van Oracle, maar die geen inbreuk maakt op de intellectuele eigendomsrechten van Oracle; en (e) resultaten van benchmark-tests vrij te geven zonder voorafgaande schriftelijke toestemming van Oracle. Iedere overzetting van Programma's is onderworpen aan de transfer-policy en - vergoeding zoals door Oracle gehanteerd. Cliënt verkrijgt uitsluitend het gebruiksrecht op de Programma's in deze verpakking welke zijn gespecificeerd in het order document of het Program Use Certificaat.

AUTEURSRECHT/EIGENDOM VAN DE PROGRAMMA'S: De Programma's zijn eigendom van Oracle en worden beschermd door auteurs- en overige intellectuele eigendomsrechten. Cliënt verkrijgt uitsluitend het recht de Programma's te gebruiken en verkrijgt noch uitdrukkelijk noch stilzwijgend andere rechten op de Programma's en de media waarop de Programma's worden verstrekt dan die aangegeven in deze voorwaarden. Alle rechten, eigendom en overige belangen, intellectuele eigendomsrechten daaronder begrepen, in of op het Programma en de media blijven voorbehouden aan Oracle of diens licentiegever.

GARANTIE EN GARANTIEBEPERKINGEN: Oracle garandeert gedurende een periode van 90 dagen vanaf de afleverdatum dat (a) tapes, diskettes of andere gegevensdragers, bij normaal gebruik, vrij zijn van gebreken in materiaal en afwerking; en (b) dat de Programma's, mits ongewijzigd, in hoofdzaak functioneren overeenkomstig de functies beschreven in de bijbehorende door Oracle geleverde documentatie, mits gebruikt op de aangewezen hardware/besturingssysteem combinatie. Oracle garandeert niet dat de Programma's voldoen aan de eisen van Cliënt, voldoen in alle combinaties die Cliënt voor gebruik selecteert, dat de werking van de Programma's ononderbroken of vrij van onvolkomenheden zal zijn, of dat alle onvolkomenheden zullen worden hersteld. Deze garanties zijn uitputtend beschreven en alle overige garanties, uitdrukkelijk dan wel stilzwijgend, zijn uitgesloten. Indien Cliënt een onvolkomenheid in een Programma rapporteert binnen de garantieperiode van 90 dagen, zal Oracle, te harer beoordeling deze onvolkomenheid herstellen, danwel Cliënt voorzien van een redelijke "workaround" procedure, of, nadat Cliënt het Programma aan Oracle heeft geretourneerd, de betaalde licentievergoeding terugbetalen. Oracle zal gebrekkige media kosteloos vervangen mits deze media aan Oracle is geretourneerd binnen de garantieperiode van 90 dagen. De hier omschreven oplossingen vormen een uitputtende opsomming van de aan Cliënt toekomende rechten uit hoofde van garantie.

BEPERKING VAN AANSPRAKELIJKHEID: De aansprakelijkheid van Oracle voor Cliënt geleden directe schade krachtens enige bepaling van deze voorwaarden zal zijn beperkt tot ten hoogste het bedrag van de licentievergoeding die Oracle uit hoofde van deze voorwaarden van Cliënt ontving. Oracle zal in geen geval aansprakelijk zijn voor enige indirecte-, of gevolgschade, daaronder begrepen gederfde winst of verlies van verwachte omzet, verlies van data of verlies van gebruik van data, geleden door Cliënt of enige derde, uit hoofde van een actie uit onrechtmatige daad of wanprestatie, afgezien van het feit of Oracle of enig andere persoon op de hoogte was van de mogelijkheid tot het ontstaan van dergelijke schade. Iedere verdere aansprakelijkheid van Oracle is uitgesloten, tenzij sprake is van opzet of grove schuld van de zijde van Oracle. Cliënt zal zich houden aan alle toepasselijke wettelijke voorschriften en regels met betrekking tot (a) het direct of indirect exporteren van de Programma's danwel direct daarvan afgeleide producten; en (b) het gebruik van de Programma's voor een doel verboden door de export wetgeving zoals onder andere doeleinden betrekking hebbende op nucleaire, chemische of biologische wapens. Deze Voorwaarden worden beheerst door Nederlands Recht. Alle geschillen voortvloeiende uit deze Voorwaarden zullen worden beslecht door de daartoe bevoegde rechter te Utrecht. Alle bepalingen van inkooporders of andere documenten waarvan Cliënt zich bij het bestellen van produkten of diensten bedient, zullen worden vervangen door deze voorwaarden.

DEFINITIES IN HET PROGRAM USE CERTIFICAAT:
Concurrent Device/Concurrent Accesses: het maximale aantal invoersystemen dat de Programma's op ieder gegeven moment gelijktijdig mag benaderen. Indien multiplexing software of hardware (zoals bijvoorbeeld een TP monitor) wordt gebruikt wordt het aantal gemeten aan het 'front end' van de multiplexer.

Cliënt: één computer die (1) tegelijkertijd slechts door een persoon wordt gebruikt, en; (2) Oracle software opgeslagen in een lokaal geheugen gebruikt danwel de software opslaat op een lokale opslag apparatuur.

Gebruiker (User): een individu die door de klant is geauthoriseerd om de Programma's te gebruiken, los van het feit of die individu de Programma's op enig moment ook actief gebruikt.

Mailbox: een punt waarvandaan electronische mail wordt ontvangen of verzonden: een dergelijk punt wordt gecreeerd wanneer een gebruikers account of een applicatie wordt aangemaakt in Oracle*Office.

English

ORACLE PROGRAM LICENSE TERMS

CAUTION: IF YOU OPEN THIS PACKAGE OR USE THE ENCLOSED SOFTWARE, THE FOLLOWING TERMS APPLY. IF THE SOFTWARE OR THESE TERMS ARE NOT ACCEPTABLE TO YOU, RETURN THE SOFTWARE WITHIN 30 DAYS TO THE COMPANY FROM WHICH YOU RECEIVED IT FOR REFUND.

ORACLE CORPORATION OR ITS SUBSIDIARY ("ORACLE") GRANTS YOU ("CUSTOMER") A LICENSE TO USE THE ENCLOSED SOFTWARE AND DOCUMENTATION ("PROGRAMS") AS INDICATED BELOW.

LICENSE: Customer shall have the right to use the Programs in the operating environment identified by Oracle, either (a) to the extent specified in an ordering document or Program Use Certificate distributed to Customer by Oracle or its distributor, or (b) if not specified, for a single user on a single computer. Customer may use the Programs solely for its own internal data processing operations. Customer may make one copy of each licensed Program for backup; rights to make additional copies, if any, may be specified in an ordering document or Program Use Certificate. No other copies shall be made without Oracle's prior written consent. Customer shall not: (a) remove any product identification, copyright notices, or other notices or proprietary restrictions from Programs; (b) use Programs for commercial timesharing, rental, or service bureau use; (c) transfer, sell, assign or otherwise convey Programs to another party without Oracle's prior written consent; (d) cause or permit reverse engineering, disassembly, or decompilation of Programs; or (e) disclose results of any benchmark tests of any Program to any third party without Oracle's prior written approval. All Program transfers are subject to Oracle's transfer policies and fees. Customer shall have the right to use only the Programs in this package that are specified in an ordering document or Program Use Certificate.

COPYRIGHT/OWNERSHIP OF PROGRAMS: Programs are the proprietary products of Oracle and are protected by copyright and other intellectual property laws. Customer acquires only the right to use Programs and does not acquire any rights, express or implied, in Programs or media containing Programs other than those specified in this License. Oracle, or its licensor, shall at all times retain all rights, title, interest, including intellectual property rights, in Programs and media.

LIMITED WARRANTIES/EXCLUSIVE REMEDIES: Oracle warrants that for 90 days from date of delivery to Customer: (a) enclosed media is free of defects in materials and workmanship under normal use; and (b) unmodified Programs will substantially perform functions described in documentation provided by Oracle when operated on the designated computer and operating system. Oracle does not warrant that: Programs will meet Customer's requirements, Programs will operate in combinations Customer may select for use, operation of Programs will be uninterrupted or error-free, or all Program errors will be corrected. These warranties are exclusive and in lieu of all other warranties, whether express or implied, including implied warranties of merchantability or fitness for a particular purpose. If Customer reports an error in a Program within the 90 day period, Oracle shall, at its option, correct the error, provide Customer with a reasonable procedure to circumvent the error, or, upon return of Programs to Oracle by Customer, refund the license fees. Oracle will replace any defective media without charge if it is returned to Oracle within the 90 day period. These are Customer's sole and exclusive remedies for any breach of warranty. This limited warranty gives you specific legal rights. You may have others, which vary from state to state and/or from country to country.

LIMITATION OF LIABILITY: ORACLE SHALL NOT BE LIABLE FOR ANY INDIRECT, INCIDENTAL, SPECIAL OR CONSEQUENTIAL DAMAGES, OR DAMAGES FOR LOSS OF PROFITS, REVENUE, DATA OR DATA USE, INCURRED BY CUSTOMER OR ANY THIRD PARTY, WHETHER IN AN ACTION IN CONTRACT OR TORT, EVEN IF ORACLE HAS BEEN ADVISED OF THE POSSIBILITY OF SUCH DAMAGES. ORACLE'S LIABILITY FOR DAMAGES HEREUNDER SHALL IN NO EVENT EXCEED THE FEES PAID BY CUSTOMER FOR THIS LICENSE.

RESTRICTED RIGHTS: Programs delivered to the U.S. Defense Dept. are delivered with Restricted Rights and the following applies: "Restricted Rights Legend: Use, duplication or disclosure by Government is subject to restrictions as currently set forth in subparagraph (c)(1)(ii) of DFARS 252-227-7013, Rights in Technical Data and Computer Software (October 1988). Oracle Corp. 500 Oracle Pkwy., Redwood City, CA, 94065. Programs delivered to a U.S. Government Agency not within the Defense, Dept. are delivered with "Restricted Rights" as defined in FAR 52.227-14, Rights in Data - General, including Alternate III (June 1987)."

Customer shall comply fully with all laws and regulations of the United States and other countries ("Export Laws") to assure that neither the Programs, nor any direct products thereof are (1) exported, directly or indirectly, in violation of Export Laws, or (2) are used for any purpose prohibited by Export Laws, including, without limitation, nuclear, chemical, or biological weapons proliferation. Oracle may audit Customer's use of the Programs. All terms of any Customer purchase order or other Customer ordering document shall be superseded by this License.

The law governing this License and all related actions will depend on where Customer receives delivery of Programs: (a) The laws of the Province of Ontario, Canada if received in Canada (except Quebec); (b) the laws of the Republic of Singapore if received in Singapore; (c) the laws of Malaysia if received in Malaysia; or (d) the laws of the State of California, U.S.A. if received in U.S.A., Australia, New Zealand, Hong Kong, Vietnam, Thailand, Philippines, Indonesia, India, Pakistan, Sri Lanka, Bangladesh, Ukraine, Croatia, Slovenia, Macedonia, Slovakia, Kazakhstan, Romania, Bulgaria, Lithuania, Latvia, Estonia, Albania, or any Country not specified elsewhere herein.

PROGRAM USE CERTIFICATE AND ORDERING DOCUMENT DEFINITIONS:

Concurrent Devices/Concurrent Accesses: the maximum number of input devices accessing the Programs at any given point in time. If multiplexing software or hardware (e.g., a TP monitor) is used, this number must be measured at the multiplexing front end.

Client: a computer which (1) is used by only one person at a time, and (2) executes Oracle software in local memory or stores the software on a local storage device.

User: an individual authorized by Customer to use the Programs, regardless of whether the individual is actively using the Programs at any given time.

Mailbox: a point from which electronic mail is sent or received; it is created when a user account or application is established in Oracle*Office.

English/Canada

ORACLE PROGRAM LICENSE TERMS

CAUTION: IF YOU OPEN THIS PACKAGE AND USE THE ENCLOSED SOFTWARE THE FOLLOWING TERMS APPLY. IF THE SOFTWARE OR THESE TERMS ARE NOT ACCEPTABLE TO YOU. RETURN THE SOFTWARE WITHIN 30 DAYS TO THE COMPANY FROM WHICH YOU RECEIVED IT FOR REFUND.

ORACLE CORPORATION CANADA INC. ("ORACLE") GRANTS YOU ("CUSTOMER") A LICENSE TO USE THE ENCLOSED SOFTWARE AND DOCUMENTATION ("PROGRAMS") AS INDICATED BELOW.

LICENSE: Customer shall have the right to use the Programs in the operating environment identified by Oracle, either (a) to the extent specified in an ordering document or Program Use Certificate distributed to Customer by Oracle or its distributor, or (b) if not specified, for a single user on a single computer. Customer may use the Programs solely for its own internal data processing operations. Customer may make one copy of each licensed Program for backup; rights to make additional copies, if any, may be specified in an ordering document or Program Use Certificate. No other copies shall be made without Oracle's prior written consent. Customer shall not: (a) remove any product identification, copyright notices, or other notices or proprietary restrictions from Programs; (b) use Programs for commercial timesharing, rental or service bureau use; (c) transfer, sell, assign or otherwise convey Programs to another party without Oracle's prior written consent; (d) cause or permit the reverse engineering, disassembly, decompilation,of Programs: or (e) disclose results of any benchmark tests of Programs to any third party without Oracle's prior written approval. All Program transfers are subject to Oracle's transfer policies and fees. Customer shall have the right to use only the Programs in this package that are specified in an ordering document or Program Use Certificate.

COPYRIGHT/OWNERSHIP OF PROGRAMS: Programs are the proprietary products of Oracle or its licensor and are protected by copyright and other intellectual property laws. Customer acquires only the right to use Programs and does not acquire any rights, express or implied, in Programs or media containing Programs other than those specified in this License. Oracle, or its licensor, shall at all times retain all rights, title, interest, including intellectual property rights, in Programs and media.

LIMITED WARRANTIES/EXCLUSIVE REMEDIES: Oracle warrants that for 90 days from date of delivery to Customer: (a) enclosed media is free of defects in materials and workmanship under normal use; and (b) unmodified Programs will substantially perform functions described in documentation provided by Oracle when operated on the designated computer and operating system. Oracle does not warrant that: Programs will meet Customer's requirements, Programs will operate in combinations Customer may select for use, operation of Programs will be uninterrupted or error-free, or all Program errors will be corrected. These warranties are exclusive and in lieu of all other warranties and conditions, whether express or implied warranties or conditions of merchantability or fitness for a particular purpose. If Customer reports an error in a Program within the 90 day period, Oracle shall, at its option, correct the error, provide Customer with a reasonable procedure to circumvent the error, or, upon return of the Programs to Oracle by Customer, refund the license fees paid. Oracle will replace any defective media without charge if it is returned to Oracle within the 90 day period. These are Customer's sole and exclusive remedies for any breach of warranty. This limited warranty gives you specific legal rights. You may have others, which vary from state to state and/or province to province.

LIMITATION OF LIABILITY: ORACLE SHALL NOT BE LIABLE FOR ANY INDIRECT, INCIDENTAL, SPECIAL OR CONSEQUENTIAL DAMAGES, OR DAMAGES FOR LOSS OF PROFITS, REVENUE, DATA OR DATA USE, INCURRED BY CUSTOMER OR ANY THIRD PARTY, WHETHER IN AN ACTION IN CONTRACT OR TORT, EVEN IF ORACLE HAS BEEN ADVISED OF THE POSSIBILITY OF SUCH DAMAGES. ORACLES LIABILITY FOR DAMAGES HEREUNDER SHALL IN NO EVENT EXCEED THE FEES PAID BY CUSTOMER FOR THIS LICENSE.

Customer shall comply fully with all laws and regulations of Canada ("Export Laws") to assure that neither the Programs, nor any direct products thereof are (1) exported, directly or indirectly, in violation of Export Laws, or (2) are used for any purpose prohibited by Export Laws, including, without limitation, nuclear, chemical, or biological weapons proliferation. Oracle may audit Customer's use of the Programs. All terms of any Customer purchase order or other Customer ordering document shall be superseded by this License.

The law governing this License and all related actions will be those laws in force in the province or Ontario, Canada.

TERRITORY: Programs may only be used by Customer in Canada. Customer agrees to ensure that neither the programs, nor any direct product there of is exported; directly or indirectly, from Canada without prior written consent of Oracle.

PROGRAM USE CERTIFICATE AND ORDERING DOCUMENT DEFINITIONS:
Concurrent Devices/Concurrent Accesses: the maximum number of input devices accessing the Programs at any given point in time. If multiplexing software or hardware (e.g. a TP monitor) is used, this number must be measured at the multiplexing front end.

Client: a computer which (1) is used by only one person at a time, and (2) executes Oracle software in local memory or stores the software on a local storage device.

User: an individual authorized by Customer to use the Programs, regardless of whether the individual is actively using the Programs at any given time.

Mailbox: a point from which electronic mail is sent or received; it is created when a user account or application is established in Oracle*Office.

English/United Kingdom

ORACLE PROGRAM LICENCE TERMS

CAUTION: IF YOU OPEN THIS PACKAGE AND USE THE ENCLOSED SOFTWARE THE FOLLOWING TERMS APPLY. IF THE SOFTWARE OR THESE TERMS ARE NOT ACCEPTABLE TO YOU RETURN THE SOFTWARE WITHIN 30 DAYS TO THE COMPANY FROM WHICH YOU RECEIVED IT FOR REFUND.

ORACLE CORPORATION UK LIMITED ("Oracle") GRANTS YOU ("Customer") A LICENCE TO USE THE ENCLOSED SOFTWARE AND DOCUMENTATION ("Programs") AS INDICATED BELOW.

LICENCE: Customer shall have the right to use the Programs in the operating environment identified by Oracle, either (a) to the extent specified in an ordering document or Program Use Certificate distributed to Customer by Oracle or its distributor, or (b) if not specified, for a single user on a single computer. Customer may use the Programs solely for its own internal data processing operations. Customer may make one copy of each licensed Program for backup; rights to make additional copies, if any, may be specified in an ordering document or Program Use Certificate. No other copies shall be made without Oracle's prior written consent. Customer shall not: (a) remove any product identification, copyright notices, or other notices or proprietary restrictions from Programs; (b) use Programs for commercial timesharing, rental or service bureau use; (c) transfer, sell, assign or otherwise convey Programs to another party without Oracle's prior written consent; (d) cause or permit the reverse engineering, disassembly, decompilation, translation or adaptation of the Programs except where Customer shall not have received from Oracle within a reasonable time after written request such information as is available to Oracle and as is necessary to create programs which are interoperable with the Programs but which do not infringe Oracle's intellectual property rights; or (e) disclose results of any benchmark tests of Programs to any third party without Oracle's prior written approval. All Program transfers are subject to Oracle's transfer policies and fees. Customer shall have the right to use only the Programs in this package that are specified in an ordering document or Program Use Certificate.

COPYRIGHT/OWNERSHIP OF PROGRAMS: Programs are the proprietary products of Oracle and are protected by copyright and other intellectual property laws. Customer acquires only the right to use Programs and does not acquire any rights, express or implied, in Programs or media containing Programs other than those specified in this Licence. Oracle, or its licensor, shall at all times retain all rights, title, interest, including intellectual property rights, in Programs and media.

WARRANTIES/EXCLUSIVE REMEDIES: Oracle warrants that for 90 days from date of delivery to Customer: (a) the enclosed media is free of defects in materials and workmanship under normal use; and (b) unmodified Programs will substantially perform functions described in documentation provided by Oracle when operated on the designated computer and operating system. Oracle does not warrant that: Programs will meet Customer's requirements, Programs will operate in combinations Customer may select for use, operation of Programs will be uninterrupted or error-free, or all Program errors will be corrected. These warranties are exclusive and in lieu of all other warranties and conditions ,whether express or implied in law, including implied conditions of merchantability or fitness for a particular purpose. If Customer reports an error in a Program within the 90 day period, Oracle shall, at its option, correct the error, provide Customer with a reasonable procedure to circumvent the error, or, upon return of the Program to Oracle by Customer, refund the licence fees paid. Oracle will replace any defective media without charge if it is returned to Oracle within the 90 day period. These are Customer's sole and exclusive remedies for any breach of warranty.

LIMITATION OF LIABILITY: Oracle shall indemnify Customer for personal injury or death caused by the negligence of Oracle or its employees. Subject thereto Oracle shall not be liable whether in contract, tort or otherwise and whether or not Oracle has been advised of the possibility of such loss for (a) consequential or indirect loss; and/or (b) loss of profits; and/or (c) loss of revenue; and/or (d) loss of business or goodwill; and/or (e) loss of, damage to or corruption of data; and/or (f) loss of availability, and Oracle's liability otherwise for direct loss or damage hereunder shall in no event exceed a total aggregate limit of liability of £250,000 sterling.

VERIFICATION: At Oracle's written request, Customer shall furnish Oracle with a signed statement: (a) verifying that the Programs and documentation are being used pursuant to the provisions of this Licence including any User limitations; and (b) listing the locations, type and serial number of any and all computer hardware on which the Programs are being utilised. Customer agrees to grant Oracle access, upon reasonable prior notice, in order to audit the use of the Programs and documentation. If such audit establishes Customer has unauthorised copies of the Programs or documentation, without prejudice to Oracle's other rights and remedies, Oracle shall have the right to charge Customer for the costs of performing the audit, in addition to recovering charges which would have been due to Oracle had Oracle licensed such copies for use.

TERRITORY: the Programs may be used by Customer within the European Union.

All terms of any Customer purchase order or other Customer ordering document shall be superseded by this Licence. Customer agrees to ensure that neither the Programs, nor any direct product thereof, is exported, directly or indirectly, from the United Kingdom without complying with all regulations relating to such export issued by the United States and United Kingdom Governments. This Licence is governed by English Law and the parties agree to submit to the exclusive jurisdiction of the English Courts.

PROGRAM USE CERTIFICATE DEFINITIONS:
Concurrent Devices/Concurrent Accesses: the maximum number of input devices accessing the Programs at any given point in time. If multiplexing software or hardware (e.g. a TP monitor) is used, this number must be measured at the multiplexing front end.

Client: a computer which (1) is used by only one person at a time, and (2) executes Oracle software in local memory or stores the software on a local storage device.

User: an individual authorised by Customer to use the Programs, regardless of whether the individual is actively using the Programs at any given time.

Mailbox: a point from which electronic mail is sent or received; it is created when a user account or application is established in Oracle*Office.

Finsk/Finland

SOPIMUS ORACLE-OHJELMAN KÄYTTÖOIKEUDESTA

VAROITUS: TÄMÄN PAKKAUKSEN AVAAMISELLA TAI OHJELMIEN KÄYTTÄMISELLÄ ILMOITATTE YMMÄRTÄVÄNNE JA HYVÄKSYVÄNNE SEURAAVAT EHDOT. LUKEKAA EHDOT HUOLELLISESTI LÄPI ENNEN PAKKAUKSEN AVAAMISTA: ELLETTE HYVÄKSY EHTOJA TAI OHJELMIA, PALAUTTAKAA PAKKAUS AVAAMATTOMANA MYYJÄLLE 30 PÄIVÄN KULUESSA, JOLLOIN TEILLE PALAUTETAAN MAKSAMANNE KAUPPAHINTA.

ORACLE FINLAND OY ("Oracle") MYÖNTÄÄ TEILLE ("asiakas") KÄYTTÖOIKEUDEN OHEISIIN OHJELMISTOTUOTTEISIIN JA DOKUMENTAATIOON ("ohjelmat") SEURAAVIEN EHTOJEN MUKAISESTI.

KÄYTTÖOIKEUS: Asiakkaalla on oikeus käyttää ohjelmia Oraclen määrittelemässä käyttöympäristössä joko (a) Oraclen tai sen jakelijan kanssa sopimassaan laajuudessa tai (b) ellei käyttöoikeudesta ei ole muuta sovittu, yhdellä käyttäjällä yhdellä tietokoneella. Asiakas saa käyttää ohjelmia ainoastaan omiin sisäisiin tietojenkäsittelytarkoituksiinsa. Asiakas saa tehdä niistä ohjelmista, joita hänellä on oikeus käyttää, yhden varmistuskopion. Lisävarmistuskopioista on sovittava myyjän kanssa. Muita kopioita ei saa tehdä ilman Oraclen etukäteen antamaa kirjallista suostumusta. Asiakas ei saa: (a) poistaa ohjelmista mitään tuotemerkkiä, tekijänoikeusmerkintää eikä muita oikeuksia määrittäviä tai muita merkintöjä, (b) käyttää ohjelmia kaupalliseen osituskäyttöön, vuokraukseen tai palvelutoimistokäyttöön, (c) siirtää, myydä, luovuttaa tai muutoin saattaa ohjelmaa kolmannelle osapuolelle ilman Oraclen etukäteen antamaa kirjallista suostumusta, (d) aiheuttaa tai sallia ohjelmien konekielisen koodin purkamista tai sen muuttamista selväkieliseksi eikä (e) paljastaa ohjelmien suorituskykytestin tuloksia kolmannelle osapuolelle ilman Oraclen etukäteen antamaa kirjallista hyväksyntää. Ohjelman siirrossa noudatetaan Oraclen siirtokäytäntöjä ja -maksuja. Asiakas saa käyttää ainoastaan niitä ohjelmia, joiden käyttöoikeudesta on sovittu,. riippumatta siitä, että tämä paketti muita ohjelmia.

OHJELMIEN TEKIJÄNOIKEUS/OMISTUSOIKEUS: Ohjelmat ovat Oraclen omaisuutta ja suojattu tekijänoikeudella ja muilla aineettomilla oikeuksilla. Asiakas saa ohjelmiin vain käyttöoikeuden. Oracle tai sen lisenssinhaltija pidättävät itsellään kaikkina aikoina kaikki oikeudet ohjelmiin ja tallennusvälineiseen.

RAJOITETUT TAKUUT JA TAKUUHYVITYKSET: Oracle vastaa tuotteiden toimituspäivästä lukien 90 päivän ajan (a) siitä, ettei oheisissa tallennusvälineissä ole materiaalista eikä ammattitaidosta johtuvia virheitä normaalissa käytössä sekä (b) siitä, että muuttamattomat ohjelmat suoriutuvat olennaisin osin niistä toiminnoista, jotka on kuvattu Oraclen toimittamassa dokumentaatiossa, kun ohjelmia käytetään sovitussa tietokoneessa ja käyttöjärjestelmässä. Oracle ei takaa, että ohjelmat vastaavat asiakkaan vaatimuksia, että ohjelma toimii kaikissa niissä yhdistelmissä, joita asiakas haluaa käyttää, että ohjelman toiminta on keskeytymätöntä tai virheetöntä tai että kaikki ohjelmavirheet korjataan. Edellä mainitut takuut ovat ainoat Oraclen myöntämät takuut ja korvaavat kaikki muut nimenomaiset tai hiljaisesti sovitut ehdot tai soveltuvuutta koskevasta takuusta. Jos asiakas ilmoittaa 90 päivän kuluessa Oraclelle ohjelmavirheestä, Oracle voi harkintansa mukaan joko korjata virheen, neuvoa asiakkaalle kohtuullisen keinon, jolla virhe voidaan kiertää, tai palauttaa asiakkaalle tämän maksamat käyttöoikeusmaksut maksut asiakkaan palauttettua ohjelmat Oraclelle. Oracle vaihtaa virheelliset tallennusvälineet maksutta, jos ne toimitetaan Oraclelle edellä määritetyn 90 päivän kuluessa. Edellä mainitut ovat asiakkaan ainoat ja yksinomaiset hyvitystavat takuutilanteissa. Tässä ilmoitetun lisäksi asiakkaalla saattaa olla muita pakottavasta lainsäädännöstä johtuvia oikeuksia, jotka vaihtelevat kussakin maassa sovellettavan lainsäädännön mukaan.

VASTUUNRAJOITUS: ORACLE EI OLE VASTUUSSA MISTÄÄN EPÄSUORISTA EIKÄ VÄLILLISISTÄ VAHINGOISTA EIKÄ ASIAKKAAN TAI MAHDOLLISEN KOLMANNEN OSAPUOLEN KÄRSIMISTÄ VOITON, TULOJEN, TIETOJEN TAI TIETOJENKÄYTÖN MENETYKSISTÄ, JOHTUIVATPA NE SOPIMUKSEN MUKAISESTA TOIMINNASTA TAI RIKKOMUKSESTA, RIIPPUMATTA SIITÄ, ONKO ASIAKKAALLE TAI MUULLE HENKILÖLLE OLISI ILMOITETTU TÄLLAISTEN VAHINKOJEN MAHDOLLISUUDESTA. ORACLEN TÄMÄN SOPIMUKSEN MUKAINEN VAHINGONKORVAUSVELVOLLISUUS EI MÄÄRÄLTÄÄN MISSÄÄN TILANTEESSA YLITÄ ASIAKKAAN TÄSTÄ KÄYTTÖOIKEUDESTA MAKSAMIA MAKSUJA.

Asiakas sitoutuu noudattamaan kaikkia vientilakeja ja -määräyksiä varmistaakseen, ettei ohjelmia tai mitään niistä suoranaisesti johtuvaa tuotetta viedä maasta lainvastaisesti, suoraan tai epäsuorasti, mukaanlukien ydin-, kemiallisten ja biologisten aseiden leviämisen rajoittamista koskevat säännökset. Tähän sopimukseen sovelletaan Suomen lakia. Oraclella on oikeus tarkastaa ohjelmien sopimuksenmukainen käyttö. Tämän sopimuksen määräykset ovat ensisijaisia asiakkaan myyjän kanssa mahdollisesti sopimiin käyttöoikeusehtoihin nähden.

OHJELMIEN KÄYTTÖÄ KOSKEVIA MÄÄRITTELYJÄ: Yhtäaikainen käyttäjä/pääte: ohjelman tiettynä hetkenä yhteydessä olevien syöttölaitteiden enimmäismäärä, kanavointiohjelmistoa tai -laitteistoa käytettäessä (TP-monitori) kanavointia käyttävien syöttölaitteiden päästä laskettuna; Asiakas (v. palvelin): tietokone, (1) jota käyttää tiettynä hetkenä vain yksi henkilö ja (2) joka ajaa Oracle-ohjelmistoa omassa muistissaan tai säilyttää ohjelmistoja paikallisella varastointipäätteellä; Käyttäjä: henkilö, jonka asiakas on valtuuttanut käyttämään Oracle-ohjelmia riippumatta siitä, käyttääkö hän ohjelmia tiettynä hetkenä; Postilaatikko: paikka, josta sähköpostia lähetetään tai johon sitä vastaanotetaan, ja joka luodaan, kun käyttäjätili tai sovellus perustetaan Oracle*Office-ohjelmistoon.

Français/Belgique, Luxembourg, Pays-Bas

CONTRAT D'UTILISATION DU LOGICIEL ORACLE

ATTENTION: L'OUVERTURE DE CET EMBALLAGE OU L'UTILISATION DU LOGICIEL INCLUS, IMPLIQUE L'ACCEPTATION DES CONDITIONS DE CE CONTRAT. AU CAS OÙ VOUS N'ACCEPTEZ PAS LE LOGICIEL OU LES CONDITIONS CI-DESSOUS, VEUILLEZ RETOURNER LE LOGICIEL ET SON EMBALLAGE À VOTRE FOURNISSEUR DANS LES 30 JOURS SI VOUS SOUHAITEZ LE REMBOURSEMENT DES FRAIS DE LICENCE PAYÉS.

ORACLE CORPORATION OU SA FILIALE ("Oracle") VOUS ("Client") OCTROIE LE DROIT D'UTILISATION DU LOGICIEL ET DE LA DOCUMENTATION ("Programmes") SELON LES CONDITIONS SUIVANTES:

LICENCE: Le Client aura le droit d'utiliser les Programmes (a) sur la combinaison hardware/système opératoire telle que stipulée dans le document de commande ou le "Certificat d'Utilisation du Logiciel" octroyé au Client par Oracle ou ses distributeurs ou (b) si les conditions d'utilisations ne sont pas plus explicites, pour un seul utilisateur sur un seul ordinateur. Le Client peut utiliser les Programmes uniquement pour les opérations de traitement de données internes. Le Client aura le droit de faire 1 (une) copie à des fins de sauvegarde, cependant le droit de faire plusieurs copies peut être specifié dans la Commande ou dans le "Certificat d'Utilisation du Logiciel". Aucune copie additionnelle n'est permise sans l'accord écrit préalable d'Oracle. Il n'est pas permis au Client de: (a) enlever toute notice d'identification du produit, de droit d'auteur, de propriété, de marque ou tout autre droit de propriété intellectuelle; (b) utiliser les Programmes à des fins de "time-sharing" commercial, de location ou de bureau de services; (c) vendre, céder ou transférer les Programmes ou de toute autre manière mettre les Programmes à disposition de tiers sans l'accord écrit préalable d'Oracle; (d) pratiquer le "reverse-engineering", la décompilation ou le désassemblage des Programmes, sauf dans le cas où le Client, après une demande écrite, n'a pas reçu d'Oracle dans délai raisonnable les informations disponibles qui sont nécessaires pour développer le logiciel compatible avec les Programmes d'Oracle mais qui ne constitue pas une violation des droits de propriétés intellectuelle d'Oracle; (e) publier les résultats de tests de Benchmark sans l'accord écrit préalable d'Oracle. Tout transfert de Programme est soumis aux politiques et frais de transfert tels que pratiqués par Oracle. Le Client reçoit le droit d'utilisation pour les Programmes inclus dans cet emballages qui sont mentionnés sur le document de commande ou le "Certificat d'Utilisation du Logiciel".

DROITS D'AUTEUR: Les Programmes sont la propriété d'Oracle et sont protégés par les réglementations en matière de droits d'auteur ainsi que toutes les autres législations applicables en matière de droit de propriété intellectuelle. Le Client reçoit exclusivement le droit d'utilisation des Programmes et ne reçoit aucun droit de propriété des Programmes ou du média sur lequel les Programmes sont distribués. Tout droit, propriété ou intérêt, y compris le droit de propriété intellectuelle, dans ou sur les Programmes reste à tout moment réservé à Oracle ou ses représentants légaux.

GARANTIE ET LIMITE DE LA GARANTIE: Oracle garantit pendant une période de 90 (nonante) jours après la date de livraison: (a) que les bandes, disquettes ou autres supports d'information ne contiennent, pour un usage normal, aucun défaut matériel ou de traitement; et (b) que le fonctionnement du logiciel, s'il reste inchangé, corresponde aux fonctions décrites dans la documentation annexe, à condition qu'il soit utilisé sur l'Unité Centrale de Traitement mentionné dans la commande. Oracle ne garantit pas que les Programmes répondront aux exigences du Client, conviendra à toutes les situations sélectionnées par le Client, ou que le fonctionnement des Programmes se fera sans interruption ou sans erreurs et imperfections, ou que toutes les fautes et imperfections seront réparées. Ces garanties sont decrites ici de manière exhaustive à l'exclusion de toute autre garantie expresse ou tacite. Au cas où le Cient rapporte une erreur dans les Programmes pendant la période de garantie de 90 jours, Oracle réparera cette erreur à ses frais, ou trouvera une solution "workaround"raisonnable, ou remboursera les redevances de Licence payées par le Client pour autant que le Client ait retourné les programmes à Oracle. Oracle remplacera gratuitement tout média défectif pour autant que celui-ci soit retourné à Oracle dans la période de garantie des 90 jours. Les solutions ci-dessus décrivent de manière exhaustive la totalité des droits du Client en matière de garantie.

LIMITE DE LA RESPONSABILITE: La responsabilité d'Oracle pour tout dommage direct subi par le Client suite à l'une des clauses de ce contrat sera limitée à un maximum équivalent au montant des redevances de Licence reçues du Client par Oracle dans le cadre de ce contrat. Oracle ne sera en aucun cas responsable de tout dommage indirect ou consecutif, y compris le manque à gagner ou la perte de chiffre d'affaire attendu, la perte de données ou d'usage, subi par le Client ou un tiers, découlant d'une action à tort ou insuffisante, que Oracle ait été informé ou non de cette possibilité de dommage. Toute autre responsabilité d'Oracle est exclue, sauf en cas de faute grave ou intentionnelle de la part d'Oracle. Le Client se conformera à toutes les prescriptions et réglementations légales applicables concernant (a) l'exportation directe ou indirecte des programmes ou d'un produit dérivé des Programmes; (b) l'utilisation des Programmes à des fins interdites par les lois de l'exportation y compris mais non exclusivement la prolifération des armes nucléaires, chimiques ou biologiques. Ces conditions sont régies par le droit des Pays-Bas. Tout litige découlant de ces conditions sera réglé par le tribunal de Utrecht, pour autant que ce tribunal est compétent. Toutes les dispositions de bon de commande ou autre document dont le Client fait usage pour commander des produits ou services, sont remplacées par le présent contrat.

DEFINITIONS DU CERTIFICAT D'UTILISATION DE PROGRAMME:
Concurrent Device/Concurrent Access: Le nombre maximum de systèmes d'entrées de données qui peut accéder au Programme à un Programme donné. S'il s'agit de Software ou Hardware "multiplexing" (par exemple un moniteur TP), le nombre sera mesuré au "front-end" du multiplexer.

Client: Un ordinateur qui: (1) est utilisé par une personne à la fois, et (2) utilise le Software Oracle en mémoire locale, ou archive le Software sur un appareil d'archivage local.

User: Un individu autorisé par le Client à utiliser les Programmes, que l'individu utilise activement ou non les Programmes à un moment donné dans le temps.

Mailbox: Un point à partir duquel du courrier électronique est envoyé ou reçu: ce point est crée lorsqu'un compte d'utilisateur est établi dans Oracle Office.

Français canadien/Québec

CONDITIONS D'UTILISATION DE LICENCE ORACLE

AVERTISSEMENT: L'OUVERTURE DE CET EMBALLAGE OU L'UTILISATION DU LOGICIEL CONTENU À L'INTÉRIEUR ENTRAÎNE VOTRE CONSENTEMENT CONTRACTUEL AUX CONDITIONS ÉNONCÉES CI-DESSOUS. SI VOUS N'ÊTES PAS SATISFAIT DU LOGICIEL OU DES CONDITIONS DE SON UTILISATION, RETOURNEZ-LE AU FOURNISSEUR DANS LES TRENTE (30) JOURS POUR OBTENIR UN REMBOURSEMENT.

LA SOCIÉTÉ D'INFORMATIQUE ORACLE DU QUÉBEC INC. ("ORACLE") CONCÈDE À VOUS (LE "CLIENT") UNE LICENCE D'UTILISATION DES PROGRAMMES ET DE LA DOCUMENTATION CI-JOINTS SELON LES CONDITIONS SUIVANTES:

LICENCE: Le client a le droit d'utiliser les programmes dans le contexte d'exploitation identifié par Oracle, soit: (a) conformément aux conditions stipulées dans le bon de commande ou le certificat d'utilisation des programmes distribués au client par Oracle ou son distributeur; ou (b), sauf indication contraire, pour un seul utilisateur sur un seul ordinateur. L'utilisation des programmes est réservée exclusivement aux opérations internes de traitement informatique effectuées par le client. Le client peut faire une copie de sauvegarde de chaque programme sous licence; les droits d'effectuer des copies additionnelles, le cas échéant, sont indiqués dans le bon de commande ou le certificat d'utilisation des programmes. Aucune autre copie ne peut être faite sans l'accord préalable écrit d'Oracle. Le client n'est pas autorisé à supprimer les identifications du produits, les avis relatifs aux droits d'auteur ou tous autres avis ou restrictions concernant la propriété intellectuelle des programmes. Le client ne peut se servir des programmes pour une utilisation commerciale en temps partagé. De plus, le client ne peut pas louer les programmes ou les utiliser dans un contexte d'impartition. Il ne peut en effectuer le transfert, la vente ou la cession sous quelque que forme que ce soit à des tiers sans l'accord préalable écrit d'Oracle. Le client s'engage à ne pas causer ou permettre l'utilisation de techniques de désassemblage, de décompilation ou de rétroconception pour les programmes. Le client ne peut divulguer les résultats d'essais sur les programmes à des tiers sans l'accord préalable écrit d'Oracle. Le transfert des programmes est assujetti à la politique et aux frais de transfert établis par Oracle.

DROITS D'AUTEUR ET DE PROPRIÉTÉ: Les programmes sont la propriété d'Oracle ou son concédant de licence et sont protégés par le droit d'auteur et les autres droits de propriété intellectuelle. Le client bénéficie seulement d'un droit d'utilisation et n'acquiert aucun droit relatif à ces programmes ou à leur support, que ce soit expressément ou tacitement, que ceux qui lui sont accordés par la présente licence. Oracle, ou son concédant de licence, conserve tout titre, tout droit d'auteur ou tout autre droit de propriété, y compris la propriété intellectuelle, sur les programmes ou leur support.

GARANTIES LIMITÉES ET RECOURS EXCLUSIFS: Oracle garantit, pour une période de 90 jours à compter de la date de livraison des programmes au client, que les programmes utilisés de façon normale sont exempts de défaut de fabrication et assume durant cette période les frais de main-d'oeuvre; que les programmes, à moins qu'ils n'aient été modifiés par l'utilisateur, permettent d'exécuter les fonctions décrites dans la documentation fournie par Oracle, lorsqu'ils sont utilisés sur le système désigné. Oracle ne garantit pas que les programmes respecteront les exigences du client, que les programmes pourront être utilisés dans les combinaisons que le client pourra choisir, que l'utilisation des programmes se fera de façon ininterrompue ou sans erreur, ou que toutes les erreurs des programmes seront corrigées. **Les garanties susmentionnées constituent les seules garanties offertes par Oracle. Elles annulent et remplacent toute autre garantie ou condition expresse ou tacite, y compris les garanties ou conditions relatives à la valeur marchande ou les garanties de satisfaction en ce qui concerne un but particulier.** Si le client signale une erreur dans les 90 jours, Oracle se réserve le droit de corriger l'erreur ou de proposer à défaut une procédure de contournement ou, sur réception des programmes, remboursera le client. Oracle remplacera tout support défectueux sans frais s'il est retourné dans les 90 jours. **Ces recours sont les seules garanties contractuelles données par Oracle.**

LIMITATION DE RESPONSABILITÉ: ORACLE NE POURRA ÊTRE TENUE RESPONSABLE DE TOUT DOMMAGE INDIRECT, ACCIDENTEL, SPÉCIAL OU ACCESSOIRE, NI DES DOMMAGES RÉSULTANT DE LA PERTE DE PROFIT, DE REVENU, DE DONNÉES OU D'UTILISATION, ENCOURUS PAR L'UNE OU L'AUTRE DES PARTIES OU PAR UNE TIERCE PARTIE, RÉSULTANT DIRECTEMENT OU INDIRECTEMENT DE L'UTILISATION DES PROGRAMMES, MÊME SI L'AUTRE PARTIE OU TOUTE AUTRE PERSONNE A ÉTÉ AVISÉE DE LA POSSIBILITÉ DE TELS DOMMAGES. LA RESPONSABILITÉ D'ORACLE POUR LES DOMMAGES N'EXCÉDERA EN AUCUN CAS LE MONTANT PAYÉ PAR LE CLIENT À ORACLE EN VERTU DE LA PRÉSENTE LICENCE.

EXPORTATION: Le client doit se conformer entièrement aux lois et règlements en vigueur au Canada (lois sur l'exportation) afin de s'assurer qu'aucun programme ou produit direct associé ne soit: (1) exporté, directement ou indirectement, en violation des lois sur l'exportation, ou (2) ne soit utilisé à des fins prohibées par les lois sur l'exportation, notamment celles concernant la prolifération des armes nucléaires, chimiques ou biologiques. La présente licence et tout ce qui en découle doivent être assujettis aux lois en vigueur dans la province du Quebec. Oracle se réserve le droit de vérifier l'utilisation des programmes par le client. La présente licence annule et remplace les conditions relatives à tous bons ou documents de commande détenus par le client.

EXPORTATION: En aucun cas, le Client ne fera l'exportation à l'extérieur du Canada de façon directe ou indirecte, des Programmes ou de toute donnée technique en rapport avec les Programmes sans une authorisation au préalable ecrit d'Oracle.

DÉFINITIONS DES CERTIFICATS D'UTILISATION DES PROGRAMMES:
Unités concurrentes/Accès concurrents: Le nombre d'unités concurrentes équivaut au nombre maximal de terminaux et d'unités d'entrée utilisés pour accéder au système désigné à un moment donné. Si des logiciels ou de l'équipement de multiplexage (par exemple, un moniteur de traitement de transactions) sont utilisés avec le système désigné, le nombre d'unités concurrentes doit correspondre au nombre de terminaux et d'unités d'entrée qui sont reliés aux unités de multiplexage.

Client: Ordinateur qui est utilisé que par une seule personne à la fois et qui exécute un logiciel Oracle en mémoire locale ou stocke le logiciel dans une unité de mémoire locale.

Utilisateur: désigne une personne autorisée par le client à utiliser les programmes installés sur les systèmes désignés.

Boîte aux lettres: Emplacement à partir duquel du courrier électronique est expédié ou est reçu; elle est créée au moment de la mise sur pied d'un compte d'un client ou d'une application dans Oracle*Office.

Français/France

CONTRAT D'UTILISATION DU LOGICIEL ORACLE

ATTENTION: L'ouverture de cet emballage ou l'utilisation du Logiciel inclus implique l'acceptation des conditions de ce contrat. Au cas où vous n'accepteriez pas les Programmes ou les conditions ci-dessous, retournez-le dans son emballage d'origine au fournisseur dans les 30 jours de la date d'acquisition pour être remboursé.

Oracle France (« Oracle ») concède à la personne en ayant fait l'acquisition (le « Client ») une licence d'utilisation des programmes d'ordinateur ci-inclus et leur documentation (le « Logiciel ») dans les conditions suivantes:

LICENCE: Le Client aura le droit d'utiliser le Logiciel dans l'environnement d'exploitation (matériel et système d'exploitation) identifié par Oracle, (a) dans la mesure stipulée soit dans le document de commande, soit dans le Certificat d'Utilisation de Logiciel émis par Oracle ou son distributeur ou (b) pour un seul utilisateur sur un seul ordinateur, à défaut de stipulations contraires. L'utilisation du Logiciel est réservée exclusivement aux opérations de traitement de données internes. Le Client aura le droit de faire une copie de sauvegarde des programmes sous licence; le droit de faire des copies additionnelles est, s'il existe, stipulé dans le document de commande ou le Certificat d'Utilisation de Logiciel. Aucune copie additionnelle n'est permise sans l'accord écrit et préalable d'Oracle. Le Client n'est pas autorisé à supprimer les identifications du Logiciel, les mentions relatives au droit d'auteur ou tous autres avis ou restrictions concernant la propriété intellectuelle du Logiciel; ni à utiliser le Logiciel à des fins de temps partagé, de location ou de service bureau; ni à vendre, céder, ou transférer le Logiciel à des tiers sous quelque forme que ce soit sans l'accord écrit et préalable d'Oracle; ni à pratiquer ou autoriser l'ingénierie à rebours, la décompilation ou le désassemblage des programmes, si ce n'est dans la mesure indispensable pour développer des programmes compatibles avec le Logiciel mais n'enfreignant pas la propriété intellectuelle qui y est attachée, et cela dans le seul cas où le Client après demande écrite à Oracle n'aurait pas reçu dans un délai raisonnable les informations disponibles et nécessaires aux fins ci-dessus; ni de diffuser ou communiquer à un ou des tiers les résultats d'essais effectués sans l'accord écrit et préalable d'Oracle. L'éventuel transfert du Logiciel sera soumis aux politiques et frais de transfert établis par Oracle. Les droits d'utilisation sont concédés au Client uniquement pour le Logiciel mentionné sur le document de commande ou le Certificat d'Utilisation de Logiciel.

DROITS D'AUTEUR: Le Logiciel est protégé par les lois relatives au droit d'auteur et aux droits de propriété intellectuelle. Le Client n'acquiert sur le Logiciel aucun droit autre que ceux expressément concédés au titre des présentes. Oracle, ou son donneur de licence, conservent tout titre, droit d'auteur ou autre droit de propriété, y compris la propriété intellectuelle, relatifs au Logiciel et son support.

GARANTIES LIMITEES ET LIMITATION DES RECOURS: Oracle garantit, pour une période de quatre-vingt-dix jours à compter de la livraison que (a) le support d'information sur lequel le Logiciel est enregistré est, en utilisation normale, exempt de défauts de fabrication; et (b) un Logiciel non modifié remplit ses fonctionnalités documentées dans l'environnement d'exploitation désigné. Oracle ne garantit pas que le Logiciel répondra aux exigences du Client, conviendra à toutes les combinaisons que le Client pourra choisir, sera utilisable sans interruptions ou erreurs, ni que toutes les erreurs puissent être corrigées. Ces garanties constituent les seules garanties offertes par Oracle, et excluent toute autre garantie explicite ou implicite. Si le Client notifie une erreur pendant la période de garantie, Oracle corrigera l'erreur ou, à défaut, proposera une procédure de contournement ou, sur réception du Logiciel, remboursera le Client. Oracle remplacera tout support défectueux sans frais s'il est retourné dans les 90 jours. Ces recours sont les seules garanties contractuelles données par Oracle.

LIMITATION DE RESPONSABILITE: Oracle ne pourra être tenue pour responsable d'aucun dommage indirect ou accessoire, y compris la perte de profits, revenus, données ou utilisation, subis par le Client ou un tiers et résultant de l'utilisation du Logiciel, qu'Oracle ait été informé ou non de la possibilité de tels dommages. Oracle sera responsable des dommages directs qui lui seraient imputables dans la limite du prix payé par le Client dans le cadre de la présente licence.

VERIFICATION: Sur demande écrite d'Oracle, le Client lui fournira une déclaration (a) attestant que l'utilisation faite du Logiciel est conforme au présent contrat, y compris quand au nombre maximum d'utilisateurs et (b) listant le(s) site(s), type(s) et numéro(s) de série des matériels sur lesquels ils sont utilisés. Le Client fournira à Oracle une possibilité raisonnable de vérification des conditions d'utilisation.

TERRITOIRE: Le Client s'assurera que le Logiciel ne puisse être exporté si ce n'est en stricte conformité avec les dispositions applicables françaises et des Etats Unis d'Amérique ou utilisé à des fins interdites par ces dispositions, telles que la prolifération des armes nucléaires, chimiques ou biologiques. Ces dispositions s'appliquent sous la loi et le droit international privé français. La compétence revient aux tribunaux français. En cas de conflit entre ce contrat et des conditions générales associées au document de commande, ce contrat prévaudra.

DEFINITIONS DU CERTIFICAT D'UTILISATION DE LOGICIEL
Poste Concurrent / Accès Concurrent: le nombre de postes concurrents équivaut au nombre maximum d'organes d'entrée de données qui peuvent accéder au Logiciel à un moment donné. Si des programmes ou matériels de multiplexage (par exemple un moniteur transactionnel) sont utilisés, le nombre de postes concurrents équivaudra au nombre d'organes d'entrée de données reliés audit programme ou matériel de multiplexage.

Client: ordinateur utilisé par une seule personne à la fois et qui exécute un Logiciel en mémoire locale ou stocke un Logiciel en mémoire locale.

Utilisateur: personne autorisée par le titulaire de la présente licence à utiliser le Logiciel dans l'environnement d'exploitation désigné.

Boîte aux Lettres: Emplacement à partir duquel du courrier électronique est expédié ou reçu. Elle est créée au moment de l'ouverture d'un compte au profit d'un Utilisateur ou d'une application dans Oracle*Office.

Deutsch/Österreich, Deutschland, Schweiz

ORACLE PROGRAMM LIZENZ BEDINGUNGEN

VORSICHT: WENN SIE DIESE VERPACKUNG ÖFFNEN ODER DIE BEIGEFÜGTE SOFTWARE NUTZEN, GELTEN DIE FOLGENDEN BESTIMMUNGEN. WENN SIE MIT DER SOFTWARE ODER DIESEN BESTIMMUNGEN NICHT EINVERSTANDEN SIND, GEBEN SIE DIE SOFTWARE INNERHALB VON 30 TAGEN ZURÜCK AN IHREN VERKÄUFER GEGEN RÜCKERSTATTUNG DES PREISES.

ORACLE GEWÄHRT IHNEN ("KUNDE") EINE LIZENZ, DIE BEIGEFÜGTE SOFTWARE UND DOKUMENTATION ("PROGRAMME") WIE FOLGEND AUFGEZEIGT ZU NUTZEN.

LIZENZ: Der Kunde hat das Recht, die Programme in der von Oracle bestimmten Betriebsumgebung entweder (a) in dem Umfang zu nutzen, wie in einem Auftragsformular oder in einem Programm-Nutzungs-Zertifikat einzeln angegeben, das von Oracle oder ihrem Distributor erteilt wird, oder (b) sofern keine Angaben erfolgt sind, die Programme für einen einzelnen Anwender auf einem einzelnen Computer zu nutzen. Der Kunde darf die Programme nur für Zwecke der eigenen internen Datenverarbeitung nutzen. Der Kunde darf eine Kopie der Programme als Backup anfertigen; das Recht zusätzliche Kopien anzufertigen muß im Auftragsformular oder im Programm-Nutzungs-Zertifikat festgelegt werden. Ohne schriftliche Genehmigung von Oracle dürfen keine weiteren Kopien angefertigt werden. Der Kunde ist nicht berechtigt: (a) Produktbezeichnungen, Urheberrechtsvermerke oder andere Vermerke sowie Eigentumsbeschränkungen in den Programmen zu entfernen; (b) die Programme für kommerzielles Timesharing, für Miete oder ein Rechenzentrum zu nutzen; (c) die Programme zu übertragen, zu verkaufen, Rechte daraus abzutreten oder sonstwie einem Dritten zu übertragen, es sei denn, Oracle genehmigt dies vorher schriftlich; (d) Dekompilierung, Dissassemblierung oder Reverse Engineering der Programme durchzuführen oder zu gestatten oder (e) Ergebnisse von Benchmark-Tests eines Programms einem Dritten offenzulegen, es sei denn, Oracle genehmigt dies vorher schriftlich. Alle Übertragun der Programme richten sich nach den Transfer Regeln und Gebühren von Oracle. Der Kunde hat das Recht, nur die Programme in dieser Verpackung zu nutzen, die in einem Auftragsformular einzeln angegeben sind.

URHEBERRECHT: Oracle ist Rechtsinhaberin der urheberrechtlich und in anderen gewerblichen Schutzrechten geschützten Programmen. Der Kunde erwirbt Nutzungsrechte nur für diejenigen Programme, die einzeln in dieser Lizenz angegeben sind. Er erwirbt keine Nutzungsrechte an solchen Programmen oder Datenträgern, die in dieser Lizenz nicht einzeln angegeben sind. Oracle bleibt jederzeit alleinige Rechtsinhaberin aller Immaterialgüterrechte an den Programmen und den Datenträgern.

GEWÄHRLEISTUNG: Oracle gewährleistet für die Dauer von 90 Tagen ab dem Datum der Lieferung: (a) daß der beiliegende Datenträger bei gewöhnlichem Gebrauch nicht mit Material- und Herstellungsfehlern behaftet ist und (b) daß die unveränderten Programme die in der zugehörigen Dokumentation beschriebenen Funktionen auf dem genau bezeichneten Computer und Betriebssystem im wesentlichen erfüllen und nicht mit Fehlern behaftet sind, die die Tauglichkeit aufheben oder mindern. Eine unerhebliche Minderung bleibt außer Betracht. Oracle kann nicht zusichern, daß die Programme alle Anforderungen des Kunden erfüllen oder daß die darin enthaltenen Funktionen in einer vom Kunden ausgewählten Kombination ununterbrochen und fehlerfrei ablaufen oder alle Programmfehler behoben werden. Die Gewährleistung für nicht erkennbare Mängel aufgrund von Hardware- bzw. Betriebssystemfehlern und für solche Programme, die der Kunden ändert oder in die er sonstwie eingreift, ist ausgeschlossen, es sei denn, der Kunde weist im Zusammenhang mit der Fehlermeldung nach, daß ein solcher Fehler oder Eingriff für den Mangel nicht ursächlich ist. Falls der Kunde innerhalb von 90 Tagen einen Programmfehler meldet, kann Oracle wahlweise den Fehler beheben, dem Kunden eine Fehlerumgehung liefern oder dem Kunden nach Rücksendung der Programme an Oracle die Lizenzgebühren zurückerstatten. Oracle ersetzt kostenlos jeden nachgewiesenen fehlerhaften Datenträger, wenn der Datenträger innerhalb der Frist von 90 Tagen an Oracle zurückgeschickt wird.

HAFTUNGSBESCHRÄNKUNG: Oracle haftet dem Kunden, gleichgültig aus welchem Rechtsgrund, für die selbst oder durch Erfüllungsgehilfen vorsätzlich oder grob fahrlässig verursachten Schäden. Eine Haftung für leichte Fahrlässigkeit besteht nur bei der Verletzung wesentlicher Vertragspflichten. In diesem Fall wird die Haftung für vertragsuntypische Schäden ausgeschlossen. Für einen einzelnen Schadensfall ist die Haftung auf maximal DM 500.000, – bzw. den entsprechenden Betrag in österreichischer oder schweizerischer Währung begrenzt. Als einzelner Schadensfall gilt die Summe der Schadensersatzansprüche aller Anspruchsberechtigten, die sich aus einer einzelnen, zeitlich zusammenhängend erbrachten, abgrenzbaren und insoweit einheitlichen Leistung ergibt.

EINGESCHRÄNKTE RECHTE: Der Kunde verpflichtet sich, die Bestimmungen und Vorschriften des Exportverwaltungsgesetzes der USA sowie die einschlägigen deutschen Ausfuhrbestimmungen zu beachten ("Export- Gesetze") und stellt sicher, daß weder die Programme noch direkte Produkte davon (1) direkt oder indirekt unter Verletzung der Export- Gesetze exportiert werden oder (2) zu dem Zwecke eingesetzt werden, den Export- Gesetze verbieten, insbesondere zur Verbreitung von Kernwaffen, chemischen oder biologischen Waffen. Es gilt das Recht der Bundesrepublik Deutschland mit Ausnahme des UN-Kaufrechts. Oracle ist berechtigt, die Nutzung der Programme durch den Kunden zu überprüfen. Diese Bedingungen haben Vorrang vor allen Geschäfts- und Einkaufsbedingungen des Kunden.

Das anwendbare Recht für diese Lizenz und alle im Zusammenhang damit stehende Handlungen bestimmt sich nach der Lieferung der Programme an den Kunden: (a) Schweizer Recht, sofern die Lieferung in der Schweiz erfolgte; (b) Deutsches Recht mit Ausnahme des UN- Kaufrechts, sofern die Lieferung in der Bundesrepublik Deutschland erfolgte; (c) Österreichisches Recht mit Ausnahme des UN-Kaufrechts, sofern die Lieferung in der Republik Österreich erfolgte.

DEFINITION DES PROGRAMM-NUTZUNGS-ZERTIFIKATS:
Concurrent Devices/Concurrent Accesses: Maximale Anzahl von Eingabegeräten, die auf die Programme zu einem bestimmten Zeitpunkt zugreifen. Sofern Multiplexe Software oder Hardware (d.h. TP Monitor) eingesetzt wird, wird die Zahl vor dem Multiplexer bestimmt.

Client: Ein Computer, der (1) nur von einer Person zu einem Zeitpunkt genutzt wird und (2), der die Oracle Software im lokalen Speicher ausführt oder die Software in lokale Eingabegeräte speichert.

User: Eine Einzelperson, die vom Kunden zur Nutzung der Programme berechtigt wird, unabhängig davon, ob die Einzelperson die Programme zu irgendeinem Zeitpunkt tatsächlich aktiv nutzt.

Mailbox: Sendet und empfängt Nachrichten; sie wird angelegt, wenn ein User oder eine Anwendungsprogramm für Oracle*Office errichtet wird.

Ελληνικά/Ελλάδα

ΠΡΟΣΟΧΗ!!! ΠΑΡΑΚΑΛΩ, ΜΗΝ ΑΝΟΙΞΕΤΕ ΤΟ ΠΑΚΕΤΟ ΑΥΤΟ ΟΥΤΕ ΝΑ ΧΡΗΣΙΜΟΠΟΙΗΣΕΤΕ ΤΑ ΠΡΟΪΟΝΤΑ ΛΟΓΙΣΜΙΚΟΥ ΚΑΙ ΤΗΝ ΤΕΚΜΗΡΙΩΣΗ ΠΟΥ ΕΣΩΚΛΕΙΟΝΤΑΙ, ΠΑΡΑ ΜΟΝΟΝ ΑΦΟΥ ΕΧΕΤΕ ΔΙΑΒΑΣΕΙ ΠΡΟΣΕΚΤΙΚΑ ΚΑΙ ΑΠΟΔΕΧΤΕΙ ΤΟΥΣ ΠΑΡΑΚΑΤΩ ΟΡΟΥΣ. ΤΟ ΑΝΟΙΓΜΑ ΤΟΥ ΠΕΡΙΤΥΛΙΓΜΑΤΟΣ ΙΣΟΔΥΝΑΜΕΙ ΜΕ ΑΠΟΔΟΧΗ ΤΩΝ ΠΙΟ ΚΑΤΩ ΟΡΩΝ ΧΡΗΣΕΩΣ ΤΟΥ ΛΟΓΙΣΜΙΚΟΥ

ΣΥΜΒΑΣΗ ΠΑΡΟΧΗΣ ΑΔΕΙΑΣ ΧΡΗΣΗΣ ΛΟΓΙΣΜΙΚΟΥ

ΜΕΤΑΞΥ: Αφενός, της ORACLE ΕΛΛΑΣ Α.Ε.Ε., που εδρεύει στην Αθήνα (11361), οδός Φωκίωνος Νέγρη 30 (στην συνέχεια η ORACLE), και

Αφετέρου, του ΠΕΛΑΤΗ. Ως "ΠΕΛΑΤΗΣ" νοείται ο αγοραστής, με τους πιο κάτω περιορισμούς, του παρόντος πακέτου.

Η εταιρία ORACLE παρέχει με το παρόν στον "ΠΕΛΑΤΗ" μόνο την άδεια χρήσης του λογισμικού και της τεκμηρίωσης που εσωκλείεται στο παρόν πακέτο και τα οποία στη συνέχεια θα αναφέρονται ως "Προγράμματα", με τους ακόλουθους όρους:

ΑΔΕΙΑ ΧΡΗΣΗΣ: Ο ΠΕΛΑΤΗΣ έχει το δικαίωμα να χρησιμοποιεί τα προγράμματα σε λειτουργική μονάδα που έχει καθορισθεί από την ORACLE είτε α) κατά τον τρόπο που καθορίζεται στο έντυπο παραγγελίας ή στην Εξουσιοδότηση Χρήσης του Προγράμματος, την οποία έχει δώσει στον πελάτη η ORACLE ή η διανομέας της, είτε β) εάν δεν έχει καθορισθεί, τα προγράμματα θα χρησιμοποιούνται από έναν μόνο χρήστη σε ένα μόνο ηλεκτρονικό υπολογιστή. Ο ΠΕΛΑΤΗΣ μπορεί να χρησιμοποιεί τα προγράμματα αποκλειστικά και μόνο για την επεξεργασία των δικών του δεδομένων. Ο ΠΕΛΑΤΗΣ μπορεί να αντιγράψει μόνο μία φορά το πρόγραμμα για το οποίο παραχωρήθηκε άδεια χρήσης, για εφεδρεία (backup). Το τυχόν δικαίωμα του ΠΕΛΑΤΗ να κάνει περισσότερα αντίγραφα του προγράμματος πρέπει να προσδιορίζεται στο έντυπο παραγγελίας ή στην Εξουσιοδότηση Χρήσης του προγράμματος. Απαγορεύεται να γίνουν άλλα αντίγραφα χωρίς την προηγούμενη έγγραφη άδεια της ORACLE. Ο ΠΕΛΑΤΗΣ απαγορεύεται να προβαίνει στις εξής ενέργειες: α) να αφαιρεί από το προγράμματο τα διακριτικά τους, τις ενδείξεις πνευματικής ιδιοκτησίας και κάθε άλλη ένδειξη ή περιορισμό σε σχέση με τα αποκλειστικά δικαιώματα της ORACLE, β) να εκμισθώνει τα προγράμματα με εμπορικό χρονομετρική ή μη μίσθωση, ή ως επιχείρηση παροχής υπηρεσιών, γ) να μεταβιβάζει, πωλεί, παραχωρεί ή με οποιοδήποτε άλλο τρόπο εκχωρεί τα προγράμματα σε τρίτον χωρίς την προηγούμενη έγγραφη συναίνεση της ORACLE, δ) ο ΠΕΛΑΤΗΣ υποχρεούται να μην προβαίνει, ούτε να επιτρέπει την αντίστροφη μετάγλωττιση (αποσυμπίληση), αποσυναρμολόγηση, αποκωδικοποίηση, μετάφραση, προσαρμογή ή διασκευή των προγραμμάτων, με εξαίρεση την περίπτωση κατά την οποία ο ΠΕΛΑΤΗΣ δεν έχει λάβει από την ORACLE μέσα σε εύλογο χρονικό διάστημα, ύστερα από έγγραφη αίτησή του, τις πληροφορίες που διαθέτει η ORACLE και οι οποίες είναι αναγκαίες για τη διαλειτουργικότητα προγραμμάτων που δημιουργεί ο ΠΕΛΑΤΗΣ με τα προγράμματα των οποίων παραχωρείται η άδεια χρήσης με το παρόν, αλλά δεν παραβιάζουν τα δικαιώματα πνευματικής ιδιοκτησίας της ORACLE και ε) να αποκαλύπτει σε τρίτους χωρίς την προηγούμενη έγγραφη έγκριση της ORACLE τα αποτελέσματα δοκιμών του προγράμματος. Για κάθε μεταβίβαση του προγράμματος ισχύει η διαδικασία μεταβίβασης και οι αμοιβές που έχουν καθορισθεί από την ORACLE. Ο ΠΕΛΑΤΗΣ έχει δικαίωμα να χρησιμοποιεί από τα προγράμματα που εσωκλείονται στο παρόν πακέτο μόνο εκείνα τα οποία καθορίζονται στο έντυπο παραγγελίας ή στην Εξουσιοδότηση Χρήσης του Προγράμματος.

ΠΝΕΥΜΑΤΙΚΗ ΙΔΙΟΚΤΗΣΙΑ/ΚΥΡΙΟΤΗΤΑ ΠΡΟΓΡΑΜΜΑΤΩΝ: Τα προγράμματα είναι προϊόντα της αποκλειστικής κυριότητας της ORACLE και προστατεύονται από το νόμο περί πνευματικής ιδιοκτησίας.

Ο ΠΕΛΑΤΗΣ αποκτά μόνο το δικαίωμα να χρησιμοποιεί τα προγράμματα και κανένα άλλο δικαίωμα, ρητό ή σιωπηρό, επί των προγραμμάτων αυτών ή επί των μέσων (υλικών φορέων) στα οποία τα προγράμματα έχουν ενσωματωθεί εκτός από αυτά που καθορίζονται στην παρούσα άδεια. Η ORACLE ή ο παρέχων σε αυτήν άδεια χρήσης λογισμικού διατηρεί πάντοτε την κυριότητα και κάθε άλλο δικαίωμα και έννομο συμφέρον, συμπεριλαμβανομένων των δικαιωμάτων πνευματικής ιδιοκτησίας, στα προγράμματα και στα μέσα.

ΕΓΓΥΗΣΕΙΣ/ΑΠΟΚΛΕΙΣΤΙΚΟΙ ΤΡΟΠΟΙ ΑΠΟΚΑΤΑΣΤΑΣΗΣ: Η ORACLE εγγυάται ότι για έξι (6) μήνες από την ημερομηνία παράδοσης στον πελάτη: α) τα μέσα (media) που εσωκλείονται στο παρόν πακέτο είναι απαλλαγμένα από ελαττώματα ποιότητας υλικού και επεξεργασίας κατά τη διάρκεια κανονικής χρήσης τους και β) τα προγράμματα, εφόσον δεν έχουν τροποποιηθεί και λειτουργούν στον καθορισμένο ηλεκτρονικό υπολογιστή και λειτουργικό σύστημα, θα εκτελούν ουσιαστικά τις λειτουργίες που περιγράφονται στην τεκμηρίωση που παρέχεται από την ORACLE. Η ORACLE δεν εγγυάται, ότι το πρόγραμμα θα ανταποκρίνεται στις απαιτήσεις του ΠΕΛΑΤΗ, ότι θα λειτουργεί σε συνδυασμό με άλλα προγράμματα που μπορεί να επιλέξει προς χρήση ο ΠΕΛΑΤΗΣ, ότι η λειτουργία του προγράμματος θα είναι αδιάκοπη ή απαλλαγμένη από σφάλματα, ούτε ότι όλα τα σφάλματα του προγράμματος θα επιδέχονται διόρθωση. Οι εγγυήσεις αυτές αποκλείουν (κάθε άλλη ευθύνη η ORACLE) και υποκαθιστούν οποιαδήποτε άλλη εγγύηση ή όρο ρητό ή σιωπηρό, συμπεριλαμβανομένων ακόμη και των σιωπηρών εγγυήσεων για την εμπορικότητα και καταλληλότητα του προγράμματος για τον συγκεκριμένο σκοπό που το προορίζει ο ΠΕΛΑΤΗΣ. Εάν ο ΠΕΛΑΤΗΣ μέσα στο χρονικό διάστημα των έξι (6) μηνών αναφέρει στην ORACLE την ύπαρξη ελαττώματος, η ORACLE θα μπορεί κατά την κρίση της, να διορθώσει το σφάλμα, να υποδεικνύει στον ΠΕΛΑΤΗ τον εύλογο κατά τις συνθήκες τρόπο για να ξεπεράσει το σφάλμα, ή, εφόσον ο ΠΕΛΑΤΗΣ επιστρέψει τα προγράμματα στην ORACLE, αυτή να του επιστρέφει την αμοιβή που έχει εισπράξει για την άδεια χρήσης. Η ORACLE θα αντικαθιστά δωρεάν όλα τα ελαττωματικά μέσα (media) εφόσον επιστρέφονται στην ORACLE μέσα σε χρονικό διάστημα έξι (6) μηνών. Η ευθύνη της ORACLE σε περίπτωση παράβασης των όρων εγγύησης περιορίζεται αποκλειστικά στις πιο πάνω υποχρεώσεις απέναντι στον ΠΕΛΑΤΗ.

ΠΕΡΙΟΡΙΣΜΟΣ ΕΥΘΥΝΗΣ: Η ORACLE σε καμμία περίπτωση δεν θα ευθύνεται για άμεσες ή έμμεσες ζημίες, θετικές ή αποθετικές, τυχηρά, ανωτέρα βία ή για περαιτέρω ζημίες συμπεριλαμβανομένου του διαφυγόντος κέρδους και της απώλειας δεδομένων ή χρήσης δεδομένων, που προκλήθηκαν στον ΠΕΛΑΤΗ ή σε τρίτον στα πλαίσια συμβατικής ή αδικοπρακτικής ευθύνης ακόμα και εάν η ORACLE ή οποιοδήποτε άλλο πρόσωπο είχε ενημερωθεί για τη δυνατότητα επέλευσης των ζημιών αυτών. Η ORACLE για ζημίες σε καμμία περίπτωση δεν θα υπερβαίνει τις αμοιβές που κατέβαλε ο ΠΕΛΑΤΗΣ για την παρούσα άδεια χρήσης.

Το παρόν συμφωνητικό υπερέχει των όρων προμηθείας του ΠΕΛΑΤΗ, καθώς και κάθε άλλου εντύπου παραγγελίας. Ο ΠΕΛΑΤΗΣ συμφωνεί να τηρεί πλήρως όλους τους νόμους και κανονισμούς προκειμένου να εξασφαλισθεί ότι αυτό το πρόγραμμα ούτε κανένα άμεσο προϊόν αυτού θα εξάγεται από την Ελλάδα άμεσα ή έμμεσα κατά παράβαση του νόμου.

Ο ΠΕΛΑΤΗΣ είναι υποχρεωμένος να τηρεί πλήρως τους νόμους και κανονισμούς που ισχύουν στις Ηνωμένες Πολιτείες και στην Ελλάδα και αναφέρονται στην εξαγωγή προϊόντων, προκειμένου να εξασφαλισθεί 1) ότι τα προγράμματα ή άλλο άμεσο προϊόν αυτών δεν θα εξάγονται στην αλλοδαπή άμεσα ή έμμεσα, κατά παράβαση των ανωτέρω νόμων και διατάξεων ή 2) ότι αυτά δεν θα χρησιμοποιούνται για σκοπό που απαγορεύεται από τους πιο πάνω νόμους και διατάξεις, συμπεριλαμβανομένης, ενδεικτικά, της εξάπλωσης των πυρηνικών, χημικών ή βιολογικών όπλων. Η παρούσα σύμβαση και κάθε άλλη συναφής συμφωνία ή ενέργεια, δικαστική ή εξώδικη θα διέπεται από το Ελληνικό δίκαιο. Η ORACLE μπορεί να ελέγχει τη χρησιμοποίηση προγραμμάτων από τον ΠΕΛΑΤΗ. Η σύμβαση αυτή υπερισχύει των όρων παραγγελίας αγοράς ή οποιουδήποτε άλλου εντύπου παραγγελίας του ΠΕΛΑΤΗ.

ΕΝΝΟΙΑ ΟΡΩΝ ΣΤΗ ΕΞΟΥΣΙΟΔΟΤΗΣΗ ΧΡΗΣΗΣ ΠΡΟΓΡΑΜΜΑΤΟΣ

Ταυτόχρονα συνδεδεμένες με το σύστημα διατάξεις/Ταυτόχρονες προσβάσεις: είναι ο ανώτατος αριθμός διατάξεων εισόδου στο σύστημα, οι οποίες έχουν πρόσβαση στα προγράμματα σε μία δεδομένη χρονική στιγμή. Εάν χρησιμοποιείται λογισμικό ή ηλεκτρονικό υλικό που επιτρέπει την πολυσύνδεση (π.χ. TP monitor), ο ανωτέρω αριθμός πρέπει να υπολογίζεται πριν από την πολυσύνδεση.

Εξυπηρετούμενος υπολογιστής: είναι ο ηλεκτρονικός υπολογιστής ο οποίος 1) χρησιμοποιείται από ένα μόνο πρόσωπο κάθε φορά και 2) εκτελεί το λογισμικό της ORACLE στην τοπική μνήμη ή αποθηκεύει το λογισμικό σε μια τοπική διάταξη αποθήκευσης.

Χρήστης: είναι το φυσικό πρόσωπο το οποίο έχει εξουσιοδοτηθεί από τον ΠΕΛΑΤΗ να χρησιμοποιεί τα προγράμματα, ανεξάρτητα εάν το φυσικό αυτό πρόσωπο χρησιμοποιεί πράγματι τα προγράμματα αυτά ή όχι σε μία δεδομένη χρονική στιγμή.

Γραμματοθυρίδα: είναι η περιοχή από την οποία στέλνονται ή η οποία λαμβάνει μηνύματα ή δεδομένα με σύστημα ηλεκτρονικού ταχυδρομείου (electronic mail) και η οποία δημιουργείται όταν λογαριασμός ή η εφαρμογή του χρήστη εγκαθίσταται στο Oracle* Office.

ΔΟΣΙΔΙΚΙΑ ΚΑΙ ΑΡΜΟΔΙΟΤΗΣ: Για κάθε διαφορά που θα προκύψει σε σχέση με το κύρος, την ερμηνεία ή την εκτέλεση του παρόντος, αποκλειστικά αρμόδια θα είναι τα Δικαστήρια της Αθήνας κάθε βαθμού και δικαιοδοσίας.

Magyar/Magyarország

AZ ORACLE PROGRAMOK LICENC FELTÉTELEI

FIGYELEM: HA KINYITJA EZT A DOBOZT VAGY HASZNÁLJA A BENNE TALÁLHATÓ SZOFTVERT, ÉLETBE LÉPNEK AZ ALÁBBI KIKÖTÉSEK. HA EZEK A FELTÉTELEK NEM ELFOGADHATÓK AZ ÖN SZÁMÁRA, KÉRJÜK, JUTTASSA VISSZA A SZOFTVERT A MEGFIZETETT DÍJ VISSZATÉRÍTÉSE ELLENÉBEN ANNAK A CÉGNEK, AMELYTŐL BESZEREZTE.

AZ ORACLE HUNGARY KFT. (A TOVÁBBIAKBAN: „ORACLE") ÖNT (A TOVÁBBIAKBAN: „VEVŐ") JELEN SZOFTVER LICENCCEL FELHATALMAZZA ARRA, HOGY A MELLÉKELT SZOFTVERT ÉS DOKUMENTÁCIÓT (EGYÜTTESEN: „PROGRAMOK") AZ ALÁBBIAKNAK MEGFELELŐEN HASZNÁLHASSA.

LICENC: A Vevő a Programok használatára az adott földrajzi Területen, kizárólag az Oracle által megadott üzemeltetési környezetben jogosult, mégpedig vagy (a) az ORACLE vagy annak disztribútora által a Vevőnek átadott megrendelési bizonylat vagy használatbavételi engedély által meghatározott mennyiségi kereteken belül, vagy (b) konkrét előírások hiányában egy számítógépen, egy felhasználóval. A Vevő a Programokat kizárólag saját belső adatfeldolgozási igényeinek kielégítésére használhatja. A Vevő biztonsági célból egy másolatot készíthet magának minden licencbe adott Programról; a további másolatok készítésének jogáról a megrendelési bizonylatban vagy a használatbavételi engedélyben történhet rendelkezés. A Programokról további másolatok az Oracle előzetes írásos beleegyezése nélkül nem készíthetők. A Vevő: (a) nem távolíthat el semmilyen megkülönböztetett termékjelzést, a szerzői jogra vonatkozó jelzést, vagy egyéb megkülönböztető vagy a szellemi tulajdonhoz kapcsolódó korlátozó jelzést a Programokból; (b) nem használhatja a Programokat többfelhasználós idősztásos üzemmódban, ha ez kereskedelmi céllal történik, illetve nem adhatja bérbe és nem használhatja számítóközpontban bérfeldolgozásra; (c) nem adhatja át, nem adhatja el, nem engedményezheti vagy semmilyen egyéb módon nem ruházhatja át a Programokat harmadik fél részére az Oracle előzetes, írásos beleegyezése nélkül; (d) nem fejtheti vissza a Programok működését, nem fejtheti vissza őket gépi kódra disassembler segítségével, nem fordíthatja őket vissza, illetve ezen tevékenységek egyikét sem engedheti meg; és (e) az Oracle előzetes írásos beleegyezése nélkül a Programok teljesítményértékelő tesztjeinek eredményeit harmadik féllel nem közölheti. A Programok átruházása csakis az Oracle idevonatkozó rendelkezései és díjai alapján történhet. A Vevő kizárólag az ebben a dobozban lévő, a használatbavételi engedélyben meghatározott Programok használatára jogosult.

SZERZŐI JOG: A Programok az Oracle szellemi termékei, és a szerzői jogi, valamint a szellemi tulajdonra vonatkozó egyéb törvények védelme alá esnek. A Vevő kizárólag a Programok felhasználásának jogát szerzi meg, és nem szerez a Programokhoz vagy a Programokat tartalmazó adathordozókhoz fűződő semmilyen kifejezett vagy hallgatólagos jogot a jelen licencfeltételekben meghatározott jogokon kívül. Az Oracle vagy az Oracle licencbe adója mindenkor fenntart minden, a Programokhoz és az adathordozóhoz fűződő jogot, jogcímet és érdekeltséget, ideértve a szellemi tulajdonra vonatkozó jogokat is.

KORLÁTOZOTT SZAVATOSSÁG/KIZÁRÓLAGOS JOGORVOSLAT: Az Oracle szavatolja, hogy a Vevő részére történő átadástól számított 90 napig (a) a mellékelt adathordozó rendeltetésszerű használat esetén kivitelezési és anyaghibáktól mentes, és hogy (b) a Programok, amennyiben azokat nem módosítják, az Oracle által adott dokumentációban leírt funkciók végrehajtására lényegileg képesek lesznek, feltéve, ha az előírt számítógépen és operációs rendszerrel használják azokat. Az Oracle nem szavatolja, hogy a Programok megfelelnek a Vevő igényeinek, hogy a Programok a Vevő által esetleg kiválasztott összetételben működni fognak, hogy a Programok megszakítatlanul vagy hibamentesen fognak működni, valamint azt sem, hogy a Programok valamennyi hibáját kijavítják. Mindezen szavatossági előírások kizárólagosak, és helyettesítenek minden egyéb szavatosságot, legyen az vagy hallgatólagos (jogszabályi), beleértve a kereskedelmi forgalmazhatóságért való és a meghatározott célra történő alkalmasságért való szavatosságot. Ha a Vevő 90 napon belül bejelenti a Program valamilyen hibáját, az Oracle belátása szerint vagy kijavítja a hibát, vagy a hiba megkerüléséhez megfelelő eljárást biztosít a Vevő részére, vagy a Vevő által visszaadott Programok ellenében megtéríti a Vevő által fizetett licencdíjat. Az Oracle ellenszolgáltatás nélkül kicserél minden hibás adathordozót, ha azt 90 napos időtartamon belül részére visszaszolgáltatták. A fent felsoroltak a Vevő egyedüli és kizárólagos jogai bármilyen szavatossági probléma esetében. Ez a korlátozott szavatosság határozza meg az Ön jogait.

A FELELŐSSÉG KORLÁTOZÁSA. AZ ORACLE NEM TARTOZIK FELELŐSSÉGGEL SEMMILYEN KÖZVETETT, ESETLEGES, KÜLÖNÖS VAGY KÖVETKEZMÉNYES KÁRÉRT, SEM A VEVŐ VAGY HARMADIK SZEMÉLY ÁLTAL ELSZENVEDETT, HASZON, JÖVEDELEM, ADAT VAGY ADATHASZNÁLAT ELVESZTÉSÉBŐL EREDŐ KÁRÉRT, TEKINTET NÉLKÜL ARRA, HOGY EZ SZERZŐDÉSES VAGY SZERZŐDÉSEN KÍVÜLI IGÉNY. AKKOR SEM, HA AZ ORACLE-T VAGY BÁRMELY MÁS SZEMÉLYT TÁJÉKOZTATTÁK AZ ILYEN KÁROK LEHETŐSÉGÉRŐL. AZ ORACLE JELEN SZERZŐDÉS SZERINTI, KÁROKOZÁSÁBÓL EREDŐ FELELŐSSÉGE SEMMILYEN ESETBEN SEM HALADHATJA MEG A VEVŐ ÁLTAL A JELEN LICENCÉRT FIZETETT DÍJAT.

TERÜLET: a „Terület" Magyarországot jelenti, kivéve, ha ezt megrendelési bizonylat vagy használatbavételi engedély másként határozza meg.

A VEVŐ beleegyezik, hogy az Amerikai Egyesült Államok és más államok összes törvényét és előírását („Exportszabályozás") teljes mértékben betartja annak biztosítására, hogy sem a Programok, sem a közvetlenül segítségükkel készült termékek (1) sem közvetlen, sem közvetett módon nem kerülnek exportálásra az Exportszabályozást megsértő módon, és (2) nem kerülnek felhasználásra az Exportszabályozás által tiltott célokra, beleértve többek közt a nukleáris, vegyi és biológiai fegyvereket korlátozó rendelkezések hatókörébe eső tevékenységeket. Jelen megállapodásra és minden hozzá kapcsolódó tevékenységre a Magyar Köztársaság törvényei vonatkoznak. Az Oracle fenntartja annak a jogát, hogy a Program használatát a Vevőnél ellenőrizze. Jelen szoftver licenc a Vevő minden esetleges korábbi megrendelésének és megrendelési bizonylatának kikötéseit felülbírálja.

A HASZNÁLATBAVÉTELI ENGEDÉLYBEN SZEREPLŐ FOGALMAK MEGHATÁROZÁSA:
Egyidejű eszközhasználat/egyidejű hozzáférések: a programhoz egy adott időpontban hozzáférő adatbeviteli eszközök száma. Ha multiplexer hardvert vagy szoftvert (pl. TP monitort) használnak, a felhasználók számát a multiplexer bemenetén kell mérni.

Ügyfél (kliens): olyan számítógép, amelyet (1) egyidőben csak egy személy használ, és (2) az Oracle szoftvert saját memóriájában futtatja és saját háttértárolóján tárolja.

Felhasználó: a Vevő által a Programok használatára feljogosított személy, függetlenül attól, hogy egy adott időpontban a programot ténylegesen használja-e vagy sem.

Postaláda (mailbox): olyan pont, amelyről/amelyre elektronikus levél továbbítható vagy fogadható; akkor keletkezik, amikor egy új felhasználó vagy alkalmazás hozzáférési jogosultságot kap az Oracle*Office-hoz.

Italiano/Italia

LICENZA D'USO DI PROGRAMMA ORACLE

**ATTENZIONE: SE APRITE QUESTO PACCHETTO O USATE IL SOFTWARE IVI CONTENUTO, SI APPLICHERANNO I SEGUENTI TERMINI E CON-
DIZIONI. SE NON ACCETTATE IL SOFTWARE O I PREDETTI TERMINI E CONDIZIONI, RESTITUITE IL SOFTWARE - ENTRO 30
GIORNI - ALLA SOCIETÀ DA CUI LO AVETE RICEVUTO PER IL RIMBORSO.**

ORACLE ITALIA S.p.A. ("ORACLE") CONCEDE A VOI ("CLIENTE") UNA LICENZA D'USO DEL SOFTWARE E DELLA DOCUMENTAZIONE
CONTENUTI NEL PACCHETTO ("PROGRAMMI") COME INDICATO OLTRE.

LICENZA: il Cliente avrà il diritto di usare i Programmi, nell'ambiente operativo identificato da Oracle: (a) nei limiti specificati in un documento di ordine o in
un Certificato di Uso di Programma distribuito al Cliente da Oracle o da un suo Distributore; o (b) se non specificati, per un singolo utente su un singolo
computer. Il Cliente potrà usare i Programmi unicamente per l'elaborazione propria di dati interni. Il Cliente potrà trarre n.1 copia per il caso di guasti, detta
copia di backup, di ciascun Programma licenziato; eventuali diritti di trarre copie ulteriori, se del caso, saranno specificati in un documento d'ordine o in un
Certificato di Uso di Programma. Non potranno essere tratte altre copie senza la previa autorizzazione scritta di Oracle. Il Cliente non potrà: (a) eliminare
dai Programmi i dati identificativi del Prodotto, i dati di copyright, e ogni indicazione dei diritti di proprietà riservata; (b) commercializzare i Programmi,
noleggiarli, usarli per erogare servizi a terzi, condividere l'uso con terzi, concedere anche parzialmente e/o temporaneamente l'uso a terzi a qualsivoglia
titolo; (c) cedere, assegnare o altrimenti trasferire, a qualsivoglia titolo, i Programmi a terzi senza il previo consenso scritto di Oracle; (d) effettuare o far
effettuare la compilazione a ritroso, detta reverse engineering, il disassemblaggio, la decompilazione dei Programmi, salvo che nonostante la propria
richiesta scritta, non abbia ricevuto da Oracle entro un termine ragionevole le informazioni, di cui Oracle medesima avesse la disponibilità, necessarie
perché altri programmi possano essere resi interattivi con i Programmi, senza peraltro violare diritti di proprietà intellettuale di Oracle; (e) rivelare i risultati di
eventuali test prestazionali di alcun Programma, senza la previa approvazione scritta di Oracle. Ogni trasferimento di Programma è soggetto alle politiche e
ai corrispettivi Oracle per il trasferimento. Il Cliente avrà il diritto di usare unicamente i Programmi all'interno di questo pacchetto specificati in un documento d'ordine o in un Certificato di Uso di Programma.

COPYRIGHT E PROPRIETÀ DEI PROGRAMMI: i Programmi sono di proprietà di Oracle e sono protetti dalle leggi sul copyright e sui diritti di proprietà
intellettuale. Il Cliente acquisisce unicamente il diritto di usare i Programmi, con esclusione di qualunque diritto, esplicito o implicito, sui Programmi e sui
supporti materiali che li contengono, diverso da quelli specificati nella presente Licenza. Oracle o il suo licenziante conserveranno sempre ogni diritto,
titolo, interesse, inclusi i diritti di proprietà intellettuale, sui Programmi e i supporti materiali.

GARANZIE, LIMITAZIONI/RIMEDI ESCLUSIVI: Oracle garantisce per il periodo di 90 giorni dalla data di invio al Cliente che: (a) il supporto materiale è
esente da difetti dei materiali e di fabbricazione, se correttamente utilizzato secondo il suo normale uso; (b) i Programmi nello stato in cui sono stati
consegnati sono sostanzialmente in grado di eseguire le funzioni descritte nella documentazione fornita da Oracle, se installati sul computer e sul sistema
operativo designati. Oracle non garantisce che i Programmi risponderanno alle esigenze o aspettative del Cliente, né che opereranno in qualunque
combinazione scelta dal Cliente per l'uso, né che le operazioni dei Programmi saranno ininterrotte o esenti da errori, né che ogni errore dei Programmi
potrà essere corretto. Qualora entro il predetto termine di 90 giorni il Cliente dia comunicazione ad Oracle di un errore di un Programma, Oracle, a propria
discrezione, correggerà l'errore, o provvederà a fornire al Cliente una procedura adeguata per superare il problema tecnico rilevato, o, dietro restituzione
dei Programmi ad Oracle da parte del Cliente, rimborserà a questi l'importo pagato per la licenza d'uso. Oracle sostituirà gratuitamente eventuali supporti
materiali difettosi che le fossero restituiti entro il medesimo termine di 90 giorni. Quanto precede limita ed esaurisce, definitivamente e senza residui, ogni
obbligo di Oracle in materia di garanzie, esplicite ed implicite, incluse le garanzie di buon funzionamento, adeguatezza legale e/o contrattuale ad un
particolare scopo, ai sensi degli artt. 1490 e segg. e 1512 Cod. Civ. Il Cliente prende atto che il regime della garanzia può variare da Paese a Paese.

LIMITI DI RESPONSABILITÀ: L'EVENTUALE RESPONSABILITÀ CONTRATTUALE E/O EXTRACONTRATTUALE DI ORACLE NON COMPRENDERÀ
IN ALCUN CASO DANNI INDIRETTI O CONSEQUENZIALI, DANNI PER PERDITA DI PROFITTI, RICAVI, DATI, USO DI DATI. PER TUTTI TALI TITOLI,
PERTANTO, IL CLIENTE NON POTRÀ DOMANDARE NÉ OTTENERE RISARCIMENTO DI SORTA DA ORACLE. FERMO QUANTO SOPRA, LA
RESPONSABILITÀ DI ORACLE PER DANNI E PREGIUDIZI DI QUALSIASI TIPO DERIVANTI O CONNESSI CON LA PRESENTE LICENZA D'USO
NON POTRÀ IN NESSUN CASO SUPERARE L'IMPORTO PAGATO DAL CLIENTE PER LA LICENZA MEDESIMA. Il Cliente si impegna a rispettare
pienamente tutte le leggi ed i regolamenti in materia di esportazione emanati dagli Stati Uniti d'America, dallo Stato Italiano e dagli altri Paesi in cui il
Cliente medesimo abbia ad esportare i Programmi ("Leggi sull'Esportazione") e garantisce che né i Programmi, né i prodotti da essi derivati saranno
direttamente o indirettamente esportati in violazione delle Leggi sull'Esportazione, o utilizzati per scopi proibiti dalle Leggi sull'Esportazione, inclusa, senza
limitazioni, la proliferazione di armi nucleari, chimiche o biologiche. La legge applicabile alla presente Licenza d'uso e alle eventuali azioni ad essa relative
è quella italiana. Oracle potrà effettuare verifiche dell'uso dei Programmi da parte del Cliente. Le disposizioni di cui alla presente Licenza prevarranno su
tutte le condizioni eventualmente contenute nell'ordine di acquisto o in altri documenti d'ordine del Cliente.

DEFINIZIONI DEL CERTIFICATO DI USO DI PROGRAMMA:
Dispositivi Concorrenti/Accessi Concorrenti: il numero massimo di dispositivi di immissione dati che accedono ai Programmi in un determinato
momento. Se vengono utilizzati un software o un hardware di gestione multipla dell'accesso (ad es. un TP monitor), il predetto numero viene determinato
con riguardo al numero consentito di accessi simultanei.

Client: un computer che viene usato da una sola persona alla volta, e che esegue il sotware Oracle in memoria locale o archivia il software in un
dispositivo di archiviazione locale.

Utente: un individuo autorizzato dal Cliente ad usare i Programmi, senza riguardo al fatto che tale individuo utilizzi attivamente i Programmi in un
determinato momento.

Mailbox: un punto da cui viene inviata o ricevuta la posta elettronica; è creato quando un utente o un'applicazione sono connessi ad Oracle*Office.

Oracle Italia S.p.A., sede legale in Roma, Via Laurentina 756, iscritta al Registro delle Societa' del Tribunale di Roma al n. 3277/93, Capitale
Sociale Lit. 20.000.000.000.= i.v., cod. fisc. 01603630599, p. IVA 04491561009.

日本語／日本

オラクル　プログラム　ライセンス条件

注意：このパッケージに含まれているディスケットの梱包を開封し、又は対象プログラムを使用した場合には、お客様が以下の「使用権許諾書」の条項を全て理解し、同意したこととさせて頂きます。以下の条項をお読みになり、同意できない場合には、包装をあけずにお買い上げの日から530日以内に販売会社にお返し下さい。その場合、お支払い済みの代金をお返し致します。

日本オラクル株式会社（以下オラクルといいます）はお客様に以下に定められたプログラム及びドキュメント（以下併せて対象プログラムといいます）を使用するライセンスを付与します。

ライセンス：お客様は、(a)注文書、又はオラクル若しくはその販売会社がお客様に配布致しましたプログラム使用証明書に規定される範囲内という条件にて、又(b) それらに規定なき場合は、単一コンピューター上で単一ユーザーという条件にて、オラクルが確認した動作環境下で対象プログラムを使用する権利を有します。お客様は自己の内部データを処理するためにのみ対象プログラムを使用できます。お客様はバックアップを目的として、各々の対象プログラムを一部複製することができます。一部を超える複製権が許諾される場合には、注文書又はプログラム使用証明書に規定されることになります。オラクルの事前の書面による承諾なく、ここで定める以上に複製を行ってはなりません。お客様は次の(a)から(e)に定めることを行ってはなりません。(a)製品表示、著作権表示又はその他の注意文言あるいは専有権に基づく制限事項を抹消すること、(b)商用のタイムシェアリング、賃与又はデータセンター用に対象プログラムを使用すること、(c)オラクルの事前の書面による承諾なく、対象プログラムを第三者に対して移転、販売、譲渡その他処分すること、(d)対象プログラムをリバース・エンジニアリング、逆アセンブル、逆コンパイルしたり、または第三者にそれらの行為を行わせること、又は(e)オラクルの事前の書面による承諾なく、対象プログラムのベンチマークテストの結果を第三者に開示すること。対象プログラムの譲渡は全て、オラクルの基準と料金に従って為されるものとします。お客様は注文書又はプログラム使用証明書に規定されているこのパッケージ内の対象プログラムのみ使用する権利を有します。

著作権：対象プログラムは日本オラクル株式会社の親会社である米国オラクル・コーポレーション（以下「米国オラクル」といいます。）が専有する製品であり、著作権及びその他の知的財産権に関する法律によって保護されております。お客様は対象プログラムを使用する権利を付与されたに過ぎず、この使用権許諾書に定める以外に、対象プログラム又はそれを含む媒体に係る一切の権利を明示的に、付与されたわけではありません。オラクル、米国オラクル又はそのライセンサーは、いかなる時に於いても、対象プログラム又は媒体に係る知的財産権を含む一切の権原、権利を保持するものとします。

限定保証：オラクルは、対象プログラムに関し、それをお客様が変更しない限り、引渡時に指定されたシステムで所期の環境において操作された場合には、それがドキュメントに記載された機能を当該引渡時点で発揮することを保証いたします。オラクルは、報告されたエラーを是正する最善の努力をいたします。

2.オラクルは、このパッケージが引渡された日から90日以内にお客様よりオラクルに返却された物理的な不具合のある対象プログラムの媒体につき、交換又は修理を保証いたします。

3.前二項の保証が、法定の瑕疵担保責任を含め、オラクルの保証内容の全てであり、オラクルは対象プログラムの商品性や特定目的への適合性については保証いたしかねます。又、対象プログラムがいかなるコンピューター・ハードウェア及び（又は）オペレーティングシステムでも適切に機能すること、お客様の要求に合致しもしくはお客様が使用するために選択できる組み合わせで作動すること、動作が中断せずもしくはプログラミング上の誤りが皆無であること、又それが完全に是正されることについても同様の取扱いとします。

責任範囲：いかなる場合でもオラクルは契約上の行為による損害かを問わず、間接的、結果的、特別もしくは付随的損害、逸失利益、使用不能であったこと、又は信用毀損について、たとえオラクルがかかる損害発生の可能性について知らされていた場合でも、お客様ないし第三者が蒙ったそれらの損害に対し、なんら責任を有しないものとします。又、データのバックアップを確保する責任はお客様にあるものとし、対象プログラム又は技術サポートの提供に起因するデータの喪失について、オラクルは一切の責任を負わないものとします。

2.　前項にかかわらず、オラクルのお客様に対する損害賠償責任は、債務不履行、法律上の瑕疵担保責任、不当利得、不法行為、その他請求原因、訴訟形態の如何にかかわらず、本契約の不履行に起因して発生した損害について、オラクルに賠償責任があるものと裁判所が認定した場合においても、オラクルの履行又は不履行の直接的結果として現実に発生した通常の損害についてのみ、お客様はオラクルにその賠償を請求できるものとします。かかるオラクルのお客様に対する損害賠償責任は、このライセンスに関してお客様が支払った金額を限度とします。

制限された権利：お客様が米国政府の防衛局 (U.S. Defense Dept.) である場合は、次の規定が適用されるものとします。
Restricted Rights Legend; Use, duplication or disclosure by the Government is subject to restrictions as currently set forth in subparagraph (c)(1)(ii) of DFARS 252-227-7013, Rights in Technical Data and Computer Software (October 1988).
Oracle Corporation, 500 Oracle Parkway, Redwood City, CA, 94065.

お客様が米国政府の防衛局 (U.S. Defense Dept.) 以外の政府機関である場合は、対象プログラムは、FAR 52.227-14, Rights in Data-General, including Alternate III (June 1987) に定める「Restricted Rights Legend」により提供されるものとします。

お客様は、対象プログラム又はその直接的製品を (1) 直接的、間接的を問わず、日本国、米国及びその他の国の全ての法律・規則(以下「輸出管理法」といいます。) に違反して輸出しないこと、又 (2) 核兵器、化学兵器、生物兵器の拡散防止に関する規定を含む輸出管理法によって禁じられている用途で使用しないことを保証すると共に、それらの諸規制等を遵守する義務があります。

本ライセンスは日本国の法律に準拠し、これに従って解釈されます。本ライセンス条件により生ずる紛争については、東京地方裁判所のみを専属的に第一番の管轄裁判所とします。オラクルはお客様の対象プログラム使用状況を監査できます。このライセンス条件はお客様の注文書又はその他の注文ドキュメントの条件に優先します。

한국어/한국

오라클 프로그램 라이센스 계약조건

주의 사항: 귀하께서 이 패키지를 개봉하시거나 동봉된 소프트웨어를 사용하실 경우, 하기 계약조건이 적용됩니다. 귀하께서 소프트웨어나 이 계약조건을 수락하지 않으실 경우에는 귀하께서 소프트웨어를 인도받은 회사로 반환하시고 대금을 환급받으시기 바랍니다.

오라클 코퍼레이션과 그 자회사("오라클")는 귀하("고객")께 동봉된 소프트웨어 및 문서("프로그램")를 사용할 수 있는 라이센스를 아래 기재된 바와 같이 부여합니다.

라이센스: 고객은 오라클이 지정하는 운영환경에서 프로그램을 사용하되, (가) 오라클 또는 그 대리점이 고객에게 제공하는 주문서나 프로그램 사용증서에 명시된 범위 내에서 사용하거나, 또는 (나)명시되어 있지 않은 경우, 단일 컴퓨터 위에서 단인 사용자용으로 사용할 수 있는 권리를 갖는다. 고객은 프로그램을 오직 자신의 내부 자료 처리 작업을 위해서만 사용할 수 있다. 그 이상의 복제 본을 만들 수 있는 권리가 있을 경우에는 주문서나 프로그램 사용증서에 명시된다. 그 밖의 여하한 복제 본도 오라클의 사전 서면 동의없이 만들 수 없다. 고객은 (가) 제품 인식표, 저작권 표시, 기타 독점권 관련 제한사항을 프로그램에서 제거하지 못하고, (나) 상업적 시 분할, 임대 ,서비스국 용도로 프로그램을 사용하지 못하며, (다) 오라클의 사전 서면 동의없이 프로그램을 타인에게 이전, 매각, 양도, 기타의 방법으로 전달하지 못하고, (라) 프로그램의 리버스엔지니어링, 디스어셈블리, 디콤파일레이션 작업을 시키거나 허락하지 못하며, (마) 오라클의 사전 서면 동의 없이 프로그램의 벤치마크 테스트 결과를 제 3자에게 공개하지 못한다. 프로그램의 양도는 양도에 관한 오라클의 방침과 요금의 규제를 받는다. 고객은 이 패키지에 동봉된, 주문서나 프로그램 사용증명서에 명시된 프로그램만 사용할 수 있는 권리를 갖는다.

프로그램 저작권/소유권: 프로그램은 오라클의 재산에 속하는 제품으로서 저작권 및 기타 지적재산권에 관한 법률에 의해 보호된다. 고객은 프로그램을 사용할 수 있는 권리를 취득할 뿐이며, 명시적으로든 묵시적으로든, 프로그램 또는 프로그램이 수록된 매체에 대해서는 이 라이센스계약에 명시된 것을 제외하고는 아무런 권리도 취득하지 않는다. 오라클 또는 오라클에 대한 라이센스 허여자는 프로그램 및 매체에 대해 항상 지적 재산권을 포함한 일체의 권리, 소유권, 이권을 보유한다.

제한적 보증/배타적 구제수단: 오라클은 고객에게 인도한 날로부터 90일 동안 (가) 동봉된 매체가 정상적으로 사용될 때 자재 및 가공 상의 결함을 나타내지 않을 것이며 (나) 수정을 가하지 않은 상태의 프로그램이 지정된 컴퓨터 및 운영환경에서 작동될 경우 대체로 오라클이 제공한 문서에 서술되어 있는 기능을 수행할 것임을 보증한다. 오라클은 프로그램이 고객의 요구를 충족하거나, 프로그램이 고객의 용도에 맞는 선택과 결합하여 작동한다거나, 프로그램의 작동에 중단이 없고 오류가 발생하지 않는다거나, 또는 모든 프로그램 오류가 교정될 것임을 보증하지는 않는다. 이 보증은 상품성에 대한 보증이나 특정 목적에 부합한다는 보증 등, 명시적이거나 묵시적인, 그 밖의 모든 보증을 배제하고 갈음한다. 고객이 90일 이내에 오류를 신고할 경우, 오라클은 그 선택에 의해, 오류를 교정해 주거나, 고객에게 오류를 극복하기 위한 합리적인 절차를 제시해 주거나, 또는 고객이 프로그램을 오라클에게 반환하는 즉시 라이센스 요금을 환급해 준다. 오라클은 결함이 있는 매체가 90일의 기간 이내에 오라클에게 반환되면 대가 없이 교환해 준다. 이는 보증 위반의 경우 고객이 갖는 유일하고 배타적인 구제수단이다. 이 제한적 보증은 귀하에게 특정의 법적 권리를 부여한다.

책임 제한: 오라클은 고객 또는 제 3자가 입은 간접적 손해, 부수적 손해, 특별 손해, 결과적 손해 또는 일실 이익, 일실 수입, 자료 상실 또는 자료사용 상실로 인한 손해에 대해서는, 계약 소송에 있어서든 불법행위 소송에 있어서든, 설령 오라클이 그와 같은 손해의 가능성에 대해 고지 받은 경우라고, 아무런 책임도 지지 않는다. 이 계약에 따른 오라클의 손해배상 책임은 여하한 경우에도 고객이 라이센스의 대가로 지급한 요금을 초과하지 않는다.

제한적 권리: 미국 국방성으로 인도되는 프로그램은 제한적 권리와 함께 인도되며 다음 규정이 적용된다. "제한적 권리 문구: 정부의 사용, 복제 또는 공개 행위에 대해서는 DFARS 252-227-7013, Rights in Technical Data and Computer Software (October 1988), Oracle Corp. 500 Oracle Pkway, Redwood City, CA 94065의 (c)(1)(ii)함에 현재 규정되어 있는 제한 사항이 적용된다. 국방성에 속하지 않는 미국 정부 기관으로 인도되는 프로그램은 FAR52.227-14. Rights in Data - General, including Alternate III (June 1987)에 정의된 "제한적 권리"와 함께 인도된다."

고객은 미합중국 및 다른 나라들의 모든 법령("수출법")을 완벽히 준수함으로써 프로그램이나 그 직접적 산물이 (1) 직접적으로든 간접적으로든 수출법에 위반하여 수출되지 않도록 하고, (2) 화생방 부기 확산 등 수출법이 금하는 목적에 사용되지 않도록 하여야 한다. 이 라이센스 계약 및 모든 관련 사항은 캘리포니아 법률에 의해 규율된다. 오라클은 고객의 프로그램 사용을 감사할 수 있다. 이 라이센스 계약은 고객의 구매 주문서 또는 고객의 기타 주문서의 모든 조건에 우선한다.

프로그램 사용 증서 정의:

동시 장치/동시 접속: 주어진 시점에 프로그램에 접속되어 있는 최대 수의 입력장치. 다중 송신 소프트웨어 또는 하드웨어(예: TP 모니터)가 사용될 경우, 이 숫자는 다중 송신 전단에서 측정하여야 한다.

클라이언트: (1) 한 시점에 한 명에 의해서만 사용되고, (2) 로컬 메모리에 들어 있는 오라클 소프트웨어를 실행하거나 로컬 저장 장치에 소프트웨어를 저장하는 컴퓨터.

사용자: 고객이 프로그램을 사용할 수 있도록 권한을 부여한 개인. 그 개인 이 어진 시점에 적극적으로 프로그램을 사용하고 있는지 여부를 불문한다.

우편함: 전자우편을 보내거나 수령하는 지점: 오라클 오피스에 사용자의 계정 또는 신청이 설치될 때 생긴다.

Norsk/Norge

ORACLE PROGRAM LISENS

ADVARSEL - HVIS DE ÅPNER DENNE PAKKEN ELLER BRUKER PROGRAMMET SOM ER I DENNE PAKKEN, ER BRUKEN UNDERLAGT BETINGELSERNE I DENNE AVTALEN. DERSOM DE IKKE KAN AKSEPTERE PROGRAMMET ELLER NEDENFORSTÅENDE BETINGELSER, BES DE OM Å RETURNERE PROGRAMMET INNEN 30 DAGER TIL DET FIRMA, FRA HVOR DE FIKK LEVERT PROGRAMMET, DERETTER VIL DE BLI REFUNDERT BETALINGEN DE MÅTTE HA GJENNOMFØRT FOR PROGRAMMET.

ORACLE NORGE AS ("Oracle") GIR DEM ("Kunden") LISENS TIL Å ANVENDE DE VEDLAGTE PROGRAM OG DOKUMENTASJON ("Program") I HENHOLD TIL NEDENFORSTÅENDE BETINGELSER.

LISENS: Kunden har rett til å bruke Programmet i det driftsmiljø, som er definert av Oracle enten (a) i henhold til de relevante ordre-dokumenter eller et Bruker sertifikat, som Kunden mottar fra Oracle eller Oracles distributør eller (b) såfremt det ikke er spesifisert gjelder denne lisensen for en enkelt bruker på en computer. Kunden må kun anvende Programmet til intern databehandling. Kunden har rett til å kopiere Programmet til backupformål. Hvis kunden har fått rett til å ta ytterligere kopier, er dette angitt i ordre-dokumentet eller Bruker-Sertifikat. Kunden har ikke rett til å ta anne kopier uten at Oracle først har gitt en skriftlig tillatelse til dette. Kunden må ikke (a) fjerne produktidentifikasjon, copyright-notater, eller andre notater eller andre immaterielle angivelser av Programmet; (b) anvende Programmet til timesharing, utleie eller service byråvirksomhet; (c) overdra, videreselge eller på annen måte overlate Programmet til en tredje person uten at Oracle på forhånd skriftlig godkjenner dette; (d) gjøre eller tillate andre å gjøre reverse engineering, rekonstruksjon eller dekompilering av Programmet, med mindre Kunden innen for rimelig tid etter Kundens skriftlige henvendelse til Oracle ikke har mottatt denne informasjon fra Oracle, som Oracle er i besittelse av og som er nødvendig for å lage et EDB-program som kan fungere sammen med Programmet, men som ikke bryter Oracle's immaterielle rettigheter; samt (e) meddele resultater fra benchmark testing av Programmet til en tredje person uten at Oracle på forhånd har gitt en skriftlig tillatelse til dette. Overflytting av Programmet til et annet driftsmiljø er underlagt Oracles regler og avgifter for overflytting av Programmet. Kunden har kun rett til å bruke Programmet i denne pakken i det omfang, som er angitt i ordre-dokumentet eller Bruker-Sertifikatet.

IMMATERIELLE RETTIGHETER/EINDOMSRETT: Oracle er innehaver av opphavsretten og andre immaterielle rettigheter til Programmet og Programmet er beskyttet av den gjeldende opphavsrettige lovgivningen. Kunden erhverver kun rett til å bruke Programmet, og erhverver således ingen utrykkelige eller underforståtte rettigheter til Programmet eller det media, som inneholder Programmet, som ikke er spesifisert under denne avtalen. Eiendomsretten og alle immaterielle rettigheter til Programmet og media forblir i alle henseender Oracles eller Oracles underleverandør.

BEGRENSNINGER AV GARANTIER/MISLIGHOLDSFORFØYNINGER: Oracle garanterer i en periode på 90 dager fra leveringstidspunkt til Kunden, at (a) det leverte media ved normal bruk er uten fabrikasjonsfeil, og at (b) Programmet, medmindre det er modifisert av Kunden, i all sin vesentlighet kan oppfylle den funksjonalitet, som er beskrevet i dokumentasjonen ved bruk på den relevante datamaskin med tilhørende operativsystem. Oracle gir ingen garanti for, at Programmet svarer til Kundens behov, at Programmet kan brukes i spesifikke kombinasjoner, som Kunden måtte velge, at driften vil være uten avbrytelser og/eller feilfri, eller at feil i Programmet vil bli rettet. Kun de ovenfor uttrykkelig angitte garantier er gjeldende for Programmet. Andre garantier, som måtte følge av deklatorisk lovgivning eller av sedvane og kotyme, er ved dette tilsidesatt. Såfremt Kunden rapporterer en feil i Programmet innen utløpet av den angitte 90 dagers garantiperiode for Programmet, kan Oracle velge enten å utbedre feilen, eller å informere Kunden om en rimelig måte, hvordan feilen kan omgås, eller såfremt Kunden returnerer Programmet til Oracle, å tilbakebetale Kunden lisensavgiften for Programmet. Oracle vil bytte defekte media uten omkostninger for Kunden, såfremt de returneres til Oracle innen utløpet av den ovenfor angivne periode på 90 dager. Overstående er de eneste misligholdsforføyninger, som Kunden kan påberope seg i forbindelse med Oracles misligholdelse av Oracles garantiforpliktelser.

ANSVARSBEGRENSNING: IKKE I NOE TILFELLE ER ORACLE ANSVARLIG FOR INDIREKTE TAP, FØLGESKADER, TAP AV FORTJENESTE, DRIFTSTAP, TAPTE DATA ELLER LIKNENDE TAP, SOM KUNDEN ELLER TREDJEMANN PÅDRAR SEG, UANSETT OM ORACLE AV KUNDEN ELLER AV TREDJEMANN MÅTTE VÆRE BLITT INFORMERT OM MULIGHETEN FOR AT SÅDANNE TAP KUNNE OPPSTÅ. ORACLES ERSTATNINGSANSVAR SKAL IKKE I NOE TILFELLE OVERSTIGE DE LISENSBETALINGER SOM ORACLE HAR MOTTATT FRA KUNDEN FOR PROGRAMMET.

Kunden aksepterer å overholde alle relevante lover og offentlige forskrifter i Norge og USA eller andre land i forbindelse med, at Kunden måtte (1) gjøre Programmet, et direkte produkt herav eller tekniske data om Programmet til gjenstand for direkte eller indirekte eksport. eller (2) måtte anvende Programmet til formål i forbindelse med spredning av atom, kjemiske eller biologiske våpen i strid med eksportlovgivningen. Denne avtalen samt tilhørende forhold er undergitt norsk rett og alle uoveren-stemmelser herunder henvises til Asker og Bærum Herredsrett. Oracle har rett til å kontrollere Kundens bruk av Programmet. Denne avtalen har prioritet for alle betingelser i Kundens inkjøpsrekvisisjon eller annet dokument.

BRUKER-SERTIFIKAT DEFINISJONER:
Samtidige Tilganger: Det maksimale antall påloggingsenheter som på ethvert tidspunkt bruker programmene samtidig. Dersom multiplexersoftware eller - hardware (f.eks. en TP-monitor) benyttes, beregnes antallet Samtidige Tilganger ved multiplexerinn-gangen.

Klient: En computer som (1) kun brukes av en person ad gangen, og som (2) utfører Oracle software i lokal hukommelse eller lagrer programmet på en lokal hukommelse eller lagrer programmet på en lokal lagringsenhet.

Bruker: En individuell person som er autorisert av Kunden til å bruke Programmet uansett om individet bruker programmet aktivt til enhver tid.

Mailbox: Et punkt hvorfra elektronisk post er sendt eller mottatt. En mailbox oppstår når en Brukerkonto eller applikasjon opprettes i Oracle*Office.

Polski/ Polska

WARUNKI LICENCJI NA PROGRAM ORACLE

UWAGA: JEŻELI TO OPAKOWANIE ZOSTANIE OTWARTE LUB ZAWARTE W NIM OPROGRAMOWANIE UŻYTE, BĘDZIE TO RÓWNOZNACZNE Z ZAAKCEPTOWANIEM PONIŻSZYCH WARUNKÓW. JEŻELI ZAŚ OPROGRAMOWANIE LUB PONIŻSZE WARUNKI SĄ NIE DO PRZYJĘCIA PROSZĘ ZWRÓCIĆ TO OPROGRAMOWANIE W CIĄGU 30 DNI DO FIRMY, KTÓRA JE DOSTARCZYŁA CELEM ZWROTU ZAPŁATY.

ORACLE POLSKA SP. Z O.O. («ORACLE») UDZIELA NABYWCY («KLIENT») LICENCJĘ NA KORZYSTANIE Z ZAŁĄCZONEGO OPROGRAMOWANIA ORAZ DOKUMENTACJI («PROGRAMY») ZGODNIE Z PONIŻSZYMI WARUNKAMI.

LICENCJA. Klientowi przysługuje prawo do korzystania z Programów na obszarze Terytorium w środowisku operacyjnym zidentyfikowanym przez Oracle albo (a) w zakresie określonym w dokumentach zamówienia lub Świadectwie Prawa Użytkowania dostarczonych Klientowi przez Oracle bądź jego dystrybutorów, albo (b) jeśli nie określono inaczej, licencja zostaje udzielona pojedynczemu użytkownikowi na pojedynczy komputer. Klient może używać Programów jedynie w celu przetwarzania danych dla własnego użytku. Klient może sporządzić jedną kopię każdego licencjonowanego Programu jako kopię zapasową; Klientowi nie przysługuje prawo sporządzania dodatkowych kopii, o ile nie jest to określone w dokumentach zamówienia lub Świadectwie Prawa Użytkowania. Klient nie może sporządzać innych kopii bez uzyskania uprzedniej pisemnej zgody Oracle. Klient nie jest uprawniony do: (a) usuwania z Programów jakichkolwiek ich cech identyfikacyjnych, ostrzeżeń o prawach autorskich lub innych zawiadomień lub ograniczeń odnośnie własności; (b) zezwalania osobom trzecim na korzystanie z Programów za odpłatnością, wynajmowania programu lub wykorzystywania Programów dla świadczenia usług biurowych; (c) przenoszenia, sprzedaży, cesji lub zbywania Programów w inny sposób na rzecz osoby trzeciej bez uprzedniej pisemnej zgody Oracle; (d) podejmowania lub zezwalania na podjęcie czynności mających na celu odtworzenie kodu źródłowego Programów (reverse engineering), rozłożenia, lub dekompilacji Programów oraz (e) ujawniania osobom trzecim rezultatów jakichkolwiek testów wydajnościowych (bench mark tests) jakiegokolwiek Programu bez uprzedniej pisemnej zgody Oracle. Klient ma prawo do korzystania tylko z Programów komputerowych w tym opakowaniu, które są wyspecyfikowane w dokumentach zamówienia lub Świadectwie Prawa Użytkowania.

PRAWA AUTORSKIE/WŁASNOŚĆ PROGRAMÓW. Programy są własnością Oracle i podlegają ochronie prawa autorskiego i innych intelektualnych praw własności. Klient nabywa tylko prawo do korzystania z Programów i nie nabywa jakichkolwiek praw, wyrażonych lub oznaczonych, w Programach lub nośnikach, zawierających Programy inne niż te określone w niniejszej licencji. Oracle lub jej licencjodawca przez cały czas zachowuje wszelkie prawa i tytuł, łącznie z intelektualnymi prawami własności, do Programów i nośnika.

OGRANICZONA GWARANCJA/WYŁĄCZNE ZASPOKOJENIE ROSZCZEŃ. Oracle gwarantuje, że w okresie 90 dni od daty dostarczenia Programu do Klienta: (a) dostarczony nośnik jest wolny od wad w materiale i w wykonaniu w warunkach normalnego korzystania z niego; oraz (b) nie zmieniony Program będzie zasadniczo wykonywać funkcje opisane w dokumentacji dostarczonej przez Oracle, o ile będzie wykonywać czynności na określonym komputerze i przy użyciu określonego systemu operacyjnego. Oracle nie gwarantuje, że: Program spełni oczekiwania Klienta, będzie działać w kombinacjach, które Klient może wybrać dla jego używania, operacje Programu będą nieprzerwane lub wolne od błędów lub że wszystkie błędy w Programie będą usunięte. Gwarancje powyższe są gwarancjami wyłącznymi i zastępują wszelkie inne gwarancje zarówno udzielone wyraźnie jak i zrozumiane, włączając w to rozumiane gwarancje handlowe oraz gwarancje, że Program jest przydatny do danego celu. Jeżeli Klient zgłosi błąd w Programie w okresie 90 dni, Oracle w zależności od swojego uznania może błąd usunąć, zapoznać Klienta z odpowiednią procedurą dla ominięcia błędu lub, pod warunkiem zwrotu Programu Oracle przez Klienta, zwrócić opłatę licencyjną. Oracle wymieni wadliwe media bez dodatkowej opłaty jeśli zostaną one zwrócone w ciągu 90 dni. Powyższe prawa Klienta są jego jedynymi i wyłącznymi prawami z tytułu naruszenia gwarancji. Ta ograniczona gwarancja daje Klientowi określone prawa.

OGRANICZENIA ODPOWIEDZIALNOŚCI. ORACLE NIE BĘDZIE PONOSIŁ ODPOWIEDZIALNOŚCI ZA JAKĄKOLWIEK POŚREDNIĄ, WYPADKOWĄ, SPECJALNĄ BĄDŹ NASTĘPCZĄ SZKODĘ LUB SZKODY ZA UTRATĘ ZYSKÓW, PRZYCHODÓW, DANYCH BĄDŹ BRAKU MOŻLIWOŚCI KORZYSTANIA Z DANYCH PONIESIONĄ PRZEZ KLIENTA LUB JAKĄKOLWIEK OSOBĘ TRZECIĄ ZARÓWNO Z TYTUŁU UMOWY LUB CZYNU NIEDOZWOLONEGO RÓWNIEŻ W PRZYPADKU GDY ORACLE LUB JAKAKOLWIEK INNA OSOBA BYŁY POINFORMOWANE O MOŻLIWOŚCI WYSTĄPIENIA TAKICH SZKÓD. W KAŻDYM PRZYPADKU ODPOWIEDZIALNOŚĆ ORACLE ZA POWYŻSZE SZKODY NIE PRZEKROCZY WYSOKOŚCI OPŁAT ZAPŁACONYCH PRZEZ KLIENTA ZA NINIEJSZĄ LICENCJĘ.

TERYTORIUM: «Terytorium» oznaczać będzie Polskę, chyba że inaczej zostało to określone w dokumentach zamówienia lub Świadectwie Prawa Użytkowania.

Klient wyraża zgodę w pełni przestrzegać postanowień prawa i innych regulacji Stanów Zjednoczonych i innych krajów («Prawo Eksportowe») dla zapewnienia, że ani Programy, ani jakiekolwiek produkty bezpośrednio z nich powstałe (1) nie są wyeksportowane, bezpośrednio lub pośrednio, z naruszeniem Prawa Eksportowego, lub (2) są używane dla innych celów zastrzeżonych przez Prawo Eksportowe, włączając bez żadnych ograniczeń, rozprzestrzenianie broni nuklearnej, chemicznej i biologicznej. Oracle może skontrolować używanie Programów przez Klienta. Wszystkie warunki jakiegokolwiek zamówienia Klienta lub innego dokumentu zamówienia zostaną zastąpione przez postanowienia niniejszej Licencji.

DEFINICJA ŚWIADECTWA PRAWA UŻYTKOWANIA:
Urządzenia jednoczesne/Dostępy jednoczesne: maksymalna liczba urządzeń mających dostęp do Programów w dowolnym momencie. Jeśli dostęp do oprogramowania lub komputerów zostaje zwielokrotniony (np. poprzez monitor TP), to tę zwielokrotnioną liczbę należy uważać za faktyczną maksymalną liczbę urządzeń, mających dostęp do Programów w dowolnym momencie.

Klient: komputer, który (1) jest używany tylko przez jedną osobę w danym momencie i (2) w którego lokalnej pamięci operacyjnej działa oprogramowanie Oracle lub jest ono składowane w lokalnej pamięci masowej.

Użytkownik: osoba upoważniona przez Klienta do używania Programów niezależnie od tego, czy osoba ta w danym momencie faktycznie ich używa.

Skrzynka Pocztowa: punkt, z którego poczta elektroniczna jest wysyłana lub otrzymywana; jest tworzony w momencie założenia użytkownikowi konta w Oracle*Office.

Português/Brasil

CONDIÇÕES DA LICENÇA DOS PROGRAMAS ORACLE

ATENÇÃO: CASO ABRA ESTA EMBALAGEM OU UTILIZE O PROGRAMA DE COMPUTADOR NELA CONTIDO, VOCÊ ESTARÁ SUJEITO(A) ÀS CONDIÇÕES ESPECIFICADAS A SEGUIR. CASO O PROGRAMA DE COMPUTADOR OU ESSAS CONDIÇÕES NÃO SEJAM ACEITÁVEIS PARA VOCÊ, QUEIRA DEVOLVER ESTE PROGRAMA DE COMPUTADOR, EM ATÉ 30 (TRINTA) DIAS, À EMPRESA DA QUAL O RECEBEU, PARA REEMBOLSO.

A ORACLE DO BRASIL SISTEMAS LTDA. ("ORACLE"), DÁ A VOCÊ ("CLIENTE") UMA LICENÇA PARA UTILIZAÇÃO DO PROGRAMA DE COMPUTADOR AQUI CONTIDO E DE SUA RESPECTIVA DOCUMENTAÇÃO ("PROGRAMAS"), CONFORME INDICADO ABAIXO.

LICENÇA: O Cliente terá o direito de usar os Programas no ambiente operacional identificado pela Oracle, ou (a) na extensão especificada em um pedido de compra, no Certificado para Uso do Programa distribuídos ao Cliente pela Oracle ou por sua distribuidora, ou, na Nota Fiscal que acompanha os Programas; ou (b) se não houver especificação, para uso de um único usuário em um único computador. O Cliente poderá usar os Programas apenas e tão somente para suas próprias e internas operações de processamento de dados. O Cliente poderá fazer uma cópia de cada Programa licenciado para efeitos de salvaguarda (backup); direitos de fazer cópias adicionais, caso haja, estarão especificados em um pedido de compra, no Certificado para Uso do Programa, ou, na Nota Fiscal que acompanha os Programas. Nenhuma outra cópia poderá ser feita sem o prévio consentimento por escrito da Oracle. O Cliente não poderá: (a) remover qualquer identificação do produto, avisos de direitos autorais, ou outros avisos ou restrições referentes à propriedade intelectual dos Programas; (b) usar os Programas para compartilhamento comercial de tempo, locação, ou utilização em bureau de prestação de serviços; (c) transferir, vender, ceder ou de qualquer outra forma transmitir os Programas a quaisquer terceiros, sem o prévio consentimento por escrito da Oracle; (d) promover ou permitir engenharia reversa, desmontagem ou decompilação dos Programas; ou (e) divulgar resultados de testes de desempenho de qualquer Programa para quaisquer terceiros sem a aprovação prévia por escrito da Oracle. Todas as transferências de Programas estão sujeitas às condições e às taxas convencionais de transferência praticadas pela Oracle. O Cliente terá o direito de usar somente os Programas contidos nesta embalagem que estiverem especificados em um pedido de compra, Certificado para Uso do Programa, ou, na Nota Fiscal que acompanha os Programas.

DIREITOS AUTORAIS/TITULARIDADE DOS PROGRAMAS: Os Programas são produtos de propriedade da Oracle Corporation e estão protegidos pela lei de direitos autorais, bem como por outras leis de proteção à propriedade intelectual. O Cliente adquire somente o direito de usar os Programas, e não adquire quaisquer outros direitos expressos ou implícitos, sobre os Programas ou meios físicos contendo os Programas, além dos que não os especificados nesta Licença. A Oracle Corporation, ou sua licenciadora, detém e deterá durante todo o tempo, todos os direitos, incluindo os direitos de propriedade intelectual, a titularidade e os interesses sobre os Programas e sobre os meios físicos.

GARANTIAS LIMITADAS/RECURSOS EXCLUSIVOS: A Oracle garante que durante 90 dias a contar da data de entrega ao Cliente: (a) os meios físicos aqui incluídos estarão livres de defeitos nos materiais e qualidade de trabalho em condições normais de uso; e que (b) Programas que se encontrem inalterados irão substancialmente desempenhar as funções descritas na documentação fornecida pela Oracle quando operados no computador e sistema operacional designados. A Oracle não garante que: os Programas irão atender aos requisitos do Cliente, que os Programas irão operar nas combinações que o Cliente possa vir a selecionar para uso, que a operação dos Programas seja ininterrupta ou livre de erros, ou que todos os erros dos Programas serão corrigidos. **Essas garantias são exclusivas e substituem todas e quaisquer outras garantias, sejam estas expressas ou implícitas em lei.** Caso o Cliente comunique um erro existente em um Programa dentro do período de 90 dias, a Oracle deverá, a seu critério, corrigir o erro, fornecer ao Cliente um procedimento razoável para que corrija esse erro, ou, por ocasião da devolução dos Programas à Oracle pelo Cliente, devolver a este último as remunerações pagas pela licença. A Oracle substituirá qualquer meio físico defeituoso, sem custo, se este for devolvido à Oracle dentro do período de 90 dias. Estes são os únicos e exclusivos recursos do Cliente por qualquer descumprimento da garantia dada. **Esta garantia limitada dá a você direitos jurídicos específicos. Você pode ter outros, previstos em lei.**

LIMITAÇÃO DE RESPONSABILIDADE: A ORACLE E/OU A ORACLE CORPORATION NÃO SERÁ RESPONSÁVEL POR QUAISQUER DANOS INDIRETOS, INCIDENTAIS, ESPECIAIS OU CONSEQÜENTES, OU RELATIVOS A LUCROS CESSANTES, OU PERDA DE RECEITA, DE DADOS OU DE USO DE DADOS, INCORRIDOS PELO CLIENTE OU POR QUAISQUER TERCEIROS, SEJA POR AÇÃO COM BASE EM CONTRATO OU POR ATO ILÍCITO, MESMO QUE A ORACLE E/OU A ORACLE CORPORATION TENHA SIDO ADVERTIDA ACERCA DA POSSIBILIDADE DA OCORRÊNCIA DE TAIS DANOS. A RESPONSABILIDADE DA ORACLE E/OU DA ORACLE CORPORATION POR QUAISQUER DANOS EM DECORRÊNCIA DESTA LICENÇA NÃO DEVERÁ, EM NENHUMA CIRCUNSTÂNCIA, EXCEDER A IMPORTÂNCIA DAS REMUNERAÇÕES PAGAS PELO CLIENTE POR ESTA LICENÇA.

DIREITOS RESTRITOS: O Cliente deverá obedecer todas as leis e regulamentos dos Estados Unidos da América do Norte e de outros países ("Leis de Exportação") para assegurar que nem os Programas, nem quaisquer produtos diretos deles decorrentes, sejam (1) exportados, direta ou indiretamente, de forma a infringir as Leis de Exportação ou (2) sejam usados para finalidades proibidas pelas Leis de Exportação, incluindo, sem limitação, proliferação de armas nucleares, químicas ou biológicas. Esta Licença e todas as ações a ela relativas serão regidas pela legislação local. A Oracle poderá auditar o uso dos Programas pelo Cliente. **Todos os termos de qualquer pedido de compra ou qualquer outro documento de pedido do Cliente são superados por esta Licença. Este contrato é regido pelas leis da República Federativa do Brasil**

DEFINIÇÕES DO CERTIFICADO DE USO DE PROGRAMA:

Dispositivos Simultâneos/Acessos Simultâneos: o número máximo de dispositivos de entrada de dados que acessam os Programas em qualquer momento determinado. Caso um programa de computador ou equipamento multiplexador esteja sendo usado (por exemplo, um monitor TP), este número deverá ser medido na saída multiplexora frontal.

Cliente: um computador que (1) é utilizado por uma só pessoa de cada vez, e (2) que roda o programa de computador da Oracle em memória local, ou armazena o programa de computador em um dispositivo de armazenamento local.

Usuário: uma pessoa autorizada pelo Cliente a usar os Programas, independentemente de estar essa pessoa usando ou não os Programas em qualquer momento determinado.

Caixa Postal: um ponto a partir do qual se envia ou recebe mensagens por correio eletrônico; a caixa postal é criada quando uma conta ou aplicação de usuário é estabelecida/cadastrada no programa Escritório Oracle (Oracle *Office).

Português/Portugal

CONTRATO DE LICENÇA DE PROGRAMA ORACLE

AVISO: Não abra este pacote nem utilize o software nele contido, salvo se previamente tiver analisado e aceite os termos que se seguem.Em caso de não aceitação do software incluso e respectivos termos gerais então deverá devolver, no prazo de 30 (trinta) dias, este pacote à empresa que lho enviou.

A ORACLE PORTUGAL ("Oracle") CONCEDE-LHE ("Cliente") UMA LICENÇA DE UTILIZAÇÃO DE SOFTWARE E RESPECTIVA DOCUMENTAÇÃO ("Programa") INCLUÍDOS NO PRESENTE PACOTE, CONFORME A SEGUIR INDICADO.

LICENÇA: O Cliente terá o direito de utilizar os Programas de acordo com o especificado na documentação de encomenda ou no Certificado de utilização dos Programas ("Autorização de Utilização") distribuído ao Cliente pela Oracle ou pelo seu Distribuidor. Se os direitos de utilização da licença não vierem especificados e explícitos numa Autorização de Utilização então esta licença deverá ser considerada como válida para um único utilizador num único computador. O Cliente poderá fazer uma cópia do Programa para efeitos de segurança; o direito à reprodução de outras cópias deverá constar da encomenda e da Autorização de Utilização. Não poderão ser efectuadas outras cópias sem o consentimento prévio escrito da Oracle. O Cliente: a)não retirará qualquer identificação do produto, avisos de direitos de autor ou outros avisos ou restrições de propriedade do Programa; b)não cederá o Programa em aluguer, locação periódica, ou service bureau; c)não transferirá, venderá, atribuirá ou cederá de qualquer forma os Programas sem o prévio acordo escrito da Oracle; d) não efectuará ou autorizará reverse engineering, dessassemblagem ou descompilação de Programas sempre que o Cliente tenha recebido da Oracle, num prazo razoável e após pedido por escrito, a informação necessária para a criação de programas de software interoperáveis com o Programa, mas que não infrinjam os direitos de propriedade intelectual da Oracle, tal como é permitido e disponível à Oracle; e)não revelará a terceiros os resultados de quaisquer testes de benchmark de Programas, salvo mediante prévio acordo escrito da Oracle. O Cliente terá o direito de utilizar apenas os Programas especificados numa Autorização de Utilização para este pacote.

DIREITOS DE AUTOR: O Programa é propriedade da Oracle e está protegido por direitos de autor. O Cliente adquire apenas o direito de utilizar o Programa não adquirindo quaisquer outros direitos de propriedade sobre este ou sobre os suportes físicos em que este se encontre reproduzido. A Oracle ou o seu licenciador manterá a todo o tempo a totalidade dos direitos, título e interesses sobre o Programa e suportes físicos.

GARANTIAS/REPARAÇÕES EXCLUSIVAS: A Oracle garante ao Cliente pelo período de 90 dias a contar da data de entrega a este: a)que os suportes magnéticos incluídos se encontram isentos de defeitos físicos e de fabrico e em condições normais de utilização ; b)que os Programas que não tenham sofrido alterações desempenharão as funções descritas na documentação fornecida pela Oracle se forem executados no computador e sistema operativo designados.A Oracle não garante: que o Programa cumprirá os requisitos do Cliente; que o Programa operará em combinações seleccionadas pelo Cliente, que a operação dos programas seja ininterrupta ou isenta de erros, ou que todos os erros do Programa sejam corrigidos. As presentes garantias são exclusivas e substituem quaisquer outras, expressas ou implícitas, incluindo garantias implícitas de comercialização e adequação para fins específicos. A Oracle substituirá quaisquer suportes físicos defeituosos, livre de encargos, se estes forem devolvidos à Oracle no prazo de 90 dias. Se o Cliente comunicar um defeito à Oracle dentro do referido período de 90 dias, esta optará por: corrigir o defeito, fornecer ao Cliente processos razoáveis para que este possa resolver o defeito ou, devolver as taxas de licença pagas por este, mediante a devolução do Programa pelo Cliente. Estas são as únicas e exclusivas reparações garantidas ao Cliente por qualquer quebra de garantia.

LIMITAÇÃO DE RESPONSABILIDADE: A ORACLE NÃO SERÀ RESPONSÁVEL POR QUAISQUER DANOS INDIRECTOS, ACIDENTAIS, ESPECIAIS OU EMERGENTES, OU POR DANOS POR PERDAS DE LUCROS, RECEITAS, DADOS OU UTILIZAÇÃO DE DADOS, SOFRIDOS PELO CLIENTE OU POR TERCEIROS, CONTRATUAL OU EXTRACONTRATUALMENTE, MESMO QUE O CLIENTE OU QUALQUER OUTRA PESSOA TENHA SIDO AVISADA DA POSSIBILIDADE DE OCORRÊNCIA DE TAIS DANOS, A RESPONSABILIDADE DA ORACLE POR DANOS NO ÂMBITO DO PRESENTE NÃO EXCEDERÀ EM CASO ALGUM AS TAXAS DEVIDAS PELAS LICENÇAS E PAGAS PELO CLIENTE.

DIREITOS RESTRITOS: Se o Programa for enviado ao Departamento de Defesa dos E.U.A., sê-lo-à com Direitos Restritos aplicando-se a seguinte menção: "utilização da Legenda de Direitos Restritos, a reprodução ou divulgação pelo Governo está sujeita às restrições à altura mencionadas no subparágrafo c) (1) (ii) do DFARS 252-227-7013, Direitos sobre Dados Técnicos e Software para Computador (Outubro de 1988). Oracle Corp 500 Oracle Pkwy., Redwood City, CA, 94065. Se o Programa for enviado a um Departamento do Governo dos E.U.A que não o da Defesa, sê-lo-à com os Direitos Restritos conforme definido no FAR 52.227-14, Direitos sobre Dados-Geral, incluindo Alternate III (Junho de 1987)". O Cliente acorda no cumprimento integral de todas as leis e regulamentos dos Estados Unidos da América e de Portugal destinados a garantir que o Programa ou qualquer produto dele resultante (1) não será exportado, directa ou indirectamente, em violação da lei (2) é usado para qualquer fim proibido pelas leis e regulamentos de Exportação, incluindo, mas não limitado, ao uso com fins de proliferação de armas nucleares, químicas ou biológicas. O presente Contrato é regulado pela Lei Portuguesa. O presente Contrato substitui na íntegra os termos de qualquer encomenda de Cliente ou outro documento de encomenda.

AUTORIZAÇÃO DE UTILIZAÇÃO - DEFINIÇÕES:

Dispositivos Concorrentes ou Acessos Concorrentes: máximo número de dispositivos em modo input que acedem aos Programas em qualquer momento de tempo. Se for utilizado software ou hardware multiplexing (i.e a monitor transaccional) este número deve ser medido no multiplexing front end.

Cliente: um computador que (1) é usado apenas por um utilizador de cada vez, e (2) executa software Oracle na memória local ou arquiva/guarda o software num mecanismo local de guarda ou arquivo.

Utilizador: um indivíduo autorizado pelo cliente a usar os Programas, independentemente de os estar a utilizar activamente ou não num qualquer momento de tempo.

MailBox ou Caixa de Correio: um ponto a partir do qual correio electrónico é enviado ou recebido; é criado quando uma conta ou aplicação de utilizador é criada no Oracle*Office.

Русский/Россия

УСЛОВИЯ ЛИЦЕНЗИИ НА ПРОГРАММЫ "ORACLE"

ВНИМАНИЕ! ЕСЛИ ВЫ ВСКРОЕТЕ ЭТОТ ПАКЕТ ИЛИ БУДЕТЕ ИСПОЛЬЗОВАТЬ НАХОДЯЩЕЕСЯ В НЕМ ПРОГРАММНОЕ ОБЕСПЕЧЕНИЕ, ТО ВСТУПАЮТ В СИЛУ НИЖЕСЛЕДУЮЩИЕ УСЛОВИЯ. ЕСЛИ ВЫ НЕ СОГЛАСНЫ С ЭТИМИ УСЛОВИЯМИ, ПОЖАЛУЙСТА, ВЕРНИТЕ В ТЕЧЕНИЕ 30 ДНЕЙ ПРОГРАММНОЕ ОБЕСПЕЧЕНИЕ В КОМПАНИЮ, ГДЕ ВЫ ЕГО ПРИОБРЕЛИ, ДЛЯ ВОЗВРАТА ДЕНЕГ.

КОМПАНИЯ "ORACLE AG" (ДАЛЕЕ - "ОРАКЛ") ПРЕДОСТАВЛЯЕТ ВАМ ("ЗАКАЗЧИКУ") ЛИЦЕНЗИЮ НА ИСПОЛЬЗОВАНИЕ ПРИЛАГАЕМЫХ ПРОГРАММНЫХ СРЕДСТВ И ДОКУМЕНТАЦИИ (ДАЛЕЕ - "ПРОГРАММЫ") В СООТВЕТСТВИИ С НИЖЕПРИВЕДЕННЫМИ УСЛОВИЯМИ.

ЛИЦЕНЗИЯ. Заказчик имеет право использовать Программы в пределах Территории и в операционной среде, указанной "Оракл" в объеме, (а) указанном в заявочном документе или Сертификате на Использование Программы, переданных Заказчику "Оракл" или дистрибьютором "Оракл", или, (б) если это не оговорено, настоящая лицензия предоставляет право использования Программ одним пользователем на одном компьютере. Заказчик имеет право использовать Программы исключительно для внутренней обработки своих данных.

Заказчик имеет право создать одну копию каждой из лицензированных Программ в качестве резервной копии; права на создание дополнительного количества копий должны оговариваться в заявочном документе или Сертификате на Использование Программы. Запрещается создавать другие копии без предварительного письменного разрешения "Оракл". Заказчик не имеет права: (а) удалять из Программ любые обозначения продукта, предупреждения об авторских правах и иные предупреждения или ограничения на использование информации, составляющей предмет собственности; (б) использовать Программы в системах разделения времени на коммерческой основе, сдавать их в аренду и использовать в сфере обслуживания; (в) передавать, продавать, переуступать Программы другому лицу и иным образом распоряжаться ими в пользу другого лица без предварительного письменного разрешения "Оракл"; (г) выполнять или разрешать восстановление исходного кода, дизассемблирование или декомпилирование Программ; или (д) разглашать результаты любых тестов производительности Программ каким-либо третьим лицам без предварительного письменного разрешения "Оракл". Все переносы Программы выполняются в соответствии с правилами "Оракл" и за определенную плату. Заказчик имеет право использовать только те программные средства из комплекта поставки, которые указаны в заявочном документе или Сертификате на Использование Программы.

АВТОРСКИЕ ПРАВА/ПРАВА СОБСТВЕННОСТИ. Программы являются продуктом, составляющим предмет собственности "Оракл", и защищены законодательством об авторских правах и другими законами об интеллектуальной собственности, в частности (не ограничиваясь этим), российским Законом об авторских правах 1993г. и Законом о правовой защите компьютерных программ и баз данных 1992г. Заказчик приобретает только права на использование Программ, не получая при этом никаких прав, прямо выраженных или подразумеваемых, на Программы и носители, на которых они записаны, кроме указанных в лицензии. "Оракл" и ее лицензиары всегда сохраняют за собой все права, титул и вещноправовой интерес, включая права на интеллектуальную собственность, на Программы и носители.

ОГРАНИЧЕННЫЕ ГАРАНТИИ И ИСКЛЮЧИТЕЛЬНЫЕ СРЕДСТВА ЗАЩИТЫ. "Оракл" гарантирует, что в течение 90 дней с даты поставки Заказчику: (а) поставляемые носители, при их нормальном использовании, не проявят дефектов, связанных с материалами и изготовлением; и (б) функциональные характеристики неизмененных Программ в основном будут соответствовать указанным в документации, предоставленной "Оракл", при условии использования Программ на указанном компьютере в указанной операционной среде. "Оракл" не гарантирует: что Программы отвечают потребностям Заказчика; что Программы будут работать в комбинации с другими программами по желанию Заказчика; что работа Программ будет бесперебойной или безошибочной, и что все ошибки, обнаруженные в Программах, будут исправлены. Указанная гарантия является исключительной и заменяет собой все иные прямо выраженные и подразумеваемые гарантии, в том числе подразумеваемые гарантии товарности или пригодности для конкретного применения. Если в течение 90-дневного срока Заказчик сообщит о наличии ошибок в Программах, "Оракл", по своему усмотрению, либо устранит ошибки, либо укажет Заказчику порядок обхода ошибки, либо, по получении Программ от Заказчика, вернет Заказчику лицензионную плату. "Оракл" заменит любой дефектный носитель бесплатно, если он возвращен "Оракл" в течение 90 дней с даты поставки. Указанные положения содержат единственные и исключительные средства защиты Заказчика в случае нарушения гарантии. Настоящая ограниченная гарантия предоставляет Вам особые юридические права.

ОГРАНИЧЕНИЕ ОТВЕТСТВЕННОСТИ. "ОРАКЛ" НЕ НЕСЕТ ОТВЕТСТВЕННОСТИ НИ ЗА КАКИЕ КОСВЕННЫЕ, СЛУЧАЙНЫЕ, СПЕЦИАЛЬНЫЕ И ПОБОЧНЫЕ УБЫТКИ, А ТАКЖЕ ЗА УПУЩЕНИЕ ПРИБЫЛИ ИЛИ ВЫГОДЫ, УТЕРЮ ДАННЫХ ИЛИ ВОЗМОЖНОСТИ ИСПОЛЬЗОВАНИЯ ДАННЫХ, ПОНЕСЕННЫЕ ЗАКАЗЧИКОМ ИЛИ ЛЮБОЙ ТРЕТЬЕЙ СТОРОНОЙ, БУДЬ ТО В РЕЗУЛЬТАТЕ НАРУШЕНИЯ КОНТРАКТНЫХ ОБЯЗАТЕЛЬСТВ ИЛИ ГРАЖДАНСКО-ПРАВОВОГО НАРУШЕНИЯ, ДАЖЕ ЕСЛИ "ОРАКЛ" БЫЛ ИЗВЕЩЕН О ВОЗМОЖНОСТИ ТАКИХ УБЫТКОВ. РАЗМЕР ОТВЕТСТВЕННОСТИ "ОРАКЛ" ПО НАСТОЯЩЕЙ ЛИЦЕНЗИИ НИ В КОЕМ СЛУЧАЕ НЕ ПРЕВЫШАЕТ РАЗМЕР ЛИЦЕНЗИОННОЙ ПЛАТЫ, ВЫПЛАЧЕННОЙ ЗАКАЗЧИКОМ ЗА ЭТУ ЛИЦЕНЗИЮ.

ТЕРРИТОРИЯ. Если иного не указано в заявочном документе или Сертификате на Использование Программы, "Территория" означает Россию.

Заказчик обязуется в полном объеме соблюдать все законы и постановления Соединенных Штатов Америки и других стран (далее - "Экспортное Законодательство") и гарантирует, что ни Программы, ни их любая прямая продукция, (1) не будут экспортироваться напрямую или косвенно в нарушение Экспортного Законодательства или (2) использоваться в любых целях, запрещенных Экспортным Законодательством, включая, но не ограничивая, распространение ядерного, химического или биологического оружия. Действие настоящей Лицензии регулируется законодательством штата Калифорния, США. "Оракл" может проводить инспекцию порядка использования Программ. Настоящая Лицензия имеет преимущественную силу над всеми условиями любого заказа на покупку Заказчика.

ОПРЕДЕЛЕНИЯ:

Одновременные пользователи/Одновременные соединения: максимальное число устройств ввода, имеющих доступ к Программам в любой выделенный момент времени. В случае использования мультиплексных программных или аппаратных средств это число должно быть определено на входе мультиплексора.

Клиент: компьютер, который (1) используется одним пользователем в каждый момент времени и (2) исполняет программное обеспечение "Оракл" в локальной памяти или хранящий программное обеспечение на локальном диске.

Пользователь: лицо, уполномоченное Заказчиком использовать Программы вне всякой зависимости от степени активности использования Программ в любой выделенный момент времени.

Почтовый ящик: место, в котором электронная почта получается или из которого отправляется: он создается когда в Oracle*Office заносится информация о пользователе или приложении.

Español/América Latina (excepto Brasil)

TÉRMINOS DE LA LICENCIA DEL PROGRAMA DE ORACLE

ADVERTENCIA: SI ABRE ESTE PAQUETE O USA EL SOFTWARE AQUÍ INCLUIDO, REGIRÁN LOS SIGUIENTES TÉRMINOS. SI NO ESTÁ DE ACUERDO CON DICHO SOFTWARE O TÉRMINOS, DEVUELVA EL SOFTWARE DENTRO DE LOS 30 DÍAS A LA COMPAÑÍA QUE SE LO ENVIÓ PARA OBTENER UN REEMBOLSO.

ORACLE CORPORATION O SU SUBSIDIARIA LOCAL (DE AQUÍ EN ADELANTE DENOMINADA "ORACLE") LE OTORGA A USTED (DE AQUÍ EN ADELANTE DENOMINADO CLIENTE) UNA LICENCIA PARA USAR EL SOFTWARE Y LA DOCUMENTACIÓN INCLUIDOS EN ESTE PAQUETE (DE AQUÍ EN ADELANTE DENOMINADOS PROGRAMAS), COMO SE ESPECIFICA A CONTINUACIÓN.

LICENCIA: El Cliente tendrá el derecho de utilizar los Programas en el entorno operativo identificado por Oracle, ya sea (a) tal como se especifica en un documento de pedido o en un Certificado para el Uso del Programa que Oracle o su distribuidor distribuya al Cliente, o (b) en caso de no especificarse, para un solo usuario en una sola computadora. El Cliente puede usar los Programas solamente para sus propias operaciones internas de procesamiento de datos. El Cliente puede hacer una copia de cada Programa licenciado a los fines de conservar una copia de respaldo. Los derechos para realizar copias adicionales, si las hubiere, se detallarán en un documento de pedido o Certificado para el Uso del Programa. No se podrá realizar ningún otro tipo de copias sin el consentimiento previo por escrito de Oracle. El Cliente no deberá: (a) quitar ninguna identificación del producto, notificaciones de derechos de autor, u otras notificaciones o restricciones de propiedad de los Programas; (b) usar los Programas con propósitos de compartimiento temporario comercial, alquiler o prestación de servicios de procesamiento de datos; (c) transferir, vender, ceder o de otra manera otorgar Programas a otra parte sin el consentimiento previo por escrito de Oracle; (d) realizar o permitir la ingeniería reversa, desmontaje o descompilación de los Programas; o (e) divulgar a terceros los resultados de cualquier prueba de conjuntos representativos de datos (benchmark tests) realizados a cualquier Programa sin la autorización previa por escrito de Oracle. Todas las transferencias de los Programas están sujetas a las tarifas y políticas de transferencia de Oracle. El Cliente tendrá el derecho de usar solamente los Programas contenidos en este paquete que estén especificados en un documento de pedido o Certificado para el Uso del Programa.

DERECHOS DE AUTOR/PROPIEDAD EXCLUSIVA DE LOS PROGRAMAS: Los Programas son productos de propiedad exclusiva de Oracle y están protegidos por la ley de derechos de autor y otras leyes de propiedad intelectual. El Cliente adquiere solamente el derecho de usar los Programas y no adquiere ningún derecho, expreso o implícito, sobre los Programas o medios que contengan Programas que no sean los especificados en esta Licencia. Oracle o su licenciante conservará, en todo momento, todos los derechos, titularidad y participación -incluyendo los derechos de propiedad intelectual- en los Programas y los medios.

GARANTÍAS LIMITADAS/RECURSOS LEGALES EXCLUSIVOS: Oracle garantiza que, por un período de 90 días a partir de la fecha de envío al Cliente: (a) los medios incluidos en este paquete no poseen defectos en los materiales o en su fabricación en condiciones de uso normales; y (b) los Programas no modificados ejecutarán substancialmente las funciones descriptas en la documentación provista por Oracle cuando se ejecuten en el sistema operativo y computadora designados. Oracle no garantiza que: los Programas reunirán los requisitos del Cliente, que los Programas funcionarán en las combinaciones que el Cliente seleccione para su uso, que la ejecución de los Programas será ininterrumpida o libre de errores, o que todos los errores de los Programas serán corregidos. **Estas garantías son exclusivas y se otorgan en lugar de todas otras garantías, ya sean expresas o implícitas por la ley.** Si el Cliente notifica a Oracle acerca de un error en un Programa dentro del período de los 90 días, Oracle habrá de, según su elección, corregir el error, ofrecer al Cliente un procedimiento razonable para solucionar el error habilidosamente, o reembolsar al Cliente las tarifas de licencia una vez que el Cliente devuelva los Programas a Oracle. Oracle reemplazará cualquier medio defectuoso, sin cargo, si éste se devuelve a Oracle dentro del período de los 90 días. **Estos son los recursos legales absolutos y exclusivos del Cliente ante cualquier violación de las garantías. Esta garantía limitada le otorga derechos legales específicos. Usted podrá poseer otros.**

LIMITACIÓN DE LA RESPONSABILIDAD: ORACLE NO SERÁ RESPONSABLE POR DAÑOS Y PERJUICIOS INDIRECTOS, ACCESORIOS, ESPECIALES O CONSECUENCIALES, O DAÑOS Y PERJUICIOS POR PÉRDIDA DE GANANCIAS, INGRESOS TOTALES, DATOS O USO DE DATOS, INCURRIDOS POR EL CLIENTE O POR UNA TERCERA PARTE, YA SEA A TRAVÉS DE UNA ACCIÓN CONTRACTUAL O EXTRACONTRACTUAL, AUN EN EL CASO EN QUE SE HAYA ADVERTIDO A ORACLE O CUALQUIER OTRA PERSONA ACERCA DE LA POSIBILIDAD DE DICHOS DAÑOS Y PERJUICIOS. LA RESPONSABILIDAD DE ORACLE POR DAÑOS Y PERJUICIOS EN VIRTUD DEL PRESENTE NO EXCEDERÁ, BAJO NINGUNA CIRCUNSTANCIA, LAS TARIFAS ABONADAS POR EL CLIENTE PARA ESTA LICENCIA.

El Cliente deberá acatar en su totalidad todas las leyes y reglamentos de los Estados Unidos de América y otros países (de aquí en adelante denominadas Leyes de Exportación) para asegurar que ni los Programas, ni ningún producto directo de los mismos, se (1) exporten, directa o indirectamente, en violación de las Leyes de Exportación o (2) sean utilizados con fines prohibidos por las Leyes de Exportación, incluyendo, pero sin limitarse a, la proliferación de armas nucleares, químicas o biológicas. Esta Licencia y todas las actividades relacionadas se regirán por las leyes locales. Oracle puede auditar el uso que el Cliente haga de los Programas. Esta Licencia anula y reemplaza todos los términos de cualquier orden de compra del Cliente o cualquier otro documento de pedido del Cliente.

DEFINICIONES DEL CERTIFICADO PARA EL USO DEL PROGRAMA:
Dispositivos Simultáneos/Acceso Simultáneo: La cantidad máxima de dispositivos de entrada con acceso a los Programas en un momento determinado. Si se utiliza software o hardware de multiplexión (por ejemplo un monitor TP), esta cantidad debe medirse en el extremo frontal de multiplexión.

Cliente: Una computadora que (1) es utilizada por una sola persona a la vez y (2) ejecuta software Oracle en la memoria local o almacena el software en un dispositivo de almacenamiento local.

Usuario: Un individuo a quien el Cliente autoriza a usar los Programas, independientemente de que el individuo esté utilizando los Programas en forma activa en algún momento.

Buzón: Un lugar desde donde se envía o recibe el correo electrónico: se crea cuando se establece una aplicación o cuenta del usuario en Oracle* Office.

Español/España

Si Vd. ha adquirido su producto ORACLE en España, el presente Contrato de Licencia será de aplicación

ADVERTENCIA: SI VD. ABRE ESTE PAQUETE O UTILIZA EL SOFTWARE ADJUNTO, LOS SIGUIENTES TERMINOS DE CONTRATO DE LICENCIA SERAN DE APLICACION. SI EL REFERIDO SOFTWARE O LOS PRESENTES TERMINOS CONTRACTUALES NO SON ACEPTABLES PARA VD., DEVUELVA EL SOFTWARE DENTRO DE 30 DIAS A LA COMPAÑIA DE QUIEN LO ADQUIRIO PARA EL REEMBOLSO DE SU IMPORTE.

ORACLE CORPORATION O SU FILIAL, ORACLE IBÉRICA, S.A. (EN ADELANTE "ORACLE"), LE CONCEDE (EN LO SUCESIVO "CLIENTE") UNA LICENCIA PARA USAR EL SOFTWARE ADJUNTO Y SU DOCUMENTACION ("PROGRAMAS") EN LA FORMA QUE A CONTINUACIÓN SE DETALLA.

LICENCIA: El Cliente tendrá el derecho de utilizar los Programas en el entorno operacional identificado por Oracle (a) hasta el grado de extensión especificado en la documentación de pedido o en el Certificado de Uso de Programa entregado al Cliente por Oracle o por su distribuidor, o, (b) en ausencia de especificación al respecto, por un único usuario y en un único ordenador. El Cliente sólo podrá utilizar los Programas para operaciones de procesamiento de sus propios datos internos. El Cliente podrá efectuar una copia de cada Programa licenciado para fines de seguridad o "backup"; los derechos para ejecutar copias adicionales, en su caso, pueden quedar especificados en la documentación de pedido o en el certificado de Uso de Programa. No se realizará ninguna otra copia sin el previo consentimiento por escrito de Oracle. El Cliente se abstendrá de: (a) eliminar cualesquiera identificaciones de producto, advertencias de copyright o de restricciones de propiedad de los Programas; (b) utilizar los Programas para fines de "timesharing" o venta por tiempo compartido, préstamo, alquiler o servicios comerciales de procesamiento de datos ("service bureau"; (c) transferir, vender, ceder o transmitir en cualquier forma los Programas a otra parte sin el previo consentimiento por escrito de Oracle; (d) realizar o permitir la realización de actividades de ingeniería inversa ("reverse engineering"), desensamblaje o descompilación de los Programas cuando el Cliente haya recibido de Oracle, dentro de un plazo de tiempo razonable a contar desde su requerimiento por escrito en tal sentido, la información suficiente, en cuanto ésta sea disponible para Oracle y en la medida de que sea necesaria para la creación de programas que sean interoperables con los Programas sin infringir los derechos de propiedad intelectual de Oracle, y; (e) revelar los resultados de cualesquiera tests "benchmark" o de banco de pruebas de cualquier Programa a cualquier tercera parte sin el previo consentimiento por escrito de Oracle. El Cliente sólo tendrá el derecho de utilizar los Programas contenidos en este paquete que aparezcan especificados en la documentación de pedido o en el Certificado de Uso del Programa.

COPYRIGHT/PROPIEDAD DE LOS PROGRAMAS: Los Programas son un producto propiedad de Oracle o de su licenciante y están protegidos por las Leyes de Copyright y otras de Propiedad Intelectual. El Cliente sólo adquiere el derecho de utilizar los Programas y no adquiere derecho alguno de propiedad sobre los mismos o sobre la media o soporte físico en el que aquéllos se contienen distinto de los especificados en el presente contrato. Oracle, o su licenciante, retendrán en todo momento toda titularidad, derechos e intereses, incluyendo los derechos de propiedad intelectual sobre los Programas y la media o soporte físico.

GARANTÍAS/RECURSOS EXCLUSIVOS: Oracle garantiza que durante un período de doce meses a contar desde la fecha de entrega al Cliente: (a) la media o soporte físico adjunto estarán libres de defectos de fabricación y material bajo un uso normal; y (b) los Programas, a menos que sean modificados, desarrollarán substancialmente las funciones descritas en la documentación entregada por Oracle cuando sean operados en el ordenador y sistema operativo designados. Oracle no garantiza que: los Programas cumplan los requerimientos del Cliente, que los Programas operen en todas las combinaciones que el Cliente pueda seleccionar para su uso, que la operación de los Programas sea ininterrumpida o libre de errores ni que todos los errores sean corregidos. Estas garantías, en la extensión permitida por la ley, son exclusivas y sustituyen a cualquier otro tipo de garantías, expresas o implícitas. Si el Cliente avisa de un defecto en los Programas dentro del período de doce meses, Oracle, a su elección, corregirá tales defectos o proveerá al Cliente con un procedimiento razonable para salvar el defecto o, contra la devolución por el Cliente de los Programas a Oracle, devolverá las tarifas de licencia. Oracle reemplazará sin cargo alguno cualquier media o soporte físico defectuoso si el mismo es devuelto a Oracle en el plazo de doce (12) meses a contar desde la fecha original de entrega. Estos constituyen los únicos y exclusivos recursos de que dispondrá el Cliente para el caso de incumplimiento de la garantía.

LIMITACIÓN DE RESPONSABILIDAD: ORACLE NO SERÁ RESPONSABLE POR CUALESQUIERA DAÑOS INDIRECTOS (INCLUYENDO DE FORMA NO LIMITATIVA LA PÉRDIDA DE BENEFICIOS, INGRESOS, DATOS O USO) EN QUE INCURRA EL CLIENTE O CUALQUIER TERCERA PARTE, SEA EN EL CURSO DE UNA RECLAMACIÓN CONTRACTUAL O POR DAÑOS, INCLUSO SI ORACLE HUBIERA SIDO ADVERTIDA DE LA POSIBILIDAD DE TALES PÉRDIDAS. LA RESPONSABILIDAD DE ORACLE POR DAÑOS Y PERJUICIOS DE CUALQUIER TIPO DERIVADOS DEL PRESENTE CONTRATO NO EXCEDERÁ EN NINGUN CASO DE LAS TARIFAS SATISFECHAS POR EL CLIENTE PARA ESTA LICENCIA. LOS PRECIOS DE ORACLE REFLEJAN LA DISTRIBUCIÓN DEL RIESGO Y LA LIMITACIÓN DE RESPONSABILIDAD AQUI CONTENIDA.

El Cliente consiente en cumplir enteramente con la normativa aplicable sobre exportación emitida por los Gobiernos Español o de los Estados Unidos de América ("Normativa de Exportación") a fin de asegurarse de que los Programas, Documentación o cualquier producto directo de los mismos (a) no son exportados, directa o indirectamente, en violación de dicha Normativa de Exportación, ni (b) son utilizados para cualquier finalidad prohibida por la Normativa de Exportación, incluyendo de forma no limitativa, la proliferación de armamento nuclear, químico o biológico. Este contrato quedará sujeto a las leyes españolas. El presente contrato prevalecerá sobre todos los términos contenidos en cualesquiera órdenes de compra del Cliente o cualesquiera otros documentos de Pedido en contradicción con los presentes términos.

DEFINICIONES DEL CERTIFICADO DE USO DE PROGRAMA:
Dispositivos Concurrentes/Accesos Concurrentes: el número máximo de dispositivos de entrada accediendo a los Programas en cualquier momento dado del tiempo. Si se utiliza software o hardware multiplexador (como por ejemplo, un monitor TP), este número debe ser medido al multiplexador "front end"

Cliente: un ordenador el cual (1) es utilizado por una sola persona al tiempo y (2) ejecuta software Oracle en su memoria local o almacena el software en un dispositivo de almacenaje local.

Usuario: un individuo autorizado por el Cliente para utilizar los programas, con independencia de si el individuo en cuestión está utilizando activamente o no los Programas en un momento dado en el tiempo.

Buzón ("Mailbox"): un punto desde el cual se puede enviar o recibir correo electrónico y que es creado cuando una cuenta de usuario o una aplicación es establecida en Oracle Office.

Svenska/Sverige

ORACLE PROGRAMVARULICENS

V I K T I G T - OM NI ÖPPNAR DENNA FÖRPACKNING ELLER ANVÄNDER DEN MEDFÖLJANDE PROGRAMVARAN GÄLLER NEDAN ANGIVNA VILLKOR FÖR DESS ANVÄNDANDE. ACCEPTERAR NI INTE PROGRAMVARAN ELLER VILLKOREN, VAR VÄNLIG ÅTERLÄMNA PROGRAMVARAN INOM 30 DAGAR TILL DET FÖRSÄLJNINGSSTÄLLE VARIFRÅN NI ERHÅLLIT PROGRAMVARAN. ÅTERBETALNING KOMMER DÅ ATT SKE.

ORACLE SVENSKA AB, NEDAN KALLAT ORACLE, UPPLÅTER OCH TILLHANDAHÅLLER TILL ER, NEDAN KALLAD KUNDEN, EN LICENS TILL BILAGDA PROGRAMVARA OCH DESS DOKUMENTATION, NEDAN KALLAD PROGRAMVARAN, PÅ NEDAN ANGIVNA VILLKOR.

LICENSEN: Kunden har rätt att använda Programvaran i den driftsmiljö, som definierats av Oracle antingen (a) i ett beställningsdokument eller Programanvändarcertfikat, som kunden mottagit av Oracle eller Oracles distributör, eller (b) om inte annat specificerats, innefattar licensen rätt för en användare att nyttja Programvaran på en dator. Kunden får endast använda Programvaran för intern databehandling. Kunden har rätt att göra en kopia av Programvaran för back-up-ändamål. Endast för det fall det framgår av beställningsdokumentet eller Programanvändartillståndet äger Kunden rätt att göra ytterligare kopior. Därutöver har Kunden ej rätt att kopiera Programvaran utan att Oracle dessförinnan skriftligen lämnat sitt medgivande därtill. Kunden skall (a) bibehålla og ej förändra märkning, uppgift om förekommande patent, upphovsrätt eller copyrightmärkning på eller i Programvaran eller på medium med vilket Programvaran göres tillgängligt för Kunden, (b) inte använda Programvaren för uthyrning, utlåning, servicebyråverksamhet eller på annat sätt tillhandahållas för användning av tredje man, (c) får inte överlåta, sälja eller på annat sätt låta annan disponera eller i övrigt förfoga över Programvaran utan att Oracle dessförinnan skriftligen lämnat tillstånd därtill, (d) inte Dekompilera Programvaran annan omfattning än vad som är nödvändigt för att åstadkomma samverkansförmåga med andra programvaror, (e) inte göra resultat av prestandamätningar "bench mark test" tillgängliga för tredje man utan Oracles skriftliga godkännande. Vid överflyttning av Programvaran till annan driftsmiljö gäller Oracles regler och avgifter för överflyttning av programvaror. Kunden har endast rätt att använda Programvaran i förpackningen som är angivna i beställningsdokumentet eller Programanvändartill-ståndet.

IMMATERIELLA RÄTTIGHETER/ÄGANDERÄTT: Oracle innehar upphovsrätt och andra immateriella rättigheter till Programvaran, och Oracles rättigheter är skyddade enligt gällande immateriellrättslig lagstiftning och lagstiftning om äganderätt. Kunden förvärvar endast rätten att använda Programvaran och förvärvar sålunda inte någon rätt, uttryckligt eller underförstått, till Programvaran eller medium, som innehåller Programvaran, om inte annat specificerats i nuvarande licens. Äganderätten och alla immateriella rättigheter till Programvaran och media tillhör i alla hänseen-den Oracle eller dess underleverantör.

BEGRÄNSNINGAR AV GARANTIER/RÄTT ATT AVHJÄLPA FEL: Under en period om 90 dagar från och med det datum som Programvaran leve-rererats till Kunden garanterar Oracle att (a) media såsom band, disketter, som tillhandahålles av Oracle, vid normalt användande ej innehåller materialfel eller andra fel, och att (b) levererad Programvara i allt väsentligt har de funktioner som angivits i dokumentationen under förutsättning att Programvaran inte modifierats och att den använts på därför avsedd dator med tillhörande operativsystem. Oracle garanterar inte att Programvaran och/eller dokumentationen motsvarar Kundens alla behov eller att programvarudokumentationen alltid kommer att fungera under sådana förhållanden där Kunden vill nyttja den. Oracle garanterar inte att Programvaran alltid fungerar felfritt, att alla fel kan avhjälpas, att Programvaran fungerar utan avbrott, att den är felfri eller att alla fel kommer att bli rättade. Oracle har inget ansvar för fel eller brister utöver vad som uttryckligen angivits i detta avtal. För det fall Kunden meddelar Oracle att fel föreligger i Programvaran innan utgången av ovan angivna garantiperiod om 90 dagar, äger Oracle rätt att välja om Oracle skall åtgärda felet, eller tillhandahålla Kunden annan rimlig möjlighet att undgå felet, eller för det fall Kunden returnerar Programvaran till Oracle, återbetala de licensavgifter som har erlagts av Kunden. Under förutsättning att Kunden returnerat defekt media till Oracle inom utgången av ovan angivna garantiperiod om 90 dagar, byter Oracle ut media som är felaktiga utan kostnad för Kunden. Kunden äger ej rätt till någon annan form av avhjälpande eller gottgörelse än vad som ovan angivits.

ANSVARSBEGRÄNSNING: ORACLE SVARAR INTE UNDER NÅGRA OMSTÄNDIGHETER FÖR INDIREKT FÖRLUST, FÖLJDSKADOR, UTEBLIVEN VINST, DRIFTSFÖRLUST, FÖRLORAD DATA ELLER LIKNANDE FÖRLUST SOM KUNDEN ELLER TREDJE MAN ÅDRAGIT SIG OAVSETT OM ORACLE AV KUNDEN ELLER AV TREDJEMAN BLIVIT INFORMERAD OM RISKEN FÖR ATT SÅDAN FÖRLUST SKULLE KUNNA UPPSTÅ. ORACLES ERSÄTTNINGSANSVAR SKALL ALDRIG ÖVERSTIGA ETT BELOPP MOTSVARANDE STORLEKEN AV DE LICENSAVGIFTER SOM KUNDEN ERLAGT FÖR PROGRAMVARAN.

Kunden skall var helt införstådd med att alla lagar och förordningar i Sverige och USA samt andre länders efterlevs för att försäkra sig om att varkan program eller andra produkter härav (1) exporteras direkt eller indirekt i strid med exportlagarna eller (2) används i något syfte som strider mot exportlagarna, vilket inkluderar utan begränsningar, spridning av kärnvapen, kemiska- eller biologiska vapan. Denna licens och alla berörda handlingar skall lyda under svensk lag. Oracle har rätt att granska Kundens användning av Programmen. Alla villkor som berörs av en inköbsorder eller annat orderdokument från Kunden skall ersättas av denna licens.

DEFINITIONER FÖR PROGRAMANVÄNDARTILLSTÅND

Samtidiga användare: Det maximala antalet inläsningsenheter, som på en given tidpunkt använder Programvaran samtidigt. Om multiplexer program- eller hårdvara användes, avgörs antalet samtidiga användare vid multiplexer-ingången.

Klient: En dator (1), som används av endast en person åt gången och (2) exekverar Oracles Programvara i ett lokal minne och lagrar Programvaran i en lokal minnesenhet.

Användare: En individuell person, som har Kundens tillstånd att använda Programvaran oavsett om det sker på en given tidpunkt.

Mailbox: En punkt varifrån elektronisk post skickas och mottages. En "mailbox" uppstår, när ett användar-id eller en applikation har upprättats i Oracle*Office.

Türkçe/Türkiye

ORACLE PROGRAM LİSANSI ŞARTLARI

UYARI: BU PAKETİ AÇAR VEYA İÇİNDEKİ BİLGİSAYAR PROGRAMINI ("YAZILIM") KULLANIRSANIZ, AŞAĞIDAKİ HÜKÜMLERE TABİ OLURSUNUZ. YAZILIMI VEYA BU HÜKÜMLERİ KABUL EDİLEMEZ BULUYORSANIZ, YAZILIMI 30 GÜN İÇİNDE ŞİRKETE GERİ GETİRİNİZ, BU DURUMDA YAZILIM GERİ ALINACAK VE PARANIZ İADE EDİLECEKTİR.

ORACLE BİLGİSAYAR SİSTEMLERİ LTD. ŞTİ. ("ORACLE") AŞAĞIDA BELİRTİLEN SINIRLAR DAHİLİNDE SİZE ("MÜŞTERİ") İLİŞİKTEKİ YAZILIMIN VE DOKÜMANTASYONUN ("PROGRAMLAR") KULLANMA LİSANSINI VERİR.

LİSANS: Müşteri (a) sipariş formunda veya Oracle yahut Oracle yetkili dağıtıcısı tarafından Müşteriye verilmiş bulunan Program Kullanma Sertifikası'nda tanımlanan sınırlar içinde veya, böyle bir tanım yoksa (b) tek bir kullanıcı tarafından ve tek bir bilgisayarda kullanılmak üzere Oracle tarafından tesbit edilmiş olan iletim sisteminde ve Ülke içinde Programları kullanma hakkına sahiptir. Müşteri, Programları sadece kendi veri işleme işlemlerinde kullanabilir. Müşteri her bir Lisanslı Programın yedekleme amacıyla sadece bir kopyasını çıkartabilir; eğer verilmişse, ek kopyalar çıkartabilmek hakkı, sipariş formunda veya Program Kullanma Sertifikası'nda mutlaka yer almalıdır. Oracle'ın açık olarak yazılı izni alınmadıkça başkaca kopya yapılamaz. Müşteri, (a) Programlardan herhangi bir ürün tanımlamasını, telif hakkı uyarısını, diğer her türlü uyarıyı veya mülkiyet kısıtlamalarını kaldıramaz, (b) Programları ticari zaman paylaşımlı sistemlerde kiralama yoluyla veya servis büro işlemlerinde kullanamaz, (c) Oracle'ın önceden yazılı kabulünü almaksızın Programları başka herhangi bir kişiye veremez, satamaz, nakledemez ya da başkaca herhangi bir şekilde devredemez, (d) Programları ters mühendislik (reverse engineer) kod formunun çevirisi (decompile) veya derlenmiş kodu çözme işlemlerine tabi tutamaz, (c) Oracle'ın önceden yazılı onayını almaksızın her türlü üçüncü kişiye herhangi bir Programın herhangi bir kontrol testi (benchmark test) sonucunu açıklayamaz. Programların devirleri Oracle'ın devir politikası ve devir ücretlerine uygun olarak yapılacaktır. Müşterinin tek ve yegane hakkı, bu paketteki Programları sipariş belgesinde veya Program Kullanma Sertifikası'nda yer aldığı şekilde kullanmaktır.

oracle/shrinkwrap.lic

TELİF HAKKI/PROGRAMLARIN MÜLKİYETİ: Programlar Oracle'ın malik olduğu ürünlerdir ve Fikir ve Sanat Eserleri Kanunu ile diğer fikri mülkiyet kanunları uyarınca korunurlar. Müşteri sadece Programları kullanmak hakkını edinmekte ve bunun dışında Programlar veya Programların yer aldığı ortam ("Ortam") üzerinde işbu Lisansta yer alanlar dışında her ne şekil ve surette olursa olsun herhangi bir hak elde etmemektedir. Oracle veya onun adına lisans verenler, Programlar ve Ortam üzerindeki fikri mülkiyet hakları da dahil olmak üzere ürün ve onun semereleri üzerindeki tüm haklara daima sahip olmaya devam edeceklerdir.

SINIRLI GARANTİ/TANINAN İMKANLAR: Oracle, Müşteriye teslimden sonraki 90 günlük süre için (a) normal kullanım halinde Programların yer aldığı ortamın malzeme ve işçilik kusuru taşımadığını ve (b) değiştirilmemiş Programların uygun bilgisayar ve işletim sistemi altında çalıştırılmak şartıyla Oracle tarafından sağlanan dokümantasyonda genel olarak tanımlanan işlevleri yerine getireceğini garanti eder. Oracle hiçbir şekilde, Programların Müşterinin ihtiyacını tam ve uygun olarak karşılayacağını, Programların Müşteri tarafından kullanılan diğer Programlarla birlikte çalışacağını, Programların çalışmasının kesintisiz, hatasız olacağını ve Programların tüm hatalarından arındırılmış olduğunu garanti etmez. Oracle tarafından verilen garantiler bu sayılanlarla sınırlı olup ticari değer veya özel bir amaca uygunluk garantisi de dahil olmak üzere kanun tarafından veya başka bir şekilde tanınan ister sarih ister zımni her şekil ve suretteki garanti ve hükmün yerine geçer. Eğer Müşteri 90 günlük süre içinde Programlarda bir hatanın bulunduğunu bildirirse, Oracle seçim hakkı kendisinde kalmak üzere hatayı giderebilir, Müşteriye hatanın giderilmesi için bir yol önerebilir veya Programların Oracle'a teslimi şartı ile lisans bedelini geri ödeyebilir. Oracle hatalı ortamı 90 günlük süre için kendisine teslim edilmiş olması koşuluyla ücretsiz olarak değiştirecektir. Tüm bunlar herhangi bir garanti ihlali durumunda Müşterinin sahip olabileceği tek ve yegane imkandır.

SORUMLULUĞUN SINIRLANMASI: ORACLE, İSTER SÖZLEŞMEDEN VEYA HAKSIZ FİİLDEN KAYNAKLANSIN, İSTER MÜŞTERİ VEYA DİĞER KİŞİNİN BÖYLE BİR ZARARA UĞRAYABİLECEĞİ ORACLE VEYA HERHANGİ BİR ÜÇÜNCÜ KİŞİ TARAFINDAN KENDİSİNE BİLDİRİLMİŞ OLSUN HER TÜRLÜ DOLAYLI, TESADÜFİ, ÖZEL VEYA ÖNEMLİ HASARLARDAN VEYA MÜŞTERİ YAHUT ÜÇÜNCÜ BİR KİŞİNİN UĞRADIĞI KAZANÇ VEYA GELİR, VERİ VEYA KULLANILAN VERİ KAYBINDAN KAYNAKLANAN HASARLARDAN SORUMLU DEĞİLDİR.

ORACLE'IN BU TÜRDEKİ HASARLARDAN SORUMLULUĞU HİÇBİR ŞEKİLDE BU LİSANS DOLAYISIYLA MÜŞTERİ TARAFINDAN ÖDENMİŞ LİSANS BEDELİNDEN FAZLA OLMAYACAKTIR.
Ülke: "Ülke" aksi açık bir şekilde sipariş belgesinde veya Program Kullanma Sertifikası'nda belirtilmediği sürece Türkiye Cumhuriyeti anlamına gelecektir.

Müşteri, Amerika Birleşik Devletleri ve Türkiye Cumhuriyetinin tüm gümrük ithalat ve ihracat mevzuatına ("Mevzuat") tamamıyla uyacaktır ve ne Programları ne de bunlardan faydalanılarak oluşturulan her türlü ürünlerin (1) Mevzuata aykırı olarak doğrudan veya dolayısıyla ihraç edilmeyeceğini veya (2) sayılanlarla sınırlı olmaksızın, nükleer, kimyasal veya biyolojik silahların yayılması da dahil olmak üzere mevzuat tarafından yasaklanmış her türlü amaçla kullanılmayacağını taahhüt etmektedir.

İşbu sözleşme ve ilgili tüm işlemler Türkiye Cumhuriyeti kanunlarına tabiidir. Oracle, Müşterinin Programları kullanmasını denetleyebilir. Müşteri tarafından verilen ürün siparişi formları veya sair Müşteri Sipariş dokümanları bu lisansın ayrılmaz parçasını oluşturur.

PROGRAM KULLANMA SERTİFİKASI TANIMLARI:

Aynı Anda Erişen Aygıt/Aynı Anda Gerçekleşen Erişimler: Herhangi bir zamanda Programlara erişen girdi aygıtlarının sayısı. Eğer çok evreli yazılım veya donanım (örneğin TP ekranı gibi) kullanılıyorsa, bu sayı çok evrelenmiş uçların sayısına göre hesaplanacaktır.

Müşteri Bilgisayar: (1) herhangi bir zamanda sadece bir kişi tarafından kullanılan ve (2) belleğinde Oracle yazılımını çalıştıran veya yazılımı iç saklama ünitesinde bulunduran bir bilgisayar.

Kullanıcı:herhangi bir zamanda Programları kullanıp kullanmadığına bakılmaksızın Programları kullanmak üzere Müşteri tarafından yetkili kılınmış kişi

Posta Kutusu: Bir kullanıcı veya Oracle Ofisinde kurulmuş bir uygulama tarafından yaratılmış elektronik postanın gönderildiği veya alındığı nokta;

Oracle WebServer Trial License

Oracle Corporation ("Oracle") giver hermed Kunden en vederlagsfri testlicens til i 60 dage regnet fra leveringsdagen at anvende Oracle WebServer Programmellet på en enkelt afviklingsmaskine med tilhørende operativsystem, hvortil Programmellet er leveret, udelukkende med henblik på evaluering af Programmellet, i overensstemmelse med de licensvilkår (Oracle Program License Terms), som er leveret sammen med dette Oracle WebServer Programmel. Programmellet er ikke til anvendelse i produktionsmiljø eller tiltænkt anvendelse i forbindelse med "live" data. Efter ovennævnte 60 dages testperiode, skal Kunden enten betale Oracle for en produktionslicens eller ophøre med at anvende og returnere eller destruere alle eksemplarer af Programmellet. Oracle leverer Programmellet "as is" uden garanti af nogen art og fraskriver sig således enhver udtrykkelig eller implicit garanti, herunder garanti for egnethed til et specifikt formål.

Oracle Corporation ("Oracle") verleent de Cliënt een kosteloze proeflicentie voor het gebruik van Oracle WebServer Programma op één enkele computer voor de Operationele Verwerkingsomgevingen waarvoor het programma verzonden is en slechts voor beoordelingsdoeleinden gedurende een periode van 60 dagen, te beginnen op de datum van levering overeenkomstig de Licentievoorwaarden van Oracle software die gedistribueerd zijn bij Oracle WebServer Programma. Het programma is niet voor productiegebruik of bedoeld voor gebruik met "live" gegevens. Na een proefperiode van 60 dagen betaalt de Cliënt Oracle óf voor een licentie voor productiegebruik óf houdt hij op met het gebruik en retourneert of vernietigt alle kopieën van het programma. Oracle biedt deze licentie op basis van de huidige conditie zonder enige vorm van garantie; Oracle wijst alle uitdrukkelijke en stilzwijgende garanties af, met inbegrip van stilzwijgende garanties van verkoopbaarheid of geschiktheid voor een bepaald doel.

Oracle Corporation ("Oracle") grants Customer a no-charge trial license to use the Oracle WebServer Program on a single computer for the Operating Environments for which the Program is shipped solely for evaluation purposes for a period of 60 days beginning on the date of delivery, in accordance with the Oracle Program License Terms distributed with this Oracle WebServer Program. The Program is not for production use or intended for use with "live" data. After the 60 day trial period, Customer shall either pay Oracle for a production use license or cease using, and return or destroy all Program copies. Oracle is providing this license on an "as is" basis without warranty of any kind; Oracle disclaims all express and implied warranties, including the implied warranties of merchantability or fitness for a particular purpose.

Oracle Corporation myöntää Asiakkaalle veloituksetta koekäyttöoikeuden Oracle WebServer -ohjelmaan. Koekäyttöoikeus on voimassa yhdessä tietokoneessa niissä käyttöympäristöissä, joihin ohjelma on toimitettu, ja ohjelmaa voidaan käyttää ainoastaan arviointitarkoitukseen. Koekäyttöoikeus on voimassa 60 päivää toimituksesta. Käyttöoikeusehdot ovat ohjelmatoimituksen mukana. Ohjelma ei ole tarkoitettu tuotantokäyttöön eikä käytettäväksi "todellisella" datalla. 60 päivän koekäyttöjakson jälkeen Asiakas voi joko maksaa Oraclelle tuotantokäyttölisenssistä tai lopettaa käytön ja palauttaa tai tuhota ohjelmakopiot. Oracle myöntää tämän käyttöoikeuden "as is" -periaatteella eikä myönnä ohjelmalle mitään takuuta; Oracle kumoaa kaikki mahdollisesti hiljaisesti tai nimenomaisesti annetut takuut mukaan lukien takuut kaupattavuudesta tai sopivuudesta tiettyyn tarkoitukseen.

Oracle France (« Oracle ») concède à la personne l'ayant commandée (le « Client ») une licence gratuite d'évaluation du Programme Oracle WebServer, sur une seule unité centrale, pour l'Environnement d'Exploitation pour lequel le Programme a été livré. Cette licence a une durée de 60 jours à compter de la date de livraison, et est sujette aux termes et conditions de la Licence de Programme Oracle livrée avec le dit Programme. Le Programme n'est pas destiné à un usage en production ni adapté au traitement de données « live ». A l'expiration de la période d'évaluation de 60 jours, le Client paiera à Oracle le prix d'une licence de production, ou cessera l'utilisation du Programme et retournera à Oracle ou détruira toutes copies du Programme. Oracle fournit le Programme dans l'état ou il se trouve (« as is ») sans garantie d'aucune nature, explicite ni implicite, y compris les garanties d'utilisation commerciale ou aptitude à satisfaire un quelconque besoin particulier.

Oracle Corporation ("Oracle") udziela Klientowi bezpłatną licencję na okres próbny na korzystanie z Programu Oracle WebServer na pojedynczym komputerze w Środowiskach Operacyjnych, dla których Program jest przeznaczony wyłącznie dla celów poznawczych, na okres 60 dni rozpoczynający się w dacie dostawy zgodnie z Warunkami Licencji Programu Oracle dostarczonymi wraz z niniejszym Programem Oracle WebServer. Program nie służy do użytku produkcyjnego ani nie jest przeznaczony do korzystania z danymi rzeczywistymi. Po upływie próbnego okresu 60-dniowego Klient powinien zapłacić Oracle opłatę za licencję na produkcyjne korzystanie z Programu, bądź zaprzestać dalszego korzystania i zwrócić, bądź zniszczyć wszelkie kopie Programu. Oracle udziela niniejszej licencji tylko wyłącznie na ten Program, który został dostarczony i w postaci w jakiej został dostarczony bez udzielania gwarancji i rękojmii jakiegokolwiek rodzaju. Oracle wyłącza wszelkie przewidziane przepisami prawa bądź dorozumiane gwarancje i rękojmie, włączając w to dorozumianą rękojmię wartości handlowej lub przydatności dla określonego celu.

A Oracle Corporation (Oracle) concede ao Cliente uma licença temporária grátis para uso do Programa Oracle WebServer num único computador para o ambiente operativo designado. Este Programa só é válido para efeitos de avaliação e teste para um período de 60 (sessenta) dias contados a partir da data de entrega, de acordo com os Termos Gerais e Condições de Licenciamento de Programas Oracle distribuídos com este Programa. Este Programa não é válido para correr em ambientes de "produção" nem deverá ser utilizado com dados "reais". No término do período de avaliação e/ou teste o Cliente poderá (i) pagar à Oracle uma licença de uso completa ou (ii) deixar de utilizar os Programas pelo que os deverá devolver ou destruir. A Oracle concede esta licença numa base "no estado actual dos programas" sem qualquer garantia de qualquer espécie; a Oracle rejeita qualquer garantia implícita ou explícita, incluindo as garantias implícitas de mercantibilidade ou adequação a um fim particular.

Корпорация Оракл ("Оракл") предоставляет Заказчику бесплатную лицензию на тестирование для использования Программы Oracle WebServer на одном компьютере в операционных средах, для которых Программа была приобретена, только для целей оценки на срок 60 дней, начиная с даты поставки, в соответствии с Условиями Лицензии на программы Оракл, распространяемыми с Программой Oracle WebServer. Программа не предназначена для промышленного использования, а также для использования с реальными данными. По окончании периода тестирования в 60 дней, Заказчик должен либо уплатить Оракл за лицензию на промышленное использование либо прекратить использование, вернуть или уничтожить все копии Программ. Оракл предоставляет настоящую лицензию на условиях "как есть" без каких-либо гарантий; Оракл отказывается от всех прямовыраженных и подразумеваемых гарантий, в том числе подразумеваемых гарантий товарности или пригодности для конкретной цели.

Корпорация Оракл ("Оракл") предоставляет Заказчику бесплатную лицензию на тестирование для использования Программы Oracle WebServer на одном компьютере в операционных средах, для которых Программа была приобретена, только для целей оценки на срок 60 дней, начиная с даты поставки, в соответствии с Условиями Лицензии на программы Оракл, распространяемыми с Программой Oracle WebServer. Программа не предназначена для промышленного использования, а также для использования с реальными данными. По окончании периода тестирования в 60 дней, Заказчик должен либо уплатить Оракл за лицензию на промышленное использование либо прекратить использование, вернуть или уничтожить все копии Программ. Оракл предоставляет настоящую лицензию на условиях "как есть" без каких-либо гарантий; Оракл отказывается от всех прямовыраженных и подразумеваемых гарантий, в том числе подразумеваемых гарантий товарности или пригодности для конкретной цели.

Oracle Svenska AB ("Oracle") upplåter till Kunden en kostnadsfri lånelicens för användning av Oracle WebServer Programvara på en enstaka dator för den Plattform på vilken Programvaran levererats. Lånelicensen innebär endast rätt att testa Programvaran för en tid av 60 dagar från leverans, i enlighet med Licensvillkoren som medföljer WebServer Programvara. Programvaran får icke användas i produktion eller på annat sätt användas för "live-data". Vid låneperiodens upphörande skall Kunden antingen betala till Oracle för en produktionslicens enligt gällande prislista, alternativt omedelbart upphöra med användningen och återsända eller förstöra samtliga kopior av Programvaran. Lånelicensen upplåts i befintligt skick utan garantier av något slag, vare sig uttryckliga eller underförstådda. Oracle har inte heller i övrigt något ansvar för användningen av Programvaran.

Oracle şirketi, "Oracle WebServer" programı ile verilen. Oracle Programı lisans şartlarına uygun olarak, teslim tarihinden başlamak üzere 60 günlük süre ile, Oracle WebServer programını tek bir bilgisayarda ve işletim çevresinde, programı değerlendirmek amacı ile kullanılması için Müşteri'ye ücretsiz bir deneme lisansı verir. Program üretim amacı ile veya canlı veriler ile kullanılamaz. 60 günlük deneme süresi sonunda Müşteri, Oracle'a ya lisans bedelini ödeyecek, veya programı kullanmayı durdurarak iade, ya da programın bütün kopyalarını imha edecektir. Oracle, bu lisansı "Olduğu gibi", ve olması gerektiği şekle ilişkin herhangi bir taahhütte bulunmadan vermektedir; Oracle, ticarete uygunluk veya özel bir amacı karşılama halleri de dahil olmak üzere, hiçbir açık veya üstü örtülü taahhüdü peşinen kabul etmemektedir.

Oracle Italia (« Oracle ») concede a voi (« Cliente ») una licenza gratuita per l'uso del Programma Oracle WebServer su un singolo elaboratore allo scopo di prova ed evaluazione esclusivamente, nel Ambiente Operativo per il quale il Programma viene consegnato, per 60 giorni dalla data di consegna, e sotto i termini e condizioni della Licenza di Programma Oracle consegnata con il Programma stesso. Il Programma non è adatto per l'uso in produzione ne per l'elaborazione di dati « live ». Al termine del periodo di evaluazione di 60 giorni di cui sopra, il Cliente sarà tenuto di pagare alla Oracle una licenza di produzione, o cessare l'uso del Programma e restituire alla Oracle o distrurre ogni copia dello stesso. Il Programma è fornito « as is », senza garanzia di nessun genere; Oracle non fornisce garanzie esplicite ne implicite, incluse le garanzie di qualisiasi adeguatezza commerciale o a uno scopo particolare.

오라클 번인 회사 ("오라클") 는 소비자에게 운영 환경에 적합한 단독 컴퓨터에서 사용할 수 있도록 오라클 웹서버 프로그램에 대한 비판매 시범 라이센스를 부여한다. 본 라이센스는 단지 제공한 프로그램을 평가할 목적으로만 사용되어야 하며, 배달된 날로부터 60일간만 사용할 수 있다. 본 오라클 웹서버 프로그램의 사용은 본 프로그램에 함께 첨부된 오라클 프로그램 라이센스 계약 조건에 준한다. 본 프로그램은 생산 목적으로 사용되어서도 안되며, "실지" 데이터와 함께 사용되어서도 절대 안된다. 60일간의 시범 기간이 끝나면, 소비자는 제품 사용 라이센스비를 오라클에게 지불한다. 그렇지 않으면, 본 제품의 사용을 중단하고 모든 프로그램과 복사품을 파기하거나 오라클에 되돌려주어야 한다. 오라클은 본 라이센스를 어떠한 종류의 보증 없이 "현 상태 그대로" 제공한다. 오라클은 상품성에 대한 묵시적 보증과 특정 목적에의 부합성을 포함한 어떠한 명시적 또는 묵시적 보증을 하지 않는다.

Oracle gir med dette Kunden en begrenset bruksrett til programvaren Oracle WebServer
Program, som følger: Programvaren kan bare anvendes på en enkelt prosessor, og bare for
det formål å teste og evalucre programvaren. Varighet av bruksrett: 60 dager fra mottak.
Programvaren kan ikke anvendes på annen plattform (operasjonssystem og maskinutstyr)
enn som det fremgår av leveransen. Vedlagte lisensbetingelser er gjeldende. Programvaren kan
ikke anvendes til produktiv bruk, inklusive bruk av aktuelle produksjons- eller driftsdate.
Efter utløp av den 60 dager lange testperioden kan Kunden velge enten å betale Oracle full
lisensavgift for programvaren og derved få rett til fortsatt bruk, eller opphøre med bruken
og makulere alt mottatt materiell. Programvaren leveres i den stand den befinner seg.
Det gis således ingen garanti forat programvaren er feilfri eller at eventuelle feil eller
mangler vil bli rettet.

Η Εταιρία Oracle παρέχει στον Πελάτη χωρίς επιβαρύνσεις την άδεια να
χρησιμοποιήσει δοκιμαστικά το Πρόγραμμα WebServer, σε ένα μόνο ηλεκτρονικό
υπολογιστή, στο Περιβάλλον των Λειτουργικών Μονάδων για τις οποίες το
Πρόγραμμα αυτό εστάλη, αποκλειστικά και μόνο προκειμένου να το αξιολογήσει,
για χρονική περίοδο 60 ημερών, η οποία αρχίζει από την ημερομηνία της παράδοσης,
σύμφωνα με τους όρους παροχής άδειας χρήσης του προγράμματος, οι οποίοι
διανέμονται μαζί με το Πρόγραμμα WebServer. Το Πρόγραμμα αυτό δεν μπορεί
να χρησιμοποιηθεί για παραγωγικούς σκοπούς ούτε παρέχεται με σκοπό να
χρησιμοποιηθεί με πραγματικά δεδομένα. Μετά την παρέλευση της δοκιμαστικής
περιόδου των 60 ημερών, ο Πελάτης έχει τη δυνατότητα είτε να καταβάλει
στην Oracle αμοιβή για την παροχή άδειας χρήσης του προγράμματος για
παραγωγικούς σκοπούς είτε να σταματήσει να το χρησιμοποιεί και να επιστρέψει ή
να καταστρέψει όλα τα αντίγραφα του Προγράμματος. Η Oracle προμηθεύει την εν
λόγω άδεια "όπως είναι" χωρίς καμμία εγγύηση οποιασδήποτε φύσης. Η Oracle
απαλλάσσεται από κάθε ρητή ή σιωπηρή εγγύηση συμπεριλαμβανομένων ακόμη
και των σιωπηρών εγγυήσεων για την εμπορικότητα ή την καταλληλότητα του
πογράμματος για ένα συγκεκριμένο σκοπό.

Az Oracle Corporation (továbbiakban "Oracle") feljogosítja a felhasználót az ingyenes
próbalicensz alapján, hogy az Oracle WebServer programot egyetlen számítógépen
használja, abban a környezetben amelyre az készült, kizárólagosan kiértékelési céllal, a
szállítás napjától kezdve 60 napos időszakban, az Oracle WebServer programmal együtt
szállított "Az Oracle programok licensz feltételei"-nek megfelelően. A program nem
használható "éles" adatokkal. A 60 napos próbaidőszak lejárta után a felhasználó vagy
kifizeti az Oracle-nek a termék használati licenszdíját vagy a továbbiakban nem használja
a programot és visszadja vagy megsemmisíti a program minden másolatát. Az Oracle ezt
a próbalicenszet bárminemű felelősségvállalás nélkül adja, nem vállal semmiféle közvetlen
vagy közvetett szavatosságot, nem szavatolja, hogy adott célra a program felhasználható.

Oracle公司授权客户在为环境运作服务的单一电脑上免费试用 Oracle WebServer 软件。
此软件供客户在交货后六十天内仅作功能评估之用，须受所附授权条件的约束。此
软件不可用于正式业务运作，也不得与日常运作数据资料混同使用。客户应于六十
天试用期满后，向本公司付款购买 此软件的正式使用权，否则应停止使用此软件，
并退还或销毁该软件的一切版本。本公司仅按软件现有实际情况提供使用权，不作
任何形式的担保，不承担任何明示或隐含的担保，其中包括关于软件之适售性或特
定用途适应性之任何隐含的担保。

本公司授權台端於乙部電腦上免費使用內附之 Oracle WebServer 軟體試用版。 此軟
體乃供台端於付運後六十天內免費試用及評估用途，一切軟體之使用均受內附授
權合約之約束。此軟體不可作生產用途，亦不得與現行數據一併使用。台端應於六
十天試用期後，向本公司付款購買此軟體之生產版，否則應停止使用此軟體，并退
還或銷毀所有軟體樣本。本公司不為其他明示或暗示擔保，其中包括軟體之通售性
或符合特定使用此授權合約目的之默示。

Společnost Oracle ("Oracle") uděluje Zákazníkovi bezplatnou zkušební licenci k použití Programu Oracle WebServer na jednom počítači pro operační systémy, pro které je Program dodáván. Tato licence se uděluje výhradně za účelem vyhodnocení na období 60 dnů počínaje datem doručení, v souladu s Podmínkami licence Programu distribuovanými společně s daným Programem Oracle WebServer. Program není určen k provoznímu použití nebo použití se „skutečnými daty." Po uplynutí lhůty 60 dnů je Zákazník povinen buď zaplatit za licenci k použití Programu, přestat Program používat nebo vrátit a zničit všechny kopie Programu. Oracle tuto licenci uděluje na Program "ve stávajícím stavu" bez jakékoli záruky. Oracle se zříká veškerých záruk, ať už vyslovených nebo implicitních, včetně implicitních záruk prodejnosti nebo vhodnosti pro konkrétní použití.

ORACLE®

Oracle Corporation
World Headquarters
500 Oracle Parkway
Redwood Shores, CA 94065
USA

Worldwide Inquiries:
Phone +1.415.506.7000
Fax +1.415.506.7200
http://www.oracle.com/

Americas Headquarters
Phone +1.415.506.7000
Fax +1.415.506.7200

Asia/Pacific Rim/India
Headquarters
Phone +65.220.5488
Fax +65.227.4098

Europe/Middle East/Africa
Headquarters
Phone +31.34.069.4211
Fax +31.34.066.5603

Japan Headquarters
Phone +81.3.5213.6666
Fax +81.3.5213.6600

To offer our customers the most complete and effective information management solutions, Oracle Corporation offers its products, along with support, education, and consulting, in more than 90 countries.

Oracle is a registered trademark of Oracle Corporation.

Copyright © Oracle Corporation 1996
All Rights Reserved

Printed in the U.S.A.
9317.1095.50K

A43753-1

About the CD-ROM

Inside the back cover is the accompanying CD for *Oracle8 PL/SQL Programming*, by Scott Urman. There are three different items on this CD:

1. Source code for the examples used in the book.

2. A demo version of SQL-Station First Edition for Windows 95 and Windows NT, by Platinum Technologies. This is a full-featured version that expires after 30 days.

3. A demo version of Oracle's WebServer, version 2.1 for Windows NT and Solaris systems. This is a full-featured version that expires after 90 days.

The organization of the CD is as follows:

readme.txt	A readme file containing the information on this page.
code/	The code directory contains the source code for all the examples used in the book. In the code subdirectory is a separate directory for each chapter, with that chapter's examples. Also in the code directory is a file called readme.txt with a full description of the contents. The file code/ch01/tables.sql will create the sample tables used for the examples. All of the code is distributed as ASCII text files which should be readable with a standard text editor on both Windows and Unix systems.
station/	The station directory contains a demo version of SQL-Station. To install it, run the setup.exe program found in the station directory. Online documentation (in HTML format) can be found in the station/info directory. For more information on SQL-Station, including pricing and ordering information, see Platinum's website at **http://www.platinum.com**. SQL-Station is discussed in Chapters 13, 14, 19, and 22 of this book.
ows-nt/ ows-sol/	These directories contain demo versions of Oracle WebServer 2.1. The ows-nt directory contains the NT version, and the ows-sol directory contains the Solaris version. To install the NT version, run setup.exe in the ows-nt directory. After installation, you should install the patch to version 2.1.0.3.2 which is found in the ows-nt/patch directory. See the readme.txt file in ows-nt/patch for more details. To install the Solaris version, follow the directions in install.txt found in the ows-sol directory. For more information on the Oracle WebServer, including pricing and ordering information, see Oracle's web site at **http://www.oracle.com**. The Oracle WebServer is discussed in Chapter 19 of this book.

The Oracle Programs are distributed according to the terms of the Trial License and Global License Terms included. They are distributed "as-is," and Oracle shall not be liable for any damages resulting from use of the CD-ROM or these Programs, including direct, indirect, incidental, special or consequential damages, or damages for loss of profits, revenue, data or data use. This is the Export Version of the Oracle Programs.

WARNING: BEFORE OPENING THE DISC PACKAGE, CAREFULLY READ THE TERMS AND CONDITIONS OF THE FOLLOWING COPYRIGHT STATEMENT AND LIMITED CD-ROM WARRANTY.

Copyright Statement

This software is protected by both United States copyright law and international copyright treaty provision. Except as noted in the contents of the CD-ROM, you must treat this software just like a book. However, you may copy it into a computer to be used and you may make archival copies of the software for the sole purpose of backing up the software and protecting your investment from loss. By saying, "just like a book," The McGraw-Hill Companies, Inc. ("Osborne/McGraw-Hill") means, for example, that this software may be used by any number of people and may be freely moved from one computer location to another, so long as there is no possibility of its being used at one location or on one computer while it is being used at another. Just as a book cannot be read by two different people in two different places at the same time, neither can the software be used by two different people in two different places at the same time.

Limited Warranty

Osborne/McGraw-Hill warrants the physical compact disc enclosed herein to be free of defects in materials and workmanship for a period of sixty days from the purchase date. If the CD included in your book has defects in materials or workmanship, please call McGraw-Hill at 1-800-217-0059, 9:00 A.M. to 5:00 P.M., Monday through Friday, Eastern Standard Time, and McGraw-Hill will replace the defective disc.

The entire and exclusive liability and remedy for breach of this Limited Warranty shall be limited to replacement of the defective disc, and shall not include or extend to any claim for or right to cover any other damages, including but not limited to, loss of profit, data, or use of the software, or special incidental, or consequential damages or other similar claims, even if Osborne/McGraw-Hill has been specifically advised of the possibility of such damages. In no event will Osborne/McGraw-Hill's liability for any damages to you or any other person ever exceed the lower of the suggested list price or actual price paid for the license to use the software, regardless of any form of the claim.

OSBORNE/McGRAW-HILL SPECIFICALLY DISCLAIMS ALL OTHER WARRANTIES, EXPRESS OR IMPLIED, INCLUDING BUT NOT LIMITED TO, ANY IMPLIED WARRANTY OF MERCHANTABILITY OR FITNESS FOR A PARTICULAR PURPOSE. Specifically, Osborne/McGraw-Hill make no representation or warranty that the software is fit for any particular purpose, and any implied warranty of merchantability is limited to the sixty-day duration of the Limited Warranty covering the physical disc only (and not the software), and is otherwise expressly and specifically disclaimed.

This limited warranty gives you specific legal rights; you may have others which may vary from state to state. Some states do not allow the exclusion of incidental or consequential damages, or the limitation on how long an implied warranty lasts, so some of the above may not apply to you.

This agreement constitutes the entire agreement between the parties relating to use of the Product. The terms of any purchase order shall have no effect on the terms of this Agreement. Failure of Osborne/McGraw-Hill to insist at any time on strict compliance with this Agreement shall not constitute a waiver of any rights under this Agreement. This Agreement shall be construed and governed in accordance with the laws of New York. If any provision of this Agreement is held to be contrary to law, that provision will be enforced to the maximum extent permissible, and the remaining provisions will remain in force and effect.

NO TECHNICAL SUPPORT IS PROVIDED WITH THIS CD-ROM.